MICROSOFT®

QUICKBASIC™

An Introduction to Computer Programming on the IBM® PC

Robert J. Bent
George C. Sethares
Bridgewater State College

D1522986

PWS Publishing Company
Boston

PWS PUBLISHING COMPANY
20 Park Plaza, Boston, MA 02116-4324

PWS Publishing Company is a division of Wadsworth, Inc.

Printed in the United States of America
10 9 8 7 6 5 4 3 2

Library of Congress Cataloging-in-Publication Data
Bent, Robert J., [date]
    QuickBASIC : an introduction to computer programming on the IBM PC
/ Robert J. Bent & George C. Sethares.
        p   cm.
    Includes index.
    ISBN 0-534-17593-7
    1. IBM Personal Computer—Programming.   2. BASIC (Computer program
language)   3. Microsoft QuickBASIC.   I. Sethares, George C., [date].
    Title.
      ‹ 8.I2596B463   1993
            —dc20

92-38635
CIP

Microsoft is a registered tra
IBM PC is a registered tradema

'icrosoft Corp.
tional Business Machines Corp.

Sponsoring Editor: *Michael Sugarman*
Editorial Assistant: *Carol Ann Benedict*
Production Editor: *Nancy L. Shammas*
Manuscript Editor: *Barbara Kimmel*
Permissions Editor: *Carline Haga*
Interior Design: *Roy R. Neuhaus*
Cover Design: *Katherine Minerva*
Cover Photo: *Lee Hocker Photography*
Art Coordinator: *Susan Haberkorn*
Photo Coordinator: *Larry Molmud*
Typesetting: *GTS Graphics*
Cover Printing: *Lehigh Press, Inc.*
Printing and Binding: *The Courier Companies, Inc.*

Preface

*T*his book is intended to serve as an introduction to computer programming in the environment of an IBM® Personal Computer (PC) system. The programming language used is Microsoft® QuickBASIC™, an extended version of BASIC implemented on IBM compatible microcomputer systems. No prior experience with computers or computer programming languages is assumed. Included are descriptions of the computing equipment you will encounter and procedures for using this equipment.

Most of the material is semitutorial and intended to be studied with a PC close at hand. For beginning programmers, hands-on experience with a real computer is the most effective way to learn about computers. The programming language QuickBASIC is described in detail and illustrated in numerous examples drawn from a wide range of application areas, including business, sports, economics, personal finance, the natural and social sciences, and mathematics. A working knowledge of elementary algebra is the only mathematics needed to understand most of the material and to complete the assignments successfully. The examples and problems involving more advanced topics in mathematics, such as the trigonometric functions, may be omitted with no loss in continuity.

■ *Organization and Coverage*

We wrote this book with two principal goals in mind. First, we felt it important to present the elements of QuickBASIC so that meaningful computer programs could be written at the earliest possible time. We adhere to the notion that one learns by doing. But the development of programming habits, both good and bad, will begin with the first programs written. For this reason, fundamental principles of program design are considered at the outset. Specifically, Chapter 2 describes the top-down approach to problem solving, illustrates the importance of input/output specification, modularization, and stepwise refinement, and the benefits to be gained by adhering to these problem-solving principles.

Our second goal was to write a book that would serve as a general introduction to programming, not just to programming language. Toward this end we have included examples that illustrate several major application areas of computer programming and that also describe important programming techniques that can be used effectively in many diverse programming situations. But a complete introduction to programming requires more than a description of application areas and programming techniques. Equally important is a consideration of the entire programming process that takes us from a problem statement to the finished product: a well-documented computer program that correctly carries out the task described in the problem statement. The approach we have taken toward achieving this objective is to consistently use the problem-solving methods introduced in Chapter 2, to introduce new programming principles as they can be appreciated in the context of the applications being considered, and to illustrate and reinforce these programming principles in the worked-out examples.

A few remarks are appropriate concerning the order in which we have introduced the elements of QuickBASIC. The INPUT statement (Chapter 5) is introduced early, before the READ and DATA statements, to emphasize the interactive nature of QuickBASIC. (The introductory material on the READ and DATA statements in Chapter 11 requires only the PRINT, DO, and LET statements.) In Chapter 6, the DO and LOOP statements are used to introduce program loops. (Loops coded with the FOR and NEXT statements are taken up in Chapter 9.) Chapter 7 expands upon the description of the PRINT statement given in Chapter 3 and introduces the PRINT USING statement. These output statements are introduced early so that well-formatted output can be illustrated in the examples and can be produced while carrying out all subsequent programming exercises. The IF and Block IF selection statements are introduced in Sections 8.1 through 8.4. The QuickBASIC statements described through Section 8.4 are taken up first because they are needed to write meaningful interactive programs. The SELECT CASE structure (Section 8.5) provides an alternative to the IF statement not allowed in previous versions of the BASIC language.

The SUB and FUNCTION procedures described in Chapter 12 represent a major improvement over previous versions of BASIC. Section 12.1, which describes SUB procedures with no parameters, can be taken up any time after the LET, PRINT, READ, and DO statements. So that a person using this book will not be tied down to the order we have chosen, the introductory material for the remaining QuickBASIC statements is presented in a way that allows these statements to be taken up in any order after Chapter 12.

■ *Acknowledgments*

A very special thanks goes to Patricia Shea, our typist, proofreader, debugger, and general assistant. Her fifteen years of cheerful cooperation are greatly appreciated. Finally, we are happy to acknowledge the fine cooperation of the staff at Brooks/Cole Publishing Company, and we especially thank Mike Sugarman, Computer Science Editor, for encouraging us to write this book.

Robert J. Bent
George C. Sethares

Contents

1
IBM Personal Computer Systems

Any electronic device that can receive, store, process, and transmit data (information)—and can also receive and store the instructions to process these data—is called a **computer.** Photo 1.1 shows an IBM personal computer (PC) with its cover removed. The *system board* shown in the photo contains many miniaturized electronic and magnetic devices, together with the circuitry interconnecting them. The system board is the computer component that can receive, store, process, and transmit data.

A **computer system** is any group of interrelated components that includes a computer as one of its principal elements. Photo 1.2 shows a complete IBM personal computer system that includes an IBM computer with two disk storage units, a detachable keyboard, and a video display screen.

A computer system has the ability to store large quantities of data, to process these data at very fast rates, and to present the results of this processing in ways that are meaningful to the task at hand. If the task is to prepare a payroll, for example, employee data will be transmitted to the computer, the computer will process these data to calculate relevant wage statistics, and the results will be presented in printed form, possibly including paychecks. This payroll example illustrates the three principal tasks involved in every computer application: data must be presented to the computer **(INPUT),** data must be processed **(PROCESS),** and results must be presented in a useful way **(OUTPUT)** (see Figure 1.1).

Today, computer applications are so numerous and widespread that it is not always easy to distinguish between tasks that we should assign to computers and tasks that we should do ourselves. Certainly, tasks requiring large numbers of numerical calculations are best delegated to computers. Computers carry out thousands of calculations per second without error; we perform but a few per minute—even with a calculator in hand—and must exercise the greatest care and concentration to avoid errors. The very first computers were built precisely for such tasks (see Photo 1.3).

Applications of the computer, however, are no longer restricted to numerical tasks. Modern computers are useful tools in many application areas that have nothing to do with arithmetic. Word processing and communications systems, for example, allow for easy storage, retrieval, editing, and transmission of most types of correspondence (see Photo 1.4).

In our rapidly changing technological society, an understanding of computers and how they are used is becoming more and more essential. But the purpose of this chapter is not to convince you that a computer can "do" many things nor even to indicate the computer applications that you will be able to carry out after completing this book. Rather, the objectives of this chapter are to introduce you to the types of computing equipment that you may encounter, to describe what a computer program is, and to introduce certain terminology that is helpful when talking about computers.

System board

Power supply

Disk storage unit

Photo 1.1   IBM Personal Computer with cover removed. *(Courtesy of IBM Corporation.)*

Photo 1.2   An IBM Personal Computer system. *(Courtesy of IBM Corporation.)*

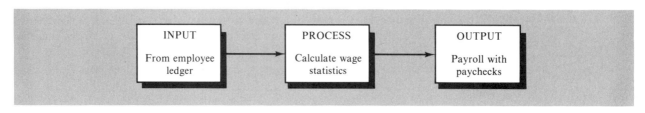

INPUT	PROCESS	OUTPUT
From employee ledger	Calculate wage statistics	Payroll with paychecks

Figure 1.1   An INPUT-PROCESS-OUTPUT diagram.

Photo 1.3   Presentation of the first UNIVAC I (first-generation UNIVersal Automatic Computer) to the Smithsonian Institution, where portions of it are now on display. Designed by John W. Mauchly and J. Presper Eckert, Jr., and built under their direction by Remington Rand Corporation, the UNIVAC I was the first commercially available electronic computer and the first computer to be used for business data processing. Unlike its predecessors, which were built for specific scientific applications, the UNIVAC I was a general-purpose computer. Early applications included the tabulation of U.S. census data—the first UNIVAC I was delivered to the U.S. Bureau of the Census in 1951—and the analysis of election returns during the 1952 presidential election. The early projection of Dwight D. Eisenhower as the winner over Adlai E. Stevenson was an impressive feat that greatly increased public awareness of computers. *(Courtesy of Sperry Corporation.)*

■ 1.1 Computer Hardware

Central to every computer system is an electronic computer whose principal function is to process data. The computer component that does this is called the **central processing unit (CPU).** The IBM's CPU is called a **microprocessor** because of its microminiaturized circuitry. The CPU contains an **arithmetic and logic unit (ALU),** consisting of circuitry that performs all the arithmetic and logical operations the computer was designed to carry out. The PC's ALU is an *integrated circuit* about the size of a fingernail and is housed in a special protective container located on the system board.* Computers such as the PC, whose CPUs are microprocessors, are called **microcomputers.**

In addition to the CPU, every computer has a **memory unit** that can store data for processing. This memory unit consists of thousands of memory locations, each with its own

---

*An integrated circuit (IC) is an electronic circuit that has been etched into a small, thin wafer of a glasslike substance, such as silicon. A single IC less than a square inch in area can contain several thousand distinct but interconnected electronic components, such as transistors and diodes.

Photo 1.4 Data terminals have replaced the typewriter as the standard office tool. With modern word processing systems, letters, memos, reports, and even entire books can be typed at terminal keyboards for transmission to a computer, which automatically stores the information on high-speed disk storage devices. The information can later be used in many ways. It can be displayed for reading on a video screen, modified by typing changes at the keyboard, formatted for output by typing special editing codes, and transmitted to an output device to obtain printed copy. If the word processing system is part of a communications system, the information can also be transmitted to other locations. *(Courtesy of Texas Instruments.)*

address. The term **random access memory (RAM)** is used when referring to a computer's memory. This term indicates that data can be obtained from or transmitted to any memory storage unit by specifying its address. The PC's RAM consists of ICs placed on the system board. It is *volatile* memory—that is, when you turn the power off, everything stored in RAM is lost. [The term **read only memory (ROM)** refers to computer memory that can be accessed but not changed. ROM is not volatile.]

Fortunately, you don't have to understand how a computer stores and processes data to make it work for you. The circuitry in a computer is not unlike that in an ordinary pocket calculator, and all who have used calculators know that no knowledge of their circuitry is needed to use them.

Data must be transmitted to the computer (*input*), and results of the processing must be returned (*output*). Devices that transfer data to and from a computer are called **input** and **output (I/O) devices.** As you learn computer programming on the PC, you are likely to encounter the following I/O devices, which serve as the principal means of communication between you and the PC:

Keyboard and **video display screen** (Photo 1.2): You transmit information to the computer simply by typing it at the keyboard, and the computer transmits the results back to you by displaying them on the video screen.

Printers: A printer serves only as an output device. A single printer can be used as the output device for many PCs.

Modern computer systems are equipped with memory storage devices other than the main memory unit. They are called **external** (or **secondary**) **storage devices** because, unlike the memory unit, they are not part of the computer. The following external storage devices are used with personal computers:

Disk storage units: Information is stored on rotating **disks** that resemble phonograph records. The disks have no grooves, however; the data are stored as sequences of magnetized spots appearing on concentric circles. Disk units (also called drives) are **random access devices;** as with RAM, the term **random access** indicates that the data stored on any part of

Photo 1.5   A $5\frac{1}{4}$-inch disk being inserted into an IBM PC disk unit. *(Courtesy of Frank Keillor.)*

a disk can be accessed directly without having to read through the entire disk to find the desired data. Your PC will have either a $3\frac{1}{2}$- or $5\frac{1}{4}$-inch disk drive. Photo 1.5 shows a disk being inserted into a $5\frac{1}{4}$-inch drive. These $5\frac{1}{4}$-inch disks are called floppy disks because they are flexible. Your PC may also come with a hard (not flexible) disk that is not removable and that can store very large quantities of data.

Cassette tape units: Information is stored on magnetic tapes (cassettes) as sequences of magnetized "spots" by using an ordinary cassette tape recorder. Data are "read" from a tape sequentially until the desired data are found. For this reason, tape units are called **sequential access devices.** Today, PCs rarely use tape units. Disk units have greater storage capacity, allow much faster access to data, and are now affordable.

Video display units, printers, tape units, disk units, and all other mechanical and electrical devices other than the computer itself are referred to as **computer peripherals.** The computer and all peripherals constitute the **hardware** of the computer system. Figure 1.2 illustrates the flow of information between a computer and its peripherals.

■ 1.2 Computer Software

The physical components, or hardware, of a computer system are inanimate objects. They cannot prepare a payroll or perform any other task, however simple, without human assistance. This assistance is given in the form of instructions to the computer. A sequence of such instructions is called a **computer program,** and a person who composes these instructions is called a **programmer.**

The precise form that instructions to a computer must take depends on the computer system being used. **BASIC** (Beginner's All-purpose Symbolic Instruction Code) is a carefully constructed English-like language used for writing computer programs.* **Microsoft**® **QuickBASIC**™ is an extended version of BASIC used with many computers, including IBM and IBM compatible computers. Instructions in the BASIC language are designed to

---

*BASIC was developed at Dartmouth College by John G. Kemeny and Thomas E. Kurtz.

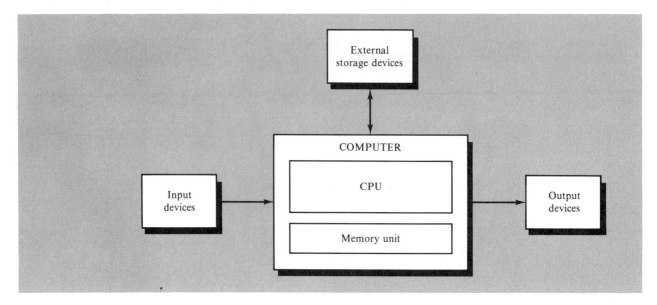

Figure 1.2   Flow of information through a computer system.

be understood by people as well as by the computer. Even the uninitiated will understand the meaning of this simple QuickBASIC program:

```
LET A=123
LET B=290
PRINT A+B
END
```

A computer is an electronic device, and it understands an instruction such as LET A = 123 in a very special way. An electronic device can distinguish between two electrical or magnetic states. Consider, for instance, an ordinary on/off switch for a light fixture. When the switch is in the "on" position, current is allowed to flow and the light bulb glows. If we denote the "on" position by the number 1 and the "off" position by the number 0, we can say that the instruction 1 causes the bulb to glow and the instruction 0 causes it not to glow. In like manner, we can envision a machine with two switches whose positions are denoted by the four codes 00, 01, 10, and 11, such that each of these four codes causes a different event to occur. It is this ability to distinguish between two distinct states that has led to the development of modern computers. Indeed, modern computers are still based on this principle. For example, each memory location in the PC's RAM can store a sequence of 0s and 1s, and one or more such sequences can be used to represent either data (in coded form) or instructions to the PC's processing unit.* These instructions are called the computer's *machine language.* Although the PC's hardware understands only these machine instructions, you will not be required to write programs in machine language. Your personal computer comes with a **translator,** which automatically translates your QuickBASIC instructions into equivalent machine language instructions that are then executed by the computer. There are two different types of translators: **interpreters** and **compilers.** An *interpreter* translates an instruction into machine code each time the instruction is to be carried out; a *compiler* translates an entire program into machine code only once.

Your QuickBASIC system may allow you to choose between an interpreter and a compiler. The interpreter is easier to use and is preferred for programs that will have limited use. If your system allows you to use QuickBASIC's compiler, you might consider using it when you write a program that will be used many times.

---

*The digits 0 and 1 are called *bits,* an acronym for "binary digit." The PC uses a sequence of eight bits, called a *byte,* to store each letter or character appearing in a program.

Photo 1.6 IBM PC system in an office setting. *(Courtesy of Stephen Barth.)*

Interpreters and compilers are themselves computer programs. They are called **systems programs** because they are an integral part of the computer system itself. The QuickBASIC programs in this book, as well as the programs you will write, are called **applications programs.** They are not an integral part of the computer system, so they are not called systems programs. All computer programs, both systems programs and applications programs, are called **computer software.**

In addition to the QuickBASIC translator, your system contains other systems programs. The most important of these are programs that allow you to use disk units as external storage devices. These include programs to store information on disks, to retrieve any infor-

Photo 1.7 IBM PC system in an educational setting. *(Courtesy of Frank Keillor.)*

mation previously stored on a disk, and to perform several other useful tasks involving disk units. Together, all systems programs designed to carry out disk operations are called the **disk operating system (DOS).**

The emergence of computer science as a new discipline has been accompanied by a proliferation of new words and expressions. Although they are useful for talking about computers, they are for the most part unnecessary if your objective is to learn a computer language such as QuickBASIC to help you solve problems. In our discussion of computer hardware and software, we have introduced only fundamental concepts and terminology. Even so, if this is your first exposure to computers, you may feel lost in this terminology. Don't be disheartened; much of the new vocabulary has already been introduced. You will become more familiar with it and recognize its usefulness as you study the material in the subsequent chapters. You will also find it helpful to reread this chapter after you have written a few computer programs.

■ *1.3 Review True-or-False Quiz*

1. Any electronic device that can process data is called a computer.   T   F
2. Input/output devices, external storage devices, and the central processing unit are called computer peripherals.   T   F
3. A computer whose central processing unit is a microprocessor is called a microcomputer.   T   F
4. The terms *microprocessor* and *integrated circuit* are used synonymously.   T   F
5. An automobile that uses a microprocessor to control the gas and air mixture is correctly referred to as a computer system.   T   F
6. Whatever information is stored in the PC's RAM is lost when the power to the PC is cut off.   T   F
7. There is a significant difference between memory units called RAM and memory units called ROM.   T   F
8. The terms *compiler* and *interpreter* are used synonymously.   T   F
9. A computer program written to solve a particular problem is called a systems program.   T   F
10. A computer system must contain at least one printer.   T   F
11. Disk storage units are called *random access devices* because information stored on a disk is accessed by randomly searching portions of the disk until the desired data are found.   T   F
12. The PC's disk operating system (DOS) is a computer system.   T   F

2
Problem Solving: Top-Down Approach

A computer program consists of a sequence of instructions to the computer. These instructions describe a step-by-step process for carrying out a specified task. Such a process is called an **algorithm.** Algorithms have been with us since antiquity: the familiar division algorithm was known and used in ancient Greece; the activities of bookkeepers have always been guided by algorithms (an algorithm to determine a tax assessment, an algorithm to calculate a depletion allowance, and so on); even the instructions for assembling a child's new toy are often given in algorithmic form.

Since a computer program describes an algorithm, the process of writing computer programs can be equated to the process of discovering algorithms. For this reason, an understanding of what is, and what is not, an algorithm is indispensable to a programmer.

In Section 2.1, we define the term *algorithm* and illustrate, with simple examples, the method of designing algorithms called the top-down approach to problem solving. In Section 2.2, we define the term *variable,* an essential concept in programming, and illustrate the use of variables in writing algorithms.

■ 2.1 Algorithms

An algorithm is a prescribed set of well-defined rules and processes for carrying out a specified task in a finite number of steps. Here is an algorithm giving instructions for completing a financial transaction at a drive-in teller port:

a. Press the call button.
b. Remove the carrier from the tray.
c. Place your transaction inside the carrier.
d. Replace the carrier.
e. Press the send button.
f. When the carrier returns, remove the transaction.
g. Replace the carrier.

To see that these seven steps describe an algorithm, we must verify that each step is well defined and that the process stops in a finite number of steps. For example, Step (a) requires that there be only one call button, Step (b) requires that there be but one tray containing a single carrier, and Step (f) requires that the carrier be returned. Having verified that each step is well defined, and having noted that the process stops after a transaction has been completed, we can be fairly confident that the seven steps do indeed describe an algorithm for the specified task.

The drive-in teller example illustrates the following three properties of an algorithm:

1. Each step must be well defined—that is, unambiguous.
2. The process must halt in a finite number of steps.
3. The process must do what is claimed.

The examples in this section are intended to help you understand what an algorithm is and to allow you to gain some practice with the process of designing algorithms. In keeping with current terminology, we will refer to this process as the **problem-solving process.** In each example, we begin with a description of the task to be performed (the **problem statement**), illustrate the essential steps in the problem-solving process, and end with an algorithm for the specified task.

EXAMPLE 1   ***Let's find an algorithm to produce a report showing the name, annual salary, and year-end bonus for each salaried employee in a firm. Employees are to receive 2% of their annual salary or $400, whichever is larger.***

To produce a bonus report, we will need to know the names and salaries of the employees. (These data are called the *input.*) To keep things as simple as possible, we'll assume that all names and annual salaries are contained in an employee ledger and are obtained simply by reading the ledger.

Since our algorithm is to produce a year-end bonus report (called the *output*), we must decide upon a format for this report. A quick reading of the problem statement suggests a report such as the following:

Year-end bonuses (1992)

Name	Salary	Bonus
Susan Andrade	27,000	540
Lester Barkley	16,500	400
.	.	.
.	.	.

To help us design a detailed algorithm to produce our bonus report, we'll begin with the following short algorithm that simply identifies what tasks must be performed:

a. Write the title and column headings for the bonus sheet.
b. Read the ledger to determine and fill in the name, salary, and bonus for each employee.

To carry out Step (a), a payroll clerk would simply copy the information from the output format already specified. To carry out Step (b), a clerk might proceed as follows:

b1. Open the employee ledger.
b2. Read the next employee's name and salary.
b3. Determine the employee's bonus.
b4. Write the employee's name, salary, and bonus on the bonus sheet.
b5. If all bonuses have not been determined, return to Step (b2).
b6. Close the ledger.

It is not difficult to see that Steps (b1) to (b6) constitute an algorithm for Step (b). Each step is well defined, and because a business can employ only a finite number of people, the algorithm will terminate in a finite number of steps. Moreover, if this algorithm is followed—without error—all employee bonuses will be determined as specified.

Although the algorithm does what was asked, the process could be made more specific by including more detail in Step (b3). Recalling the method specified for calculating bonus amounts, we can substitute the following for Step (b3):

b3.1. Multiply the salary by 0.02 to obtain a tentative bonus.
b3.2. If the tentative bonus is less than $400, set the bonus to $400; otherwise, make the bonus equal to the tentative bonus.

Making this change, or *refinement,* we obtain the following more detailed algorithm for Step (b):

b1. Open the employee ledger.
b2. Read the next employee's name and salary.
b3.1. Multiply the salary by 0.02 to obtain a tentative bonus.
b3.2. If the tentative bonus is less than $400, set the bonus to $400; otherwise, make the bonus equal to the tentative bonus.
b4. Write the employee's name, salary, and bonus on the bonus sheet.
b5. If all bonuses have not been determined, return to Step (b2).
b6. Close the ledger.

Our final detailed algorithm consists of eight steps—Step (a) followed by this seven-step algorithm for carrying out Step (b).

REMARK

In this example, we started with a problem statement describing the task to be carried out (produce a year-end bonus report) and ended with an algorithm describing how to accomplish this task. The steps you take while designing an algorithm are called a **problem analysis.** For simple problems, a description of the input and output may lead directly to a final algorithm. For more complicated problems, a thorough analysis of alternative approaches to a solution may be required. In any case, the term *problem analysis* refers to the process of designing a suitable algorithm.

The method used to design an algorithm for Example 1 illustrates three important principles of problem solving:

1. Begin by describing the input (information needed to carry out the specified task) and the output (the results that must be obtained). In the example, we described the input as salary information to be read from the employee ledger and the output as a table showing the names, salaries, and bonus amounts for the employees. An essential first step in the problem-solving process is to read and understand the problem statement. It is unlikely that a correct algorithm will be found if the task to be performed is not understood exactly. *Giving a clear and precise description of the input and output is an effective way to acquire an understanding of a problem statement.*

2. Identify individual subtasks that must be performed while carrying out the specified task. In Example 1, we identified the following two subtasks:

a. Write the title and column headings for the bonus sheet.
b. Read the ledger to determine and fill in the name, salary, and bonus for each employee.

If a complicated task can be broken down into simpler, more manageable subtasks, the job of writing an algorithm can often be simplified significantly: you simply describe the order in which the subtasks are to be carried out. This was especially easy to do in Example 1—simply carry out Subtask (a) followed by Subtask (b). The process of breaking down a task into simpler subtasks is called **problem segmentation** or **modularization**—the subtasks are sometimes called **modules.** As in Example 1, the details of how to carry out these modules can be worked out after an algorithm has been found.

3. If more details are needed in an algorithm, include the additional details separately for each step. In Example 1, we started with a two-step algorithm:

a. Write the title and column headings for the bonus sheet.
b. Read the ledger to determine and fill in the name, salary, and bonus for each employee.

Next, we include more detail in Step (b) by breaking it down into these six steps:

b1. Open the employee ledger.
b2. Read the next employee's name and salary.
b3. Determine the employee's bonus.
b4. Write the employee's name, salary, and bonus on the bonus sheet.

b5. If all bonuses have not been determined, return to Step (b2).
b6. Close the ledger.

Finally, we include more detail in the algorithm by rewriting Step (b3) as follows:

b3.1. Multiply the salary by 0.02 to obtain a tentative bonus.
b3.2. If the tentative bonus is less than $400, set the bonus to $400; otherwise, make the bonus equal to the tentative bonus.

The important thing to notice is that we introduced details into the algorithm by refining the steps separately—that is, by breaking down the individual steps one at a time—and not by combining steps or otherwise changing the algorithm. This method of designing a detailed algorithm is called the **method of stepwise refinement.** You begin with a simple algorithm that contains few details but that you know is correct. If necessary, you refine one or more of the steps to obtain a more detailed algorithm. If even more detail is needed, you refine one or more of the steps in the derived algorithm. By repeating this process of stepwise refinement, you can obtain an algorithm with whatever detail is needed. Moreover, however complicated the final algorithm, you can be sure that it is correct simply by knowing that you started with a correct algorithm and that each step was refined correctly.

The approach to problem solving used in Example 1 is called the **top-down approach** to problem solving or the **top-down design** of algorithms. The expression *top-down* comes from using the methods of modularization and stepwise refinement. You start at the top (the problem statement), break that task down into simpler tasks, then break those tasks into even simpler ones, and continue the process, all the while knowing how the tasks at each level of refinement combine, until the tasks at the lowest (final) level contain whatever detail is desired. The advantages to be gained by adhering to the three problem-solving principles of the top-down approach will become more evident as you work through the examples and problems in this book. The following example should help you better understand these three principles and their application.

EXAMPLE 2   *A wholesale firm keeps a list of the items it sells in a card file. For each item, there is a single card containing a descriptive item name, the number of units in stock (this can be zero), the number of the warehouse in which the item is stored, and certain other information that will not concern us. Our task is to prepare a list of out-of-stock items for each warehouse.*

PROBLEM ANALYSIS   The problem statement says that a separate list of out-of-stock items is needed for each warehouse. Thus, we will need to know the warehouse numbers. Let's assume we are told there are three warehouses numbered 127, 227, and 327. With this information, we can include these numbers as input rather than reading through the entire card file to determine them. We can now specify the input and output for our algorithm:

Input: Warehouse numbers 127, 227, and 327.
Card file: one card for each item.

Output: Three reports formatted as follows:

WAREHOUSE 127
(Out-of-stock items)

Hammers—Model 2960
Hammers—Model 3375
Saws—Model 1233
:
:

WAREHOUSE 227
(Out-of-stock items)
:
:

WAREHOUSE 327
(Out-of-stock items)
:
:

Having given a precise description of the input and output, we should determine what subtask or subtasks must be performed. The problem statement specifies that three reports are to be produced, one for each warehouse. If we arrange things so that reports are produced one at a time (this is the common practice when using computers), we can use the same procedure for each report. Specifically, for each warehouse number W, we will carry out the following subtask (named R for report):

Subtask R. Prepare the report for warehouse W.

Of course, we will need to include details describing how to carry out this subtask. But even without these details, we can write a simple algorithm that obviously is correct:

THE ALGORITHM

a. Assign 127 to W.
b. Carry out Subtask R.
c. Assign 227 to W.
d. Carry out Subtask R.
e. Assign 327 to W.
f. Carry out Subtask R.

Notice that Subtask R specifies that a report is to be prepared. As in Example 1, we can break this subtask down into two subordinate subtasks R1 and R2 as follows:

R1. Write the report header for warehouse W.
R2. Read through the card file to complete the report.

At this point, we should recognize that Step R1 requires no additional details—the output specification shows how the report header should be formatted. We should, however, include more details in Step R2. In the following algorithm for Subtask R, Steps R2.1 to R2.4 show one way to carry out Step R2:

 R1. Write the report header for warehouse W.
R2.1. Turn to the first card.
R2.2. Read the warehouse number (call it N) and the units-on-hand figure (call it U).
R2.3. If N = W and U = 0, read the item name and write it on the report.
R2.4. If there is another card, turn to it and continue with Step R2.2.

Our final algorithm for the given problem statement consists of two parts: the original six-step algorithm [Steps (a)–(f)] that tells us when (but not how) to carry out Subtask R and the five-step algorithm (Steps R1, R2.1–R2.4) that shows us how Subtask R can be accomplished.

REMARK

Let's review the problem analysis carried out in this example:

Input/output specification. Our attempt to give a precise description of the input and output led us to include the warehouse numbers 127, 227, and 327 as input. As a consequence, the final algorithm is simpler than what would have been obtained had we begun by reading the entire card file just to determine the warehouse numbers.

Modularization. Our attempt to identify subtasks led us to conclude that there was but one major subtask, namely,

Subtask R. Prepare the report for warehouse W.

By using this subtask, it was easy to write an algorithm [Steps (a)–(f)] that lacked only the details needed to carry out Subtask R.

Stepwise refinement. Our next job was to show how to carry out Subtask R. We began by breaking it down into these two subordinate subtasks:

R1. Write the report header for warehouse W.
R2. Read through the card file to complete the report.

Notice that this two-step refinement of Subtask R represents an application of the principle of modularization applied to Subtask R. At this point we recognized that only Step R2 was lacking in details. We supplied these details by writing a short four-step algorithm (Steps R2.1–R2.4) for Step R2.

■ 2.2 Variables

Algorithms can often be stated clearly if symbols are used to denote certain values. Symbols are especially helpful when used to denote values that may change during the process of performing the steps in an algorithm. The symbols W, N, and U used in Example 2 illustrate this practice.

A value that can change during a process is called a **variable.** A symbol used to denote such a variable is the *name* of the variable. Thus W, N, and U in Example 2 are names of variables. It is common practice, however, to refer to the *symbol* as being the variable itself, rather than just its name. For instance, Step (a) of the algorithm for Example 2 says to assign 127 to W. Certainly this is less confusing than saying "assign 127 to the variable whose name is W."

The following two examples further illustrate the use of variables in algorithms.

EXAMPLE 3　　*Let's find an algorithm to determine the largest number in a list of numbers.*

PROBLEM ANALYSIS

Input:　　A list of numbers.

Output:　　The largest number in the list.

One way to determine the largest number in a list of numbers is to read the numbers one at a time, remembering only the largest of those already read. To help us give a precise description of this process, let's use two symbols:

LGST to denote the largest of the numbers already read
NUM to denote the number currently being read

The following algorithm can now be written:

a. Read the first number and denote it by LGST.
b. Read the next number and denote it by NUM.
c. If NUM is larger than LGST, assign NUM to LGST.
d. If all numbers have not been read, go to Step (b).
e. Write the value of LGST and stop.

To verify this algorithm for the list of numbers

　　　4, 5, 3, 6, 6, 2, 1, 8, 7, 3

we simply proceed step by step through the algorithm, always keeping track of the latest values of LGST and NUM. An orderly way to do this is to complete an assignment table, as follows:

Algorithm step	LGST	NUM	Output
a	4		
b		5	
c	5		
b		3	
b		6	
c	6		
b		6	
b		2	
b		1	
b		8	
c	8		
b		7	
b		3	
e			8

REMARK 1

If the numbers were written on a sheet of paper, you could look them over and select the largest. This process is heuristic, however, and does not constitute an algorithm.* To see that this is so, imagine many hundreds of numbers written on a large sheet of paper. In this case, attempting to select the largest simply by looking over the numbers could easily result in an error. What we need is an orderly process that will ensure that the largest number is selected. Examining numbers one at a time, as in this algorithm, is such an orderly process.

REMARK 2

The task of finding the largest number in a list of numbers occurs as a subtask in many programming problems. When confronted with such a problem, you can use Steps (a)–(d) of the given algorithm to carry out the subtask. Should you need to find the smallest rather than the largest number, simply change the word *larger* in Step (c) to *smaller.*

EXAMPLE 4

Find an algorithm to prepare a depreciation schedule for a delivery van that costs $18,000, has a salvage value of $2,000, and has a useful life of 5 years. Use the straight-line method.

[The straight-line method assumes that the value of the van will decrease by one-fifth of $16,000 (cost − salvage value) during each of the 5 years.]

PROBLEM ANALYSIS

For each year, let's agree to write one line showing the year, the depreciation allowance for that year, the cumulative depreciation (sum of yearly depreciations to that point), and the book value (cost − cumulative depreciation) at the end of the year. We can now describe the input and output.

Input: The purchased item (van), its cost ($18,000), salvage value ($2,000), and useful life (5 years).

---

*A **heuristic process** is one involving exploratory methods. Solutions to problems are discovered by a continual evaluation of the progress made toward the final result. For instance, suppose you come upon an old map indicating that a treasure is buried in the Black Hills. You may be able to work out a plan that you know will lead to the location shown on the map. *That's an algorithm.* However, suppose you can find no such plan. Determined to find the location or to verify that the map is fake, you decide on a first step in your search, with no idea of what the next step will be. *That's exploratory.* Carrying out this first step may suggest a second step, or it may lead you nowhere, in which case you would try something else. Continuing in this manner, you may eventually find the location, or you may determine that the map is a fake. But it is also possible that the search will end only when you quit. Whatever the outcome, the process is heuristic. Someone else using this process will undoubtedly carry out entirely different steps and perhaps reach a different conclusion.

Output: A report formatted as follows:

Depreciation value—van

	Cost: $18,000 Life: 5 years		Salvage: $2,000 Method: Straight-Line	
Year	Depreciation allowance	Cumulative depreciation	Book value
1993	$3,200	$3,200	$14,800
1994	3,200	6,400	11,600
⋮	⋮	⋮	⋮

It is not difficult to write an algorithm to produce this report if we leave out the details.

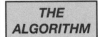

a. Look up the current year, item name, cost, salvage value, and useful life.
b. Write the report title and column headers.
c. Determine and write the table values.

Steps (a) and (b) require no additional details—they are explained in the input/output description. To carry out Step (c) by hand, you might proceed as follows:

1. Determine the depreciation allowance for 1 year.
2. Subtract the depreciation allowance from the book value (initially the cost).
3. Add the depreciation amount to the cumulative depreciation (initially zero).
4. Write one line showing the year, the depreciation allowance for that year, the cumulative depreciation, and the book value at the end of the year.
5. Return to Step (2) until the schedule is complete.

To allow us to write a concise, detailed algorithm describing how to carry out Step (c), let's choose variable names to denote the various values of interest.

$$\text{ITEM} = \text{name of purchased item}$$
$$\text{BV} = \text{book value (the initial book value is the cost)}$$
$$\text{SV} = \text{salvage value}$$
$$\text{Y} = \text{useful life in years}$$
$$\text{D} = \text{depreciation allowance for 1 year } [D = (BV - SV)/Y]$$
$$\text{C} = \text{cumulative depreciation (initially zero)}$$
$$\text{CY} = \text{current year}$$

In the following detailed algorithm, Steps (c1) to (c7) tell how to accomplish Step (c). [Note that Step (a) has been changed only by the use of variable names in place of descriptive names.]

a. Look up (input) values for CY, ITEM, BV, SV, and Y.
b. Write the report title and column headers.
c1. Start with $C = 0$.
c2. Calculate $D = (BV - SV)/Y$.
c3. Subtract D from BV.
c4. Add D to C.
c5. Write one line showing CY, D, C, and BV.
c6. Add 1 to CY.
c7. Return to Step (c3) until the schedule is complete.

For the input specified in the problem statement and with 1993 as the current year, this algorithm leads to the following depreciation schedule:

Depreciation schedule—van

	Cost: $18,000 Life: 5 years		Salvage: $2,000 Method: Straight-Line	
Year	**Depreciation allowance**	**Cumulative depreciation**	**Book value**	
1993	$3,200	$3,200	$14,800	
1994	3,200	6,400	11,600	
1995	3,200	9,600	8,400	
1996	3,200	12,800	5,200	
1997	3,200	16,000	2,000	

REMARK

It is not often that a problem statement exactly describes the task to be carried out. Problem statements are written in a natural language, such as English, and thus are subject to the ambiguities inherent in natural languages. Moreover, they are written by people, which means that they are subject to human oversight and error. Since an algorithm describes a precise, unambiguous process for carrying out a task, the task to be performed must be clearly understood. If it appears ambiguous, the ambiguities must be resolved. If it appears that one thing is being asked but another is actually desired, the difference must be resolved. For instance, the problem statement in the present example asks for only a very limited algorithm (a book value of $18,000, a salvage value of $2,000, and a useful life of 5 years) when what is really desired is the more general algorithm that has a wider application.

■ 2.3 Problems

Problems 1–4 refer to the following algorithm for completing an invoice:

   a. Let AMOUNT = 0.
   b. Read QUANTITY and PRICE of an item.
   c. Add the product QUANTITY × PRICE to AMOUNT. $AMOUNT = QUANTITY \times PRICE + AMOUNT$
   d. If there is another item, go to Step (b); otherwise, continue with Step (e).
   e. If AMOUNT is greater than $500, subtract the product 0.05 × AMOUNT from AMOUNT.
   f. Record the value AMOUNT.
   g. Stop.

 1. What interpretation could be given to the product appearing in Step (e)?
 2. What purpose would you say is served by Step (e)?
 3. If the values (10, $3), (50, $8), and (25, $12) are read by Step (b), what value will be recorded by Step (f)?
 4. If the values (100, $2) and (50, $1) are read by Step (b), what value will be recorded by Step (f)?

Problems 5–8 refer to the following algorithm, which is intended for use by a payroll clerk as a preliminary step in the preparation of a payroll:

   a. Read the next time card.
   b. Let H = number of hours worked.
   c. If H is not greater than 32, assign 0 to G and B and go to Step (f); otherwise, continue with the next step.
   d. Evaluate 6 × (H − 32) and assign this value to both G and B.
   e. Let H = 32.
   f. Evaluate 4 × H and add this value to G.
   g. Write the values G and B on the time card.
   h. If there is another time card, go to Step (a); otherwise, stop.

 5. If the numbers of hours shown on the first four time cards are 20, 32, 40, and 45, respectively, what amounts will be written on these cards?
 6. What is the base hourly rate for each employee?
 7. What is the overtime rate?

   8. Explain Step (c).

In Problems 9–12, what will be printed when each algorithm is carried out?

   9. a. Let SUM = 0 and N = 1.
   b. Add N to SUM.
   c. Increase N by 1.
   d. If N ≤ 6, return to Step (b).
   e. Print the value SUM and stop.
   10. a. Let PROD = 1 and N = 1.
   b. Print the values N and PROD on one line.
   c. Increase N by 1.
   d. Multiply PROD by N.
   e. If N ≤ 5, return to Step (b).
   f. Print the values of N and PROD on one line.
   g. Stop.
   11. a. Let A = 1, B = 1, and F = 2.
   b. If F > 50, print the value F and stop.
   c. Assign the values of B and F to A and B, respectively.
   d. Evaluate A + B and assign this value to F.
   e. Return to Step (b).
   12. a. Let NUM = 56, SUM = 1, and D = 2.
   b. If D is a factor of NUM, add D to SUM and print D.
   c. Increase D by 1.
   d. If D ≤ NUM/2, return to Step (b).
   e. Print the value SUM and stop.

Explain why the step-by-step processes given in Problems 13 and 14 do not describe algorithms.

   13. a. Let SUM = 0 and N = 1.
   b. Add N to SUM.
   c. Divide N by 2.
   d. If SUM < 2, go to Step (b).
   e. Stop.
   14. a. Let N = 0.
   b. Increase N by 10.
   c. Divide N by 2.
   d. If N < 10, go to Step (b).
   e. Stop.

In Problems 15–24, write an algorithm to carry out each specified task.

   15. A retail store's monthly sales report shows, for each item, the cost, the sale price, and the number sold. Prepare a three-column report with the column headings ITEM, GROSS SALES, and INCOME.
   16. Each of several 3 × 5 cards contains an employee's name, social security number, job classification, and date hired. Prepare a report showing the names, job classifications, and complete years of service for employees who have been with the company for more than 10 years.
   17. A summary sheet of an investor's stock portfolio shows, for each stock, the corporation name, the number of shares owned, the current price, and the earnings as reported for the most recent year. Prepare a six-column report with the column headings CORP. NAME, NO. OF SHARES, PRICE, EARNINGS, EQUITY, and PRICE/EARNINGS. Use this formula:

   Equity = number of shares × price

   18. Each of several cards contains a single number. Determine the sum and the average of all the numbers. (Use a variable N to count how many cards are read and a variable SUM to keep track of the sum of numbers already read.)
   19. Each of several cards contains a single number. On each card, write the letter G if the number is greater than the average of all the numbers; otherwise, write the letter L. (You must read through the cards twice: once to find the average and again to determine whether to write the letter G or the letter L on the cards.)

20. A bank pays interest on savings accounts at an annual rate of R percent compounded monthly. Prepare a two-column report with the headings MONTH and BALANCE that shows how a single deposit of DEP dollars will grow, month by month, over the next three years. (If the balance at the beginning of a month is BAL dollars, the interest earned for that month is R/12 percent of BAL.)

21. Prepare a two-column report as described in Problem 20 for a newly opened savings account in which a person makes a deposit of DEP dollars at the beginning of each month for the next three years.

22. You are assigned the task of writing a book report. Your teacher has specified the subject area and you and the teacher must agree on the book to be read. Describe a process you could follow while completing the assignment. Begin with the selection of a book title and end with the task of handing in the final typewritten report. After you have finished, discuss whether your process describes an algorithm.

23. A local supermarket has installed a check validation machine. To use this service, a customer must have an identification card containing a magnetic strip and a four-digit code. Instructions showing how to insert the identification card into a special magnetic-strip reader appear on the front panel. To validate a check, a customer must present the identification card to the machine, enter the four-digit code, enter the amount of the check, and place the check, blank side toward the customer, in a clearly labeled punch unit. To begin this process, the CLEAR key must be pressed and, after each of the two entries has been made, the ENTER key must be pressed. Prepare an algorithm giving instructions for validating a check.

24. Write an algorithm describing the steps to be taken to cast a ballot in a national election. Assume that a person using this algorithm is a registered voter and has just entered the building in which voting is to take place. While in the voting booth, the voter should simply be instructed to vote. No instructions concerning the actual filling out of a ballot are to be given.

■ *2.4 Flowcharts*

The following diagram is a pictorial representation of a simple algorithm to recognize whether an input value is 5.

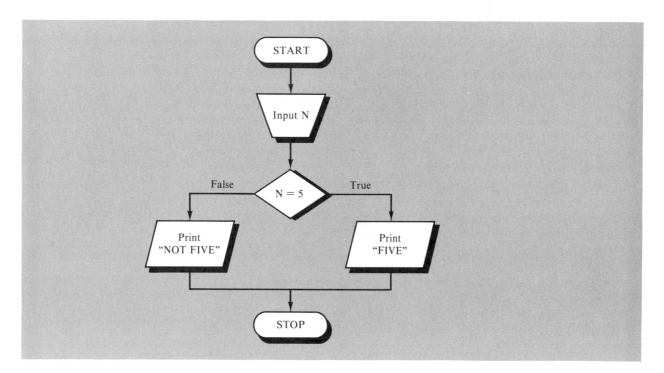

Such a pictorial representation of the sequence of steps in an algorithm (or in a computer program) is called a **flow diagram** or **flowchart.** Flowcharts serve two purposes:

1. Standard graphic symbols (called **flowchart symbols**) can be used to describe pictorially those processes that may be difficult to understand when described with words. In this book, we will give a written description of each QuickBASIC instruction; for the more complicated instructions, we will also include flow diagrams to help clarify the action caused by those instructions.

2. It is sometimes easier to discover how to carry out a complicated task (that is, to discover an algorithm) when flowcharts are used in addition to worded descriptions. This use of flowcharts is called **flowcharting.** Although many programmers feel that flowcharting has outlived its usefulness, there are situations in which the use of flow diagrams can help in the discovery of algorithms. If you have trouble writing an algorithm, you might find that a flow diagram is just what you need to get at the root of the problem.

Some of the components used to construct flowcharts are shown in Examples 5, 6, and 7. In each flowchart, arrows connect the different types of symbols to describe the action of an algorithm. It is the common practice to direct the flow either from top to bottom or from left to right, as in the examples. A brief description of the flowchart symbols* used in the example flowcharts is given in Table 2.1.

EXAMPLE 5 *Here is a flowchart that describes how to find the largest number in a list of numbers. The flowchart describes the same process as does the written algorithm in Example 3.*

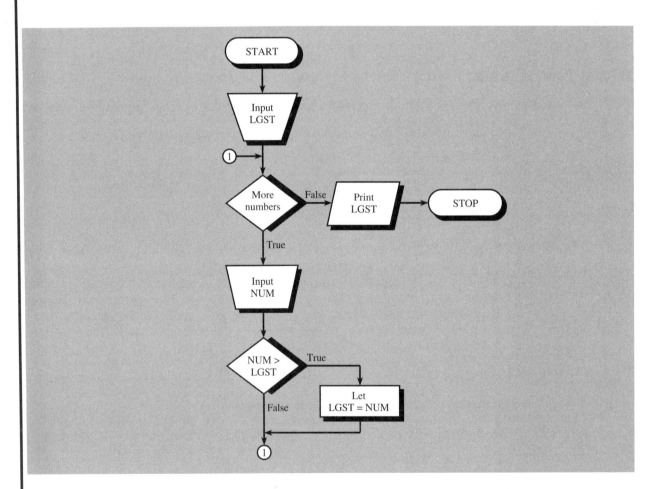

*The flowchart symbols used in this book are described in "Flowcharting with the ANSI Standard: A Tutorial," by Ned Chapin, *Computer Surveys,* Vol. 2, No. 2, June 1970. ANSI is an acronym for "American National Standards Institute."

Table 2.1   Flowchart Symbols

The symbol	Its use
(rounded rectangle)	To designate the start and end of an algorithm.
(rectangle)	To describe the assignment of values to variables. If the values are the results of simple computations, the formulas are included.
(trapezoid)	To describe the input. (In programming, this symbol is used for input values typed at the keyboard during the execution of a program. As shown in Chapter 11, a different symbol is used for input from some other source.)
(parallelogram)	To describe the output.
(diamond)	To designate a decision that is to be made.
(subprocess box)	To describe a subprocess to be carried out. (A flowchart that displays the steps in such a subprocess will often involve more than one of the other flowchart symbols.)
(circle)	A connector—used so that flow from one segment of a flowchart to another can be displayed and also to avoid drawing long lines.

EXAMPLE 6   *Here is a flowchart that describes how to prepare a three-column report showing the equivalent hourly and weekly pay rates (HRLY and WKLY) for the annual salary amounts of $15,000 to $25,000, in increments of $1,000. A normal work week is 40 hours.*

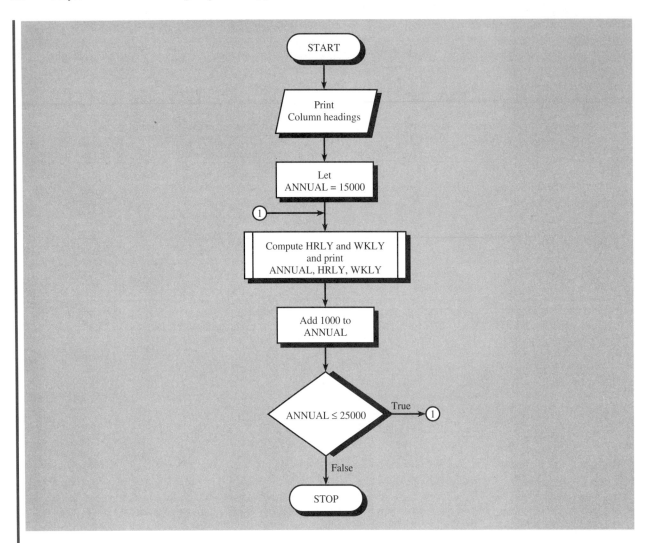

The design of the flowchart symbol

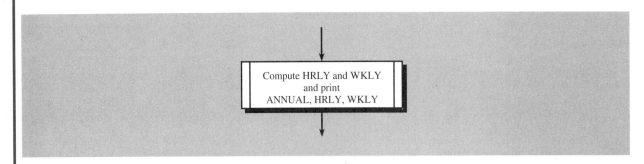

indicates a process that is somewhat more involved than a simple calculation or an input/output action. This one specifies computations and printing. To include details in the flowchart to show how to compute HRLY and WKLY, we would replace this flowchart symbol with a more detailed flow diagram, such as

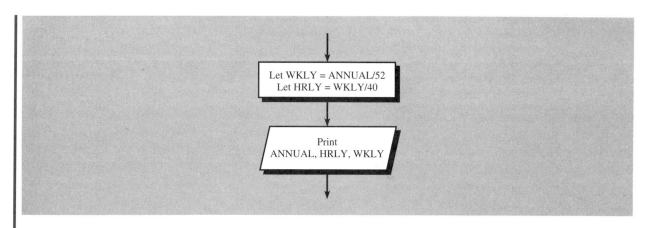

REMARK

When two or more actions are indicated in a single box, they are carried out from top to bottom.

EXAMPLE 7

Here is a flowchart for an algorithm to assign a letter grade to the variable G for any score S in the range from 0 to 100. Although this flowchart is somewhat more involved than the flowcharts in Examples 5 and 6, its action is not difficult to discern.

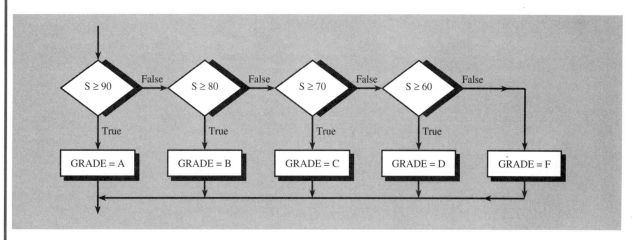

Notice that the comparison $S \geq 80$ is made only if $S \geq 90$ is false—that is, only if $S < 90$. Thus, the grade B is selected only if the value of S is a number from 80 to 90, but not 90. A similar remark applies to the comparisons $S \geq 70$ and $S \geq 60$.

■ 2.5 Structured Algorithms

The rest of this book concerns the discovery of algorithms for computer programs and how to write these algorithms in the QuickBASIC language. The process of writing a computer program that carries out the steps in an algorithm is called **coding the algorithm.**

The algorithms considered to this point take one of two forms:

1. An English-like step-by-step process describing how to carry out a specific task. The descriptions are kept brief by using a mixture of English and the programming language being used. The term **pseudocode** refers to such descriptions.

2. A flowchart displaying the steps to be carried out.

In the pseudocode form, the individual steps will often correspond to program segments. For example, the following three steps describe an algorithm for a computer program to calculate the sum of the squares of all integers from 1 to N.

a. Input N.
b. Calculate the sum S of the first N squares.
c. Print S and stop.

If you can see how to code Step (b), there is no need to include more detail in this algorithm. However, if it is not obvious to you how to code Step (b), you can try to rewrite the step in more detail. Here is one way to do this:

b1. Let S = 0.
b2. For J = 1, 2, 3, . . . , N, add J^2 to S.

This process of rewriting a single step in an algorithm to include more detail is an application of the *method of stepwise refinement* described in Section 2.1 and illustrated in Examples 1, 2, and 4.

The same process of refinement can be used with flowcharts. For the summing example just considered, you could have begun by writing the flowchart segment on the left:

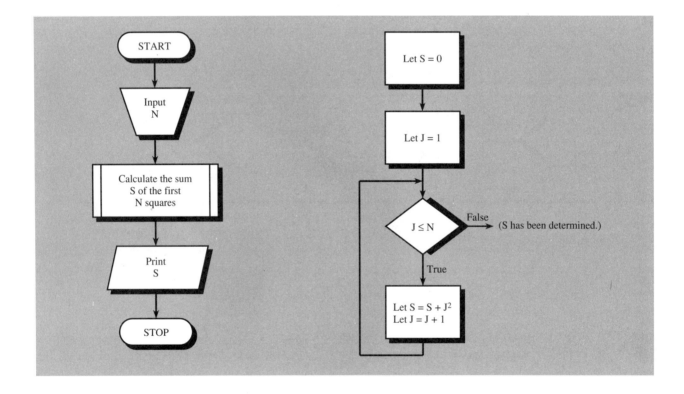

As before, if coding this flowchart is easy for you, there is no need to include more detail. However, if it is not clear how to code the box that calculates S, you should try to rewrite this step by including more detail. The flowchart segment on the right shows a way to do this.

When writing an algorithm, whether in pseudocode or as a flowchart (or in Quick-BASIC), you will encounter the following situations:

1. Two or more tasks are to be carried out in sequence (Figure 2.1).
2. One of two tasks is to be selected depending on a specified condition. It may be that one of the two tasks is to do nothing (Figure 2.2).
3. A task is to be carried out repeatedly (Figure 2.3).

Figure 2.1 Sequence.

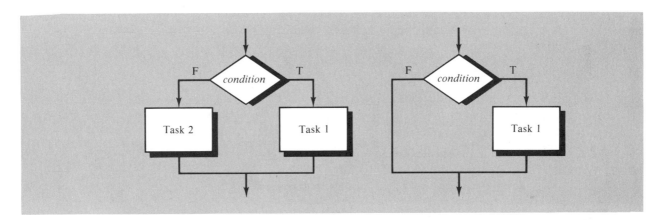

Figure 2.2 Selection.

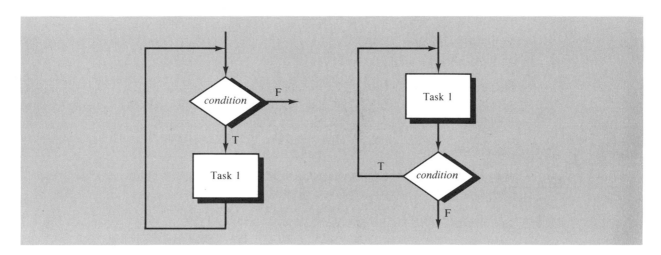

Figure 2.3 Repetition.

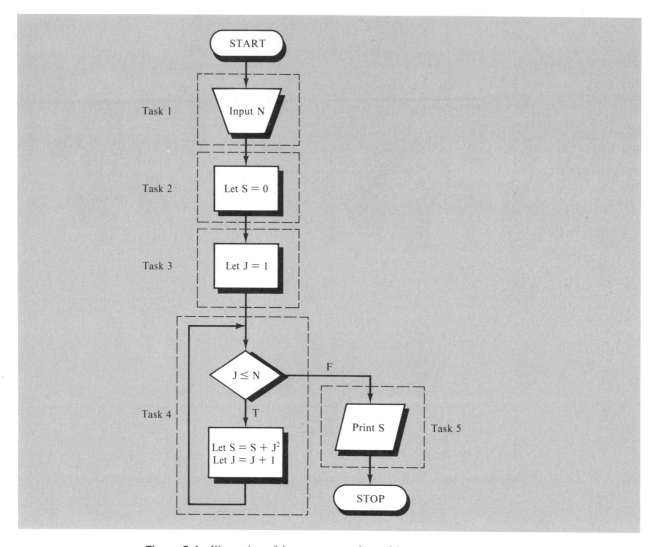

Figure 2.4 Illustration of the sequence and repetition constructs.

These three control structures are referred to as **structured programming constructs.** It has been shown that any algorithm can be written using only these constructs.* The diagram in Figure 2.4 shows how two of these constructs (*sequence* and *repetition*) are used in the flowchart to calculate the sum

$$S = 1^2 + 2^2 + 3^2 + \cdots + N^2$$

Note that Task 4 is an instance of the construct *repetition,* whereas the entire program is simply the *sequence* of Tasks 1 through 5 in that order. Note also that the task being repeated within Task 4 is a sequence of two variable assignments.

The diagram in Figure 2.5 shows that the flowchart of Example 7 involves only *selection* constructs:

Task 1 tests S ≥ 90 to select between GRADE = A and Task 2.
Task 2 tests S ≥ 80 to select between GRADE = B and Task 3.
Task 3 tests S ≥ 70 to select between GRADE = C and Task 4.
Task 4 tests S ≥ 60 to select between GRADE = D and GRADE = F.

* "Flow Diagrams, Turing Machines and Languages with Only Two Formation Rules," By Corrado Bohm and Giuseppe Jacopini, *Commun. ACM,* 9 (May 1966), pp. 366–371.

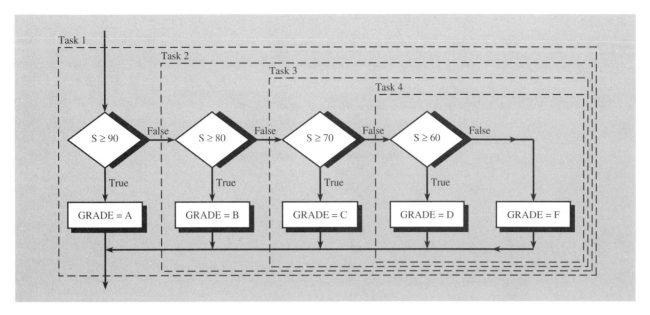

Figure 2.5 Illustration of selection constructs.

Algorithms written using only the constructs *sequence, selection,* and *repetition* are called **structured algorithms.** The process of writing such algorithms is called **structured programming,** and the resulting programs are called **structured programs.**

Notice that each of the three constructs has exactly one entry point and exactly one exit point. This means that an entire algorithm (or program) can be broken down into blocks, with each block having but one entry point and one exit point. We say that the algorithm or program is **block structured.** Since each block will perform a known task, the individual blocks can be tested separately, thus significantly simplifying the task of verifying the correctness of the entire algorithm or program. When confronted with significant programming tasks that require large programs, this method of testing is not only useful, but is also essential.

As you work through the material in the chapters that follow, you will learn that QuickBASIC contains instructions that make it easy to code the sequence, selection, and repetition constructs. If you write an algorithm using only these constructs, you should find the task of coding the algorithm as a QuickBASIC program reasonably routine.

■ *2.6 Problems*

Construct a flowchart for each algorithm shown in Problems 1–5. In each case use only the sequence, selection, and repetition constructs presented in Section 2.5.

1. **a.** Input values for N, R, and T.
   b. If $N \le 40$, let $S = N \times R$. Otherwise, let $S = 40 \times R + (N - 40) \times (1.5) \times R$.
   c. Reduce S by the amount $S \times T$.
   d. Print S and stop.
2. **a.** Input values for A and B.
   b. If A and B have the same sign (the condition for this is $A \times B > 0$), print POSITIVE or NEGATIVE according to whether A and B are positive or negative.
   c. If either A or B is 0, print FINI and stop; otherwise, repeat Step (a).
3. **a.** Input an integer N.
   b. If $N = 0$, stop.
   c. Print BETWEEN if N is between 70 and 80, exclusive; otherwise, print NOT BETWEEN.
   d. Input another integer N and continue from Step (b).

    4. a. Input values for X, Y, and Z.
      b. If X < Y, print Y − X and go to Step (d).
      c. Print Z − X only if X < Z.
      d. Print X, Y, and Z.
      e. Stop.
    5. a. Input a value for N.
      b. If N is less than or equal to 0, go to Step (g).
      c. If N > 100, print VALUE IS TOO LARGE and go to Step (f).
      d. If N > 70 print GOOD and go to Step (g).
      e. If N > 50 print OK; otherwise, print RATHER LOW.
      f. Input another value for N and continue from Step (b).
      g. Print GOODBYE and stop.

■ 2.7 Review True-or-False Quiz

    1. The terms *algorithm* and *process* are synonymous.   T   F
    2. A computer program should describe an algorithm.   T   F
    3. The expression *heuristic process* refers to an algorithm.   T   F
    4. It is always easier to verify the correctness of an algorithm that describes a specific task than the correctness of a more general algorithm.   T   F
    5. The term *variable* refers to a value that can change during a process.   T   F
    6. The expressions *input/output specification, modularization,* and *stepwise refinement* refer to principles of problem solving.   T   F
    7. A *problem analysis* is the process of discovering a correct algorithm.   T   F
    8. The *method of stepwise refinement* is a method of problem solving in which successive steps in an algorithm are combined to produce an algorithm that is easier to read.   T   F
    9. *Top-down design* involves the process of *stepwise refinement.*   T   F

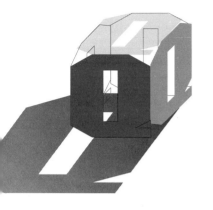

3
A First Look at QuickBASIC

We must communicate with a computer before it will perform any service for us. The medium for this communication is the computer program—for our purposes, a sequence of statements (instructions to the computer) in the English-like language BASIC. The extended version of BASIC that we use in this book is Microsoft QuickBASIC.

In this chapter, we discuss some topics vital to understanding how a QuickBASIC computer program must be written. These include the following: names of numerical and character string variables allowed; how to write numerical expressions in a form suitable for computer evaluation; how the LET, PRINT, and END statements are used; and how comments can be included in programs. In the next chapter, we explain how you get a completed program into the computer and how you cause its statements to be carried out, that is, executed.

Here is a BASIC program whose purpose is described in its first line:

```
' PROGRAM TO AVERAGE THREE NUMBERS

'    X,Y,Z denote the numbers to be added.
'       AV denotes their average.

LET X = 43                    'First number
LET Y = 27                    'Second number
LET Z = 23                    'Third number
LET AV = (X + Y + Z) / 3      'Their average
PRINT "AVERAGE IS"; AV        'Display the result.
END
```

If a computer carries out the instructions in this program, it will produce the following output:

```
AVERAGE IS 31
```

This program uses three words, called **keywords,** from the QuickBASIC language: LET, to associate certain numerical values with certain symbols (for example, LET X = 43 associates 43 with the symbol X); PRINT, to display the results; and END, to terminate the program. QuickBASIC executes the LET, PRINT, and END statements in the order in which they appear in the program.*

---

*Early versions of BASIC require line numbers to determine the order in which statements are carried out by the computer. QuickBASIC allows line numbers, but they have nothing to do with the order in which statements are executed. They are allowed only so that programs written in earlier versions of BASIC can be executed by the QuickBASIC system. Line numbers are not used in this book. QuickBASIC also allows meaningful character string line labels. The use of labels to mark specific locations in a program is illustrated in Section 11.3 (DATA statement) and in Section 16.3 (ON ERROR GOTO statement).

The program also includes comments that explain the various parts of the program. Each single apostrophe character (') begins a comment, which consists of everything from the apostrophe to the end of the line. Comments cause no action during program execution. The use of comments in QuickBASIC programs is discussed further in Section 3.7.

Unlike a natural language such as English, a programming language must not allow ambiguities. The computer must do precisely what it is instructed to do. For this reason, great care must be taken to write statements precisely according to the QuickBASIC **syntax** (rules of grammar). The following sections describe how LET, PRINT, END, and comments can be used to write admissible QuickBASIC programs. A complete treatment of these topics is not intended at this time; our immediate goal is to provide you with minimal information that you will need to understand and to write some QuickBASIC programs.

■ *3.1 Numerical Constants and Variables*

QuickBASIC allows you to write numbers as in ordinary arithmetic and also in a special E form.

Numerical form			Examples		
Integer	726	29234	−726	+423	0
Decimal	726.	−133.50	−726.	+423.	0.201
E form	27.3E4	2.6E−1	1E03	−136E12	1.234E−15

Almost all of your numerical work in QuickBASIC will deal with *integers* and *decimals*. Integers are numbers with no decimal point, and decimals are numbers in which a decimal point appears. The use of commas and dollar signs in numbers is not allowed; using 29,234 to represent 29234 will result in an error.

The E form (exponential form) may be new to you. The letter E in 27.3E4 stands for "exponent." Its meaning is *times 10 to the power.* Thus 27.3E4 means 27.3 times 10 to the power 4 or, in more mathematical symbols, 27.3×10^4. Hence,

$$27.3E4 = 27.3 \times 10^4 = 27.3 \times 10000 = 273000$$

Similarly,

$$2.6E{-}3 = 2.6 \times 10^{-3} = 2.6 \times .001 = .0026$$

Note that you could obtain the final result 273000 of 27.3E4 by moving the decimal point in 27.3 *four* places to the *right,* and you could obtain the result .0026 of 2.6E−3 by moving the decimal point in 2.6 *three* places to the *left.*

Although you may choose to use only integers and decimals in your programs, QuickBASIC will display both very large numbers and certain numbers close to zero in the E form. For example, the QuickBASIC statement

```
PRINT 1/12
```

will display the value of 1/12 as 8.33333E−02, and not .0833333.

The general form for an exponential constant, together with its meaning, is

$$n\mathrm{E}m = n \times 10^m$$

where *n* can be any integer or decimal, but *m* must be an integer (no decimal point). The values of the other exponential constants shown in the preceding table are:

$$
\begin{aligned}
1\mathrm{E}03 &= 1000 \\
-136\mathrm{E}12 &= -136000000000000 \quad\text{(12 zeros)} \\
1.23\mathrm{E}{-}15 &= .00000000000000123 \quad\text{(14 zeros)}
\end{aligned}
$$

To form names for numerical variables, QuickBASIC allows character strings containing up to forty letters, digits, and periods. The first character must be a letter. Certain words (such as LET, PRINT, and END), are part of the QuickBASIC language. They are called

reserved words and cannot be used as variable names. A complete list of the QuickBASIC reserved words is given in Appendix B.

Admissible variable names	Inadmissible variable names	
X	3RD	(begins with a digit)
SUM	S−200	(contains a dash)
LAST.NAME	LAST NAME	(contains a space)
COUNT3	COLOR	(COLOR is a reserved word)
DEPT.17	.PCT.	(begins with a period)

The variables just described are called **single-precision variables.** They can be used to store numerical values with seven-digit accuracy. In addition to the single-precision variables, QuickBASIC provides three other types of numerical variables: **integer variables, long integer variables,** and **double-precision variables.** The character strings that are used as names of variables are called **identifiers.** In QuickBASIC, an identifier is any sequence of characters allowed as the name of a single-precision variable, with a possible additional character ($, %, &, #, or !) as the last character (thus, up to 41 characters in all).

The suffix $ indicates a string variable, as explained in Section 3.2. The other suffixes indicate numerical variables, as shown in Table 3.1. As mentioned in Section 1.2, the term *byte* denotes the amount of memory that the computer uses to store a single character.

Table 3.1 Numerical Types in QuickBASIC

Numerical Type	Suffix	Description	Memory
Integer	%	−32,768 to 32,767	2 bytes
Long integer	&	−1,427,483,648 to 1,427,483,647	4 bytes
Single-precision	! or none	7-digit accuracy	4 bytes
Double-precision	#	15- or 16-digit accuracy	8 bytes

If a number that is not an integer is assigned to an integer variable (suffix % or &), it is first rounded to the nearest integer. (A number ending with .5 is rounded to the nearest even integer.) Thus, the three statements

```
LET A% = 14.625
LET B% = 12.5
LET C% = 12.5000001
```

associate 15 with A%, 12 with B%, and 13 with C%.

The identifiers A, A%, A&, and A# are names of different variables. QuickBASIC has no trouble distinguishing among them (even though we might). As indicated in Table 3.1, QuickBASIC allows you to use the suffix ! to indicate the type of a single-precision numerical variable. You will need to know this because, even though you do not include it, QuickBASIC sometimes includes this suffix in your programs. Unlike A, A%, A&, and A#, the identifiers A and A! are not names of different variables—they are simply two names for the same single-precision numerical variable.

■ *3.2 String Constants and Variables*

A **string constant** is a sequence, or **string,** of characters enclosed in quotation marks. The following are string constants:

```
"Income"          "NANCY JONES"
"X="              "567"
"19 April 1775"   "*****"
"SUM "            "   DISCOUNT"
```

The *value* of a string constant is the sequence of all characters, including blanks, appearing between the quotes. Thus the value of the string constant "NANCY JONES" is the 11-character string NANCY JONES, and the value of "SUM " is the 4-character string consisting of SUM followed by a blank character. A string may contain as few as zero (null string) or as many as 32,767 characters.

Variables whose values are strings are called **string variables.** Identifiers with the suffix $ are names of string variables. Thus B$, NAMES$, A45$, and S.S.N.$ are admissible names of string variables, but NAME$ is not—NAME is a reserved word.

■ *3.3 Arithmetic Operations and Expressions*

QuickBASIC uses the following symbols to denote the usual arithmetic operations:

QuickBASIC symbol	Operation	Priority
^	Exponentiation	1
−	Negation	2
*	Multiplication	3
/	Division	3
+	Addition	4
−	Subtraction	4

Any meaningful combination of constants, variable names, and operation symbols is called an **expression.** The order in which the operations in an expression are performed is determined first by the indicated priority and then, within the same priority class, from left to right.

EXAMPLE 1   *In the following expressions, the circled numbers indicate the order in which the operations will be performed by the computer.*

    ① ②
a. $5 - 4 + 3 =$
    1   $+ 3 =$
       4

Since + and − have the same priority, they are performed from left to right. Note that performing the + first gives the different value −2.

    ③ ① ②
b. $2 + 6/4 * 3 =$
    $2 + 1.5 * 3 =$
    $2 + \quad 4.5 \quad =$
    6.5

Since / and * have the same priority, they are performed from left to right. Note that performing the * first gives the different value 2.5.

    ③   ①   ④   ②
c. $5 * 2 \,\char94\, 2 + 3 \,\char94\, 2$

Performing these operations one at a time, we obtain:

    $5 * 2 \,\char94\, 2 + 3 \,\char94\, 2 =$
    $5 * \quad 4 \quad + 3 \,\char94\, 2 =$
    $5 * \quad 4 \quad + \quad 9 \quad =$
    $20 \qquad\quad + \quad 9 \quad =$
             29

    ② ①
d. $- 5 \,\char94\, 2 =$
    -25

Since exponentiation (^) has the highest priority, it is performed first. Thus this expression, the negative of the square of 5, results in the value −25. Note that performing the − first gives the different value 25.

Parentheses may be used in numerical expressions, just as in ordinary algebra. They are used to override the usual order in which operations are performed. If you need the negation of the sum of A and B, for example, you can use the expression −(A + B). Parentheses may also be used to clarify the meaning of numerical expressions. For example, 5/2 * 3 and (5/2) * 3 have the same meaning, but the second form is less likely to be misinterpreted.

EXAMPLE 2   *In this table, A = 3, B = −2, and C = 4:*

Expression	Value of expression
A/(2*B)	−0.75
A/2*B	−3
−(A+C)	−7
−A+C	1
(B+C)/(C−A)	2
B+C/C−A	−4
(B+C)^(−2)	0.25
(−B)^C	16
−B^C	−16
B^C	16

Roots of numbers may be indicated by using the exponentiation operator ^. Recall from algebra that

$$\sqrt{9} = 9^{1/2} = 3$$

In QuickBASIC, we write this as

9 ^ (1/2)   or   9 ^ 0.5

EXAMPLE 3   *In this table, M = 4 and N = 5:*

Algebraic expression	QuickBASIC expression	Value
$\sqrt{M}$	M^(1/2)	2
$\sqrt{M + N}$	(M+N)^0.5	3
$\sqrt[3]{2M}$	(2*M)^(1/3)	2
$\sqrt[3]{7 + MN}$	(7+M*N)^(1/3)	3
$6\sqrt{5 + M - N}$	6*(5+M−N)^0.5	12

CAUTION   QuickBASIC is not designed to take roots of negative numbers. For example, the cube root of −8 is −2, but the expression (−8) ^ (1/3) will not give this value. Expressions such as A ^ B will result in an error if A is negative and B is not an integer.

QuickBASIC also provides two additional operations to perform **integer division;** the first finds the *integer quotient,* and the second finds the *integer remainder* when one integer is divided by another.

QuickBASIC symbol	Illustration	Meaning
\	a\b	Find quotient when *a* is divided by *b*.
MOD	a MOD b	Find remainder when *a* is divided by *b*.

Note: If either *a* or *b* is not an integer, it is rounded to the nearest integer before the operation is performed.

In elementary school, before you learned about decimals, you probably divided 11 by 4 as follows:

$$\begin{array}{r} 2 \quad \text{quotient} \\ 4\overline{)11} \\ 8 \\ \hline 3 \quad \text{remainder} \end{array}$$

This is precisely the division accomplished by \ and MOD. Thus $11\backslash4 = 2$ and $11 \text{ MOD } 4 = 3$. You could use $200\backslash17$ to determine the number of 17-cent adapters that could be purchased for 2 dollars and 200 MOD 17 to determine the change in cents.

EXAMPLE 4   *In this table, A = 7, B = 2, C = 8.61, and D = 3.4:*

Expression	Value	
A\B	3	
A MOD B	1	
B\A	0	
B MOD A	2	
C\D	3	(C and D are first rounded.)
C MOD D	0	

Table 3.2 gives the order of precedence for all arithmetic operations used by QuickBASIC in evaluating numerical expressions.

Table 3.2   Priority of arithmetic operations

QuickBASIC symbol	Operation	Priority
^	Exponentiation	1
−	Negation	2
* /	Multiplication, division	3
\	Integer quotient	4
MOD	Integer remainder	5
+ −	Addition, subtraction	6

EXAMPLE 5   *In this table, M = 5, N = 8.9, and P = 3.2:*

Expression	Value of expression
M+N\P	8
(M+N)\P	4
P+N MOD M	7.2
2*M MOD P+1	2
21\M MOD P/2	0

3.4 Problems

1. *Evaluate the following.*

   a. 2+3*5   b. 5*7−2   c. −4+2
   d. −(4+2)   e. −3*5   f. −3^2
   g. 1+2^3*2   h. 6/2*3   i. 1/2/2
   j. −2*3/2*3   k. 2^2^3   l. −3*(4+0.1)

m. −2^2∗3   **n.** 1.23E7   **o.** 75E−5

p. 9^1/2   **q.** 9^0.5   **r.** (2+(3∗4−5))^0.5

s. 3∗4 MOD 5   **t.** 8\3 MOD 2   **u.** 2^3\2+1

2. *For A = 2, B = 3, and X = 2, evaluate each of the following.*

a. A+B/X   **b.** (A+B)/2∗X   **c.** B/A/X

d. B/(A∗X)   **e.** A+X^3   **f.** (A+B)^X

g. B^A/X   **h.** B+A/B−A   **i.** A^B+X

j. B^(X/A)   **k.** −A^B   **l.** (−A)^B

m. (B∗X+1) MOD A   **n.** A^B\B   **o.** B∗X MOD A∗X

3. *Some of the following are not admissible QuickBASIC expressions. Explain why. (Be sure to check the table of reserved words.)*

a. (Y+Z)X   **b.** X2∗36   **c.** A∗(2.1−7B)   **d.** SUM∗SUM

e. KEY∗7   **f.** −(A+2B)   **g.** 2X^2   **h.** X2^2

i. X−2^2   **j.** A12+B3   **k.** −9^0.5   **l.** A2−(−A2)

4. *Write QuickBASIC expressions for these arithmetic expressions.*

a. $0.06P$ **b.** $5x + 5y$ **c.** $a^2 + b^2$

d. $\dfrac{6}{5a}$ **e.** $\dfrac{a}{b} + \dfrac{c}{d}$ **f.** $\dfrac{a + b}{c + d}$

g. $ax^2 + bx + c$ **h.** $\sqrt{b^2 - 4ac}$ **i.** $(x^2 + 4xy)/(x + 2y)$

5. *Write equivalent QuickBASIC expressions without using parentheses.*

a. ((X+1)+Y)   **b.** (A+B)∗(A−B)   **c.** A∗(A∗(A+B)+1)

d. (A∗B)/C   **e.** A/(B∗C)   **f.** X∗(X∗(X∗(X+D)+C)+B)+A

g. P^(Q∗R)   **h.** 1/(A∗B∗C∗D)

■ *3.5 The LET Statement: Assigning Values to Variables*

In Section 3.3 you learned how to write numerical expressions in a form acceptable to the computer. Now we will show you how to instruct the computer to evaluate such expressions.

A QuickBASIC statement is a combination of one or more keywords, variables, expressions, and operators that QuickBASIC treats as a single unit. For example,

```
LET A = 2 + 5
```

is a QuickBASIC statement, called a LET statement, that will cause the computer to evaluate the sum 2 + 5 and then assign this value to the variable A. A QuickBASIC program is a collection of QuickBASIC statements.

The general form of our first QuickBASIC statement, the LET statement, is

LET **v** = **e**

or, more simply,

v = **e**   (LET is optional.)

where **v** denotes a variable name and **e** denotes a QuickBASIC expression that may simply be a constant. This statement directs the computer to evaluate the expression **e** and then assign this value to the variable **v.** Only numerical values may be assigned to numerical variables and only string values to string variables.

The examples that follow illustrate the use of LET statements in programs. (How programs are typed at the keyboard and how they are executed is explained in Chapter 4.) In each program shown, the statements are executed by the computer in the order in which they appear in the program. Soon you will encounter QuickBASIC statements that control the order of execution of other statements in the program.

EXAMPLE 6   **Assignment of numerical values:**

	After execution of each statement	
The program	**Value of P**	**Value of Q**
LET P=12	12	0
LET Q=P/2+1	12	7
LET P=Q/2+1	4.5	7
LET Q=P/2+1	4.5	3.25
END	4.5	3.25

REMARK 1   Note that a zero value is shown for Q following execution of the first line. QuickBASIC assigns a value of zero to all numerical variables at the time of program execution. This *initial* value is retained by each variable until the variable is reassigned a value by the program. The statement LET P = 12 assigns only the value of 12 to P. Thus, at this point, Q still retains its initial value of zero.

REMARK 2   The END statement causes program execution to terminate. The END statement in this example is optional—program execution will automatically halt whenever the PC runs out of statements to execute. It is common practice, however, to write programs so that the last statement carried out is an END statement. The END statement in this example serves this purpose.

REMARK 3   Newly written programs must be tested; they seldom do what they were meant to do. You must find and correct all errors. The errors are called **bugs.** The expressions *testing a program* and *debugging a program* mean the same thing. A useful debugging technique is to pretend that you are the computer and then prepare a table of successive values of program variables as in this example. Such a table is called a **trace of the program** or, more simply, a **trace.**

EXAMPLE 7   **Assignment of string values:**

	After execution of each statement		
The program	**Value of A$**	**Value of B$**	**Value of C$**
LET A$="AND"	AND		
LET B$="SO"	AND	SO	
LET C$=B$	AND	SO	SO
LET B$=A$	AND	AND	SO
LET A$=C$	SO	AND	SO
END	SO	AND	SO

REMARK 1   Strings appearing in LET statements *must* be quoted. Note, however, that it is the *string* and not the *quoted string* that is assigned to the variable.

REMARK 2   Although no values are shown for B$ and C$ following execution of the first line, Quick-BASIC assigns an initial **null string** (written " ") to each string variable.

The QuickBASIC statement

LET N=N+1

does not mean that N is equal to N + 1 (since that is impossible). It means that the expression N + 1 is *evaluated* and this value is *assigned* to the variable N. For example, the effect of the two programming lines

```
LET N=5
LET N=N+1
```

is that the value 6 is assigned to N. Similarly, the statement

```
LET S=S+Y
```

evaluates S + Y and then assigns this new value to S. Thus, the statement

```
LET N=N+1
```

increases the value of N by 1, and the statement

```
LET S=S+Y
```

increases the value of S by Y.

EXAMPLE 8 *In this table, S = 3, Y = −2, H = −4, Z = 6, and M = 10:*

Statement	After execution
LET S=S+Y	S has the value 1.
LET H=H+2*Z	H has the value 8.
LET M=2*M−Z	M has the value 14.

◼ 3.6 The PRINT Statement

Every computer language must be designed so that the results can be made available in a usable form. The QuickBASIC statements PRINT and LPRINT meet this requirement: PRINT is used to direct output to the PC's display screen, and LPRINT is used to direct the output to a printer. The examples in this section illustrate the PRINT statement.

The simplest form of the PRINT statement is

PRINT **e**

where **e** denotes any string or numerical expression. When executed, this statement displays the value of the expression **e** and then causes a RETURN to be executed—that is, the screen cursor is positioned at the beginning of the next display line for subsequent output. Here are four admissible PRINT statements.

```
PRINT "THIS IS A MESSAGE."
PRINT 3−8*7
PRINT X
PRINT A$
```

If X has the value 723.45 and A$ has the string value END OF MESSAGE, the preceding four statements will produce the following output:

```
THIS IS A MESSAGE.
−53
 723.45
END OF MESSAGE
```

QuickBASIC displays 723.45 with a leading blank as shown. This is the sign position, which is left blank when positive numbers are displayed.

As illustrated in the next example, you can use the PRINT statement to display more than one value on a line or to create a blank line separating output values.

EXAMPLE 9   ***Displaying labels for output values.***

```
'       AUTOMOBILE SALES TAX PROGRAM

PRINT "TAXATION DEPARTMENT"
PRINT
LET PRICE = 7295
PRINT "PRICE:"; PRICE
PRINT "SALES TAX:"; .05 * PRICE
END
```

When this program is executed, it will produce the following output:

```
TAXATION DEPARTMENT

PRICE: 7295
SALES TAX: 364.75
```

The first PRINT statement displays the first line of output and leaves the cursor positioned at the left margin of the second display line. The PRINT statement with no expression displays nothing, but it causes the cursor to move to the left margin of the next display line. This creates the blank line shown in the output. Each of the statements

```
PRINT "PRICE:"; PRICE
```

and

```
PRINT "SALES TAX:"; .05 * PRICE
```

displays a numerical value preceded by a label identifying what this value represents. Separating two expressions in a PRINT statement by a semicolon, as in these two statements, causes the two values to be displayed next to each other—the blank space preceding each number in the output is the sign position mentioned previously.*

REMARK   In this program, string constants are included in PRINT statements to display a heading (TAXATION DEPARTMENT) and two labels (PRICE: and SALES TAX:) that identify the numerical output values. You can also use string *variables* for this purpose. For instance, if you replace the statement

```
PRINT "PRICE:"; PRICE
```

with

```
LET P$ = "PRICE:"
PRINT P$; PRICE
```

the program will produce exactly the same output as before.

■ 3.7 Comments as Part of a Program

In the preceding examples, we used the single apostrophe character (') to include comment lines in programs. In early versions of BASIC, the keyword REM was used for this purpose. The two program lines

```
REM comment
```

and

```
'  comment
```

are equivalent. These statements are both referred to as *REM statements* or as *comment lines*.

---

*The forms of the PRINT statement described in this section are adequate for many programming tasks. Chapter 7 presents a more detailed description of how QuickBASIC allows you to format your output values.

The example program shown at the beginning of this chapter illustrates that you can include a comment on a line that contains another statement. Simply follow the statement with a single apostrophe and then the comment. Because of the limited width of display screens, such comments should be kept short.

EXAMPLE 10 *Typical uses of comments.*

```
' PROGRAM TO DETERMINE THE RATE OF RETURN
' GIVEN THE CURRENT PRICE AND EARNINGS

'      P denotes the price of the security.
'      E denotes the recent annual earnings.
'      R denotes the rate of return.

'Calculate the rate of return R.

LET P = 80.25                'Assign price.
LET E = 6.55                 'Assign earnings.
LET R = 100 * E / P          'Find rate of return.

'Display the results.

PRINT "PRICE:"; P            'Price.
PRINT "EARNINGS:"; E         'Earnings.
PRINT "RATE OF RETURN:"; R   'Rate of return.
END
```

Program output:
```
PRICE: 80.25
EARNINGS: 6.55
RATE OF RETURN: 8.161994
```

In the program, comments are used for four different purposes: to give a brief description of the program (first two lines); to describe the values represented by the program variables (next three lines); to describe the action of groups of statements (the group of three LET statements and the group of three PRINT statements); and to describe the action of individual QuickBASIC statements. Using comments in these four ways is an excellent programming practice. Your programs will be easier to read and to understand, easier to modify (should that be required), and easier to test.

REMARK QuickBASIC allows blank program lines. They are used, as in this example, to separate one section of a program from another.

The comments in a program and the quoted messages in PRINT statements are intended for two different audiences. Comments give information to people who actually read the program, whereas the messages in PRINT statements give information to users of the program. The needs of these two audiences are very different. For instance, a *reader* of your program may want to understand how the program carries out its task, but the *user* would be interested only in the results. To illustrate, consider the following comment line:

```
'CALCULATE THE GROSS PAY G.
```

This informs the reader of the program that the gross pay is denoted by G and that the programming lines that follow this comment will calculate this value. A user of the program, however, has no need for this information. To assist the user, you would include a statement such as

```
PRINT "GROSS PAY $"; G
```

so that the output value G is labeled in a meaningful way. You would not use

```
PRINT "G=$"; G
```

The user neither cares nor needs to know that G is used to denote the gross pay. Messages in PRINT statements should never presume that a user has read the program and is familiar with the variable names.

Good programming practice dictates that you include clarifying comments for someone reading your program, as well as messages in PRINT statements that are useful to the program user.

EXAMPLE 11   *Here are two programs to calculate and display exactly the same numerical values. Program A gives no information to the reader concerning the purpose of the program nor to the user as to what the output values represent. Program B gives useful information to both the reader and the user.*

Program A
```
LET H = 38
LET R = 7.32
LET G = H * R
PRINT H
PRINT R
PRINT G
END
```

Program output:
```
38
7.32
278.16
```

Program B
```
' PROGRAM TO COMPUTE GROSS PAY
'    H denotes hours worked.
'    R denotes hourly rate.

'Calculate the gross pay.

LET H = 38               'Assign hours.
LET R = 7.32             'Assign rate.
LET G = H * R            'gross pay.

'Display the results.

PRINT "Hours worked:"; H    'Hours worked
PRINT "Hourly rate:"; R     'Rate of pay
PRINT "Gross pay:"; G       'Gross pay
END
```

Program output:
```
Hours worked: 38
Hourly rate: 7.32
Gross pay: 278.16
```

■ 3.8 Multiple-Statement Programming Lines

You can include more than one QuickBASIC statement in a programming line—simply separate the statements with colons, and the statements will be executed from left to right. Thus, the following multiple-statement line will assign 5 to A, 7 to B, and then display their sum:

```
LET A = 5: B = 7: PRINT A + B
```

If a multiple-statement line contains a comment, everything that follows the apostrophe character (or the keyword REM) is part of the comment. Thus, the following two multiple-statement lines are admissible, but they are not equivalent:

```
PRINT X: REM Print the result.
'Print the result. : PRINT X
```

The first will display the value of X. The second is simply a comment and will cause no action during program execution. As illustrated in the earlier examples, you would probably write the first line in the equivalent (but easier to read) form

```
PRINT X     'Print the result.
```

The overuse of multiple-statement lines tends to clutter a program and obscure its meaning. As you progress in your study of programming, you may find situations in which they can be used to your advantage. In most situations, however, they are unnecessary and are best avoided.

■ *3.9 Problems*

1. *Write LET statements to perform the indicated tasks.*

   a. Assign the value 7 to M.
   b. Increase the value assigned to B by 7.
   c. Double the value assigned to H.
   d. Assign the value of the expression $(A - B)/2$ to C2.
   e. Assign the tenth power of $1 + R$ to A.
   f. Decrease the value assigned to X by twice the value assigned to Y.
   g. Assign the string COST to C$.
   h. Replace the value of A$ by the string DOE, JANE.
   i. Store the contents of P$ in Q$.
   j. Assign the string ***** to S$.

2. *Which of these are inadmissible LET statements? Explain. (Be sure to check the table of reserved words.)*

   ```
   a. LET X=(A+B)C          b. LET M=A1-A2
   c. LET A+B=S             d. LET DEPT#5=17
   e. LET A3=A*A*A          f. LET 5M=2+7*X
   g. LET X=1.23E5          h. LET Y%=X+0.5
   i. LET Z=4E2.5           j. LET AREA=LENGTH*WIDTH
   k. LET SUM=SUM+NEXT      l. LET DIFF=FIRST-SECOND
   m. LET A$=SAMMY          n. LET NAME$="JANE DOE"
   o. LET P$=Y$             p. LET "DEPT#7"=D$
   q. LET M="MONTHLY RENT"  r. LET D$="A+B+5"
   ```

3. *Which of these are inadmissible PRINT statements? Explain. (Be sure to check the table of reserved words.)*

   ```
   a. PRINT SO-AND-SO       b. PRINT SO.AND.SO
   c. PRINT "5+13=";5+13    d. PRINT SPACE$;X
   e. PRINT "RATE-OF-RETURN" f. PRINT SEVEN$;7
   g. PRINT WIDTH           h. PRINT "FINAL RESULT";AVERAGE
   ```

4. *Show the output of each program.*

   ```
   a. LET A=5               b. LET P=100
      LET B=A+2               LET R=8
      LET C=A+B               LET I=R/100
      PRINT "RESULT";C        LET A=P+I*P
      END                     PRINT "AMOUNT=";A
                              END

   c. LET X=0               d. LET A=2
      LET X=X-1               LET B=6
      LET Y=X^2+3*X           LET A=2*A
      PRINT "RESULT";Y        LET B=B/2
      END                     LET C=(A^2+B^2)^(1/2)
                              PRINT "RESULT";C
                              END
   ```

```
e. LET L=10          'Length    f. LET L$="LIST PRICE"
   LET W=5           'Width        LET D$="DISCOUNT"
   LET H=4           'Height       LET S$="SELLING PRICE"
   LET V=L*W*H       'Volume       LET L=45
   PRINT "VOLUME";V                LET D=(10/100)*L
   LET L=W : H=W                   LET S=L-D
   PRINT "BE CAREFUL."             PRINT L$;L
   PRINT "VOLUME";V                PRINT D$;D
   END                            PRINT S$;S
                                   END

g. PRINT "BOBBY LOVES"          h. LET A%=7 : B%=5
   LET M$=MARY."                   LET B%=A%/B%
   LET B$="BARB."                  LET M=A%+B%
   LET B$=M$                       PRINT M\5
   LET M$=B$                       PRINT M MOD 3+1
   PRINT M$                        END
   END
```

5. *Complete the tables of values as in Examples 4 and 5.*

	A	B	C

```
a. LET A=1 : B=2 : C=1
   LET C=C+B
   LET A=B^2
   LET B=C-B+A
   LET C=C-1 : B=A*B
   LET A=A/C : C=B/A+1
   END
```

	N	Output

```
b. LET N=1 : PRINT N
   LET N=N*(N+1) : PRINT N
   LET N=N*(N+1) : PRINT N
   LET N=N*(N+1) : PRINT N
   END
```

	X	Y	Z	Output

```
c. LET X=0
   LET Y=X+7
   LET Z=Y+X^2
   PRINT Z
   LET X=Z
   LET Y=X*Y*Z
   PRINT Y
   END
```

6. *Prepare tables showing the successive values of all variables and the output.*

```
a. LET S=0 : A=25              b. LET X=1.5
   LET S=S+A : PRINT S            LET Y=3/(2*X+2)
   LET S=S+A : PRINT S            PRINT Y
   LET S=S/2 : PRINT S            LET X=-X
   END                           PRINT X
                                 PRINT Y
                                 END
```

```
c. LET N=130    'COUNT
   LET C=3.00   'COST
   LET S=1.2*C  'SELLING PRICE
   LET G=N*S : PRINT "SALES";G
   LET P=G-N*C : PRINT "PROFIT";P
   END
```

```
d. PRINT "NTH POWERS OF 10"
   LET A=10 : P=10
   PRINT "FOR N=1";P
   LET P=A*P
   PRINT "FOR N=2";P
   LET P=A*P
   PRINT "FOR N=3";P
   LET P=A*P
   PRINT "FOR N=4";P
   REM "END OF TABLE"
   END
```

■ *3.10 Review True-or-False Quiz*

1. Parentheses may be used only to override the usual order in which numerical operations are performed by the computer. T F
2. $(A + B)^{0.5}$ and $(A + B)^{1/2}$ have the same meaning. T F
3. 2/3 is a numerical constant in QuickBASIC. T F
4. 1.0E1 = 10. T F
5. If A = 3, the statement LET 1+A^2=B1 assigns the value 10 to the variable B1. T F
6. LET A3=A3*A3 is a valid QuickBASIC statement. T F
7. LET M="1984" is a valid QuickBASIC statement. T F
8. LET X=X+1 is a valid QuickBASIC statement but will result in an error because there is no number X for which X = X + 1. T F
9. PRINT HARRY is a valid QuickBASIC statement, but it will not display the name HARRY. T F
10. PRINT A+B : PRINT A*B is a valid program line. T F
11. LET INT=A+B : PRINT INT is a valid program line. T F
12. The program line LET A=5 : B=A assigns the same value to both A and B. T F
13. NUM# is an admissible variable name. T F
14. The program line

```
    X=2   'Assign X : PRINT X^5   'Display 5th power
```

will display the number 32. T F

4
First Session
at the Keyboard

*I*n Chapter 3, we presented examples of QuickBASIC programs that were ready to be typed at the PC keyboard. The purpose of this chapter is to guide you during your first session at the QuickBASIC keyboard. Sections 4.1 and 4.2 describe the keyboard and explain how to get QuickBASIC up and running. Sections 4.3 through 4.8 show how QuickBASIC programs are entered at the keyboard and explain how to carry out certain necessary operations, such as executing programs, saving programs, and retrieving programs that were previously saved. In Section 4.9, we show how to use QuickBASIC's Immediate Mode capability, and in Section 4.10, we show how you can get printed copy of programs and program output. Section 4.11 sets forth a five-step approach to problem solving on the computer that can be used with many of the programming tasks you will first encounter.

To get the most out of this chapter, you are urged to read through the material quickly to get a general idea of what is involved, and then to read it again, this time being sure to try the examples on your computer.

■ 4.1 The PC Keyboard

The keys on the PC keyboard are organized into three general areas. The middle portion, labeled *typewriter keyboard* in Figure 4.1, is much like an ordinary typewriter keyboard. Most of your typing will be in this area. The keys to the right (labeled *Numeric keypad* in Figure 4.1) are not used to include numbers in your programs—the top row of the typewriter keyboard is used for this purpose. As explained in Section 4.3, an important use of the numeric keypad keys is to move the screen cursor to any character in the program that you are currently working on. The keys labeled F1 to F10 (they may be along the top of your keyboard) are special purpose keys. For example, your QuickBASIC system may allow you to use function key F1 to obtain information about the QuickBASIC language. The use of some of the function keys will be explained as the need arises.

To get started, you should understand how to use the following special keys; they are used in DOS and in QuickBASIC:

This is the **Enter key.** When typing a new program, end each line by pressing this key. Other uses of the Enter key will be explained in what follows.

This is the **Shift key.** It is used to type uppercase letters. The Shift key is also used in combination with other keys to carry out certain tasks. While typing a program, you can use any combination of upper- and lowercase letters. QuickBASIC keywords, however, will be changed to uppercase letters; everything else will be left as typed.

44

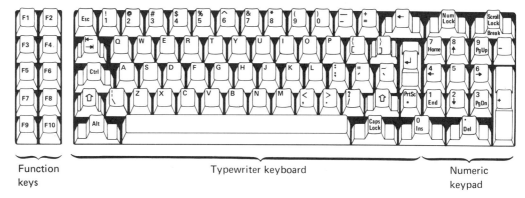

Function
keys
Typewriter keyboard
Numeric
keypad

Figure 4.1 The IBM PC keyboard.

 This key is an ON/OFF switch: press it once to type all uppercase letters; press it again to return to lowercase. This key affects only the letter keys; you must still use the shift key to obtain the top characters on those keys that type two characters.

 This key, located just above the Enter key, is the **backspace key.** It is used to erase the character just before the cursor.

 PrtSc stands for **Print Screen.** Pressing PrtSc while holding down the shift key will produce a printed copy of the current screen display. In Section 5.2, we show how you can use the PrtSc key to obtain a printed copy of the output produced by a program, even if the output does not fit on the screen.

All keys on the PC keyboard are **typematic;** that is, they repeat as long as you hold them down. You should find this keyboard feature to be very helpful.

■ *4.2 Getting QuickBASIC Up and Running*

How you load QuickBASIC depends on the computer system you are using. The following are two common methods for doing this. (However, your computer center may require a different method.) Both methods assume that the disk operating system (DOS) has been loaded as described in Appendix A.

1. Loading QuickBASIC from a hard drive:
    a. Insert a formatted disk on which you will save your programs in drive A and close the drive door.
    b. Type A: and press the Enter key to obtain the DOS prompt A:\>. This step causes QuickBASIC to use the disk in drive A as the storage disk for your programs.
    c. Type QB and press the Enter key.* (Your system may use QBI or some other name.)
2. Loading QuickBASIC from a disk in drive A:
    a. Insert a disk that contains QuickBASIC (most likely, a file named QB.EXE or QBI.EXE) in drive A and close the drive door.
    b. Type A: and press the Enter key to obtain the DOS prompt A:\>.
    c. Type QB (or QBI) and press the Enter key.

---

*If Step 1.c does not give you QuickBASIC, your computer center uses a different method for loading Quick-BASIC. If you are using a home computer with a hard drive and QuickBASIC is installed in drive C, you can change the file named AUTOEXEC.BAT so that Step 1.c will load QuickBASIC. (You should find AUTO-EXEC.BAT in the root directory of drive C.) This file contains a line beginning with the word path. Use a word processor to add the eight characters ;c:\qb45 to this line. (QB45 indicates the name of the directory that contains the QuickBASIC system.) Having done this, Step 1.c should give you QuickBASIC.

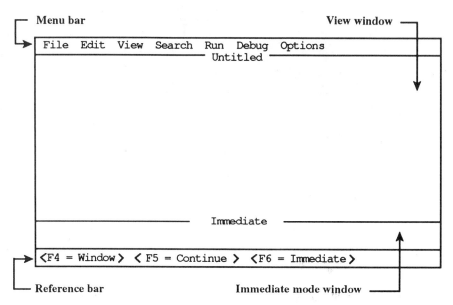

Figure 4.2   The QuickBASIC main menu screen

    d. Replace the QuickBASIC disk in drive A with a formatted disk on which you will save your programs.

    When QuickBASIC has been loaded into memory, you will get a QuickBASIC **main menu screen** similar to that shown in Figure 4.2. If your screen also contains a display box beginning "Welcome to Microsoft QuickBASIC," press the Esc key to clear the box from the screen.

    The top line of the main menu screen is called the **menu bar.** It contains the names (File, Edit, View, and so on) of menus you will use as you write, execute, and modify programs. Below the menu bar are two windows: the larger upper window is the **view window**—your QuickBASIC programs are displayed in this window; the smaller lower window is the **immediate mode window.** The bottom line is called the **reference bar.** It displays information that you should find helpful.

    After QuickBASIC has been loaded, you will find that some keys that we have not yet mentioned will take on a new meaning. In what follows, you can use the following four keys as described (other special keys will be described as they are needed).

 This key, located in the lower-right corner of the keyboard, is the **Delete key.** It erases the character at the cursor. Another use of the delete key is shown in Section 4.6.

 This key is the **Tab key.** When typing a program, you can use this key just as you do the tab key on a typewriter, or you can use *Shift Tab* to tab to the left. (Another use of the Tab key is explained in what follows.)

Ctrl stands for **control.** This key is used in combination with other keys to carry out certain necessary operations.

 Ins stands for **insert.** This key is used to toggle between **insert mode** and **overwrite mode.** The following chart explains the difference.

Mode	Cursor	Action
Insert	Blinking underscore character	Typed character is inserted at the cursor position.
Overwrite	Blinking block character	Typed character replaces the character at the cursor position.

At this point, whatever you type will appear in the View window. QuickBASIC, how-ever, assumes that you are typing a program, and it will display an error message if you enter lines that are not allowed in the QuickBASIC language. To see that this is so, type a line of text (any line will do), and then press the Enter key. If what you type is not allowed, QuickBASIC will display an appropriate message. For example, if you type the line

```
This is a sentence.
```

and press the Enter key, the following will appear on your screen:

```
┌─────────────────────────────────────┐
│   Expected: end-of-statement         │
├─────────────────────────────────────┤
│    < OK >        < Help >            │
└─────────────────────────────────────┘
```

This is an error message. For now, press the Esc key and continue on to Section 4.3, which explains in detail how to type programs and how to respond to error messages.

■ *4.3 Entering a New Program at the Keyboard*

When you first enter QuickBASIC, the View window is clear and you can immediately type a new program. The program you type will remain untitled, as indicated by the caption *Untitled* at the top of the View window. (You will name it when you save it, as explained in Section 4.7.) If the View window is not clear, you must clear it before you begin to type. This is accomplished with the *New Program* command. To issue this command (or any other QuickBASIC command), you will need to understand the effect of the following two keys:

Alt   Pressing this key selects the menu bar and highlights the first letter of each menu name. To select one of these menus, type the corresponding highlighted letter.

Esc   Pressing this key (called the **Escape key**) cancels the effect of the previous QuickBASIC command and returns you to the main menu screen. In some situations, you will have to press the Esc key more than once to get the main menu screen.

To issue the New Program command, press the Alt, F, and N keys, in that order.

Alt key   Selects the menu bar and highlights the first letter of each menu name.

F key   Displays the *File* menu and highlights a single letter in each option. The following options, and possibly others, will be in this menu:

        (N)ew Program
        (O)pen Program. . .
        Save (A)s. . .
        (P)rint. . .
        E(x)it

        The letters enclosed in boxes are the highlighted letters.

N key   Selects the *New Program* option.

You can issue the New Program command (Alt F N) even if no changes have been made in the View window. You will have a clear View window and can begin typing your program. If changes were made before typing Alt F N, QuickBASIC will display the following dia-logue box:

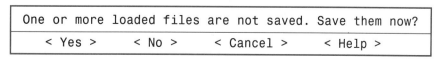

```
┌────────────────────────────────────────────────────────────┐
│  One or more loaded files are not saved. Save them now?     │
├────────────────────────────────────────────────────────────┤
│   < Yes >       < No >       < Cancel >       < Help >      │
└────────────────────────────────────────────────────────────┘
```

When confronted with a dialogue box, you will use the Tab key and possibly the arrow keys (in the numeric keypad) to select your response to QuickBASIC. If you do not want to save the changes you made, press the Tab key to highlight the *No* response, and then press the Enter key. QuickBASIC will erase the dialogue box and leave you with a clear View window, just as when you first entered QuickBASIC.

You should now have a clear View window. Notice that the cursor is at the left margin of the first line in the View window. Notice also the two numbers 00001:001 at the far right of the reference bar; these indicate the position of the cursor by row and column. Here is a program that you can now type at the keyboard.

```
' First session with QuickBASIC
' Find sum and product.
let a=5
let b=8
let sum=a+b
let product=a*b
end
```

Each character you type is displayed in the View window at the cursor position. End each line by pressing the Enter key. The program you are typing—that is, the program displayed in the View window—is called the **current program.**

As you are typing, you will notice that QuickBASIC makes some changes in what you have typed. For instance, when you press the Enter key after typing the line

```
let a=5
```

QuickBASIC will change the line to

```
LET a = 5
```

QuickBASIC always changes lowercase QuickBASIC keywords to uppercase and inserts missing spaces before and after operational symbols. It may also detect a syntax error (a violation of QuickBASIC's rules of grammar) and ask you to respond to a query. Suppose, for example, that you type

```
let b—8
```

rather than

```
let b=8
```

When you press the Enter key, QuickBASIC will display the dialogue box

```
┌─────────────────────────────────────┐
│  Expected: variable=expression       │
├─────────────────────────────────────┤
│    < OK >      < Help >              │
└─────────────────────────────────────┘
```

and will highlight the part of the line that caused the error (sometimes the dialogue box will cover the highlighted characters). At this point, you can accept the default response OK by pressing the Enter key. QuickBASIC will clear the dialogue box and you can then correct the error.

In addition to the Del, Backspace, and other special keys described earlier, you will find the keys shown in Table 4.1 helpful as you enter or modify programs. They cause **pure cursor moves**—that is, they change the position of the cursor but do not change the program in any way.

Since the program that you entered contains no PRINT statements, it will produce no output. To rectify this situation, PRINT statements that display the sum and product should be inserted. We will illustrate one way to insert new lines into a program. As you become familiar with QuickBASIC, you will discover other ways to do this. To display the sum with a PRINT statement inserted between the two lines

```
LET sum = a + b
LET product = a * b
```

Table 4.1 **Numeric keypad cursor-moving keys**

Key	Effect
↑	Moves cursor up one line
→	Moves cursor right one character
↓	Moves cursor down one line
←	Moves cursor left one character
Home	Moves cursor to start of line
End	Moves cursor to end of line
PgDn	Moves cursor down one page and displays the new page
PgUp	Moves cursor up one page and displays the new page

move the cursor to the end of the first LET statement, and then press the Enter key. (To move the cursor to the end of a line, first use the arrow keys to move it to any position on the line, and then press the End key.) This will insert a blank line between the two LET statements with the cursor in the first position.

```
LET sum = a + b

LET product = a * b
```

Now type the following, but do not press the Enter key:

```
PRINT "Sum is"; sum
```

If you press the Enter key after typing this statement, you will obtain an unwanted blank line after the PRINT statement. No harm is done; to remove unwanted lines from a program—even blank lines—move the cursor to any position on the line and type Ctrl Y (hold down the Ctrl key and press Y). You can now repeat the procedure to insert the line

```
PRINT "Product is"; product
```

just after the LET statement that calculates the product. After you do this, the display in the View window should be as follows:

```
' First session with QuickBASIC
' Find sum and product.
LET a = 5
LET b = 8
LET sum = a + b
PRINT "Sum is"; sum
LET product = a * b
PRINT "Product is"; product
END
```

■ *4.4 Spacing and the Length of a Programming Line*

As mentioned in the preceding section, QuickBASIC will sometimes change what you type at the keyboard. For example, QuickBASIC will change

```
LET A=5*(B+C)
```

to

```
LET A = 5 * (B + C)
```

by inserting a space before and after the symbols =, *, and +. If you type the same statement as

```
LETA=5*(B+C)
```

QuickBASIC will change it to

```
LETA = 5 * (B + C)
```

which is an admissible QuickBASIC statement, but it's not the one intended. QuickBASIC has interpreted LETA as the name of a variable, and it will proceed as if this were a LET statement (with the optional keyword LET omitted) to assign the value of the expression $5 * (B + C)$ to the variable LETA.

While typing your programs, you must observe two rules concerning QuickBASIC keywords, variables, and constants:

1. You must use a space to separate QuickBASIC keywords from other parts of the statement. If you don't, QuickBASIC may display a dialogue box to alert you to the error or, as just shown, you may inadvertently have typed what is a syntactically correct statement, but not the one intended.

2. You must not insert spaces within QuickBASIC keywords, variables, or constants. If you do, QuickBASIC may or may not detect the error. For instance, if you incorrectly type

```
PRINT A V
```

to display the value of the variable AV, QuickBASIC will change the statement to

```
PRINT A; V
```

If you notice the change, you can fix it. If not, your program will execute, but will produce incorrect results.

Other than adhering to these two rules concerning the use of spaces while typing keywords, variables, and constants, you can include extra spaces to improve the readability of your programs. Following are the two most common uses of extra spaces to improve program readability.*

1. Comments that you type on lines that contain other QuickBASIC statements should be aligned in a way that makes them easy to read. In most cases, this means aligning them on the apostrophe characters that begin the comments. Perhaps the best time to decide what comment to include on a line is while you are typing the line. After you finish typing a program, you can use the arrow keys, Del key, and spacebar to align (or realign) the comments.

2. As you learn more about the QuickBASIC language, you will find many situations in which you can improve the readability of your programs by indenting statements or groups of statements. To indent a QuickBASIC statement, simply move the cursor to the position for the first character, and then type the statement. If you press the Enter key after typing an indented line, QuickBASIC will position the cursor on the next line at the same level of indentation. Thus, subsequent lines will be indented in the same way. To begin a new line at the left margin, simply press the Home key.

In some situations (other than the two just mentioned), QuickBASIC may remove extra spaces or make some other change in your spacing, but no harm will have been done. For instance, QuickBASIC will change

```
LET   A = 5   :   B = 7
```

to

```
LET A = 5:     B = 7
```

by removing one of the two spaces between LET and A and moving the colon left as shown.

Each line of QuickBASIC's View window can display at most 78 characters at a time. For this reason, it is common practice to use only programming lines with 78 or fewer characters. Should you type a longer line, the entire screen will scroll to the left one position

---

*As will be explained in Chapter 11, you can also use extra spaces to align data that you include in DATA statements in any way you wish.

for each additional character you type. The leftmost characters will scroll off the screen, just as the top line is scrolled off the screen when you type more than eighteen lines. The PgUp and PgDn keys that allow you to move up or down one page at a time can be used with the Ctrl key to move right or left one screen width at a time. The key combination Ctrl PgUp gives you the next screen (to the right), and Ctrl PgDn gives you the previous screen (to the left).

■ *4.5 Running QuickBASIC Programs*

To run the current program, press the Alt, R, and S keys, in that order:

Alt key	Select the menu bar.
R key	Display the *Run* menu and highlight a single letter of each option.
S key	Select the *Start* option. This causes the program to be executed.

We issued this Run command for the previously entered sum and product program, and we obtained the following output:

```
Sum is 13
Product is 40
```

QuickBASIC uses the normal DOS screen as the output screen. The output is displayed just below whatever was on that screen when you issued the Run command. To display your output beginning at the top of an otherwise clear screen, include CLS in your programs before any PRINT statements. To see the current contents of the output screen at any time, press function key F4. Press F4 again, or almost any other key, to get back the main menu screen.

■ *4.6 Making Corrections*

During a session at the keyboard, you will most likely make occasional typing errors. As mentioned previously, you can change any line in a program by moving the cursor to the appropriate position and making the deletions and/or insertions needed. As we have already mentioned, you can erase an entire line by moving the cursor to the line and typing the key combination Ctrl Y.

QuickBASIC does not detect all syntax errors as you type your program. For example, QuickBASIC will not display an error message when you make the following rather obvious typing error:

```
PRINNT AVERAGE
```

Only when you attempt to run the program will QuickBASIC display the dialogue box

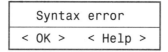

and highlight the part of the program line that caused the error.∗ Whenever you obtain this error message, you can press the Enter key to accept the default response OK. QuickBASIC will erase the dialogue box, and you can then correct the error and run the program again.

∗In Chapter 12, you will learn how to define the identifier PRINNT so that the statement PRINNT AVERAGE is a correct QuickBASIC statement. QuickBASIC allows you to define PRINNT either before or after you have typed the line PRINNT AVERAGE. Thus, when the incorrect PRINT statement is typed, it is not a syntax error— QuickBASIC does not miss them. When the program is executed, however, the incorrect PRINT statement violates the QuickBASIC syntax because you did not define the identifier PRINNT.

As illustrated in the following example, error messages are sometimes displayed even though a program contains no syntax errors.

EXAMPLE 1   *Here is a syntactically correct program with an error.*

The following program is designed to compute the ratio

$$\frac{\text{Cost} + \text{markup}}{\text{Cost} - \text{markup}}$$

```
' C Denotes the cost.
' M Denotes the markup.

LET C = 100
LET M = 100
LET R = (C + M) / (C - M)
PRINT "RATIO ="; R
END
```

If you run this program, QuickBASIC will display the following error message:

```
    Division by zero
  < OK >    < Help >
```

If you press the Enter key to accept the Ok response, the line

```
LET R = (C + M) / (C - M)
```

will be highlighted. The error message says that an attempt was made to divide by zero (something that is not allowed). This means that the denominator $(C - M)$ was zero when the statement was executed. Programming errors that cause error messages during program execution are called **run-time errors.**

Unfortunately, error messages are not always displayed when incorrect programs are run. The following program contains an error that the computer will not detect.

EXAMPLE 2   *Here is a program that incorrectly calculates a square root.*

```
' Calculate the square root
' of the sum A + B + C.

' This program is syntactically correct
' but does not give the correct result.

LET A = 5
LET B = 8
LET C = 12
LET ROOT = (A + B + C) ^ 1 / 2
PRINT "Square root of the sum is"; ROOT
END
```

Program output:
```
Square root of the sum is 12.5
```

The computer does precisely what you *instruct* it to do; it does not do what you *meant* it to do. The programming error in the LET statement that calculates ROOT is an error in the *logic* of the program; it is not a syntax or run-time error. Such programming errors can sometimes be very difficult to find.

In addition to cursor-moving keys shown in Table 4.1, QuickBASIC provides several key combinations for program editing. The key combinations shown in Table 4.2 are useful when you need to move or delete blocks of code.

Table 4.2 Moving and deleting blocks of code

Key(s)	Effect
Shift-down arrow	Marks (highlights) program lines to be moved or deleted. Repeat the Shift-down arrow key combination to mark additional lines.
Shift-up arrow	Same as Shift-down arrow, except that text above the line containing the cursor is marked.
Del	Deletes marked text. If text has not been marked, the character at the cursor is deleted.
Shift-Del	Deletes marked text after moving it to a buffer called the Clipboard. The previous contents of the Clipboard are erased.
Shift-Ins	Inserts text from the Clipboard at the cursor position.

■ *4.7 Saving Your Programs and Leaving QuickBASIC*

To save the current program, press the Alt, F, and A keys, in that order:

Alt key	Select the menu bar.
F key	Display the *File* menu.
A key	Select the *Save As. . .* option.

QuickBASIC will display a *Save As* dialogue box similar to the one shown in Figure 4.3. Type a name for your program and press the Enter key. QuickBASIC will save your program with this name and erase the dialogue box. Your program remains the current program, with its name displayed at the top of the View window.

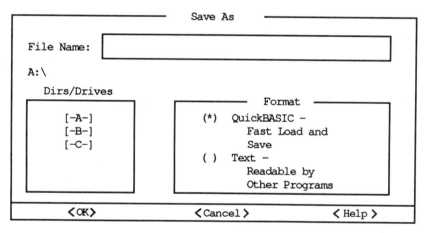

Figure 4.3 The *Save As. . .* dialogue box

The following points concerning the Save As option are significant:

1. The graphic A:\ shown in Figure 4.3 beneath the words *File Name* indicates the default directory into which QuickBASIC places the name of the program you are saving. Recall that drive A was the active drive when we loaded QuickBASIC as described in Section 4.2.

2. To save a program and to place its name in a directory other than the one indicated in the Save As box, type the complete pathname for the file, as explained in Appendix A.6.

3. If you use the Save As command and type the name of a file that already exists in the default directory, QuickBASIC will display the following dialogue box:

```
    File already exists. Overwrite?
< Yes >    < No >    < Cancel >    < Help >
```

If you press the Enter key to accept the default response Yes, the current program will replace the program currently stored under the same name. If you select No (press the Tab key and then the Enter key), QuickBASIC will display the Save As dialogue box again so that you can type another name. You can also press the Esc key to cancel the Save As command.

To leave QuickBASIC and return to DOS, press the Alt, F, and X keys, in that order:

Alt key	Select the menu bar.
F key	Display the *File* menu.
X key	Select the *Exit* option.

If you issue this Exit command before you save the program you were working on, QuickBASIC will give you another chance to save your program.

4.8 Retrieving Programs from a Disk

To retrieve a previously saved program, press the Alt, F, and O keys, in that order:

Alt key	Select the menu bar.
F key	Display the *File* menu.
O key	Select the *Open Program . . .* option.

QuickBASIC will display an *Open Program* dialogue box similar to that in Figure 4.4. You can specify a file name in two ways: you can simply type it, or you can use the Tab and arrow keys to select from the file names displayed in box labeled *Files*. These are the names of QuickBASIC programs that are currently in the default directory. To select from this list, press the Tab key to move the cursor into the Files box, and then use one or more arrow keys to highlight the file name you want.

After specifying a file name, press the Enter key. QuickBASIC will load the program into memory as the current program. At this point, you can run the program and change it, if necessary, just as you would if you were typing the program for the first time. If changes are made, use the Save As . . . command to save the modified version under the same name or a new one.

The following points concerning the Open Program option are significant:

1. The graphic A:\ shown in Figure 4.4 beneath the words *File Name* indicates the default directory from which QuickBASIC obtains programs. (Recall that drive A was the active drive when we loaded QuickBASIC as described in Section 4.2.)

2. To retrieve a program from a directory other than the one indicated in the Open Program box, type the complete pathname for the file, as explained in Appendix A.6.

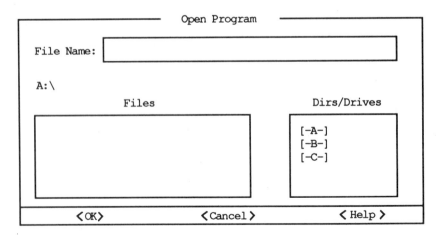

Figure 4.4   The *Open Program. . .* dialogue box

3. When using the Open Program option, you will sometimes get the following dialogue box after you have specified a file name and pressed the Enter key:

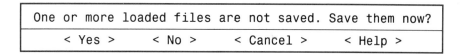

```
┌──────────────────────────────────────────────────────────┐
│ One or more loaded files are not saved. Save them now?     │
├──────────────────────────────────────────────────────────┤
│    < Yes >       < No >        < Cancel >      < Help >    │
└──────────────────────────────────────────────────────────┘
```

This will happen if you have made changes to the View window but have not used the Save As option to save the changes. (This can happen even if the View window appears to be empty—you may have pressed the space bar; that is a change.) If you choose the No response, QuickBASIC will clear the dialogue box from the screen and load the program whose name you specified. If you choose the Yes response, QuickBASIC will display the Save As dialogue box. You would then type a name for the current program and press the Enter key. QuickBASIC will save the current program, and then load the program that you selected for the Open Program option.

■ *4.9 Immediate and Deferred Execution Modes*

In QuickBASIC, each line you type in the View window is entered as a programming line and is not executed until a RUN command has been issued. This is called **deferred execution mode**—execution of the statement (or statements) contained in the line is deferred until later.

If you type a programming line with the cursor in the Immediate Mode window, it is executed as soon as you press the Enter key. (Function key F6 is used to toggle back and forth between the View and Immediate Mode windows.) Thus, if you type

```
cls:print 3+4
```

in the Immediate Mode window and press the Enter key, the value 7 will be displayed on the first line of an otherwise clear output screen.

Following are four ways you can use QuickBASIC's immediate mode capability. You will discover other uses as you learn more about the QuickBASIC language.

1. Execute CLS in immediate mode before running a program. This will ensure that the program output will be displayed beginning at the top of a clear screen.

2. If you are not sure how a QuickBASIC statement works, you can experiment by executing the statement in immediate mode. For example, if you need to know whether the statement

```
PRINT "SALLY";"JONES"
```

will display SALLY JONES with a separating space, simply execute the statement in immediate mode and find out.

3. After a program has been run, QuickBASIC retains the values of all variables. Thus, if your program produces incorrect results, you can use PRINT statements to examine these final values. This information may be just what you need to locate the error.

4. Disk files can be deleted by using the DOS command DEL as described in Appendix A.4. They can also be deleted by executing QuickBASIC's KILL statement in immediate mode. To delete the file LAB3.BAS from the disk in drive A, type

```
KILL"A:LAB3.BAS"
```

in the Immediate Mode window and press the Enter key. If drive A is the default drive, the drive designation is not needed. To delete a file from a different directory, use the complete pathname as explained in Appendix A.6. (The KILL statement can also be included in a QuickBASIC program.)

■ *4.10 Directing Output to the Printer*

Thus far in your work at the PC, every character typed by you at the keyboard, or generated as the result of some action by the computer, has appeared only on the display screen. Often, though, you will want a printed copy of your program or its output. For this, your PC must be equipped with a printer, connected by cable to an adapter at the rear of the computer.

To obtain a printed copy of the current program, be sure your printer is set to ON LINE and then press the Alt, F, and P keys, in that order:

Alt key	Select the menu bar.
F key	Display the *File* menu.
P key	Select the *Print* option.

QuickBASIC will display a dialogue box similar to the following:

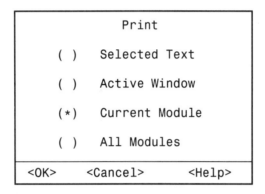

```
                    Print

        ( )    Selected Text

        ( )    Active Window

        (*)    Current Module

        ( )    All Modules

  <OK>      <Cancel>        <Help>
```

You can use the up or down arrow key to select from the four options shown. Most often, however, you will press the Enter key to accept *Current Module,* the default option. This option prints the entire current program. (The *Selected Text* option prints the programming line specified by the current cursor position. The *Active Window* option prints a single program unit, as explained in Chapter 12. The *All Modules* option is not used in this book; it concerns programs that occupy more than one disk file.)

If your printer is not turned on and set to ON LINE, one of two things can happen:

1. If the printer is off, QuickBASIC displays an *Out of paper* dialogue box. If this happens, press the Esc key to cancel the print command, turn on the printer, and try again.
2. If the printer is on but not set to ON LINE, QuickBASIC displays a *Waiting for printer* message in the reference bar at the bottom of the screen. In this case, press the printer's ON LINE button, and printing will begin.

There are three ways to obtain printed copy of the output produced by a program:

1. Use the LPRINT statement in place of the PRINT statement and run your program as usual. For example, the statement

```
LPRINT "THIS GOES TO THE PRINTER"
```

will print THIS GOES TO THE PRINTER on the printer but will not display it on the screen. To print and display the string BOTH PLACES, you can use the two statements

```
PRINT "BOTH PLACES"
LPRINT "BOTH PLACES"
```

2. As mentioned in Section 4.1, you can use the **PrtSc key** to obtain a printed copy of whatever appears on the display screen. You simply press the PrtSc key while holding down the shift key. Thus, if the output produced by your program fits on the output screen, you can run your program and then use the key combination Shift PrtSc to print the output.

3. The third method of obtaining printed copy is explained in Section 5.2. The method allows you to obtain printed copy of everything that is displayed during program execution—even if it does not fit on the output screen.

■ *4.11 On Writing Your First Program*

You are now ready to write your first program. Since a computer program is an algorithm (that is, a set of instructions to the computer to carry out a specified task), the principles of algorithm design described in Chapter 2 are also principles of program design. They will help you design algorithms that are both correct and easily translated into QuickBASIC programs. Following is a brief summary of these principles.

1. *Input/output specification.* Begin by describing the input (information needed to carry out the specified task) and the output (the results to be obtained and the form in which they should appear). Giving a clear and precise description of the input and output is an effective way to acquire an understanding of a problem statement. This principle of program design should be observed even for the relatively simple problems you will first encounter. The experience you gain while identifying and describing the input and output for simple problems will help you when you are confronted with problems that are not so simple.

2. *Modularization.* Identify individual subtasks that must be performed while carrying out the specified task. As illustrated in Chapter 2, the job of writing an algorithm (or program) is often simplified if the given task is broken down into simpler, more manageable subtasks. The importance of this principle of program design will become increasingly more evident as you learn more of the QuickBASIC language and are confronted with more substantial programming problems.

3. *Stepwise refinement.* As illustrated in Chapter 2, you begin with a simple algorithm that contains few details but is known to be correct. (This initial algorithm can be a one-step algorithm describing the task to be carried out.) If necessary, you refine (break down) one or more of the steps to obtain a more detailed algorithm. If even more detail is needed, refine one or more steps in the derived algorithm. This process of stepwise refinement is repeated until you obtain an algorithm with whatever detail you need. The significance of this approach is that you can be sure that the final detailed algorithm is correct just by knowing that you started with a correct algorithm and that each step was refined correctly. As with modularization, the value of this principle of program design will become increasingly more evident as you progress in your study of programming.

The development of programming habits, both good and bad, begins with your first program. The following five-step approach to programming is presented to help you get started. It is not a complete description of the programming process but is adequate for many programming tasks, including those you will first encounter. Example 3 illustrates the application of this five-step process. At the end of this chapter you will be asked to write some programs. To learn good programming habits from the start, you should follow this five-step approach to programming.

1. *Be sure that you thoroughly understand what is being asked in the problem statement.* A good way to do this is to identify the following items:

Input: Data to be presented to the computer for processing.

Output: The results called for in the problem statement. This may involve identifying what the output values are and in what form they are to be displayed.

2. *Identify what, if any, mathematical equations will be needed.* For example, to find the total cost C, including the 5% sales tax, of a television set listed at L dollars, you could use the equation

$$C = L + 0.05 \times L$$

3. *Devise a step-by-step process (algorithm) that, if carried out, will result in a correct solution.* For simple programming tasks, this step usually is not difficult. For example, to find the total cost of the television set referred to above, you could use the following algorithm:

a. Assign a value to L.
b. Calculate $C = L + 0.05 \times L$.
c. Print the result C and stop.

4. *Write the program statements to carry out the algorithm you have described.* This is called **coding the program.** Be sure to include adequate and meaningful comments.

5. *Test the program.* This means running it to test for syntax errors and also to convince yourself that the program produces correct results.

EXAMPLE 3

Write a program to calculate the simple interest and the amount due for a loan of P dollars, at an annual interest rate R, for a time of T years. Use the program to find the interest and amount due when P = $600, R = 0.1575, and T = 2.

A quick reading of this problem statement shows that the input and output values are as follows:

Input: P, R, and T.

Output: Simple interest and the amount due.

We should all recognize the familiar formulas that govern this situation:

Simple interest: $SI = P \times R \times T$

Amount due: $AMT = P + SI$

Knowing these formulas, we can write the following algorithm:

a. Assign values to P, R, and T.
b. Calculate the interest SI and the amount due AMT.
c. Display the results (SI and AMT) and stop.

THE PROGRAM

```
'          SIMPLE INTEREST PROGRAM

'     P denotes the loan amount.
'     R denotes the annual interest rate.
'     T denotes term of the loan in years.

'Assign values to P, R, AND T.
LET P = 600
LET R = .1575
LET T = 2

'Calculate the interest SI and amount due AMT.
LET SI = P * R * T
LET AMT = P + SI

'Display the results.
PRINT "INTEREST:    "; SI
PRINT "AMOUNT DUE: "; AMT
END
```

Program output:
```
INTEREST:    189
AMOUNT DUE: 789
```

REMARK 1

To find the interest and amount due for other loans, simply change the values assigned to P, R, and T. To test the program, try values for P, R, and T for which you know the results. For instance, P = 100, R = 0.06, and T = 1 should yield

```
INTEREST: 6
AMOUNT DUE: 106
```

Another good test would be P = 1, R = 0, and T = 1, which should yield

```
INTEREST: 0
AMOUNT DUE: 1
```

In Chapter 5 you will see how different values can be assigned to P, R, and T without having to retype programming lines.

REMARK 2

Notice that the three comments

```
'Assign values to P, R, and T.
'Calculate the interest SI and amount due AMT.
'Display the results.
```

correspond to the three steps in the algorithm written for this example. Not only does this emphasize how the coding process follows from the algorithm, but it also suggests that each step in an algorithm should contain enough detail so that it can be coded easily. Writing your algorithms according to this principle and using the individual steps as comments are excellent programming practices.

■ *4.12 Problems*

In Problems 1–6, the programs contain one or more bugs—either syntax errors (violations of the QuickBASIC rules of grammar) or programming errors (errors in the logic of a program). Find each error and tell which type of error it is. Then correct the programs, and show the output that will be generated if the corrected programs are run.

1.
```
'PROGRAM TO COMPUTE
'SIX PERCENT OF $23,000
LET D=23,000
LET R=6
LET R*D=A
PRINT "ANSWER IS";A
END
```

2.
```
'PROGRAM TO AVERAGE
'TWO NUMBERS
LET N1=24
LET N2=15
LET A=N1+N2/2
PRINT AVERAGE IS;A
END
```

3.
```
'SALES TAX PROGRAM
'T=TAX RATE : T=5
'P=PRICE : P=120
LET S=P+(T/100)*P
PRINT "TOTAL COST:";S
END
```

4.
```
'PROGRAM TO FIND SOLUTION X
'TO THE FOLLOWING EQUATION:
'    35X+220=0
LET A=35
LET B=220
LET A*X+B=0
PRINT "SOLUTION IS";X
END
```

5.
```
'PROGRAM TO SWAP THE VALUES OF A$ AND B$
LET A$="STOCK"
LET B$="BOND"
PRINT "A$=";A$
PRINT "B$=";B$
REM INTERCHANGE A$ AND B$.
```

```
LET A$=B$
LET B$=A$
PRINT "A$=";A$
PRINT "B$=";B$
END
```

6. ```
'PROGRAM TO COMPUTE THE EXCISE TAX ON TWO CARS
'VALUED AT V DOLLARS. IF THE RATE IS $66 PER $1000.
LET V=4500
LET R=66/1000
LET T=V*R
PRINT TAX ON FIRST CAR IS T
LET V=5700
PRINT TAX ON SECOND CAR IS T
END
```

*Write a program for each of the tasks listed below. Be sure to follow the guidelines suggested in Section 4.11. Use PRINT statements to label all output values, and be sure to include adequate comments.*

7. Compute the selling price S for an article whose list price is L if the rate of discount is D percent.
8. Compute the original price if an article is now selling at S dollars after a discount of D percent.
9. Compute the state gasoline tax in dollars paid by a driver who travels M miles per year if the car averages G miles per gallon and the tax is T cents per gallon.
10. Find the commission C on sales of S dollars if the rate of commission is R percent.
11. Find the principal P that, if invested at a rate of interest R for time T years, yields the simple interest I. (Recall that $I = P \times R \times T$.)
12. Compute the weekly salary, both gross G and net N, for a person who works H hours a week for D dollars an hour (no overtime). Deductions are S percent for state taxes and F percent for federal taxes.
13. Compute the batting average A of a baseball player who has S singles, D doubles, T triples, and H home runs in B times at bat. (A = number of hits/B.)
14. Compute the slugging percentage P of the baseball player who is described in Problem 13. (P = total bases/B.)
15. Find the total cost C of four tires if the list price of each is L dollars, the federal excise tax is E dollars per tire, and the sales tax is S percent.
16. Compute the total cost C of a table listed at L dollars selling at a discount of D percent if the sales tax is S percent.
17. Convert degrees Celsius to degrees Fahrenheit [F = (9/5)C + 32]. Run the program for several values of C, including C = 0 and C = 100.
18. Convert degrees Fahrenheit to degrees Celsius. Run the program for several values of F, including F = 0, F = 32, and F = 212.
19. Convert pounds L to grams G (1 oz = 28.3495 g).
20. Convert grams G to pounds L.
21. Convert yards Y to meters M. Run for several values of Y, including 1760 (1 in. = 2.54 cm).
22. Convert meters M to yards Y. Run for several values of M, including 1 and 1000.
23. Compute the area of a triangle of base B and height H.
24. Compute both the circumference and the area of a circle given the radius. Use $\pi = 3.14159$.
25. Solve the equation AX + B = 0. Run the program for several values of A and B, including the case A = 0.
26. Find the total taxes T on the McCormick property assessed at D dollars if the rate is R dollars per 1,000. If the community uses X percent of all taxes for schools, find how much of the McCormick tax is spent for schools.
27. The market value of a home is M dollars, the assessment rate is A percent of the market value, and the tax rate is R dollars per 1,000. Compute the property tax.
28. Compute the volume and surface area of a rectangular solid.
29. Compute the area of a triangle whose sides are $a$, $b$, and $c$. [Heron's formula for such a triangle is

$$A = \sqrt{s(s - a)(s - b)(s - c)}, \text{ where } s = (a + b + c)/2.]$$
```

30. A tin can is H inches high and the radius of its circular base is R inches. Calculate the volume and surface area. (Volume = area of base × height. Curved surface area = circumference of base × height.)

31. The equation

$$A = P \times \left(1 + \frac{R}{C}\right)^{N \times C}$$

is an alternative form of the compound interest formula that gives the amount A in an account after N years on an investment of P dollars at the annual interest rate R if interest is compounded C times per year. Use this formula in a program to help you determine the better investment: $1,000 for one year at 8% compounded semiannually or $1,000 for one year at 7.75% compounded daily. (Note that, for the rate 8%, R must be 8/100 or 0.08 and not 8.)

■ 4.13 Review True-or-False Quiz

1. The Home key is used to move the cursor to the beginning of a program.   T F

2. CLS is an admissible QuickBASIC statement.   T F

3. If you make a typing error while entering a program, QuickBASIC will respond immediately with an error message.   T F

4. A line can be deleted from a QuickBASIC program by typing the key combination Ctrl Y while the cursor is positioned anywhere on the line.   T F

5. Programming lines exceeding 78 characters cannot be used in QuickBASIC programs.   T F

6. A program containing no syntax errors can cause error messages to be displayed.   T F

7. The program statement `PRINT "13(2+3) = 500"` contains a syntax error.   T F

8. The line

```
LET A=5000 : R=12.5 : PRINT R*A
```

will display 12.5% of 5,000.   T F

9. Coding a program involves determining the programming lines to carry out a known algorithm.   T F

10. Pressing the End key will move the cursor to the end of the current line.   T F

11. The Save As option can be used to save several versions of the same program with different file names.   T F

12. The Open Program option can be used to load QuickBASIC programs from any disk directory.   T F

13. Function key F4 is used to display the output screen.   T F

14. Whenever you press Function key F6, the cursor will appear in the Immediate Mode window.   T F

5
Interacting with the Computer

Most computer programs are written to process input data that will be different each time a program is run. The LET statement is not intended as a means for presenting such data to the computer. As we have mentioned, the use of LET statements to assign input values to variables requires that you retype these statements each time you run the program for different input data. If a program is to process 100 different input values, you would have to type 100 LET statements. Not only is this inconvenient, but it also means that only those who know how to write correct LET statements can use the program. This violates an important rule of programming: the users of a program should not be required to have any knowledge of programming.

The QuickBASIC language includes several statements intended specifically for data input. In this chapter, we discuss the INPUT statement, which allows you to type values for variables during program execution. Thus, by using INPUT statements to obtain data from the keyboard, you will be able to run your programs for different input data without having to change programming lines in any way. In a sense, the INPUT statement allows you to *interact* with the computer while a program is running—the computer displays a message (PRINT statement) concerning the value or values to be typed, you type the input value or values, and then the computer processes the input data and displays the results. As you progress in your study of QuickBASIC, you will learn other ways to effect meaningful "dialogues" between the user and the computer.

■ 5.1 The INPUT Statement

The INPUT statement is best illustrated by example. (The general forms for the INPUT statement are shown at the end of this section.)

EXAMPLE 1 *Here is a program to display the square of any number typed at the keyboard.*

```
PRINT "TYPE A NUMBER."
INPUT NUM
LET SQUARE = NUM ^ 2
PRINT "SQUARE IS"; SQUARE
END
```

When QuickBASIC executes the statement

```
INPUT NUM
```

it displays a question mark followed by a blank space (QuickBASIC's input prompt), and nothing further takes place until you type a number and press the Enter key. QuickBASIC assigns the number you typed to NUM, and only then does program execution continue. If you run this program and type the number 13 for NUM, you will obtain this screen display:

```
TYPE A NUMBER.      (Displayed by the computer)
? 13                (You type 13 and press the Enter key)
SQUARE IS 169       (Displayed by the computer)
```

REMARK 1   When you type a value in response to an INPUT statement, QuickBASIC uses the value only when you press the Enter key. Thus, if you notice a typing error before pressing the Enter key, you can correct it. The act of pressing the Enter key is called **entering** the value.

REMARK 2   It is a common practice to capitalize only the first letter of each variable name or, if the name contains more than one word, the first letter of each word—for instance, Num and Square instead of NUM and SQUARE. In this book, we use all uppercase letters in variable names to help identify them in the text that accompanies the examples.

You can use an INPUT statement to obtain more than one value from the keyboard. The statement

```
INPUT X, Y, Z
```

displays the question mark, and you must enter three values separated by commas. If you enter 5,3,24 (that is, type 5,3,24 and then press the Enter key), 5 will be assigned to X, 3 to Y, and 24 to Z. If you don't enter exactly three values, QuickBASIC will display

```
?Redo from start
```

You must then reenter all three values.

EXAMPLE 2   *Here is a program to compute the cost C of renting a car for D days and driving it M miles. The rental rate is $26 per day and 31¢ per mile.*

```
PRINT "ENTER NUMBER OF DAYS AND NUMBER"
PRINT "OF MILES, SEPARATED BY A COMMA."
INPUT D, M
LET C = 26 * D + .31 * M
PRINT
PRINT "TOTAL COST:"; C
END
```

When you run this program, you will obtain this display:

```
ENTER NUMBER OF DAYS AND NUMBER
OF MILES, SEPARATED BY A COMMA.
?
```

At this point, simply follow the instructions and type two numbers separated by a comma. Let's complete this run as follows.

```
? 3,253          (You type underlined characters.)

TOTAL COST: 156.43
```

REMARK 1   The first two PRINT statements display a message telling the user how to respond when the input prompt ? is encountered. Without this explanation, a user would have no way of knowing what to type. It is a cardinal rule of programming never to confront the person using the program with an unexplained input prompt.

REMARK 2   The statement

```
PRINT
```

in the program produces no output, but it does cause a RETURN to be executed. This results in the blank line in the output after the input values are typed. If you include the statement

```
PRINT : PRINT
```

in your program, two blank lines will appear in the output.

Although the PRINT statements in the previous example instruct the user how to respond to the input prompt, a user might incorrectly type 253,3 instead of 3,253. This will cause 253 to be assigned to D and 3 to M, and incorrect results will follow. To prevent such errors, use a separate INPUT statement for each keyboard entry. Thus, instead of writing

```
PRINT "ENTER NUMBER OF DAYS AND NUMBER"
PRINT "OF MILES, SEPARATED BY A COMMA."
INPUT D, M
```

you might write

```
PRINT "NUMBER OF DAYS"
INPUT D
PRINT "NUMBER OF MILES"
INPUT M
```

With this change, the program will produce the following display:

```
NUMBER OF DAYS
? 3                        (You type underlined character.)
NUMBER OF MILES
? 253                      (You type underlined characters.)

TOTAL COST: 156.43
```

You can often improve the readability of your output by having an input value appear on the same line as the message identifying this value. In QuickBASIC, you can accomplish this in two ways:

1. If you end a PRINT statement with a semicolon, the RETURN normally occurring after execution of the PRINT statement is suppressed. Thus, if you type 358 in response to the programming lines

```
PRINT "WEEKLY INCOME";
INPUT WI
```

your screen will display

```
WEEKLY INCOME? 358
```

2. You can include the message identifying what is to be input as part of the INPUT statement. Simply place the quoted string after the keyword INPUT and separate it from any variables whose values are to be input with a semicolon or comma. The statement

```
INPUT "WEEKLY INCOME"; WI
```

is equivalent to the two statements

```
PRINT "WEEKLY INCOME";
INPUT WI
```

If you use a comma instead of the semicolon, QuickBASIC's input prompt (? followed by a blank space) is not displayed.

Thus, if you type 358 in response to the statement

```
INPUT "WEEKLY INCOME: $",W1
```

your screen will display

```
WEEKLY INCOME: $358
```

EXAMPLE 3   *Determine the yearly income and savings of a person whose weekly income and average monthly expenses are given.*

Two values must be specified (weekly income and monthly expenses), and two values must be determined (yearly income and savings). Let's agree to use the following variable names:

Input: WI = weekly income
            ME = monthly expenses

Output: YI = yearly income (note that YI = 52 × WI)
            YS = yearly savings (note that YS = YI − 12 × ME)

An algorithm for solving this problem can now be written:

a. Assign values to WI and ME.
b. Determine yearly income and savings.
c. Display the results.

Before this algorithm can be coded, you must decide how to assign values to WI and ME. Available are the LET and INPUT statements. Since we may use this program for different weekly incomes and monthly expenses, the decision is easy: use INPUT statements.

THE PROGRAM

```
' PROGRAM TO FIND YEARLY INCOME AND SAVINGS
' GIVEN THE WEEKLY INCOME AND MONTHLY EXPENSES

'Get input from the keyboard.
INPUT "WEEKLY INCOME? $", WI
INPUT "MONTHLY EXPENSES? $", ME

'Compute income and savings.
LET YI = 52 * WI                    'Yearly income
LET YS = YI - 12 * ME               'Yearly savings

'Display the results.
PRINT
PRINT "YEARLY INCOME:  $"; YI
PRINT "YEARLY SAVINGS: $"; YS
END
```

Program output:
```
WEEKLY INCOME? $350
MONTHLY EXPENSES? $1300

YEARLY INCOME:   $ 18200
YEARLY SAVINGS:  $ 2600
```

REMARK

Notice that the yearly income and savings amounts are displayed with a space between the dollar sign and the output value. This is the sign position that QuickBASIC leaves blank when a PRINT statement displays a positive number. In Chapter 7, you will learn how to display dollar amounts without this awkward space. Indeed, you will be able to display the last two lines of output as

```
YEARLY INCOME:   $18,200.00
YEARLY SAVINGS:   $2,600.00
```

EXAMPLE 4

This example shows that the INPUT statement can be used to input string values for string variables.

```
INPUT "NAME"; N$
INPUT "DATE"; D$
PRINT
PRINT "NEW MEMBER:       "; N$
PRINT "INITIATION DATE: "; D$
END
```

Program output:
```
NAME? STEVE MARTIN
DATE? MAY 1993

NEW MEMBER:       STEVE MARTIN
INITIATION DATE: MAY 1993
```

Notice that in the run shown in Example 4, we typed the two input strings STEVE MARTIN and MAY 1993 without quotation marks. Unlike strings in PRINT and LET statements (which must always be quoted), strings typed in response to INPUT statements must be quoted only in two situations:

1. When significant blanks begin or end the input string. If such a string is not enclosed in quotation marks, the leading and trailing blanks are ignored.

2. When a comma is included in the input string. QuickBASIC uses the comma as a delimiter (separator) of input values. If you type

```
MARTIN, STEVE
```

in response to the statement

```
INPUT "NAME"; N$
```

QuickBASIC will display the message

```
?Redo from start
```

because you typed two input values (MARTIN and STEVE), but only one variable N$ is included in the INPUT statement. However, typing

```
"MARTIN, STEVE"
```

instructs the PC that all characters between the quotes, including the comma and the blank, constitute the string being input. When typing strings in response to INPUT statements, it is always correct to quote the input strings, even when quotes are not required.

The preceding examples illustrate the general forms of the INPUT statement:

INPUT **input list**
INPUT quoted string; **input list**
INPUT quoted string, **input list**

where **input list** denotes a list of variable names separated by commas. (Most often, just one variable name will be included.) When executed, the first form displays a question mark followed by a blank space; the second displays the included string, and then the question mark and blank space; and the third displays only the included string. In each case, you must respond by typing a value for each variable in the input list. The values you type must be separated by commas, and their types (numerical or string) must agree with the types of the input variables.

The necessity of using quotation marks for string input values that contain commas, leading blanks, or trailing blanks can be avoided by using the LINE INPUT statement. The statement

```
LINE INPUT A$
```

will assign an entire line of input (terminated by pressing the Enter key) to the string variable A$. The line you type can contain commas, leading blanks, and trailing blanks. The ? is not displayed by LINE INPUT statements, but you can include it or any other characters in a string prompt. For example, the statement

```
LINE INPUT "TYPE ANYTHING:"; A$
```

will display only

```
TYPE ANYTHING:
```

If you complete this line as follows

```
TYPE ANYTHING:   A, B, and C are letters.
```

and press the Enter key, every character you entered (including the three leading blanks) will be assigned to A$. Following is the program of Example 4, with LINE INPUT replacing INPUT.

EXAMPLE 5   ***Here is an illustration of LINE INPUT.***

```
LINE INPUT "NAME?"; N$
LINE INPUT "DATE?"; D$
PRINT
PRINT "NEW MEMBER:       "; N$
PRINT "INITIATION DATE: "; D$
END
```

Program output:
```
NAME?MARTIN, STEVE
DATE?MAY, 1993

NEW MEMBER:       MARTIN, STEVE
INITIATION DATE: MAY, 1993
```

Notice that the 13-character input value MARTIN, STEVE is assigned to N$, and the 9-character input value MAY, 1993 is assigned to D$.

REMARK   If you want a blank space to separate the input prompts NAME? and DATE? from what you type, you can use the string prompts "NAME? " and "DATE? " in the LINE INPUT statements. Remember, QuickBASIC does not display its input prompt (? space) with LINE INPUT statements.

■

■ *5.2 More on Printed Copy*

To obtain printed copy of all output produced by PRINT statements, you can follow each PRINT statement with an LPRINT statement that prints the same values that are displayed by the PRINT statement. Doing this, however, does not give you a printed copy of input values typed at the keyboard, nor of any input prompts you include in your INPUT statements. If all of the output produced by a program fits on the display screen, you can use the Shift PrtSc key combination (see Section 4.1) to get a printed copy of the output screen. This will include all input prompts and all user input.

To obtain printed copy when the output does not fit on the output screen, you must press the key combination Ctrl PrtSc in response to an INPUT statement, either in immediate mode or while the program is executing. Steps (a) through (e) that follow show how to do this. After you have carried out these five steps, everything that is displayed on the output screen will also be printed. In particular, if you run a program, all output will be printed as well as being displayed.

a. Turn on your printer.
b. Press function key F6 to move the cursor to the Immediate Mode window.
c. Type INPUT A$ and press the Enter key.
d. Press the key combination Ctrl PrtSc exactly once (you will hear a prolonged beep) and then press the Enter key.
e. Press a key to return to the main menu screen.

With the hard copy mode activated [that is, after you carry out Steps (a) through (e)], the printed output of each program you run will begin with the *Press any key to continue* message. If you include extra PRINT statements at the beginning of a program, this message will not clutter your printed copy. To cancel the hard copy mode, repeat the same five steps.

■ *5.3 Problems*

Complete the following partial program so that it will perform the tasks specified in Problems 1–23.

```
PRINT " (A short program description goes here.) "
PRINT
INPUT "          ", X
LET A =
PRINT "          "; A
```

Be sure that the program description, input prompt, and output label you write are appropriate for the problem being solved. Do not refer to the variable names X and A in these messages.

1. Determine how much $100 earning 6% interest compounded annually will be worth in X years [value after X years is $100(1 + 0.06)^X$].
2. Determine the commission earned by a salesperson who sells a $625 television set if the rate of commission is X percent.
3. Determine the total cost of an article whose selling price is X dollars if the sales tax is 4.5%.
4. Determine the weekly salary of a part-time employee working X hours at $4.47 per hour (no overtime).
5. Determine the cost per driving mile for a car that averages 19.2 miles per gallon if gasoline costs X cents per gallon.
6. Determine the average of the four grades for a student who has received grades of 73, 91, 62, and X on four exams.
7. Determine the equivalent hourly salary, assuming a 40-hour week, for a worker whose annual salary is X dollars.
8. Determine the amount of sales for a salesperson whose commission is X dollars if the rate of commission is 14%.
9. For a single taxpayer whose taxable income X is more than $17,850, the federal tax due is $2,667.50 plus 28% of the amount by which X exceeds $17,850. Determine the tax due for such a taxpayer.
10. Determine the amount that must be invested at X percent simple interest to yield $1,000 at the end of 1 year.
11. Convert dollars to yen (1 dollar = 133.84 yen).
12. Convert yen to dollars.
13. Convert dollars to deutsch marks (1 dollar = 1.8045 deutsch marks).
14. Convert deutsch marks to dollars.
15. Convert deutsch marks to yen.
16. Convert yen to deutsch marks.
17. Determine the area of a circle given its diameter.
18. Determine the diameter of a circle given its area.
19. Convert inches to centimeters (1 in. = 2.54 cm).
20. Convert centimeters to inches.
21. Convert degrees to radians (1 degree = $\pi/180$ radians; use π = 3.14159).
22. Convert radians to degrees.
23. Determine the distance A to the horizon as viewed over a smooth ocean from a vantage point X feet above sea level. (Consider the right triangle in the following diagram.)

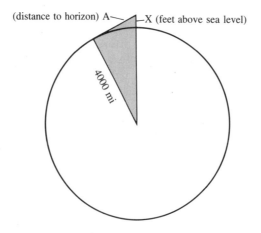

(distance to horizon) A—   —X (feet above sea level)

4000 mi.

Write a program to perform each task specified in Problems 24–32. In addition to displaying meaningful input prompts and output labels, each program should display an appropriate title or other brief description of the task it carries out.

24. For any three numbers A, B, and C, determine the three sums A + B, A + C, and B + C, and find the average of these sums.
25. For any three numbers P, Q, and R, determine the mean M, the differences P − M, Q − M, and R − M, and the sum of these differences.
26. Semester grades are based on three 1-hour tests and a 2-hour final examination. The 1-hour tests are weighted equally, and the final counts as two 1-hour tests. (All exams are graded from 0 to 100.) Determine the semester average for a student whose grades are G1, G2, G3, and F (F for final).
27. Janet and Jim are bricklayers. In 1 hour Janet can lay J1 bricks and Jim can lay J2. Determine how long it will take both of them to complete a job if the number of bricks required is known.
28. A baseball player is to be paid P dollars the first year of a 3-year contract. Find the total dollar value of the contract over 3 years if the contract calls for an increase of I percent the second year and J percent the third year.
29. Determine the yearly gross pay, net pay, combined tax deductions, and retirement deductions for a person whose monthly salary is given. The combined tax rate is R percent, and 6% of the gross salary is withheld for retirement.
30. A manufacturer produces three items that sell for $550, $620, and $1,750. A profit of 10% is realized on items selling below $1,000, and 15% is realized on all other items. Determine the profit before and after taxes for a particular year, given the quantity of each item sold. The current tax rate on profits is R percent.
31. The monthly payment M on a loan of L dollars at the annual rate R for T years is given by

$$M = \frac{L \times R/12}{1 - (1 + R/12)^{-12 \times T}}$$

    The Hendersons apply for a $65,000 mortgage for 25 years at an annual rate of 12.5%. Determine their monthly payment and the total amount repaid to the bank during the lifetime of their mortgage. (R must be .125, not 12.5.)
32. Determine driving expense statistics for Charlene's parents, who are visiting her at college. They note that at the outset of the trip, the odometer reads M1 miles and the tank is full. Just before returning, they fill the tank with G1 gallons of gasoline at a cost of C1 dollars. After they arrive home, the tank is filled again, this time taking G2 gallons at a cost of C2 dollars. The odometer now reads M2 miles. The output should be as follows:

```
GALLONS OF GASOLINE _____
COST OF GASOLINE _____
NUMBER OF MILES DRIVEN _____
COST PER DRIVING MILE _____
MILES PER GALLON OF GASOLINE _____
```

    Try your program using 12,347 and 12,903 for odometer readings, and 13.4 gallons at $16.07 and 12.7 gallons at $15.61 as the two purchases. These values are to be typed during program execution.

■ *5.4 Review True-or-False Quiz*

1. The PRINT and INPUT statements provide the means for two-way communication between a user and a running program.   T F
2. QuickBASIC allows you to type 3/4 in response to the statement INPUT X.   T F
3. QuickBASIC allows you to type 3/4 in response to the statement INPUT X$.   T F
4. It is never correct to type THORPE , JIM in response to an INPUT statement.   T F

5. If you type the ten characters "QuickBASIC" in response to the statement

```
INPUT "Language", L$
```

the screen display will contain the line

```
Language? QuickBASIC
```
T F

6. The statement INPUT B, A$ is admissible.   T F
7. The statement INPUT A; B; C is admissible.   T F
8. The statement INPUT "COST"; C is admissible.   T F
9. Quotation marks must always be used when a string is included in a LET statement or a PRINT statement or is typed in response to an INPUT statement.   T F
10. If you type the five characters "A,B,C" in response to the statement

```
LINE INPUT "LETTERS"; L$
```

the screen display will contain the line

```
LETTERSA,B,C
```
T F

11. If you follow each PRINT statement in a program with an LPRINT statement that prints the same values, you will obtain a printed copy of the screen display produced when the program is run.   T F

6
A First Look at Loops

*A*ll programs presented up to this point have executed sequentially from the first line to the last. In this chapter, we show how you can override this normal sequential order. Specifically, we show how you can direct the computer to execute sections of a program repeatedly (this is called **looping**), and thus cause it to perform many hundreds of calculations with only a few programming lines. In addition, we describe a form of the PRINT statement that is sometimes useful for generating reports in tabular form. (A complete description of the PRINT statement is given in Chapter 7.)

In this chapter, we show how QuickBASIC's DO and LOOP statements are used to code loops, called DO loops. We introduce the DO and LOOP statements in Section 6.1 by showing how you can use them to transform the computer into a useful and rapid calculator. The rest of the chapter concerns the use of DO loops in QuickBASIC programs. Section 6.2 shows how you can modify a DO statement by adding a WHILE condition that controls looping. In Section 6.3, we show how any WHILE condition can be replaced by an equivalent UNTIL condition that in some situations will give you a more readable program. Section 6.5 describes DO loops in which the LOOP statement instead of the DO statement is modified by a WHILE or UNTIL condition. That section also discusses those situations in which you should modify the DO statement, and those situations in which LOOP should be modified.

The methods of coding loops described in this chapter are adequate for all programming applications. An alternative method, which in many special situations is more convenient, uses the FOR and NEXT statements. To keep this introductory chapter on loops as simple as possible, the construction of loops with FOR and NEXT statements is taken up later (in Chapter 9).

QuickBASIC statements that control the order in which other statements in a program are executed are called **control statements.** The DO, LOOP, FOR, and NEXT statements are the control statements that QuickBASIC provides for coding loops.

■ *6.1 The Computer as a Calculator: The DO and LOOP Statements*

If you need to calculate 6% of several different amounts, you can type and run these lines:

```
DO
    INPUT "AMOUNT"; A
    PRINT "6% OF AMOUNT IS"; .06 * A
LOOP
```

The keywords DO and LOOP are always used together to indicate the beginning and the end of a loop. Used as they are here, they cause the computer to execute repeatedly the three statements

```
INPUT "AMOUNT"; A
PRINT "6% OF AMOUNT IS"; .06 * A
PRINT
```

that appear between them. We issued the Run command and typed the values 43, 100, and 89 to obtain this display:

```
AMOUNT? 43
6% OF AMOUNT IS 2.58

AMOUNT? 100
6% OF AMOUNT IS 6

AMOUNT? 89
6% OF AMOUNT IS 5.34

AMOUNT?
```

If you need 6% of other amounts, simply type the amounts one at a time. Notice, however, that the programming lines do not provide a means for stopping execution. You must stop it manually. To do this, use Ctrl-Break: press the Break key (top right key) while holding down the Ctrl key. Program execution will terminate and QuickBASIC will return to the main menu screen. If you need to reread the output screen, simply press function key F4.

The use of the DO and LOOP statements to execute other statements repeatedly can transform the computer into a very fast and useful calculator. The following is another example of using the computer as a calculator. [The values $N * (N + 1)/2$ in this example are called IRS values because they are used in certain tax calculations.]

```
LET N = 10
DO
    PRINT "NUMBER"; N
    PRINT "IRS VALUE"; N * (N + 1) / 2
    PRINT
    LET N = N + 1
LOOP
```

These statements produce the following screen display:

```
NUMBER 10
IRS VALUE 55

NUMBER 11
IRS VALUE 66

NUMBER 12
IRS VALUE 78

NUMBER 13
IRS VALUE 91

NUMBER 14          (You type Ctrl-Break.)
```

Unlike the loop in the previous example, this loop contains no INPUT statement to slow it down, so the results may be scrolled off the output screen before you can read them. In such situations, you can use **Ctrl-NumLock:** press the **NumLock** key (just to the left of the Break key) while holding down the Ctrl key. This will stop program execution temporarily, giving you all the time you need to read what is on the screen. To continue execution, press a key—almost any key will do. To stop the program and get back to the main menu screen, use Ctrl-Break—if Ctrl-NumLock is in effect, you must first press a key.

The two loop examples in this section illustrate how you can transform the computer into a useful and rapid calculator. They do not show you how to code loops for computer programs. A program loop must be written in a way that allows program execution to continue after the loop has carried out its task. In a typical program, a loop performs a specific task that is needed later in the program. The sections that follow show how to use the DO and LOOP statements to code program loops.

■ *6.2 DO Loops*

QuickBASIC provides the keywords WHILE and UNTIL that can be used with the DO and LOOP statements to code loops that allow program execution to continue after the loops have carried out their tasks. Program loops written with DO statements are called **DO loops.** In this section, we explain and illustrate the following form of a DO loop. (Other ways to code DO loops are described in Sections 6.3 and 6.5.)

```
DO WHILE condition
    - - - - - - - - -      (statements to be repeated)
    - - - - - - - - -
    - - - - - - - - -
    - - - - - - - - -
LOOP
```

As will be explained in what follows, *condition* denotes a QuickBASIC expression that is either true or false. The statements between the DO and LOOP statements are executed repeatedly as long as the *condition* is true—that is, while the condition is true. The statements that are repeated are called the **body of the loop** and *condition* is called the **WHILE condition.**[*]

EXAMPLE 1   *Here is a program to display the IRS values N * (N + 1)/2 for N = 6, 12, 18, and 24.*

```
LET N = 6
DO WHILE N <= 24
    PRINT "NUMBER:"; N
    PRINT "IRS VALUE:"; N * (N + 1) / 2
    PRINT
    LET N = N + 6
LOOP
END
```

Program output:
```
NUMBER: 6
IRS VALUE: 21

NUMBER: 12
IRS VALUE: 78

NUMBER: 18
IRS VALUE: 171

NUMBER: 24
IRS VALUE: 300
```

[*] With early versions of BASIC, WHILE loops are coded by using the keywords WHILE and WEND. If we leave out the keyword DO and change LOOP to WEND, we have a BASIC WHILE loop. Although QuickBASIC allows us to code loops in this way, we will consistently use DO and LOOP. A loop coded as a DO loop is easily changed to any of the other DO loop forms allowed in QuickBASIC. Thus, if after writing a program we discover that it would have been better to code a particular DO loop in one of the other forms, it will be a simple matter to make the change.

The WHILE condition N <= 24 is how you write N ≤ 24 in QuickBASIC. The DO statement instructs the computer to execute the body of the loop

```
PRINT "NUMBER"; N
PRINT "IRS VALUE"; N * (N + 1) / 2
PRINT
LET N = N + 6
```

repeatedly while the condition N <= 24 is true. Thus, the action of this program is as follows:

The first line assigns the initial value 6 to N; the DO statement tests the condition N <= 24. Since 6 <= 24 is true, execution continues with the two PRINT statements, which display the number 6 and the corresponding IRS value 21. The next PRINT statement causes a blank line in the output, and the LET statement increases N from 6 to 12. The LOOP statement instructs the computer to test the WHILE condition again. This looping continues until N increases from 24 to 30. When this happens, the WHILE condition N <= 24 is false so that program control passes to the line immediately following the LOOP statement, which in this program halts program execution.

REMARK 1   This program provides for no interaction between the user and the computer. It simply displays the specified output and halts when it has finished. The user doesn't have to stop execution manually.

REMARK 2   The DO and LOOP statements in this program set up a loop in which four statements are executed repeatedly. Indenting these statements as shown in the program listing improves the readability of the program. Other situations in which indentations should be used to improve the readability of your programs will be mentioned as they arise.

REMARK 3   One of the statements in the body of the loop must eventually make the condition N <= 24 false; otherwise, the result will be an infinite loop, one that must be stopped manually. The statement

```
LET N = N + 6
```

serves this purpose in this program.

EXAMPLE 2   *Here is a program to determine the sum S of any number of input values.*

```
PRINT "TYPE NUMBERS TO BE ADDED, ONE PER LINE."
PRINT "TYPE 0 WHEN ALL NUMBERS HAVE BEEN TYPED."
LET S = 0
INPUT X
DO WHILE X <> 0
   LET S = S + X
   INPUT X
LOOP
PRINT "THE SUM IS"; S
END
```

Program output:
```
TYPE NUMBERS TO BE ADDED, ONE PER LINE.
TYPE 0 WHEN ALL NUMBERS HAVE BEEN TYPED.
? 25
? 30
? -10
? 15.75
? 0
THE SUM IS 60.75
```

The first two lines of the program instruct the user; the LET statement assigns the starting value 0 to the sum S. (It is a good programming practice to include this LET statement even though the PC automatically assigns the initial value 0 to S. By including this statement, your program will be easier to understand because it shows explicitly that S starts out as 0.)

The first INPUT statement displays the first ?, and we enter 25 for X. Since the WHILE condition X <> 0 is true (X <> 0 is how you write X ≠ 0 in QuickBASIC), the two statements

```
LET S = S + X
INPUT X
```

that comprise the body of the DO loop are executed. The LET statement adds 25 to S, and the INPUT statement displays the prompt ? for the next input value. We enter 30, and the WHILE condition X <> 0 is tested again. This looping continues until we enter the value 0 for X. When this happens, the condition X <> 0 is false, and program control passes out of the loop to the PRINT statement that displays the final result.

The programs in Examples 1 and 2 use WHILE conditions to compare numerical values. The next example uses a WHILE condition to compare string values.

EXAMPLE 3   *Here is a program to produce a printed report as described in the first three lines of the program.*

```
PRINT "PROGRAM TO ENTER THREE TEST SCORES"
PRINT "FOR EACH STUDENT TO OBTAIN A PRINTED"
PRINT "REPORT OF NAMES AND SEMESTER AVERAGES."
PRINT
PRINT "GET PRINTER ONLINE BEFORE CONTINUING."
PRINT
INPUT "Class"; C$
PRINT
LPRINT C$                               'Printer output
LPRINT
INPUT "NAME ($ when done)"; N$
DO WHILE N$ <> "$"
   INPUT "THREE SCORES:", S1, S2, S3
   PRINT N$; (S1 + S2 + S3) / 3        'Screen output
   LPRINT N$; (S1 + S2 + S3) / 3       'Printer output
   PRINT
   INPUT "NAME ($ when done)"; N$
LOOP
END
```

We ran this program to produce the following screen and printer output.

Screen output:
```
PROGRAM TO ENTER THREE TEST SCORES
FOR EACH STUDENT TO OBTAIN A PRINTED
REPORT OF NAMES AND SEMESTER AVERAGES.

GET PRINTER ONLINE BEFORE CONTINUING.

Class? CS100-02

NAME ($ when done)? James Corbett   (Underlined characters are typed by the user.)
THREE SCORES:72,75,78
James Corbett 75

NAME ($ when done)? Tamara D'Costa
THREE SCORES:80,84,88
Tamara D'Costa 84
```

```
NAME ($ when done)? Melissa Myers
THREE SCORES:66,76,86
Melissa Myers 76

NAME ($ when done)? $
```

Printer output:
```
CS100-02

James Corbett 75
Tamara D'Costa 84
Melissa Myers 76
```

Notice that the statement

```
INPUT "NAME ($ when done)"; N$
```

appears twice in the program: in the body of the loop and also before the DO statement. Including this statement in the body of the loop serves two purposes: (1) it is necessary so that the user can obtain an average for many students, and (2) it allows the user to type $ to cause an exit from the loop so that the program will stop. Including the same INPUT statement before the DO statement is also necessary. It allows the user to type a name to get the loop started or to type $, if, after reading the program description displayed by the first three PRINT statements, it is decided that this is not the program wanted.

For the reasons given in the preceding example, the statement

```
INPUT "NAME ($ when done)"; N$
```

appears both in the body of the DO loop and before the loop is entered. In Example 2, for slightly different reasons, the statement INPUT X appears twice, in the same way. Including the same INPUT statement both before a DO statement and in the body of the loop is typical of many loops that begin with DO WHILE.

In Example 3, we used the statement

```
DO WHILE N$ <> "$"
```

to continue looping as long as the condition N\$ $<>$ "\$" is true. This condition is called a **relational expression**—it is true if the "not equals" symbol correctly describes the *relationship* between N\$ and "\$". Similarly, the WHILE condition X $<>$ 0 in Example 2 tests if the symbol $<>$ correctly describes the relationship between X and 0. In Example 1, we used the relational expression N $<=$ 24 to test if the symbol $<=$ correctly describes the relationship between N and 24. The symbols that QuickBASIC allows in relational expressions are as follows:

QuickBASIC symbol	Arithmetic symbol	Meaning
=	$=$	Equal
<	$<$	Less than
>	$>$	Greater than
<>	$\neq$	Not equal to
<=	$\leq$	Less than or equal to
>=	$\geq$	Greater than or equal to

Here are some correctly written DO statements:

DO statement	Meaning
DO WHILE X>50	Continue looping if X is greater than 50.
DO WHILE 2*N+1<=75	Continue looping if the value of $2 * N + 1$ is less than or equal to 75.
DO WHILE T$="YES"	Continue looping if the string value of T$ is YES.

Each of the WHILE conditions shown is a single relational expression. QuickBASIC allows you to use the keywords OR and AND to write conditions that involve two or more comparisons. For example, the statement

```
DO WHILE N > 0 AND N < 100
```

will cause looping to continue if N is a positive number less than 100. The statement

```
DO WHILE C$ = "A" OR C$ = "B"
```

will cause looping to continue if C$ has either the value A or the value B. The use of AND and OR (and other keywords that are used in making comparisons) is considered in detail in Chapter 8.

A good use of string comparisons involves testing a user's response to input prompts that require string input. We did this in Example 3 by using the statement

```
DO WHILE N$ <> "$"
```

to end the loop when the user types $ for N$. If user input is to be compared to string constants that contain letters, special considerations are required. For example, the DO loop in the program segment

```
INPUT "Type YES to continue: ", N$
DO WHILE N$ = "YES"
    ----------------
    ----------------
    ----------------
    INPUT "Type YES continue: ", N$
LOOP
```

will be repeated as long as the user types YES—that is, as long as the WHILE condition N$ = "YES" is true. However, it is likely that a user will type Yes (or yes), instead of YES. These are different strings; QuickBASIC distinguishes between upper- and lowercase letters included in strings. To allow the user to respond in either upper- or lowercase letters (or both), you can use QuickBASIC's case conversion function UCASE$. If **s** denotes a string, QuickBASIC obtains a value for the expression UCASE$(**s**) by using all characters in **s,** but it converts any lowercase letters in **s** to uppercase letters; the string **s** is not changed. [LCASE$(**s**) obtains its value by converting uppercase letters in **s** to lowercase.] Thus, to allow the user to type the word YES by using any combination of upper- and lowercase letters, change the DO statement to

```
DO WHILE UCASE$(N$) = "YES"
```

The DO loop, with this change, is used in the program of Example 4.

We have illustrated the use of the relational symbols = and <> to test whether two strings are the same. String comparisons involving the relational symbols <, <=, >, and >= are discussed in Chapter 14.

The next example illustrates that DO loops can be **nested**—that is, the statements being repeated in one DO loop can contain another DO loop.

EXAMPLE 4   *Here is a program whose purpose is described in the first two lines of the program.*

```
PRINT "THIS PROGRAM IS FOR ADDING ANY LISTS OF"
PRINT "OF NUMBERS YOU TYPE AT THE KEYBOARD."
PRINT
INPUT "Type YES to continue: ", N$
DO WHILE UCASE$(N$) = "YES"
    PRINT
    PRINT "TYPE NUMBERS TO BE ADDED, ONE PER LINE."
    PRINT "TYPE 0 WHEN ALL NUMBERS HAVE BEEN TYPED."
    LET S = 0
    INPUT X
    DO WHILE X <> 0
      LET S = S + X
      INPUT X
    LOOP
```

```
           PRINT "THE SUM IS "; S
           PRINT
           INPUT "Type YES to continue: ", N$
     LOOP
     END
```

Program output:
```
THIS PROGRAM IS FOR ADDING ANY LISTS OF
OF NUMBERS YOU TYPE AT THE KEYBOARD.

Type YES to continue: yes

TYPE NUMBERS TO BE ADDED, ONE PER LINE.
TYPE O WHEN ALL NUMBERS HAVE BEEN TYPED.
? 23
? 39
? 0
THE SUM IS  62

Type YES to continue: Yes

TYPE NUMBERS TO BE ADDED, ONE PER LINE.
TYPE O WHEN ALL NUMBERS HAVE BEEN TYPED.
? —15
? 25
? —30
? 0
THE SUM IS —20

Type YES to continue: no
```

Except for a few PRINT statements (those that describe the program and those that cause blank lines in the output), this program contains no new QuickBASIC code. The outer DO loop that allows the user to determine many sums during a single program run is identical to the DO loop shown in the discussion that precedes this example, with the condition N$ = "YES" changed as mentioned in the discussion. The code included in this outer DO loop to determine the sum of numbers typed at the keyboard is identical to the code in the program of Example 2.

REMARK 1   In the run shown, we stopped the program by typing no in response to the prompt

```
     Type YES to continue:
```

We could have stopped the program by typing anything other than YES (or the seven other ways to type yes using upper- and lowercase letters). Indeed, we could simply have pressed the Enter key, assigning the null string to N$.

REMARK 2   Notice the two levels of indentation in the program. By indenting the body of each DO loop, it is easy to see where each loop begins and ends. Indeed, the screen positions under each keyword DO are blank spaces down to the keyword LOOP that ends the loop.

Programming tasks often involve generating reports in tabular form. These reports usually consist of one or more columns of data, each with a descriptive column heading. In the next example, we use a loop containing a PRINT statement of the form

PRINT expression1,expression2,expression3

to display the values in a three-column salary report. It is the commas in this PRINT statement that cause the values of the expressions to line up in columns. We also use PRINT statements of the same form to display the column headings. A more detailed description of the use of commas in PRINT statements is given in Chapter 7.

EXAMPLE 5

Prepare a report showing the weekly and annual salaries for persons working 40 hours a week if their hourly rates are $7.50, $7.60, $7.70, . . . , $8.50.

The formulas needed for this task are simple. If HRS and RATE denote the hours worked and hourly rate, respectively, the weekly pay WKLY and equivalent annual salary ANNUAL are given by the formulas

```
WKLY = HRS x RATE
ANNUAL = 52 x WKLY
```

The hourly rates 7.50, 7.60, 7.70, and so on should not be input. Since successive values of RATE will differ by the same amount, 0.10, you can start with RATE = 7.50 and simply keep adding 0.10 to RATE (LET RATE = RATE + 0.10) to get the other values. Thus, the program will have no input. The output is simply a three-column table showing successive values obtained for RATE, WKLY, and ANNUAL.

THE ALGORITHM

a. Display column headings.
b. Let HRS = 40 and RATE = 7.50.
c. Repeat the following while RATE ≤ 8.50.

   c1. Evaluate WKLY = HRS × RATE.
   c2. Evaluate ANNUAL = 52 × WKLY.
   c3. Display RATE, WKLY, and ANNUAL.
   c4. Add 0.10 to RATE.

d. Stop

THE PROGRAM

```
' ************* SALARY REPORT PROGRAM *************

'         HRS = HOURS WORKED
'        RATE = HOURLY PAY RATE
'        WKLY = EQUIVALENT WEEKLY SALARY
'      ANNUAL = EQUIVALENT ANNUAL SALARY

PRINT "HOURLY RATE", "WEEKLY SALARY", "ANNUAL SALARY"
PRINT "-----------", "-------------", "-------------"
LET HRS = 40
LET RATE = 7.5
DO WHILE RATE <= 8.5
   LET WKLY = HRS * RATE
   LET ANNUAL = 52 * WKLY
   PRINT RATE, WKLY, ANNUAL
   LET RATE = RATE + .1
LOOP
END
```

Program output:

HOURLY RATE	WEEKLY SALARY	ANNUAL SALARY
7.5	300	15600
7.6	304	15808
7.7	308	16016
7.8	312	16224
7.9	316	16432
8	320	16640
8.099999	324	16848
8.2	328	17056
8.3	332	17264
8.400001	336	17472

Notice that a last line for the hourly rate 8.5 is missing, even though the WHILE condition RATE <= 8.5 says to repeat the loop again when RATE has the value 8.5. Why this happens and how to prevent it from happening is discussed following this example.

REMARK

The DO loop displays the table values. Since column headings must be displayed first and only once, the PRINT statements that do this must be executed before the loop is entered.

To understand why the preceding program does not display a last line for the RATE value 8.5, you need to know something about how the computer stores numbers. Your computer will store integers exactly, but in most cases it will store only close approximations of numbers with fractional parts—just as you might use 0.66666 or 0.66667 for 2/3. The number 0.10 is one of the numbers your computer does not store exactly. To see that this is so, you can type and run these lines (you'll have to halt execution manually; R will never be exactly 1):

```
LET R = 0
DO WHILE R <> 1
    PRINT R
    LET R = R + .1
LOOP
```

The program of Example 5 repeatedly adds this approximation of 0.10 to the starting value RATE = 7.5 to obtain the approximations 8.099999 and 8.400001 for 8.1 and 8.4, respectively, as shown in the output. If you run the program and then execute the statement PRINT RATE in immediate mode, QuickBASIC will display the final value of RATE as 8.500001 and not as 8.5. With this RATE value, the WHILE condition RATE <= 8.5 is false, and looping stops.

In light of what has just been said, you should compare numbers for equality only if they are known to be integers. To correct the program of Example 5, you can store the hourly rates as cents rather than as dollars, and then repeatedly add 10 instead of 0.10. The following modification of the DO loop uses the integer variable RATE% to store the hourly rate amounts in cents. As mentioned in Chapter 3, RATE% and RATE are different variables.

```
LET RATE% = 750                'Hourly rate in cents
DO WHILE RATE% <= 850
    LET RATE = RATE% / 100     'Convert RATE% to dollars.
    LET WKLY = HRS * RATE
    LET ANNUAL = 52 * WKLY
    PRINT RATE, WKLY, ANNUAL
    LET RATE% = RATE% + 10
LOOP
```

We ran the modified program and obtained the following correct output:

HOURLY RATE	WEEKLY SALARY	ANNUAL SALARY
7.5	300	15600
7.6	304	15808
7.7	308	16016
7.8	312	16224
7.9	316	16432
8	320	16640
8.1	324	16848
8.2	328	17056
8.3	332	17264
8.4	336	17472
8.5	340	17680

We conclude this section with an example that illustrates the following programming practices that we have been stressing:

1. To discover a correct algorithm for a given problem statement, carry out a complete problem analysis, and record it in writing. The first step should be to determine precisely what is being asked. Determining the input and output values is a good way to begin.

2. Use PRINT statements (or INPUT statements containing string prompts) to tell the user what values are to be input during program execution. Also, use PRINT statements to label all output values. The precise form of these statements is usually determined during the coding process—that is, after the algorithm has been described.

3. Use comments to make your program more readable and to clarify what is being done at every point.

EXAMPLE 6

A man lives in a large house with many rooms. He wants to paint the walls and ceiling of each room, but before buying paint, he naturally needs to know how much paint is necessary. On the average, each window and door covers 20 square feet. According to the label, each quart of paint covers 110 square feet. Write a program that will allow the man to enter the dimensions of each room and the number of doors and windows in each room and then determine how many quarts of wall paint and how many quarts of ceiling paint he needs for that room.

PROBLEM ANALYSIS

Although this problem statement is somewhat lengthy, it should not be difficult to identify the input and output:

Input: Name of each room.
Length, width, and height of each room.
Number of doors and windows in each room.

Output: Quarts of wall paint and quarts of ceiling paint needed for each room.

To determine how many quarts of wall paint are needed for a particular room, we must determine the wall area (in square feet) to be covered and divide this value by 110, since 1 quart of paint covers 110 square feet. Similarly, the amount of ceiling paint is obtained by dividing the ceiling area by 110.

Before attempting to write an algorithm for carrying out this task, let's choose variable names for the values of interest. This will allow us to write a concise algorithm by using variable names rather than verbal descriptions for these values.

ROOM$ = name of the room in question
L, W, H = length, width, and height of ROOM$ (in feet)
DW = total number of doors and windows in ROOM$
AW = area of all walls in ROOM$ including door and window space
  $[AW = 2 \times (L + W) \times H]$
ADW = area of the DW doors and windows $(ADW = 20 \times DW)$
AC = area of a ceiling $(AC = L \times W)$
QWP = quarts of wall paint needed $[QWP = (AW - ADW)/110]$
QCP = quarts of ceiling paint needed $(QCP = AC/110)$

For each room (ROOM$), we must carry out the following task, which we call Task R. (Note that the order in which the steps are to be taken is just how you might carry out this task with tape measure, pencil, and paper.)

Task R:

R1. Enter values for L, W, H, and DW.
R2. Determine the areas AW, ADW, and AC.
R3. Determine the number of quarts of wall and ceiling paint needed (QWP and QCP).
R4. Display the values of QWP and QCP.

In the following algorithm for the task given in the problem statement, we instruct the user to enter END for the room name (ROOM$) when all results have been obtained.

THE ALGORITHM

a. Enter a value for ROOM$.
b. Repeat the following until ROOM$ is END.
    b1. Carry out Task R.
    b2. Enter a value for ROOM$.
c. Stop.

<table>
<tr><td>

**THE
PROGRAM**

</td><td>

```
PRINT "PAINT CALCULATION PROGRAM"
PRINT
PRINT "WHEN DONE, TYPE END FOR ROOM NAME."
PRINT
INPUT "ROOM NAME"; ROOM$
DO WHILE UCASE$(ROOM$) <> "END"
    INPUT "LENGTH"; L
    INPUT "WIDTH"; W
    INPUT "HEIGHT"; H
    INPUT "TOTAL NUMBER OF WINDOWS AND DOORS"; DW

    '   -------------- CALCULATE AREAS -----------------

    LET AW = 2 * (L + W) * H      'Area of walls
    LET ADW = 20 * DW             'Area of doors and windows
    LET AC = L * W                'Area of ceiling

    '   ------- QUARTS OF WALL AND CEILING PAINT ---------

    LET QWP = (AW - ADW) / 110  'Quarts of wall paint
    LET QCP = AC / 110          'Quarts of ceiling paint

    '   -------- DISPLAY RESULTS FOR ROOM ROOM$ -----------

    PRINT "QUARTS OF WALL PAINT"; QWP
    PRINT "QUARTS OF CEILING PAINT"; QCP
    PRINT

    '   ----------- GET NEXT ROOM NAME OR END -------------

    INPUT "ROOM NAME"; ROOM$
LOOP
END
```

Program output:
```
PAINT CALCULATION PROGRAM

WHEN DONE, TYPE END FOR ROOM NAME.

ROOM NAME? KITCHEN
LENGTH? 13
WIDTH? 13
HEIGHT? 9
TOTAL NUMBER OF WINDOWS AND DOORS? 5
QUARTS OF WALL PAINT 3.345455
QUARTS OF CEILING PAINT 1.536364

ROOM NAME? FRONT BEDROOM
LENGTH? 12
WIDTH? 9
HEIGHT? 9
TOTAL NUMBER OF WINDOWS AND DOORS? 4
QUARTS OF WALL PAINT 2.709091
QUARTS OF CEILING PAINT .9818182

ROOM NAME? END
```

</td></tr>
</table>

Here are three points concerning the use of DO loops that were not specifically mentioned in this section.

1. A program must contain the same number of DO statements as LOOP statements.
2. If the program segment to be repeated in a DO loop contains any part of a second DO loop, then it must contain the entire second DO loop.

3. The PC detects errors in DO loop constructions only during program execution. If a DO without a correctly matched LOOP is encountered, the PC displays the message

```
DO without LOOP
```

Similarly, LOOP without a correctly matched DO produces the message

```
LOOP without DO
```

■ *6.3 The UNTIL Condition*

QuickBASIC allows you to replace any WHILE condition with an equivalent UNTIL condition. The DO statement

```
DO WHILE X <> 0
```

used in the summing program of Example 2 can be replaced by the statement

```
DO UNTIL X = 0
```

The first statement says to continue looping while X is not 0; the second says to continue looping until X is 0. These are simply two different ways of saying the same thing; thus, the two DO statements are simply two different ways to code the same loop. The following pairs of equivalent DO statements show how each of the other DO statements used in Section 6.2 can be coded by specifying an UNTIL condition (the condition that must be true for looping to stop) instead of a WHILE condition (the condition that must be true for looping to continue).

Example 1:
```
DO WHILE N <= 24
DO UNTIL N > 24
```
Example 3:
```
DO WHILE N$ <> "$"
DO UNTIL N$ = "$"
```
Example 4:
```
DO WHILE UCASE$(N$) = "YES"
DO UNTIL UCASE$(N$) <> "YES"
```
Example 5:
```
DO WHILE RATE% <= 850
DO UNTIL RATE% > 850
```
Example 6:
```
DO WHILE UCASE$(ROOM$) <> "END"
DO UNTIL UCASE$(ROOM$) = "END"
```

The choice between WHILE and UNTIL should be dictated by consideration of which form will give the more readable program. This means, of course, that the decision is subjective. To illustrate, consider the Paint Calculation program in Example 6 of the preceding section. At that point, we had available only WHILE conditions, so we used the statement

```
DO WHILE UCASE$(ROOM$) <> "END"
```

for loop control. There are reasons, however, for using the equivalent statement

```
DO UNTIL UCASE$(ROOM$) = "END"
```

This statement is perhaps a little easier to read. You will also notice that the third line of the program

```
PRINT "WHEN DONE, TYPE END FOR ROOM NAME."
```

says how to stop, not how to continue. A similar statement applies to Step (b) of the algorithm:

b. Repeat the following until ROOM$ is END.

For these reasons, we would be inclined to use an UNTIL condition. However, just as two programmers will write different programs for the same task, one may decide that a WHILE condition gives the more readable program, and the other may decide to use UNTIL for the same reason. Both can be correct.

■ 6.4 Problems

1. *Show the output of each program.*

a.
```
LET S=0
LET N=1
DO WHILE N < 25
   LET S=S+N
   PRINT N,S
   LET N=2*N
LOOP
PRINT N
END
```

b.
```
LET K=1 : P=1
DO WHILE P < 1000
   PRINT K,P
   LET K=K+1 : P=K*P
LOOP
END
```

c.
```
LET A=128
LET N=0
DO UNTIL A<=1
   LET N=N+1
   LET A=A/2
   PRINT N,A
LOOP
END
```

d.
```
LET A=1
LET B=0
DO UNTIL B>8
   LET FIB=A+B
   PRINT FIB
   LET A=B
   LET B=FIB
LOOP
END
```

2. *If A = 1, B = 2, and C = 3, which of the following relational expressions are true?*

a. A+B<=C   **b.** A+B=C

c. 3<>C   **d.** A*B*C>=6

e. A/C=.333   **f.** 3-(C/B)=3-C/B

3. *Explain what is wrong with each statement. The problem may be a syntax error, or the statement may serve no useful purpose.*

a. DO WHILE X < X - 0

b. DO WHILE A$ = OK

c. DO WHILE A*A >= 0

d. DO UNTIL "DONE"

e. DO UNTIL X$ <> "YES" OR X$ <> "NO"

f. DO UNTIL X < 100 OR X > 0

Write a program to display each table described in Problems 4–11. Begin each program with a PRINT statement describing the table. If a table has more than one column, display column headings.

4. The first column contains the number of miles (1, 2, 3, . . . , 10), and the second column gives the corresponding number of kilometers (1 mile = 1.6093 kilometers).

5. The first column contains the number of miles (A, A + 1, A + 2, . . . , B) and the second column gives the corresponding number of kilometers. Values for A and B are to be input.

6. The first column contains the temperature in degrees Celsius from −10 to 30 in increments of 2, and the second column gives the corresponding temperature in degrees Fahrenheit [F = (9/5)C + 32].

7. The first column contains the temperature in degrees Celsius from A to B in increments of D, and the second column gives the corresponding temperature in degrees Fahrenheit. Values for A, B, and D are to be input.

8. The first column gives the list price of an article ($25, $50, $75, . . . , $300), and the second gives the corresponding selling price after a D percent discount. A value for D is to be input.

9. Ucall Taxi charges $1.05 for a ride plus 18 cents for each tenth of a mile. The first column gives the number of miles (0.1, 0.2, 0.3, . . . , 2.0), and the second gives the total charges.

10. The first column contains the number of years (n = 1, 2, 3, . . . , 15) and the second shows the amount to which an initial deposit of A dollars has grown after n years. The interest rate is R percent compounded annually. (The value of A dollars after one year is $(1 + R/100) \times A$.) Values for A and R are to be input.

11. A two-column table showing the values of n and $\sqrt{n}$ for the n values A, A + 1, A + 2, . . . , B. Values for A and B are to be input.

In Problems 12–17, write a program to perform each specified task.

12. A list of numbers is to be typed at the keyboard. After each number is typed, the program should cause two values to be displayed: a count of how many numbers have been typed, and the average of all numbers entered to that time. The program should halt when the user types 0.

13. A program should continually request two numbers of the user. After each pair of numbers is entered, the program should cause two values to be displayed: the product of the two numbers just typed, and the average of all products to that point. The program should halt when either of the two numbers is 0. (Note that A*B=0 is an appropriate condition for halting.)

14. A person wishes to determine the dollar amount of any collection of U.S. coins simply by specifying how many of each type of coin are included. Your program should assist the user in this task. After the value of any collection is determined, the program should ask the user whether to continue or halt.

15. Division of one positive integer A by another positive integer B is often presented in elementary school as repeated subtraction. Write a program to input two positive integers A and B, and determine the quotient Q and the remainder R by this method. The program should halt if either A or B is 0.

16. Two numbers X and Y are to be typed. If the sum of X and Y is greater than 42, the computer should display the message SUM IS GREATER THAN 42. If the sum is not greater than 42, increase X by 10, decrease Y by 3, display these new X and Y values, and again check to see if the sum is greater than 42. This process should be repeated until the message SUM IS GREATER THAN 42 is displayed. When this happens, the user should be able to type two new values for X and Y or end the program.

17. For any loan of L dollars at the annual rate R for T years, display a four-column report as follows:

Column 1: Month number	(1 through 12 × T)
Column 2: Interest	Interest for the month
Column 3: Principal	Amount of the month's payment used to reduce the balance
Column 4: Balance	Amount owed at end of the month

Allow the user to obtain reports for any number of loans during a single program run. (Suggestions: First calculate the monthly payment M by using the formula given in Problem 31 of Section 5.2. If you use B to denote the running balance, the interest for a month is R/12 × B, the payment on the principal is M minus the interest, and the new balance is B minus the principal.)

6.5 *LOOP Statement Modifier*

In this section, we show how you can cause the computer to test a loop condition after first executing the body of the loop. To this point, every program loop has tested the loop condition before executing the body of the loop. Sometimes it is important to make this test before entering a loop. For instance, the program of Example 4 contains these lines:

```
PRINT "THIS PROGRAM IS FOR ADDING ANY LISTS OF"
PRINT "OF NUMBERS YOU TYPE AT THE KEYBOARD."
PRINT
INPUT "Type YES to continue: ", N$
DO WHILE UCASE$(N$) = "YES"
    .
    .
    . (Program segment to add lists of numbers)
    .
    .
LOOP
END
```

When this program is run, the PRINT statements display a description of the program, and the INPUT statement displays the prompt

```
Type YES to continue:
```

After reading the program description, a user might realize that the wrong program was run and type NO. The DO statement will immediately transfer control out of the loop to the END statement and the user can select a different program. By making the loop test before entering the loop, we do not require this user to enter a list of numbers before ending program execution.

In many situations, it makes sense to test the loop condition after the first execution of the body of the loop. To illustrate, consider the following program used in Example 1 to display IRS values for the numbers N = 6, 12, 18, and 24.

```
LET N = 6
DO WHILE N <= 24
    PRINT "NUMBER:"; N
    PRINT "IRS VALUE:"; N * (N + 1) / 2
    PRINT
    LET N = N + 6
LOOP
END
```

Since the body of the loop must be executed at least once (for N = 6), it makes sense to test the loop condition at the end of the loop.

QuickBASIC allows you to modify the LOOP statement, instead of the DO statement, with a WHILE or UNTIL condition. If you do this, QuickBASIC will execute the body of the loop once, and then test the loop condition. Thus, you can write the program shown as follows:

```
LET N = 6
DO
    PRINT "NUMBER:"; N
    PRINT "IRS VALUE:"; N * (N + 1) / 2
    PRINT
    LET N = N + 6
LOOP WHILE N <= 24
END
```

There is no difference in the effect of these two programs. The only difference is in how QuickBASIC carries out the task. In either version of the program, you can replace WHILE N <= 24 with UNTIL N > 24.

A situation in which it makes good sense to modify the LOOP rather than the DO statement involves validating user input. Suppose, for example, that you want to require the user to respond to a prompt by typing YES or NO (in either uppercase, lowercase, or both). The following DO loop will ensure that the input variable R$ is YES or NO:

```
DO
    INPUT "Enter YES or NO: ", R$
    LET R$ = UCASE$(R$)
LOOP UNTIL R$ = "YES" OR R$ = "NO"
```

If you want to require that the user respond to a prompt by typing either 1, 2, or 3, you can use this DO loop:

```
DO
    INPUT "Enter 1, 2, or 3: ", R
LOOP UNTIL R = 1 OR R = 2 OR R = 3
```

As you learn more about QuickBASIC, you will find many programming situations in which similar loops can be used to validate user input.

The next example illustrates another situation in which it makes good sense to test a loop condition after the body of the loop has been executed once. The example involves compound interest calculations.

EXAMPLE 7

A local bank pays interest at the annual rate of R percent compounded yearly. Let's write a program to show how a single deposit of A dollars grows until it doubles in value.

Input: R = annual percentage rate
A = amount of the single deposit

Output: A table showing the account balance, year by year, until the balance is at least twice the initial deposit. A two-column table with the column headings **YEAR** and **BALANCE** is appropriate. Let's use the following variables for the values to be displayed in the table:

YEAR = year number (initially 0, at the time of the deposit)
BAL = account balance (initially, the deposit amount A)

It is not difficult to write an algorithm for the specified task if we leave out the details:

a. Input values for A and R.
b. Display the column headings YEAR and BALANCE.
c. Calculate and display the table values.

Steps (a) and (b) are not new to us. To carry out Step (c), we must decide how to carry out the required compound interest calculations. First, notice that the problem statement specifies that the annual rate R is a percentage. This means that we must use R/100 instead of R in any calculations. In particular, if the balance at the beginning of a year is BAL, the interest earned for that year is (R/100)×BAL. Thus, the balance at the end of the year is BAL+(R/100)×BAL or, equivalently, BAL×(1+R/100). In the program, we then use the statement

```
LET BAL = BAL * (1 + R / 100)
```

to assign this new balance to BAL. To improve program readability, we use the additional variable

TARGET = double the amount of the initial deposit

```
INPUT "AMOUNT OF DEPOSIT"; A
INPUT "ANNUAL PERCENTAGE RATE"; R
PRINT
PRINT "YEAR", "BALANCE"
PRINT
LET YEAR = 0                          'Year of deposit
LET TARGET = 2 * A                    'Double deposit amount
LET BAL = A                           'Initial balance
DO
    LET YEAR = YEAR + 1               'Move on one year.
    LET BAL = BAL * (1 + R / 100)     'Balance at end of year
    PRINT YEAR, BAL                   'Display one line of table.
LOOP UNTIL BAL >= TARGET
END
```

Program output:
```
AMOUNT OF DEPOSIT? 1000
ANNUAL PERCENTAGE RATE? 7.5

YEAR          BALANCE

1             1075
2             1155.625
3             1242.297
4             1335.469
5             1435.629
6             1543.302
7             1659.049
8             1783.478
9             1917.239
10            2061.031
```

REMARK 1   The problem statement says to show how the single initial deposit grows until it doubles in value. Since the starting value of BAL is A, it does not exceed TARGET, so at least one pass through the loop is needed. Thus, we place the loop condition at the end of the loop.

REMARK 2   The expression 1 + R/100 is evaluated on each pass through the DO loop. It isn't necessary to do this. Simply include the statement

```
LET FACTOR=1+R/100
```

before the DO statement and change 1 + R/100 in the loop to FACTOR.

REMARK 3   Notice that the program uses the UNTIL condition

```
BAL >= TARGET
```

to end the loop when BAL > TARGET or BAL = TARGET. As mentioned following Example 5 of Section 6.2, computers store only close approximations of most numbers that are not integers. If, by chance, you type input values for A and R for which a balance BAL is reached that is a little less than TARGET but close enough to be regarded as double the initial deposit (for instance, BAL = 1999.99999, with TARGET = 2000), the program will display this balance and then, since BAL >= TARGET is false, will repeat the loop one more time causing an extra and unnecessary line of output. To prevent such incorrect output, you can use BAL > TARGET − .00001 as the UNTIL condition.

■ 6.6 Problems

1. *Show the output of each program.*

a.
```
LET N=1
LET C=0
DO
    LET N=3*N
    LET C=C+1
    PRINT C, N
LOOP WHILE N<50
END
```

b.
```
LET NUM=50
LET COUNT=0
DO
    LET NUM=NUM\2
    LET COUNT=COUNT+1
    PRINT COUNT,NUM
LOOP WHILE NUM>1
END
```

c.
```
LET X=1
LET Y=2
DO
    LET X=X+Y
    LET Y=X-Y
    PRINT X, Y
LOOP UNTIL X+Y>15
END
```

d.
```
LET X=5
DO
    PRINT X
    LET X=X-1
LOOP UNTIL X=1
PRINT X
DO
    LET X=X+1
    PRINT X
LOOP UNTIL X=5
END
```

e.
```
LET A$="A"
LET B$="B"
LET C$="C"

DO
    PRINT A$,B$,C$
    LET T$=A$
    LET A$=B$
    LET B$=T$
```

```
        PRINT A$,B$,C$
        LET T$=C$
        LET C$=A$
        LET A$=T$
     LOOP UNTIL T$="A"
     END
```

Write a program to display each table described in Problems 2–12. Begin each program with a PRINT statement describing the table. If a table has more than one column, display column headings.

2. The first column contains the number of dollars (1, 2, 3, . . . , 10), and the second column gives the corresponding number of yen (1 dollar = 146.55 yen).

3. The first column gives the amount of sales (500, 1,000, 1,500, . . . , 5,000), and the second gives the commission at a rate of R percent. A value for R is to be input.

4. The first column contains the principal (50, 100, 150, . . . , 500), and the second column gives the corresponding simple interest for 6 months at an annual interest rate of R percent. A value for R is to be input.

5. A two-column table showing how a single deposit of A dollars grows until it doubles in value. The annual interest rate is R percent compounded monthly.

6. Interest is earned at the annual rate R percent, compounded quarterly. Produce a table showing how a single deposit of A dollars will grow, quarter by quarter, until it doubles in value. R and A are to be input.

7. A one-column table (list) containing the terms of the arithmetic progression a, a + d, a + 2d, a + 3d, . . . , a + 10d. Values for a and d are to be assigned by the user.

8. A one-column table (list) of the terms of the geometric progression, a, ar, ar^2, ar^3, . . . , ar^{10}. Values for a and r are to be assigned by the user.

9. A two-column table showing the values of n and 2^n for n = 1, 2, 3, . . . , 16.

10. The first column contains the radius of a circle in inches (1, 2, 3, . . . , 15), and the second and third columns give the circumference and area of the circle.

11. The first column shows the radius in inches (1.0, 1.1, 1.2, . . . , 2.5) of the circular bottom of a tin can; the second gives the volume of the can if its height is H inches. (H must be input.)

12. You require an accurate sketch of the graph of

$$y = \sqrt{1.09}x^3 - \sqrt[3]{8.51}x^2 + (1.314/1.426)x - 0.8$$

on the interval $1 \le x \le 3$. To make this task easier, produce a table of the x and y values where the values of x are in increments of 0.1.

In Problems 13–15, write a program to perform each task specified.

13. A young man agrees to begin working for a company at the very modest salary of a penny per week, with the stipulation that his salary will double each week. What is his weekly salary at the end of six months and how much has he earned?

14. Find the total amount credited to an account after four years if $25 is deposited each month at an annual interest rate of 5.5% compounded monthly.

15. Mary deposits $25 in a bank at the annual interest rate of 6% compounded monthly. After how many months will her account first exceed $27.50?

■ *6.7 Review True-or-False Quiz*

1. String constants appearing in relational expressions must be quoted.   T F

2. If the statements

```
     PRINT "FIRST","SECOND","THIRD"
     PRINT A,B,C
```

appear in a loop, all A, B, and C values will be displayed in columns with the headings FIRST, SECOND, and THIRD.   T F

3. If the statement

```
PRINT X,Y
```

appears in a loop, the column of X values and the column of Y values will be aligned
according to decimal points.   T   F

4. The UNTIL condition is always the condition that must be true for looping to continue.   T   F

5. A program must contain exactly the same number of DO statements as LOOP
statements.   T   F

6. The statement

```
DO WHILE X$<>"55"
```

contains a syntax error.   T   F

7. The following is an infinite loop:

```
DO
    INPUT C$
LOOP WHILE C$<>"YES" OR C$<>"N"
```
                                                                                      T   F

8. The following loop will display the integers 1 to 10, and no other numbers.

```
LET N=0
DO
    LET N=N+.1
    PRINT 10*N
LOOP UNTIL N=1
```
                                                                                      T   F

9. The output from a program will not be changed by replacing the single line

```
DO WHILE X>5
```

by

```
DO UNTIL X<=5
```
                                                                                      T   F

7
More on the PRINT Statement

Up to now we have been working with very limited forms of the PRINT statement. As a consequence, we have had little control over the format of the output generated by a program. In this chapter, we'll show how you can display many string and numerical values on a line (Sections 7.1 and 7.2) and how the spacing functions TAB and SPC can be used to specify precise positions along a line for these values (Section 7.4). In Section 7.6, we describe the PRINT USING statement, an extended form of the PRINT statement that provides a convenient way to specify an exact format for all output values.

All of the material in this chapter can be used whether the output from your programs is directed to the display screen or to a printer. For printer output, simply use LPRINT and LPRINT USING.

■ *7.1 Displaying More Values on a Line*

When you first enter QuickBASIC, the PC is set to display (or print) a maximum of 80 characters per line. This maximum of 80 can be changed by using the WIDTH statement in either immediate or deferred execution mode. The statement

    WIDTH 40

clears the screen and changes the screen width to 40 somewhat larger characters. The statement

    WIDTH 80

clears the screen and changes the screen width back to 80 (40 and 80 are the only screen widths allowed).

To use the WIDTH statement for a printer, you can use the statement

    WIDTH **device, n**

where **device** denotes the name associated with the printer (most likely, "LPT1:"), and **n** denotes an integer from 0 to 255. Thus, if your printer allows 132-character lines, you can use

    WIDTH "LPT1:",132

To change back to 80, you would use

    WIDTH "LPT1:",80

In our discussion of the PRINT (and LPRINT) statements, we will assume that the line width is 80 and that the *character positions* are numbered 1 through 80. We will also continue to use the expression *display line* when referring to a line of output, whether displayed on the screen or printed by the printer.

When programming in QuickBASIC, we consider a line to be divided into units called **print zones** or **tab fields.** In QuickBASIC, the zones are as follows:

Zone 1	Zone 2	Zone 3	Zone 4	Zone 5
1–14	15–28	29–42	43–56	57–80

The statement PRINT A,B,C,D,E will display the values of the five variables, one per zone. QuickBASIC interprets *commas* in PRINT statements as instructions to *move to the beginning of the next print zone.* Thus, the two commas in the statement

```
PRINT,,A
```

instruct the computer to skip *two* print zones and display the value of A in zone 3.

EXAMPLE 1   *Displaying numerical values.*

```
LET A = 20
LET B = −3
LET C = .123
PRINT , , A, B, C
END
```

Program output:

Zone 1	Zone 2	Zone 3	Zone 4	Zone 5
		20	−3	.123

When a numerical value is displayed, the first position in its zone is reserved for the sign of the number. However, if the number is positive or zero, the sign is omitted and the first position is left blank. Thus, 20 and .123 are displayed with a leading blank, but −3 is not.

You can include more than five variables separated by commas in a PRINT statement. If you do this, you will obtain five values on the first line, and the remaining values will be displayed on subsequent lines, five to the line.

Commas can be used in PRINT statements to separate string as well as numerical expressions. Strings are displayed beginning in the *first* position of a zone.

EXAMPLE 2   *Displaying string values.*

```
PRINT "FIRST COLUMN", "THE SECOND COLUMN", "THIRD COLUMN"
PRINT "FIRST NUMBERS", "SECOND NUMBERS", "THIRD NUMBERS"
END
```

Program output:

Zone 1	Zone 2	Zone 3	Zone 4
FIRST COLUMN	THE SECOND COLUMN		THIRD COLUMN
FIRST NUMBERS	SECOND NUMBERS		THIRD NUMBERS

The string THE SECOND COLUMN displayed by the first PRINT statement uses all 14 positions in zone 2 and 3 positions from zone 3. This means that the next string must start in zone 4. The string SECOND NUMBERS displayed by the second PRINT statement uses all 14 positions in zone 2. Whenever the 14th position of a zone is used, the next zone is skipped.

REMARK

If the string variables A$, B$, and C$ have the values FIRST COLUMN, THE SECOND COLUMN, and THIRD COLUMN, respectively, the statement

```
PRINT A$, B$, C$
```

produces the same output as the first PRINT statement in the program.

Many values can be displayed on a single line if we use *semicolons* instead of commas to delimit (separate) the variables in a PRINT statement. If this is done, zones will be ignored and the output values will be displayed right next to each other. It is important to note, however, that whenever a *numerical* value is displayed, part of the display is a blank space following the last digit of the number. This means that one space will always separate numbers, with a possible second space if a number is not negative (the sign position). As many numbers will be displayed on a line as will fit. If the PRINT statement of Example 1 is changed to

```
PRINT A;B;C;A;B;C
```

the output will be

```
20 -3  .123  20 -3  .123
```

If *string constants* or *string variables* are separated by semicolons in a PRINT statement, the output will be merged. For example, if A$ = "TO", B$ = "GET", and C$ = "HER!!!", the two statements

```
PRINT A$;B$;C$
```

and

```
PRINT "TO";"GET";"HER!!!"
```

will both produce the same output

```
TOGETHER!!!
```

If spaces are desired, they must be included as part of a string. Or, you can write

```
PRINT A$;" ";B$;" ";C$
```

A PRINT statement, whether it uses semicolons or commas as delimiters, may contain any combination of constants, variables, and expressions. In the next example, we use a single PRINT statement to display the values of two string expressions ("PERCENT OF" and "IS") and three numerical expressions (R, A, and A * R/100).

EXAMPLE 3

Here is a program further illustrating the use of semicolons in PRINT statements.

```
INPUT "ENTER A NUMBER. ", A
LET R = 5
DO WHILE R <= 8
   PRINT R; "PERCENT OF"; A; "IS"; A * R / 100
   LET R = R + 1
LOOP
END
```

Program output:
```
ENTER A NUMBER. 500
5 PERCENT OF 500 IS 25
6 PERCENT OF 500 IS 30
7 PERCENT OF 500 IS 35
8 PERCENT OF 500 IS 40
```

■ *7.2 Suppressing the RETURN*

It often happens that a program contains a loop in which a new output value is determined each time the loop is executed. If the PRINT statement is of the form

```
PRINT T
```

successive values of T will be displayed on separate lines. However, if you terminate this print line with a comma or a semicolon, more than one value will be displayed on each line: five if a comma is used, and as many as will fit on the line if a semicolon is used.

EXAMPLE 4   *Displaying many values per line.*

```
LET N = 1
DO WHILE N <= 14
    LET T = 2 * N - 1
    PRINT T;
    LET N = N + 1
LOOP
PRINT
PRINT "THAT'S ALL FOLKS!"
END
```

Program output:
```
 1   3   5   7   9   11   13   15   17   19   21   23   25   27
THAT'S ALL FOLKS!
```

When the last number (27) is displayed by the statement

```
PRINT T;
```

the semicolon prevents the cursor from being positioned at the beginning of the next line. The statement

```
PRINT
```

just after the loop causes a RETURN, so that subsequent output (THAT'S ALL FOLKS!) is displayed at the left margin of a new line.

■

EXAMPLE 5   *Here is a program to display a row of N dashes.*

```
INPUT "HOW MANY DASHES"; N
LET K = 0
DO WHILE K < N
    PRINT "-";
    LET K = K + 1
LOOP
PRINT
END
```

Program output:
```
HOW MANY DASHES? 19
- - - - - - - - - - - - - - - - - - -
```

REMARK   QuickBASIC includes a function called STRING$ that allows you to replace the five lines following the INPUT statement with the single statement

```
PRINT STRING$(N, "-")
```

The value of the expression PRINT STRING$(N, "−") is a string consisting of N dashes. If N is 0, the string consists of zero dashes; that is, it is the *empty string*. You can replace the dash with any other character. For instance, the value of STRING$(N, "?") is a string with N question marks. A complete description of the STRING$ function is given in Section 10.4.

■

■ *7.3 Problems*

1. *Show the exact output (line by line and space by space) of each program.*

   a.
   ```
   PRINT "BASEBALL'S HALL OF FAME"
   PRINT "COOPERSTOWN, NY ";
   PRINT "13326"
   END
   ```

   b.
   ```
   PRINT "PASCA";
   PRINT "GOULA RIVER"
   PRINT "BAYOU";
   PRINT " COUNTRY, U.S.A."
   END
   ```

   c.
   ```
   LET X=5
   LET Y=X+3
   PRINT X;"TIMES";Y;"=";X*Y
   END
   ```

   d.
   ```
   LET N=0
   DO WHILE N<=35
       PRINT N,
       LET N=N+5
   LOOP
   PRINT "FINI"
   END
   ```

   e.
   ```
   LET X=5
   DO
       PRINT "IF A=";
       PRINT X;
       PRINT "A+2=";
       PRINT X+2,
       LET X=X+5
       PRINT
   LOOP UNTIL X=20
   END
   ```

2. *Assuming that X = 1 and Y = 2, write PRINT statements to produce the following output. No numbers are to appear in the PRINT statements.*

   a. 1 / 2 = .5   **b.** X + Y = 3   **c.** X − 2 = −1
   d. SCORE: 2 TO 1   **e.** DEPT. NO. 5   **f.** BLDG 4.25

3. *The following programs fail to do what is claimed. Correct them.*

   a.
   ```
   'A PROGRAM TO DISPLAY
   'TEA FOR TWO
   PRINT "TEA";"FOR";"TWO"
   END
   ```

   b.
   ```
   'A PROGRAM TO DISPLAY
   'Sleeping Bear Dunes
   PRINT "Sleeping";
   PRINT "Bear";
   PRINT "Dunes"
   END
   ```

c. ```
   'A PROGRAM TO DISPLAY
   '7A7A7A
   LET X=1
   DO WHILE X<=3
       PRINT 7;"A"
       LET X=X+1
   LOOP
   END
   ```

d. ```
   'A PROGRAM TO DISPLAY
   '1   2   3
   '4   5   6
   LET X=1
   DO WHILE X<=3
       PRINT X;
       LET X=X+1
   LOOP
   DO WHILE X<=6
       PRINT X;
       LET X=X+1
   LOOP
   END
   ```

Write a program to perform each task specified in Problems 4–8.

4. Fifteen years ago, the population of Easton was 3,571; it is currently 7,827. Find the average increase in population per year. The output should be

```
FIFTEEN YEARS POPULATION INCREASE IS _____.
THIS REPRESENTS AN AVERAGE INCREASE OF _____ PER YEAR.
```

5. An item has a list price of L dollars but is on sale at a discount of D percent. Find the selling price. The output should be

```
LIST PRICE $ _____
DISCOUNT OF _____ PERCENT IS $ _____
SELLING PRICE $ _____
```

6. The wholesale price of a car is W dollars and the markup is P percent. Determine the retail price. The output should be

```
WHOLESALE PRICE IS _____ DOLLARS.
MARKUP IS _____ PERCENT.
RETAIL PRICE IS _____ DOLLARS.
```

7. A manufacturer produces an item at a cost of C dollars per unit and sells each unit for S dollars. In addition to the cost of C dollars per unit, a fixed yearly cost of F dollars must be absorbed in the manufacture of the item. The number of units that must be sold in 1 year to break even (breakeven volume) is given by the formula

$$\text{Breakeven volume} = \frac{F}{S - C} \text{ units}$$

Your program is to process several sets of input values C, S, and F and end when the user types 0 as the cost per unit amount. The output for each set of input values should be

```
COST PER UNIT? _____
FIXED COST PER YEAR? _____
PRICE PER UNIT? _____
_____ UNITS MUST BE SOLD TO BREAK EVEN.
THIS REPRESENTS _____ DOLLARS IN SALES.
```

8. If A = 2, B = 5, C = 4, and D = 3, the algebraic expression (AX + B)(CX + D) can be written in the following two ways:

$$(2X + 5)(4X + 3) = 8X \wedge 2 + 26X + 15$$

Your program should produce such a display for any four input values A, B, C, and D.

Write a program to produce each display specified in Problems 9–14. Use the function STRING$, where appropriate.

9. Display a row containing M dashes followed by the string THE END. M is to be input.
10. Display THE END beginning in column position N. N is to be input.

11. Display a square array of asterisks with M rows and M columns. M is to be input.
12. Display a square array of # symbols with N rows and N columns. The display is to begin in column position P. N and P are to be input.
13. Display a square array of asterisks with 12 rows and 12 columns. The design is to be centered on the screen.
14. Display a rectangular array of + signs with R rows and C columns. The design is to be centered on the screen. R and C are to be input.

■ *7.4 The TAB and SPC Functions*

By using the semicolon in PRINT statements, you can specify exact positions for your output values. However, as you probably found while writing the programs for the preceding problem set, this process can be cumbersome. To alleviate this difficulty, QuickBASIC provides the spacing functions TAB and SPC. Both of these functions are used with PRINT and LPRINT statements. TAB(n) specifies that the next output value is to commence in column position n, and SPC(n) specifies that n spaces are to be skipped before displaying the next item.

EXAMPLE 6   *Here is an illustration of the TAB and SPC functions.*

```
PRINT "12345678901234567890"
PRINT
PRINT TAB(7); "WET"
PRINT TAB(6); "PAINT"
PRINT
PRINT "BEWARE!"; SPC(4); "ATTACK DOG"
END
```

Program output:
```
12345678901234567890

      WET
     PAINT

BEWARE!    ATTACK DOG
```

REMARK

Note the use of semicolons in the PRINT statements. Remember that a comma specifies that subsequent output is to commence at the beginning of the next print zone.

Several TAB and SPC functions may be included in a single PRINT statement. For example, the lines

```
PRINT "12345678901234567890"
PRINT TAB(8); "ONE"; SPC(4); "TWO"
```

will produce the output

```
12345678901234567890
       ONE    TWO
```

Note that SPC(4) says to skip four spaces; it does not say to move ahead four spaces. Similarly, if N = 3 and A = 1.234 the statements

```
PRINT "123456789012345678901234567890"
PRINT A; SPC(N); 10*A; SPC(N); 100*A
```

will produce the output

```
123456789012345678901234567890
 1.234    12.34     123.4
```

with exactly five spaces separating the three output values. The first of the five spaces is produced because a numerical value has just been displayed, the next three are caused by SPC(N) with N = 3, and the last is due to the suppressed plus sign of the next value.

We now give the general form of the TAB and SPC functions. In what follows, WIDTH denotes the current width (usually 80) of an output line.

TAB(**n**)   **n** denotes a numerical expression whose value is rounded, if necessary, to obtain an integer N. The effective tab position is determined as follows.

1. If $1 \leq N \leq$ WIDTH, the tab position is N.
2. If $N \leq 0$, the tab position is 1.
3. If $N >$ WIDTH, the tab position is N MOD WIDTH.
   (Note that the effective tab position is always from 1 to WIDTH.)

An attempt to tab to a position to the left of the current cursor position will result in a display on the following line. For example, the statement

```
PRINT TAB(30); "A"; TAB(10); "B"
```

will cause B to be displayed in position 10 of the line following A.

You can place TAB(**n**) at the end of a PRINT statement so that subsequent output will be displayed on the the same line. If you do not type a semicolon after TAB (**n**), QuickBASIC will insert one there.

SPC(**n**)   **n** denotes a numerical expression whose value is rounded, if necessary, to obtain an integer N. The number of spaces to be skipped is determined as follows.

1. If $0 < N <$ WIDTH, N spaces are skipped.
2. If $N \leq 0$, no spaces are skipped.
3. If $N \geq$ WIDTH, N MOD WIDTH spaces are skipped.
   (Note that you can skip at most WIDTH $-$ 1 positions.)

If there are insufficient spaces on the current line, the SPC function can cause a display on the next line. For example, if WIDTH = 80, the statement

```
PRINT TAB(30); "A"; SPC(60); "B"
```

will display A in position 30, and then skip 60 spaces—the 50 that follow A and the first 10 of the next line. Thus, B is displayed in position 11 of the line following A.

As with TAB, you can place SPC(**n**) at the end of a PRINT statement, so that subsequent output can be displayed on the same line.

The following three examples further illustrate the TAB and SPC functions.

EXAMPLE 7   *Here is an illustration of the TAB function:*

```
PRINT "1234567890"
PRINT "----------"
LET K = 0
DO
    LET K = K + 1
    PRINT TAB(K); -3 * K
LOOP UNTIL K = 5
END
```

Program output:
```
1234567890
----------
-3
 -6
  -9
   -12
    -15
```

On each pass through the DO loop, TAB(K) causes the value of $-3*K$ to be displayed beginning in column position K, as shown.

EXAMPLE 8   *Here is an illustration of the SPC function:*

```
PRINT "12345678"
PRINT "--------"
LET K = 0
DO
    LET K = K + 1
    PRINT "N"; SPC(K); "N"; SPC(5 - K); "N"
LOOP UNTIL K = 5
END
```

Program output:
```
12345678
--------
NN      N
N N     N
N  N    N
N   N   N
N    N N
N      NN
```

EXAMPLE 9   *Here we see TAB and SPC in one PRINT statement:*

```
PRINT "12345678901234567890"
LET T = 8: S = 5
DO WHILE T <= 10
    PRINT TAB(T); "*"; SPC(S); "*"
    LET T = T + 1: S = S - 2
LOOP
PRINT TAB(11); "*"
END
```

Program output:
```
12345678901234567890
       *     *
        *   *
         * *
          *
```

On each pass through the DO loop,

```
TAB(T);"*"
```

causes an asterisk to be displayed in column position T, and

```
SPC(S);"*"
```

causes a second asterisk to be displayed after skipping S positions.

REMARK   This program can be simplified by replacing SPC(S) by TAB(22 - T) and deleting the variable S entirely. The simplified program will produce exactly the same output.

■ *7.5 Problems*

1. *Show the exact output of each program.*

a.
```
PRINT TAB(5);"SALES";TAB(15);"COMMISSION"
PRINT TAB(5);"-----";TAB(15);"----------"
LET SALES=2000
DO WHILE SALES<=5000
    LET COMM = 0.10*SALES
    PRINT TAB(5);SALES;TAB(17);COMM
    LET SALES=SALES+500
LOOP
END
```

b.
```
LET B$="BASIC"
LET N=1
DO WHILE N<=3
    PRINT B$;SPC(N)
    LET N=N+1
LOOP
PRINT B$
END
```

c.
```
PRINT "1234567890"
LET T=0
DO WHILE T<=4
    PRINT TAB(2*T+1);-T
    LET T=T+1
LOOP
PRINT "THAT'S ENOUGH";
END
```

d.
```
PRINT "7777777"
N = 2: S = 5
DO
    PRINT TAB(S); N + S
    N = N + 1: S = S - 1
LOOP UNTIL S = 0
END
```

e.
```
PRINT "1234567890"
LET X=0
DO
    LET X=X+1
    PRINT SPC(2*X);"*"
LOOP UNTIL X=4
END
```

f.
```
LET X=0
PRINT TAB(5);"X";SPC(10);"X^2"
DO WHILE X<4
    PRINT
    LET X=X+1
    PRINT TAB(4);X;SPC(9);X^2;
LOOP
END
```

2. *Write a single PRINT statement for each task. (Use the TAB and SPC functions.)*
   a. Display the letter B in position 6 and the digit 3 in position 10.
   b. Display the values of X, 2X, 3X, and 4X on one line about equally spaced.

c. Display your name centered on an 80-character line.

d. Display seven zeros equally spaced along an 80-character line. The first zero is to be in position 2 and the last in position 80.

e. Display seven zeros as in part (d) except that the first zero is to be in position 1 and the last in position 79.

Write a program to perform each task specified in Problems 3–8. (Use the TAB and SPC functions.)

3. Display your name on one line, street and number on the next line, and city or town and state on the third line. Your name should be centered on a line, and successive lines should be indented.

4. Display a row of 15 A's beginning in position 21 and a row of 13 B's centered under the A's.

5. Display a rectangular array of asterisks with five rows and eight columns. The display is to be centered.

6. Display a square array of # symbols with M rows and M columns. M is to be input. The display is to be centered.

7. Display the numbers 1, 10, 100, 1000, 10000, 100000, and 1000000 in a column that lines up on the right.

8. Display the numbers .33333, 3.3333, 33.333, 333.33 and 3333.3 in a column so that the decimal points line up.

■ 7.6 *The PRINT USING Statement*

Consider the following simple program with output.

```
' Display column headings.
PRINT TAB(2); "N"; TAB(9); "1/N^2"
PRINT
' Display table values.
LET N = 1
DO WHILE N <= 10
    PRINT TAB(1); N; TAB(8); 1 / N ^ 2
    LET N = N + 1
LOOP
END
```

Program output:
```
N       1/N^2

1       1
2       .25
3       .1111111
4       .0625
5       .04
6       2.777778E-02
7       2.040816E-02
8       .015625
9       1.234568E-02
10      .01
```

Even though the TAB function is used to control the output format, the second column appears rather cluttered. The PRINT USING statement provides a simple way to rectify this situation. It not only includes the variables and expressions whose values are to be displayed, but also specifies the exact format to be used for these output values. The following example illustrates the two forms of the PRINT USING statement.

EXAMPLE 10 *Each of parts (a) and (b) contains a program segment to produce the output:*

ASSETS INCREASED BY 23.5 PERCENT.

a.
```
LET F$ = "ASSETS INCREASED BY ##.# PERCENT."
LET A = 23.478
PRINT USING F$; A
```

The PRINT USING statement displays the value of A in the form specified by the contents of a string variable (F$ in this example). The specification ##.# included in F$ says to display the value of A by using two positions to the left and one to the right of the decimal point. The value 23.487 of A is rounded to fit the specification ##.#.

b. LET A = 23.487
   PRINT USING "ASSETS INCREASED BY ##.# PERCENT."; A

This PRINT USING statement, which is equivalent to the one shown in part (a), does not require a separate statement to assign the form of the output to a string variable. The output format is simply enclosed in quotation marks and placed immediately after the keywords PRINT USING.

Both forms of the PRINT USING statement shown in Example 10 are included in the general form

   PRINT USING **s ; expressions**

where **s** denotes a string variable (F$ in Example 10.a), or a string constant (as in Example 10.b); and **expressions** denotes a list of numerical or string expressions separated by semicolons.

The string value of **s** is called the **output format.** It consists of strings and other format specifications that determine the exact form of the output. In Example 10, the output format consists of the specification ##.# and the two strings ASSETS INCREASED BY and PERCENT. Each pound symbol in ##.# specifies a position for a possible digit. Any strings included in an output format are displayed exactly as they appear, including any blanks.

The next two examples further illustrate the use of strings and pound symbols as format specifications.

EXAMPLE 11   *If X = 453, the program segment*

   PRINT "12345678901234567890"
    M$ = "ITEM NUMBER #####"
   PRINT USING M$; X

will cause the display

   12345678901234567890
   ITEM NUMBER   453

The first line of output is included for reference only. The format specification ##### in the string M$ is used to specify how 453 is to appear in the output. Since 453 uses only three of the possible five positions, it is displayed *right justified;* that is, it appears in the rightmost three positions reserved by the specification. (Notice that only one space precedes ##### in the format string M$, whereas three spaces precede 453 in the output.)

EXAMPLE 12   *If A = 42.237 and B = 25, the program segment*

   PRINT "12345678901234567890"
    H$ = "####.## ####.##"
   PRINT USING H$; A; B

will cause the display

   12345678901234567890
    42.24   25.00

This example illustrates two points: numbers are rounded (not truncated) to fit a format specification (42.237 is rounded to 42.24), and all positions specified to the right of the decimal point will be displayed (25, the value of B, is displayed as 25.00).

REMARK

If the value of B is 12345, the output will be

```
12345678901234567890
42.24 %12345.00          ·
```

The % symbol tells you that the specification ####.## is inadequate for the output value 12345. Note that QuickBASIC does, however, display the correct value of B.

QuickBASIC allows two other formatting characters that can be used with pound symbols and periods in numerical format specifications:

1. Place $$ just to the left of a numerical format specification. The numerical output value will be displayed with a single $ just before the leftmost digit. If A = 495.37, the program segment

```
LET F$ = "EQUITY IS $$###.##"
PRINT USING F$; A
```

will cause the display

```
EQUITY IS  $495.37
```

The two characters $$ specify two additional positions for the output value. In all, $$###.## specifies eight positions for the output value $495.37, which requires only seven. Thus, $495.37 is displayed with a leading blank. The other space separating IS from $495.37 is the space that follows IS in the format string.
    If A = 7.45, the display will be

```
EQUITY IS    $7.45
```

The output $7.45 is displayed right justified in the eight positions specified by $$###.##.

2. Place a single comma anywhere to the left of the decimal point in a numerical format specification. The output value will be displayed with a comma to the left of every third digit as required—for instance, 2,253,000.1234 instead of 2253000.1234. If A = 2756.13825, the two lines

```
LET F$ = "EQUITY IS $$#,###.##"
PRINT USING F$; A
```

will cause the display

```
EQUITY IS  $2,756.14
```

IF F$ = "EQUITY IS $$####,.##" (a common way to insert the comma), the output will be exactly the same.

The preceding examples show how the pound symbol, period, dollar sign, and comma are used to specify exact forms for *numerical* output values. You can also specify exact forms for *string* output values:

!	specifies that only the first character of the string is to be displayed.
&	specifies that the entire string is to be displayed.
\n spaces\	specifies that the first 2 + n characters of the string are to be displayed. Thus, two characters and an additional character for each space between the backslashes will be displayed: 2 characters for no spaces, 3 characters for 1 space, and so on. If you specify more positions than needed, the output string is displayed *left justified* with trailing blanks. If you specify too few positions, the output string is truncated on the right.

EXAMPLE 13   *Here is a program illustrating string format specifications.*

```
LET S$ = "AMOUNT DUE"
LET D = 35.91
LET A$ = "! ##.##"
LET B$ = "& ##.##"
LET C$ = "\    \ ##.##"
LET D$ = "\              \ ##.##"
LET Z$ = "12345678901234567890"
PRINT Z$
PRINT USING A$; S$; D
PRINT USING B$; S$; D
PRINT USING C$; S$; D
PRINT USING D$; S$; D
END
```

Program output:
```
12345678901234567890
A 35.91
AMOUNT DUE 35.91
AMOUNT 35.91
AMOUNT DUE      35.91
```

Each PRINT USING statement contains the two output variables S$ (AMOUNT DUE) and D (35.91). The output format A$ specifies that only the first character A of S$ be displayed, whereas B$ displays the entire string.

Since specification C$ does not provide sufficient positions for S$ (it provides only 2 + 4 = 6 positions), the string AMOUNT DUE is truncated on the right to fit the specification. Thus only the first six characters, AMOUNT, are displayed.

D$ provides 2 + 12 = 14 positions for the 10-character string S$. Thus, the string AMOUNT DUE is displayed left justified; that is, it appears in the leftmost 10 positions reserved by the format specifications.

REMARK   Note that *numerical* output values are displayed *right* justified (see Example 11), whereas *string* output values are displayed *left* justified.

The PRINT USING statement is especially useful when you have to produce reports in which the columns must line up on the decimal points. The next two examples illustrate this use of the PRINT USING statement.

EXAMPLE 14   *Here is an improved version of the program shown at the beginning of the section.*

```
' Assign heading and format strings.
LET H$ = " N        1/N^2"
LET F$ = "##       #.####"
' Display column headings.
PRINT H$
PRINT
' Display table values.
LET N = 1
DO WHILE N <= 10
   PRINT USING F$; N; 1 / N ^ 2
   LET N = N + 1
LOOP
END
```

Program output:
```
    N      1/N^2

    1      1.0000
    2      0.2500
    3      0.1111
    4      0.0625
    5      0.0400
    6      0.0278
    7      0.0204
    8      0.0156
    9      0.0123
   10      0.0100
```

Notice that the second column in the output now lines up according to the decimal points and that the exponential forms of numbers are not displayed. The format specification #.#### in F$ controls this.

REMARK

■

Note that each number in the second column, other than the first, is displayed with 0 just before the decimal point. If we had used the format specification .####, the leading zeros would not be displayed, but then the first value 1.0000 would appear as %1.0000.

EXAMPLE 15   *Here is a program to produce property tax tables.*

```
' ***************** PROPERTY TAX PROGRAM **********************

' THIS PROGRAM PRODUCES PROPERTY TAX TABLES
' BASED ON THE FOLLOWING INPUT VALUES:

'     P     PROPERTY IS ASSESSED AT P PERCENT OF MARKET VALUE.
'    L,H    LOWEST AND HIGHEST MARKET VALUES FOR TAX TABLE.
'           (SHOWN FROM LOWEST TO HIGHEST IN INCREMENTS OF $100.)
'     R     TAX RATE IN DOLLARS PER THOUSAND.

' ***************** DATA ENTRY SECTION ************************

INPUT "ASSESSMENT PERCENT"; P
INPUT "LOWEST AND HIGHEST MARKET VALUES"; L, H
INPUT "TAX RATE PER THOUSAND"; R

' **** DISPLAY COLUMN HEADINGS AND ASSIGN FORMAT STRING F$ *****
PRINT
PRINT " MARKET      ASSESSED     TOTAL    SEMIANNUAL    MONTHLY"
PRINT "  VALUE       VALUE        TAX        BILL         BILL"
  F$ = "######.##    ######.##    ####.##    ####.##     ###.##"
PRINT

' *********** CALCULATE AND DISPLAY TABLE VALUES **************

LET MV = L                                    'Market value.
DO WHILE MV <= H
  LET AV = (P / 100) * MV                      'Assessed value
  LET TX = AV * R / 1000                       'Tax for one year
  PRINT USING F$; MV; AV; TX; TX / 2; TX / 12  'Display a line.
  LET MV = MV + 100                            'New market value
LOOP
END
```

Program output:
```
ASSESSMENT PERCENT? 87
LOWEST AND HIGHEST MARKET VALUES? 12400,13400
TAX RATE PER THOUSAND? 56.45
```

MARKET	ASSESSED	TOTAL	SEMIANNUAL	MONTHLY
VALUE	VALUE	TAX	BILL	BILL
12400.00	10788.00	608.98	304.49	50.75
12500.00	10875.00	613.89	306.95	51.16
12600.00	10962.00	618.80	309.40	51.57
12700.00	11049.00	623.72	311.86	51.98
12800.00	11136.00	628.63	314.31	52.39
12900.00	11223.00	633.54	316.77	52.79
13000.00	11310.00	638.45	319.22	53.20
13100.00	11397.00	643.36	321.68	53.61
13200.00	11484.00	648.27	324.14	54.02
13300.00	11571.00	653.18	326.59	54.43
13400.00	11658.00	658.09	329.05	54.84

Here are two points concerning the use of PRINT USING statements that have not been mentioned, but that you may find helpful.

1. Placing a semicolon or comma at the end of a PRINT USING statement has the same effect as placing a *semicolon* at the end of a PRINT statement. Thus, the loop

```
LET N = 1
DO WHILE N <= 3
    PRINT USING "COLUMN#    "; N;
    LET N = N + 1
LOOP
```

will produce the output

```
Column1   Column2   Column3
```

2. If an output format contains *fewer* format specifications than output values, the *output format* is repeated. Thus,

```
PRINT USING "#";1;2;3;4;5
```

will produce the output

```
12345
```

If separating spaces are desired, you can use " #" or "# " instead of "#".

Here is a simple way to code the loop shown in point (1):

```
PRINT USING "Column#    ";1;2;3
```

This single statement produces exactly the same output as the loop.

■ 7.7 Problems

1. *Show the exact output for each program.*
   a.
```
LET N=9
DO
    PRINT USING "##.##";N
    LET N=N/2
LOOP WHILE N>1
END
```

   b.
```
LET B$="BOAT"
PRINT USING "RIVER\  \";B$
PRINT USING "      \  \SWAIN";B$
END
```

```
c. 'STOCK FRACTION VALUES
   LET F$="  #/#=##.# CENTS"
   LET D=8
   LET N=1
   DO WHILE N<=7
       LET V=N/D*100
       PRINT USING F$;N;D;V
       LET N=N+2
   LOOP
   END
```

```
d. LET Y$="TIME## A= #.##"
   LET J=1
   DO
       LET A=0.004*J
       PRINT USING Y$;J;A
       LET J=J+1
   LOOP UNTIL J=4
   END
```

```
e. 10 LET A=23.60
   20 LET W$="1234567890"
   30 LET X$="  ##.##"
   40 PRINT W$
   50 PRINT USING X$;A
   60 PRINT TAB(3);A
   70 END
```

```
f. LET A$="EYELIDS"
   LET B$="POPULAR"
   LET C$="\ \"
   PRINT USING C$;B$;
   PRINT USING C$;A$
   END
```

```
g. LET A$="BOBBY"
   LET B$="JUDITH"
   LET C$="\   \ LOVES \    \"
   LET D$="\   \ LOVES \ \"
   PRINT USING C$;A$,B$
   PRINT USING D$;B$,A$
   END
```

```
h. LET F$="\ \-\   \ ##    "
   LET T$="TAXATION"
   LET R$="RATE"
   LET R=15
   DO
       PRINT USING F$;T$,R$,R;
       LET R=R+10
   LOOP UNTIL R>35
   END
```

Write a program to perform each task specified in Problems 2–6.

2. Display the numbers 1, 10, 100, 1000, 10000, 100000, and 1000000 in a column that lines up on the right.

3. An employer is considering giving all employees a flat across-the-board raise R in addition to a percentage increase P. P and R are to be input. A three-column report with the column headings PRESENT SALARY, AMOUNT OF RAISE, and NEW SALARY is to be displayed. The first column is to list the possible salaries from $20,000 to $25,000 in increments of $500. Columns must line up on the decimal points.

4. Produce a six-column tax table showing 5%, 6%, 7%, 8%, 9%, and 10% for the amounts $100 to $300 in increments of $25. The table should have a centered title, and each column should be labeled appropriately. Columns must line up on the decimal points.

5. Produce a table showing 1%, 2%, 3%, . . . , 8% of the values from 10¢ to $2 in increments of 10¢. Your table should have nine columns, each with a column heading, and all columns are to line up on the decimal points.

6. Agaze Motors offers a new-car buyer a 4-year loan at an annual rate of R percent after a 25% down payment. Write a program to determine the monthly payment if the cost of the car is input. Part of the monthly payment is for interest and part is used to reduce the principal. Interest is charged only on the unpaid principal. The program should produce a table with four columns showing the month number, the interest for the month, the amount by which the principal is reduced, and the loan balance after the payment is made. Columns must line up on the decimal point. Conclude the table with one line indicating the total amount of interest paid during the four years. (See Problem 31 of Section 5.3 for the monthly payment formula.)

■ *7.8 Review True-or-False Quiz*

1. A semicolon in a PRINT statement always causes a separation of at least one space between the items being displayed.   T   F

2. If you want to suppress the RETURN following execution of a PRINT statement, you must end the PRINT statement with a semicolon.   T   F

3. The statement WIDTH 40 will change both the screen and printer line widths to 40 characters.   T   F

4. The statement PRINT,X,,Y is an admissible QuickBASIC statement.   T   F

5. The statements

```
PRINT STRING$(5,"*");
PRINT STRING$(5,"-")
```

will display 5 asterisks followed by 5 dashes, all on one line.   T   F

6. The program line

```
PRINT : PRINT TAB(20);"X"
```

will display the letter X in column position 21.   T   F

7. The two program statements

```
PRINT
PRINT "1";TAB(5);"5"
```

will cause the digits 1 and 5 to be displayed in column positions 1 and 5, respectively.   T   F

8. The statement

```
PRINT "GOOD";TAB(6);"GRIEF"
```

will always cause the same output as the statement

```
PRINT "GOOD GRIEF"
```
                                                                                                     T   F

9. The statement PRINT USING "CLASS###";5 will cause the output CLASS5.   T   F

10. If A = 1234.567, the statement

```
PRINT USING "VALUE###.##";A
```

will produce the display

```
VALUE 234.56
```
                                                                                                     T   F

11. IF A$ = "ABC" the statement

```
PRINT USING "! \\ &";A$;A$;A$
```

will produce the display

```
A AB ABC
```
                                                                                                     T   F

12. PRINT USING "A#";1;2;3 will produce the display A1A2A3.   T   F

8
The Computer as a Decision Maker

All of the programs shown in the preceding chapters share a common characteristic. In each program, the computations performed on data do not depend on the particular data values but are the same whatever these values are. For instance, to calculate the weekly gross salary WKLY of a person who works hours HRS at the hourly rate RATE dollars, we used the statement

```
LET WKLY = HRS * RATE
```

(See Example 5 of Chapter 6.) In practice, however, you would take overtime into consideration, and a different formula would be necessary should the overtime rate apply. If time and a half is paid for hours over 32, an appropriate LET statement for hours over 32 would be

```
LET WKLY = 32 * RATE + (HRS - 32) * (1.5 * RATE)
```

It is in this sense that a computer makes *decisions.* You code the program so that the computer tests a condition (in this case, HRS $\leq$ 32) and selects one of two alternative actions, depending on whether the condition is true or false.

In QuickBASIC, the principal decision-making tool is the IF statement. Sections 8.1 and 8.4 describe the two types of IF statements (single-line IF and Block IF) allowed in QuickBASIC. Section 8.5 describes the SELECT CASE decision structure, an alternative to the Block IF structure for making multiple-branch decisions. Relational expressions and other logical expressions are taken up in greater detail in Section 8.2.

■ *8.1 The Single-Line IF Statement*

The simplest, and most often used, forms of the single-line IF statement are:

IF *condition* THEN *statement*
IF *condition* THEN *statement1* ELSE *statement2*

The first executes *statement* if *condition* is true and does nothing if *condition* is false. The second executes *statement1* if *condition* is true and *statement2* if *condition* is false. Thus, the statement

```
IF X > 0 THEN PRINT "POSITIVE"
```

will display POSITIVE if X > 0 and will do nothing otherwise. In either case, control passes to the statement on the line that follows this IF statement. The statement

```
IF X > Y THEN PRINT X ELSE PRINT Y
```

will display the value of X if X > Y, and the value of Y otherwise; thus, this IF-THEN-ELSE statement displays the larger of the values of X and Y.

The next four examples illustrate the use of these two forms of the IF statement in coding algorithms that call for the selective execution of QuickBASIC statements. The general form of the single-line IF statement is given following Example 5.

EXAMPLE 1   *Here is a program to display 6% of any input value, but only if the input value is positive:*

```
INPUT "AMOUNT (0 when done)"; A
DO WHILE A <> 0
   IF A > 0 THEN PRINT "6% TAX IS"; .06 * A
   PRINT
   INPUT "AMOUNT (0 when done)"; A
LOOP
END
```

Program output:
```
AMOUNT (0 when done)? 100
6% TAX IS 6

AMOUNT (0 when done)? 43
6% TAX IS 2.58

AMOUNT (0 when done)? 0
```

After each value for A other than 0 is input, the condition A > 0 is tested. If it is true, the PRINT statement following the keyword THEN is executed. If it is false, the PRINT statement is not executed. In either case, control passes to the next line, which in this example prompts the user for another input value. The loop is repeated until the user enters 0 for A.

The next example shows that the statement that follows the keyword THEN does not have to be a PRINT statement. It can, in fact, be any QuickBASIC statement.

EXAMPLE 2   *Here is a program to count how many of three input values are greater than the average of all three.*

```
'      A SIMPLE COUNTING PROGRAM

'   X,Y, AND Z DENOTE THE INPUT VALUES.
'   A DENOTES THEIR AVERAGE.
'   C COUNTS INPUT VALUES THAT EXCEED A.

PRINT "ENTER THREE NUMBERS."
PRINT
INPUT "FIRST NUMBER "; X
INPUT "SECOND NUMBER"; Y
INPUT "THIRD NUMBER "; Z
LET AV = (X + Y + Z) / 3

' Begin counting.
LET C = 0
IF X > AV THEN LET C = C + 1
IF Y > AV THEN LET C = C + 1
IF Z > AV THEN LET C = C + 1

' Display results.
PRINT
PRINT "AVERAGE OF THE THREE NUMBERS:"; AV
PRINT "COUNT OF INPUT VALUES EXCEEDING THIS AVERAGE:"; C
END
```

Program output:
```
ENTER THREE NUMBERS.

FIRST NUMBER ? 79
SECOND NUMBER? 70
THIRD NUMBER ? 85
AVERAGE OF THE THREE NUMBERS: 78
COUNT OF INPUT VALUES EXCEEDING THIS AVERAGE: 2
```

The three INPUT statements accept input values for X, Y, and Z, and the LET statement that follows these INPUT statements assigns their average to AV. For the input values shown, $(79 + 70 + 85)/3 = 78$ is assigned to AV.

The second part of the program sets the counter C to 0, and then the three IF statements compare X, Y, and Z with the average AV. For each of the conditions $X > AV$, $Y > AV$, and $Z > AV$ that is true, the statement LET $C = C + 1$ is executed, increasing C by 1. For the input values shown (79, 70, and 85), the first condition is true, the second is false, and the third is true. Thus, the C value 2 is attained.

The last part of the program displays the average AV and the count C obtained in the second part of the program.

REMARK 1   The first time the statement LET $C = C + 1$ is executed, it increases the value of C from 0 to 1; the second time, from 1 to 2. Thus, the statement LET $C = C + 1$ actually does the counting. The use of such "counting" statements is widespread in computer programming.

REMARK 2   Since the keyword LET is optional, we could have written the three IF statements in the more concise form:

```
IF X>A THEN C=C+1
IF Y>A THEN C=C+1
IF Z>A THEN C=C+1
```

EXAMPLE 3   *Here is another counting program. The purpose of the program is explained in its comments.*

```
' THIS PROGRAM EXAMINES EACH PAIR OF SCORES
' ENTERED AT THE KEYBOARD TO FIND THREE COUNTS:

'    FIRST  = number of pairs with first score the larger
'    SECOND = number of pairs with second score the larger
'     SAME  = number of pairs with scores the same

'Initialize necessary counters.
LET FIRST = 0
LET SECOND = 0
LET SAME = 0

'Find counts from keyboard input.
PRINT "ENTER TWO SCORES PER LINE."
PRINT
INPUT "(0,0 when done)"; X, Y
DO UNTIL X = 0 AND Y = 0
   IF X > Y THEN FIRST = FIRST + 1
   IF X < Y THEN SECOND = SECOND + 1
   IF X = Y THEN SAME = SAME + 1
   INPUT "(0,0 when done)"; X, Y
LOOP

'Display the results.
PRINT
PRINT "PAIRS WITH FIRST SCORE LARGER:  "; FIRST
PRINT "PAIRS WITH SECOND SCORE LARGER: "; SECOND
PRINT "PAIRS IN WHICH SCORES ARE EQUAL:"; SAME
END
```

Program output:
```
ENTER TWO SCORES PER LINE.

(0,0 when done)? 72,72
(0,0 when done)? 65,83
(0,0 when done)? 67,92
(0,0 when done)? 55,79
(0,0 when done)? 0,0

PAIRS WITH FIRST SCORE LARGER:    0
PAIRS WITH SECOND SCORE LARGER:   3
PAIRS IN WHICH SCORES ARE EQUAL:  1
```

This program consists of four parts. The first simply describes the program. The comment that begins each of the other three parts describes the task being carried out.

REMARK 1

For each pair X,Y of input values (other than 0,0), the three IF statements in the DO loop execute exactly one of the three LET statements

```
FIRST = FIRST + 1
SECOND = SECOND + 1
SAME = SAME + 1
```

This happens because, for any two numbers X and Y, exactly one of the conditions $X > Y$, $X < Y$, and $X = Y$ is true.

REMARK 2

On each pass through the DO loop, the computer will make all three comparisons in the three IF statements

```
IF X > Y THEN FIRST = FIRST + 1
IF X < Y THEN SECOND = SECOND + 1
IF X = Y THEN SAME = SAME + 1
```

even though only one of the conditions can be true. Thus, if the first condition $X > Y$ is true, the program will add 1 to the count FIRST and proceed to make the other two comparisons, even though they will not be true. In Sections 8.4 and 8.5, we show how to code the selections in these three IF statements so that the computer will not make such unnecessary comparisons. However, the program in this example is very easy to read, and this justifies having the computer do a little extra work. You would code this program in a different way only if doing so would improve its readability.

Examples 4 and 5 illustrate applications of the IF-THEN-ELSE form of the single-line IF statement.

EXAMPLE 4

Here is a program to find the total of any list of numbers that do not exceed 100 in value.

```
PRINT "PROGRAM TO ADD LISTS OF NUMBERS. INPUT"
PRINT "VALUES LARGER THAN 100 ARE REJECTED."
PRINT
PRINT "ENTER NUMBERS ONE PER LINE."
PRINT
LET S = 0                          'Start with zero sum.
INPUT "(0 when done)"; X
DO UNTIL X = 0
   IF X <= 100 THEN S = S + X ELSE PRINT "IGNORED!!!"
   INPUT "(0 when done)"; X
LOOP
PRINT
PRINT "TOTAL IS"; S
END
```

Program output:
```
PROGRAM TO ADD LISTS OF NUMBERS. INPUT
VALUES LARGER THAN 100 ARE REJECTED.
```

```
ENTER NUMBERS ONE PER LINE.

(0 when done)? 80
(0 when done)? 60
(0 when done)? 5000
IGNORED!!!
(0 when done)? 50
(0 when done)? 0

TOTAL IS 190
```

For each input value X other than 0, the IF statement in the DO loop executes the LET statement S = S + X if X <= 100. If X > 100, the PRINT statement following the keyword ELSE is executed to display the message IGNORED!!!, and the value of X is not used.

REMARK

If the intent of the program were to add lists of positive numbers, we could change the condition X <= 100 in the IF statement to X <= 100 AND X > 0.

EXAMPLE 5

Let's write a program to find the total of all recent deposits to a checking account and the total of all recent checks written. After the totals have been found, we will update the previous checking-account balance.

PROBLEM ANALYSIS

The problem statement says to update a previous balance; hence, the input must include the current balance as well as the recent deposit and check amounts.

Input: The current checking account balance
                  The amount of each deposit and each check

Output: The total of all deposits
                  The total of all checks
                  The new balance

The following steps show how you might carry out the specified task with pencil and paper:

1. Start with the deposit and check totals set to zero.
2. Get the current balance.
3. Repeat these two steps for each transaction:
  3.1 Read the amount and type of the transaction.
  3.2 If the transaction is a deposit, add the amount to the deposit total; otherwise, add it to the check total.
4. Add the deposit total to the account balance, and subtract the check total.

Although this algorithm is intended for humans, it is easily modified as a program algorithm. For example, Step 3.1 says to read the transaction type. To do this, we will ask the user to respond to the following prompt:

```
DEPOSIT or CHECK (D or C)?
```

Step 3 also requires that we specify a condition for continuing (or ending) the repetition. To accomplish this, we will prompt the user for the amount of a transaction, but we will specify that 0 should be entered after all transactions have been made.

Let's choose variable names and rewrite the algorithm in a concise and easy-to-code form.

BAL	Checking account balance
AMT	Amount of a transaction
T$	Transaction type indicator (D or C)
DEP	Total of all deposits
CHK	Total of all checks

THE ALGORITHM

a. Set DEP and CHK equal to 0.
b. Input BAL.
c. Input AMT.

   d. Do the following until AMT = 0:

   d1. Input T$.
   d2. If T$ is D, add AMT to DEP; otherwise, add AMT to CHK.
   d3. Input AMT.

   e. Add DEP to BAL, and subtract CHK from BAL.
   f. Display DEP, CHK, and BAL.

THE PROGRAM

```
PRINT "CHECKBOOK BALANCE PROGRAM"
PRINT
LET DEP = 0
LET CHK = 0

'Keyboard input section.
INPUT "CURRENT BALANCE"; BAL
PRINT
INPUT "AMOUNT OF TRANSACTION (0 when done)"; AMT
DO UNTIL AMT = 0
    INPUT "DEPOSIT or CHECK (D or C)"; T$
    IF UCASE$(T$) = "D" THEN DEP = DEP + AMT ELSE CHK = CHK + AMT
    PRINT
    INPUT "AMOUNT OF TRANSACTION (0 when done)"; AMT
LOOP

'Display results.
PRINT
PRINT USING "TOTAL OF ALL DEPOSITS: $$#####.##"; DEP
PRINT USING "TOTAL OF ALL CHECKS:   $$#####.##"; CHK
PRINT USING "NEW CURRENT BALANCE:   $$#####.##"; BAL + DEP - CHK
END
```

Program output:
```
CHECKBOOK BALANCE PROGRAM

CURRENT BALANCE? 32.50

AMOUNT OF TRANSACTION (0 when done)? 400
DEPOSIT or CHECK (D or C)? d

AMOUNT OF TRANSACTION (0 when done)? 25.59
DEPOSIT or CHECK (D or C)? c

AMOUNT OF TRANSACTION (0 when done)? 50.00
DEPOSIT or CHECK (D or C)? c

AMOUNT OF TRANSACTION (0 when done)? 0

TOTAL OF ALL DEPOSITS:    $400.00
TOTAL OF ALL CHECKS:       $75.59
NEW CURRENT BALANCE:      $356.91
```

For each transaction amount AMT entered at the keyboard, the body of the DO loop prompts the user for the transaction type T$ (D or C). The IF statement adds AMT to the deposit total DEP if T$ is D (or d); otherwise, AMT is added to the check total CHK. In either case, the next statement (PRINT) causes a blank output line, and the user is prompted for the next transaction amount, or 0.

REMARK 1   If the user enters something other than D, d, C, or c for the transaction type T$, AMT will be treated as a check [the condition UCASE$(T$) = "D" will be false] and will be added to the check total CHK. One way to ensure that this will not happen is to place the INPUT statement for T$ in a loop, such as

```
DO
    INPUT "DEPOSIT or CHECK (D or C)"; T$
LOOP UNTIL UCASE$(T$) = "D" OR UCASE$(T$) = "C"
```

You will learn other ways to handle this problem in Sections 8.4 and 8.5.

REMARK 2

This program does not update the balance BAL as each transaction is entered because this requirement was not specified in the problem statement. However, the program is easily modified to do this. A simple way to make the change is to use BAL in the last PRINT USING statement (instead of BAL + DEP − AMT), and to insert the following IF statement in the DO loop either just before or just after the existing IF statement

```
IF UCASE$(T$) ="D" THEN BAL = BAL + AMT ELSE BAL = BAL - AMT
```

(You will learn two better ways to code the same thing in Sections 8.4 and 8.5.) With this change, you can follow the two IF statements with

```
PRINT USING "NEW BALANCE IS $$#####.##"; BAL
```

to display the running balance just after each transaction is entered.

The preceding examples illustrate common uses of single-line IF statements of the form

IF *condition* THEN *statement*
IF *condition* THEN *statement1* ELSE *statement2*

QuickBASIC allows you to include more than one statement following the keywords THEN and ELSE. The general form of the single-line IF statement is

IF *condition* THEN *thenblock* [ELSE *elseblock*]

where *thenblock* and *elseblock* denote one or more statements separated by colons. The part in brackets is optional. If the *condition* is true, the statements immediately following the keyword THEN (the THEN block) are executed. If *condition* is false, the statements that follow the keyword ELSE (the ELSE block) are executed. In either case, control passes to the program statement on the next line.

The following short program illustrates the form

If *condition* then *statement1* : *statement2*

EXAMPLE 6

Here is a program whose task is described in the first two comment lines.

```
'This program displays the integers
'from 10 to 30, seven to the line.

LET N = 10                'Next number to be displayed
LET C = 0                 'Current line number count

DO
    PRINT N;
    LET C  = C + 1
    IF C = 7 THEN PRINT : C = 0
    LET N = N + 1
LOOP WHILE N <= 30
PRINT
END
```

Program output:
```
10  11  12  13  14  15  16
17  18  19  20  21  22  23
24  25  26  27  28  29  30
```

The first two statements in the body of the DO loop display the value of N, without causing a RETURN, and add one to C. Thus, C counts how many numbers have been displayed in the current output line. The third statement, the IF statement, makes the comparison C = 7 to determine whether the current output line contains 7 numbers. If it does—that is, if C = 7—the THEN block

```
PRINT : C = 0
```

is executed, resetting the counter C to 0, but only after causing a RETURN so that subsequent output will appear on the next output line.

REMARK

If you change the 7 in the IF statement to 4, numbers will be displayed 4 to the line. If you insert the statement

```
INPUT "How many numbers per line"; P
```

before the loop, and change the IF condition to C = P, numbers will be displayed, P per line.

Although QuickBASIC allows you to write long single-line IF statements, doing so will result in programs whose action is difficult to follow. Indeed, statements with more than 78 characters do not fit on the screen (see Section 4.4).

In Sections 8.4 and 8.5, we describe QuickBASIC's Block IF and SELECT CASE statements, which provide alternatives to the single-line IF statement while coding algorithms that specify the selective execution of statements or groups of statements. By using Block IF and SELECT CASE statements as described, you will never have to write long programming lines. Moreover, their use will often significantly simplify the coding process while giving you programs whose action is easy to follow.

■ 8.2 Logical Expressions

A **logical expression** is an expression that is either *true* or *false*. The relational expressions encountered to this point are either true or false; hence, they are logical expressions. QuickBASIC allows you to write *compound* logical expressions by using the logical operators AND, OR, and NOT.* We have illustrated the use of AND and OR in several of the worked-out examples. The following example illustrates the NOT operator and further illustrates the AND and OR operators. Definitions of all logical operators allowed in Quick-BASIC are given in Tables 8.1 through 8.6. In each table, **le₁** and **le₂** denote logical expressions.

Table 8.1   The AND operator

le_1	le_2	(le_1) AND (le_2)
True	True	True
True	False	False
False	True	False
False	False	False

Table 8.2   The OR operator

le_1	le_2	(le_1) OR (le_2)
True	True	True
True	False	True
False	True	True
False	False	False

Table 8.3   The NOT operator

le_1	NOT (le_1)
True	False
False	True

Table 8.4   The XOR operator

le_1	le_2	(le_1) XOR (le_2)
True	True	False
True	False	True
False	True	True
False	False	False

Table 8.5   The EQV operator

le_1	le_2	(le_1) EQV (le_2)
True	True	True
True	False	False
False	True	False
False	False	True

Table 8.6   The IMP operator

le_1	le_2	(le_1) IMP (le_2)
True	True	True
True	False	False
False	True	True
False	False	True

*QuickBASIC also allows the logical operators XOR (exclusive OR), EQV (equivalent), and IMP (implies). These are described in Tables 8.4, 8.5, and 8.6, but are not otherwise illustrated in this book.

EXAMPLE 7 *Here are illustrations of the logical operators AND, OR, and NOT.*

a. The logical expression

```
C$ = "YES" OR C$ = "NO"
```

is true if either of the relational expressions C$ = "YES" and C$ = "NO" is true. Thus, the given logical expression is true if C$ has the string value YES or the string value NO; otherwise, it is false. [If C$ is obtained from the keyboard with an INPUT statement, you should replace C$ with UCASE$(C$).]

b. The logical expression

```
A < B AND B < C
```

is true if *both* of the relational expressions A $<$ B and B $<$ C are true; otherwise, it is false. Notice that this logical expression is true when the values of A, B, and C are in ascending order. In every other case, the logical expression is false.

c. The logical expression

```
X >= A OR X >= B
```

is true when either or both of the relational expressions X $>=$ A and X $>=$ B are true. Thus, this logical expression is true if X is at least as large as either A or B—that is, if X is at least as large as the smaller of A and B.

d. If SMALL $<$ LARGE, the logical expression

```
X < SMALL OR X > LARGE
```

is true if X is either less than SMALL or greater than LARGE—that is, if X is not in the range from SMALL to LARGE.

e. The logical expression

```
NOT (A < B)
```

is true if the relational expression A $<$ B is false, and it is false if A $<$ B is true. Note that the logical expression NOT (A $<$ B) is equivalent to the relational expression A $>=$ B. [Two logical expressions are equivalent if each always has the same value (true or false) as the other.]

A logical expression may contain more than one logical operator. For example, the expression

```
M=0 OR A<B AND A<C
```

is admissible. The order in which the OR and AND operators are carried out, however, matters. For instance, if M has the value 0, the expression

```
M=0 OR (M<5 AND M>1)
```

is true, whereas the expression

```
(M=0 OR M<5) AND·M>1
```

is false. If parentheses are not included, QuickBASIC uses the following priorities:

Logical operator	Priority
NOT	1
AND	2
OR	3
XOR	4
EQV	5
IMP	6

In any logical expression, the order in which the logical operators are performed is determined first by the indicated priority and then, in any priority class, from left to right. As with arithmetic expressions, parentheses may be used to override this order or simply to clarify what order is intended. Thus, the logical expression

```
M=0 OR A<B AND A<C
```

is equivalent to the expression

```
M=0 OR (A<B AND A<C)
```

If you want the OR to be performed first, you must use parentheses and write

```
(M=0 OR A<B) AND A<C
```

The following example illustrates the importance of being able to make more than one comparison in a logical expression. The example shows how the use of the logical operators AND, OR, and NOT can simplify an otherwise difficult coding task and, at the same time, significantly improve the readability of the program.

EXAMPLE 8

Here are three illustrations of the use of compound logical expressions.

a.
```
DO
    INPUT "ENTER THREE NUMBERS, SMALLEST TO LARGEST: ", A, B, C
LOOP UNTIL A <= B AND B <= C
```

If a program requires the user to enter three numbers from smallest to largest, this loop can be used to reject invalid input. To better appreciate the importance of the logical operators, you should write a similar loop without using logical operators.

b.
```
IF NOT (A$ = B$ OR B$ = C$ OR A$ = C$) THEN PRINT "DIFFERENT"
```

This IF statement will display DIFFERENT if the string values of A\$, B\$, and C\$ are all different. The IF statement is easily written without using the NOT operator, but if you do this, what you get will be less readable. [The relational symbol <> (you will need three of them) tends to clutter a program more than the simpler equals symbol does.]

c.
```
IF A < B AND B < C AND C < D THEN PRINT "IN ORDER"
```

This one IF statement determines whether four numbers are in increasing order. As an informative exercise, we suggest that you write a program segment to do what this IF statement does, but without using logical operators. However you do this, what you write will be more complicated than the given IF statement, and will probably be much more difficult to read.

REMARK

The parentheses in the IF statement given in Part (b) are necessary to override the order in which QuickBASIC carries out logical operators in the absence of parentheses. The two expressions

```
NOT (A$ = B$ OR B$ = C$ OR A$ = C$)
```

and

```
NOT A$ = B$ OR B$ = C$ OR A$ = C$
```

are not equivalent. The second is evaluated by QuickBASIC as if it were

```
(NOT A$ = B$) OR B$ = C$ OR A$ = C$
```

(NOT has priority over OR.) But, if A\$, B\$, and C\$ are all equal, this logical expression is true, whereas the expression

```
NOT (A$ = B$ OR B$ = C$ OR A$ = C$)
```

is false.

We conclude this section by giving the order in which QuickBASIC carries out the operations in any logical, numerical, or string expression. As always, parentheses can be used to override this order. In any expression, the operations are carried out from highest to lowest priority, and operations having the same priority are carried out from left to right. Note that the arithmetic operators come first, then the relational operators, and finally the logical operators.

BASIC operators		Priority
^		1
—	(negation)	2
* /		3
\	(integer division quotient)	4
MOD	(integer division remainder)	5
+ —	(subtraction)	6
> >= < <= <> =		7
NOT		8
AND		9
OR		10
XOR		11
EQV		12
IMP		13

■ *8.3 Problems*

1. *If A = 1, B = 2, and C = 3, which of the following logical expressions are true?*

   a. A<B OR A>C

   b. A<C AND A+B=C

   c. (A>B OR B>C) AND C=3

   d. A=B OR 2*B—1=C

   e. NOT (A>B OR C>A)

   f. NOT (A>B) OR NOT (C>A)

   g. NOT (A>B) AND NOT (C>A)

2. *Write a single-line IF statement to perform each task.*
   a. Display OK if R is either 7 or 11.
   b. Assign the smaller of A and B to C.
   c. Increase C by 1 if X is larger than both A and B.
   d. Display BETWEEN if S is a number from 2 to 8.
   e. Display BAD DATA if P is not in the range from 50 to 75.
   f. Decrease D by 1 if R is in the range from 0 to 100 but is not 50.
   g. Display CONTINUE if R is not 2, 7, 11, or 12.
   h. Display TRY AGAIN if C$ is not Y, y, N, or n.
   i. Display C$, but only if its contents spell the word *red* or the word *blue*.
   j. Display X$, but only if all letters in X$ are in uppercase.
   k. Display Y$, but only if letters in X$ are all in uppercase or all in lowercase.
   l. Display NO LETTERS if A$ contains no letters of the alphabet.

3. *Show the output of each program.*

   a.
   ```
   LET A = 3
   LET B = 5
   LET C = A + B
   IF A < 5 THEN A = A + 2 ELSE C = C - 2
   PRINT A; B; C
   IF A < 5 THEN A = A + 2 ELSE C = C - 2
   PRINT A; B; C
   END
   ```

   b.
   ```
   LET X = 5: C = 0
   DO
       LET C = C + 1
       PRINT C; X
   ```

```
          IF X < 10 THEN X = X + 10
          IF X > 10 THEN X = X - 3
       LOOP UNTIL X < 10
       PRINT C; X
       END

   c. LET X = 10: Y = X
       DO
          IF X > 10 THEN X = X - 5 ELSE X = X + 10
          PRINT X; Y
       LOOP UNTIL Y = X
       END

   d. LET L = 22: C = 0
       DO WHILE L < 40 OR L > 60
          IF L < 40 THEN L = L + 50: C = C - 1
          IF L > 60 THEN L = L - 10: C = C + 1
          PRINT C; L
       LOOP
       END

   e. LET P = 10
       DO
          LET P = P + 1
          PRINT P;
          IF P \ 5 = P / 5 THEN PRINT
       LOOP UNTIL P = 25
       PRINT "ENOUGH"
       END
```

In Problems 4–14, write a program for each task specified. Begin each program with PRINT statements that give a brief description of the program. A one-line description is often enough. For instance, you could have your program for Problem 4 begin by displaying this line:

```
   PROGRAM TO CALCULATE COST OF SENDING TELEGRAMS.
```

4. The cost of sending a telegram is $1.35 for the first 10 words and 9¢ for each additional word. Find the cost if the number of words is input. Have the program stop only if zero words are specified.

5. If the wholesale cost of an item is under $100, the markup is 20%. Otherwise, the markup is 30%. Determine the retail price for an item whose wholesale cost is given. The program should stop only if 0 is entered as the wholesale cost.

6. Several pairs (X, Y) of numbers are to be input. Any pair with $X = Y$ serves as the EOD tag. Determine and display counts of how many pairs satisfy $X < Y$ and how many pairs satisfy $X > Y$. The user should be able to stop the program after reading the program description without having to type any numbers.

7. A person earns R dollars an hour with time and a half for all hours over 32. Determine the gross pay for a T-hour week. R and T are to be input, and the program should stop only if 0 is entered for R. The user should not be required to enter a T value for the R value 0.

8. A finance charge is added each month to the outstanding balance on all credit card accounts at Knox Department Store. If the outstanding balance is not greater than $33, the finance charge is 50¢; otherwise, it is 1.5% of the outstanding balance. Find the finance charge if the outstanding balance is input. The program should stop only if an outstanding balance of zero is entered.

9. Input a list of numbers whose last value is 9999. Display the smallest and largest values in the list excluding the 9999. After each input list, ask the user whether there is another list.

10. Each salesperson earns a base weekly salary of $185. In addition, if a salesperson's total weekly sales exceed $1,000, a commission of 5.3% is earned on any amount up to $5,000 and 7.8% is earned on any amount in excess of $5,000. Determine the weekly pay, before deductions, for any salesperson whose total weekly sales amount is input. Use an EOD tag to terminate the program.

11. A company payroll clerk needs a computer program to assist in preparing the weekly payroll. For each employee, the clerk is to enter the hours worked H, the hourly pay rate R, the federal tax rate F, the state tax rate S, and the Social Security rate T. The clerk needs to know the gross pay, the net pay, and the amount of each deduction. Employees receive time and a half for each hour worked over 40 hours.

12. A number is to be typed. If it is between 7 and 35 inclusive, display BETWEEN. If it is less than 7, increase it by 5; if it is greater than 35, decrease it by 5. In either case, display the value obtained, and check to see if this new value is between 7 and 35. Repeat the process until BETWEEN is displayed. After displaying a brief program description, ask the user to respond to the prompt, SHALL I CONTINUE (Y or N)? The program should continue only if the user specifies Y. After the program processes a numerical input value as described, the same prompt (or a similar one) should be displayed to allow the user either to continue or to stop the program.

13. Several pairs of scores are to be entered at the keyboard. Your program is to find and display the total obtained by using the smaller score in each pair. Use a prompt, such as the one described in Problem 12, to allow the user to continue with the program or to stop it.

14. Write a program as described in Problem 13, but this time, find two totals: the total obtained by using the larger score in each pair, and the total obtained by using the smaller score.

■ 8.4 The Block IF Structure

QuickBASIC provides the Block IF structure as an alternative to the single-line IF statement. In many situations, the use of the Block form, instead of the single-line form, will significantly simplify the task of coding an algorithm and, at the same time, give you programs whose action is easy to follow.

The simplest forms of the Block IF structure are as follows:

IF *condition* THEN

_____ (THEN block: executed if *condition* is true)

END IF

IF *condition* THEN

_____ (THEN block: executed if *condition* is true)

ELSE

_____ (ELSE block: executed if *condition* is false)

END IF

In the first form, if the *conditon* is true, the block of statements following THEN (the THEN block) is executed, and control passes to the line after END IF. If the *condition* is false, control passes to the line after END IF without executing the THEN block. Thus, the Block IF structure

```
IF R$ = "NEW" THEN
    INPUT "LAST NAME"; LAST$
    INPUT "FIRST NAME"; FIRST$
    INPUT "TELEPHONE"; PHONE$
END IF
```

will execute the three INPUT statements (the THEN block) if R$ has the string value NEW and will do nothing if R$ is not NEW.

In the second form (the IF-THEN-ELSE form), the THEN block is executed if the *condition* is true, and the ELSE block is executed if it is false. In either case, control passes to the line after END IF. Thus, the Block IF structure

```
IF T$ = "DEPOSIT" THEN
    LET DEPTOTAL = DEPTOTAL + AMOUNT
    LET BALANCE = BALANCE + AMOUNT
ELSE
    LET CHKTOTAL = CHKTOTAL + AMOUNT
    LET BALANCE = BALANCE - AMOUNT
END IF
```

will execute the two LET statements following THEN if T$ has the string value DEPOSIT. These two LET statements add AMOUNT to DEPTOTAL and to BALANCE. If T$ does not have the string value DEPOSIT, the two statements following ELSE are executed. These two LET statements add AMOUNT to CHKTOTAL and then subtract it from BALANCE.

Notice that we indented the statements in each THEN block and each ELSE block, as is common practice. Doing so significantly improves the readability of Block IF structures.

It is also common practice to refer to a Block IF structure as a Block IF statement, even though it will always consist of more than one statement (usually, one on each line).

EXAMPLE 9   *Parts (a) and (b) show how the readability of two of the single-line IF statements used in the earlier examples might be improved by coding them as Block IF statements. Writing the other single-line IF statements as Block IF statements would probably not improve their readability. You may wish to examine them to see whether you agree.*

a. Single-line IF statement (Example 4):

```
IF X <= 100 THEN S = S + X ELSE PRINT "IGNORED!!!"
```

Equivalent Block IF statement:

```
IF X <= 100 THEN
    S = S + X                'Add it to S.
ELSE
    PRINT "IGNORED!!!"       'Don't use X.
END IF
```

This example illustrates that Block IF statements allow clarifying comments for statements in the THEN and ELSE blocks. A single-line IF statement allows only one comment at the end of the IF statement.

b. Single-line IF statement (Example 5):

```
IF UCASE$(T$) = "D" THEN DEP = DEP + AMT ELSE CHK = CHK + AMT
```

Equivalent Block IF statement:

```
IF UCASE$(T$) = "D" THEN
    DEP = DEP + AMT          'AMT is a deposit.
ELSE
    CHK = CHK + AMT          'AMT is a check.
END IF
```

In Remark 2 of Example 5, we suggested using the two single-line IF statements

```
IF UCASE$(T$) = "D" THEN DEP = DEP + AMT ELSE CHK = CHK + AMT
IF UCASE$(T$) = "D" THEN BAL = BAL + AMT ELSE BAL = BAL - AMT
```

to keep a running balance BAL. These two single-line IF statements are better written as one Block IF statement. Here is one way to do this:

```
IF UCASE$(T$) = "D" THEN
    DEP = DEP + AMT          'AMT is a deposit.
    BAL = BAL + AMT          'Add it to balance.
ELSE
    CHK = CHK + AMT          'AMT is a check.
    BAK = BAL - AMT          'Subtract it from balance.
END IF
```

When we coded the program of Example 5, we used the short variable names T$, DEP, AMT, and CHK so that the single-line IF statements would not be excessively long. With the shorter lines obtained by using Block IF statements, you can often improve the readability of your programs by choosing more meaningful variable names, even if they happen to be a little longer.

Each IF statement considered to this point takes a course of action based on *one* condition, the condition included between the keywords IF and THEN. Many programming tasks will require that your programs test a *sequence* of conditions (rather than just one), and take a particular course of action depending on which one is true. For example, suppose commissions on sales are determined by the table

Sales	Commission rate
Up to $3,000	8%
Next $2,000	9%
Additional amounts	13%

and your program must find the commission COMM for any sales amount SALES. A different formula will be needed for each of the sales amount ranges:

```
SALES <= 3000
SALES > 3000 and SALES <= 5000
SALES > 5000
```

Hence, the statements that your program executes to calculate COMM will depend on which of these conditions is true.

QuickBASIC allows an extended form of the Block IF statement that helps you code tasks that require testing such sequences of conditions. In the following general form, *statementblock-1, statementblock-2, . . . , statementblock-n,* and *elseblock* denote QuickBASIC statements or blocks of statements:

```
IF condition-1 THEN
    statementblock-1
ELSEIF condition-2 THEN
    statementblock-2
            .
            .
            .
ELSEIF condition-n THEN
    statementblock-n
ELSE                        (These two lines
    elseblock                are optional.)
END IF
```

The action is as follows: The conditions are tested in order, beginning with *condition-1,* until one is found to be true. If *condition-1* is true, *statementblock-1* is executed, and control passes immediately to the line after END IF. If *condition-2* is the first true condition, *statementblock-2* is executed, and so on. If none of the conditions is true, the ELSE block, if present, is executed before passing to the line following END IF. The following flow diagram describes the action of a Block IF statement that selects one of three statement blocks or an ELSE block.

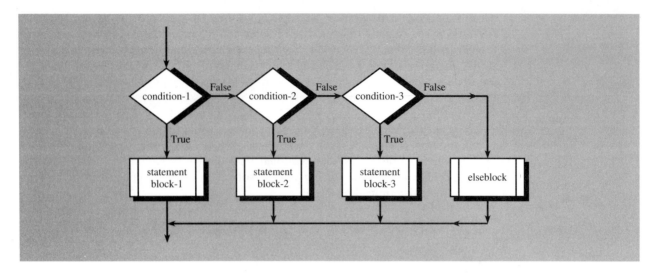

EXAMPLE 10   *Here is a Block IF statement to find the commission on sales when commissions are determined as in the preceding commission rate table.*

```
IF SALES <= 3000
   COMM = .08 * SALES
ELSEIF SALES <= 5000
   COMM = .08 * 3000 + .09 * (SALES - 3000)
ELSE
   COMM = .08 * 3000 + .09 * 2000 + .13 * (SALES - 5000)
END IF
```

The formula for SALES <= 3000 is straightforward. The second category in the table specifies that sales from $3,000 to $5,000 earn a commission of 8% on the first $3,000, plus 9% on the excess (SALES − 3000). This gives the formula in the ELSEIF block. For sales over $5,000, the table specifies a commission of 8% of $3,000, plus 9% of $2,000, plus 13% of the excess (SALES − 5000). This gives the formula in the ELSE block.

REMARK   We wrote the lengthy formulas for COMM to clarify how they were determined. Having done this, you could do the arithmetic and write the ELSEIF and ELSE blocks as

```
COMM = 240 + .09 * (SALES - 3000)
COMM = 420 + .13 * (SALES - 5000)
```

EXAMPLE 11   *Let's write a program to determine the semester grade of each student whose name, midsemester exam grade, and final exam grade are entered at the keyboard. The program is to calculate the numerical average of the two grades, and then display a letter grade based on the following table:*

Numerical average	Letter grade
90 or above	A
In the 80s	B
In the 70s	C
In the 60s	D
Below 60	F

PROBLEM ANALYSIS

Input: A name and two grades for each student

Output: A letter grade for each student

Since letter grades must be determined for more than one student, we need a loop. To end the loop, we'll require that the user enter END when prompted for a student's name. The following variable names will allow us to write a concise algorithm:

```
     NAME$  A student's name
       MID  Midsemester exam grade
     FINAL  Final exam grade
```

a. Input NAME$.
b. Repeat the following until NAME$ is END:

    b1. Input MID and FINAL.
    b2. Determine and display letter grade for NAME$.
    b3. Input next NAME$.

To find the correct letter grade, we need to determine which range of values includes the student's numerical average AV. One way to do this is to test the following conditions:

For letter grade A:	$AV >= 90$
For letter grade B:	$AV >= 80$ AND $AV < 90$
For letter grade C:	$AV >= 70$ AND $AV < 80$
For letter grade D:	$AV >= 60$ AND $AV < 70$
For letter grade F:	$AV < 60$

If you include these, in the order shown, as conditions in a Block IF statement, the comparisons $AV < 90$, $AV < 80$, and $AV < 70$ will not be needed. For instance, if $AV = 82$, the second condition

```
AV >= 80 AND AV < 90
```

will be true. But to get to the second condition, the first, $AV >= 90$, must be false; that is, AV must be less than 90. So we don't need $AV < 90$ in this second condition. For similar reasons, we don't need $AV < 80$ and $AV < 70$. In the program, we will also omit the last condition $AV < 60$ by using ELSE instead of ELSEIF.

```
' PROGRAM TO DETERMINE LETTER GRADES

'     NAME$ = NAME OF STUDENT
'       MID = MIDSEMESTER GRADE
'     FINAL = FINAL EXAM GRADE
'        AV = NUMERICAL AVERAGE
'        G$ = LETTER GRADE

INPUT "NAME (END when done)"; NAME$
DO UNTIL UCASE$(NAME$) = "END"
   INPUT "MIDSEMESTER GRADE"; MID
   INPUT "FINAL EXAM GRADE"; FINAL
   LET AV = (MID + FINAL) / 2

   IF AV >= 90 THEN
      G$ = "A"
   ELSEIF AV >= 80 THEN
      G$ = "B"
   ELSEIF AV >= 70 THEN
      G$ = "C"
   ELSEIF AV >= 60 THEN
      G$ = "D"
   ELSE
      G$ = "F"
   END IF

   PRINT "AVERAGE: "; AV
   PRINT "FINAL GRADE: "; G$
   PRINT
   INPUT "NAME(END when done)"; NAME$
LOOP
END
```

Program output:
```
NAME (END when done)? FRANK
MIDSEMESTER GRADE? 75
```

```
FINAL EXAM GRADE? 63
AVERAGE:  69
FINAL GRADE: D

NAME (END when done)? AMY
MIDSEMESTER GRADE? 86
FINAL EXAM GRADE? 77
AVERAGE:  81.5
FINAL GRADE: B

NAME(END when done)? END
```

■ 8.5 *The SELECT CASE Structure*

We have just seen how the Block IF structure gives programs the ability to choose one of many courses of action. The choice is based on testing a sequence of conditions until one is found to be true or until all are found to be false. In this section, we describe the SELECT CASE structure that allows programs to choose one of many courses of action based on testing the value of a single numerical or string expression, rather than on testing a sequence of conditions.

As with Block IF structures, SELECT CASE structures contain more than one QuickBASIC statement—usually one per line. It is common practice, however, to call them SELECT CASE statements, just as Block IF structures are called Block IF statements. Here is a SELECT CASE statement that will selectively execute one of four PRINT statements. The selection is based on the current value of the variable L$ included in the first line.

```
SELECT CASE L$
    CASE "A"
        PRINT "1st LETTER"
    CASE "B"
        PRINT "2nd LETTER"
    CASE "C"
        PRINT "3rd LETTER"
    CASE ELSE
        PRINT "Bad Value - must be A, B, or C."
END SELECT
```

If L$ = "A", the statement following CASE "A" is executed to produce the display 1st LETTER. Similarly, 2nd LETTER is displayed if L$ = "B", and 3rd LETTER if L$ = "C". If L$ has a value other than the three values A, B, and C specified in the CASE statements, the statement following CASE ELSE is executed to produce the display

```
Bad value - must be A, B, or C
```

This SELECT CASE statement bases its selection on the value of the string expression L$. The following SELECT CASE statement shows that selection can be based on the value of a numerical expression. It also shows that a CASE statement can contain more than one value and that more than one statement can be executed each time that a match is found.

```
SELECT CASE RATING
    CASE 1, 2, 3, 4
        LET RESPONSE$ = "POOR"
        LET TOTAL = TOTAL + 1
    CASE 5, 6, 7
        LET RESPONSE$ = "OK"
        LET TOTAL = TOTAL + 5
    CASE 8, 9
        LET RESPONSE$ = "GOOD"
        LET TOTAL = TOTAL + 8
    CASE 10
        LET RESPONSE$ = "PERFECT"
        LET TOTAL = TOTAL + 10
```

```
    CASE ELSE
        LET RESPONSE$ = "MUST BE 1 TO 10"
END SELECT
```

Including the variable RATING in the first line specifies that selections will be based on the current numerical value of RATING. Notice that the first CASE statement specifies four values (1, 2, 3, and 4), the second specifies three values, and the third specifies two values. Notice also that the statement block that follows each CASE statement other than CASE ELSE contains two statements that will be executed if the value of RATING matches a value in the CASE statement. As with most SELECT CASE statements, the action is easy to follow. For instance, if the current value of RATING is 8, a match is made with the 8 that is specified in the CASE statement

```
    CASE 8, 9
```

and the two-line statement block

```
    LET RESPONSE$ = "GOOD"
    LET TOTAL = TOTAL + 8
```

that follows this CASE statement is executed, assigning the string GOOD to the variable RESPONSE$ and adding 8 to the variable TOTAL. If the value of RATING is not one of the values specified in the CASE statements (that is, if RATING is not an integer from 1 to 10), the statement that follows CASE ELSE is executed to assign the string value MUST BE 1 TO 10 to the variable RESPONSE$, while leaving TOTAL unchanged.

In both examples of SELECT CASE statements, the expressions included in each CASE statement are constant expressions: string constants in the first example and numerical constants in the second. As shown in the second example, two or more expressions must be separated by commas. The list of all expressions in a CASE statement is called its **expression list.** As we explain shortly, QuickBASIC allows expressions other than constants in an expression list.

The preceding examples illustrate the form of SELECT CASE statements. In the following general form, *expression* denotes a numerical or string expression; *expressionlist-1, expressionlist-2, . . . , expressionlist-n* denote lists of expressions separated by commas; and *statementblock-1, statementblock-2, . . . , statementblock-n,* and *elseblock* denote blocks of one or more QuickBASIC statements.

```
SELECT CASE expression
    CASE expressionlist-1
        statementblock-1
    CASE expressionlist-2
        statementblock-2
              .
              .
              .
    CASE expressionlist-n
        statementblock-n
    CASE ELSE            (These two lines
        elseblock        are optional.)
END SELECT
```

The action is as follows: *expression* is evaluated, and this value is compared with the values specified by the expression lists, in order beginning with *expressionlist-1.* If a match is found with a value in *expressionlist-1, statementblock-1* is executed and control passes immediately to the line after END SELECT. If a match is first found with a value in *expressionlist-2, statementblock-2* is executed, and so on. If no match is found, *elseblock* (if present) is executed, and control passes to the line after END SELECT.

As does the Block IF structure, the SELECT CASE structure includes one or more statement blocks, but executes either one or none of these blocks. The major difference between Block IF and SELECT CASE is that SELECT CASE makes its selection by examining the value of a single expression, whereas Block IF makes its selection by testing a sequence of conditions. With SELECT CASE, the CASE statement

CASE *expressionlist*

serves the same purpose that the ELSEIF statement

ELSEIF *condition*

serves in Block IF statements. Although you can always use Block IF for selection, there are many situations in which using SELECT CASE will simplify the coding process, as well as give you a more readable program. If you are coding an algorithm that requires the selective execution of two or more subtasks, and if you can find a variable (or other expression) with values that specify which subtask to execute, you should consider using a SELECT CASE statement.

The following example shows one way to code the program of Example 11 by using SELECT CASE instead of Block IF for selection.

EXAMPLE 12   *Here is a program to determine the semester letter grade for each student whose name, midsemester exam grade, and final exam grade are entered at the keyboard.*

```
' PROGRAM TO DETERMINE LETTER GRADES

'    NAME$ = NAME OF STUDENT
'      MID = MIDSEMESTER GRADE
'    FINAL = FINAL EXAM GRADE
'       AV = NUMERICAL AVERAGE
'       G$ = LETTER GRADE

INPUT "NAME (END when done)"; NAME$
DO UNTIL UCASE$(NAME$) = "END"
   INPUT "MIDSEMESTER GRADE"; MID
   INPUT "FINAL EXAM GRADE"; FINAL
   LET AV = (MID + FINAL) / 2
   LET AV% = AV \ 10                'Integer division

   SELECT CASE AV%
      CASE 9, 10
         G$ = "A"
      CASE 8
         G$ = "B"
      CASE 7
         G$ = "C"
      CASE 6
         G$ = "D"
      CASE 0, 1, 2, 3, 4, 5
         G$ = "F"
      CASE ELSE
         G$ = "AVERAGE IS NOT 0 TO 100!!!"
   END SELECT

   PRINT "AVERAGE: "; AV
   PRINT "FINAL GRADE: "; G$
   PRINT
   INPUT "NAME(END when done)"; NAME$
LOOP
END
```

Program output:
```
NAME (END when done)? FRANK
MIDSEMESTER GRADE? 75
FINAL EXAM GRADE? 63
AVERAGE:  69
FINAL GRADE: D

NAME(END when done)? AMY
MIDSEMESTER GRADE? 866
FINAL EXAM GRADE? 77
```

```
AVERAGE:  471.5
FINAL GRADE: AVERAGE IS NOT 0 TO 100!!!

NAME(END when done)? AMY
MIDSEMESTER GRADE? 86
FINAL EXAM GRADE? 77
AVERAGE:   81.5
FINAL GRADE: B

NAME(END when done)? END
```

REMARK 1   If all averages are in the range 0 to 100 (the program was written with this in mind), the action of this program is identical to the action of the program given in Example 11. The two programs, however, handle values outside this range differently. The program of Example 11 assigns A to G$ if AV > 100. The SELECT CASE statement assigns A to G$ for these high values of AV up to 110, but for AV >= 110, the string AVERAGE IS NOT 0 TO 100!!! is assigned to G$. The SELECT CASE statement assigns this same string to G$ if AV < 0, whereas the program of Example 11 assigns F to G$ for negative averages.

REMARK 2   The statement CASE 0, 1, 2, 3, 4, 5 can be written CASE 0 TO 5 as explained in what follows.

In the three SELECT CASE statements considered to this point, the expressions included in each CASE statement are constant expressions: "A", "B", and "C" in the first SELECT CASE statement, the integers 1 to 10 in the second, and the integers 0 to 10 in Example 12. QuickBASIC allows you to include expressions other than constant expressions in CASE statements. For example, you can use any numerical or string expression to specify values for CASE statements:

CASE statement	Values specified
CASE 1, 3, -1, -3	1, 3, -1, and -3
CASE X, Y	The current values of X and Y
CASE "P", "Q", "END"	P, Q, and END
CASE A$, B$	The current values of A$ and B$

You can also use a single expression to specify an entire range of numerical or string values.

1. *Ranges of numerical values.* Ranges of values are specified by using the keywords TO and IS. If *expression1* and *expression2* denote numerical expressions whose values are E1 and E2,

   expression1 TO *expression2*

specifies all numbers from E1 up to E2. If E1 > E2, no values are specified.

   1 TO 7   specifies all numbers (not just integers) from 1 to 7.
   25 TO 72 specifies all numbers from 25 up to 75.
   75 TO 25 specifies no numbers. It makes no sense to use this.

If *relop* denotes one of the relational operators (=, <, <=, >, >=, <>), and *expression* denotes a numerical expression,

   IS *relop expression*

specifies all numbers N for which N *relop expression* is true.

   IS > 100 specifies all numbers greater than 100.
   IS <> 5 specifies all numbers not equal to 5.
   IS = 5   specifies 5, (Simply write 5 instead of this.)

Following are some CASE statements whose expression lists include one or more expressions that specify ranges of numerical values.

CASE statement	Range of values specified
CASE 0 TO 10	All numbers (not just integers) in the range 0 to 10
CASE 0 TO 10, 90 TO 100	All numbers in the ranges 0 to 10 and 90 to 100
CASE IS > 50	All numbers greater than 50
CASE IS < 5, IS > 10	All numbers that are either less than 5 or greater than 10
CASE 25 TO 75, IS <> 50	All numbers; IS <> 50 specifies all numbers other than 50, but 50 is specified by 25 to 75
CASE 6, 7, IS < 0	6, 7, and any number less than 0

2. Ranges of string values. Ranges of string values are also specified by using the keywords TO and IS. If *expression1* and *expression2* denote string expressions whose values are S1 and S2,

> *expression1* TO *expression2*

specifies all strings from S1 to S2—that is, all strings S for which S1 <= S and S <= S2. How QuickBASIC orders strings is explained in Section 14.5. At this point, it is enough to know that two words are ordered as they are in the dictionary if both consist entirely of uppercase letters or if both consist entirely of lowercase letters.

"A" TO "C"   specifies the uppercase letters A to C, and no other uppercase letters. It does, however, specify many other strings.

If *relop* denotes a relational operator and *expression* denotes a string expression,

> IS *relop expression*

specifies all strings S for which S *relop expression* is true.

IS <= "M"   specifies the uppercase letters A to M, and no other uppercase letters. It does, however, specify many other strings.

Following are some CASE statements with expression lists that include one or more expressions that specify ranges of string values:

CASE statement	Uppercase letters included among the strings specified
CASE "B" TO "E", "Z"	B, C, D, E, Z
CASE "A", IS >= "X"	A, X, Y, Z
CASE "M" TO "A"	Specifies no strings
CASE IS < "D", IS > "X"	A, B, C, Y, Z
CASE "A" TO "Z", IS <> "N"	All letters A to Z. It makes no sense to use this CASE statement. It specifies all strings: IS <> "N" gives all strings other than N, but N is given by "A" to "Z".

The use of the keywords TO and IS to specify ranges of values for CASE expressions can significantly simplify many coding tasks and, at the same time, give you programs that are quite easy to read. To illustrate, the next example shows how the Block IF statement presented in Example 10 can be coded as a SELECT CASE statement whose action is very easy to follow. We do not suggest that you always try to avoid the Block IF structure in favor of SELECT CASE. There are many situations in which Block IF is needed and others in which it is simply more appropriate than SELECT CASE.

EXAMPLE 13   *Here are two ways to find the commission on sales, when commissions are determined by this table:*

Sales	Commission rate
Up to $3,000	8%
Next $2,000	9%
Additional amounts	13%

Following is the Block IF statement given in Example 10 (with the improvement suggested in the remark):

```
IF SALES <= 3000 THEN
    LET COMM = .08 * SALES
ELSEIF SALES <= 5000 THEN
    COMM = 240 + .09 * (SALES - 3000)
ELSE
    COMM = 420 + .13 * (SALES - 5000)
END IF
```

Here is a SELECT CASE statement to do the same thing:

```
SELECT CASE SALES
    CASE 0 TO 3000
        COMM = .08 * SALES
    CASE 3000 TO 5000
        COMM = 240 + .09 * (SALES - 3000)
    CASE ELSE
        COMM = 420 + .13 * (SALES - 5000)
END SELECT
```

Notice that the Block IF statement uses the condition SALES <= 5000 to specify the range 3,000 to 5,000. This is correct only because the condition will not be tested if the first condition, SALES <= 3000, is true. With SELECT CASE, both of the ranges 0–3,000 and 3,000–5,000 are shown explicitly in the CASE statements.

We conclude this section with an example that further illustrates the application of the SELECT CASE and Block IF structures.

EXAMPLE 14   *A program is desired for the following game. Two players alternate typing a letter from A to E. The computer assigns a point value (unknown to the players) for each letter typed according to the table given. The first player to accumulate a total of 15 points or more wins.*

Letter chosen	Point value
A	3
B	2
C	2
D	1
E	2
Any other	0

PROBLEM ANALYSIS

The input and output values for this problem are as follows:

Input: A sequence of letters alternately typed by two players.

Output: The scores of the two players when one of them has achieved a score of 15 or more.

The problem statement requires that we assign a point value to any letter typed at the keyboard. The SELECT CASE structure is ideally suited for such a task. Indeed, if the input value is assigned to the variable LETTER$, the following SELECT CASE statement will assign its point value to the variable POINTVALUE:

```
SELECT CASE UCASE$(LETTER$)
   CASE "A"
      POINTVALUE = 3
   CASE "B", "C", "E"
      POINTVALUE = 2
   CASE "D"
      POINTVALUE = 1
   CASE ELSE
      POINTVALUE = 0
END SELECT
```

When writing a program for a game between two or more players, it is common practice to use the same QuickBASIC code to handle the input of each player. This is accomplished by including the code in a loop. For the game described in the problem statement, we must keep two scores, so there must be a way to tell which score to change. One way to do this is to use a string variable that contains the name of the current player, and then base the decision on the current value of this variable. In addition to this string variable, we will need numerical variables for the two scores (the total points accumulated by each player). The following variable names are appropriate:

PLAYER$	Current player's name
TOTAL 1	Accumulated score of first player
TOTAL2	Accumulated score of second player

Although we could use two INPUT statements to require that the players enter their names at the keyboard, let's keep things as simple as possible by using the names PLAYER1 and PLAYER2, with PLAYER1 going first.

In light of the preceding analysis, it is not difficult to write an algorithm for the game specified in the problem statement.

THE ALGORITHM

a. Display game instructions.
b. Set TOTAL1 and TOTAL2 to 0.
c. Set PLAYER$ to PLAYER1.
d. Repeat the following until TOTAL1 or TOTAL2 is 15 or more:
  d1. Input PLAYER$'s choice of a letter.
  d2. Find the point value of this letter.
  d3. Add the point value to PLAYER$'s score.
  d4. Assign the other player (PLAYER1 or PLAYER2) to PLAYER$.
e. Display the results and stop.

Writing code for Steps (a), (b), (c), and (e) is routine. Step (d1) requires only an INPUT statement, and Step (d2) is accomplished by the SELECT CASE statement already written. As suggested in the problem analysis, Step (d3) can be coded as follows:

```
IF PLAYER$ = "PLAYER1" THEN
   TOTAL1 = TOTAL1 + POINTVALUE
ELSE
   TOTAL2 = TOTAL2 + POINTVALUE
END IF
```

However, Step (d4) also requires examining PLAYER$. If PLAYER$ is PLAYER1, we must assign PLAYER2 to PLAYER$; otherwise, we must assign PLAYER1 to PLAYER$. Thus, we can accomplish Step (d4) by inserting the appropriate LET statements in the same Block IF statement.

```
'*************** TWO PLAYER GUESSING GAME *******************

PRINT "Two players alternate in typing a letter from A to E."
PRINT "The computer assigns a point value (unknown to players)"
PRINT "to each letter. The first player to accumulate a total"
PRINT "of 15 or more points wins."
PRINT

LET TOTAL1 = 0                          'Score for PLAYER1
LET TOTAL2 = 0                          'Score for PLAYER2
LET PLAYER$ = "PLAYER1"                 'First player
DO UNTIL TOTAL1 >= 15 OR TOTAL2 >= 15   '15 or more wins.
   PRINT PLAYER$; "'S CHOICE ";         'Prompt PLAYER$.
   INPUT LETTER$                        'PLAYER$'s choice

   SELECT CASE UCASE$(LETTER$)          'Determine point
      CASE "A"                          ' value for
         POINTVALUE = 3                 ' LETTER$.
      CASE "B", "C", "E"
         POINTVALUE = 2
      CASE "D"
         POINTVALUE = 1
      CASE ELSE
         POINTVALUE = 0
   END SELECT

   IF PLAYER$ = "PLAYER1" THEN          'Credit proper player.
      TOTAL1 = TOTAL1 + POINTVALUE      'Add to PLAYER1 total.
      PLAYER$ = "PLAYER2"               'Next player
   ELSE
      TOTAL2 = TOTAL2 + POINTVALUE      'Add to PLAYER2 total.
      PLAYER$ = "PLAYER1"               'Next player
   END IF

LOOP

PRINT                                   'Display winner
IF TOTAL1 >= 15 THEN                    'and final scores.
   PRINT "PLAYER1 WINS"; TOTAL1; "TO"; TOTAL2
ELSE
   PRINT "PLAYER2 WINS"; TOTAL2; "TO"; TOTAL1
END IF
END
```

Program output:

```
Two players alternate in typing a letter from A to E.
The computer assigns a point value (unknown to players)
to each letter. The first player to accumulate a total
of 15 or more points wins.

PLAYER1'S CHOICE ? D
PLAYER2'S CHOICE ? A
PLAYER1'S CHOICE ? E
PLAYER2'S CHOICE ? H
PLAYER1'S CHOICE ? B
PLAYER2'S CHOICE ? B
PLAYER1'S CHOICE ? C
PLAYER2'S CHOICE ? D
PLAYER1'S CHOICE ? C
PLAYER2'S CHOICE ? E
PLAYER1'S CHOICE ? A
PLAYER2'S CHOICE ? D
PLAYER1'S CHOICE ? A

PLAYER1 WINS 15 TO 9
```

■ *8.6 Problems*

1. *Show the output of each program.*

a.
```
LET X=5 : Y=7
LET X=X+1 : Y=Y-2
IF X=6 AND Y=7 THEN
    PRINT X+Y
ELSE
    PRINT Y-X
END IF
END
```

b.
```
LET X=1
DO WHILE X<=4
    IF X>2 THEN
        PRINT X;X^2
    ELSEIF X<2 THEN
        PRINT X;X-1
    ELSE
        PRINT X;X+1
    END IF
    LET X=X+1
LOOP
END
```

c.
```
LET X=10
DO UNTIL X=0
    IF X>6 THEN
        LET X=X-2
    ELSEIF X>3 THEN
        LET X=X-3
    ELSE
        LET X=X-1
    END IF
    PRINT X
LOOP
END
```

d.
```
LET A=5
DO
    SELECT CASE A
        CASE 2,4,6,7
            PRINT"XXX"
        CASE 1,3,5,8
            PRINT"YYY"
        CASE ELSE
            PRINT "ZZZ"
    END SELECT
    LET A=A+1
LOOP UNTIL A=10
END
```

e.
```
LET R=0
DO UNTIL R>10
    SELECT CASE R
        CASE 3 TO 5, 7 TO 9
            PRINT "A";
        CASE 2, 10
            PRINT "B";
        CASE IS < 2, IS > 10
            PRINT "C";
        CASE ELSE
            PRINT "D";
    END SELECT
    LET R=R+2
LOOP
END
```

2. *Show the output of this program using the input data given in parts (a), (b), and (c).*
   a. K=15, M=8
   b. K=8, M=15
   c. K=6, M=−14

```
INPUT K, M
IF K >= M THEN
    IF M > 0 THEN
        LET K = K - 5
        LET M = M + K
    ELSE
        LET M = 10 - M
    END IF
```

```
   ELSEIF M - K > 5 THEN
      LET M = M - 10
   ELSE
      LET K = M - K
   END IF
   PRINT K; M
```

3. *Write a Block IF statement to carry out each task.*
   a. Display the larger of X and Y, and add this larger value to TOTAL.
   b. If A$ = "BOTH", display the values of both X and Y; otherwise, display the smaller of X and Y.
   c. Display the values of X and Y on two lines, with the smaller value first. However, if X = Y, display this common value only once.
   d. Display the gross salary and, if there is overtime, the part of this amount that represents overtime. The salary is for an H-hour week at D dollars per hour, with time and a half for hours over 40.
   e. Display POOR, GOOD, or EXCELLENT, depending on whether the value of GRADE is, respectively, less than 50, from 50 to 80, or above 80.
   f. Display ALL UC, ALL LC, or UC AND LC, depending on whether the letters in X$ are, respectively, all in uppercase, all in lowercase, or in some of each.

4. *Write a SELECT CASE statement to carry out each specified task.*
   a. Display ELEMENTARY SCHOOL, MIDDLE SCHOOL, HIGH SCHOOL, or COLLEGE, depending on whether LEVEL$ has, respectively, a string value of E, M, H, or C.
   b. Determine the hourly pay rate RATE given the job classification CLASS$.

Job classification	Hourly pay rate
A	$ 5.25
B	$ 7.95
C	$11.45
D	$14.50

   c. Display the complete state name for the six New England states given the abbreviation ABBREV$.

State	Abbreviation
Connecticut	CT
Maine	ME
Massachusetts	MA
New Hampshire	NH
Rhode Island	RI
Vermont	VT

   d. The cost for an order of 2-quart syrup containers is determined as follows:

Quantity	Price per container
1–49	99¢
50–99	89¢
100–199	75¢
200 or more	62¢

   Determine the cost for an order of QTY containers.

In Problems 5–14, write a program to perform each task specified. Be sure to write each program so that the user can try any number of input values during a single program run.

5. For any two numbers M and N, display POSITIVE if both are positive and NEGATIVE if both are negative; otherwise, display NEITHER.
6. For any three numbers input, display ALL NEGATIVE if all are negative, ALL POSITIVE if all are positive, and NEITHER in all other cases.
7. Using the information in the following table, find the tax due for a single taxpayer whose taxable income I is less than $89,560.

Taxable income I	Tax due
$0 < I \leq 17,850$	15% of I
$17,850 < I \leq 43,150$	2677.50 + 28% of (I − 17,850)
$43,150 < I \leq 89,560$	9761.50 + 33% of (I − 43,150)

8. Change Fahrenheit temperatures to Celsius and Celsius temperatures to Fahrenheit. Enter a letter (F or C to indicate the given scale) and a temperature, and then change this temperature to the other scale $[F = (9/5)C + 32]$.
9. A salesperson's monthly commission is determined according to the following schedule:

Net sales	Commision rate
Up to $10,000	6%
Next $4,000	7%
Next $6,000	8%
Additional amounts	10%

Determine the monthly commission given the total monthly sales.

10. Determine the number of days in the month MONTH if values for MONTH (1, 2, . . . , 12) and YEAR are input. (Be sure to take leap years into account. A year is a leap year if it is divisible by 4; but if it is a century year it must be divisible by 400. Integer division will help.)
11. A firm has four job classification codes, as shown in Problem 4(b). The firm also pays time and a half for all hours over 40. Determine the week's salary and, if there is overtime, the part of the salary that represents overtime pay, for any employee whose name, job classification, and hours worked this week are entered at the keyboard. If the user enters Tibor Alexis, d, 10, the output should be:

```
Employee:  TIBOR ALEXIS
Overtime:  none
Total pay: $145.00
```

12. Write a program as described in Problem 11, but this time have all output printed as well as displayed on the screen.
13. (Electric bill problem) Given the following information, produce a short report for each customer, showing the customer number, total number of kilowatt-hours (kWh) used, and total monthly bill. The charges are computed according to the following schedule: $1.41 for the first 14 kWh, the next 85 kWh at $0.0389/kWh, the next 200 at $0.0214/kWh, the next 300 at $0.0134/kWh, and the excess at $0.0099/kWh. In addition, there is a fuel-adjustment charge of $0.0322/kWh for all kilowatt-hours used.

Customer number	Previous month's reading	Current reading
0516	25,346	25,973
2634	47,947	48,851
2917	21,342	21,652
2853	893,462	894,258
3576	347,643	348,748
3943	41,241	41,783
3465	887,531	888,165

The report for each customer should appear as

```
Custom number _____
Kilowatt-hours used _____
Monthly bill _____
```

14. The guessing game program of Example 14 calls the two participants in the game PLAYER1 and PLAYER2. Make changes in the program that allow the computer to ask for the actual names of the players and to refer to these names (rather than to PLAYER1 and PLAYER2) in the output. Be sure to allow many games during a single program run. Have the loser of each game go first in the next game, if there is a next game.

■ *8.7 Review True-or-False Quiz*

1. The statement

```
IF X>0 THEN PRINT "GOOD" ELSE PRINT "BAD"
```

is equivalent to the two statements

```
IF X>0 THEN PRINT "GOOD"
IF X<=0 THEN PRINT "BAD"
```
                                                                              T   F

2. The statement

```
IF A=B THEN PRINT A : C=C+1
```

is equivalent to the two statements

```
IF A=B THEN PRINT A
LET C=C+1
```
                                                                              T   F

3. If A = 1 and B = 2, this IF statement will print 3.

```
IF B=1 AND A>B OR B<3 THEN PRINT A+B
```
                                                                              T   F

4. The statement

```
IF A>5 THEN IF A<10 THEN PRINT A
```

is equivalent to the statement

```
IF A>5 AND A<10 THEN PRINT A
```
                                                                              T   F

5. These two logical expressions are equivalent:

```
NOT (A=1 AND B=2)
A<>1 OR B<>2
```
                                                                              T   F

6. The statement

```
IF A=1, 2, OR 3 THEN PRINT "OK"
```

will display OK if A has the value 1, 2, or 3.
                                                                              T   F

7. The statement

```
IF A<B<C THEN PRINT "IN ORDER"
```

can be used to determine whether the values A, B, and C are in increasing order.   T F

8. The statement

```
IF A<B THEN C=A ELSE C=B
```

is equivalent to

```
IF A<B THEN
   LET C=A
ELSE
   LET C=B
END IF
```
                                                                                                    T F

9. The statement

```
IF A>0 THEN
  PRINT "OK"
ELSEIF A<0 THEN
  PRINT "OK"
END IF
```

will always display OK.   T F

10. The statement

```
SELECT CASE R
   CASE 1 TO 5
      PRINT "BAD"
   CASE 6 TO 9
      PRINT "GOOD"
END SELECT
```

will display BAD if R is in the range 1 to 5 and will display GOOD if R is in the range
6 to 9.   T F

11. The statement

```
SELECT CASE X
   CASE 0 TO 10, IS <> 5
      PRINT X
   CASE ELSE
      PRINT "BAD"
   END SELECT
```

will display the value of X if X is a number from 0 to 10 other than 5 and will display
BAD for any other X value.   T F

12. The statement

```
IF X<0 THEN
      PRINT "N"
ELSEIF X>0 THEN
      PRINT "P"
ELSE
      PRINT Z
END IF
```

is equivalent to

```
SELECT CASE X
   CASE IS < 0
      PRINT "N"
   CASE IS > 0
      PRINT "P"
   CASE 0
      PRINT "Z"
END SELECT
```
                                                                                                    T F

9
Loops Made Easier

So far, we have coded each program loop as a DO loop, specifying for each loop either a WHILE or UNTIL condition to control looping. In this chapter, we describe the FOR loop structure that controls looping in a different and, in many cases, more convenient way. A FOR loop is coded by using a FOR and NEXT statement instead of a DO and LOOP statement. Unlike DO loops, in which the statements being repeated determine when the repetition will stop, a FOR loop repeatedly executes a block of QuickBASIC statements a definite number of times. QuickBASIC determines this number from a starting value, ending value, and increment value that you specify in the FOR statement. As explained and illustrated in this chapter, there are many situations in which the use of a FOR loop instead of a DO loop will both simplify the coding process and give you a more readable program.

■ *9.1 FOR Loops*

Here is a program to display the integers from 1 to 5:

Program 1
```
LET N = 1
DO WHILE N <= 5
   PRINT N;
   LET N = N + 1
LOOP
END
```

Program output:
```
 1   2   3   4   5
```

The same thing can be accomplished by the following program:

Program 2
```
FOR N = 1 TO 5
   PRINT N;
NEXT
END
```

This program instructs the computer to execute the PRINT statement five times, once for each integer N from 1 to 5. In QuickBASIC, Program 2 is equivalent to Program 1. Thus the action of Program 2 can be described as follows:

a. The FOR statement assigns an initial value of 1 to N.
b. N is compared with the terminal value 5. If N > 5, control passes to the line following

the NEXT statement. The loop has been satisfied. If N ≤ 5, control passes to the line following the FOR statement.

  c. The PRINT statement displays the current value of N.

  d. When the NEXT statement is encountered, N is increased by 1, and the comparison in Step (b) is repeated.

The following examples further illustrate the use of the FOR and NEXT statements to construct loops. To clarify the meaning of the FOR loops, we have written each program in two equivalent ways—with and without the FOR and NEXT statements. The general form for FOR loops is given following Example 3.

EXAMPLE 1   *Here is a program to calculate and display the price of one, two, three, four, five, and six items selling at seven for $1.00.*

```
LET U = 1 / 7      'Unit price        LET U = 1 / 7       'Unit price
LET F$ = "#  #.##"                    LET F$ = "#  #.##"
FOR K = 1 TO 6                        LET K = 1
   LET P = U * K                      DO WHILE K <= 6
   PRINT USING F$; K; P                  LET P = U * K
NEXT K                                   PRINT USING F$; K; P
END                                      LET K = K + 1
                                      LOOP
                                      END
```

Output produced by either program:

```
1   0.14
2   0.29
3   0.43
4   0.57
5   0.71
6   0.86
```

The FOR loop instructs the computer to execute the statements

```
LET P=U*K
PRINT USING F$;K,P
```

six times, once for each integer K from 1 to 6. These two statements are called the **body** or **range** of the loop. It is an excellent programming practice to indent the body of each FOR loop to improve program readability.

EXAMPLE 2   *Here is a loop to display the numbers -4, -2, 0, 2, 4, 6.*

```
FOR J = -4 TO 6 STEP 2      LET J = -4
   PRINT J;                 DO WHILE J <= 6
NEXT J                         PRINT J;
END                            LET J = J + 2
                            LOOP
                            END
```

Output produced by either program:

```
-4 -2  0  2  4  6
```

The starting value for J is −4. Including STEP 2 in the statement

```
FOR J=-4 TO 6 STEP 2
```

specifies that J is to be increased by 2 each time NEXT J is encountered. Thus, the FOR loop instructs the computer to execute the statement

```
PRINT J;
```

for the successive J values −4, −2, 0, 2, 4, and 6.

EXAMPLE 3   *Here is a loop to display the numbers 5, 4, 3, 2, 1.*

```
FOR N = 5 TO 1 STEP -1       LET N = 5
   PRINT N;                  DO WHILE N >= 1
NEXT N                          PRINT N;
END                             LET N = N - 1
                             LOOP
                             END
```

Output produced by either program:
```
5   4   3   2   1
```

This example illustrates that negative increments are allowed. The initial value of N is 5 and, after each pass through the loop, N is *decreased* by 1 (STEP -1). As soon as N attains a value *less* than 1 (as specified in the FOR statement), control passes out of the loop to the statement following the NEXT statement.

The general form of a FOR loop is

FOR **v**   = **a** TO **b** STEP **c**
.
.   (Body of the loop)
.

NEXT **v**

where **v** denotes a *simple* numerical variable name* and **a, b,** and **c** denote arithmetic expressions. (IF STEP **c** is omitted, **c** is assumed to have the value 1.) **v** is called the **control variable,** and the values of **a, b,** and **c** are called the **initial, terminal,** and **step** values, respectively. The action of a FOR loop is described by the following flow diagrams.

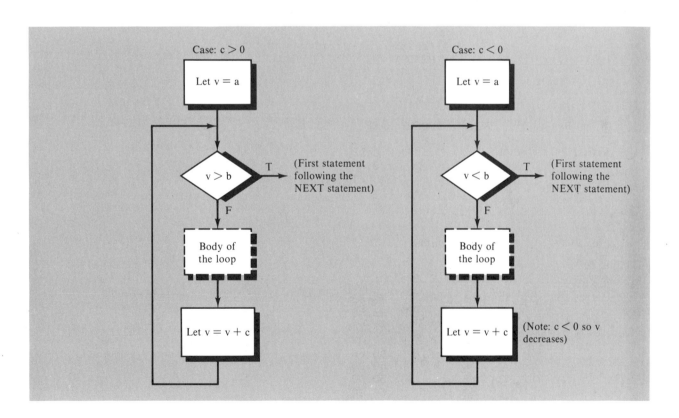

*The numerical variables considered to this point are called *simple* to distinguish them from the **subscripted** variables considered in Chapter 15.

In each FOR loop shown in Examples 1 through 3, the control variable appears in a statement in the body of the loop. The next example shows that you are not required to do this. Indeed, in many cases, as in this one, the control variable serves only as a counter.

EXAMPLE 4   ***Here is a loop to display a row of N dashes***

```
FOR I = 1 TO N
    PRINT "-";
NEXT I
```

Of course, N must be assigned a value before the FOR statement is executed. If N is 15, a row of 15 dashes will be displayed.

REMARK 1   If the terminal value N is 0, then the entire loop will be skipped, since the initial value I = 1 will be greater than the terminal value N = 0.

REMARK 2   As shown in Example 5 of Section 7.2, you can replace this FOR loop with the equivalent statement

```
PRINT STRING$(N, "-");
```

In the next example, we use a FOR loop to produce a table of values. This is a common application of FOR loops. The example also illustrates that the initial, terminal, and step values of a FOR loop do not have to be integers.

EXAMPLE 5   ***Here is a program to produce a table showing the 5.5%, 6%, 6.5%, . . . , 9% discount on any amount A typed at the keyboard. The maximum discount, however, is $50.***

```
' **** DISCOUNT CALCULATIONS ****

'    A = AMOUNT
'    R = PERCENT DISCOUNT RATE
'    D = DISCOUNT AMOUNT

INPUT "AMOUNT"; A
PRINT
PRINT "PERCENT RATE    DISCOUNT"
 F$ = "    ##.#          ##.##"
FOR R = 5.5 TO 9 STEP .5
   LET D = R / 100 * A
   IF D > 50 THEN LET D = 50
   PRINT USING F$; R; D
NEXT R
END
```

Program output:
```
AMOUNT? 725

PERCENT RATE    DISCOUNT
    5.5         39.88
    6.0         43.50
    6.5         47.13
    7.0         50.00
    7.5         50.00
    8.0         50.00
    8.5         50.00
    9.0         50.00
```

The FOR statement specifies that the control variable R is to range from 5.5 to 9, with 0.5 as the increment. For the R values 5.5, 6.0, and 6.5, the discount values determined by

```
LET D = R / 100 * A
```

do not exceed 50; hence, the statement LET D = 50 is not executed. When R is 7.0, 7.5, 8.0, 8.5, and 9.0, however, the D values do exceed 50, so the statement LET D = 50 is executed, as shown in the output.

REMARK 1 Special care must be taken when writing FOR loops with initial, terminal, or step values that are not integers. As we have mentioned previously (Examples 5 and 7, Chapter 6), the computer stores only close approximations for most numbers that are not integers. The loop in this example causes no difficulty because 0.5 is one of the fractional numbers that computers store exactly. If we had used STEP 0.1 instead of STEP 0.5, however, the control variable R would have taken on only close approximations to the values 5.6, 5.7, 5.8, . . . , 9. We ran the program with STEP .1 and did not obtain output for R = 9. Executing the statement PRINT R in immediate mode, we obtained 9.000001, and not 9, as the final value of R. Since 9.000001 is not in the range 5.5 to 9, the loop was not repeated to produce a last line for the percent rate R = 9. To avoid such awkward situations, many programmers use only integers for the initial, terminal, and step values in FOR loops. To write the program in this example so that the control variable R takes on only integer values, you can make these two changes:

```
FOR R=55 TO 80 STEP 5
   LET D=R/1000*A
```

If increments of 0.1 instead of 0.5 are required, you can simply use STEP 1 rather than STEP 5.

REMARK 2 The last five lines of output are not necessary; they simply display the maximum discount allowed. The program would be improved if, instead of displaying these five lines, it displayed a concluding message, such as

```
HIGHER PERCENTS GIVE THE DISCOUNT: $50.00
```

One way to accomplish this would be to rewrite the program with a DO loop instead of the FOR loop. If you do this, you will need to specify a loop condition that allows looping to continue only if D < 50 and R <= 9. Another way to accomplish the same thing is to use QuickBASIC's EXIT FOR statement. If QuickBASIC encounters EXIT FOR while executing the body of a FOR loop, it immediately transfers control out of the loop to the statement after the NEXT statement that closes the loop. If you replace the two statements

```
IF D > 50 THEN LET D = 50
PRINT USING F$; R; D
```

by the Block IF statement

```
IF D < 50 THEN
   PRINT USING F$; R; D
ELSE
   PRINT
   PRINT "HIGHER PERCENTS GIVE THE DISCOUNT: $50.00"
   EXIT FOR
END IF
```

the modified program will exit the FOR loop if D attains a value 50 or more, but only after displaying the HIGHER PERCENTS message. We ran the modified program twice, entering 725 and 425 for A, to obtain the following two displays:

```
AMOUNT? 725                                    AMOUNT? 425

PERCENT RATE   DISCOUNT                        PERCENT RATE   DISCOUNT
      5.5         39.88                              5.5         23.38
      6.0         43.50                              6.0         25.50
      6.5         47.13                              6.5         27.63
                                                     7.0         29.75
HIGHER PERCENTS GIVE THE DISCOUNT: $50.00            7.5         31.88
                                                     8.0         34.00
                                                     8.5         36.13
                                                     9.0         38.25
```

In this section, we have described and illustrated the syntax that must be used in writing FOR loops. Although the examples also illustrate certain situations in which loops are best coded as FOR loops, more needs to be said on this topic.

You may have noticed that all FOR loops share a common characteristic: the number of times the body of the loop must be executed to satisfy the loop (this is called the **iteration count** of the loop) can be determined before the loop is entered. For example, the statement

```
FOR N=1 TO 500
```

initiates a loop with iteration count 500, the statement

```
FOR N=1 TO 20 STEP 4
```

initiates a loop with iteration count 5 (the five N values are 1, 5, 9, 13, and 17), and if M has been assigned a positive integer value,

```
FOR K=1 TO M
```

initiates a loop with iteration count M.

There is a simple formula for determining the iteration count for any FOR loop. If **i, t,** and **s** denote the initial, terminal, and step values, respectively, the iteration count is the larger of the two values

$$\left[\frac{t - i + s}{s} \right] \text{ and } 0$$

where the expression in brackets is truncated, if necessary, to obtain an integer.

FOR statement	i, t, s	(t − i + s)/s	Iteration count
FOR N=1 TO 20 STEP 3	1, 20, 3	$(20 - 1 + 3)/3 = 7\frac{1}{3}$	7
FOR K=1 TO 1000	1, 1000, 1	$(1000 - 1 + 1)/1 = 1000$	1000
FOR L=2 TO 100 STEP 50	2, 100, 50	$(100 - 2 + 50)/50 = 2.96$	2
FOR M=20 TO 1 STEP −3	20, 1, −3	$(1 - 20 + (-3))/(-3) = 7\frac{1}{3}$	7
FOR P=10 TO 1	10, 1, 1	$(1 - 10 + 1)/1 = -8$	0
FOR R=5.5 TO 8 STEP 0.5	5.5, 8, 0.5	$(8 - 5.5 + 0.5)/0.5 = 6$	6

A common method used by computers to process FOR statements is first to calculate the iteration count, and then to use a counter to control looping. An exit from the loop occurs when the predetermined number of passes has been made.* Loops that are controlled by such counters are called **counter-controlled loops.** Thus, every FOR loop that does not contain an EXIT FOR statement to terminate the loop prematurely is a counter-controlled loop.

The worked-out examples in this section and in the preceding discussion of counter-controlled loops suggest the following guideline concerning the use of FOR loops.

Use a FOR loop only if both of the following conditions are met:

1. *The number of times the loop will be repeated can be determined before the loop is entered.* It isn't necessary that you determine this count, but it is necessary that you know it can be determined. For instance, to produce a report showing the equivalent annual salaries for people working at the hourly rates 4.00, 4.25, 4.50, . . . , 9.00, we could use a FOR loop beginning

```
FOR H=4 TO 9 STEP 0.25
```

---

*The flow diagrams shown after Example 3 explain the effect of a FOR loop, but they are not intended to describe exactly how the computer causes this effect. For instance, our description of the action caused by the statement FOR R = 5.5 to 9 STEP 0.5 suggests that the computer first assigns 5.5 to R, and then compares R with the terminal value 9. Although this helps us understand the effect of the FOR statement, it does not necessarily correspond to what actually happens.

We would not determine the iteration count, but it is obvious that it can be determined simply by counting the H values. As an example of a loop that should not be coded as a FOR loop, suppose that we must find the smallest of these hourly rates that gives an equivalent annual salary of $11,500 or more. In this case, an iteration count cannot be determined without actually performing some calculations—that is, without entering the loop. Thus, we would code the loop as a DO loop, specifying that looping should continue only if SALARY < 11500.

2. *A meaningful control variable can be found for the loop.* If you determine the iteration count C for a loop, you can use a counter, say N, as the control variable and use a FOR loop beginning

```
FOR N=1 TO C
```

Such a counter, however, is not always meaningful. For instance, in Example 5 we used a FOR loop beginning

```
FOR R=5.5 TO 9 STEP 0.5
```

to display R percent discounts. The iteration count for the loop is

$$\frac{9 - 5.5 + 0.5}{0.5} = \frac{4}{0.5} = 8$$

But it would not be particularly meaningful to code the loop by using

```
FOR N=1 TO 8
```

The control variable R, however, is meaningful—it denotes the discount rate.

Following are some points concerning the use of FOR loops that were not raised explicitly in this section:

1. The initial, terminal, and step values are determined once, when the FOR statement is executed, and cannot be altered within the body of the loop.
2. Although the control variable can be modified inside the FOR loop, don't do it. The resulting program may be very difficult to understand.
3. When a FOR loop has been satisfied (that is, when an exit is made via the NEXT statement), the value of the control variable is the first value not used.
4. FOR loops can be nested. (This is the subject of Section 9.3.)

■ *9.2 Problems*

1. *Show the output of each program.*

a.
```
FOR J=2 TO 4
    PRINT J+2
NEXT J
END
```

b.
```
FOR N=5 TO -3 STEP -4
    PRINT N
NEXT N
END
```

c.
```
LET C=0
LET X=1
FOR Q=1 TO 4.9 STEP 2
    LET C=C+1
    LET X=X*Q
NEXT Q
PRINT "TIMES THROUGH LOOP=";C
PRINT X
END
```

d.
```
FOR I=1 TO 3
    PRINT "+";
NEXT I
FOR J=5 TO 7
    PRINT "/";
NEXT J
END
```

e.
```
FOR J=2 TO 2
    PRINT "LOOP"
NEXT J
END
```

f.
```
FOR J=5 TO 1
    PRINT "LOOP"
NEXT J
END
```

g.
```
LET X = 1 : Y = 3
FOR N = X TO Y
    LET X = 2 * X + Y
    LET Y = X - Y
    PRINT X; Y
NEXT N
END
```

h.
```
FOR N=1 TO 4
    PRINT USING "ITEM# ";N;
NEXT N
PRINT
FOR N=1 TO 4
    PRINT USING "###    ";N;
NEXT N
END
```

i.
```
PRINT "123456789"
FOR V=1 TO 4
    PRINT TAB(V);"V";TAB(10-V);"V"
NEXT V
PRINT TAB(5);"V"
END
```

2. *Each of the following programs contains an error—either a syntax error that will cause an error message or a programming error that the computer will not recognize but that will cause incorrect results. In each case, find the error and tell which of the two types it is.*

a.
```
' 6 PERCENT PROGRAM
FOR N=1 TO 6
    INPUT X
    PRINT X,.06*X
NEXT X
END
```

b.
```
' COUNT THE POSITIVE
' NUMBERS TYPED
FOR I=1 TO 10
    LET C=0
    INPUT N
    IF N>O THEN C=C+1
NEXT I
PRINT C;"ARE POSITIVE."
END
```

c.
```
' SUMMING PROGRAM
LET S=0
FOR X=1 TO 4
    INPUT X
    LET S=S+X
NEXT X
PRINT "SUM IS";S
END
```

d.
```
' DISPLAY THE NUMBERS
' 1 3 6 10 15
LET S=1
FOR N=1 TO 15 STEP S
    PRINT N
    LET S=S+1
NEXT N
END
```

In Problems 3–13, write a program for each task specified.

3. A positive integer N is to be entered, followed by N numbers. Determine the sum and average of the N numbers.

4. A positive integer N is to be entered, followed by N numbers. Determine how many of the N numbers are negative, how many are positive, and how many are 0.

5. Display the integers from 1 to 72, eight to the line.

6. Display the integers from 1 to 72, eight to the line, equally spaced.

7. A program is needed to assist grade-school students with their multiplication tables. After an initial greeting, the computer should ask the student to type a number from 2 to 12 so that products involving this number can be practiced. (Call this number N, but don't confuse the student with this information.) Next, the student should be asked to answer the questions $2 \times N = ?$, $3 \times N = ?, \ldots, 12 \times N = ?$ Of course, the *value* of N should be displayed, not the letter N. If a question is answered correctly, the next question should be asked; if not, the question should be repeated. If the same question is answered incorrectly twice, the correct answer should be dis-

played and then the next question should be asked. After all questions pertaining to N have been answered, display the student's score and give the student the choice of trying another multiplication table or stopping. (*Suggestion:* Write the code that prompts the student for an answer twice: once for the first answer, and again for the possible second try.)

8. Produce a two-column table with column headings showing P percent of the amounts $1, $2, $3, . . . , $20. P is to be input.

9. Prepare a report showing the effect of a flat across-the-board raise of F dollars in addition to a percentage increase of P percent on the salaries $20,000, $20,500, $21,000, . . . , $30,000. F and P are to be input. Include three columns labeled PRESENT SALARY, RAISE, and NEW SALARY.

10. Evaluate the following sums. If a value for N is required, it is to be input.

   a. $1 + 3 + 5 + 7 + \cdots + 51$
   b. $1 + 2 + 3 + \cdots + N$
   c. $1 + 3 + 5 + 7 + \cdots + (2N - 1)$
   d. $2 + 5 + 8 + 11 + \cdots + K$, where $N - 3 < K <= N$
   e. $(.06) + (.06)^2 + (.06)^3 + \cdots + (.06)^N$
   f. $1 + 1/2 + 1/3 + 1/4 + \cdots + 1/N$
   g. $1 + 1/4 + 1/9 + 1/16 + \cdots + 1/N^2$
   h. $1 + 1/2 + 1/4 + 1/8 + \cdots + 1/2^N$
   i. $1 - 1/2 + 1/3 - 1/4 + \cdots - 1/100$
   j. $4[1 - 1/3 + 1/5 - 1/7 + \cdots + (-1)^{N+1}/(2N - 1)]$

11. Produce a two-column table with the headings N and $1 + 2 + 3 + \cdots + N$. The first column is to show the N values 1, 2, 3, . . . , 20, and the second is to show the indicated sums. [*Hint:* The second column value for row N(N > 1) is simply N plus the previous sum.]

12. For any positive integer N, the product $1 \times 2 \times 3 \times \cdots \times N$ is denoted by the symbol N! and is called N factorial. Also, zero factorial (0!) is defined to be 1. (Thus, 0! = 1! = 1.) Produce a two-column table with column headings showing the values of N and N! for N = 0, 1, 2, . . . , 10. [*Hint:* For N > 0, N! = (N - 1)! × N.]

13. Produce a table of x and y values on the interval $0 \leqslant x \leqslant 10$, if y is given by

$$y = \begin{cases} x^2 & \text{if } x \leqslant 3 \\ 12 - x & \text{if } 3 < x \leqslant 7 \\ 2x - 9 & \text{if } x > 7 \end{cases}$$

and x is in increments of 0.5. (*Suggestion:* Use a Block IF or SELECT CASE case statement to select the correct formula for y by testing which of the three intervals 0 to 3, 3 to 7, or greater than 7 contains each of the specified values of x.)

■ *9.3 Nested Loops*

It is permissible, and often desirable, to have one FOR loop contained in another. When nesting loops in this way, there is one rule that must be observed:

If the body of one FOR loop contains either the FOR or the NEXT statement of another loop, it must contain both of them. This is illustrated in Figure 9.1.

EXAMPLE 6   *Here is an illustration of nested FOR loops.*

```
FOR I = 1 TO 3
   FOR J = 1 TO 5
      PRINT I;
   NEXT J
   PRINT
NEXT I
END
```

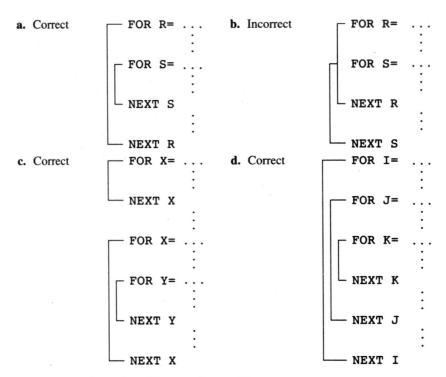

Figure 9.1   Correctly and incorrectly nested loops.

Program output:
```
1   1   1   1   1
2   2   2   2   2
3   3   3   3   3
```

The first statement starts the outer loop, the I-loop. The body of this loop consists of all statements up to NEXT I. The first three of these statements, the inner J-loop, display the value of I five times on one line, leaving the cursor positioned at the end of that line. The PRINT statement causes a RETURN to be executed, so that subsequent output will appear on a new line. Since the body of the I-loop is repeated for the successive I values 1, 2, and 3, the program produces three lines of output as shown.

REMARK   Since the J-loop (the inner loop) is short and performs such a simple and well-defined task (displays a single digit five times), you may find it convenient to replace those three lines by the equivalent multiple-statement line

```
20 FOR J=1 TO 5 : PRINT I; : NEXT J
```

As shown in Section 9.1, the value of the control variable of a FOR loop can be used in the body of the loop in any way you wish. In the preceding example, the control variable I was used to supply output values; in the next example, we use the control variable of an outer loop to supply the terminal value for an inner loop.

EXAMPLE 7   *Here is a program to display five lines containing the word BASIC—once in the first row, twice in the second, and so on.*

```
FOR ROW = 1 to 5        'ROW counts the rows.
    FOR COL = 1 TO ROW  'COL counts the times per row.
        PRINT "BASIC ";
    NEXT COL
    PRINT
NEXT ROW
END
```

Program output:

```
BASIC
BASIC BASIC
BASIC BASIC BASIC
BASIC BASIC BASIC BASIC
BASIC BASIC BASIC BASIC BASIC
```

To display the output nearer the center of the screen, you can use the TAB function. To cause the output of each row to begin in column position 20, for example, simply insert the statement

```
PRINT TAB(20):
```

between the two FOR statements. This statement causes the cursor to move to position 20 so that the inner loop will begin its output at position 20.

Nested FOR loops are especially useful when tables must be prepared in which the rows and columns each correspond to equally spaced data values. We conclude this chapter with an example illustrating one such application of nested loops.

EXAMPLE 8

Prepare a table showing the possible raises for salaried employees whose salaries are $20,000, $21,000, $22,000, . . . , $27,000. A raise is to consist of a flat across-the-board increase and a percentage increase of either 2, 3, or 4%.

PROBLEM ANALYSIS

Let's agree on the following variable names.

SALARY = present salary ($20,000, $21,000, . . . , $27,000)
FLAT = flat across-the-board increase (to be input)
PERCENT = percentage increase (2, 3, 4%)
RAISE = amount of raise for a given SALARY, FLAT, and PERCENT

The formula governing this situation is

$$\text{RAISE} = (\text{PERCENT}/100) * \text{SALARY} + \text{FLAT}$$

For each SALARY, we must display three possible raises RAISE—one for each of the indicated percentages PERCENT. Thus a four-column table is appropriate, the first showing the present salary SALARY and the others showing the three possible raises. The following program segment can be used to display these values.

```
FOR SALARY=20000 TO 27000 STEP 1000
    PRINT SALARY,
    FOR PERCENT=2 TO 4
        LET RAISE=(PERCENT/100)*SALARY+FLAT
        PRINT RAISE,
    NEXT PERCENT
    PRINT
NEXT SALARY
```

All that remains is to include an INPUT statement, so that a value can be typed for FLAT, and to add the PRINT statements needed to display a title for the table and appropriate column headings. We will use PRINT USING rather than PRINT statements to align the columns by decimal point.

THE PROGRAM

```
PRINT "              SALARY INCREASE SCHEDULE"
PRINT
INPUT "ACROSS THE BOARD INCREASE "; FLAT
PRINT
PRINT "              -- ADDITIONAL PERCENTAGE INCREASE --"
PRINT
PRINT " SALARY      2 PERCENT     3 PERCENT     4 PERCENT"
PRINT
LET D$ = "  #####.##"
LET E$ = "        ####.##"
```

```
        FOR SALARY = 20000 TO 27000 STEP 1000
           PRINT USING D$; SALARY;
           FOR PERCENT = 2 TO 4
              LET RAISE = (PERCENT / 100) * SALARY + FLAT
              PRINT USING E$; RAISE;
           NEXT PERCENT
           PRINT
        NEXT SALARY
        END
```

Program output:

```
                    SALARY INCREASE SCHEDULE

ACROSS THE BOARD INCREASE ? 700

                    -- ADDITIONAL PERCENTAGE INCREASE --

        SALARY        2 PERCENT      3 PERCENT      4 PERCENT

        20000.00       1100.00        1300.00        1500.00
        21000.00       1120.00        1330.00        1540.00
        22000.00       1140.00        1360.00        1580.00
        23000.00       1160.00        1390.00        1620.00
        24000.00       1180.00        1420.00        1660.00
        25000.00       1200.00        1450.00        1700.00
        26000.00       1220.00        1480.00        1740.00
        27000.00       1240.00        1510.00        1780.00
```

9.4 Problems

1. *Show the output of each program.*

a.
```
FOR I=1 TO 3
   FOR J=2 TO 3
      PRINT J;
   NEXT J
NEXT I
END
```

b.
```
FOR J=9 TO 7 STEP -2
   FOR K=4 TO 9 STEP 3
      PRINT J+K;
   NEXT K
NEXT J
END
```

c.
```
FOR X=1 TO 4
   FOR Y=X+1 TO 5
      PRINT Y;
   NEXT Y
   PRINT
NEXT X
END
```

d.
```
LET X=0
FOR P=1 TO 6
   FOR Q=2 TO 7
      FOR R=2 TO 4
         LET X=X+1
      NEXT R
   NEXT Q
NEXT P
PRINT X
END
```

e.
```
LET F$="## "
FOR R=7 TO 13 STEP 2
   FOR C=1 TO 3
      PRINT USING F$;R;
   NEXT C
   PRINT
NEXT R
END
```

2. *Each of the following programs contains an error—either a syntax error that will cause an error message to be displayed, or a programming error that the computer will not recognize but that will cause incorrect results. In each case, find the error and tell which of the two types it is.*

a.
```
' DISPLAY PRODUCTS.
FOR I=1 TO 3
FOR J=2 TO 4
PRINT I;"TIMES";J;"=";I*J
NEXT I
NEXT J
END
```

b.
```
' DISPLAY SUMS.
FOR A=3 TO 1
FOR B=4 TO 1
PRINT A;"PLUS";B;"=";A+B
NEXT B
NEXT A
END
```

c. A program to display
```
1  2
1  3
1  4
2  3
2  4
3  4
```
```
FOR I=1 TO 4
FOR J=2 TO 4
IF I<>J THEN PRINT I;J
NEXT J
NEXT I
END
```

d. A program to display
```
XXXXX
 XXXX
  XXX
   XX
    X
```
```
FOR R=1 TO 5
FOR C=1 TO 5
IF R>=C THEN PRINT "X";
IF R<C THEN PRINT " ";
NEXT C
NEXT R
END
```

3. *Produce the following designs.*

a.
```
1
2 2
3 3 3
4 4 4 4
5 5 5 5 5
```

b.
```
5 5 5 5 5
4 4 4 4
3 3 3
2 2
1
```

c.
```
1
1 2
1 2 3
1 2 3 4
1 2 3 4 5
```

d.
```
1
2 1
3 2 1
4 3 2 1
5 4 3 2 1
```

In Problems 4–15, write a program to perform each task specified.

4. Produce a tax-rate schedule showing the 4, 5, 6, and 7% tax on the dollar amounts $1, $2, $3, ..., $20.

5. Prepare a table showing the interest earned on a $100 deposit for the rates 0.05 to 0.08 in increments of 0.01 and for times 1, 2, ..., 8 years. Interest is compounded annually $[I = P(1 + R)^N - P]$.

6. Prepare the table for Problem 5 except that rates are to be in increments of 0.005 instead of 0.01.

7. Present the information required in Problem 6 by producing seven short tables, one for each interest rate specified. Label each of these tables and also the information contained in the tables.

8. For each of the tax rates 5, $5\frac{1}{8}$, $5\frac{1}{4}$, $5\frac{3}{8}$, and $5\frac{1}{2}$%, produce a table showing the tax on the dollar amounts, $1, $2, $3, ..., $20. Each of the five tables is to have an appropriate title and is to contain two labeled columns—the first showing the dollar amounts $1, $2, $3, ..., $20 and the second showing the corresponding tax amounts.

9. Produce a listing of all three-digit numbers whose digits are 1, 2, or 3. Spaces are not to appear between the digits of the numbers. (*Hint:* Use triple-nested loops with control variables I, J, and K ranging from 1 to 3. If I, J, and K are the digits, the number is $100 \times I + 10 \times J + K$.)

10. Produce a listing of all three-digit numbers as described in Problem 9. If no digit is repeated in a number, however, it is to be preceded by an asterisk. Thus a portion of your display should be as follows.

```
              .
              .
              .
            121
            122
           *123
            131
           *132
            133
              .
              .
              .
```

11. Let's define an operation whose symbol is & on the set A = {0, 1, 2, 3, 4, 5} as follows. The "product" of two integers **i** and **j** is given by

$$i \,\&\, j = \text{the remainder when } i \times j \text{ is divided by 6}$$

Write a program to display a table showing all possible "products" of numbers in the set A. The table values should be labeled as follows:

```
    &   0   1   2   3   4   5
    --- --- --- --- --- --- ---
    0
    1
    2
    3
    4
    5
```

12. Determine the largest value that the expression $XY^2 - X^2Y + X - Y$ can assume if X and Y can be any integers from 1 to 5, inclusive.

13. Find the maximum and minimum values of the expression $3X^2 - 2XY + Y^2$ if X and Y are subject to the following constraints.

$$X = -4, -3.5, -3, \ldots, 4$$

$$Y = -3, -2.5, -2, \ldots, 5$$

14. The expression $X^3 - 4XY + X^2 + 10X$ is to be examined for all integers X and Y between 1 and 5 to determine those pairs (X, Y) for which the expression is negative. All such pairs are to be displayed, together with the corresponding negative value of the expression.

15. Find all pairs of integers (X, Y) that satisfy the following system of inequalities.

$$2X - Y < 3$$

$$X + 3Y \geq 1$$

$$-6 \leq X \leq 6$$

$$-10 \leq Y \leq 10$$

The solutions are to be displayed as individual ordered pairs (X, Y). (*Hint:* The last two conditions give the initial and terminal values of FOR loops.)

■ *9.5 Review True-or-False Quiz*

1. If a group of statements is to be executed several times in a program, it is always a good practice to use a FOR loop.   T F

2. If a loop begins with the statement FOR K = 1 to 35, the variable K must occur in some statement before the NEXT K statement is encountered.   T F

3. The statement FOR J = X to 10 STEP 3 is valid even though X may have a value that is not an integer.   T F

4. In the statement FOR N = 15 to 200 STEP C, C must be a positive integer.   T F

5. The initial, terminal, and step values in a FOR loop cannot be changed in the body of the loop.   T F

6. The control variable in a FOR loop can be changed in the body of the loop; moreover, doing so represents a good programming practice.   T F

7. The control variable of a loop containing a loop may be used as the initial, terminal, or step value of the inner loop.   T F

8. Some loops must be coded by using the FOR and NEXT statements.   T F

9. The statement FOR X = Y TO Z STEP W contains a syntax error.   T F

10. The statement FOR X$ = "A" TO "Z" contains a syntax error.   T F

11. All counter-controlled loops are best coded as FOR loops.   T F

10
More on Screen Displays

QuickBASIC allows much greater control of the display screen than shown in the preceding chapters. In this chapter, we describe how the LOCATE statement can be used to specify *any* screen position for your output without affecting the rest of the screen (Section 10.1). We also show how the COLOR statement can be used to create reverse image and blinking displays and, if your screen allows color, to specify colors for all output values (Section 10.3). Finally, in Section 10.4 we show how certain nonstandard characters, such as

☺   ♥   ◆   ♣   ♠   →   æ   ½   Σ   π   ≤

and many others, can be included in your screen displays.

■ 10.1 The Cursor Moving Statement: LOCATE

The LOCATE statement allows you to move the cursor to any position on the PC's display screen without affecting the current screen display. (This is called a **pure cursor move.**) For example, the two statements

```
LOCATE 20,5
PRINT "A"
```

will display the letter A in the fifth character position of display line 20. The statement LOCATE 20,5 moves the cursor up or down (depending on the current display line) to line 20, and left or right to position 5. Since the two statements shown are so closely related, you may sometimes want to use the multiple-statement line

```
LOCATE 20, 5: PRINT "A"
```

Any numerical expression can be used to specify positions in the LOCATE statement. For example, if L = 20 and P = 5, the previous line can be changed to

```
LOCATE L, P: PRINT "A"
```

EXAMPLE 1 *Here is a program to produce the following screen display beginning at position 30 of display line 10:*

```
IBM PC
 IBM PC
  IBM PC
   IBM PC
```

<table>
<tr><td>

THE PROGRAM

</td><td>

```
CLS                          'Clear screen
LET L = 10                   'Starting line
LET C = 30                   'Starting Column
FOR N = 0 TO 3
   LOCATE L + N, C + N       'Pure cursor move
   PRINT "IBM PC";           'Output
NEXT N
END
```

</td></tr>
</table>

When N = 0, the LOCATE statement causes a pure cursor move to screen position 10,30 (position 30 on line 10); when N = 1, the move is to screen position 11,31; and so on.

REMARK 1

Without the CLS statement, you may end with a cluttered output screen. The output will be displayed over whatever happens to be on the screen when the RUN command is entered.

REMARK 2

Exactly the same screen display will be produced if the FOR statement is changed to

```
130 FOR N=3 TO 0 STEP -1
```

With this change, the output will be displayed from the bottom line up. However, it will happen so fast that you will not notice the difference.

REMARK 3

Notice that the PRINT statement ends with a semicolon. In this program, the output would be the same without the semicolon. However, if we were to direct output to screen line 24, a PRINT statement without a final semicolon would cause a RETURN, and everything on screen lines 1–24 would scroll up one line. Situations that can lead to unwanted scrolling are discussed following Example 3.

EXAMPLE 2

Here is a program to display BASIC at the four corners and the center of the output screen.

```
CLS
LET B$ = "BASIC"
LOCATE 1, 1: PRINT B$;        'Top left corner
LOCATE 1, 76: PRINT B$;       'Top right corner
LOCATE 13, 38: PRINT B$;      'Center of screen
LOCATE 24, 1: PRINT B$;       'Bottom left corner
LOCATE 24, 76: PRINT B$;      'Bottom right corner
END
```

REMARK 1

As mentioned above, the semicolon in

```
PRINT B$;
```

is necessary on both lines that direct output to screen 24. If it were not present, lines 1 through 24 would scroll upward, and the display intended for screen line 1 would be lost.

REMARK 2

When this program stops, the screen will contain the program output and also the prompt

```
Press any key to continue
```

on screen line 25, which somewhat tarnishes the display. As you have probably already discovered, you can clear this prompt by pressing a key and then pressing function key F4 to display the output screen again, but without the prompt.

The program of Example 2 does not use screen line 25 for output. When a program stops, any display on line 25 is erased when QuickBASIC displays the *Press any key to continue* prompt. (Unlike lines 1 to 24, line 25 is never scrolled upward.) One way to prevent losing output that appears in line 25 is to keep the program from ending. You can do this conveniently with the **INKEY$ variable,** a string variable that is part of the QuickBASIC language. It causes the program to read a single character from the keyboard for its value. (You just press the key.) If the loop

```
DO WHILE INKEY$ = "": LOOP
```

is included in a program, a value will be read from the keyboard and assigned to INKEY\$. If that value is the null string "" (that is, no character has been typed), the condition INKEY\$ = "" is true and looping continues. This process will continue until some character is typed (it will not be displayed). INKEY\$ will at that point take the typed character as its value, the condition INKEY\$ = "" will be false, and control will pass to the next line, allowing the program to continue. Thus, including this one-line loop is an effective method of delaying further execution of a program for as long as desired. In the present instance, it can prevent the prompt from being displayed by delaying the execution of the END statement.

To illustrate this use of INKEY\$, the program

```
CLS
LOCATE 1, 1: PRINT "FIRST LINE"
LOCATE 25, 1: PRINT "LAST LINE";
DO WHILE INKEY$ = "": LOOP
END
```

will display the strings FIRST LINE on line 1 and LAST LINE on line 25, without any other character appearing anywhere on the screen. This display will remain on the screen until a key is pressed.

The LOCATE statement will position the cursor at a location on the screen whether or not a character is already displayed at that location. Thus, the statements

```
LET A$="COMPUTER"
LET B$="IBM"
LOCATE 15,5 : PRINT A$
LOCATE 15,5 : PRINT B$
```

will display the string COMPUTER beginning at the fifth position on display line 15, and then will display the string IBM beginning at this same location. The effect is to display the characters IBMPUTER. If the intent is to replace one string by a second, you must make sure that blanks are displayed over positions in the first string that are not used by the second. Here are two ways to do this for the given example.

1. Include the line

```
LOCATE 15,5 : PRINT STRING$(8," ")
```

to "erase" COMPUTER by displaying enough blank characters over it.

2. Use PRINT USING rather than PRINT statements:

```
LET A$="COMPUTER"
LET B$="IBM"
LET F$="\        \"
LOCATE 15,5 : PRINT USING F$;A$
LOCATE 15,5 : PRINT USING F$;B$
```

Remember that string output values are displayed left justified with trailing blanks. Thus, the value IBM of B\$ is displayed with five trailing blanks that "erase" PUTER.

There are many coding situations in which you should erase old screen displays before generating new ones. Many involve the use of the PRINT statement to display new information in specified screen positions, as just illustrated. Another situation concerns displays produced because of INPUT statements. Suppose, for example, that the programming line

```
LOCATE 20,1 : INPUT "AMOUNT";AMT
```

is included in a loop and that the user enters 5239.46 for AMT. The display on screen line 20 will be

```
AMOUNT? 5239.46
```

If the amount 5239.46 is not erased before the INPUT statement is encountered a second time, the user will be confronted with the preceding display and not with the desired prompt

```
AMOUNT?
```

If, this time, the user types 467 and presses the Enter key, 467 will be assigned to AMT, but the display will be

```
AMOUNT? 4679.46
```

and not

```
AMOUNT? 467
```

To ensure that such confusing (and erroneous) information will not appear in the display, you could precede

```
LOCATE 20,1 : INPUT "AMOUNT";AMT
```

by

```
LOCATE 20,1 : PRINT STRING$(20," ")
```

to erase the old amount before prompting the user for a new one.

EXAMPLE 3   *Here is a program segment that prompts the user for an input value from 50 to 80 and that rejects any other values.*

```
DO
    LOCATE 10, 1                       'Location of input
    PRINT STRING$(29, " ")            'Erase any old input.
    LOCATE 10, 1
    INPUT "AMOUNT (50-80)"; AMT        'Enter amount AMT.
    IF AMT < 50 OR AMT > 80 THEN
        LOCATE 10,30                   'Position for message
        PRINT "BAD INPUT - REENTER";   'The message
    END IF
LOOP UNTIL AMT >= 50 AND AMT <= 80
LOCATE 10, 30                          'Position of message
PRINT STRING$(20, " ")                 'Make sure it's clear
' (PROGRAM CONTINUATION)
```

As indicated by the comments, the first four lines erase any previous input and prompt the user by displaying the prompt

```
AMOUNT (50-80)?
```

on screen line 10. If the value entered for AMT is not in the range 50 to 80, the Block IF statement (its condition will be true) displays the message

```
BAD INPUT - REENTER
```

also on line 10, but to the right of the input value. The WHILE condition in the loop statement will also be true, so the loop will be repeated. When the user enters a value for AMT that is in the range 50 to 80, the Block IF statement does nothing (its condition will be false). The WHILE condition will also be false, so control will pass to the statement following the LOOP statement. As indicated by the comments, the last two lines ensure that the message BAD INPUT − REENTER is erased. If no such message is displayed, these two lines simply display blanks on screen positions that are already blank.

The general form of the LOCATE statement is

LOCATE **l, p**

where **l** and **p** denote numerical expressions. The values of **l** and **p** are rounded, if necessary, to obtain integers (call them L and P). If L is in the range 1−25, and P is in the range 1−80 (1−40 if WIDTH 40 is in effect), the cursor is moved to position P of display line L. If either L or P is outside the specified range, a fatal illegal function call error occurs. (*Note:* If output is directed to a printer, LOCATE has no effect whatsoever.)

In Examples 1 and 2, we mentioned two ways in which unwanted scrolling can occur and explained how to avoid the scrolling. We now summarize these and other situations in which unwanted scrolling can be avoided.

1. (See Example 2.) If a PRINT statement with no terminating semicolon causes output to screen line 24 or 25, lines 1–24 will scroll upward, and the top line will scroll off the screen. Placing a semicolon at the end of each PRINT statement resolves this difficulty.

2. Unwanted scrolling may occur if an INPUT statement is executed while the cursor is on screen line 24 or 25. The scrolling occurs when you press the Enter key after typing the input. One way to avoid this scrolling is to use a LOCATE statement to position the cursor on one of screen lines 1–23 before each INPUT statement. QuickBASIC provides another method: place a semicolon just after the keyword INPUT. For instance, the following programming line allows you to enter a value for AMT on line 24 with no scrolling:

```
LOCATE 24,1 : INPUT; "ENTER AMOUNT";AMT
```

Another important application of the LOCATE statement is in programming tasks that require you to modify screen displays by displaying new information over old information without affecting the rest of the screen. We conclude this section with an example illustrating this use of LOCATE.

EXAMPLE 4   ***Selective modification of a screen display.***

The program given in this example consists of three parts as indicated by the comments. The first part simply assigns string values to certain string variables. The second part displays this table:

```
- - - - - - - - - - - - -
ITEM PERCENT
  1   10.00
  2   10.00
  3   10.00
  4   10.00
  5   10.00
- - - - - - - - - - - - -
```

The third part allows a user to enter different percent figures for one or more of the five items numbered 1 through 5.

```
'    **********************************************
'    * ASSIGN STRING CONSTANTS AND OUTPUT FORMAT *
'    **********************************************

LET DASHES$ = "--------------"
LET HEADER$ = " ITEM PERCENT "
LET FORMAT$ = "  #    ###.##  "
LET BLANKS$ = STRING$(79, " ")

'    ************************
'    * DISPLAY A SHORT TABLE *
'    ************************

CLS                                  'Clear the screen.
LOCATE 5, 15: PRINT DASHES$;
LOCATE 6, 15: PRINT HEADER$;            'Column headers
FOR N = 1 TO 5
   LOCATE 6 + N, 15: PRINT USING FORMAT$; N; 10;    'Table values
NEXT N
LOCATE 6 + N, 15: PRINT DASHES$;

'    *****************************************************
'    * PROMPT FOR NEW PERCENT FIGURES AND CHANGE TABLE *
'    *****************************************************

LOCATE 19, 1: PRINT "TO CHANGE A PERCENT, TYPE ITEM NUMBER."
LOCATE 20, 1: PRINT "MUST BE 1 TO 5; ELSE PROGRAM HALTS."
LOCATE 22, 1: INPUT "ENTER ITEM NUMBER: ", N%
```

```
      DO WHILE 1 <= N% AND N% <= 5
         LOCATE 23, 1: INPUT "ENTER NEW PERCENT: ", P
         LOCATE 6 + N%, 15: PRINT USING FORMAT$; N%; P;    'Change P.
         LOCATE 22, 1: PRINT BLANKS$;                      'Erase old
         LOCATE 23, 1: PRINT BLANKS$;                      'input values.
         LOCATE 22, 1: INPUT "ENTER ITEM NUMBER: ", N%
      LOOP
      END
```

The action caused by the third section of the program is as follows.

1. The first two lines display the instructions

```
      TO CHANGE A PERCENT, TYPE ITEM NUMBER.
      MUST BE 1 TO 5; ELSE PROGRAM HALTS.
```

on display lines 19 and 20. These instructions stay on the screen during the entire input session.

2. The next line displays the input prompt

```
      ENTER ITEM NUMBER: _
```

on display line 22, and if the user types a value for N% from 1 to 5, the DO loop is entered; otherwise, the program stops.

3. The first statement in the DO loop displays the prompt

```
      ENTER NEW PERCENT:
```

and waits for the user to enter a new percent for item number N%.

4. The next line

```
      LOCATE 6 + N%, 15: PRINT USING FORMAT$; N%; P;    'Change P.
```

makes the specified change in the table. The last three lines

```
      LOCATE 22, 1: PRINT BLANKS$;                      'Erase old
      LOCATE 23, 1: PRINT BLANKS$;                      'input values.
      LOCATE 22, 1: INPUT "ENTER ITEM NUMBER: ", N%
```

of the DO loop erase the previous two input lines and prompt the user for another item number.

REMARK   When the given program is run, the user will have to respond to the two input prompts

```
      ENTER ITEM NUMBER: _
      ENTER NEW PERCENT: _
```

The only thing that will draw the user's attention to either of these prompts is the blinking cursor. In QuickBASIC, there are several better ways to draw attention to a particular prompt. You can display it in reverse image (black on white rather than white on black), in blinking characters, or in color, if you have a color monitor. How all of this can be done is explained in Section 10.3.

■ *10.2 Problems*

1. *Describe the screen displays produced by each program.*

a.
```
CLS
LET B$="BASIC"
LET M=2
FOR N=0 TO 10 STEP 5
   LOCATE M,40-N : PRINT B$;
   LOCATE M,40+N : PRINT B$
   LET M=M+1
NEXT N
END
```

b.
```
CLS
LET A$="IBM"
FOR N=1 TO 5 STEP 2
   LOCATE N,20+N : PRINT A$
   LOCATE 10-N,20+N : PRINT A$
NEXT N
END
```

c.
```
CLS
LET R=15 : C=8
FOR N=0 TO 6
   LOCATE R+N,C : PRINT "H   H"
NEXT N
LOCATE R+3,C+1 : PRINT "HHH"
END
```

d.
```
FOR TIME=0 TO 50
   CLS
   FOR N=10 TO 15
      LOCATE N,15 : PRINT "GOOD"
   NEXT N
   CLS
   FOR N=10 TO 15
      LOCATE N,20 : PRINT "GRIEF"
   NEXT N
NEXT TIME
CLS : END
```

Write a program to produce each screen display described in Problems 2–9. Use the LOCATE statement. (Be sure to avoid the scrolling problems cited in this section.)

2. Display the word COMPUTER near the four corners and then at the approximate center of the screen. Be sure that the top line is not scrolled off the screen when the program halts.

3. Display X's along all four edges of the screen. Then display your name near the center of the screen. Be sure that the entire display remains when the program halts.

4. Display your name and address, centered on an otherwise clear screen.

5. Display a square block containing 36 X's at the center of the screen.

6. Successively display the digits 0 through 9 in the 36-character block described in Problem 5. Be sure to clear the screen after each 36-character block is displayed. After this process has been repeated 20 times, the program should halt with a clear screen.

7. Display the following table approximately centered on the screen.

```
RANGE    COUNT    WEIGHT
-----------------------
 0-10      0        1
11-20      0        1
21-30      0        1
31-40      0        1
41-50      0        1
```

8. Display the table shown in Problem 7 and then prompt the user to enter five counts in place of the five 0s and five weights in place of the five 1s.

9. Display the table in Problem 7 and then allow the user to make selective changes in the count and weight columns. (For instance, you could require the user to enter 31,COUNT to specify that the count in the fourth line is to be changed.) Whatever dialogue you set up between the user and the computer, be sure to program an orderly exit from the program when the user indicates that all desired changes have been made.

■ 10.3 The COLOR Statement

Your video display unit is connected to the PC through one of two types of connectors:

1. The Color/Graphics Monitor Adapter* or
2. The Monochrome (black and white only) Display and Parallel Printer Adapter.

If your PC is equipped with the first of these adapters and your display unit is a color monitor, you will be able to use any of the 16 colors listed in Table 10.1 during your sessions at the computer. You can also create reverse image and blinking screen displays. If your PC is equipped with the second of these adapters, you will be limited to black-and-white displays, but you will still have the capability of reverse image and blinking screen displays. All of this is accomplished with the COLOR statement.

Table 10.1   Colors for screen displays

Number	Color	Number	Color
0	Black	8	Gray
1	Blue	9	Light blue
2	Green	10	Light green
3	Cyan (medium blue)	11	Light cyan
4	Red	12	Light red
5	Magenta (purple)	13	Light magenta
6	Brown	14	Yellow
7	White	15	High-intensity white

The COLOR statement can include three numbers: the first sets the foreground color (the color of the actual characters), the second sets the background color (the box that contains the character), and the third sets the color of the border screen:

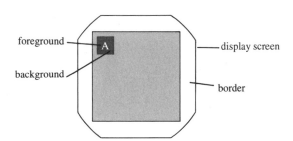

For example, type COLOR 4,1,2 in immediate mode. The border screen is set immediately to green (2), and the prompt *Press any key to continue* appears in red (4) on a blue (1) background. Any characters from a previous display remain in white on a black background. The COLOR statement affects only displays generated after the COLOR statement has been executed. Now, clear the screen with CLS. This colors the entire interior portion of the screen blue (1—the new background color).

When you first load QuickBASIC, the color is automatically set to 7,0,0, white foreground with a black background and a black border screen. Having the same background and border color makes these two regions indistinguishable. We will call this color combination the *normal* screen. To return to this normal screen, type

```
COLOR 7,0,0 : CLS
```

The CLS statement removes any previous display and leaves the entire screen black.

---

*Some PCs are equipped with enhanced graphics adapters that allow greater color and graphics capabilities than we discuss in this book.

EXAMPLE 5 *Here is a program to display the PC's 16 colors, one at a time.*

```
CLS
PRINT "This program will display the PC's 16 colors - black first."
PRINT "To pass from one color to the next, press any key."
PRINT "Press any key to begin."
DO WHILE INKEY$ = "": LOOP          'Wait for a key.
FOR N = 0 TO 15
   COLOR N, N, 0
   CLS
   DO WHILE INKEY$ = "": LOOP     'Wait for a key.
NEXT N
COLOR 7, 0, 0: CLS                'Normal screen
END
```

The first five lines clear the screen, display instructions, and wait for a key to be pressed. When a key is pressed, the FOR loop executes the three lines

```
COLOR N, N, 0
CLS
DO WHILE INKEY$ = "": LOOP    'Wait for key.
```

for the successive N values 0, 1, 2, up to 15. The COLOR statement specifies color code N for both the background and the foreground. The border color remains black (0). The CLS statement clears the display area, leaving it in the color specified by N. The DO loop keeps the display from changing until a key is pressed. When this happens, NEXT N increases N by 1, and the body of the FOR loop is repeated with this N value. This process continues until all 16 colors have been displayed.

REMARK It is important to note that once a color is set by a COLOR statement it remains so until another COLOR statement changes it. Thus, the final line

```
COLOR 7, 0, 0: CLS
```

returns the screen to the normal white on black and ends the program with a clear screen, showing only the prompt Press any key to continue.

EXAMPLE 6 *Here is a program to display three lines in three different colors.*

```
CLS
'Display output in blue on a white background.
COLOR 1, 7, 0
LOCATE 4, 25
PRINT "    BLUE - A PRIMARY COLOR   "

'Display output in yellow on a white background.
COLOR 14, 7, 0
LOCATE 8, 25
PRINT "  YELLOW - A PRIMARY COLOR   "

'Display output in green on a white background.
COLOR 2, 7, 0
LOCATE 12, 25
PRINT "  GREEN - MIX BLUE AND YELLOW "

'Return to a normal screen after a key is pressed.
DO WHILE INKEY$ = "": LOOP
COLOR 7, 0, 0: CLS
END
```

The action of this program is explained in its four comment lines.

Selected lines of text in a screen display can be highlighted by displaying them in reverse image—for instance, black characters on a white background (COLOR 0,7,0) instead of white on black (COLOR 7,0,0). In general, if the active color specification is

```
COLOR A,B,C
```

change it to

```
COLOR B,A,C
```

to display text in reverse image.

EXAMPLE 7   *Here is a program to allow the user to specify which of five lines is to be displayed in reverse image.*

```
'Display five messages.
COLOR 7, 0, 0
CLS           'Normal screen
FOR N% = 1 TO 5
    LOCATE 4 + N%, 10
    PRINT "Message number"; N%
NEXT N%

'Allow the user to select a message.
LOCATE 1, 1
INPUT "Enter 1, 2, 3, 4, or 5 : ", N%
IF N% >= 1 AND N% <= 5 THEN
    COLOR 0, 7, 0
    LOCATE 4 + N%, 10: PRINT "Message number"; N%
    COLOR 7, 0, 0
END IF
END
```

If the user enters 4 in response to the input statement, the screen display will be as follows:

```
Enter 1, 2, 3, 4, or 5 : 4

        Message number 1
        Message number 2
        Message number 3
        Message number 4        ← reverse image
        Message number 5
```

In the first part of the program, the FOR loop displays the five messages. Each line is displayed beginning at position 10, as specified by

```
LOCATE 4 + N%, 10
```

Since the FOR loop uses the successive values 1, 2, 3, 4, and 5 for N%, the line number 4 + N% specifies the successive lines 5, 6, 7, 8, and 9 for these messages.

The second part of the program begins by prompting the user for a value of N%. Because of the statement

```
LOCATE 1, 1
```

that precedes the INPUT statement, the prompt and the value entered by the user appear on the top line of the screen, above the five messages. The statement

```
COLOR 0, 7, 0
```

causes any subsequent output to be displayed as black characters on a white background. Thus, the two statements

```
LOCATE 4 + N%, 10: PRINT "Message number"; N%
COLOR 7, 0, 0
```

first display the message on line 4 + N% again, but this time in reverse image characters, and then return the screen to normal.

The preceding example shows how display lines can be changed from normal to reverse image and back to normal. An excellent application of this technique is to highlight each prompt to the user of a program, but only at the time that the prompt requires some action by the user. Another way to draw attention to a particular screen line is to display it in blinking characters.

Blinking characters are displayed in any color simply by adding 16 to the foreground color. Thus,

```
COLOR 23,0,0
```

will cause each subsequent character to be displayed in blinking white (7 + 16 = 23) on a black (0) background. Similarly,

```
COLOR 18,7,4
```

will cause subsequent characters to be displayed in blinking green (2 + 16 = 18) on white (7) with a red (4) border.

QuickBASIC can operate in text mode and in several graphics modes. We have been operating in *text mode*. This means that only text—that is, sequences of characters such as letters, +, −, and so on—is displayed or printed. The form of the COLOR statement described in this section is for text mode only. COLOR as used in the two graphics modes is explained in Chapter 19.

The general form of the COLOR statement as used in *text mode* is

COLOR **fore,back,bord**

where **fore, back,** and **bord** denote numerical expressions that are rounded, if necessary, to integer values that we'll call FORE, BACK, and BORD. These integers specify the foreground, background, and border colors, respectively. The following rules apply:

1. FORE should be in the range 0 to 31. The numbers 0 to 15 specify the foreground colors, and adding 16 causes displayed characters to blink on and off.
2. BACK should be in the range 0 to 7. Only these eight colors can be used for the background.
3. BORD should be in the range 0 to 15. The border color is changed as soon as the COLOR statement is executed.
4. Each of the color parameters **fore, back,** and **bord** is optional. Omitting a color parameter means it will not be changed.

EXAMPLE 8   *In this table assume the current color specifications are 5,3,4.*

COLOR statement	Equivalent COLOR statements		
COLOR 6,3,4	COLOR 6,3	COLOR 6,,4	COLOR 6
COLOR 5,3,7	COLOR 5,,7	COLOR,3,7	COLOR,,7
COLOR 7,3,6	COLOR 7,,6		

EXAMPLE 9   *Here is a program to illustrate reverse image and blinking displays on any screen.*

```
CLS
LET ND$ = "Normal display"
LET BD$ = "Blinking display"
LET RID$ = "Reverse image display"
LET BRID$ = "Blinking reverse image display"
COLOR 7, 0, 0
PRINT "*** "; : PRINT ND$; : PRINT " ***"
PRINT "*** "; : COLOR 23, 0, 0: PRINT BD$; : COLOR 7, 0, 0: PRINT " ***"
PRINT "*** "; : COLOR 0, 7, 0: PRINT RID$; : COLOR 7, 0, 0: PRINT " ***"
PRINT "*** "; : COLOR 16, 7, 0: PRINT BRID$; : COLOR 7, 0, 0: PRINT " ***"
END
```

■ *10.4 The IBM PC Display Characters*

Your PC is capable of displaying a wide variety of characters on its video screen. Some you have already seen; others will be introduced in this section. A table showing all of the IBM PC characters is given in Appendix C. Following is the portion of the table that shows the familiar characters used in QuickBASIC.

Numeric code	Character	Numeric code	Character	Numeric code	Character	Numeric code	Character
032	(space)	056	8	080	P	104	h
033	!	057	9	081	Q	105	i
034	"	058	:	082	R	106	j
035	#	059	;	083	S	107	k
036	$	060	<	084	T	108	l
037	%	061	=	085	U	109	m
038	&	062	>	086	V	110	n
039	'	063	?	087	W	111	o
040	(	064	@	088	X	112	p
041	)	065	A	089	Y	113	q
042	*	066	B	090	Z	114	r
043	+	067	C	091	[	115	s
044	,	068	D	092	\	116	t
045	−	069	E	093	]	117	u
046	.	070	F	094	^	118	v
047	/	071	G	095	−	119	w
048	0	072	H	096	`	120	x
049	1	073	I	097	a	121	y
050	2	074	J	098	b	122	z
051	3	075	K	099	c	123	{
052	4	076	L	100	d	124	¦
053	5	077	M	101	e	125	}
054	6	078	N	102	f	126	~
055	7	079	O	103	g	127	⌂

You will note that each character is paired with a positive integer called its numeric code. For instance, "A" is associated with numeric code 65, "a" with 97, "5" with 53, and so on. These are, incidentally, the numeric codes of the *American Standard Code of Information Interchange* (ASCII).

In addition to these standard characters, Appendix C shows other characters that can be displayed on the IBM PC video screen. Following are some of these characters with their numeric codes.

Numeric code	Character	Numeric code	Character
001	☺	169	⌐
003	♥	170	¬
004	♦	171	½
005	♣	219	■
006	♠	220	▬
145	æ	221	▮
146	Æ	227	π
147	ô	228	Σ
148	ö	234	Ω

All of the characters shown in Appendix C are called **display characters,** since they can be displayed on the monitor. (You will note that Appendix C shows the numeric codes 0–255, but that not all of these correspond to display characters. In particular, numeric codes 0, 7, 9–13, and 28–31 have special meanings, as indicated in the table.)

There are no individual keys to press for many of the PC display characters. All, however, can be included in your screen displays. In what follows, we show ways to do this.

The Character Function CHR$

If **n** denotes an integer from 0 to 255, the value of the expression CHR$(**n**) is the character with numeric code **n.** Thus,

```
PRINT CHR$(3);CHR$(4);CHR$(5);CHR$(6)
```

will produce the screen display

♥ ♦ ♣ ♠

Similarly, the loop

```
FOR N=224 TO 235 : PRINT CHR$(N); : NEXT N
```

will display (see Appendix C):

αβΓπΣσμτΦθΩδ

EXAMPLE 10   *Here is a program to display the English alphabet in upper- and lowercase letters.*

```
CLS
FOR K = 65 TO 90
    PRINT CHR$(K); CHR$(K + 32);
NEXT K
FOR L = 1 TO 5
    PRINT CHR$(7);
NEXT L
END
```

Program output:
AaBbCcDdEeFfGgHhIiJjKkLlMmNnOoPpQqRrSsTtUuVvWwXxYyZz

The numeric code for each lowercase letter is 32 more than the code for the same letter in uppercase. Thus, when K is 65, Aa is displayed; when K is 66, Bb is displayed; and so on.

The argument *n* in CHR$(**n**) can be any of the numeric codes 0–255. As shown in Appendix C, numeric code 7 corresponds to a beep. Thus, the second FOR loop causes the PC's speaker to beep five times. [Early computer output devices had a bell rather than a speaker. For this reason, CHR$(7) is sometimes called the *bell character.*]

The following short program illustrates how the special characters can be combined to create a screen display different from the usual line-by-line displays.

EXAMPLE 11   *Here is a program to produce the screen display:*

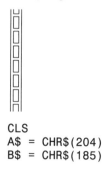

```
CLS
A$ = CHR$(204)
B$ = CHR$(185)
```

```
     FOR N = 1 TO 7
        PRINT A$; B$
     NEXT N
     END
```

Numeric code 204 corresponds to the character

and numeric code 185 corresponds to

When displayed next to each other, you get

Displaying seven of these pairs of characters, one under the other, gives the display shown.

The Alt Key

If you use CHR$ to include display characters in a QuickBASIC program, the characters do not actually appear in the program. For instance, the representation CHR$(204) of the character

appears in the program of Example 10, but not the character itself. QuickBASIC allows you to use the Alt key (just to the left of the space bar) and the numeric keypad (the rightmost part of the keyboard) to include a picture of most of the display characters in your programs. (With the Alt key, you can include all of the display characters with numeric codes 32 to 255, and some of those with codes less than 32.) To enter a character, type its numeric code on the numeric keypad while holding down the Alt key. When you release the Alt key, the character will be inserted in your program at the cursor position. For example, you can assign the block symbol (code 219) to the string variable BLOCK$ by using either of the following statements:

```
     LET BLOCK$ = CHR$(219)     ' ■ symbol
     LET BLOCK$ = "■"           'Alt/219
```

Simply type the line as usual, and when you get to the block symbol, use Alt/219. To assign the name of the fraternity ΣN to the variable CLUB$, use

```
     LET CLUB$="ΣN"
```

To type Σ you must use Alt/228. Although you can use Alt/78 for N, it is easier simply to type N.

You can even respond to INPUT statements with any characters that can be entered with the Alt key. Thus, you can respond to the question mark caused by

```
     INPUT CLUB$
```

with ΣN, or ΓΣ, or any other character string that can be entered at the keyboard.

EXAMPLE 12

Here is a program to produce the screen display:

```
     '   A$ IS A 5 CHARACTER STRING.
     LET A$ = "╠═══╣"   'Alt/204,Alt/205,Alt/205,Alt/205,Alt/185
     '   B$ IS ANOTHER 5 CHARACTER STRING.
     LET B$ = "║   ║"   'Alt/186,space,space,space,Alt/186
```

```
CLS
PRINT TAB(10); B$
PRINT TAB(10); A$
PRINT TAB(10); B$
END
```

The String Function STRING$

If **n** and **c** denote integers in the range 0–255 and **S$** denotes a string expression then

STRING$(**n,c**) is the string that repeats **n** times the character whose numeric code is **c.**
STRING$(**n,S$**) is the string that repeats **n** times the first character of **S$.**

We have already illustrated the second of these two forms. For instance, we have used

```
PRINT STRING$(N,"-")
```

to display a row of N dashes. Since we know how to enter special characters by using the Alt key, we can write

```
PRINT STRING$(N,"♦")
```

to display a row of N diamond symbols.

The first form STRING$(**n,c**) includes the numeric code **c** of the character to be repeated. Thus, STRING$(5,4) has the value

♦♦♦♦

since 4 is the numeric code of the diamond symbol. Similarly, the statement

```
PRINT STRING$(N,4)
```

will display a row of N diamonds.

EXAMPLE 13 *Use the block character ■ (numeric code 219) to display a rectangle W positions wide and R rows high:*

PROBLEM ANALYSIS

To display the required figure all that is needed is to:

1. Draw the first row
2. Draw R − 2 rows
3. Draw the last row

To draw the first and last rows, simply display ■ W times. Let BLOCK$ = "■" and print STRING$(W,BLOCK$).

To draw each of the other rows, display ■, then W − 2 blanks and ■ again. Let BLANK$=" " and print BLOCK$;STRING$(W − 2,BLANK$);BLOCK$.

THE PROGRAM

```
CLS
INPUT "How many positions wide (3 to 79)"; W
DO WHILE W < 3 OR W > 79
    INPUT "How many positions wide (3 to 79)"; W
LOOP
INPUT "How many rows high (3 to 18)"; R
DO WHILE R < 3 OR R > 18
    INPUT "How many rows high (3 to 18)"; R
LOOP
PRINT
```

```
LET BLOCK$ = "■"                              'Code 219
LET BLANK$ = " "
LET A$ = STRING$(W, BLOCK$)
LET B$ = STRING$(W - 2, BLANK$)
PRINT A$                                      'First row
FOR N = 1 TO R - 2                            'Middle rows
   PRINT BLOCK$; B$; BLOCK$
NEXT N
PRINT A$                                      'Last row
END
```

Program output:
```
How many positions wide (3 to 79)? 8
How many rows high (3 to 18)? 4
```

REMARK

The LET statements that assign values to A$ and B$ can be replaced by

```
LET A$=STRING$(W,219)
LET B$=STRING$(W-2,32)
```

STRING$(W − 2,32) can also be written SPACE$(W − 2).

EXAMPLE 14   *Here is a program to display 16 horizontal bars showing the 16 PC colors.*

```
CLS
PRINT TAB(37); "COLORS"
PRINT
LET BAR$ = STRING$(20, 219)                   'Code 219 is ■.
FOR N = 0 TO 15
   COLOR 7, 0, 0: PRINT TAB(25); N;           'Display number of bar.
   COLOR N, 0, 0: PRINT TAB(30); BAR$         'Display bar in color.
NEXT N
COLOR 7, 0, 0                                 'Normal screen
END
```

REMARK

The first bar (color 0) cannot be seen because the background color is also black. Its number, however, is seen—all numbers are displayed in the normal white on black.

■ 10.5 Problems

1. *Describe the screen display produced by each program.*

a.
```
COLOR 7,0,0
CLS
FOR N=1 TO 5
   PRINT "NORMAL"
NEXT N
COLOR 0,7,0
FOR N=1 TO 5
   PRINT TAB(7);"REVERSE"
NEXT N
COLOR 7,0,0
END
```

b.
```
COLOR 7,0,0
CLS
FOR T=1 TO 5
   LOCATE 10+T,38
   PRINT "BASIC"
NEXT T
COLOR 23
LOCATE 13,38
PRINT "BASIC"
COLOR 7
END
```

c. COLOR 7,0,0
```
   COLOR 7,0,0
   CLS
   COLOR 0,7
   FOR R=1 TO 10
      FOR C=1 TO 5
         PRINT TAB(2*C);" ";
      NEXT C
      PRINT
   NEXT R
   COLOR 7,0
   END
```

d.
```
   COLOR 0,7,0
   CLS
   ROW$=STRING$(80," ")
   FOR K=0 TO 15
      COLOR 0,K
      LOCATE K+1,1
      PRINT ROW$
   NEXT K
   COLOR 7,0,0
   END
```

2. *Describe the screen display produced by each program. (These displays involve the PC special characters.)*

a.
```
   COLOR 7,0,0
   CLS
   FOR Y=1 TO 5
      PRINT STRING$(Y,219)
   NEXT Y
   END
```

b.
```
   COLOR 7,0,0
   CLS
   FOR N=1 TO 5
      PRINT TAB(6-N);STRING$(N,219)
   NEXT N
   END
```

c.
```
   COLOR 0,7,0
   CLS
   LET L$=CHR$(169)
   LET R$=CHR$(170)
   PRINT
   FOR N=1 TO 3
      PRINT L$;R$;
   NEXT N
   COLOR 7,0,0
   END
```

d.
```
   COLOR 0,7,0 : CLS
   LET A$="■ ■ ■ ■"    'Alt/219
   LET B$=" ■ ■ ■ "
   COLOR 4,0,0
   FOR N=1 TO 2
      PRINT A$ : PRINT B$
   NEXT N
   PRINT A$
   COLOR 7,0,0
   END
```

In Problems 3–7, write a program for each task specified. The PC special characters described in Section 10.4 are not required.

3. Color the entire display area white, and then display your name and address in black characters centered on the screen.

4. Color the entire display area white, and then display the following five lines (in black characters) centered on screen lines 6–10. The first line is to be displayed in reverse image characters.

```
   This is line 1
   This is line 2
   This is line 3
   This is line 4
   This is line 5
```

5. First produce the display described in Problem 4. Then use the bottom portion of the screen to instruct the user to type an integer from 0 to 5. If the user types a number 1–5, the line currently in reverse image should be displayed in black characters on a white background, the line specified by the user should appear in reverse image, and the user should be instructed to type another number. This process should be repeated until the user types 0.

6. Display the five lines shown in Problem 4 in black characters on a white background, with the first line displayed in blinking characters. The user should then be able to cause the current blinking line to stop blinking and the next one to start blinking, simply by pressing any key other than 0. If line 5 is the blinking line, the next one is line 1. When the user presses the 0 key, the program is to halt.

7. A user should be allowed to type up to ten dollar amounts in the range −9999.99 to 9999.99 to obtain their sum. The value 0, when typed, is to indicate that all numbers have been entered. The screen display is to be as follows.

a. All interaction between user and computer is to take place in screen lines 20–23.

b. As the user types input values (other than 0), they are to be displayed in a column in the top portion of the screen with negative amounts appearing in red (reverse image if your screen does not allow color).

c. After all numbers have been entered, a row of dashes is to be displayed under the column of numbers.

d. The sum is to be displayed under the row of dashes. All numbers in the column, including the sum, are to line up by decimal points. (Use a PRINT USING statement with the specification #####.## to display all numbers.)

In Problems 8–11, write a program for each task specified. You should use the PC special display characters.

8. Color the entire screen white, and then use the block character (numeric code 219) to color in black a rectangular region 15 blocks high and 25 blocks wide, centered on the screen.

9. For integers L and H, with L in the range 1–80 and H in the range 1–22, use the block character (code 219) to color in black a rectangular region H blocks high and L blocks wide, centered on the screen. The user is to enter values for L and H during program execution.

10. Produce a table showing the numeric codes 128–255, each with its corresponding display character. Use eight double columns labeled CODE CHAR, so that the entire table will fit on the screen. (You should find the PRINT USING statement helpful.)

11. Produce a table as in Problem 10 for the numeric codes 0–127. However, display the block character (CHR$(219)) for each of the numeric codes 0, 7, 9–13, and 28–31. As mentioned previously, these have the special meanings shown in Appendix C.

■ *10.6 Review True-or-False Quiz*

1. The statement LOCATE 5,9 will cause the next output value to be displayed beginning in position 9 of display line 5. T F

2. The programming line

```
LOCATE 12,6 : PRINT "BASIC"
```

will cause five blanks followed by the word BASIC to be displayed on screen line 12. T F

3. The programming line

```
LOCATE 24,1 : PRINT "DONE"
```

will display DONE on screen line 24 and will not affect screen lines 1–23. T F

4. The LOCATE statement is necessary for output to appear on screen line 25. T F

5. If all output is produced by using LPRINT statements, the LOCATE statement can be used to specify print positions along a line. T F

6. The programming line

```
DO WHILE INKEY$ <> ".": LOOP
```

will cause the computer to loop until the period key is pressed. T F

7. The statement COLOR 0,7,0 will cause subsequent output to be displayed in black characters on a white background. T F

8. The statement COLOR 16,7,7 will cause subsequent output to be displayed in blinking black characters on a white background. T F

9. Colors specified in a COLOR statement remain in effect until another COLOR statement is encountered or until program execution terminates, whichever comes first. T F

10. The expression *reverse image* always means that characters are displayed in black letters on a white background. T F

11. The statement COLOR,,7 is admissible. When executed, the border screen is immediately colored in white. T F

12. The programming line

    ```
    CLS : COLOR 0,7,7
    ```

    will cause the entire screen to be colored in white.   T   F

13. Any of the IBM PC display characters can be displayed by using the statement
    PRINT CHR$(N), where N denotes the numeric code of the character to be displayed.   T   F

14. Any of the IBM PC display characters can be displayed by using the Alt key together
    with the numeric keypad.   T   F

15. Any of the IBM PC display characters can be displayed by using the statement
    PRINT STRING$(1,N), where N denotes the numeric code of the character to be
    displayed.   T   F

11
Data as Part of a Program

*T*o this point, we have used only LET and INPUT statements to assign values to variables. QuickBASIC provides alternative ways of presenting data to the computer. In this chapter, we describe three statements: the DATA statement, which allows you to include data as part of your programs; the READ statement, which is used to assign these data to variables; and the RESTORE statement, which allows you to "read" these data more than once during a single program run.

As you work through the examples in this chapter, you will see that these statements often provide a convenient, and sometimes necessary, alternative to the LET and INPUT statements.

■ *11.1 The READ and DATA Statements*

These two statements are best illustrated by example. The general forms that must be used for READ and DATA statements, together with rules governing their use, are given following Example 4.

EXAMPLE 1   *Here is a program to "read" two numbers and display their sum.*

```
READ A
READ B
PRINT "VALUES:"; A; B
PRINT "SUM:"; A + B
DATA 17,8
END          ← data pointer
```
(handwritten annotations: Input or Read, Do while, Input or Read, Loop)

Program output:
```
VALUES: 17  8
THEIR SUM: 25
```

The DATA statement contains the numbers to be added. The first READ statement assigns the first of these (17) to A, and the second READ statement assigns the second (8) to B. When the DATA statement is encountered, it is ignored; DATA statements allow you to include data as part of your programs, but cause no action during program execution.

REMARK   You can replace the two READ statements

```
READ A
READ B
```

by the single statement

```
READ A,B
```

This statement obtains the first datum (17) for the first variable (A) and the second (8) for the second variable (B).

EXAMPLE 2   **Here is a program to "read" and display three strings.**

```
READ A$, B$, P$
PRINT B$; " "; A$; P$
END
DATA FLIES,TIME,.
```

Program output:
```
TIME FLIES.
```

The READ statement assigns the first datum (FLIES) to A$, the second (TIME) to B$, and the third (a period) to P$. The PRINT statement then produces the output shown.

REMARK 1   Both upper- and lowercase letters are allowed in DATA statements. Thus the DATA line could be written

```
DATA flies,Time,.
```

to produce the output

```
Time flies.
```

REMARK 2   Notice that the DATA statement appears after the END statement. DATA statements cause no action during program execution and can be placed anywhere in your programs.

Note that the strings in the DATA line of Example 2 are not in quotation marks. Strings must be quoted only if:

1. they contain significant leading or trailing blanks. (If not quoted, these blanks are ignored.)
2. a comma or colon appears in the string. (The comma is used to delimit the constants contained in the DATA lines and the colon to separate statements.)

It is always correct to enclose strings in quotation marks.

EXAMPLE 3   *Here is a program to illustrate quoted and unquoted strings in DATA lines.*

```
' Read and display these data:
DATA 1234567,VI,"   AL",TO GO
DATA "CLARK,JACK",'NOT A COMMENT
DATA END-OF-DATA

READ Z$
DO UNTIL Z$ = "END-OF-DATA"
    PRINT Z$
    READ Z$
LOOP
END
```

Program output:
```
1234567
VI
   AL
TO GO
CLARK,JACK
'NOT A COMMENT
```

Quotes are needed for " AL" because of the leading blanks and for "CLARK, JACK" because of the comma. Quotes are not needed for the string TO GO because the blank is not a leading or trailing blank.

REMARK 1   Note that the string 1234567 is displayed without a leading blank. When the READ statement obtains the value 1234567 for the *string* variable Z$, the computer stores it as seven distinct characters. This would not be so if 1234567 were assigned to a *numerical* variable. The statement

```
LET Z=1234567
```

stores the numbers 1234567 in a special binary form that the computer uses to store numerical values.

REMARK 2   Note also that the string 'NOT A COMMENT that ends the DATA statement containing "CLARK,JACK" is treated just as any other datum. An apostrophe character (') appearing in a DATA statement is treated as any other character. To end a DATA statement with a comment, use :' or :REM.

The last datum (END-OF-DATA) in the preceding example is called an *end-of-data* (EOD) *tag*. It is not displayed in the output, but serves only to cause an exit from the loop. An attempt to execute a READ statement after all data have been read causes an error condition that terminates program execution. Should this happen, the READ statement that caused the error will be highlighted, and the following dialogue box will be displayed:

```
┌─────────────────────────────┐
│        Out of DATA          │
├─────────────────────────────┤
│  < OK >       < Help >      │
└─────────────────────────────┘
```

At this point, you can press the Enter key to accept the default response OK.

As illustrated in the next example, you can avoid out-of-data errors by including a data count as the first datum instead of an end-of-data tag as the last. The example also illustrates that both string and numerical data can be included in a single DATA statement, and a single READ statement can be used to read values for both string and numerical variables.

EXAMPLE 4   *Here is a program to produce a table that summarizes the information contained in DATA statements.*

```
' Display column headings

PRINT "NAME","SCORE1","SCORE2","AVERAGE"
PRINT

' Read data and display table values

READ N                    'Student count
LET COUNT=1               'Data counter
DO WHILE COUNT <= N
   READ STUDENT$, SCORE1, SCORE2
   LET AV = (SCORE1 + SCORE2) / 2
   PRINT STUDENT$, SCORE1, SCORE2, AV
   LET COUNT = COUNT + 1
LOOP
END                       'Program exit

'Student names and scores

DATA 4                    :'Number of students
DATA CARL,71,79
DATA MARLENE,82,88
DATA SUZANNE,89,62
DATA WILLIAM,58,96
```

Program output:

NAME	SCORE1	SCORE2	AVERAGE
CARL	71	79	75
MARLENE	82	88	85
SUZANNE	89	62	75.5
WILLIAM	58	96	77

The first READ statement (READ N) assigns the first datum (4) to the variable N. This N is then used in the WHILE condition COUNT $<=$ N to ensure that exactly four names with their corresponding scores are read and processed.

REMARK

Note that the variable COUNT serves as a counter for the WHILE loop that reads and displays the table values. Thus, the loop is a counter-controlled loop, as described in Section 9.1, and is more conveniently coded as a FOR loop.

The general forms of the READ and DATA statements are as follows:

READ   List of variables separated by commas
DATA   List of constants separated by commas

The following rules govern the use of these two statements:

1. As many DATA lines as desired may be included in a program, and as many values as will fit may appear on each line. The values must be *constants.*

2. All values appearing in the DATA lines constitute a single list called the **data list.** The order in which data appear in this list is precisely the order in which they appear in the program.

3. When a READ statement is executed, the variables appearing are assigned successive values from the data list. You must write your READ and DATA statements so that only numerical values are assigned to numerical variables and only string values to string variables. The data appearing in DATA lines constitute a *single* data list; no special treatment is given to string constants. The execution of a READ statement will attempt to assign the next value in this list to the variable being assigned. If this next value is not of the same type as the variable, either an error message will be displayed or your program will simply produce incorrect results.

4. It is not necessary that all data values be read. However, an attempt to read more data than appear in DATA lines will result in an error condition that causes an Out-of-data message and program execution to stop. Errors that stop program execution are called **fatal errors.**

5. If a DATA statement is encountered during program execution, the statement is ignored and control passes to the next statement. Thus, DATA lines may appear anywhere in the program, although you should position them to make your programs more readable. Placing them near the end of a program is a common practice. If DATA lines will never be changed, it is sometimes better to place them just after the READ statements that read the data.

In flowcharting, the symbol

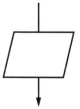

is used to designate any input or output that is carried out automatically with no user interaction. The PRINT and READ statements designate such actions; hence, this symbol is used for both of these statements. You will recall that we have used the flowchart symbol

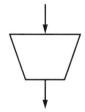

for all INPUT statements. In flowcharting, this symbol is used to designate any process that requires user interaction, thus causing a temporary halt in execution. The INPUT statement does precisely this—the program waits until you enter data at the keyboard.

There is no flowchart symbol for DATA statements. DATA statements simply provide a means of presenting data to the computer for processing. When encountered during program execution, they cause nothing to happen. Thus, they have no place in a flowchart, whose purpose is to describe the flow of activity in a program.

We conclude this section with another example illustrating the use of an EOD tag. Using an EOD tag as the last datum, rather than a count as the first, relieves us of the burden of counting the values in a data list.

EXAMPLE 5

In this example, we are given the results of a golf tournament and must produce a two-column table showing the names and total scores of all golfers. We must also tell how many golfers are tied for the lead (lowest total score). If there is a single winner, however, the winner's name and total score are to be displayed instead of the count. The results of the tournament are given to us in DATA lines as follows:

```
DATA BROUHA,70,72,68,69
DATA HERMAN,66,68,73,76
DATA MITCHELL,66,75,72,74
DATA NICKLAUS,73,70,70,65
DATA SANDERS,73,73,71,72
DATA SMYTHE,68,72,77,68
DATA XXX
```

PROBLEM ANALYSIS

Producing a two-column table as specified in the problem statement is not new to us. After displaying a title and column headings, we can process the DATA lines one at a time to produce the table values.

In addition to producing the table, the problem statement says that we must find the lowest total score and count how many golfers have achieved this lowest score. Moreover, if there is a winner, we'll need that winner's name. This short analysis suggests that we use variable names for the following values:

N$	=	player's name
S1,S2,S3,S4	=	scores for player N$
TTL	=	total score for N$
LOW	=	lowest total score
WIN$	=	winner's name
CNT	=	count of players with lowest score

Each time we read N$ and the four scores S1, S2, S3, and S4, we will calculate TTL = S1 + S2 + S3 + S4 and display N$ and TTL. Then, if TTL = LOW, we have another player with the best score LOW, so we'll add 1 to CNT. If TTL < LOW, we have a new lowest score, so we'll assign TTL to LOW, assign N$ to WIN$, and set CNT to 1. Since the first player's total TTL will be the lowest score to that point, we'll start with LOW = a large number to ensure that TTL < LOW will be true for the first player.

THE ALGORITHM

a. Display a title and column headings.
b. Initialize: LOW = 9999.
c. Read N$ (first player's name).

    d. Repeat the following as long as N$ <> "XXX":

        d1. Read S1, S2, S3, S4.

        d2. Calculate their sum TTL.

        d3. Display N$ and TTL.

        d4. If TTL = LOW, add 1 to CNT.

        d5. If TTL < LOW, assign TTL to LOW, N$ to WIN$, and set CNT to 1.

        d6. READ N$ (next player's name).

    e. Display the lowest score LOW.

    f. If CNT = 1, display winner's name WIN$; otherwise, display CNT.

    g. Stop.

THE PROGRAM

```
' GOLF TOURNAMENT PROGRAM

'     N$          PLAYER'S NAME
'     S1-S4       SCORES FOR N$
'     TTL         TOTAL SCORE FOR N$
'     LOW         LOWEST SCORE
'     WIN$        WINNER'S NAME
'     CNT         NUMBER OF PLAYERS WITH LOW SCORE


' Display title and column headings.

PRINT "  GOLF TOURNAMENT"
PRINT "   (ROUNDS 1-4)"
PRINT
PRINT "PLAYER", "TOTAL"
PRINT


' Read data to produce table values
' and to find LOW, CNT, AND WIN$.

LET LOW = 9999                  'Larger than all scores
READ N$                         'First player's name
DO WHILE N$ <> "XXX"
   READ S1, S2, S3, S4          'Scores
   LET TTL = S1 + S2 + S3 + S4  'Add the scores.
   PRINT N$, TTL                'Output
   IF TTL = LOW THEN            'Tie for lead?
      CNT = CNT + 1             'Increase count.
   ELSEIF TTL < LOW THEN        'New leader?
      LET LOW = TTL             'New low score
      LET WIN$ = N$             'Leader's name
      LET CNT = 1               'Only one leader
   END IF
   READ N$                      'Next player's name
LOOP


' Display final results.

PRINT
PRINT "BEST FOUR-ROUND TOTAL:"; LOW
IF CNT = 1 THEN
   PRINT "TOURNAMENT WINNER: "; WIN$
ELSE
   PRINT CNT; "PLAYERS ARE TIED FOR THE LEAD."
END IF


' Data: Names and scores for four rounds
DATA BROUHA,70,72,68,69
DATA HERMAN,66,68,73,76
DATA MITCHELL,66,75,72,74
DATA NICKLAUS,73,70,70,65
DATA SANDERS,73,73,71,72
DATA SMYTHE,68,72,77,68
DATA XXX
```

Program output:

```
GOLF TOURNAMENT
  (ROUNDS 1-4)

PLAYER        TOTAL

BROUHA         279
HERMAN         283
MITCHELL       287
NICKLAUS       278
SANDERS        289
SMYTHE         285


BEST FOUR-ROUND TOTAL: 278
TOURNAMENT WINNER: NICKLAUS
```

11.2 Problems

1. *Show the output of each program.*

a.
```
READ X
DO WHILE X>=0
   LET Y=X-5
   PRINT X;Y
   READ X
LOOP
DATA 2,5,0,-1
END
```

b.
```
READ A,B$,M$
LET M$=B$
PRINT M$;
READ A,B$,M$
LET M$=B$
LET B$=M$
PRINT B$
DATA 6,CAT,MOUSE
DATA 8,"WOMAN","MAN"
END
```

c.
```
LET N=0
READ X
DO WHILE X<>9999
   LET N=N+1
   PRINT X
   READ X
LOOP
PRINT N
DATA 7,3,18,-5,9999
END
```

d.
```
LET B=0
READ V
DO WHILE V<>0
   IF V<25 OR V>75 THEN
      PRINT "BAD VALUE:";V
      LET B=B+1
   END IF
   READ V
LOOP
IF B=0 THEN
   PRINT "DATA ARE OK."
ELSE
   PRINT B;"BAD VALUES."
END IF
END
DATA 36,42,71,22,63,68,84,51,0
```

2. *Find and correct the errors in these programs.*

a.
```
READ X,X$
PRINT X$;X
DATA "1";A
END
```

b.
```
READ Y;Z$
PRINT Z$;" OF ";Y
DATA 42,SUMMER
END
```

c.
```
READ B$
DO WHILE B$<>GOODBYE
    READ B$
LOOP
PRINT B$
DATA HELLO,BYE,GOODBYE
END
```

d.
```
READ N$,A,B,C
PRINT "NAME: ";N$
PRINT "AVERAGE:"(A+B+C)/3
DATA TOM DOOLEY,JR
DATA 85,81,76
END
```

3. *The following programs do not do what they claim. Find and correct all errors.*

a.
```
'    DISPLAY SQUARES OF
'    12,37,21,96.
DO WHILE A<>999
    READ A
    LET A=A*A
    PRINT A
    READ A
LOOP
DATA 12,37,21,96
DATA 999
END
```

b.
```
'    AVERAGE N NUMBERS.
READ X
DO WHILE X<>1E-30
    LET SUM=0
    LET SUM=SUM+X
LOOP
PRINT "AVERAGE IS";SUM/N
DATA 18,23,17,22
DATA 1E-30
END
```

c.
```
'    COUNT DATA VALUES,
'     BUT NOT 999.
LET C=0
DO WHILE V<999
    READ V
    LET C=C+1
LOOP
PRINT "DATA COUNT:";C
DATA 275,863,947,1262
DATA 1344,2765,999
END
```

In Problems 4–11, write a program to perform each task specified.

4. Read values from DATA lines two at a time. Display each pair of values, their sum, and their average on one line. Run your program using the following DATA lines. The last two values $(-1,-1)$ are to be used to detect the end of the data.

```
DATA 70,80,90,65,75,85
DATA 50,40,65,80,78,76
DATA 62,60,65,50,60,85
DATA 35,45,60,90,96,92
DATA -1,-1
```

5. Read values three at a time from DATA lines and display them only if the third is greater than the average of the first two. Run your program using the data in Problem 4. (Change only the last DATA statement.)

6. Read values three at a time from DATA lines and display them only if they are in ascending order. Use the data in Problem 4.

7. Find how many of the numbers appearing in DATA lines lie between 40 and 60, inclusive, and determine the average of these numbers. Use the data in Problem 4.

8. A list of scores in the range 0 to 100 is to be examined to determine the following counts:

> C1 = number of scores less than 40
> C2 = number of scores between 40 and 60, inclusive
> C3 = number of scores greater than 60

Determine these counts for any list appearing in DATA lines. Use the data in Problem 4.

9. A list of scores in the range 0 to 100 is to be examined to determine the following counts:

> C1 = number of scores less than 20
> C2 = number of scores less than 40 but at least 20
> C3 = number of scores less than 60 but at least 40
> C4 = number of scores less than 80 but at least 60
> C5 = number of scores not less than 80

Determine these counts for any list appearing in DATA lines. Use the data in Problem 4.

10. A candidate for political office conducted a preelection poll. Each voter polled was assigned a number from 1 to 3 as follows:

> 1 = will vote for candidate
> 2 = leans toward candidate but still undecided
> 3 = all other cases

Tally the results of this poll. Use DATA lines to present the data to the computer.

11. Modify Problem 10 by assigning two values to each voter. The first is as stated; the second is to designate whether the voter is female (F) or male (M). There are now six counts to be determined. (Use READ A,S$ to read the two values assigned to a voter.)

For Problems 12–16, write programs to produce reports as specified. Make sure each report has a title and each column has an appropriate heading. All data are to be presented in DATA lines.

12. The following DATA lines show the salaries for all salaried employees in a small firm. [The first value (10) denotes how many salaries are listed.]

```
DATA 10
DATA 19923,20240,20275,21390,22560
DATA 22997,23423,24620,29240,32730
```

Prepare a report showing the effect of a flat across-the-board raise of R dollars in addition to a percentage increase of P percent. R and P are to be input. Include three columns labeled PRESENT SALARY, RAISE, and NEW SALARY.

13. The following DATA lines show the annual salaries for all salaried employees in a firm. Each salary amount is followed by a count of the number of employees earning that amount. This firm has a salary step schedule. [The values 0,0 are end-of-data tags.]

```
DATA 19020,4,20250,8,22330,16,22940,30
DATA 23570,21,24840,86,25920,28,26520,7
DATA 0,0
```

Prepare a three-column report as in Problem 12. In addition, conclude the report by displaying the total cost to the owners of the old salary package, the total cost of the new salary package, the total dollar amount of all raises (the difference of the previous two figures), and the overall percent increase that this amount represents.

14. Given the following information, produce a three-column report showing the employee number, monthly sales, and commission for each employee if the commission rate for each person is 6%.

Employee number	Monthly sales
018266234	$4,050
026196551	6,500
034257321	3,750
016187718	3,640
023298049	7,150

15. Given the following information, produce a four-column report showing the employee name, the monthly sales, the commission rate, and the total commission for each employee.

Employee number	Monthly sales	Commission rate
Hart	$28,400	2 %
Wilson	34,550	2.5 %
Brown	19,600	3 %
Ruiz	14,500	2 %
Jensen	22,300	3.25%
Grogan	31,350	1.5 %

16. (Electric bill problem) Given the following information, produce a report showing the customer number, total number of kilowatt-hours (kWh) used, and total monthly bill. The charges are computed according to the following schedule: $1.41 for the first 14 kWh, the next 85 kWh at $0.0389/kWh, the next 200 at $0.0214/kWh, the next 300 at $0.0134/kWh, and the excess at $0.0099/kWh. In addition, there is a fuel-adjustment charge of $0.0322/kWh for all kilowatt-hours used.

Customer number	Previous month's reading	Current reading
0516	25,346	25,973
2634	49,947	48,851
2917	21,342	21,652
2853	893,462	894,258
3576	347,643	348,748
3943	41,241	41,783
3465	887,531	888,165

■ *11.3 The RESTORE Statement*

We have described a *data list* as the list of all data values appearing in all DATA lines in a program. Associated with a data list is a conceptual *pointer* indicating the value to be read by the next READ statement. The pointer is initially set to the first value in the list; then each time a value is read, the pointer moves to the next value. The statement

    RESTORE

positions this pointer back to the beginning of the data list (the first DATA line) so that the values can be read again. The statement

    RESTORE **labelname**

positions the pointer to the first datum in the programming line with the string label **labelname**. String labels must begin with a letter and must contain only letters, digits, and periods. When assigning a string label to a line, you must end the label with a colon. The following are correctly labeled DATA statements:

```
MONTHS: DATA JAN,FEB,MAR,APR,MAY,JUN
        DATA JUL,AUG,SEP,OCT,NOV,DEC
DAYS:   DATA SUN,MON,TUE,WED,THU,FRI,SAT
```

EXAMPLE 6 *This example illustrates the action caused by the two forms of the RESTORE statement.*

The program segment

```
READ A
RESTORE
READ B, C
RESTORE
READ D, E, F
PRINT A; B; C; D; E; F
DATA 1,2,3,4,5,6
```

produces the output

```
1  1  2  1  2  3
```

The first RESTORE statement positions the data pointer at the first datum (1), and the statement READ B,C reads the first two values (1 and 2) for B and C. The second RESTORE statement again positions the pointer at the first datum, and the statement READ D,E,F reads the first three values (1, 2, and 3) for D, E, and F. The PRINT statement produces the output shown. The final three values (4, 5, and 6) are simply not used by this program segment.

The program segment

```
RESTORE MONTHS
READ A$, B$
RESTORE WEEKDAYS
READ C$, D$
PRINT A$; " "; B$; " "; C$; " "; D$
WEEKDAYS: DATA MON,TUE,WED,THU,FRI
MONTHS:   DATA JAN,FEB,MAR,APR,MAY
```

produces the output

```
JAN FEB MON TUE
```

Following are two examples that illustrate typical ways in which the RESTORE statement is used.

EXAMPLE 7 *Here is a program to display two lists obtained from a single data list.*

```
PRINT "SCORES 70 OR MORE:";    'First display all
FOR N = 1 TO 10                'numbers 70 or more.
   READ X
   IF X >= 70 THEN PRINT X;
NEXT N
PRINT
RESTORE
PRINT "SCORES LESS THAN 70:";  'Next display those
FOR N = 1 TO 10                'less than 70.
   READ X
   IF X < 70 THEN PRINT X;
NEXT N
PRINT
END

' Data list containing 10 numbers:
DATA 78,84,65,32,93,58,88,76,68,83
```

Program output:
```
SCORES 70 OR MORE: 78  84  93  88  76  83
SCORES LESS THAN 70: 65  32  58  68
```

The comments describe what this program does. Since all numbers 70 or greater must be displayed before any number less than 70 is displayed, the data must be examined twice. The RESTORE statement makes this possible.

REMARK
■

Without the RESTORE statement, 10 variables would be needed for the 10 numbers that appear in the DATA line. With the RESTORE statement, only one (X) is needed.

EXAMPLE 8   *Here is a program to search a list for any value typed at the keyboard.*

```
'            ON MIXING COLORS

'     X$ = A color included in DATA lines
'     Y$ = Information about the color X$
'     C$ = A string input value
'
PRINT "THIS PROGRAM GIVES INFORMATION ABOUT COLORS."
PRINT "ALL ENTRIES YOU MAKE MUST BE IN UPPERCASE."
PRINT
INPUT "COLOR (TYPE END TO STOP)"; C$
DO WHILE C$ <> "END"
   READ X$, Y$                              'Search for
   DO WHILE X$ <> C$ AND X$ <> "XXX"        'color C$.
      READ X$, Y$
   LOOP
   IF X$ = "XXX" THEN                       'Display output.
      PRINT C$; " IS NOT IN MY LIST OF COLORS."
   ELSE
      PRINT Y$                              'Color info.
   END IF
   RESTORE                                  'Prepare
   PRINT                                    'for next
   INPUT "COLOR (TYPE END TO STOP)"; C$     'input.
LOOP
END                                         'Program exit

' Data: Colors and color information
DATA WHITE, USED FOR TINTING
DATA BLACK, USED FOR SHADING
DATA YELLOW, A PRIMARY COLOR
DATA RED, A PRIMARY COLOR
DATA BLUE, A PRIMARY COLOR
DATA ORANGE, MIX YELLOW AND RED.
DATA GREEN, MIX YELLOW AND BLUE.
DATA PURPLE, MIX RED AND BLUE.
DATA PINK, MIX RED AND WHITE.
DATA GRAY, MIX BLACK AND WHITE.
DATA MAGENTA, MIX RED WITH A SPECK OF BLACK.
DATA XXX,YYY
```

Program output:
```
THIS PROGRAM GIVES INFORMATION ABOUT COLORS.
ALL ENTRIES YOU MAKE MUST BE IN UPPERCASE.

COLOR (TYPE END TO STOP)? BLUE
A PRIMARY COLOR

COLOR (TYPE END TO STOP)? MAGENTA
MIX RED WITH A SPECK OF BLACK.

COLOR (TYPE END TO STOP)? AQUA
AQUA IS NOT IN MY LIST OF COLORS.

COLOR (TYPE END TO STOP)? END
```

The list of colors being searched for the color C$ consists of every other datum—we use READ X$,Y$ to read the data and compare the input value C$ with X$, a color, and not with Y$ that contains information about the color.

When the value read for X$ is the input value C$ or the EOD tag XXX, the while condition

```
X$ <> C$ AND X$ <> "XXX"
```

is false and control passes out of the WHILE loop to the IF statement, which displays the output. If X$ = "XXX", the input value C$ is not one of the colors included in the DATA lines, and a message indicating this fact is displayed. If X$ <> "XXX", then X$ = C$ is one of the included colors, and Y$, which contains information about this color, is displayed.

The programming lines with the comment *Prepare for next input* restore the data pointer to the first datum and prompt the user for another color. This process is repeated until the user types END.

REMARK

Note that the information in DATA lines does not represent input data in the usual sense. Rather, it represents more or less permanent data that the program uses while processing other information (values typed at the keyboard). This represents a common usage of DATA statements.

■ *11.4 Problems*

1. *Show the output of each program.*

a.
```
LET I=2
DO WHILE I<=6
    READ Y
    PRINT Y
    LET I=I+2
LOOP
RESTORE
DATA 9,3,5,8,12
END
```

b.
```
FOR I=1 TO 4
    READ X
    IF X=5 THEN RESTORE
    PRINT X
NEXT I
DATA 3,5,8,9,6
END
```

c.
```
READ A$,B$,C$
RESTORE
READ D$
PRINT B$;C$;D$
DATA HEAD,ROB,IN,HOOD
END
```

d.
```
READ A1,A2,A3
PRINT A1;A2;A3
RESTORE
READ A3,A2,A1
PRINT A3;A2;A1
DATA 10,20,30
END
```

e.
```
FOR J=1 TO 4
    READ A$,S
    IF A$<>"BURNS" THEN PRINT A$;S ELSE RESTORE
NEXT J
DATA ALLEN,40,BURNS,36
DATA CASH,38,DOOR,40
END
```

In Problems 2–8, write a program to carry out each task described.

2. Allow a user to type several words and determine whether they appear in the DATA lines. For each word typed, display the message IS IN THE LIST or IS NOT IN THE LIST, whichever is appropriate. Let the user end the run by typing DONE. Try your program by using the following DATA statements, and inform the user that conjunctions are to be typed. (You may wish to add to the data list.)

```
'    SOME CONJUNCTIONS
DATA ALTHOUGH,AS,BUT,HOWBEIT,HOWEVER
DATA IF,OR,SINCE,THOUGH,YET
DATA END-OF-DATA
```

3. Several pairs of values are included in DATA lines. The first value in each pair represents an item code, and the second represents the current selling price. Allow a user to type several item codes to obtain the current selling prices. In an incorrect code is typed, an appropriate message should be displayed. Allow the user to end the run by typing DONE. Use the following data lines:

```
'    ITEM CODES WITH PRICES
DATA X100,12.39,X110,17.97,X120,23.55,X130,20.50
DATA Y100,72.60,Y110,85.00,Y120,97.43
DATA XXX,0
```

4. A list of numbers appears in DATA lines in ascending order. Allow a user to type a number. If the number appears in the list, all numbers in the list up to but not including it should be displayed. If it doesn't appear, a message to that effect should be displayed. In either case, let the user enter another number. If 0 is typed, the run should terminate. Use the following DATA lines and inform the user that the numbers are in the range 1 to 50.

```
DATA 1,3,6,9,13,18,24,31,39,48
DATA 0
```

5. A wholesale firm has two warehouses, designated A and B. During a recent inventory, the following data were compiled:

Item	Warehouse	Quantity on hand	Average cost/unit
6625	A	52,000	$ 1.954
6204	A	40,000	3.126
3300	B	8,500	19.532
5925	A	22,000	6.884
0220	B	6,200	88.724
2100	B	4,350	43.612
4800	A	21,500	2.741
0077	A	15,000	1.605
1752	B	200	193.800

Prepare a separate inventory report for each warehouse. Each report is to contain the given information and show the total cost represented by the inventory of each item.

6. Use the inventory data shown in Problem 5 to prepare an inventory report for the warehouse whose entire stock represents the greater cost to the company.

7. The O'Halloran Shoe Company wants to know the average monthly income for its retail store and the number of months in which the income exceeds this average. Carry out this task with the following DATA lines, which give the 12 monthly income amounts:

```
DATA 13200.57,11402.48,9248.23,9200.94
DATA 11825.50,12158.07,11028.40,22804.22
DATA 18009.40,12607.25,19423.36,24922.50
```

8. I. M. Good, a candidate for political office, conducted a preelection poll. Each voter polled was assigned a number from 1 to 5 as follows:

1 = will vote for Good
2 = leaning toward Good but still undecided
3 = will vote for Shepherd, Good's only opponent
4 = leaning toward Shepherd but still undecided
5 = all other cases

The results of the poll are included in DATA lines as follows:

```
DATA 1,1,2,5,3,5,1,2
DATA 5,5,2,  . . .
     .
     .
     .
DATA 0
```

Write a program that displays two tables as follows:

```
                TABLE 1
                    FOR    LEANING
    GOOD
    SHEPHERD
                TABLE 2
                    FOR OR     PERCENTAGE OF TOTAL
                    LEANING    NUMBER OF PEOPLE POLLED
    GOOD
    SHEPHERD
    OTHERS
```

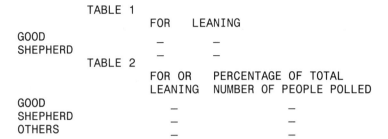

■ *11.5 Review True-or-False Quiz*

1. The READ and DATA statements provide the means to present data to the computer without having to type them during program execution.   **T** F

2. DATA statements must follow the READ statements that read the data values.   T **F**

3. The line

   ```
   DATA 5,-3E2,7+3,12
   ```

   contains a syntax error.   T F   T F

4. A *pointer* is a special value appearing in a data list.

5. It is not necessary to read an entire data list before the first value can be read for a second time.   **T** F

6. At most one RESTORE statement may be used in a QuickBASIC program.   T **F**

7. The READ and DATA statements can be useful when no interaction between the computer and the user is required.   **T** F

8. When we include a string in a DATA statement, quotation marks are sometimes necessary.   **T** F

9. It is sometimes useful to assign values to both string variables and numerical variables using the same READ statement.   **T** F

10. The following are correctly written DATA lines:

    ```
    SCORES:  DATA 73,79,81,89,92
    CUTOFFS: DATA 60,70,80,90
    ```
       T F

11. The statement

    ```
    DATA M,T,W,X,F    'weekdays
    ```

    contains exactly five data values, each consisting of a single letter.   T **F**

12
QuickBASIC
Procedures

*I*n the worked-out examples to this point, we have stressed the importance of the three principles of problem solving: *input/output specification, modularization,* and *stepwise refinement.* The QuickBASIC language features introduced in this chapter concern the second of these, modularization.

Modularization. Identify individual subtasks that must be performed while carrying out the specified task. The job of designing an algorithm is often simplified if the given task is broken down into simpler, more manageable subtasks.

The following are typical examples of subtasks that you may encounter:

1. Display contents of data lines in tabular form.
2. Display the equivalent hourly, weekly, and monthly pay rates for any annual salary amount.
3. Determine the count and sum of any set of numbers entered at the keyboard.
4. Find the average of all numbers in a data list.
5. Find the monthly payment for a loan, given the amount, interest rate, and term.
6. Sort a list of names into alphabetical order. (The topic of sorting is taken up in Chapters 15 and 18.)

QuickBASIC provides the means to code each subtask as a separate entity, called a **program unit.** This is accomplished with the SUB and FUNCTION statements. By using these two statements as described in this chapter, you will organize your programs into separate program units. The part of a program that contains the first executable statement is called the **main unit.** To this point, all programs have consisted only of a main unit. Each program unit other than the main unit:

1. contains code for a single subtask.
2. has a name by which it is referenced (executed).
3. can be referenced from the main unit or any other unit.
4. can be tested separately.

Section 12.1 shows how to use the SUB statement to create program units called **SUB procedures (subroutine procedures).** Section 12.2 introduces the topic of **menu-driven programs** and shows how to code menu-driven programs by using SUB procedures. Section 12.4 describes a more general form of the SUB statement and explains how information is passed between program units. Essentially everything that is said about SUB procedures applies also to **FUNCTION procedures,** which are created by using the FUNCTION statement described in Section 12.5.

■ *12.1 A First Look at SUB Procedures*

In this section, we consider the simplest form of the SUB statement,

SUB **pname**

where **pname** denotes a string of letters, digits, and periods beginning with a letter. **pname** is the *name* of the procedure.

Here is a SUB procedure named DELIMITER.* (The steps that you must take to enter procedures at the keyboard are explained following Example 1.)

```
SUB DELIMITER
   PRINT
   PRINT STRING$(30,"-")
   PRINT STRING$(30,"-")
   PRINT
END SUB
```

This procedure displays a four-line delimiter that can be used to highlight key portions of an output document. The first line of the delimiter is blank, the next two contain thirty dashes, and the fourth is blank. The QuickBASIC statement

```
CALL DELIMITER
```

will cause the procedure to be executed. Thus, the three statements

```
CALL DELIMITER
PRINT "TODAY'S STARTING LINEUP"
CALL DELIMITER
```

will cause the output

```
------------------------------
------------------------------

TODAY'S STARTING LINEUP

------------------------------
------------------------------
```

You will notice that the procedure DELIMITER consists entirely of PRINT statements and contains no variables. Example 1 shows that you are not restricted in this way. Indeed, every executable QuickBASIC statement (statement that causes some action during program execution) can be used in procedures.

EXAMPLE 1   *Here is a program that uses a procedure DISPLAY.WORDS to display any data list ending with the EOD tag END-OF-LIST.*

```
' Display these colors:

DATA BLUE,GREEN,ORANGE,RED,YELLOW
DATA END-OF-LIST

LET A$ = "DISPLAY PROGRAM"        'Program begins here.
PRINT A$
PRINT
CALL DISPLAY.WORDS                'Execute procedure
PRINT
PRINT "Sign off --- "; A$
END                               'Program ends.
```

---

* It is common practice to capitalize only the first letter of each word in a procedure name. In this book, we use all uppercase letters to help identify procedure names that appear in the text accompanying the examples. As mentioned in Chapter 4, uppercase letters are used in variable names for the same reason.

```
SUB DISPLAY.WORDS
   READ A$
   DO UNTIL A$ = "END-OF-LIST"
      PRINT A$; " ";
      READ A$
   LOOP
   PRINT
END SUB
```

Program output:
```
DISPLAY PROGRAM

BLUE GREEN ORANGE RED YELLOW

Sign off --- DISPLAY PROGRAM
```

The main program unit (all but the SUB procedure) assigns the string DISPLAY PROGRAM to A$, and then displays the first line of the output followed by a blank line. The statement

```
CALL DISPLAY.WORDS                    'Execute procedure
```

executes the procedure to produce the list of colors, and program control returns to the statement following the CALL statement. The final two PRINT statements produce a blank line and the final line shown in the output.

REMARK   Notice that the same variable (A$) is used in the main unit and in the procedure. The last line of output shows that A$ in the main unit retains its value DISPLAY PROGRAM, even though the procedure ends with A$ equal to the string END-OF-LIST. In QuickBASIC, variables appearing in a program unit have meaning only to that unit. No conflict in usage arises if the same variable names are used in other units.

In light of the REMARK in Example 1, you can see that there is no communication between the main program unit and the procedure DISPLAY.WORDS; all variables that appear in a program unit have meaning (or scope) only in that unit. The expression **local variable** means precisely this. Thus, all variables in a program unit are local variables.* (How you can pass information between program units is explained in Section 12.4.)

There are certain steps that you must understand when you are typing programs that contain procedures. We illustrate these steps by showing how you can enter the program in Example 1 at the keyboard.

1. Issue the NEW program option (Alt F N) to ensure that you are beginning a new program.
2. Type the main program unit.
3. Type the following on its own line:

```
SUB DISPLAY.WORDS
```

When you press the Enter key, the lines

```
SUB DISPLAY.WORDS

END SUB
```

will appear on an otherwise clear screen, with the cursor positioned at the left margin of the blank line.
4. Type the rest of the procedure. When you are finished, only the procedure is displayed. To display the main unit, proceed to Step 5.
5. Press Function key F2. You will obtain a display similar to that shown in Figure 12.1. In this display, *Untitled* (we did not name the program) and DISPLAY.WORDS are the names of the two program units. *Untitled* is highlighted, so press the Enter key and the main unit will appear in place of the procedure.

_____

*QuickBASIC contains statements to designate variables as global variables, a term that indicates that they have the same meaning in every program unit. Global variables are not used in this book.

```
                              Subs
Choose program item to edit
 ┌──────────────────────────────────────────────────────────┐
 │ Untitled                                                   │
 │    DELIMITER                                               │
 │                                                            │
 │                                                            │
 │                                                            │
 │                                                            │
 └──────────────────────────────────────────────────────────┘
Untitled is the Main Module

< Edit in active >                              < Cancel >

< Delete >                                      < Help >
```

Figure 12.1   Dialogue box showing program units (Function key F2)

You can now use the program as you would any other program. For instance, you can run it (Function key F5 or Alt R S), print it (Alt F P), or save and name it (Alt F A). These commands can be issued whether the main unit or a procedure is currently being displayed. When you save the program shown, QuickBASIC will insert the line

```
DECLARE SUB DISPLAY.WORDS ()
```

at the very beginning of the program. This statement informs the QuickBASIC system that DISPLAY.WORDS is the name of a procedure. The meaning of the parentheses at the end of the DECLARE statement is explained in Section 12.4.

Following are other actions that you may need to carry out:

1. **Modify a unit.** Use F2 to display the unit, and then make the changes.
2. **Add a new procedure.** Type SUB followed by its name on an otherwise blank line. It doesn't matter which program unit is currently being displayed.
3. **Delete a program unit.** Use F2 to display the screen shown in Figure 12.1, use the up-arrow or down-arrow keys to highlight the unit to be deleted, use the Tab key to select the Delete option, and then press the Enter key. If you delete the main program unit, you will delete all procedures as well. [You are, in effect, issuing the NEW program option (Alt F N).]
4. **Execute a procedure.** Use F6 to select *Immediate mode* and then enter CALL *pname* (*pname* denotes the name of the procedure that you wish to execute). It doesn't matter which program unit is currently being displayed.

A procedure may be called from within another procedure. Following is a schematic representation of a program that does this. The action of the program is indicated by the arrows labeled a, b, c, and d.

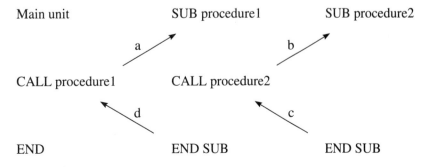

Example 2 illustrates the method: having one procedure call another is a common programming practice.

EXAMPLE 2   *Here is a program to produce a printed report for each employee whose name and annual salary are included in DATA lines. Two procedures are used: REPORTS, which produces the printed reports after the user turns on the printer; and DELIMITER, which prints an output delimiter (DELIMITER is the procedure considered at the outset of this chapter, but with each PRINT changed to LPRINT). The procedure REPORTS calls the procedure DELIMITER.*

```
PRINT "SALARY REPORT PROGRAM"
PRINT
PRINT "This program prints a short salary report for"
PRINT "each employee included in the DATA lines."
PRINT
PRINT "Press a key when printer is on."
DO WHILE INKEY$ = "": LOOP        'Wait for key.
CALL REPORTS                      'Begin printing.
END


' Data: Names and annual salaries
DATA S.J. BRYANT,18500
DATA T.S. ENDICOTT,25700
DATA END,0


SUB DELIMITER

   ' This procedure prints an output delimiter.
   LPRINT
   LPRINT STRING$(30, "-")
   LPRINT STRING$(30, "-")
   LPRINT
END SUB


SUB REPORTS

   ' This procedure prints a short report
   ' for each employee in a data list of
   ' names and annual salaries.

   ' The procedure assumes that END,0
   ' ends the data list.

   READ N$, S                     'First employee
   DO UNTIL N$ = "END"
      LET WK = S / 52             'Weekly salary for N$
      CALL DELIMITER
      LPRINT USING "EMPLOYEE NAME: &"; N$
      LPRINT USING "ANNUAL SALARY: ##,###.##"; S
      LPRINT USING "WEEKLY SALARY:  #,###.##"; WK
      CALL DELIMITER
      READ N$, S                  'Next employee
   LOOP
END SUB
```

Program output:
(Screen display)

```
SALARY REPORT PROGRAM

This program prints a short salary report for
each employee included in the DATA lines.

Press any key when printer is on.
```

(Printed copy)

```
------------------------------
------------------------------

EMPLOYEE NAME: S.J. BRYANT
ANNUAL SALARY: 18,500.00
WEEKLY SALARY:    355.77

------------------------------
------------------------------


------------------------------
------------------------------

EMPLOYEE NAME: T.S. ENDICOTT
ANNUAL SALARY: 25,700.00
WEEKLY SALARY:    494.23

------------------------------
------------------------------
```

REMARK 1 Note that the procedure REPORTS is called in only one program line. This means that we can delete the line

```
CALL REPORTS                    'Begin printing.
```

and, in its place, insert the QuickBASIC code included in the procedure. The resulting program will be shorter but not necessarily better. By using a procedure, we do not force a person reading the program to read through the details of how a report is produced. The comment in the CALL statement tells the reader that a report will be produced but leaves out the details. A reader who needs more details would simply read the procedure.

REMARK 2 Programming applications that call for lengthy reports are not uncommon. If confronted with such a programming task, examine the requirements carefully to see whether the long report in fact consists of several short reports that are to be repeated several times. Program segments that produce such short reports are often ideal candidates for procedures.

REMARK 3 An important advantage in using procedures is that your programs can be modified more easily should a change be needed. For instance, if the program shown must be altered to display other information about each employee, only the procedure REPORTS needs to be changed. You may sometimes find that a method used to carry out a particular task is inefficient and needs to be improved. If the task is coded as a procedure, the entire procedure can be replaced with more efficient code, with no need to modify the rest of the program.

REMARK 4 Notice the order of the program units in the program listing. When you press Function key F2, the list of program units shows first the name of the main unit, and then the names of the procedure units in alphabetical order. When you use the Print command (Alt F P), the program units are displayed in this order.

12.2 Menu-Driven Programs

Many programming applications require a program that can carry out several tasks but that will perform only those specified by the user. In such situations, it is natural to write a **menu-driven program.** This means that the program displays a list of the options available to the user (this is the **menu**) and permits the user to select options from the list.

It is customary to include two special options in each menu-driven program: an option to end the program and one to display instructions to the user. The following algorithm can be used for many menu-driven programs:

Algorithm for menu-driven programs

a. Display instructions to the user. (This step may be omitted if one of the options in the menu is to display instructions.)

b. Repeat the following until the end option has been selected:

b1. Display the menu.

b2. Specify an option at the keyboard.

b3. Carry out the specified task.

You will greatly simplify the task of coding menu-driven programs by using procedures to carry out the specified options. Suppose you must code a program with this menu:

```
MENU:

        1    To end the program
        2    To carry out Task A
        3    To carry out Task B
```

If you use a SUB procedure for each task and another to display the menu (we'll assume they are named TASKA, TASKB, and MENU), you can include the following in the main program unit to allow the user to select tasks:

```
DO
   CALL MENU                        'Display the menu.
   INPUT "Option number"; OP        'Keyboard selection
   SELECT CASE OP

       CASE 1:                      'Program exit
       CASE 2: CALL TASKA           'Carry out Task A.
       CASE 3: CALL TASKB           'Carry out Task B.
       CASE ELSE: PRINT "Invalid option - reenter."

   END SELECT
LOOP UNTIL OP = 1
END
```

Of course, you will have to write the SUB procedures. The procedure MENU is easy; it will consist entirely of PRINT statements. Thus, the only possible difficulty in writing menu-driven programs will be in writing QuickBASIC code for the procedures that carry out the individual tasks.

We included the line

```
CASE 1:                      'Program exit
```

which says to do nothing if OP = 1 so that the CASE ELSE statement will not display the Invalid option message when the End option is selected. If you want to carry out some action after the user selects Option 1, you can place the necessary code in the CASE 1 section of the SELECT CASE statement, or you can insert it just after the LOOP statement and before the END statement so that the DO loop used for option selection will not appear cluttered. If the action to be carried out after the user selects Option 1 is significant, you can include the necessary code in a procedure, say in a procedure named ENDTASK, and write

```
CASE 1: CALL ENDTASK         'Program exit
```

This will leave the main program unit uncluttered. Moreover, the program will now handle this task in the same way that it handles every other task.

Example 3 illustrates the simple structure of menu-driven programs. The program is designed to assist the user in carrying out simple- and compound-interest calculations.

EXAMPLE 3   ***Here is a menu-driven program to perform interest calculations.***

The main program unit allows the user to choose options from this menu:

```
TYPE AN OPTION AS FOLLOWS:

    1    TO END THE PROGRAM
    2    FOR INSTRUCTIONS
    3    FOR SIMPLE INTEREST
    4    FOR COMPOUND INTEREST
```

As shown in the SELECT CASE statement, each option, including the End option, is carried out in a procedure.

**THE
PROGRAM**

```
'                   MENU-DRIVEN PROGRAM
'
' This program performs simple interest
' and compound interest calculations.

DO
    CALL MENU                              'Display the menu.
    INPUT "OPTION? ", OP                   'Keyboard selection
    SELECT CASE OP

        CASE 1: CALL END.MESSAGE           'End program option
        CASE 2: CALL INSTRUCTIONS          'Display instructions.
        CASE 3: CALL SIMPLE.INTEREST       'Simple interest
        CASE 4: CALL COMPOUND.INTEREST     'Compound interest

        CASE ELSE
            PRINT "Invalid option!!!"
    END SELECT
LOOP UNTIL OP = 1                          'Loop until End option
END

SUB COMPOUND.INTEREST

    ' CHOICE 4 : COMPOUND INTEREST OPTION
    PRINT
    INPUT "AMOUNT OF INVESTMENT"; P
    INPUT "RATE OF INTEREST AS PERCENT"; R
    INPUT "NUMBER OF TIMES COMPOUNDED PER YEAR"; T
    LET AMT = P * (1 + R / 100 / T) ^ T
    PRINT USING "COMPOUND INTEREST: $$#######.##"; AMT — P
END SUB


SUB END.MESSAGE

    ' CHOICE 1 : END OPTION
    PRINT
    PRINT "PROGRAM TERMINATED."
END SUB

SUB INSTRUCTIONS

    ' CHOICE 2 : DISPLAY INSTRUCTIONS
    PRINT
    PRINT "THIS PROGRAM COMPUTES EITHER THE SIMPLE OR THE"
    PRINT "COMPOUND INTEREST ON A ONE-YEAR INVESTMENT. YOU"
    PRINT "MUST CHOOSE THE METHOD OF CALCULATION AND ENTER"
    PRINT "THE NECESSARY INFORMATION."
END SUB
```

```
SUB MENU

    ' DISPLAY THE MENU
    PRINT
    PRINT "TYPE AN OPTION AS FOLLOWS:"
    PRINT
    PRINT "    1    TO END THE PROGRAM"
    PRINT "    2    FOR INSTRUCTIONS"
    PRINT "    3    FOR SIMPLE INTEREST"
    PRINT "    4    FOR COMPOUND INTEREST"
    PRINT
END SUB

SUB SIMPLE.INTEREST

    ' CHOICE 3 : SIMPLE INTEREST OPTION
    PRINT
    INPUT "AMOUNT OF INVESTMENT"; P
    INPUT "RATE OF INTEREST AS PERCENT"; R
    PRINT USING "SIMPLE INTEREST: $$#######.##"; P * R / 100
END SUB
```

The following display was produced when we ran this program, selecting options 2, 5 (invalid), 4, and 1, in that order.

```
TYPE AN OPTION AS FOLLOWS:

    1    TO END THE PROGRAM
    2    FOR INSTRUCTIONS
    3    FOR SIMPLE INTEREST
    4    FOR COMPOUND INTEREST

OPTION? 2

THIS PROGRAM COMPUTES EITHER THE SIMPLE OR THE
COMPOUND INTEREST ON A ONE-YEAR INVESTMENT. YOU
MUST CHOOSE THE METHOD OF CALCULATION AND ENTER
THE NECESSARY INFORMATION.

TYPE AN OPTION AS FOLLOWS:

    1    TO END THE PROGRAM
    2    FOR INSTRUCTIONS
    3    FOR SIMPLE INTEREST
    4    FOR COMPOUND INTEREST

OPTION? 5
Invalid option!!!

TYPE AN OPTION AS FOLLOWS:

    1    TO END THE PROGRAM
    2    FOR INSTRUCTIONS
    3    FOR SIMPLE INTEREST
    4    FOR COMPOUND INTEREST

OPTION? 4

AMOUNT OF INVESTMENT? 100
RATE OF INTEREST AS PERCENT? 9.125
NUMBER OF TIMES COMPOUNDED PER YEAR? 365
COMPOUND INTEREST:        $9.55
```

```
TYPE AN OPTION AS FOLLOWS:

   1    TO END THE PROGRAM
   2    FOR INSTRUCTIONS
   3    FOR SIMPLE INTEREST
   4    FOR COMPOUND INTEREST

OPTION? 1

PROGRAM TERMINATED.
```

A significant advantage in using procedures to carry out the options in menu-driven programs is that new options are easily added. We illustrate by adding to the program of Example 3 an option that allows the user to find the total of any column of numbers typed at the keyboard. Finding the sum of a column of numbers is not new to us. The code in the following SUB procedure shows one way to carry out the task:

```
SUB FIND.TOTAL

    PRINT "Enter the numbers, one per line."
    PRINT
    LET TOTAL = 0                 'No numbers yet
    INPUT "(0 when done)? ",N     'First number
    DO UNTIL N = 0                'Is it 0?
       LET TOTAL = TOTAL + N       'No. Add it to TOTAL
       INPUT "(0 when done)? ",N   'Next number
    LOOP
    PRINT "TOTAL IS"; TOTAL       'Display the total.
END SUB
```

To include this option in the program of Example 3, you can type the procedure FIND.TOTAL and add just two other lines to the program: add

```
CASE 5 : CALL FIND.TOTAL         'To find column totals
```

to the SELECT CASE statement in the main program unit, and add

```
PRINT "    5    TO ADD COLUMNS OF NUMBERS"
```

to the procedure MENU that displays the menu. The modified program will allow you to select any of the options in the expanded menu.

12.3 Problems

In Problems 1–4, show the output produced when the given procedure is called. Assume that READ statements will read data from these data lines:

```
'Data: Item name, Quantity, Cost
DATA CROWBAR, 40, 5.00
DATA RIP SAW, 10, 7.50
DATA TAPE25, 100, 4.45
DATA TAPE50, 25, 10.00
DATA YARDSTICK, 100, 2.79
DATA XXX, 0, 0
```

1. SUB AAA
```
    RESTORE
    READ X$
    DO WHILE X$ <> "XXX"
       READ A,B
       IF A < 50 THEN PRINT X$
       READ X$
    LOOP
END SUB
```

2. SUB BBB

```
    RESTORE
    C = 0
    DO
        READ X$
        C = C + 1
    LOOP UNTIL X$ = "XXX"
    PRINT "Last datum: ";X$
    PRINT "Data count: ";C-1
    END SUB
```

3. SUB CCC

```
    RESTORE
    X = 0 : Y = 0
    READ X$,A,B
    DO WHILE X$ <> "XXX"
        Y = Y + A : X = X + 1
        PRINT A
        READ X$,A,B
    LOOP
    PRINT X;Y
    END SUB
```

4. SUB DDD

```
    RESTORE
    T = 0
    READ X$,A,B
    DO WHILE X$ <> "XXX"
        AMT = A * B : T = T + AMT
        PRINT X$,AMT
        READ X$,A,B
    LOOP
    PRINT USING "TOTAL $$####.##"; T
    END SUB
```

In Problems 5–10 write a SUB procedure to carry out each task. Test each procedure, either by calling it with QuickBASIC's immediate mode facility, or by including the CALL statement in the main program unit and issuing the RUN command. If data are required, you must include them in the main program unit.

5. Display a two-column table with the column headings NUMBER and SQUARE ROOT. Display the integers 1 to 20 in the first column, and display their square roots in the second. Align columns by decimal points and display square roots with four decimal positions.

6. Find and display the sum and average of any list of numbers typed at the keyboard.

7. Find and display the largest and smallest of any list of numbers typed at the keyboard.

8. Display the data shown in Problem 1 in tabular form with appropriate column headings. Display dollar amounts with two decimal positions. Align numerical values in the table by their decimal points.

9. Use the data shown in Problem 1 to produce a two-column report with the headings ITEM and TOTAL COST. The total cost is simply the product Quantity × Cost. The TOTAL COST column must align by decimal points with the amounts displayed to two decimal positions.

10. Read the data shown in Problem 1 to find and display the name and total cost of the item with the greatest total cost.

In Problems 11–15, write a menu-driven program to allow the user to carry out any or all of the specified tasks.

11. While studying the current day's receipts, a bookkeeper must perform numerous calculations to answer certain questions. Write a menu-driven program to assist the bookkeeper in obtaining answers to these questions.
    a. What is the selling price of an item whose list price and discount percent are known?
    b. What is the discount percent for an item whose list and selling prices are known?
    c. What is the list price of an item whose selling price and discount percent are known?

12. An investor must carry out several calculations while assessing the performance of the family's current stock portfolio. These include finding the equity (paper value) given the number of shares and the current price; and finding the profit (or loss) for a holding given the total price paid for all shares, the number of shares owned, and the current selling price. Write a menu-driven program to assist the investor in carrying out these calculations.

13. First write a menu-driven program as described in Problem 12. Then modify it by including a new option: allow the investor to find the sum of any column of numbers typed at the keyboard.

14. A menu-driven program is desired that will allow students to practice addition, multiplication, or taking powers. If addition is chosen, have the computer prompt the student for two numbers, and then ask for their sum. If the correct answer is typed, have the computer say so. If the answer is not correct, display the correct answer. In either case, allow the student to try another addition or to return to the menu. Handle multiplication (of two numbers) the same way. If the student chooses to practice powers, have the computer ask for a number whose powers are to be found. If the student types 3, have the computer display, in order,

    ```
    WHAT IS 3 TO THE POWER 2?
    WHAT IS 3 TO THE POWER 3?
    WHAT IS 3 TO THE POWER 4?
         .
         .
         .
    WHAT IS 3 TO THE POWER 10?
    ```

    Ask each question, however, only if the previous answer is correct. If an answer is incorrect, display the correct answer. Congratulate a student successful to high powers, perhaps in a way reflective of how high the power. In any case, allow the student to try powers of another number or to return to the menu.

15. First write a menu-driven program as described in Problem 14. Then modify it by adding an option so that the student can practice summing three numbers as well as two.

■ *12.4 Communication Between Program Units*

QuickBASIC allows two forms of the SUB statement:

    SUB **pname**
    SUB **pname(plist)**

where **pname** denotes the name of the SUB procedure and **plist** denotes a list of variable names separated by commas. The variables are called **parameters** and **plist** is the **parameter list.**

    If no communication is needed between program units, the first form is adequate; this form is described in Section 12.1. The second form should be used if you must transmit data to a procedure, or if the procedure must transmit data back to the program unit that calls it. The parameters (variables in **plist**) are used for this purpose. The passing of values to and from a procedure is sometimes called **parameter passing.**

    We illustrate the passing of values to a procedure with the following slight modification of the procedure DELIMITER that we used in Section 12.1 to display a four-line delimiter to highlight key portions of an output document.

```
SUB HIGHLIGHT (N)
   PRINT
   PRINT STRING$(N,"-")
   PRINT STRING$(N,"-")
   PRINT
END SUB
```

The statement

```
CALL HIGHLIGHT(30)
```

passes the value 30 to the parameter N, and the procedure is executed to display an output delimiter with each line of dashes containing thirty dashes. If the variable DASHES has the value 30, the statement

```
CALL HIGHLIGHT(DASHES)
```

does the same thing. The value of DASHES (30 in this case) is called the **actual argument** because it supplies an actual value for the parameter N. It is common practice to refer to the variable DASHES as the *argument,* even though the actual argument is its value. The five lines

```
LET A$="TODAY'S LINEUP"
LET DASHES=LEN(A$)            'LEN gives character count of A$
CALL HIGHLIGHT(DASHES)
PRINT A$
CALL HIGHLIGHT(DASHES)
```

pass the value of DASHES (14 because A$ contains 14 characters) to the parameter N to produce the display

```
 --------------
 --------------


TODAY'S LINEUP

 --------------
 --------------
```

The SUB statement used to define the procedure HIGHLIGHT contains a single parameter, the numerical variable N. Thus, each CALL to the procedure includes a single argument of the same type. We used the numerical constant 30 and the numerical variable DASHES as arguments.

The parameter list in a SUB statement can contain any number of variables separated by commas. When calling a procedure, the CALL statement must include the same number of arguments as there are parameters in the SUB statement, and each argument must be of the same type as the corresponding parameter.

The foregoing discussion concerning the procedure HIGHLIGHT explains how values are passed to a procedure. Specifically, the value of any expression used as an argument in a CALL statement is passed as the value of the corresponding parameter in the SUB statement. However, if the argument is a variable (and only in this case), the communication between the variable argument and the parameter is a two-way communication. This is how information is passed back from a procedure to the program unit that called it. The following example illustrates the method.

EXAMPLE 4   *Here is a program to produce a table that shows the equivalent hourly and weekly pay rates for certain annual salary amounts.*

```
' Display headings and assign format string F$.

PRINT "ANNUAL SALARY   HOURLY RATE   WEEKLY RATE"
PRINT "--------------  -----------   -----------"
 F$ = "  ######.##       ###.##        ####.##    "
```

```
' Display equivalent hourly and weekly
' rates for the annual salary amounts
' $20,000 to $25,000 in steps of $500.

FOR ANNUAL.SALARY = 20000 TO 25000 STEP 500
   CALL HR.WK.RATES(ANNUAL.SALARY, HOURLY, WEEKLY)
   PRINT USING F$; ANNUAL.SALARY; HOURLY; WEEKLY
NEXT ANNUAL.SALARY
END


SUB HR.WK.RATES (ANNUAL, PERHOUR, PERWEEK)
   LET PERWEEK = ANNUAL / 52      '52 weeks per year
   LET PERHOUR = PERWEEK / 40     '40-hour weeks
END SUB
```

Program output:

```
ANNUAL SALARY    HOURLY RATE    WEEKLY RATE
- - - - - - - -    - - - - - - -    - - - - - - -
   20000.00           9.62          384.62
   20500.00           9.86          394.23
   21000.00          10.10          403.85
   21500.00          10.34          413.46
   22000.00          10.58          423.08
   22500.00          10.82          432.69
   23000.00          11.06          442.31
   23500.00          11.30          451.92
   24000.00          11.54          461.54
   24500.00          11.78          471.15
   25000.00          12.02          480.77
```

The main program unit consists of two segments, as indicated by the comments. For each value of ANNUAL.SALARY, the body of the FOR loop calls the procedure HR.WK.RATES with the statement

```
CALL HR.WK.RATES(ANNUAL.SALARY, HOURLY, WEEKLY)
```

Because each argument in the CALL statement is a variable, the correspondences between arguments and parameters are two-way correspondences:

Main unit		Procedure
ANNUAL.SALARY	$\longleftrightarrow$	ANNUAL
HOURLY	$\longleftrightarrow$	PERHOUR
WEEKLY	$\longleftrightarrow$	PERWEEK

The first time the procedure is called, we have

Main unit			Procedure
ANNUAL.SALARY =	20000	=	ANNUAL
HOURLY =	0	=	PERHOUR
WEEKLY =	0	=	PERWEEK

QuickBASIC automatically assigns the value 0 to HOURLY and WEEKLY when the RUN command is issued. Thus, when the procedure is first called, the corresponding parameters PERHOUR and PERWEEK also have the value 0.

The procedure then executes the two statements

```
LET PERWEEK = ANNUAL / 52      '52 weeks per year
LET PERHOUR = PERWEEK / 40     '40-hour weeks
```

Because of the two-way correspondence, these changes in PERWEEK and PERHOUR are also changes in WEEKLY and HOURLY, respectively. At this point, we have

Main unit			Procedure
ANNUAL.SALARY =	20000	=	ANNUAL
HOURLY =	9.62	=	PERHOUR
WEEKLY =	384.62	=	PERWEEK

Control then passes back to the main program unit with these three values for ANNUAL.SALARY (this wasn't changed), HOURLY, and WEEKLY, respectively, as shown in the first line of output values.

REMARK 1

We used variable arguments in the CALL statement to set up two-way correspondences between the three arguments and the three parameters. However, the only passing of values actually needed are as follows (arrowheads indicate the direction in which values must be passed):

ANNUAL.SALARY $\rightarrow$ ANNUAL
HOURLY $\leftarrow$ PERHOUR
WEEKLY $\leftarrow$ PERWEEK

In QuickBASIC, the only way to return values from a SUB procedure to a calling unit is to set up a two-way correspondence between variables in the calling unit and variables in the procedure. Thus, we used the variable arguments HOURLY and WEEKLY in the CALL statement so that the calculated values of the corresponding parameters PERHOUR and PERWEEK would be returned to the main program unit as the values of HOURLY and WEEKLY, respectively.

REMARK 2

By using the variable argument ANNUAL.SALARY in the CALL statement, we set up a two-way correspondence between ANNUAL.SALARY and the parameter ANNUAL. But, as noted in REMARK 1, a two-way correspondence is not needed; we need only pass the value of ANNUAL.SALARY to the parameter ANNUAL. To cause a one-way correspondence from ANNUAL.SALARY to the parameter ANNUAL, simply enclose ANNUAL.SALARY in parentheses:

```
CALL HR.WK.RATES((ANNUAL.SALARY), HOURLY, WEEKLY)
```

The argument (ANNUAL.SALARY) is regarded by QuickBASIC as a numerical expression other than a variable, so the correspondence between argument and parameter is one-way; that is, the value of the argument (ANNUAL.SALARY) is passed to the parameter ANNUAL.

We have shown how you can cause one-way and two-way communication between arguments in a CALL statement and their corresponding parameters in the procedure being called: for two-way communication, the arguments must be variables; for one-way communication, they must be expressions other than variables. To understand how QuickBASIC effects these two ways of passing values between program units, you need to know that QuickBASIC associates an *address* with each program variable—the address of the memory storage unit where values for the variable are stored. Whenever a variable is encountered during program execution, QuickBASIC uses its address to locate the storage unit for that variable. If the variable appears in an expression, QuickBASIC uses the value stored in this storage unit. If the variable is being assigned a value (for instance, in a LET, INPUT, or READ statement), the value is copied into this storage unit.

Two-way communication. If an argument in a CALL statement is a variable, the address associated with that variable is used as the address of the corresponding parameter. Thus, when the procedure modifies the parameter, it is actually changing the value of the variable argument. This method of passing values between program units is called **passing by reference;** the parameter *references* the storage unit that stores values of the variable argument.

One-way communication. If an argument in a CALL statement is an expression other than a variable, QuickBASIC evaluates the argument, copies this value into an unused memory storage unit, and associates the address of this storage unit with the parameter that corresponds to the argument. Thus, any changes to the parameter are changes to this storage unit. Because its address is not associated with any other program variable (the storage unit was unused), changing the parameter does not change any other program variable. This method is called **passing by value.**

When you save the program shown in Example 4, the QuickBASIC system will automatically insert the line

```
DECLARE SUB HR.WK.RATES (ANNUAL!, PERHOUR!, PERWEEK!)
```

as the first line of the main program unit. As explained in Section 3.2, the character ! ending each variable indicates that the variable is a single-precision real variable. When you issue the RUN command, the QuickBASIC system examines DECLARE statements to determine how many parameters are included and what type they are. If you don't want the exclamation symbols, simply delete them—no harm is done. As mentioned in Section 12.1, when you save a procedure that has no parameters, QuickBASIC inserts a DECLARE statement that ends with (). The empty parentheses inform the system that the procedure in the DECLARE statement has no parameters. Do not delete (). If you do, you will get the following dialogue box when you attempt to issue the RUN command:

```
┌─────────────────────────────┐
│  Argument-count mismatch     │
├─────────────────────────────┤
│   < OK >      < Help >       │
└─────────────────────────────┘
```

Should this happen, press the Enter key to accept the default response OK, and then insert () at the end of the DECLARE statement. You can type your own DECLARE statements, but we recommend that you let QuickBASIC insert them for you.

Following are two examples that further illustrate the use of procedures with parameters. Example 5 shows an alternative way to code the program in Example 2 of Section 12.1. The modified version produces screen rather than printer output, and shows that you can include string parameters as well as numerical parameters in SUB statements. Example 6 shows an application for an airline charter service.

EXAMPLE 5

(from Example 2 of Section 12.1) Here is a program to display a short report for each employee whose name and annual salary are included in DATA statements. The program includes a procedure REPORT to display a report for any employee whose name and salary are passed to the procedure. The procedure REPORT calls a second procedure DELIMITER that displays a four-line output delimiter.

```
'          SALARY REPORT PROGRAM

' Produce salary reports from these data:

DATA S.J. BRYANT,18500
DATA T.S. ENDICOTT,25700
DATA END-OF-DATA

DECLARE SUB DELIMITER ()
DECLARE SUB REPORT (EMPLOYEE$, SALARY!)

' Read data and display reports.

READ N$                          'First name (or END-OF-DATA)
DO UNTIL N$ = "END-OF-DATA"
   READ A                        'Annual salary of N$
   CALL REPORT(N$, A)            'Display a report for N$.
   READ N$                       'Next name (or END-OF-DATA)
LOOP
END
```

```
             SUB DELIMITER

                 'This procedure displays an output delimiter.

                 PRINT
                 PRINT STRING$(30, "-")
                 PRINT STRING$(30, "-")
                 PRINT

             END SUB


             SUB REPORT (EMPLOYEE$, SALARY!)

                 ' This procedure displays a short report given:
                 '
                 '    EMPLOYEE$ = an employee's name
                 '    SALARY    = the employee's annual salary

                 CALL DELIMITER            'Display a delimiter.

                 PRINT USING "EMPLOYEE NAME: &"; EMPLOYEE$
                 PRINT USING "ANNUAL SALARY: ##,###.##"; SALARY
                 PRINT USING "WEEKLY SALARY:  #,###.##"; SALARY / 52

                 CALL DELIMITER            'Display a delimiter.

             END SUB
```

Program output:

```
    ------------------------------
    ------------------------------

    EMPLOYEE NAME: S.J. BRYANT
    ANNUAL SALARY: 18,500.00
    WEEKLY SALARY:    355.77


    ------------------------------
    ------------------------------



    ------------------------------
    ------------------------------

    EMPLOYEE NAME: T.S. ENDICOTT
    ANNUAL SALARY: 25,700.00
    WEEKLY SALARY:    494.23


    ------------------------------
    ------------------------------
```

REMARK   You may have noticed that the DECLARE statements appear after the DATA statements. We allowed QuickBASIC to insert them at the beginning, and then moved them. In Quick-BASIC, DECLARE statements must not be preceded by any executable statements. We were able to move them because DATA statements and comments are not executable statements.

EXAMPLE 6   ***Charter service example—an illustration of procedures.***

An airline charter service estimates that ticket sales of $1,000 are required to break even on a certain excursion. It thus makes the following offer to an interested organization. If 10 people sign up, the cost will be $100 per person. For each additional person, the cost per person will be reduced by $3. Produce a table showing the cost per customer and the profit to the airline for N = 10, 11, 12, . . . , 30 customers. In addition, display a message giving the maximum possible profit for the airline and the number of customers that gives this profit. Use column headings underlined by a row of dashes.

We must produce a three-column table showing the number of customers, the corresponding cost per customer, and the corresponding profit to the airline. Thus, for each value of N from 10 to 30 (the number of customers), we must calculate two values:

C = cost per person (C = 130 − 3 × N)
P = profit to the airline (P = N × C − 1000)

The problem statement also specifies that the three-column cost and profit table be followed by a message giving two values:

NMAX = number of people yielding a maximum profit to the airline
PMAX = the maximum profit

The following algorithm describes one way to produce the required output.

a. Display column headings.
b. Start with PMAX = 0
c. For N = 10 to 30, do the following:

    c1. Determine C and P.
    c2. Display N, C, and P in the table.
    c3. Adjust NMAX and PMAX, if necessary.

d. Display a message showing NMAX and PMAX.
e. Stop.

Step (c3) is included to determine NMAX and PMAX. To carry out this step, we will compare the profit P for N customers with PMAX, the largest profit obtained to that point. If P is larger than PMAX, we will assign P to PMAX and N to NMAX. To keep the main part of the program as uncluttered as possible, we'll do this in a procedure CHECK.MAX. Finally, it is not difficult to see that the output will not fit on a 24- or 25-line screen. Hence we will produce a printed report by using LPRINT and LPRINT USING statements.

```
PRINT "               CHARTER SERVICE PROGRAM"
PRINT
PRINT "This program prints a table of airline excursion rates"
PRINT "and finds the maximum possible profit for the airline."
PRINT "Press any key after printer is turned on."

DO WHILE INKEY$ = "": LOOP                  'Wait for key.


'Display column headings and assign output format strings.

LPRINT "PASSENGERS         COST/PERSON         AIRLINE PROFIT"
LPRINT "-------------------------------------------------------"
  F$ = "    ##              ###.##               ####.##     "
  G$ = " ## PASSENGERS YIELD A MAXIMUM PROFIT OF$$###          "
  H$ = "-------------------------------------------------------"


'Display table values and maximum possible profit.

   'PMAX denotes maximum possible profit.
   'NMAX denotes number of customers giving this max profit.

LET PMAX = 0                            'Start with max of 0.
FOR N = 10 TO 30                        'Number of customers
   LET C = 130 - 3 * N                  'Cost per person
   LET P = N * C - 1000                 'Profit to airline
   LPRINT USING F$; N; C; P             'Print one line of table.
   CALL CHECK.MAX(N, P, PMAX, NMAX)     'Check for new max profit.
NEXT N
LPRINT H$                       'Row of dashes
LPRINT USING G$; NMAX; PMAX     'Maximum profit message
LPRINT H$                       'Row of dashes
END
```

```
SUB CHECK.MAX (N, P, PMAX, NMAX)

    'This procedure checks the profit P for N
    'customers for a possible new maximum profit.
    '
    '     PMAX = Current maximum profit amount
    '     NMAX = Number of customers giving this maximum profit

    IF P > PMAX THEN PMAX = P: NMAX = N

END SUB
```

Program output:

(Screen display)

```
                    CHARTER SERVICE PROGRAM
This program prints a table of airline excursion rates
and finds the maximum possible profit for the airline.
Press any key after printer is turned on.
```

(Printer output)

PASSENGERS	COST/PERSON	AIRLINE PROFIT
10	100.00	0.00
11	97.00	67.00
12	94.00	128.00
13	91.00	183.00
14	88.00	232.00
15	85.00	275.00
16	82.00	312.00
17	79.00	343.00
18	76.00	368.00
19	73.00	387.00
20	70.00	400.00
21	67.00	407.00
22	64.00	408.00
23	61.00	403.00
24	58.00	392.00
25	55.00	375.00
26	52.00	352.00
27	49.00	323.00
28	46.00	288.00
29	43.00	247.00
30	40.00	200.00

```
22 PASSENGERS YIELD A MAXIMUM PROFIT OF $408
```

REMARK   If, at a later date, the airline decides to offer a different excursion package, you can change the two lines

```
LET C = 130 - 3 * N          'Cost per person
LET P = N * C - 1000         'Profit to airline
```

which determine the cost per customer (C) and profit to the airline (P) for N passengers. If you suspect that the airline will be offering many different excursion packages, you should consider using a procedure to determine C and P. If you do this, any method specified by the airline for determining C and P—even complex methods that may require many programming lines—can be handled simply by replacing the procedure with a new one. No change would be required in the rest of the program, except possibly changing the name in a CALL statement.

We conclude this section with four comments concerning the use of procedures that are not otherwise discussed in this chapter.

1. The keyword CALL is optional. However, if you omit CALL, you must also omit the parentheses that enclose the argument list. Thus, the statement

```
CALL CHECK.MAX(N, P, PMAX, NMAX)
```

used in the program of Example 6 can be written in the equivalent form

```
CHECK.MAX N, P, PMAX, NMAX
```

In this book, we will always include the keyword CALL when calling a SUB procedure. The word CALL tells you explicitly that a procedure is to be executed; without it, you may have to guess.

2. The examples in this chapter include procedures that call other procedures. In QuickBASIC, a procedure can call itself. The use of procedures that call themselves involves an advanced method of problem solving called *recursion,* which is illustrated in Section 18.3.

3. In Chapter 15 (Arrays), we describe the array data structure that allows you to store large amounts of data under a single name, called the *array name.* As explained in Chapter 15, array arguments are always passed by reference; that is, the communication between arguments and parameters that represent arrays is always two-way communication.

4. In Chapter 16 (Data Files), we introduce *fixed-length* string variables—variables that always contain the same number of characters. All string variables used to this point are *variable-length* variables, which means that you can assign them strings of varying lengths. QuickBASIC does not allow fixed-length string variables as parameters in procedures.

12.5 FUNCTION Procedures

Sections 12.1 and 12.4 explain how to code subtasks as SUB procedures. If the purpose of a subtask is to determine a single value, the common practice is to code it as a FUNCTION procedure, as explained in this section, rather than as a SUB procedure. Following is a FUNCTION procedure whose purpose (that is, *function*) is described in the comment lines. [To enter a FUNCTION procedure at the keyboard, enter its first line (the FUNCTION statement), and then follow the steps shown in Section 12.1 for entering a SUB procedure.]

```
FUNCTION PAY.FOR.WEEK (H, R)

    ' Calculate the week's pay for an
    ' H hour week at R dollars an hour.
    ' (Time-and-a-half for hours over 32)

    IF H > 32 THEN
        LET OVERTIME = 1.5 * R * (H - 32)
        LET PAY.FOR.WEEK = 32 * R + OVERTIME
    ELSE
        LET PAY.FOR.WEEK = R * H
    END IF

END FUNCTION
```

The FUNCTION statement includes the name PAY.FOR.WEEK of the FUNCTION procedure and two parameters, H and R. The parameters are used to pass values to the FUNCTION procedure in precisely the same way that values are passed to SUB procedures. In a program that contains this FUNCTION procedure, the statement

```
LET PAY = PAY.FOR.WEEK(30, 8)
```

assigns the value 240 (30 × 8) to the variable PAY. It obtains this value as follows:

1. The arguments 30 and 8 are passed to the FUNCTION procedure as the values of the parameters H and R.
2. The statements in the FUNCTION procedure are executed to obtain the value 240 for the variable PAY.FOR.WEEK.

3. The value 240 of PAY.FOR.WEEK is passed back as the value of the expression PAY.FOR.WEEK (30, 8). (Notice that the FUNCTION procedure assigns a value to the name PAY.FOR.WEEK of the function: this difference between FUNCTION and SUB procedures is explained shortly.)

4. The statement LET PAY = PAY.FOR.WEEK(30, 8) assigns the value 240 of PAY.FOR.WEEK(30, 8) to the variable PAY.

The expression PAY.FOR.WEEK(30, 8) in the statement

```
LET PAY = PAY.FOR.WEEK(30, 8)
```

is a numerical expression and can be used just as any other numerical expression is used. For example, the statement

```
PRINT "Equivalent annual amount:"; 52 * PAY.FOR.WEEK(30, 8)
```

produces the output

```
Equivalent annual amount: 12480
```

QuickBASIC obtains the value 240 for PAY.FOR.WEEK (30, 8) as before and multiplies this value by 52 to obtain the value 12480 for the expression 52 * PAY.FOR.WEEK (30, 8). If HRS = 30 and RATE = 8, the following statement does the same thing:

```
PRINT "Equivalent annual amount:"; 52 * PAY.FOR.WEEK (HRS, RATE)
```

The expressions PAY.FOR.WEEK (30, 8) and PAY.FOR.WEEK (HRS, RATE) are **calls** to the FUNCTION procedure PAY.FOR.WEEK. A call to a FUNCTION procedure is called a **function reference.**

You can also write string functions—that is, FUNCTION procedures that return string values. Here is a string function whose purpose is described in the comment lines. The function has no parameters; it returns a value that depends on keyboard input, not on data passed to it when it is referenced.

```
FUNCTION KEYBOARD.INPUT$

' This function returns Y or N when keyboard
' input for LETTER$ is Y,y,N,or n. Other
' input values LETTER$ are rejected.

   DO
      INPUT "Enter Y or N: ", LETTER$
      LETTER$ = UCASE$(LETTER$)
   LOOP UNTIL LETTER$ = "Y" OR LETTER$  = "N"

   LET KEYBOARD.INPUT$ = LETTER$

END FUNCTION
```

In a program that contains this FUNCTION procedure, the statement

```
LET RESPONSE$ = KEYBOARD.INPUT$
```

references the function to obtain a string value Y or N for the function reference KEYBOARD.INPUT$. The LET statement assigns this string to the variable RESPONSE$. Similarly, the function reference KEYBOARD.INPUT$ in the Block IF statement

```
IF KEYBOARD.INPUT$ = "Y" THEN
   PRINT "You answered yes."
ELSE
   PRINT "You answered no."
END IF
```

returns a value Y or N for the function reference KEYBOARD.INPUT$ to produce one of the output lines

```
You answered yes.
You answered no.
```

depending on whether Y or N is returned.

As mentioned at the outset of this section, it is common practice to use FUNCTION procedures instead of SUB procedures if the subtask to be performed is to find a single value; the functions PAY.FOR.WEEK and KEYBOARD.INPUT$ do this. Other than this difference in usage, there is only one way in which FUNCTION and SUB procedures differ: the variable name that appears in a FUNCTION statement (the function's name) is assigned a value by using a LET statement. (Unless you are an experienced programmer, the name of any function you write should appear only in the FUNCTION statement and to the left of the equal sign in LET statements.) In the numerical function PAY.FOR.WEEK, the two statements

```
LET PAY.FOR.WEEK = 32 * R + OVERTIME
LET PAY.FOR.WEEK = R * H
```

are used to assign a numerical value to the function name PAY.FOR.WEEK. The first is executed if $H > 32$, and the second is executed if $H \leq 32$. In the string function KEYBOARD.INPUT$, the statement

```
LET KEYBOARD.INPUT$ = LETTER$
```

assigns the value of LETTER$ (Y or N) to the function name KEYBOARD.INPUT$.

As with SUB procedures, QuickBASIC allows two forms of the FUNCTION statement:

FUNCTION **fname**
FUNCTION **fname** (**plist**)

where **fname** denotes the name of the FUNCTION procedure, and **plist** denotes the parameter list. As just mentioned, the name **fname** is assigned a value by a LET statement included between the FUNCTION and END FUNCTION statements. In contrast to SUB procedures, a FUNCTION procedure has a type. We used a numerical variable name for the function PAY.FOR.WEEK because it returns a numerical value, and we used a string variable name for the function KEYBOARD.INPUT$ because it returns a string.

A common use of FUNCTION procedures is to search a data list for specified values. Here is an example of a search function. Its purpose is explained in the comment lines.

```
FUNCTION SEARCH.DATA$ (Y$)

   ' Search data lists that end with
   ' the EOD-tag END-OF-LIST for Y$
   ' and return the value:
   '
   '       FOUND     if Y$ is in list
   '   NOT FOUND     if Y$ is not in list

   RESTORE                          'Start search at beginning.
   DO                               'Begin search for Y$.
      READ X$                       'Read an item.
   LOOP UNTIL X$ = Y$ OR X$ = "END-OF-LIST"

   IF X$ = "END-OF-LIST" THEN       'Search is complete.
      SEARCH.DATA$ = "NOT FOUND"    'Y$ not found.
   ELSE
      SEARCH.DATA$ = "FOUND"        'Y$ found.
   END IF

END FUNCTION
```

If the variable WORD$ has been assigned a value, the two statements

```
LET STATUS$=SEARCH.DATA$(WORD$)
PRINT STATUS$
```

will display FOUND if WORD$ is included in the DATA statements and NOT FOUND if it is not included. The single statement

```
PRINT SEARCH.DATA$(WORD$)
```

does the same thing. In each case, the function returns a string value for the string expression SEARCH.DATA$(WORD$).

The function SEARCH.DATA$ is easily modified to search data organized other than as a simple list of values. For instance, the following search function searches paired data, as explained in the comment lines.

```
FUNCTION SEARCH.PAIRED.DATA$ (ITEM$)

   ' This function searches any data list of paired data
   ' terminated by a pair with END-OF-LIST as first value.
   '
   ' If ITEM$ is the first item in a pair, the function
   ' returns the second string of the pair; otherwise,
   ' the value NOT FOUND is returned.

   RESTORE                          'Start search at beginning.
   DO                               'Begin search for ITEM$.
      READ X$, Y$                   'Next item pair.
   LOOP UNTIL X$ = ITEM$ OR X$ = "END-OF-LIST"

   IF X$ = "END-OF-LIST" THEN                'Search complete
      SEARCH.PAIRED.DATA$ = "NOT FOUND." 'Not found
   ELSE
      SEARCH.PAIRED.DATA$ = Y$              'Found
   END IF

END FUNCTION
```

If C$ has been assigned the string value MAGENTA, and if the DATA statements contain the pair of values

```
MAGENTA, MIX RED WITH A SPECK OF BLACK.
```

the statement

```
PRINT SEARCH.PAIRED.DATA$(C$)
```

will display

```
MIX RED WITH A SPECK OF BLACK.
```

If the DATA statements do not contain a pair with MAGENTA as the first value, the PRINT statement will display

```
NOT FOUND.
```

Notice that the comments in the two search functions SEARCH.DATA$ and SEARCH.PAIRED.DATA$ say nothing about what the data represent. They refer only to the organization of the data and how the data list is terminated. We did this so that the same functions could be used without change for different programming applications. Writing FUNCTION and SUB procedures in this way is a common and useful programming practice. Example 7 illustrates two applications of the function SEARCH.PAIRED.DATA$.

EXAMPLE 7 *Parts (a) and (b) of this example contain programs that search lists of paired data. In each example, we show only the main program unit. The function SEARCH.PAIRED.DATA$ is exactly as shown in the foregoing discussion.*

a. An application of the function SEARCH.PAIRED.DATA$ in a program that displays information about colors typed at the keyboard. (This program is a modification of the program given in Example 8 of Section 11.3.)

```
'          ON MIXING COLORS
'
' This program uses the function SEARCH.PAIRED.DATA$
' to search the following DATA lines for colors
' typed at the keyboard.

'Data: Colors and color information
DATA WHITE, USED FOR TINTING
DATA BLACK, USED FOR SHADING
```

```
            DATA YELLOW, A PRIMARY COLOR
            DATA RED, A PRIMARY COLOR
            DATA BLUE, A PRIMARY COLOR
            DATA ORANGE, MIX YELLOW AND RED.
            DATA GREEN, MIX YELLOW AND BLUE.
            DATA PURPLE, MIX RED AND BLUE.
            DATA PINK, MIX RED AND WHITE.
            DATA GRAY, MIX BLACK AND WHITE.
            DATA MAGENTA, MIX RED WITH A SPECK OF BLACK.
            DATA END-OF-LIST, XXX

            DECLARE FUNCTION SEARCH.PAIRED.DATA$ (ITEM$)

            PRINT "THIS PROGRAM GIVES INFORMATION ABOUT COLORS."
            PRINT "ALL ENTRIES YOU MAKE MUST BE IN UPPERCASE."
            PRINT
            INPUT "COLOR (TYPE END TO STOP)"; C$        'Keyboard input
            DO UNTIL C$ = "END"

                'Search DATA for the color C$ and display
                'corresponding description or a not found message.

                PRINT "DESCRIPTION: "; SEARCH.PAIRED.DATA$(C$)
                PRINT                                   'Prepare for
                INPUT "COLOR (TYPE END TO STOP)"; C$    'next input.
            LOOP
            END
```

Program output:

```
THIS PROGRAM GIVES INFORMATION ABOUT COLORS.
ALL ENTRIES YOU MAKE MUST BE IN UPPERCASE.

COLOR (TYPE END TO STOP)? BLUE
DESCRIPTION: A PRIMARY COLOR

COLOR (TYPE END TO STOP)? MAGENTA
DESCRIPTION: MIX RED WITH A SPECK OF BLACK.

COLOR (TYPE END TO STOP)? AQUA
DESCRIPTION: NOT FOUND.

COLOR (TYPE END TO STOP)? END
```

b. An application of the function SEARCH.PAIRED.DATA$ in a program that displays the arrival time for any flight whose number is typed at the keyboard.

```
    ' This program uses the function SEARCH.PAIRED.DATA$
    ' to search the following DATA lines for flight
    ' numbers typed at the keyboard.

    'Data: Flight numbers and arrival times
    DATA 53,"8:15 AM"
    DATA 172,"9:20 AM"
    DATA 122,"11:30 AM"
    DATA 62,"2:20 PM"
    DATA 303,"4:45 PM"
    DATA 291,"6:15 PM"
    DATA END-OF-LIST,X

    DECLARE FUNCTION SEARCH.PAIRED.DATA$ (ITEM$)

    PRINT "THIS PROGRAM GIVES FLIGHT ARRIVAL TIMES."
    PRINT
    INPUT "Flight (0 when done)? ", FLIGHT$    'Keyboard input
    DO UNTIL FLIGHT$ = "0"

        'Search DATA for the flight number FLIGHT$
        'and display the arrival time ARRIVAL$.
```

```
          LET ARRIVAL$ = SEARCH.PAIRED.DATA$(FLIGHT$)
          PRINT "Arrival time is "; ARRIVAL$
          PRINT                                 'Prepare for
          INPUT "Flight (0 when done)?", FLIGHT$ ' next input.
     LOOP
     END
```

Program output:
```
THIS PROGRAM GIVES FLIGHT ARRIVAL TIMES.

Flight (0 when done)? 53
Arrival time is 8:15 AM

Flight (0 when done)? 303
Arrival time is 4:45 PM

Flight (0 when done)? 127
Arrival time is NOT FOUND.

Flight (0 when done)? 172
Arrival time is 11:30 AM

Flight (0 when done)? 0
```

REMARK 1

The quotation marks used in the DATA statements are required because QuickBASIC uses the colon (:) as a separator when two or more QuickBASIC statements are included in a single programming line.

REMARK 2

Notice that the flight number typed at the keyboard is assigned to the string variable FLIGHT$, rather than to a numerical variable. We did this because the flight number had to be passed to the string parameter ITEM$ in the function SEARCH.PAIRED.DATA$. If you pass a numerical argument to a string parameter, you will get the dialogue box:

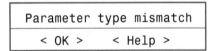

```
┌─────────────────────────────┐
│   Parameter type mismatch   │
├─────────────────────────────┤
│    < OK >      < Help >     │
└─────────────────────────────┘
```

There are several ways to copy a procedure from one program to another. We illustrate one method by copying a procedure OLDPROCEDURE currently in program OLDPROG as a procedure in program NEWPROG.

1. If you are working on NEWPROG, save it.
2. Load (Alt F O) OLDPROG and use Function key F2 to display OLDPROCEDURE.
3. Use the Shift and down-arrow keys to highlight each line other than the SUB and END SUB (or FUNCTION and END FUNCTION) lines, and then press the key combination Shift-Del to move the highlighted lines to the clipboard.
4. Press the key combination Shift-Ins. This will restore the procedure as a safety precaution for the next step.
5. Load (Alt F O) NEWPROG. (If you did not restore the procedure in Step 4, do not allow QuickBASIC to save OLDPROG.)
6. Type the SUB (or FUNCTION) statement for OLDPROCEDURE on an otherwise clear line. Your display will show only the SUB and END SUB (or FUNCTION and END FUNCTION) statements.
7. Press the key combination Shift-Ins. The QuickBASIC code for the procedure will be displayed. OLDPROCEDURE is now part of your program NEWPROG.

12.6 Problems

Problems 1–9 reference the following SUB and FUNCTION procedures.

```
SUB SUB1 (A, B, C, S, L)          SUB SUB2 (A, B, C)
   LET S = A: L = B                  IF A > B THEN A = B
   IF S > B THEN S = B               IF A > C THEN A = C
   IF L < C THEN L = C            END SUB
END SUB

SUB SUB3 (A)                      SUB SUB4
   FOR N = 1 TO A                    DO
      PRINT N; FCN3(1, N, 1)            READ A, B, C
   NEXT N                              PRINT A; B; C; FCN1(A, B, C)
END SUB                              LOOP UNTIL A = 0
                                  END SUB

FUNCTION FCN1 (A, B, C)           FUNCTION FCN2 (A, B, C)
   LET X = A                         IF A < B THEN A = B
   IF X < B THEN X = B               IF A < C THEN A = C
   IF X < C THEN X = C               LET FCN2 = A
   LET FCN1 = X                   END FUNCTION
END FUNCTION

FUNCTION FCN3 (A, B, C)
   LET S = 0
   FOR X = A TO B STEP C
      LET S = S + X
   NEXT X
   FCN3 = S
END FUNCTION
```

In Problems 1–6, show the values of the indicated variables after the given program segment is executed.

1. LET X = 7: Y = 9: Z = 3   **2.** LET S = 8: T = 4: U = 5
   CALL SUB1(X, Y, Z, U, V)   CALL SUB1(S, T, U, A, B)

   X =   S =
   Y =   T =
   Z =   U =
   U =   A =
   V =   B =

3. LET X = 4: Y = 9: Z = 7   **4.** LET X = 5: Y = 7: Z = 9
   CALL SUB2(X, Y, Z)   LET A = FCN1(X, Y, Z)

   X =   A =
   Y =   X =
   Z =   Y =
                                       Z =

5. LET X = 5: Y = 7: Z = 9   **6.** LET X = 1: Y = 3: Z = 1
   LET A = FCN2(X, Y, Z)   LET A = FCN3(X, Y, Z)

   A =   A =
   X =   X =
   Y =   Y =
   Z =   Z =

In Problems 7–9, show the output produced when the CALL statement is executed.

7. DATA 9, 3, 2, 4, 6, 3, 0, 2, 4
   CALL SUB4

8. LET N = FCN1(3, 1, 2)
   CALL SUB3(N)

9. CALL SUB3(FCN1(3,1,2))

In Problems 10–20, write a SUB or FUNCTION procedure to carry out each task: a FUNCTION procedure if the task is to return a single value; a SUB procedure otherwise. In each case, test the procedure by using QuickBASIC's immediate mode facility or by writing a short main program unit that references the procedure.

10. For any number N, return the string OK if N is in the range 0–100, and return the string BAD DATA in every other case.
11. Return the sum of the next N values that appear in DATA lines. (You may assume that only numbers appear in the DATA lines.)
12. For any string C$, return a value 0 to 4, as in the following table.

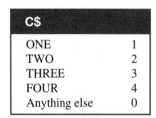

C$	
ONE	1
TWO	2
THREE	3
FOUR	4
Anything else	0

13. Given the following data, produce a two-column table showing each job classification code with the hourly pay rate for that job classification:

```
' EACH DATA LINE GIVES THESE THREE VALUES:

'     A JOB CLASSIFICATION CODE,
'     THE CORRESPONDING HOURLY PAY RATE,
'     THE NUMBER OF EMPLOYEES WITH THIS JOB CLASSIFICATION

DATA A1101, 6.75, 12
DATA A1343, 7.85, 8
DATA F4423, 9.25, 23
         .
         .
         .
DATA END, 0, 0
```

14. Given data as in Problem 13, return a count of the total number of employees.
15. Given data as in Problem 13, return the amount of the total annual payroll for the firm.
16. Given data as in Problem 13, return the hourly pay rate for any job classification code passed as an argument. If the argument is not a valid job classification code, return the value 0.
17. N! (read "N factorial") is defined as the product

$$N! = 1 \times 2 \times 3 \times \cdots \times N$$

if N is a positive integer and as 1 if N = 0. Return N! for any N. When you test your procedure, run it for several input values to determine the largest for which the procedure gives correct answers. Also, find the largest input value that does not cause a fatal error.
18. Determine the greatest common divisor (GCD) of the two positive integers A and B. Use the following algorithm (and convince yourself that it works):
   a. Start with G = smaller of A and B.
   b. While G is not a factor of both A and B, subtract 1 from G.
   c. Return the value of G; it is the greatest common divisor.
19. Use the following algorithm to find the GCD of two positive integers A and B:
   a. Let R = integer remainder when A is divided by B.
   b. While R is not 0, assign B to A and R to B.
   c. LET G = B

d. Return the value of G; it is the greatest common divisor. The algorithm in Problem 18 can be slow for large numbers; this algorithm, called the Euclidean algorithm, is very fast.

In Problems 20–24, write a program for each task specified.

20. The following DATA lines show the names and annual salaries of all employees in a small firm:

```
DATA SAUL JACOBS,23500,PAUL WINFIELD,29000
DATA MARIA KARAS,30000,SILVIA STORM,26400
DATA RAOUL PARENT,31400,RICHARD KELLY,28000
DATA PATTY SAULNIER,22000,MARTHA BRADLEY,31400
DATA XXX,0
```

Calculate and display the total annual payroll of the firm, and then display a report showing the names and salaries of those whose salary exceeds the average annual salary for all employees. Use a FUNCTION procedure to return the total annual payroll amount and a SUB procedure to produce the specified report.

21. Include the data in Problem 20 in a program that displays a two-column table showing precisely the given information and displays after this table a message telling which employee (or employees) has the highest salary. Use three procedures: a SUB procedure to display the two-column table, a FUNCTION procedure to return the highest salary amount, and a SUB procedure to display the concluding message. Each of the three procedures should read the data while carrying out its task.

22. An apple orchard occupying 1 acre of land now contains 25 apple trees, and each tree yields 450 apples per season. For each new tree planted, the yield per tree will be reduced by 10 apples per season. How many additional trees should be planted so that the total yield is as large as possible? Produce a table showing the yield per tree and the total yield if N = 1, 2, 3 . . . , 25 additional trees are planted. Use column headings underlined by a row of dashes. Separate the message telling how many additional trees to plant from the table by a row of dashes. Use a procedure to keep track of the greatest total yield and the number of additional trees that give this greatest yield.

23. An organization can charter a ship for a harbor cruise for $9.75 a ticket, provided that at least 200 people agree to go. However, the ship's owner agrees to reduce the cost per ticket by 25¢ for each additional 10 people who sign up. Thus if 220 people sign up, the cost per person will be $9.25. Write a program to determine the maximum revenue the ship's owner can receive if the ship's capacity is 400 people. Moreover, prepare a table showing the cost per person and the total amount paid for N = 200, 210, 220, . . . , 400 people. Use column headings underlined by a row of dashes. The maximum revenue the ship's owner can receive should be displayed following the table and separated from it by a row of dashes. Use a procedure to keep track of the greatest revenue amount and the number of passengers that give this greatest revenue.

24. A merchant must pay the fixed price of $1 a yard for a certain fabric. From experience, the merchant knows that 1,000 yards will be sold each month if the material is sold at cost and also that each 10¢ increase in price means that 50 fewer yards will be sold each month. Write a program to produce a table that shows the merchant's profit for each selling price from $1 to $3 in increments of 10¢. Also, display a message giving the selling price that will maximize the profit. Use a procedure to keep track of the greatest profit amount and the selling price that gives this greatest profit.

In Problems 25–36, write a menu-driven program to carry out the specified tasks. In each program, be sure to include an option to end the program. Typically, the SUB procedures that carry out the options in a menu-driven program will have no parameters. The program, however, may include other procedures that do have parameters. These will be FUNCTION and SUB procedures called by the procedures that carry out the options. Be sure to use such procedures, where appropriate, while writing the menu-driven programs specified in these problems.

25. Following are last year's monthly income figures for the Garruga Dating Service. Include these data in DATA lines for a program that allows the user to obtain one or more of the following:
   a. A two-column table showing precisely the given information.
   b. The total income for last year.

c. A two-column table showing each month and the amount by which the income for the month exceeds the average monthly income. (Some of these amounts will be negative.)

January	18,000	July	20,000
February	13,500	August	22,650
March	11,200	September	18,500
April	16,900	October	12,500
May	20,500	November	9,250
June	22,200	December	11,300

26. First write a program as specified in Problem 25, and run it to make sure that it works. Then modify the program so that the user also can obtain a list of the months for which the income amount exceeds a value that is entered by the user.

27. Following is a table containing information about employees of the Mendosa Publishing Company. Include this information in DATA lines for a program that will carry out, at the request of the user, any of the following tasks:

a. Display precisely the given information.

b. Display the names of all employees who have been with the company for at least Y years.

Name	Age	Years of service
Lia Brookes	22	1
Mary Crimmins	27	3
Lee Marston	46	18
Joe Nunes	58	9
Paul Reese	23	2
Jean Saulnier	34	12
Jesse Torres	68	21
Mara Walenda	32	7

28. First, write a program as specified in Problem 27, and run it to make sure that it works. Then modify the program so that it will also carry out, at the request of the user, the following additional tasks:

a. Display the names of all employees.

b. Display the average age and average years of service of all employees.

29. The accompanying table describes an investor's stock portfolio. Include this information in DATA lines for a menu-driven program that allows the user to obtain one or more of these reports: a four-column report showing precisely the given information; a three-column report showing each stock name with its current value (numbers of shares × current price) and its value at the close of business last month; and a short report showing the name and current value of the stock whose current value is greatest.

Name of stock	Number of shares	Last month's closing price	Current closing price
STERLING DRUG	800	16.50	16.125
DATA GENERAL	500	56.25	57.50
OWEN ILLINOIS	1,200	22.50	21.50
MATTEL INC	1,000	10.75	11.125
ABBOTT LAB	2,000	33.75	34.75
FED NATL MTG	2,500	17.75	17.25
IC GEN	250	43.125	43.625
ALO SYSTEMS	550	18.50	18.25

30. First, write a menu-driven program as described in Problem 29. Then, modify the program so that it will also display a simple list that shows only the names of the companies in which stock is owned.

31. The accompanying table contains information about employees of the Libel Insurance Company. Include this information in DATA lines for a menu-driven program that allows the user to obtain one or more of these reports: a five-column report showing precisely the given information; a two-column report showing the name and years of service of each person who has been with the company for at least Y years (the procedure that produces this report should prompt the user for Y); and a short report showing the total payroll amount for men and that for women.

Name	Sex	Age	Years of service	Annual salary
J. R. Adamson	M	47	13	20,200.00
P. M. Martell	F	33	6	14,300.00
J. D. Carlson	F	41	15	23,900.00
S. T. Chang	M	22	2	21,400.00
R. T. Richardson	M	59	7	29,200.00
M. E. Thompson	F	25	3	13,000.00
C. B. Rado	M	33	13	21,500.00
O. L. Lawanda	F	28	4	33,400.00
C. Hartwick	M	68	30	25,500.00
C. Cleveland Barnes	M	35	6	14,300.00
M. L. Chou	F	21	3	19,200.00

32. First, write a menu-driven program as described in Problem 31. Then, modify the program so that it will display two additional options: one to display a list of employee names, and another to display the average age of all employees.

33. The following DATA statements give the name, weight in pounds, height in inches, and sex for each child born during the current month. Write a menu-driven program to allow the user to obtain, selectively, this information: a list of all names, the average length of all males and of all females, and a list of children's names whose weight exceeds whatever value is typed at the keyboard.

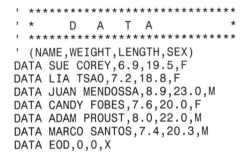

```
'  ******************************
'  *     D  A  T  A          *
'  ******************************
'  (NAME,WEIGHT,LENGTH,SEX)
DATA SUE COREY,6.9,19.5,F
DATA LIA TSAO,7.2,18.8,F
DATA JUAN MENDOSSA,8.9,23.0,M
DATA CANDY FOBES,7.6,20.0,F
DATA ADAM PROUST,8.0,22.0,M
DATA MARCO SANTOS,7.4,20.3,M
DATA EOD,0,0,X
```

34. First, write a program as described in Problem 33. Then, modify it by adding an option that produces a report showing all of the given information.

35. A clothing manufacturer has retail outlets in Miami, Orlando, Chicago, Austin, Seattle, and Montreal. Each month, the company compiles a report showing three amounts for each location: the month's sales, payroll, and building maintenance costs. Here is last month's report:

Location	Sales	Payroll	Maintenance
Miami	$45,000	$15,000	$ 3,000
Orlando	27,000	16,000	2,000
Chicago	64,000	14,000	5,000
Austin	88,000	24,000	5,000
Seattle	28,000	15,000	6,000
Montreal	98,000	32,000	23,000

Write a menu-driven program to allow the user to obtain, selectively, this information: the current month's report and a report showing the sales/payroll ratio for each retail outlet.

36. First, write a program as described in Problem 35. Then, modify it by adding an option that gives the total sales, total payroll, and the total maintenance costs for the current month.

■ *12.7 Review True-or-False Quiz*

1. The expressions *program unit* and *procedure* have the same meaning.   T F

2. There is nothing wrong with the following procedure:

```
SUB RESPONSE$
    INPUT "Answer YES or NO: ",RESPONSE$
END SUB
```
   T F

3. To test a procedure, you must write a main program unit that references the procedure, and then issue the RUN command.   T F

4. Variables that appear in procedures are, by default, local variables.   T F

5. Every procedure must involve at least one variable.   T F

6. If an argument that appears in a CALL statement is a variable, the communication between the argument and the corresponding parameter in the procedure is a two-way communication.   T F

7. If an argument in a FUNCTION reference is a variable, the value of the variable is passed to the procedure as the value of the corresponding parameter; but changes to the parameter are not passed back as changes to the variable argument.   T F

8. If a procedure named SUBNAME assigns the value 15 to a variable named A, the two statements

```
CALL SUBNAME((A))
PRINT A
```

will display the value 15.   T F

9. QuickBASIC handles parameter passing for SUB and FUNCTION procedures in exactly the same way.   T F

10. Character strings allowed as names of numerical and string variables are allowed as names of FUNCTION and SUB procedures.   T F

11. The following procedure contains an error that will halt program execution.

```
FUNCTION MAX (X, Y)
    LET MAX = X
    IF Y > MAX THEN MAX = Y
END FUNCTION
```
   T F

13
Numerical Functions

QuickBASIC is designed to assist you in manipulating both numerical and string data. For this reason, the language includes several functions, called **built-in functions,** to carry out automatically many common calculations with numbers and operations with strings. Section 13.1 describes and illustrates certain built-in numerical functions and presents a table that shows all such functions that are available in QuickBASIC. The built-in functions used with string data are described in Chapter 14. These two chapters on functions can be taken up in either order.

In addition to the built-in functions, QuickBASIC allows you to define your own functions—functions that you may need but that are not part of the language. FUNCTION procedures, as described in Section 12.5, provide this capability. An alternative to FUNCTION procedures, and one that you may find convenient in certain limited situations, uses the DEF FN statement and is described in Section 13.3.

■ 13.1 Built-in Numerical Functions

A list of the QuickBASIC numerical functions is provided in Table 13.1. These functions are an integral part of the language and can be used in any QuickBASIC program. In this section we'll illustrate the square root function SQR, the absolute value function ABS, the integer conversion functions INT, CINT, and FIX, and the sine function SIN. The RND function (which is used somewhat differently from the other numerical functions) is considered in Chapter 17. The first sections of the RND chapter are written so that the material can be taken up at this time, should that be desired.

The Numerical Function SQR

SQR is called the **square root function.** Instead of writing N ^ 0.5 to evaluate the square root of N, you can write SQR(N). The principal advantage in doing this is that your programs will be easier to read—SQR(N) is English-like, whereas N ^ 0.5 is not. For instance, to evaluate the algebraic expression

$$\sqrt{\frac{S}{N-1}}$$

you can write

SQR(S/(N − 1))

Table 13.1   QuickBASIC numerical functions

Function	Purpose
ABS(x)	Gives the absolute value of x.
INT(x)	Gives the greatest integer less than or equal to x.
FIX(x)	Converts x to an integer by truncating.
CINT(x)	Converts x to an integer by rounding.
CLNG(x)	Converts x to a long integer by rounding.
CSNG(x)	Converts x to a single-precision value.
CDBL(x)	Converts x to a double-precision value.
SGN(x)	Returns the value 1 if x is positive, -1 if x is negative, and 0 if x is zero.
SQR(x)	Calculates the principal square root of x if $x \geq 0$; results in an error if x is negative.
RND(x)	Returns a pseudorandom number between 0 and 1 (see Chapter 17).
SIN(x)	Calculates the sine of x, where x is in radian measure.
COS(x)	Calculates the cosine of x, where x is in radian measure.
TAN(x)	Calculates the tangent of x, where x is in radian measure.
ATN(x)	Calculates the arctangent of x; $-\pi/2 <$ ATN(x) $< \pi/2$.
LOG(x)	Calculates the natural logarithm $\ln(x)$; x must be positive.
EXP(x)	Calculates the exponential e^x, where $e = 2.71828\ldots$ is the base of the natural logarithms.

instead of

$(S/(N - 1), {}^\wedge 0.5$

From left to right, the SQR form of the expression reads "evaluate the square root of $S/(N - 1)$," whereas the exponential reads "evaluate $S/(N - 1)$ to the one-half power." (See Problem 15 in Section 13.2 for an application of the expression $\sqrt{S/(N - 1)}$.

EXAMPLE 1   *Here is an illustration of the SQR function.*

```
PRINT "NUMBER", "SQUARE ROOT"
PRINT "------", "-----------"
FOR N = 10 TO 20
  PRINT N, SQR(N)
NEXT N
END
```

Program output:

```
NUMBER      SQUARE ROOT
------      -----------
  10          3.162278
  11          3.316625
  12          3.464102
  13          3.605551
  14          3.741657
  15          3.872983
  16          4
  17          4.123106
  18          4.24264
  19          4.358899
  20          4.472136
```

The Numerical Function ABS

ABS is the **absolute value function:** for example, ABS(-3) $= 3$, ABS(7) $= 7$, and ABS($4 - 9$) $= 5$. In general, if **e** denotes a numerical expression, then ABS(**e**) is the absolute value of the value of the expression **e**.

EXAMPLE 2   ***Here is an illustration of the ABS function.***

```
' Program to find the absolute value
' of the sum of any two input values.

PRINT "TYPE TWO NUMBERS PER LINE."
PRINT "TYPE 0,0 TO STOP."
PRINT
INPUT "FIRST PAIR ", X, Y
DO UNTIL X = 0 AND Y = 0
   LET Z = ABS(X + Y)
   PRINT "ABSOLUTE VALUE OF SUM:"; Z
   PRINT
   INPUT "NEXT PAIR ", X, Y
LOOP
END
```

Program output:
```
TYPE TWO NUMBERS PER LINE.
TYPE 0,0 TO STOP.

FIRST PAIR 7,3
ABSOLUTE VALUE OF SUM: 10

NEXT PAIR 5,-9
ABSOLUTE VALUE OF SUM: 4

NEXT PAIR 0, -92.7
ABSOLUTE VALUE OF SUM: 92.7

NEXT PAIR 0,0
```

This program could have been written without using the ABS function. For example, if the statement

```
LET Z = ABS(X + Y)
```

were replaced by the two lines

```
LET Z = X + Y
IF Z < 0 THEN Z = -Z
```

the resulting program would work in the same way as the original. The first version is better—its logic is transparent, whereas the logic of the second version is somewhat obscure. As a general rule you should use the built-in functions supplied with your system. Not only will your programs be easier to code, but they will also be easier to understand and hence simpler to debug or modify, should that be required.

A common application of the ABS function is in problems that require examining numerical data to determine how they deviate from a specified number. The following example illustrates this use of the ABS function.

EXAMPLE 3   ***A data list contains two items for each of 10 retail stores: the current week's sales figure preceded by the store's identification code. Let's write a program to identify those stores with sales that deviate from the average sales by more than 20% of the average sales amount.***

PROBLEM ANALYSIS

The problem statement specifies the following input and output:

Input: Identification code and current sales for each store.

Output: A report identifying those stores with sales that deviate from the average sales by more than 20% of the average sales figure. Let's prepare a two-column report with title and column headings as follows:

```
STORES WITH SIGNIFICANTLY
HIGH OR LOW SALES FOR THE WEEK.

STORE CODE     WEEK'S SALES
----------     ------------
     •              •
     •              •
     •              •
```

To determine whether a store should be included in this report, we must compare the store's sales with the average sales of all stores. Thus, before attempting to prepare the report, we should first find the average sales figure. The following algorithm contains few details but shows precisely what must be done. In the algorithm, we use these variable names:

CODE$ = identification code of a store
SALES = current sales for store with code CODE$
AVG   = average sale of all stores
DEV   = 20% of AVG

THE ALGORITHM

a. Determine AVG and DEV.
b. Prepare a report showing CODE$ AND SALES for each store whose current sales (SALES) differs from AVG by more than DEV.

To find the deviation of SALES from AVG, we could subtract SALES from AVG or AVG from SALES, depending on whether AVG is larger or smaller than SALES. Since we are interested only in how close SALES is to AVG, not which is larger, we will simply examine the absolute value of SALES − AVG (the two expressions SALES − AVG and AVG − SALES differ only in their signs). Thus, CODE$ and SALES for a particular store will be included in the report only if the logical expression

```
ABS(SALES-AVG)>DEV
```

is true.

THE PROGRAM

```
' Program to produce a report showing retail
' stores with significantly high or low sales.

'        COUNT     Number of stores
'        CODE$     Identification code of a store
'        SALES     Current sales for store CODE$
'          AVG     Average sales of all stores
'          DEV     20 percent of AVG

' --------------------------------------------
' Read data to determine AVG, DEV, and COUNT.

LET SUM = 0
LET COUNT = 0
READ CODE$, SALES
DO UNTIL CODE$ = "XXX"
   LET COUNT = COUNT + 1
   LET SUM = SUM + SALES
   READ CODE$, SALES
LOOP
LET AVG = SUM / COUNT
LET DEV = .2 * AVG              'Specify 20% deviation.

' --------------------------------------------
'    Produce the specified report.

PRINT "STORES WITH SIGNIFICANTLY"
PRINT "HIGH OR LOW SALES FOR THE WEEK."
PRINT
PRINT "STORE CODE", "WEEK'S SALES"
PRINT "----------", "------------"
RESTORE
```

```
FOR N = 1 TO COUNT
   READ CODE$, SALES
   IF ABS(SALES - AVG) > DEV THEN PRINT CODE$, SALES
NEXT N
END


' -------------------------------------------------
'            D    A    T    A
DATA BX14, 21000, AX17, 16000, BX19, 12500
DATA BY12, 25740, AY33, 14480, AX11, 28700
DATA BX09, 20400, AY04, 14200, BX27, 15200
DATA XXX, 0
```

Program output:

```
STORES WITH SIGNIFICANTLY
HIGH OR LOW SALES FOR THE WEEK.

STORE CODE     WEEK'S SALES
----------     ------------
BX19            12500
BY12            25740
AY33            14480
AX11            28700
AY04            14200
```

The Numerical Functions INT, FIX, and CINT

If **e** denotes a numerical expression, and E denotes its value, then:

1. The value of INT(**e**) is the greatest integer less than or equal to E. For example, INT(2.6) = 2, INT(7) = 7, INT(7 − 3.2) = 3, and INT (−4.35) = −5. For this reason, INT is called the **greatest-integer function.**
2. The value of FIX(**e**) is obtained by truncating E. Thus, FIX(2.6) = 2, FIX(7) = 7, FIX (7 − 3.2) = 3, and FIX(−4.35) = −4. (For expressions **e** with positive values, INT and FIX are equivalent.)
3. The value of CINT(**e**) is obtained by rounding E to the nearest integer, provided this value is in the range −32768 to 32767. If E is not in this range, an Overflow error occurs. Thus, CINT(2.6) = 3, CINT(7) = 7, CINT(−4.35) = −4, and CINT(42345.6) results in an Overflow error. A number ending with .5 is rounded to the nearest even integer.

If a program requires integer input, you can use INT to detect input values that are not integers. This common use of INT is illustrated in the following example.

EXAMPLE 4   *Here is a program segment to reject numerical input values that are not integers.*

```
DO
   INPUT "HOW MANY APPLES HAVE YOU"; C
LOOP UNTIL C = INT(C)
```

If the user types a number that is not an integer, the condition C = INT(C) will be false, and the INPUT statement will be repeated so that another number can be entered.

REMARK   To inform the user why the prompt

```
HOW MANY APPLES HAVE YOU?
```

is displayed a second time and also to reject meaningless negative input values, you could use lines such as these:

```
INPUT "HOW MANY APPLES HAVE YOU"; C
DO UNTIL C = INT(C) AND C >= 0
   PRINT "PLEASE ENTER A COUNT."
   INPUT "HOW MANY APPLES HAVE YOU"; C
LOOP
```

Should the user now enter an improper number, the message

```
PLEASE ENTER A COUNT.
```

will be displayed before the user is prompted a second time. Note that 0 as an input value is both allowed and meaningful.

To round *any* number (not just those numbers in the range -32768 to 32767, which can be handled by CINT), you can use the INT function. For example, suppose X satisfies the inequalities

$$40136.5 \le X < 40137.5$$

Then $X + 0.5$ satisfies the inequalities

$$40137 \le X + 0.5 < 40138$$

and we see that

$$INT(X+0.5) = 40137.$$

That is, to round a number X to the nearest integer, use the expression

```
INT(X+0.5)
```

A slight modification of this method of rounding to the nearest integer can be used to round to any decimal position. We illustrate by rounding the number $X = 42567.382$ to the nearest tenth to obtain 42567.4.

Expression	Value	Comment
X	42567.382	Number to be rounded.
10 * X	425673.82	Move decimal point to the right.
INT(10 * X + 0.5)	425674	Round to nearest integer.
INT(10 * X + 0.5)/10	42567.4	Move decimal point back.

Thus to round X to the nearest tenth, use the expression

```
INT(10*X+0.5)/10
```

If you are sure that all numbers involved will be in the range -32768 to 32767, you can use CINT (10*X)/10. Note, however, that 10*X, not just X, must be in the restricted range. The safest policy is to use INT.

If you change each 10 in the expression INT(10 * X + 0.5)/10 to 100, X will be rounded to two decimal positions; if you use 1000, it will be rounded to three; and so on. You are limited only because the PC keeps a fixed number of significant digits when numbers are stored in memory.

For more work with rounding numbers, see Problem 5 in Section 13.2.

EXAMPLE 5   *Here is a program that uses INT to round the values 1/7, 2/7, 3/7, . . . , 6/7 to five decimal places.*

```
PRINT " N", "    N/7"
PRINT
FOR N = 1 TO 6
   LET N.ROUNDED = INT(100000 * N / 7 + .5) / 100000
   PRINT N, N.ROUNDED
NEXT N
END
```

Program output:

```
N               N/7

1               .14286
2               .28571
3               .42857
4               .57143
5               .71429
6               .85714
```

REMARK

You may have noticed that the INT function is not needed to produce this table—simply replace the two lines in the body of the FOR loop with the single line

```
PRINT USING " #               .#####"; N; N / 7
```

This program illustrates, however, that INT can be used to assign rounded values to variables, something that cannot be done with the PRINT USING statement.

In Example 4 we saw that the condition C = INT(C) is true if C is an integer and false if it is not. Thus, if N is any integer, the condition

```
N/2 = INT(N/2)
```

will be true precisely when N/2 is an integer—that is, when N is divisible by 2. Similarly, if N and D are any integers (with D not 0), the condition

```
N/D = INT(N/D)
```

is true precisely when N/D is an integer—that is, when N is divisible by D.

Relational expression	Truth value
63/7 = INT(63/7)	True
6/4 = INT(6/4)	False
INT(105/15) = 105/15	True
INT(100/8) <> 100/8	True

Here we must add a word of caution. In QuickBASIC, the condition

```
N/D=INT(N/D)
```

is used to determine whether N/D is an integer only if both N and D are integers. If either is not an integer, you may get unexpected results. For instance, the condition

```
9/.3=INT(9/.3)
```

is false even though the fraction 9/.3 has the integer value 30. To see that this is so, type the immediate mode statement

```
PRINT 9/.3,INT(9/.3)
```

The PC will display 30 and 29. The reason for this discrepancy is that computers use an internal representation of numbers that does not allow all numbers to be stored exactly. As mentioned previously, .1 is one of these numbers; so is .3. Thus, calculations involving .3 as well as .1 may not be exact. The following short program with output produced by an IBM Personal Computer further illustrates this situation:

```
PRINT " X", "X/.1", "INT(X/.1)"
PRINT
FOR X = 2 TO 2.5 STEP .1
    PRINT X, X / .1, INT(X / .1)
NEXT X
END
```

Program output:

```
X               X/.1            INT(X/.1)

2               20              19
2.1             21              20
2.2             22              21
2.3             23              22
2.4             24              23
2.5             24.99999        24
```

EXAMPLE 6   ***Here is a program to display the integers from 1 to 28, seven numbers per line.***

```
FOR N = 1 TO 28
   PRINT USING "####"; N;
   IF N / 7 = INT(N / 7) THEN PRINT
NEXT N
END
```

Program output:

```
 1    2    3    4    5    6    7
 8    9   10   11   12   13   14
15   16   17   18   19   20   21
22   23   24   25   26   27   28
```

The only statement that moves the cursor to the next display line is the PRINT statement that follows the keyword THEN. This PRINT statement is executed only when the condition N/7 = INT(N/7) is true. As shown in the output, this happens when N is 7, 14, 21, and 28.

The INT function has many applications. We have shown that it can be used to validate user input (Example 4), to round numbers (discussion preceding Example 5), and to test for divisibility of one number by another (Example 6). As you work through the examples and problems in this and subsequent chapters, you will find that the INT function is a valuable programming tool that can be used to simplify many programming tasks.

In the next example, we give a detailed analysis for a prime number program. The example illustrates the use of the SQR and INT functions and also discusses simple ways to speed up program execution, should that be important.

EXAMPLE 7   ***Write a program to tell whether an integer typed at the keyboard is a prime number.***

Let N denote the number to be tested. A number N is prime if it is an integer greater than 1 whose only factors are 1 and N. To determine whether a number N is prime, you can divide it successively by 2, 3, . . . , N − 1. If N is divisible by none of these, then N is a prime. It is not necessary to check all the way to N − 1, however, but only to the square root of N. Can you see why? We will use this fact.

Let's construct a flowchart to describe this process in detail. Since all primes are at least as large as 2, we will reject any input value that is less than 2. Thus, we can begin our flowchart as follows:

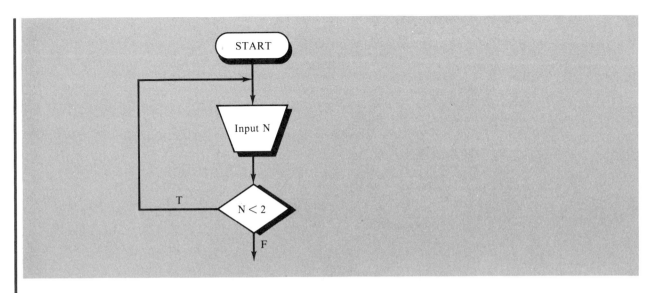

Next, we test all integers from 2 to $\sqrt{N}$ as possible factors of N. If we test them in the order D = 2, 3, 4, and so on, we can stop testing when $D > \sqrt{N}$ or when D is a factor of N. Thus, we can add the following segment to our partial flowchart:

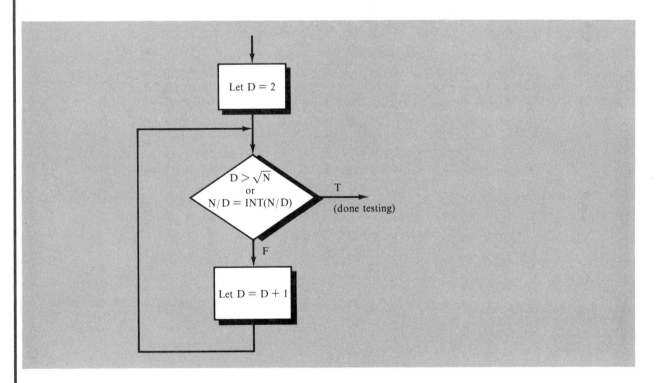

When we are done testing, we can be sure that N is prime if the last D value satisfies the condition $D > \sqrt{N}$, since this means that no factor less than or equal to $\sqrt{N}$ was found. On the other hand, if this last D value does not satisfy the condition $D > \sqrt{N}$, then it must satisfy the only other condition, N/D = INT(N/D), that can get us out of the loop. This means that D is a factor of N that lies between 2 and $\sqrt{N}$, inclusive; that is, N is not prime. Thus we can now complete the flowchart as follows.

PRIME NUMBER FLOWCHART

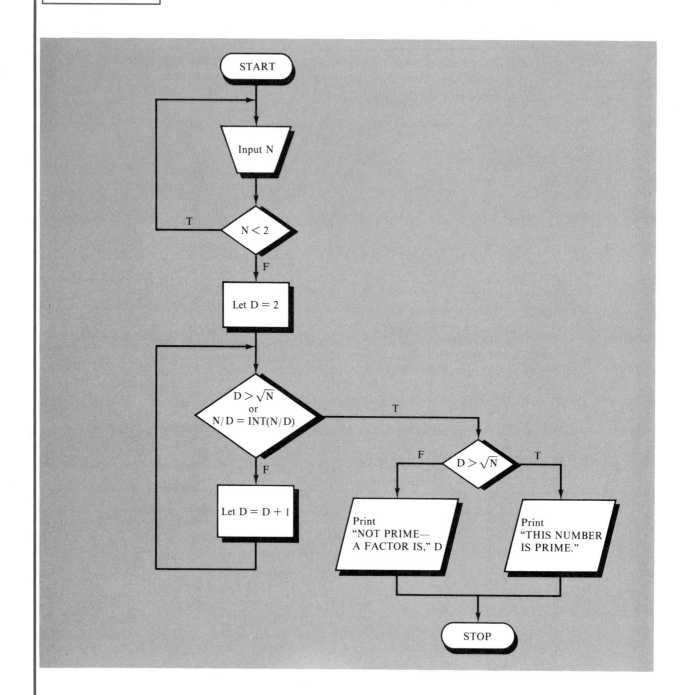

REMARK

It is tempting to say that N is not a prime if the last value of D is a factor of N—that is, if N/D = INT(N/D) is true. If you use this condition (instead of the condition D > $\sqrt{N}$) to complete the flowchart, you will find that you have a bug. You should find it. (*Suggestion:* When debugging a program, test it for *extreme* values of any input variables. In this problem, the smallest value that the program will actually test is N = 2, so 2 is an extreme value.)

THE PROGRAM

```
DO
    INPUT "TYPE AN INTEGER: ", N
LOOP WHILE N < 2
```

```
LET D = 2
DO UNTIL D > SQR(N) OR N / D = INT(N / D)
   LET D = D + 1
LOOP

IF D > SQR(N) THEN
   PRINT "THIS NUMBER IS PRIME."
ELSE
   PRINT "NOT PRIME - A FACTOR IS"; D
END IF
END
```

Program output for N = 253009:
```
TYPE AN INTEGER: 253009
NOT PRIME - A FACTOR IS 503
```

Program output for N = 765767:
```
TYPE AN INTEGER: 765767
THIS NUMBER IS PRIME.
```

REMARK 1

When we ran this program for the input value 253009, we had to wait approximately 6 seconds for the output to be displayed. For the input value 765767, we had to wait about 11.5 seconds. The PC spent essentially all of this time executing the second DO loop. It is often possible to reduce execution time significantly by making small changes in a loop. Here are two ways to improve the prime number program:

1. Treat D = 2 as a special case before the loop is entered, and use the loop to test only the odd numbers D = 3, 5, 7, . . . , SQR(N). This will cut execution time in half.
2. On each pass through the second loop, the PC must calculate SQR(N) anew. This takes time. To avoid these calculations, include the line

    ```
    LET ROOTN = SQR(N)
    ```

    and change all the other occurrences of SQR(N) to ROOTN. The change in the DO statement is the important one, because it is in the loop. By making these changes, we obtained execution times of approximately 4.5 seconds and 7.5 seconds instead of 6 seconds and 11.5 seconds, respectively. When we made this change in addition to the change in Step 1, the execution times were further reduced to approximately 2.5 seconds for the input value 253009 and 4.5 seconds for 765767.

REMARK 2

If this program is run, there is no guarantee that the user will type an integer. The first DO loop ensures that the prime number algorithm will not be carried out for N < 2, but if 256.73 is input, the algorithm will produce a silly result. To avoid this, you can change the WHILE condition N < 2 to

```
N < 2 OR INT(N) <> N
```

The Trigonometric Functions

If **e** denotes a numerical expression, then SIN(**e**), COS(**e**), TAN(**e**), and ATN(**e**) evaluate the sine, cosine, tangent, and arctangent of the value of **e**. If the value of **e** denotes an angle, this value must be in radian measure.

EXAMPLE 8

Here is a program to determine SIN(D) for D = 0, 5, 10, . . . , 45°.

Since D denotes an angle in degrees, it must be changed to radian measure. Recalling the correspondence

$$1 \text{ degree} = \pi/180 \text{ radians}$$

we must multiply D by $\pi/180$ to convert to radian measure.

```
PRINT "DEGREES          SINE"
PRINT "-------          ------"
 F$ = "  ##            #.####"
LET PI = 3.14159
FOR DEGREE = 0 TO 45 STEP 5
   LET Y = SIN(PI / 180 * DEGREE)
   PRINT USING F$; DEGREE; Y
NEXT DEGREE
END
```

Program output:

```
DEGREES        SINE
-------        ------
      0        0.0000
      5        0.0872
     10        0.1736
     15        0.2588
     20        0.3420
     25        0.4226
     30        0.5000
     35        0.5736
     40        0.6428
     45        0.7071
```

EXAMPLE 9

Given side a and angles A and B in degrees, use the law of sines to determine side b of the following triangle:

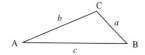

PROBLEM ANALYSIS

The law of sines states that

$$\frac{a}{\sin A} = \frac{b}{\sin B}$$

Solving for b, we obtain

$$b = \frac{a \sin B}{\sin A}$$

Since the angles A and B will be given in degrees, they must be changed to radian measure as required by the function SIN. In the following program, A1 and B1 denote the sides *a* and *b*, respectively.

THE PROGRAM

```
' APPLICATION OF LAW OF SINES

CONST PI = 3.14159

' -----------------------------------
'            KEYBOARD INPUT

INPUT "ANGLE A IN DEGREES: ", A
INPUT "ANGLE B IN DEGREES: ", B
INPUT "SIDE OPPOSITE ANGLE A: ", A1

' -----------------------------------
' CONVERT A AND B TO RADIANS AND FIND
' LENGTH B1 OF SIDE OPPOSITE ANGLE B.

LET A = PI / 180 * A
LET B = PI / 180 * B
LET B1 = A1 * SIN(B) / SIN(A)
PRINT
PRINT "THE SIDE OPPOSITE ANGLE B HAS LENGTH"; B1
END
```

Program output:
```
ANGLE A IN DEGREES: 28
ANGLE B IN DEGREES: 42
SIDE OPPOSITE ANGLE A: 2

THE SIDE OPPOSITE ANGLE B HAS LENGTH 2.850569
```

■ *13.2 Problems*

1. *Evaluate the following QuickBASIC expressions.*

   a. `ABS(3*(2-5))`   **b.** `ABS(-3*(-2))`
   c. `ABS(2-30/3*2)`   **d.** `INT(26.1+0.5)`
   e. `INT(-43.2+0.5)`   **f.** `100*INT(1235.7/100+0.5)`
   g. `CINT(123.6)`   **h.** `CINT(-123.6)`
   i. `FIX(123.6)`   **j.** `FIX(-123.6)`
   k. `ABS(INT(-3.2))`   **l.** `INT(ABS(-3.2))`

2. *Evaluate the following with* A $= -4.32$, B $= 5.93$, *and* C $= 2864.7144$.

   a. `INT(ABS(A))`   **b.** `ABS(INT(A))`
   c. `INT(B+0.5)`   **d.** `INT(A+0.5)`
   e. `INT(C+0.5)`   **f.** `10*INT(C/10+0.5)`
   g. `100*INT(C/100+0.5)`   **h.** `1000*INT(C/1000+0.5)`
   i. `INT(1000*C+0.5)/1000` **j.** `CINT(ABS(A))`
   k. `FIX(ABS(A))`   **l.** `CINT(10*B)`

3. *Show the output for each program.*

   a.
   ```
   FOR N=0 TO 4
       LET X=N*(N-1)
       LET Y=ABS(X-8)
       PRINT N, Y
   NEXT N
   END
   ```
   b.
   ```
   LET X=1.1 : Y=X
   DO WHILE X<1.5
       LET Z=INT(Y)
       PRINT Y,Z
       LET Y=X*Y
   LOOP
   END
   ```

   c.
   ```
   FOR X=3 TO 10
       PRINT "X";
       IF X/4=INT(X/4) THEN PRINT
   NEXT X
   END
   ```

   d.
   ```
   FOR X=3 TO 10
       PRINT "X";
       IF X\4=INT(X/4) THEN PRINT
   NEXT X
   END
   ```

   e.
   ```
   FOR X=3 TO 10
       PRINT X;
       IF X\4=CINT(X/4) THEN PRINT
   NEXT X
   END
   ```

   f.
   ```
   LET N=63 : D=1
   DO
       IF N/D=INT(N/D) THEN PRINT D;
       LET D=D+1
   LOOP UNTIL D>N/2
   END
   ```

g.
```
LET M=24
FOR D=2 TO 23 STEP 3
    PRINT "*";
    IF M/D=INT(M/D) THEN PRINT
NEXT D
END
```

h.
```
LET S=13.99
DO
    LET R=INT(100*S+0.5)/100
    PRINT USING "##.### ##.##";S;R
    LET S=S+0.003
LOOP WHILE S<14
END
```

4. *Write a single QuickBASIC statement for each task:*
  a. For any two numbers A and B, display EQUAL if the absolute value of their sum is equal to the sum of their absolute values.
  b. For any two integers M and N, display DIVISIBLE if M is divisible by N.
  c. Display OK if X is a positive integer. (All you know about X is that it is a number.)
  d. Add 1 to COUNT if the integer K is divisible by either 7 or 11.
  e. Cause a RETURN to be executed if the integer L is even and also divisible by 25.
  f. For any integers A, B, and C, display OK if C is a factor of both A and B.

5. *Using the INT function, write a single QuickBASIC statement that will round the value of X:*
  a. to the nearest hundredth.
  b. to the nearest thousandth.
  c. to the nearest hundred.
  d. to the nearest thousand.

In Problems 6–15, write a program for each task specified. For tasks that require keyboard input, a user should be able to try different input values without having to rerun the program.

6. Find the sum and the sum of the absolute values of any input list. Display the number of values in the list as well as the two sums.
7. The deviation of a number N from a number M is defined to be ABS(M − N). Find the sum of the deviations of the numbers 2, 5, 3, 7, 12, −8, 43, −16 from M = 6. (M and the list of numbers are to be input during program execution. Use an EOD tag to end each list.)
8. Find the sum of the deviations of numbers X from INT(X) where the X's are input.
9. Find the sums S1 and S2 of any input list. S1 is the sum of the numbers, and S2 is the sum of the numbers each rounded to the nearest integer. Display both sums and also the number of values in the list.
10. Determine all positive factors of a positive integer N input at the keyboard. (Include the factors 1 and N.)
11. A list of integers is to be input. Any integer less than 1 serves as the EOD tag. Display the sum and count of the even input values and also the sum and count of the odd ones.
12. Display the exact change received from a purchase of P dollars if an amount D is presented to the salesclerk. Assume that D is at most $100. The change should be given in the largest possible denominations of bills and coins, but $50 and $2 bills cannot be used. If P = 26.68 and D = 100, for example, the change D − P = 73.32 would be:

  3 $20 bills, 1 $10 bill, 3 $1 bills, 1 quarter, 1 nickel, and 2 pennies

Suggestion: If C denotes the change in pennies, then C/2000 gives the number of $20 bills. You would then let C = CMOD 2000 and proceed to the next lower denomination. Because computers store some numbers only approximately, you must not use the statement LET C = 100 ∗ (D − P) to get C. Rather, use the statement

```
LET C=CINT(100*(D−P))
```

and explain the reason for adding 0.1.

13. The Apex Gas Station is running a special on cut glassware that regularly costs $3.29. The sale price of the glassware is determined by the number of gallons of gasoline purchased according to this table:

Number of gallons purchased	Sale price of glassware
Less than 10	Regular price
From 10 to 15	Twenty percent is deducted from regular price for each whole numbered gallon over the minimum of 10
More than 15	Free

Apex sells three grades of gasoline:

Grade	Code	Price per gallon
Regular unleaded	U	$1.179
Unleaded Plus	P	$1.259
Super unleaded	S	$1.399

Write a program that prompts the user to enter the code for the grade of gasoline and the number of gallons purchased. Then, have it display the sale price of the glassware and ask the user (Y or N) whether the glassware will be purchased. After the user enters a response, display the cost of the gasoline purchase and the total cost of the transaction.

14. Last year's sales report of the RJB Card Company reads as follows:

January	$32,350	July	$22,000
February	$16,440	August	$43,500
March	$18,624	September	$51,400
April	$26,100	October	$29,000
May	$30,500	November	$20,100
June	$28,600	December	$27,500

Display the average monthly sales and a short report showing the month and the monthly sales for those months for which the sales deviate from the average by more than P percent. Have the user enter a value for P.

15. Find the mean M and standard deviation D of a set of numbers contained in DATA lines. Use the following method to compute D. If the numbers are $x_1, x_2, x_3, \ldots, x_n$, then $D = \sqrt{S2/(n-1)}$, where

$$S2 = (x_1 - M)^2 + (x_2 - M)^2 + \cdots + (x_n - M)^2$$

In Problems 16–25, write a program for each task specified. (These are for the mathematically inclined reader.)

16. Determine all prime numbers that do not exceed N. N is to be input.

17. Determine all prime numbers between A and B. A and B are to be input and are to be rejected if either is not a positive integer.

18. Display the prime factorization of any positive integer greater than 1 typed at the keyboard. For example, if 35 is input, the output should be $35 = 5 * 7$; if 41 is input, the output should be 41 IS PRIME; if 90 is input, the output should be $90 = 2 * 3 * 3 * 5$.

19. Write a program to input a decimal constant that contains fewer than five fractional digits, and display it as a quotient of two integers. For example, if 23.79 is input, the output should be 2379/100. (Remember, the computer may store only a close approximation of the input value. Be sure that your program works in all cases.)

20. Write a program to input a decimal constant as in Problem 19 and display it as a quotient of two integers that have no common factors. For example, if 4.40 is input, the output should be 22/5.

21. If a, b, and c are any three numbers with $a \neq 0$, the quadratic equation

$$ax^2 + bx + c = 0$$

can be solved for x by using the formula

$$x = \frac{-b \pm \sqrt{b^2 - 4ac}}{2a}$$

If $b^2 - 4ac > 0$, the formula gives two solutions: if $b^2 - 4ac = 0$, it gives one solution. If $b^2 - 4ac < 0$, however, there are no real solutions. Your program is to solve the quadratic equation for any input values a, b, and c, with $a \neq 0$.

22. The distance d of a point (x, y) in the xy-plane from the line $ax + by + c = 0$ is given by

$$d = \frac{|ax + by + c|}{\sqrt{a^2 + b^2}}$$

Write a program to input the coefficients a, b, and c, and compute the distance d for any number of points (x, y) typed at the keyboard. Be sure that all input requests and all output values are labeled. End the program when $a = 0$ and $b = 0$.

23. Produce a two-column table showing the value of X and the cotangent of X for all values of X from zero to $\pi/2$ in increments of 0.05. (The case X = 0 must get special treatment.)

24. Refer to the diagram in Example 9, and write a program to determine side c if sides a and b and angle C are given. [Use the law of cosines: $c^2 = a^2 + b^2 - 2ab \cos(C)$.]

25. An object moves so that its distance d from a fixed point P at time t is

$$d = \frac{1}{1 - 0.999 \cos t}$$

Produce a table (with column headings) of the d values for t between zero and 2π in increments of 0.1.

■ 13.3 User-Defined Functions: The DEF FN Statement

In addition to providing the built-in functions, QuickBASIC allows you to define and name your own functions. These functions, called **user-defined functions,** can be referenced in any part of your program, just as the built-in functions are referenced.

Usually, user-defined functions are written as FUNCTION procedures, as described in Section 12.5. However, if a function evaluates a single expression, you may find it more convenient to define it by using the DEF FN statement. We illustrate with a simple example of a function that rounds values to two decimal places. The statement

```
DEF FNR (X) = INT(100 * X + .5) / 100
```

defines a function named FNR whose value for any number X is X rounded to the nearest hundredth (recall that the expression to the right of the equals sign rounds X to two decimal places). The keyword DEF is an abbreviation for DEFINE, and FN stands for FUNCTION. The variable X is a **formal parameter;** it serves only to define the function. The function FNR is referenced just as the built-in functions and FUNCTION procedures are referenced. Thus, to reference (or call) FNR, you must use the form

FNR(**argument**)

where **argument** denotes a numerical expression whose value is to be substituted for X in the function definition. If the expression FNR(943.828) appears in a program, its value will be 943.83. Similarly, if Y = 943.828, then FNR(Y) will again have the value 943.83. The program in Example 10 uses this user-defined function to round calculated values before they are displayed.

The function FNR is called a **single-statement function** because it is defined by using only one QuickBASIC statement, the DEF FN statement that specifies the expression to be evaluated. If you need to define a function whose value cannot be determined by evaluating a single expression, you should code it as a FUNCTION procedure.*

EXAMPLE 10   *Here is a program to illustrate the DEF FN statement.*

```
' ------------------------------------------------
' FUNCTION DEFINITION: ROUND TO NEAREST CENT.

DEF FNR (X) = INT(100 * X + .5) / 100


' ------------------------------------------------
'          BEGIN PROGRAM EXECUTION.

INPUT "ENTER AN AMOUNT (0 TO STOP ): ", AMT
DO UNTIL AMT = 0
   INPUT "ENTER A PERCENT: ", PCT
   LET RESULT = (PCT / 100) * AMT
   PRINT PCT; "PERCENT OF"; AMT; "IS"; FNR(RESULT)
   PRINT
   INPUT "ENTER AN AMOUNT (0 TO STOP ): ", AMT
LOOP
END
```

Program output:
```
ENTER AN AMOUNT (0 TO STOP ): 100
ENTER A PERCENT: 12.625
 12.625 PERCENT OF 100 IS 12.63

ENTER AN AMOUNT (0 TO STOP ): 154.49
ENTER A PERCENT: 6
 6 PERCENT OF 154.49 IS 9.27

ENTER AN AMOUNT (0 TO STOP ): 0
```

The advantages in writing FUNCTION procedures apply also to the use of functions defined with the DEF FN statement. The following points are significant:

1. A program that contains a user-defined function is easily modified to treat different functions. For example, if you change the DEF FN statement in the preceding program to

   ```
   DEF FNR (X) = INT(1000 * X + .5) / 1000
   ```

   values will be rounded to three decimal places.
2. The expression defining a function is written only once, even though it may be used several times in a program.
3. By assigning a name to an expression, you can often write programs so that they are easier to read and so that their logic is simpler to follow.

A program can contain any number of user-defined functions. In the next example, we use two: a function to convert centimeters to inches and another to convert inches to feet.

---

*In early versions of BASIC, functions that cannot be defined in a single DEF FN statement are coded as **multiple-statement functions** by using DEF FN and FN END statements. In QuickBASIC, such functions are coded as FUNCTION procedures.

EXAMPLE 11   *Here is a program to produce a table that shows conversions from centimeters to inches and to feet.*

```
' ----------------------------------------------
'           FUNCTION DEFINITIONS

DEF FNI (C) = C / 2.54    'Centimeters to inches
DEF FNF (I) = I / 12      'Inches to feet

' ----------------------------------------------
'          DISPLAY CONVERSION TABLE.

PRINT "CENTIMETERS      INCHES      FEET"
 F$ = "    ###          ##.##       #.##"
PRINT
FOR CENT = 10 TO 100 STEP 10
   LET INCH = FNI(CENT)
   LET FEET = FNF(INCH)
   PRINT USING F$; CENT; INCH; FEET
NEXT CENT
END
```

Program output:

```
CENTIMETERS     INCHES     FEET

        10        3.94     0.33
        20        7.87     0.66
        30       11.81     0.98
        40       15.75     1.31
        50       19.69     1.64
        60       23.62     1.97
        70       27.56     2.30
        80       31.50     2.62
        90       35.43     2.95
       100       39.37     3.28
```

REMARK   The formal parameters C and I used in the function definitions could have been any simple numerical variable names. Formal parameters are sometimes called **dummy variables** because they serve only to define functions; they have meaning only in the function definitions. No conflict in usage will occur if they are used later in the program for some other purpose. For example, if the first DEF FN statement is changed to

```
DEF FNI (CENT) = CENT / 2.54    'Centimeters to inches
```

the program will behave just as before. In contrast, the variables CENT and INCH in the function references FNI(CENT) and FNF(INCH) in the FOR loop supply actual values to the functions. As with FUNCTION procedures, they are called **actual arguments** or, more simply, **arguments.**

You can include more than one parameter in a function definition. For example, the statement

```
DEF FNI (P, R) = P * R / 100
```

defines a function whose value for any numbers P and R is P * R/100. If the expression FNI(2000,10) is used in the program, its value will be $2000 \times 10/100 = 200$. Similarly, if the variables A and B have the values 2000 and 10, respectively, then FNI(A,B) will again have the value 200.

EXAMPLE 12   *Charges at a car rental agency are $14 a day plus 32¢ a mile. The following program calculates the total charge if the number of days D and the total mileage M are typed at the keyboard.*

```
DEF FNCHARGE (D, M) = 14 * D + (.32) * M
INPUT "HOW MANY DAYS"; D
```

```
INPUT "HOW MANY MILES"; M
PRINT "CHARGE:"; FNCHARGE(D, M)
END
```

Program output:
```
HOW MANY DAYS? 3
HOW MANY MILES? 523
CHARGE: 209.36
```

As mentioned previously, the functions FNR, FNI, FNF, and FNCHARGE used in Examples 10 through 12 are called *single-statement* functions because each is defined by using *one* QuickBASIC statement. The general form of the DEF FN statement for single-statement functions is

DEF FNname (plist) = expr

where **name** denotes any string allowed as a variable name, **plist** denotes a list of parameters (one or more simple variables separated by commas), and **expr** denotes an expression that defines a function of the parameters in **plist.** The expression **expr** and the function name **name** must match in type—that is, both numerical or both string. (Single-statement string functions are illustrated in Section 14.7.) The function is referenced by using the form

FNname (arglist)

where **arglist** denotes a list of arguments (one or more numerical or string expressions separated by commas). The arguments supply values for the parameters in the function definition. Their number and types must agree with the number and types of the parameters.

The following rules govern the use of functions defined by DEF FN statements.

1. DEF FN statements can appear only in the main program unit.
2. The DEF FN statement that defines a function must be executed before the function is referenced.
3. A user-defined function can be referenced as an operand in QuickBASIC expressions that appear in any program unit.
4. The expression **expr** used in a DEF FN statement can involve variables other than the parameters. When such a function is referenced, the current values of these variables (their values in the main program unit), are used in the evaluation. Thus, if the function EVAL is defined by

```
DEF FNEVAL (S) = 5 * S + T
```

and if the last value assigned to T in the main program unit is 1000, the statement

```
PRINT FNEVAL (7)
```

will display the value 1035 ($5 \times 7 + 1000 = 1035$).
5. The expression **expr** used in a DEF FN statement can involve other functions. Thus, the two lines

```
DEF FNY (X) = X + 3
DEF FNZ (S) = S * FNY (S)
```

are allowed. The reference FNZ(4) will have the value 28:

```
FNZ(4) = 4 * FNY(4) = 4 * (4 + 3) = 28
```

6. DEF FN statements cannot be used in immediate mode.

■ *13.4 Problems*

1. *Each of these short programs contains an error—either a syntax error that will cause an error message or a programming error that the computer will not recognize but that will cause incorrect results. In each case, find the error and tell which of the two types it is.*

a.
```
' DISPLAY 6 PERCENT
' OF ANY NUMBER.
DEF FNZ(U)=.06*U
INPUT X
LET V=FNZ(U)
PRINT V
END
```

b.
```
' A TABLE OF SQUARES
DEF FNS(I)=X^2
FOR I=1 TO 9
    LET S=FNS(I)
    PRINT I,S
NEXT I
END
```

c.
```
' BONUS CALCULATION
DEF BONUS(S)=200+0.02*S
INPUT "SALARY: ",S
LET B=BONUS(S)
PRINT "BONUS IS";B
END
```

d.
```
' DISPLAY RECIPROCALS.
' OF 1,2,3, . . . ,10
DEF FNR(X)=X/N
LET X=1
FOR N=1 TO 10
    PRINT FNR(N)
NEXT N
END
```

2. *Show the output of each program:*

a.
```
DEF FNR(X)=100*INT(X/100+0.5)
FOR I=1 TO 3
    READ S
    PRINT FNR(S)
NEXT I
DATA 227.376,1382.123,7.125
END
```

b.
```
DEF FNY(X)=1+1/X
LET X=2
FOR I=1 TO 3
    LET X=FNY(X)-1
    PRINT X;
NEXT I
END
```

c.
```
DEF FNQ(A)=A+1
DEF FNR(A)=A+2
FOR X=0 TO 3
    LET A=FNR(FNQ(X))
    PRINT X;A
NEXT X
END
```

d.
```
DEF FNA(X,Y)=X/Y
FOR I=1 TO 2
    FOR J=1 TO 4
        PRINT FNA(J,I);
    NEXT J
    PRINT
NEXT I
END
```

e.
```
DEF FNI(P,R,T)=P*R/100*T
LET T=1/2
LET P=1000
FOR R=2 TO 5
    PRINT FNI(P,R,T)
NEXT R
END
```

3. *Write a single-statement function that:*

a. gives the total cost of an article listed at L dollars if the sales tax is 5%.
b. gives the simple interest earned in 3 months on $100 at an annual tax rate of R percent.
c. gives the cost of covering a floor whose length and width (in feet) are L and W, respectively, if the covering costs $12.95 per square yard.
d. gives the excise tax on a car assessed at E dollars if the tax rate is $27 per thousand.
e. converts degrees Celsius to degrees Fahrenheit [F = (9/5)C + 32].
f. converts degrees Fahrenheit to degrees Celsius.
g. converts feet to miles.
h. converts kilometers to miles (1 mi = 1609.3 m).
i. converts miles to kilometers.
j. rounds X to the third decimal place.
k. gives the average speed in miles per hour for a trip of D miles that takes T hours.
l. gives the selling price if an article whose list price is X dollars is selling at a discount of Y percent.
m. gives the cost in dollars of a trip of X miles in a car that averages 15 mph if gasoline costs Y cents per gallon.
n. gives the area of a circle of radius R.
o. gives the volume of a sphere of radius R.
p. gives the sine of an angle A degrees.

In Problems 4–14 write a program to perform each task specified.

4. Produce a three-column table showing the conversions from feet F to miles and then to kilometers for the values F = 1,000, 2,000, 3,000, . . . , 20,000. All output values are to be rounded to three decimal places. Write user-defined functions to perform the two conversions required and to do the rounding.

5. Produce a three-column table showing the conversions from grams G to ounces and then to pounds (1 oz = 28.3495 g) for G = 20, 40, 60, . . . , 400. All output values are to be rounded to three decimal places. Employ a user-defined function to do the rounding.

6. Produce a four-column table as follows. The first column is to contain the mileage figures 10 miles, 20 miles, . . . , 200 miles. The second, third, and fourth columns are to give the time in minutes required to travel these distances at the respective speeds 45 mph, 50 mph, and 55 mph. All output values are to be rounded to the nearest minute. Write user-defined functions to calculate the times and to do the rounding.

7. Following is the weekly inventory report of a sewing-supply wholesaler:

Item	Batches on hand Monday	Batches sold during week	Cost per batch	Sales price per batch
Bobbins	220	105	8.20	10.98
Buttons	550	320	5.50	6.95
Needles—1	450	295	2.74	3.55
Needles—2	200	102	7.25	9.49
Pins	720	375	4.29	5.89
Thimbles	178	82	6.22	7.59
Thread—A	980	525	4.71	5.99
Thread—B	1424	718	7.42	9.89

Produce a three-column report showing the item names, the number on hand at the end of the week, and the income per item. Denoting the markup by M and the quantity sold by Q, use a function FNP(M,Q) to calculate the income figures.

8. Using the inventory report shown in Problem 7, produce a five-column report showing the item names, the cost per batch, the sales price per batch, the dollar markup per batch, and the percent markup per batch. Denoting the markup by M and the cost by C, use a function FNA(M,C) to calculate the percent figures in the fifth column (M/C × 100 gives the required percentage). In addition, use a function to round the percentages to the nearest whole number.

9. Each salesperson for the Mod Dress Company is paid $140 a week plus 4.875% of all sales. Using the following sales figures, produce a five-column report showing the name, total sales, base pay, commission, and gross pay for each salesperson. All money amounts are to be rounded to the nearest cent.

| Name | Total sales for the week | |
	Type-1 items	Type-2 items
Barnes, James	$ 7826.28	$1198.42
Colby, Irene	415.92	2092.50
Cole, Bruce	2606.95	700.40
Drew, Nancy	350.42	301.27
Hilton, Lynn	1300.23	1521.32
Moore, Warren	268.92	399.92
Rich, Steven	2094.50	227.03
Skinner, Kerry	1102.37	303.52

10. Assume that a salesperson for the Mod Dress Company is paid $230 a week plus a commission of 3.125% on all Type-1 sales and 5.875% on all Type-2 sales. However, a salesperson whose total sales do not exceed $700 receives only the base pay of $230. Using the sales figures given

in Problem 9, produce a five-column report showing the name, base pay, Type-1 commission, Type-2 commission, and gross pay for each salesperson. All money amounts are to be rounded to the nearest cent.

11. Produce a three-column table showing the values of t, x, and y for $t = 0, 1, 2, \ldots, 10$, where $x = 5(1 + t)$ and $y = \sqrt{x^2 + 1}$. Determine x and y with user-defined functions.

12. Determine the area in square centimeters of any rectangle whose length and width in inches are typed by the user. Use a function to convert inches to centimeters.

13. Write a user-defined function FNAC(L) to determine the area of a circle with circumference L. Also write a function FNAS(L) to determine the area of a square with perimeter L. Use these two functions in a program to produce a three-column table showing L and the values of FNAC(L) and FNAS(L) for L = 1, 2, 3, ..., 10. Values are to be rounded to three decimal places.

14. A thin wire of length L is cut into two pieces of lengths L1 and L2. One piece is bent into the shape of a circle and the other into a square. Decide how the wire should be cut if the sum of the two enclosed areas is to be as small as possible. (Use the functions described in Problem 13.) How should the wire be cut if the sum of the areas is to be as large as possible?

13.5 Review True-or-False Quiz

1. If a QuickBASIC function exists that performs a needed task, you should use it even if it is a simple matter to write your own programming lines to perform this task.   T F
2. INT(5/2) <> 5/2.   T F
3. ABS(INT(−2.3)) = INT(ABS(−2.3)).   T F
4. INT(X) = FIX(X)   T F
5. CINT(42564.8) = 42565   T F
6. If A = ABS(INT(A)), then A is a positive integer.   T F
7. If N and D are positive numbers but not necessarily integers, QuickBASIC allows you to use the relational expression INT(N/D) = N/D to determine whether dividing N by D gives an integer.   T F
8. The relational expression INT(N) = N is true if N is either 0 or a positive integer and is false in all other cases.   T F
9. If the statement DEF FNC(P) = 2 * P + 2 appears in a program, then the function FNC may be referenced as often as desired and in exactly the same way as any built-in function is referenced.   T F
10. If the variable Y is used as a formal parameter in a DEF FN statement, then Y may be used elsewhere in the program for a different purpose.   T F
11. If FNF(X) is defined in a program, you may also define the function FNC(X) = 2 + FNF(X).   T F
12. The expression SIN(37 * 3.14159/180) may be used to find the sine of 37 degrees.   T F

14
More on Processing String Data

String processing is a major application area for computers. For this reason, modern programming languages are designed to simplify tasks that require processing string data. In this chapter, we describe the QuickBASIC functions and operations used with string data.

In Sections 14.1 through 14.3, we show how programming tasks that require examining parts of strings or combining given strings to build new ones can be carried out by using the string functions LEFT$, RIGHT$, and MID$, the string-related functions LEN and INSTR, and the concatenation operator +. In Section 14.5 we discuss how computers store string data and explain how this knowledge allows you to give meaning to string comparisons involving the relational operators <, <=, >, and >=. To this point, strings have been compared only to determine whether they are equal (=) or not equal (<>). In Section 14.6, we describe the conversion functions CHR$, ASC, STR$, and VAL and show how they can be used effectively for many programming tasks that would otherwise be very difficult. In Section 14.7, we return to the topic of user-defined functions begun in Chapter 13 and show how you can use the DEF FN statement to write your own string and string-related functions.

■ 14.1 String and String-Related Functions

This section describes four of the most useful functions included in QuickBASIC. The first determines the length of a string, and the other three are used to examine individual characters or groups of characters in a string.

The Length Function LEN

If **s** denotes a string, then LEN(**s**), read length of **s**, is the number of characters contained in **s**. Thus LEN("JOHN AND MARY") has the value 13. If Z$ = "JOHN AND MARY", then LEN(Z$) also has the value 13. As always, blanks are counted as characters. The **s** in LEN(**s**) is called the *argument* of the function and must be enclosed in parentheses as shown.

EXAMPLE 1   *Here is a program to display only the strings that contain exactly three characters:*

```
FOR I = 1 TO 6
   READ X$
   IF LEN(X$) = 3 THEN PRINT X$
NEXT I
DATA "THE", "I DO", "ONE", "OLD ", "THREE", "127"
END
```

Program output:
```
THE
ONE
127
```

Note that "I DO" has four characters—three letters and an embedded blank. Similarly, "OLD " has a trailing blank character.

EXAMPLE 2   *Here is a program to display a column of words lined up on the right:*

```
' Read words and display them right justified.

PRINT "12345678901234567890"     'For reference

READ A$
DO UNTIL A$ = "XXX"
   PRINT TAB(15 - LEN(A$)); A$
   READ A$
LOOP
END
DATA A,SHORT,LIST,OF,WORDS,XXX
```

Program output:
```
12345678901234567890
              A
          SHORT
           LIST
             OF
          WORDS
```

The TAB function tabs to position 15−1 for the letter A, to position 15−5 for SHORT, and so on. This effectively displays the column of words with the last character of each word in column position 14.

The String Function LEFT$

If **s** denotes a string and **n** an integer from 0 to LEN(**s**), then LEFT$(**s,n**) is the string consisting of the first **n** characters of **s**. Thus, LEFT$("JOHN AND MARY",4) has the value JOHN. If A$ = "JOHN AND MARY" and N = 4, then LEFT$(A$,N) also has the value JOHN. If N = 0, LEFT$(A$,N) is the null string. (How QuickBASIC handles LEFT$(**s,n**) when **n** is not an integer from 0 to LEN(**s**) is explained following Example 4.)

EXAMPLE 3   *Here is a program that extracts strings with the LEFT$ function.*

```
LET Y$ = "SEVEN"
FOR N = 1 TO LEN(Y$)
   PRINT LEFT$(Y$, N)
NEXT N
END
```

Program output:
```
S
SE
SEV
SEVE
SEVEN
```

EXAMPLE 4   *Here is a program that displays only words that begin with the prefix typed by the user.*

```
INPUT "TYPE A PREFIX: ", P$
PRINT
PRINT "WORDS BEGINNING WITH THE PREFIX "; P$; ":"
PRINT
```

```
FOR K = 1 TO 13
   READ A$
   IF LEFT$(A$, LEN(P$)) = P$ THEN PRINT TAB(6); A$
NEXT K
END
DATA ENABLE,ENACT,ENGAGE,ENSURE,ENDORSE
DATA HYPERACTIVE,HYPERMYSTICAL,HYPERNEUROTIC,HYPERPURE
DATA UNAFRAID,UNDO,UNEVEN,UNFOLD
```

Program output:
```
TYPE A PREFIX: UN

WORDS BEGINNING WITH THE PREFIX UN:

      UNAFRAID
      UNDO
      UNEVEN
      UNFOLD
```

REMARK
If you enter the prefix HYPER for P$, the IF condition

```
LEFT$(A$,LEN(P$))=P$
```

compares the first five characters of A$ with HYPER. But when the value UNDO is read for A$, A$ will have only *four* characters. As we explain following this example, LEFT$("UNDO",5) is the four-character string UNDO. Thus, with P$ = "HYPER" and A$ = "UNDO", the IF condition is false and UNDO is not displayed, as it shouldn't be. Thus, the program will work for any prefix you enter, not only for prefixes with fewer letters than the words in the DATA lines.

We have explained how the computer assigns to LEFT$(**s**,**n**) a substring of **s** in cases where **n** is an integer from 0 to LEN(**s**). If **n** is not an integer in this range, the PC rounds **n**, if necessary, to obtain an integer, say N. Then:

1. If N is greater than LEN(**s**) but no greater than 32767, LEFT$(**s**,**n**) is **s**.
2. If N is not in the range 0–32767, a fatal error occurs.

The String Function RIGHT$

If **s** denotes a string and **n** an integer from 0 to LEN(**s**) then RIGHT$(**s**,**n**) is the string consisting of the last **n** characters in **s**. Thus RIGHT$("JOHN AND MARY",4) has the value MARY, and RIGHT$("JOHN AND MARY",0) is the null string.

If **n** is not an integer from 0 to LEN(**s**), it is rounded, if necessary—say to N. N must be in the range 0–32767. If LEN(**s**) ≤ N ≤ 32767, then RIGHT$(**s**,**n**) is **s**.

EXAMPLE 5   *Here is a program that extracts strings with the RIGHT$ function.*

```
LET Y$ = "SEVEN"
FOR N = 1 TO LEN(Y$)
   PRINT RIGHT$(Y$, N)
NEXT N
END
```

Program output:
```
N
EN
VEN
EVEN
SEVEN
```

The String Function MID$

There are two forms of the MID$ function: If **s** denotes a string and **m** and **n** denote integers, then

1. MID$(**s,m,n**) is the string of **n** characters from **s** beginning with the **m**th character of **s**.
2. MID$(**s,m**) is the string consisting of all characters in **s** from the **m**th character on.

In the following illustration, A$ = "JOHN AND MARY":

Expression	Its value	Length of its value
MID$(A$,6,3)	AND	3
MID$(A$,6)	AND MARY	8
MID$(A$,6,8)	AND MARY	8
MID$(A$,6,1)	A	1
MID$(A$,6,0)	null string	0

EXAMPLE 6   *Here is a program to illustrate the two forms of the MID$ function.*

```
LET Y$ = "ABCD"
FOR K = 1 TO LEN(Y$)
    PRINT MID$(Y$, K, 1), MID$(Y$, K)
NEXT K
END
```

Program output:
```
A          ABCD
B          BCD
C          CD
D          D
```

REMARK   The use of MID$(Y$,K,1) to extract the Kth character of Y$ represents a common use of the MID$ function. The next example further illustrates this use of MID$.

EXAMPLE 7   *Here is a program to count the number of A's in a string A$ of any length.*

```
INPUT "TYPE ANY STRING"; A$
LET C = 0                      'Count of A's
FOR K = 1 TO LEN(A$)
    IF MID$(A$, K, 1) = "A" THEN C = C + 1
NEXT K
PRINT "NUMBER OF A'S IS"; C
END
```

Program output:
```
TYPE ANY STRING? ABRACADABRA
NUMBER OF A'S IS 5
```

The following special cases should be understood. When QuickBASIC encounters MID$(**s,m,n**) or MID$(**s,m**), it rounds **m** and **n**, if necessary, to obtain integers—say M and N.

M must be in the range 1–32767
N must be in the range 0–32767

If M and N are in these ranges, then:

1. If M > LEN(**s**), both forms give the null string.
2. If there are fewer than N characters from the Mth character of **s** on, MID$(**s,m,n**) gives the same substring as MID$(**s,m**); that is, all characters of **s** from the Mth character on.

MID$ as a Statement

You can also use MID$ to replace characters in one string by characters from another. The *statement*

```
MID$(T$, M, N) = S$
```

replaces N characters in T$, beginning at position M, by the first N characters in S$. The argument N may be omitted if the intention is to replace a portion of T$ with all of S$. Thus,

```
MID$(T$, M) = S$
```

is equivalent to

```
MID$(T$, M, LEN(S$)) = S$
```

Special cases are handled as follows:

1. If LEN(S$) is less than N, only LEN(S$) characters are replaced.
2. N can be in the range 0–32767.
3. The length LEN(T$) is never changed.
4. M *must* be in the range 1 to LEN(T$).

EXAMPLE 8   *This example illustrates MID$ as a statement.*

```
LET T$ = "abcdefgh"    'String to be changed
PRINT T$               'Display it.
LET S$ = "XYZ"         'Source of replacement characters

MID$(T$, 2, 1) = S$    'Change T$ beginning in position 2.
PRINT T$
MID$(T$, 8, 2) = S$    'Change T$ beginning in position 8.
PRINT T$
MID$(T$, 4) = S$       'Change T$ beginning in position 4.
PRINT T$
END
```

Program output:
```
abcdefgh
aXcdefgh
aXcdefgX
aXcXYZgX
```

The action of the three MID$ statements is as follows:

```
MID$(T$,2,1) = S$ changes T$ from abcdefgh to aXcdefgh
MID$(T$,8,2) = S$ changes T$ from aXcdefgh to aXcdefgX
  MID$(T$,4) = S$ changes T$ from aXcdefgX to aXcXYZgX
```

■ 14.2 Combining Strings (Concatenation)

The **concatenation operator +** allows you to combine two or more strings into a single string. Thus the statement

```
LET X$ = "PARA" + "MEDIC"
```

assigns the string PARAMEDIC to the variable X$. Similarly, if A$ = "PARA" and B$ = "MEDIC" the statement

```
LET X$ = A$ + B$
```

does exactly the same thing.

EXAMPLE 9   *Here is a program to illustrate the concatenation operator.*

```
LET X$ = "BIOLOGY"
LET Y$ = "ELECTRONICS"
LET Z$ = LEFT$(X$, 3) + RIGHT$(Y$, 4)
PRINT Z$
END
```

Program output:
```
BIONICS
```

Using only the functions LEFT$ and RIGHT$, we could have caused BIONICS to be displayed by the statement

```
PRINT LEFT$(X$, 3); RIGHT$(Y$, 4)
```

but we could not have assigned the string BIONICS to the variable Z$.

EXAMPLE 10   *Here is a program to assign the contents of A$ to B$, but in reverse order. For instance, if A$ = "AMNZ", then B$ will contain "ZNMA."*

```
INPUT "ENTER ANY STRING: ", A$     'Keyboard input
LET B$ = ""                        'Null string

' Using the concatenation operator, append the
' characters of A$, from last to first, to B$.

FOR K = LEN(A$) TO 1 STEP -1
   LET B$ = B$ + MID$(A$, K, 1)
NEXT K
PRINT A$; " IN REVERSE ORDER IS "; B$
END
```

Program output:
```
ENTER ANY STRING: RORRIM
RORRIM IN REVERSE ORDER IS MIRROR
```

The statement LET B$ = "" ensures that the program enters the FOR loop that appends letters to B$ with nothing in B$.

REMARK 1   The MID$ function allows you to display a string in reverse order. The concatenation operator is what allows you to assign the new string to B$.

REMARK 2   The program shown in this example illustrates the principal reason that programming languages allow the empty string. When you wish to determine a numerical sum by adding a list of numbers, you begin with a sum of zero; when you wish to build a new string by concatenating a list of characters or strings, you begin with the empty string.

14.3 The Search Function INSTR

Searching a string for a specific character or sequence of characters is a common programming task. For this reason, QuickBASIC provides the INSTR function to search one string for another automatically. For example, you can use

```
LET P = INSTR(1, A$, " ")
```

to determine the position P of the first blank in A$. The number 1 instructs the computer to begin the search with the first character in A$.

The general forms of the INSTR function are:

INSTR(**n, s, t**)
INSTR(**s, t**)

where **s** and **t** denote string expressions, and **n** denotes a numerical expression whose value is rounded to an integer that we'll also call **n**. The expression INSTR(**n, s, t**) has an integer value determined as follows. The string **s** is searched, beginning at position **n**, for the first occurrence of the string **t**. If **n** is omitted, the search begins at position 1.

1. If **t** is found, INSTR returns the first position in **s** at which the match occurs. Thus the expression

   ```
   INSTR("STOCKS AND BONDS", "ND")
   ```

   has the value 9; the search for ND begins in position 1 and is successful at position 9. The expression

   ```
   INSTR(10, "STOCKS AND BONDS", "ND")
   ```

   has the value 14; the search for ND begins in position 10 and is successful at position 14.

2. If **t** is not found, INSTR returns the value 0.
3. If **n** > LEN(**s**), INSTR returns the value 0.
4. The rounded value **n** must be in the range 1 to 32767.

EXAMPLE 11   *Here is a program to search the words in DATA lines for any string input at the keyboard.*

```
INPUT "FOR WHAT STRING ARE YOU LOOKING"; S$
PRINT
PRINT "THESE WORDS CONTAIN THE SPECIFIED STRING:"
READ WORD$
DO WHILE WORD$ <> "XXX"
   IF INSTR(WORD$, S$) > 0 THEN PRINT TAB(10); WORD$
   READ WORD$
LOOP
END
DATA THEORIZE,GUESS,HYPOTHESIZE,CONJECTURE
DATA XXX
```

Program output:
```
FOR WHAT STRING ARE YOU LOOKING? THE

THESE WORDS CONTAIN THE SPECIFIED STRING:
        THEORIZE
        HYPOTHESIZE
```

EXAMPLE 12   *Here is a program to interchange the first and last names given in the string EMILY DICKINSON.*

```
LET A$ = "EMILY DICKINSON"      'Assign name
PRINT A$                        'Display it.

LET P = INSTR(A$, " ")          'Position of blank

IF P = 0 THEN
   PRINT A$; " contains no blank."
ELSE
   LET F$ = LEFT$(A$, P - 1)    'Assign first name.
   LET L$ = MID$(A$, P + 1)     'Assign last name.
   LET A$ = L$ + ", " + F$      'Combine them.
   PRINT A$                     'Display new form.
END IF
END
```

Program output:
```
EMILY DICKINSON
DICKINSON, EMILY
```

REMARK

The technique illustrated in this example has two immediate applications: it gives you additional control over the precise form of your output, and it allows you to alphabetize a list of names even if first names are given first. Simply interchange first and last names, and then use a standard sorting algorithm to alphabetize your list (see Section 15.5).

EXAMPLE 13   *This example shows how INSTR can be used to allow abbreviations for input values.*

```
' --------------------------------------------------------
'   Assign a list of words to the string variable S$.

LET S$ = " APPLE   BANANA LEMON   PEACH   PLUM   "

' --------------------------------------------------------
'   Display words from abbreviations typed at keyboard.

INPUT "Enter an abbreviation (XXX to stop):", A$
LET A$ = UCASE$(A$)
DO UNTIL A$ = "XXX"
   LET P = INSTR(S$, " " + A$)
   IF P > 0 THEN
      PRINT A$; " stands for "; MID$(S$, P, 7)
   ELSE
      PRINT "Invalid abbreviation."
   END IF
   PRINT
   INPUT "Enter an abbreviation (XXX to stop):", A$
   LET A$ = UCASE$(A$)
LOOP
END
```

Program output:
```
Enter an abbreviation (XXX to stop):LE
LE stands for   LEMON

Enter an abbreviation (XXX to stop):PLU
PLU stands for   PLUM

Enter an abbreviation (XXX to stop):P
P stands for   PEACH

Enter an abbreviation (XXX to stop):XXX
```

Each word in S$ is preceded by a blank. Since the INSTR function searches S$ for the string " " + A$, this blank ensures that the abbreviation typed will be matched only with the beginnings of words included in S$. For instance, LE is matched with the LE in LEMON and not with the first occurrence of LE in APPLE.

Each word in S$ uses exactly 7 positions: the leading blank, the letters in the word, and trailing blanks, if needed. This ensures that the string MID$(S$,P,7) will give the entire word corresponding to the abbreviation typed by the user.

Note that the input value P gives PEACH, the first word in S$ that begins with P. To ensure that abbreviations are unique, you can require abbreviations with more than one letter.

REMARK

In this program, the input values APPLE, BANANA, LEMON, PEACH, and PLUM (or their abbreviations) give the respective P values 1, 8, 15, 22, and 29. You can check that the value of the expression $1 + (P - 1)/7$ for these P values is 1, 2, 3, 4, and 5, respectively. When using the SELECT CASE statement (Section 12.2), you may find that this method of assigning the numbers 1, 2, 3, and so on to different string input values can be helpful.

■ *14.4 Problems*

1. *Show the output of each program.*

a.
```
LET A$="CYBERNETIC"
PRINT LEFT$(A$,LEN(A$)/2)
END
```

b.
```
LET B$="A TO Z"
PRINT RIGHT$(B$,1);" TO ";LEFT$(B$,1)
END
```

c.
```
LET A$="CONSTRUCTION"
LET B$="SULTAN OF SWAT"
LET C$=LEFT$(A$,3)+LEFT$(B$,5)+RIGHT$(A$,4)
PRINT C$
END
```

d.
```
LET A$="BIOLOGY"
LET B$="PHYSICS"
LET C$=LEFT$(A$,3)
FOR I=1 TO LEN(B$)
    LET C$=C$+MID$(B$,I,1)
NEXT I
PRINT C$
END
```

e.
```
LET SP$=" "                'Space
READ X$
LET A=1 : B=INSTR(A,X$,SP$)
DO WHILE B>0
    PRINT MID$(X$,A,B-A)
    LET A=B+1 : B=INSTR(A,X$,SP$)
LOOP
PRINT MID$(X$,A)
DATA "Great Salt Lake Desert, Utah"
END
```

f.
```
LET S$="-ADD -LIST-STEP-STOP"
FOR K=1 TO 7
    READ C$
    IF LEN(C$) >=3 THEN
        LET P=INSTR(1,S$,"-"+C$)
        IF P>0 THEN PRINT MID$(S$,P+1,4)
    END IF
NEXT K
DATA ADD,LIST,STOP,START,S,ST,STE
END
```

g.
```
LET S$="-ADD -LIST-STEP-STOP"
FOR K=1 TO 4
    READ C$
    LET P=INSTR(1,S$,"-"+C$)
    LET N=1+(P-1)/5
    PRINT N;C$
NEXT K
DATA STEP,LIST,STOP,ADD
END
```

2. *Write a single QuickBASIC statement to perform each of the following tasks.*
  a. Display the first character of A$.
  b. Display the second character of A$.
  c. Display the last character of A$.
  d. Display the first three characters of A$.
  e. Display the last three characters of A$.
  f. Display the first and last characters of A$.
  g. Increase N by 1 if A$ and B$ have the same number of characters.
  h. Display the first character in A$ only if it's the same as the last character in A$.
  i. Assign the string SAME to X$ if the first two characters in A$ are the same.
  j. Display the string COMMA if A$ contains a comma. (Use INSTR.)
  k. Display the string NO SPACES if A$ contains no spaces. (Use INSTR.)
  l. Assign the first N characters of A$ to B$.
  m. A$ is a two-letter string. Interchange these letters to obtain the string B$.
  n. Interchange the first two characters in S$ to obtain T$.
  o. Create a string F$ consisting of the first three characters of G$ and the last three characters of H$.
  p. Display the string OK if the first character of A$, the second character of B$, and the third character of C$ spell "YES".
  q. Replace the fourth character of A$ by the character Y.

In Problems 3–15, write a program for each task specified.

3. Display any five-character string typed at the keyboard in reverse order. If the string does not contain exactly five characters, display nothing. Allow the user to try many strings, and stop the program when the user types DONE.
4. Display any string typed at the keyboard in reverse order. Stop the program when the user types DONE.
5. Examine all strings that appear in DATA lines to determine and display those that begin with whatever letter is input. Allow the user to try different letters during a single run, and stop the program when * is typed.
6. The user types two five-letter words. Compare them letter by letter. If two corresponding letters are different, display a dollar sign; otherwise, display the letter. If CANDY and CHIDE are typed, for example, the output should be C$$D$.
7. The user types two words to obtain a listing of those letters in the second word that are also in the first. If the user types STRING and HARNESS, for example, the output should be RNSS, since these four letters in the second word HARNESS are also in the first word STRING.
8. The user types a string that contains two words separated by a comma. Display the two words in reverse order without the comma. If the user types "PUCKETT,KIRBY", for example, the output should be KIRBY PUCKETT. Stop the program only when the user types DONE.
9. Include a list of names, with last names last, in DATA lines. Produce a listing of the names with last names first followed by a comma. Run your program with the given DATA lines. Note that

```
    BRICE, MARY ELLEN
```

is how MARY ELLEN BRICE should be displayed. You may assume that *last* names contain no blanks.

```
    DATA MARY ELLEN BRICE,MARK BRONSON,MARIA MANDELA
    DATA LIZ WALKER,LI-JUAN WEI,SUE ANN TILTON
    DATA ART ROBELLO,RONALD MACDONALD
    DATA END-OF-DATA
```

10. Input a string and change all occurrences of the letter Y to the letter M.
11. Read a list of words from DATA lines to determine the average number of letters per word.
12. Read a list of words from DATA lines, and display only the words with exactly N letters. N is to be input by the user, who should be allowed to try several different values for N during a single program run.

13. Read a list of strings appearing in DATA lines to determine how many times a particular letter or other character appears in this list. The letter or character is to be input by the user, who should be allowed to try several different characters during the same run. Stop the program if the user types END.

14. Display the words that appear in an English sentence, one per line. You may assume that words are separated by exactly one space, that the sentence ends with a period, and that no other punctuation is used. The sentence is to be input into a string variable. Stop the program only when the user types DONE. If the input sentence does not contain a period, inform the user of this fact. Try your program with the sentences

```
ALL GAUL IS DIVIDED INTO THREE PARTS.
WHERE IS THE PERIOD?
```

15. Carry out the task described in Problem 14 with the following difference: words may be separated by more than one space and may be followed by a comma, semicolon, or colon; and sentences may end with a period or a question mark. Inform the user if a sentence does not end with a period or question mark. Try your program with these sentences:

```
ALLOWED COMMANDS ARE ADD, LIST, STEP, AND STOP.
YOU MAY USE THE FOLLOWING: ADD, LIST, AND STOP.
IS ALL GAUL DIVIDED INTO THREE PARTS?
THERE IS NO PERIOD
```

■ *14.5 The QuickBASIC Character Set*

QuickBASIC allows several operations with string data that we have yet to explain. For instance, although we have used relational expressions such as A$ = B$ and A$ <> B$ to determine whether two strings are identical, we have not compared strings by using the other relational operators <, <=, >, and >=. As we explain shortly, there are many programming situations that require making such string comparisons. To understand these and other operations with strings described in Section 14.6, you will need some knowledge of how a computer stores string data in memory.

Whenever a program requires the use of a string, each character of the string is assigned a numerical value called its **numeric code.** It is these numerical values that are compared. As we would expect, the numeric code for the letter A is smaller than that for B, the numeric code for B is smaller than that for C, and so on. But it is not only letters that can be compared; each character has its own unique numeric code so that any two characters may be compared. One character is less than a second character if the numeric code of the first is less than the numeric code of the second.

The **ordering sequence** (or **collating sequence**) of numeric codes for the QuickBASIC character set is the ASCII (American Standard Code of Information Interchange) ordering sequence given in Appendix C. As mentioned in Section 10.4, many of these codes correspond to characters that are used only in screen displays. In this section, we will use only characters that are the same whether displayed on the screen or printed by a printer. These are shown in Table 14.1, which is included here for easy reference.

Using this ASCII ordering sequence, we have;

"G" < "P" since 71 < 80
"4" < "Y" since 52 < 89
"$" < "^" since 36 < 94
"8" < "?" since 56 < 63
"M" < "m" since 77 < 109
"Z" < "a" since 90 < 97

If strings that contain more than one character are to be compared, they are compared character by character beginning at the left. Strings that consist of uppercase letters of the alpha-

Table 14.1   **ASCII numeric codes 32–127**

Numeric code	Character	Numeric code	Character	Numeric code	Character	Numeric code	Character
032	(space)	056	8	080	P	104	h
033	!	057	9	081	Q	105	i
034	"	058	:	082	R	106	j
035	#	059	;	083	S	107	k
036	$	060	<	084	T	108	l
037	%	061	=	085	U	109	m
038	&	062	>	086	V	110	n
039	'	063	?	087	W	111	o
040	(	064	@	088	X	112	p
041	)	065	A	089	Y	113	q
042	*	066	B	090	Z	114	r
043	+	067	C	091	[	115	s
044	,	068	D	092	\	116	t
045	−	069	E	093	]	117	u
046	.	070	F	094	^	118	v
047	/	071	G	095	—	119	w
048	0	072	H	096	`	120	x
049	1	073	I	097	a	121	y
050	2	074	J	098	b	122	z
051	3	075	K	099	c	123	{
052	4	076	L	100	d	124	¦
053	5	077	M	101	e	125	}
054	6	078	N	102	f	126	~
055	7	079	O	103	g	127	⌂

bet are ordered just as they would appear in a dictionary, as are strings consisting only of lowercase letters. Here are some relational expressions and their truth values:

Relational expression	Truth value
"AMA" > "AM"	True
"Bat" < = "BAT"	False
"13N" < "14N"	True
"M24" < "M31"	True
"B2" < "A59"	False
"sect" > "Zen"	True
UCASE$ ("sect") > UCASE$ ("Zen")	False
"BEAL TOM" < "BEALS TOM"	True

In the last expression, the fifth character in "BEAL TOM" is the blank character (ASCII code 32), whereas the fifth character in "BEALS TOM" is S (ASCII code 83). Since 32 < 83, the relational expression is true. Note that "sect" > "Zen" is true even though sect appears before Zen in the dictionary.

EXAMPLE 14   *Here is a program segment to interchange the word contents of W1$ and W2$ if they are not in alphabetical order.*

```
'Interchange W1$ and W2$ if they
'are not in alphabetical order.

IF UCASE$(W1$) > UCASE$(W2$) THEN SWAP W1$, W2$

'Program continuation
```

The contents of W1$ and W2$ are in alphabetical order if UCASE$(W1$) ≤ UCASE$(W2$). Thus, the IF statement says to swap the contents of W1$ and W2$ if they are not in order. The statement

```
SWAP W1$, W2$
```

performs the same task as the three statements:

```
LET T$ = W1$
LET W1$ = W2$
LET W2$ = T$
```

REMARK

A program segment that interchanges two words when they are not in alphabetical order can be used in larger program segments (or procedures) to alphabetize lists of any length. Before doing this, you will need to understand how lists can be stored conveniently. This topic is covered in Chapter 15.

■

EXAMPLE 15

Here is a program to read both upper- and lowercase words that appear in DATA lines and display those that begin with a letter D to M.

```
PRINT "WORDS WITH FIRST LETTER D TO M:"
PRINT
READ W$                              'First word
DO WHILE W$ <> "END OF LIST"
    LET F$ = LEFT$(W$, 1)            'First letter in W$
    LET F$ = UCASE$(F$)                 'Convert to uppercase.
    IF F$ >= "D" AND F$ <= "M" THEN PRINT TAB(5); W$
    READ W$                          'Next word
LOOP
END
DATA WHITE,BLACK,YELLOW,RED,BLUE,ORANGE,GREEN
DATA pink,gray,magenta,beige,brown,violet,lime
DATA END OF LIST
```

Program output:
```
WORDS WITH FIRST LETTER D TO M:

    GREEN
    gray
    magenta
    lime
```

Each word from the data list is read into W$ and compared with the EOD tag END OF LIST. As indicated by the comments, the two LET statements in the DO loop assign the first letter of W$ to F$ and change this letter to uppercase. The IF statement then causes W$ to be displayed if its first letter F$ is a letter from D to M.

REMARK

The two statements

```
LET F$ = LEFT$(W$, 1)
LET F$ = UCASE$(F$)
```

can be replaced by the equivalent single statement

```
LET F$ = UCASE$(LEFT$(W$, 1))
```

■

■ *14.6 QuickBASIC Conversion Functions*

A **conversion function** is a function that converts values from one data type to another.

The function CHR$ described in Section 10.4 is an example of a conversion function; it converts integer numeric codes to characters. In this section, we describe three other conversion functions: the ASC function, which converts characters to their numeric codes, and the

STR$ and VAL functions, which are used to convert between numbers and strings whose contents denote numbers. As illustrated in the examples, conversion functions provide a convenient way to code several string-related programming tasks.

The ASCII Function ASC

The ASC function converts the first character in a string to its numeric code. For example, ASC("BROOK") = 66, the numeric code for B, and ASC("brook") = 98, the code for b. When used with a one-character string, ASC converts the character to its numeric code. Thus ASC("A") = 65 and ASC("+") = 43.

You will recall that CHR$ converts each numeric code to its corresponding character. Moreover, if N denotes a valid numeric code and if A$ denotes a single character, then

$$ASC(CHR\$(N)) = N \quad \text{and} \quad CHR\$(ASC(A\$)) = A\$$$

Thus, ASC and CHR$ are inverses of each other, provided that only valid numeric codes and single-character strings are used.

EXAMPLE 16   *Here is a program to find the position in the alphabet of letters typed at the keyboard.*

```
' This program displays the position in the
' alphabet of letters typed at the keyboard.

INPUT "Type a letter ($ to stop): ", L$        'Keyboard input
DO UNTIL L$ = "$"
   LET L$ = UCASE$(L$)                          'Convert to uc.
   IF L$ >= "A" AND L$ <= "Z" THEN              'Is it a letter?
      LET N = ASC(L$) - ASC("A") + 1            'Yes - display
      PRINT "Its position is"; N                ' its position.
   ELSE
      PRINT "Not a letter."                     'Not a letter
   END IF
   PRINT
   INPUT "Type a letter ($ to stop): ", L$      'Keyboard input
LOOP
END
```

Program output:
```
Type a letter ($ to stop): C
Its position is 3

Type a letter ($ to stop): z
Its position is 26

Type a letter ($ to stop): 5
Not a letter.

Type a letter ($ to stop): $
```

For each input value L$ (other than $, which ends the program), the first two lines in the DO loop convert L$ to uppercase and test whether L$ is in the alphabetical range A to Z. If it is, the THEN block

```
LET N = ASC(L$) - ASC("A") + 1
PRINT "Its position is"; N
```

is executed. The numeric codes for the uppercase letters A to Z are 65 to 90, respectively. Thus, for the first input value C, we have ASC(L$) = 67, so N = ASC(L$) − ASC("A") + 1 gives N = 67 − 65 + 1 = 3, the correct position for C.

REMARK 1   Since the numeric codes for A to Z are 65 to 90, it would be correct (but not necessarily better) to replace the IF condition with

```
ASC(L$) >= 65 AND ASC(L$) <= 90
```

REMARK 2

If the user enters CAT for L$, the program will display its position as 3. Remember, ASC(L$) gives the numeric code of the first character in L$. To handle input strings with more than one character, simply change the IF condition to

```
L$ >= "A" AND L$ <= "Z" AND LEN(L$) = 1
```

The Value Function VAL

The VAL function converts a string whose contents represent a number to its numerical form. After ignoring leading blanks, it converts a string up to its first nonnumerical character into its numerical value. For example:

Quick BASIC statement	Value assigned to A
LET A = VAL(" 29.04")	29.04
LET A = VAL("537.2 FEET")	537.2
LET A = VAL(" 1.234E2XYZ")	123.4
LET A = VAL("THREE")	0
LET A = VAL("−123")	−123
LET A = VAL("+123")	123

If no number occurs before the first nonnumerical character, VAL gives the value 0. Thus VAL("THREE") = 0 as shown.

EXAMPLE 17 *This example illustrates the VAL function.*

```
' This program reads the following data
' to find the total number of tools.

'    12345678901234567890         'For data alignment
DATA HAMMERS 320 SHELF X
DATA PLIERS  100 SHELF L
DATA SAWS     57 SHELF B
DATA END OF DATA

LET TOTAL = 0                     'Start with 0 total.
READ X$
DO WHILE X$ <> "END OF DATA"
   LET ITEM$ = LEFT$(X$, 8)       'Get item name.
   LET C$ = MID$(X$, 9, 3)        'Get the count as string.
   PRINT ITEM$; C$                'Display item and count.
   LET TOTAL = TOTAL + VAL(C$)    'Add count to TOTAL
   READ X$
LOOP
PRINT "-----------"
PRINT "TOTAL   "; TOTAL
END
```

Program output:
```
HAMMERS 320
PLIERS  100
SAWS     57
-----------
TOTAL   477
```

For each value read for X$ (other than END OF DATA), the first two statements in the DO loop

```
LET ITEM$ = LEFT$(X$, 8)       'Get item name.
LET C$ = MID$(X$, 9, 3)        'Get the count as string.
```

assign the first 8 characters of X$ to ITEM$ and assign characters 9, 10, and 11 to C$. Thus, for X$ = "HAMMERS 320 SHELF X", we have

```
ITEM$ = "HAMMERS "
   C$ = "320"
```

The PRINT statement then displays these two strings, as shown in the output, and the line

```
TOTAL = TOTAL + VAL(C$)
```

converts the string C\$ = "320" to the numerical value 320 and adds it to TOTAL. This process is carried out for each datum to give the total shown in the output.

The String Function STR$

The function STR\$ reverses the process just described for VAL—it converts a numerical value to a string. If the number is positive, the string representation has a leading blank. For example, the statements

```
LET A$ = STR$(-234.6)
LET B$ = STR$(234.6)
```

assign the six-character string "−234.6" to A\$ and assign the six-character string " 234.6" to B\$. If you need to display a positive numerical value X without the leading blank, you can use

```
PRINT MID$(STR$(X), 2)
```

For instance, the two lines

```
LET A=15.37 : B=10
PRINT MID$(STR$(A),2);"+";MID$(STR$(B),2);"=";MID$(STR$(A+B),2)
```

produce the output

```
15.37+10=25.37
```

with no blank spaces, as there would be if we had used

```
PRINT A; "+"; B; "="; A + B
```

EXAMPLE 18 *Here is a program to display the individual digits in any number, positive or negative.*

```
INPUT "Type a number (0 to stop): ", X
DO UNTIL X = 0
   LET X$ = STR$(X)                        'Convert to string.
   PRINT "Its digits are ";
   FOR K = 2 TO LEN(X$)
      LET D$ = MID$(X$, K, 1)              'Kth position
      IF D$ <> "." THEN PRINT D$; " ";     'Display digit
   NEXT K
   PRINT : PRINT
   INPUT "Type a number (0 to stop): ", X
LOOP
END
```

Program Output:
```
Type a number (0 to stop): -102.9
Its digits are 1 0 2 9

Type a number (0 to stop): +123.005
Its digits are 1 2 3 0 0 5

Type a number (0 to stop): 12345
Its digits are 1 2 3 4 5

Type a number (0 to stop): 0
```

■ *14.7 User-Defined Functions Involving String Data*

QuickBASIC allows you to use the DEF FN statement to define your own string and string-related functions. To illustrate, the statement

```
DEF FNNAME$ (A$, B$) = A$ + " " + B$
```

defines a string function called FNNAME$ whose value for any two strings A$ and B$ is the concatenation of the strings with a separating blank. To reference (or *call*) this function, you must use the form

FNNAME$(**string1**,**string2**)

where **string1** and **string2** denote string expressions whose values are to be substituted for A$ and B$ in the function definition. Thus, if FIRST$ = "CLYDE" and SECOND$ = "DREXLER", the statement

```
PRINT FNNAME$(FIRST$, SECOND$)
```

will display

```
CLYDE DREXLER
```

An example of a user-defined string-related function is

```
DEF FNP(L$) = ASC(UCASE$(L$)) - ASC("A") + 1
```

This statement defines a numerical function FNP that gives the position in the alphabet of any letter L$ (see Example 16, Section 14.6).

The general form of the DEF FN statement given in Section 13.3 applies to both numerical and string functions. As with numerical functions, string functions that cannot be defined with a single expression should be coded as FUNCTION procedures. The following examples illustrate how two of the programming tasks considered previously might be coded by using single-statement, user-defined functions.

EXAMPLE 19   *Here is a program to display the names read from DATA lines in two ways, first name first and last name first.*

```
'***************************************************
'                 FUNCTION DEFINITIONS

DEF FNFIRSTLAST$ (A$, B$) = B$ + " " + A$
DEF FNLASTFIRST$ (A$, B$) = A$ + ", " + B$


'***************************************************
'  DISPLAY COLUMN HEADINGS AND ASSIGN FORMAT STRING

PRINT "FIRST LAST            LAST FIRST"
PRINT "-------------------   -------------------- "
F$ = "\                  \   \                  \ "

'***************************************************
'        READ DATA AND DISPLAY TABLE VALUES

READ C$, D$
DO WHILE C$ <> "XXXX"
   PRINT USING F$; FNFIRSTLAST$(C$, D$); FNLASTFIRST$(C$, D$)
   READ C$, D$
LOOP
END

'*********************
'    D   A   T   A
DATA WORTHY,JAMES
DATA DIVAC,VLADE
```

```
DATA GREEN,A.C.
DATA SCOTT,BYRON
DATA THREATT,SEDALE
DATA XXXX,ZZZZ
```

Program output:

```
FIRST LAST                 LAST FIRST
-------------------        -------------------
JAMES WORTHY               WORTHY, JAMES
VLADE DIVAC                DIVAC, VLADE
A.C. GREEN                 GREEN, A.C.
BYRON SCOTT                SCOTT, BYRON
SEDALE THREATT             THREATT, SEDALE
```

EXAMPLE 20   ***Here is a program to display the letters of the alphabet.***

```
'-------------------------------------------
' Function to return Nth letter of alphabet

DEF FNLETTER$ (N) = CHR$(N + ASC("A") - 1)
'-------------------------------------------

PRINT "THE ALPHABET:"
FOR P = 1 TO 26
    PRINT FNLETTER$(P);
NEXT P
END
```

Program output:
```
THE ALPHABET:
ABCDEFGHIJKLMNOPQRSTUVWXYZ
```

To display the alphabet in lowercase letters, simply change ASC("A") in the function definition to ASC("a").

■ *14.8 Problems*

1. *Show the output for each program.*

a.
```
FOR I=1 TO 3
    READ A$,B$
    IF A$<=B$ THEN PRINT A$
NEXT I
DATA M,MO,A,AA,M,KANT
END
```

b.
```
FOR J=1 TO 3
    READ C$,D$
    IF C$>D$ THEN C$=D$
    PRINT C$;D$
NEXT J
DATA CAT,DOG,7,10,MAN,BEAST
END
```

c.
```
LET M$="MIDDLE"
FOR N=1 TO 4
    READ A$
    IF A$>M$ AND A$<"ZZZ" THEN A$="LAST"
    PRINT A$
NEXT N
DATA HARRY,ALICE,PAUL,ROSE
END
```

d.
```
LET A$="31"
LET B$="31"
PRINT A$;"+";B$;"=";
PRINT VAL(A$)+VAL(B$)
END
```

e.
```
LET L$="E"
LET N=ASC(L$)-ASC("A")+1
PRINT L$;N
END
```

f. LET D$="7"
   LET N=ASC(D$)-ASC("0")
   PRINT D$;N
   END

g. FOR K=48 to 58
      PRINT CHR$(K);
   NEXT K
   END

h. 'W=NUMBER OF WINS
   'G=NUMBER OF GAMES PLAYED
   LET W=42
   LET G=63
   LET B$=STR$(W)+" WINS AND "
   LET C$=STR$(G-W)+" LOSSES GIVES A PERCENTAGE OF "
   LET D$=STR$(INT(1000*W/G+0.5)/1000)
   PRINT B$;C$;D$
   END

i. DEF FNXT$(D$)=CHR$(ASC(D$)+1)
   FOR N-1 TO 7
      READ X$
      PRINT FNXT$(X$);
   NEXT N
   DATA B,N,Q,Q,D,B,S
   END

j. DEF FNPRE$(X$)=CHR$(ASC(X$)-1)
   LET L$=":"
   FOR N=1 TO 10
      LET L$=FNPRE$(L$)
      PRINT L$;
   NEXT N
   END

k. DEF FNV(X$)=VAL(LEFT$(X$,2))
   LET COUNT=0
   FOR N=1 TO 3
      READ A$
      LET COUNT=COUNT+FNV(A$)
   NEXT N
   PRINT "COUNT:";COUNT
   DATA 12 DUCKS
   DATA 15 GEESE
   DATA 20 GULLS
   END

In Problems 2–11, write a program for each task specified.

2. Include a list of English words in DATA lines. First, display those words beginning with a letter from A to M; then display the rest.

3. Write a program that contains the following DATA lines:

```
DATA 9
DATA MARIAN EVANS,JAMES PAYN,JOSEPH CONRAD
DATA EMILY DICKINSON,HENRY THOREAU,JOHN PAYNE
DATA JOHN FOX,MARY FREEMAN,GEORGE ELIOT
```

Read the names twice. On the first pass, display only those names with a last name beginning with a letter from A to M. Display the remaining names on the second pass.

4. For any string typed at the keyboard, display THE FIRST CHARACTER IS A LETTER or THE FIRST CHARACTER IS NOT A LETTER, whichever message is correct. Allow the user to type many strings during a single program run, and stop the program when $ is typed.

5. Include a list of English words in DATA lines. Allow a user to type any two words to obtain a listing of all words alphabetically between them. Stop the program when both input words are the same.

6. Repeat Problem 5, but this time, assume that the words are in alphabetical order and make use of this fact.

7. For any input string, display two columns. The first column is to contain the characters in the string and the second their numeric codes. Allow the user to try many strings during a single program run.

8. Input any decimal number and display its digits backward. For example, if 764.38 is typed, the output should be 83467; if −124.6 is typed, the output should be 6421.

9. Display any word typed at the keyboard with its first letter uppercase and all other letters lowercase. However, if a character other than a letter is included, display nothing and allow the user to enter another word. Stop the program only when the user types DONE.

10. Each of the following DATA lines includes a person's name, the hours worked this week, and the hourly wage. (The first line is for reference only, and the last contains the EOD tag.)

```
'      12345678901234567890123 4567890
DATA HARRY SMITHSON     36     8.25
DATA SUSAN COREY        25     6.00
DATA ABIGAIL ADAMS      32     6.85
DATA BERT REGIS         32     7.00
DATA EMERSON FOSDICK    40     9.50
DATA BART BARTLETT      20     5.25
DATA END-OF-DATA
```

Produce a four-column report showing the name, hours worked, hourly rate, and gross pay for each person. Time and a half is earned for all hours over 32.

11. Input two positive integers A and B for which A < B. The program should display the decimal expansion of A/B to N places where the positive integer N is also input during program execution. For example, if 1, 8, and 10 are input for A, B, and N, respectively, the output should be .1250000000.

■ *14.9 Review True-or-False Quiz*

1. If A is any number, LEN(A) will give the number of digits in A.   T F

2. If LEN(X$) = LEN(Y$), then X$ = Y$.   T F

3. LEN(X$ + Y$) = LEN(X$) + LEN(Y$)   T F

4. B$ = LEFT$(B$,LEN(B$)).   T F

5. Although it may be convenient to use the functions LEFT$ and RIGHT$, they are not necessary. The function MID$ can always be used in their place.   T F

6. If X$ = "MADAM", then MID$(X$,3,3) has the value "D".   T F

7. The statement

```
    IF A$>="A" AND A$<="Z" THEN PRINT "OK"
```

will display OK whenever the first character in A$ is an uppercase letter of the alphabet.   T F

8. The statement PRINT CHR$(1) will display the letter A.   T F

9. ASC("Z") − ASC("A") = 25   T F

10. ASC("3") = ASC("2") + 1   T F

11. ASC(CHR$(32)) = 32   T F

12. VAL(STR$(55.23)) = 55.23   T F

13. CHR$(ASC("a") + 32) = "A"   T F

14. The statement

```
    IF STR$(VAL(A$))=A$ THEN PRINT "OK"
```

will display OK whatever the value of A$.   T F

15. The statement

```
    IF VAL(STR$(N))=N THEN PRINT "OK"
```

will display OK whatever the numerical value of N, even if N has a negative value.   T F

15
Arrays

In this chapter, you will encounter several programming situations for which the numerical and string variables we have been using are inadequate. To illustrate, suppose that many words are contained in a data list and you must determine counts of the number of words that begin with each letter of the alphabet so that these counts can be used later in the program. If only the numerical variables considered to this point were available, you would need 26 different variable names, one for each of the 26 counts. If, instead of words, the data list contains integers in the range 1–100 and you must determine counts of the number of 1s, of 2s, of 3s, and so on, you would need 100 different variables, one for each of the 100 counts. Certainly, writing a program with 100 (or even 26) different variable names would be a long and tedious task.

To be useful, a programming language must provide the means for handling such problems efficiently. QuickBASIC meets this requirement with the inclusion of the **array** data structure. As you work through the material in this chapter, you will learn how an array can be used to store an entire collection of values under a single name and how the values stored in an array are referenced simply by specifying their positions in the array. The array data structure not only provides the means to resolve the difficulties cited, but it also provides a way to simplify significantly many programming tasks involving both large and small quantities of data.

In Sections 15.1 and 15.2 we explain how data are placed into arrays and how these data are referenced, and we illustrate how arrays can be used in certain programming tasks that involve lists of numbers or lists of strings. In Section 15.4, we show how arrays are passed between calling units and procedures, and in Section 15.5, we describe a sorting algorithm that can be used to rearrange string data into alphabetical order, or numerical data into either ascending or descending order. The application of arrays in programming tasks that involve tables of values (other than lists) is taken up in Sections 15.7 and 15.9.

■ 15.1 One-Dimensional Arrays

A **one-dimensional array**, or list, is an ordered collection of items in the sense that there is a first item, a second item, and so on. For example, if you took five quizzes during a semester and received grades of 71, 83, 96, 77, and 92, you have a list in which the first grade is 71, the second grade is 83, and so forth. In mathematics, we might use the following subscripted notation:

$$g_1 = 71$$
$$g_2 = 83$$

$$g_3 = 96$$
$$g_4 = 77$$
$$g_5 = 92$$

Since the QuickBASIC character set does not include such subscripts, the notation is changed to the following:

$$G(1) = 71$$
$$G(2) = 83$$
$$G(3) = 96$$
$$G(4) = 77$$
$$G(5) = 92$$

We say that the *name* of the array is G, that G(1), G(2), G(3), G(4), and G(5) are **subscripted variables,** and that 1, 2, 3, 4, and 5 are the *subscripts* of G. G(1) is read **G sub 1,** and in general G(N) is read **G sub N.** G(1), G1, and G are all different variables and can be used in the same program; the computer has no problem distinguishing among them, even though we might.

The array G can be visualized as follows:

	1	**2**	**3**	**4**	**5**
G	71	83	96	77	92

The name of the array appears to the left, the subscripts are above each entry, and the entries are inside, just below their subscripts. Names that are acceptable for simple variables are also admissible array names.

To declare to the computer that your program will use the subscripted variables G(1) through G(5), you would include the DIM (for **dimension**) statement

```
DIM G(1 TO 5)
```

so that it is encountered before any of the subscripted variables are referenced. Early versions of QuickBASIC require the form

```
DIM G(5)
```

The general forms of the DIM statement are given and explained in detail in Section 15.2. If you include the statement

```
DIM G(1 TO 100)      [or DIM G(100)]
```

your program can reference any or all of the subscripted variables G(1) through G(100).

The value of a subscripted variable—that is, an entry in an array—is referenced in a program just as values of simple variables (variables with no subscripts) are referenced. For example, the two LET statements

```
LET G(1)=71
LET G(2)=G(1)+12
```

assign 71 to the subscripted variable G(1) and 83 to G(2); that is, 71 and 83 are assigned as the first and second entries of array G. To allow the user to enter a value for G(1) at the keyboard, you can use the statement

```
INPUT G(1)
```

The principal advantage in using subscripted variables is that the subscripts can be specified by using variables or other numerical expressions, rather than just integer constants. For instance, if N has the value 3, then G(N) refers to G(3), G(2 * N) refers to G(6), and G(2 * N − 1) refers to G(5). It is common practice to refer to *subscript expressions* such as N, 2 * N, and 2 * N − 1 as the subscripts, even though the actual subscripts are the integer values of these expressions.

EXAMPLE 1   *Here is a program segment to assign values to G(1), G(2), G(3), G(4), and G(5).*

```
DIM G(1 TO 5)
FOR J = 1 TO 5
    READ G(J)
NEXT J
DATA 71,83,96,77,92
```

On each pass through the loop, the index J of the loop serves as the subscript. The first time through the loop, J has the value 1, so the READ statement assigns the first data value 71 to G(1). Similarly, G(2) through G(5) are assigned their respective values during the remaining four passes through the loop.

REMARK 1   To allow the user to enter the five array values at the keyboard, you can use

```
FOR J=1 TO 5
    INPUT G(J)
NEXT J
```

REMARK 2   Having assigned five values to array G—that is, to the subscripted variables G(1) through G(5)—you can process these values just as you process any other numerical variables. For instance, if you need to find and display the sum of the five entries in G, you can continue the program by writing

```
LET SUM = 0
FOR J = 1 TO 5
    LET SUM = SUM + G(J)
NEXT J
PRINT "SUM OF THE 5 QUIZ SCORES:"; SUM
```

REMARK 3   Notice that we use the same control variable (J) for each FOR loop. Although we could have used different control variables, there is no good reason for doing so. There is reason, however, for using the same one. In each loop, J serves the *same* purpose—it provides subscripts for array G; hence, the program will be easier to read if the *same* name is used.

Just as with simple variables, values assigned to subscripted variables are retained until they are changed in another programming line. Thus, individual entries in an array can be changed without affecting the rest of the array. For instance, if G has been assigned values as in Example 1

	1	2	3	4	5
G	71	83	96	77	92

the statement

```
LET G(1) = G(5)
```

will assign the value 92 of G(5) to G(1) but will not change G(5). The modified array will be as follows [note that the previous value 71 of G(1) is lost]:

	1	2	3	4	5
G	92	83	96	77	92

EXAMPLE 2   *Here is a program segment that modifies each entry of the array G, and then stores the resulting values in a second array M, but in the reverse order.*

```
'Increase array G entries by 2.

FOR K = 1 TO 5
    LET G(K) = G(K) + 2
NEXT K
```

```
'Create array M.

DIM M(1 TO 5)
FOR K = 1 TO 5
   LET M(K) = G(6 - K)
NEXT K
```

Let's assume that before the execution of this program segment, values are read into array G as in Example 1. Pictorially,

	1	2	3	4	5
G	71	83	96	77	92

The first FOR loop adds 2 to each entry in G:

	1	2	3	4	5
G	73	85	98	79	94

The second FOR loop creates a new array M. For K = 1, the assignment statement is LET M(1) = G(5); for K = 2, LET M(2) = G(4); and so on. Thus, after execution of this second loop, M is as follows:

	1	2	3	4	5
M	94	79	98	85	73

REMARK 1   The two DIM statements

```
DIM G(1 TO 5)
DIM M(1 TO 5)
```

can be combined into the single statement

```
DIM G(1 TO 5), M(1 TO 5)
```

REMARK 2   Creating new arrays that are modifications of existing arrays is a common programming task. In this example, the entries in the array M are a rearrangement of the entries in array G. Note that the creation of array M by the second FOR loop in no way modifies the existing array G.

REMARK 3   Although it is common practice to refer to the symbols G(K), M(K), and G(6 − K) as variables, remember that the actual variable names are G(1), G(2), G(3), and so on. Each time the LET statements are executed, K has a particular value that indicates which of these variables is being referenced.

The subscript expression that appears within the parentheses to indicate the position in an array (K and 6 − K in Example 2 and J in Example 1) can be any QuickBASIC numerical expression. Thus the following are all admissible:

```
A(7)              X(I + 1)
B(7 + 3/2)        Z(100 − N)
```

When the computer encounters a subscript, the subscript is evaluated; if it is not an integer, it is rounded to the nearest integer.

QuickBASIC allows string arrays for storing strings as well as numerical arrays for storing numbers. The only difference is that string array names must end with a $. The use of subscripts is the same as for numerical arrays.

EXAMPLE 3   *Here is a program segment to read string values into the string array DAY$.*

```
DIM DAY$(1 TO 7)
FOR N = 1 TO 7
   READ DAY$(N)
NEXT N
DATA SUNDAY,MONDAY,TUESDAY,WEDNESDAY
DATA THURSDAY,FRIDAY,SATURDAY
```

When N is 1, the first datum SUNDAY is read into DAY$(1); when N is 2, MONDAY is read into DAY$(2); and so on. At this point, we can use the string values stored in DAY$—that is, the values of the subscripted variables DAY$(1) through DAY$(7)—just as the values of any string variables can be used. For instance, if we continue the program with the statements

```
INPUT "ENTER DAY OF WEEK (1-7): ", D
PRINT "YOU SELECTED "; DAY$(D); "."
```

and enter 7 in response to the INPUT statement, the computer will display

```
ENTER DAY OF WEEK (1-7): 7
YOU SELECTED SATURDAY.
```

REMARK 1   Since the variable D used in the INPUT and PRINT statements represents a day of the week (1–7), we could have used the more descriptive name DAY. Had we done this, the PRINT statement would have been written

```
PRINT "YOU SELECTED "; DAY$(DAY); "."
```

The computer has no difficulty with the expression DAY$(DAY). It correctly interprets DAY as the name of a simple numerical variable whose value gives the position (subscript) of an entry in the string array DAY$. Thus, with DAY = 7, DAY$(DAY) refers to DAY$(7).

REMARK 2   The array DAY$ can be pictured as shown previously for array G:

	1	2	3	4	5	6	7
DAY$	SUNDAY	MONDAY	TUESDAY	WEDNESDAY	THURSDAY	FRIDAY	SATURDAY

There is no special significance in the placement of the array entries along a line. You may find it more convenient to think of the array as follows:

DAY$

1	SUNDAY
2	MONDAY
3	TUESDAY
4	WEDNESDAY
5	THURSDAY
6	FRIDAY
7	SATURDAY

The two diagrams contain the same information.

In each of Examples 1–3, we used a FOR loop to read values into an array. If you know exactly how many values are to be stored in an array, a FOR loop provides the most convenient way to do it. Thus, if a table of values to be read into one or more arrays appears in

DATA statements, and if the DATA are preceded by a data count, you would read the count into a simple numerical variable and use its value as the terminal value of a FOR loop that reads the data into the array or arrays.

The next two examples illustrate a common method used to store data in arrays when the data are given in DATA lines that end with an EOD tag rather than being preceded by a count.

EXAMPLE 4   *Here is a program segment to read a list of words into an array named WORDS$.*

```
' -----------------------
'     D   A   T   A

DATA RED, BLUE, YELLOW
DATA GREEN, PURPLE, VIOLET
DATA XXX

' ---------------------------------
' Read data into the array WORDS$
' and find the word count COUNT.

DIM WORDS$(1 TO 20)                'Declare array
LET COUNT = 1                      'Array subscript
READ WORDS$(COUNT)                 'Read first word.
DO UNTIL WORDS$(COUNT) = "XXX"
   LET COUNT = COUNT + 1           'Next subscript.
   READ WORDS$(COUNT)              'Read next word.
LOOP

' ----------------------------------------------------
' Subtract 1 from COUNT to get actual word count.

LET COUNT = COUNT - 1
```

The variable COUNT provides the successive subscripts 1, 2, 3, and so on for the statement

```
READ WORDS$(COUNT)
```

Each value read by this statement is compared with the EOD tag XXX. If WORDS$(COUNT) is not XXX, the two statements in the body of the DO loop increase COUNT by 1 and read the next word into the next array position.

When the EOD tag is read, we have WORDS$(COUNT)="XXX". Thus, the UNTIL condition is true and program control passes to the statement that follows the LOOP statement. At this point, COUNT and the array WORDS$ are as follows (notice that the EOD tag XXX is in position COUNT of array WORDS$):

COUNT = 7   (One more than the number of words)

WORDS$

1	RED
2	BLUE
3	YELLOW
4	GREEN
5	PURPLE
6	VIOLET
7	XXX

The statement

```
LET COUNT = COUNT - 1
```

then decreases COUNT by 1 so that COUNT gives the number of values read into the array WORDS$, exclusive of the EOD tag XXX. In any subsequent processing of array WORDS$, we can use COUNT to denote its size. For example, we could display the words stored in array WORDS$ with this FOR loop:

```
FOR W = 1 TO COUNT
    PRINT WORDS$(W)
NEXT W
```

REMARK   The statement DIM WORDS$(1 TO 20) allows the program to use the subscripted variables WORDS$(1), WORDS$(2), up to WORDS$(20). Since the program stores the EOD tag XXX in the array, nineteen words at most can be included in the DATA statements. If more words are included, the program will execute the statement.

```
READ WORDS$(COUNT)
```

with COUNT = 21. This will cause a fatal *Subscript out of range* error. In many situations, the simplest way to avoid such a fatal error is to specify very large subscripts in DIM statements—for example, use DIM WORDS$(1 TO 1000). Another way to avoid the fatal error is explained following Example 5.

EXAMPLE 5   *Here is a program segment to read numerical and string data into arrays.*

```
'------------------------------------------------
'       DATA: Information on incoming flights.

' Flight number, Point of origin, Arrival time
DATA 53,  MIAMI,    "8:15 AM"
DATA 172, ATLANTA,  "9:20 AM"
DATA 122, NEW YORK, "11:30 AM"
DATA 62,  MONTREAL, "2:20 PM"
DATA 303, HOUSTON,  "4:45 PM"
DATA 291, CHICAGO,  "6:15 PM"
DATA 0


'------------------------------------------------
'               Declare arrays.

DIM FLIGHT(1 TO 50)     'Array of flight numbers
DIM ORIGIN$(1 TO 50)    'Array of points of origin
DIM ARRIVE$(1 TO 50)    'Array of arrival times


'------------------------------------------------
'       Read flight information into arrays.

LET COUNT = 1                           'Array subscript
READ FLIGHT(COUNT)                      'First flight number
DO UNTIL FLIGHT(COUNT) = 0
    READ ORIGIN$(COUNT), ARRIVE$(COUNT) 'Flight info
    LET COUNT = COUNT + 1               'Increase subscript
    READ FLIGHT(COUNT)                  'Next flight number
LOOP

LET COUNT = COUNT - 1                   'Actual data count
```

As in the program of Example 4, the variable COUNT provides the successive subscripts 1, 2, 3, and so on. In this program, the first READ statement (just before the DO loop) reads a flight number and compares it with the EOD tag 0 before reading the point of origin and arrival time for the flight. Since the first flight number, 53, is not 0, the DO loop is entered.

The three statements in the body of the loop read the point of origin and arrival time into ORIGIN$(COUNT) and ARRIVE$(COUNT), increase the subscript COUNT by 1, and read the next flight number. The loop is repeated until the EOD tag 0 is read for FLIGHT(COUNT).

REMARK 1 In this example, the information for each flight consists of three values: the flight number, the point of origin, and the arrival time. When reading such grouped data into arrays, it is common practice to read one of the values [we read FLIGHT(COUNT)] in each group and test it for an EOD tag before reading the other values.

REMARK 2 The quotation marks used in the DATA statements are required, since QuickBASIC uses the colon (:) as a separator when two or more statements are included in a single programming line.

QuickBASIC allows you to use numerical expressions other than constants to specify ranges of subscripts for arrays. For example, if the variable COUNT has the value 6, the statement

```
DIM WORDS$(1 TO COUNT)
```

specifies that the integers 1 to 6 are allowed as subscripts for the array WORDS$. Thus, if the data in the program of Example 4 were given as

```
' ------------------------
'    D   A   T   A

DATA 6
DATA RED, BLUE, YELLOW
DATA GREEN, PURPLE, VIOLET
```

we could use the two statements

```
READ COUNT              'Word count
DIM WORDS$(1 TO COUNT)  'Declare array
```

to declare an array WORDS$ with exactly the subscripts needed. Moreover, the following simplified loop will now read the data into array WORDS$:

```
FOR K = 1 TO COUNT
   READ WORDS$(COUNT)
LOOP
```

Arrays whose subscript ranges are specified by numerical expressions other than constants are called **dynamic arrays**: the computer allocates memory space for the arrays *dynamically,* that is, during program execution. Memory space for arrays whose subscript ranges are specified by numerical constants (as in Examples 1 through 4) is allocated before program execution begins. Such arrays are called **static arrays.**

Data to be read into dynamic arrays do not have to be preceded by a data count. You can read the data to determine the data count, declare the necessary array or arrays dynamically, and then read the data a second time, this time storing the values in the array or arrays. The following program segment illustrates the method.

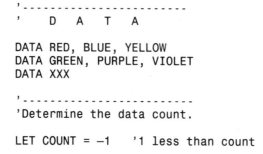

```
'-------------------------
'    D   A   T   A

DATA RED, BLUE, YELLOW
DATA GREEN, PURPLE, VIOLET
DATA XXX

'-------------------------
'Determine the data count.

LET COUNT = -1   '1 less than count
```

```
DO
   LET COUNT = COUNT +1
   READ W$
LOOP UNTIL W$ = "XXX"

'--------------------------
'Declare array WORDS$ and
'read data into WORDS$.

DIM WORDS$(1 TO COUNT)
RESTORE
FOR N = 1 TO COUNT
   READ WORDS$(COUNT)
NEXT N
```

■ *15.2 The DIM Statement (Declaring Arrays)*

As illustrated in the preceding examples, the DIM statement specifies the names and sizes of arrays. The size of an array is the number of values it can store. Thus, DIM G(1 TO 5) specifies an array G of size 5—the five values are stored with the subscripted variables G(1) to G(5). If N = 5, DIM G(1 TO N) also specifies an array G of size 5. An array for which only one subscript is specified (variables with more than one subscript are considered in Section 15.8) is called a **one-dimensional** array. Thus, the statement

```
DIM G(1 TO 5), DAY$(1 TO 7)
```

specifies a one-dimensional numerical array G of size 5 (subscripts 1 to 5) and a one-dimensional string array DAY$ of size 7 (subscripts 1 to 7). To use common terminology, we say that the arrays G and DAY$ have been **declared** or that they have been **dimensioned.**

In early versions of QuickBASIC, the DIM statement shown above must be written

```
DIM G(5), DAY$(7)
```

This statement specifies a one-dimensional array G of size 6 (the 6 subscripts are 0 to 5 instead of 1 to 5) and a one-dimensional array DAY$ of size 8 (subscripts 0 to 7). If you will not need the subscripted variables G(0) and DAY$(0), you can either ignore them or use the statement

```
OPTION BASE 1
```

to specify 1 as the smallest subscript. The general form of the OPTION BASE statement is

OPTION BASE **n**

where **n** denotes either 0 or 1. If you use the OPTION BASE statement, it must be executed before any arrays are used.

The general form of the DIM statement, as it applies to the declaration of one-dimensional arrays (lists), is

DIM **arraylist**

where **arraylist** denotes a list of one or more array declarations separated by commas. The array declarations have either of the two forms

name(**expr1** TO **expr2**)
name(**expr**)

where **name** denotes the name of the array being declared (any string allowed as the name of a simple variable); and **expr, expr1,** and **expr2** denote numerical constants or expressions whose values (rounded to integers, if necessary) specify the subscript ranges for the arrays. If the rounded values of **expr, expr1,** and **expr2** are E, E1, and E2, respectively, the declaration

name(**expr1** TO **expr2**)

declares an array named **name** with subscripts from E1 to E2. E1 must be less than or equal to E2. The declaration

name(expr)

is equivalent to **name**(0 TO **expr**) unless OPTION BASE 1 is used, in which case it is equivalent to **name**(1 TO **expr**).

E1 and E2 must be in the integer range -32768 to 32767 and E must be in the range 0 to 32767. Limits on array sizes are also imposed by the amount of memory available and by the maximum of 64K (65,535) bytes that QuickBASIC allows for *static arrays* (those dimensioned by using positive integer constants). These limitations, however, should not be a problem. For instance, since single-precision numerical values require four bytes (see Section 3.1), each single-precision static array is limited to $65,535 \backslash 4 = 16,383$ subscripts. This array size should be more than adequate.

Following are six additional points concerning the use of DIM statements and arrays:

1. QuickBASIC does not require DIM statements for arrays whose subscripts will be in the range 0 to 10. If any of the subscripted variables A(0) through A(10) is referenced in a program that does not declare A in a DIM statement, QuickBASIC, by default, will declare A as if the program included the statement DIM A(10). Thus, the DIM statements in Examples 1 through 3 are not actually required. It is excellent programming practice, however, to use DIM statements to declare all arrays. Doing so will make your programs easier to read, since DIM statements explicitly establish which variable names represent arrays and indicate their sizes.

2. A DIM statement must be executed before any reference is made to the array (or arrays) being dimensioned. The customary practice is to place DIM statements near the beginning of a program (or program unit—see list item 4), unless they are used for dynamic storage allocation.

3. When an array is dimensioned, either explicitly or implicitly by usage as mentioned in list item 1, its entries are initialized: numerical array entries initialize to 0, and string array entries initialize to the null string.

4. DIM statements can be used to declare local arrays in SUB and FUNCTION procedures. Each time the procedure is called, QuickBASIC allocates memory space for any arrays declared in DIM statements. When control returns to the calling unit, this memory space is freed—we say that the array is **deallocated.** Deallocating an array allows the name of the array to be declared again in a DIM statement; thus, the procedure can be called many times.

5. The size of a dynamic array (but not a static array) can be changed by using the REDIM statement. For example, if a dynamic array A of size 50 has been dimensioned with the statements

```
LET N = 50
DIM A(1 TO N)
```

it can be redimensioned to size 100 by using

```
REDIM A(1 TO 100)
```

or

```
LET N = 100
REDIM A(1 TO N)
```

Using REDIM with a static array causes a fatal *Duplicate definition* error.

6. If **name** denotes the name of a static array (an array dimensioned by using only integer constants in the DIM statement), the statement

ERASE name

will reinitialize all of its entries—numerical array entries to zero and string array entries to the null string. Thus, if A has been dimensioned with the statement

```
DIM A(1 to 100)
```

you can use

```
ERASE A
```

instead of

```
FOR N = 1 TO 100
   LET A(N) = 0
NEXT N
```

The ERASE statement deallocates dynamic arrays; it does not reinitialize them. To reinitialize a dynamic array, use the REDIM statement.

At the outset of this chapter, we mentioned that arrays can be used effectively in programming tasks that require us to determine many counts. The following example illustrates this use of arrays.

EXAMPLE 6   *Several lists of integers in the range 1 to 100 are·contained in DATA statements. The first datum is a count of the number of lists included, and each list ends with the end-of-list tag 0. Let's write a program to produce, for each list, a frequency table showing how many of each integer are included.*

PROBLEM ANALYSIS

Input: Several lists of numbers, as described in the problem statement. For example,

```
DATA 2    : 'Number of lists
DATA 80,80,80,80,80,60,60,50
DATA 50,50,45,45,50,50,50,32
DATA 0
DATA 95,95,95,95,90,90,90,88
DATA 75,75,75,75
DATA 0
```

Output: A frequency table for each list. Let's agree to display a two-column table with the headings DATUM and FREQUENCY. Let's also precede each frequency table with a title that indicates the list numbers (List 1 and List 2 for the DATA shown).

For each list, we must find 100 counts: the number of 1s, the number of 2s, and so on. Let's use FREQ(1), FREQ(2), and so on up to FREQ(100) to store these counts. Each value that appears in the DATA lines must be read to determine which of the 100 integers it is. If it is 87, then FREQ(87) must be increased by 1; if it is 24, then FREQ(24) must be increased by 1. To accomplish this for any value in the DATA lines, we can use the statements

```
READ X
LET FREQ(X) = FREQ(X) + 1
```

If we allow 0 as a subscript for the array FREQ, no harm is done by these two statements, even if X is the end-of-list tag 0. We simply will not use FREQ(0) in any other way. Thus, we can use the DO loop

```
DO
   READ X
   LET FREQ(X) = FREQ(X) + 1
LOOP UNTIL X = 0
```

to process the numbers in a single list. This brief analysis should make it easy to code the following algorithm.

THE ALGORITHM

a. Declare array FREQ with subscripts 0 to 100.
b. Read the number (LISTCOUNT) of lists.

c. Repeat the following for each list.

    c1. Read data to determine the frequency counts.

    c2. Display the frequency table.

d. Stop.

To carry out Step c1, we must start with zero counts. If we declare FREQ as a static array, we can use ERASE FREQ to initialize the counts (see list item 6 preceding this example). The actual counting for Step (c1) in the algorithm is accomplished by the DO loop shown above.

The other steps in the algorithm are routine: Step (a) requires only a DIM statement; Step (b) a READ statement; Step (c) a FOR statement; and for Step (c2), we can use a FOR loop with control variable N (ranging from 100 down to 1) to display N and the corresponding count FREQ(N) but suppress the output if FREQ(N) $= 0$—that is, if N is not in the list.

```
DIM FREQ(0 TO 100)    'Static array of counters
READ LISTCOUNT        'Number of lists

FOR LISTNUM = 1 TO LISTCOUNT

    ERASE FREQ           'Clear frequency counts.

    '----------------------------------------
    'Read X and add 1 to FREQ(X) until
    'end of list tag 0 is encountered.
    '----------------------------------------
    DO
        READ X
        LET FREQ(X) = FREQ(X) + 1
    LOOP UNTIL X = 0


    '------------------------------------------
    'Display frequency table number LISTNUM.
    '------------------------------------------
    PRINT "Frequencies for list"; LISTNUM
    PRINT
    PRINT "DATUM", "FREQUENCY"
    PRINT "-----", "---------"
    FOR N = 100 TO 1 STEP -1
        IF FREQ(N) > 0 THEN PRINT N, FREQ(N)
    NEXT N
    PRINT
NEXT LISTNUM
END
```

Program output (for data shown in the Problem Analysis):

```
Frequencies for list 1

DATUM          FREQUENCY
-----          ---------
80             5
60             2
50             6
45             2
32             1


Frequencies for list 2

DATUM          FREQUENCY
-----          ---------
95             4
90             3
88             1
75             4
```

■ *15.3 Problems*

1. *Show the output of each program.*

a.
```
DIM X(1 TO 4)
LET N=2
READ X(N),X(1)
FOR N=1 TO 2
    PRINT X(N)
NEXT N
DATA 4,5,7,3
END
```

b.
```
DIM X$(1 TO 7)
LET N=1
READ X$(N)
DO UNTIL X$(N)="."
    PRINT " ";X$(N)
    LET N=N+1
    READ X$(N)
LOOP
PRINT X$(N)
DATA TO,BE,OR,NOT,TO,BE,.
END
```

c.
```
DIM M(1 TO 7)
READ J
FOR J=5 TO 7
    READ M(J)
NEXT J
READ B,C
FOR K=B TO C
    PRINT M(K);
NEXT K
DATA 2,9,8,4,6,6,3
END
```

d.
```
DIM A$(1 TO 4)
FOR J=1 TO 4
    READ X$
    IF X$<>"HAT" THEN A$(J)=X$
NEXT J
FOR J=1 TO 4 STEP 2
    PRINT A$(J);
NEXT J
DATA IRAN,TOP,GATE,HAT
END
```

e.
```
READ C
DIM F$(1 TO C),L$(1 TO C)
FOR K=1 TO C
    READ F$(K),L$(K)
NEXT K
FOR K=C TO 1 STEP -1
    PRINT L$(K);", ";F$(K)
NEXT K
DATA 4
DATA JOHN,CASH,ELTON,JOHN
DATA JOHN,DENVER
DATA JOHN,PAYCHECK
END
```

In Problems 2–7, write a program for each task specified. In each program use a single numerical array or a single string array.

2. Input a list of numbers of undetermined length, and display the values in reverse order. Use an EOD tag to terminate the input list. (You may assume that the input list will contain fewer than 20 numbers.)

3. Input a list of words of undetermined length, and display them in reverse order. Use an EOD tag to terminate the input list. (You may assume that the input will contain fewer than 20 words.)

4. First read a list of words from DATA lines into a string array. Then allow the user to enter letters, one at a time, to obtain a list of those words that begin with the letter typed. The program should halt only when the user types DONE.

5. Input five numbers into an array B as follows: assign the first value to B(1) and B(10), the second to B(2) and B(9), and so on. Then display the array B and input five more values in the same way. Continue this process until the user types 0. When this happens, stop program execution with no further output.

6. Input a list of undetermined length into array A and display three columns as follows: Column 1 contains the input list in the order typed; Column 2 contains them in reverse order; and Column 3 contains the averages of the corresponding numbers in Columns 1 and 2. You may assume that the input list will contain fewer than 20 numbers.

7. Produce the following designs. Begin each program by reading the needed strings A, B, C, and so on, into an array from DATA lines. Use the arrays to produce the designs.

   a. A
   　　BB
   　　CCC
   　　DDD
   　　EEEEE
   　　FFFFFF

   b. ABCDEFG
   　　BCDEFG
   　　CDEFG
   　　DEFG
   　　EFG
   　　FG
   　　G

   c. A A A A
   　　B B B
   　　C C C C
   　　D D D
   　　E E E E

   d. 　　A
   　　BBB
   　　CCCCC
   　　DDDDDDD
   　　EEEEEEEEE

In Problems 8–21, write a program for each task specified. Use one or more arrays in each program.

8. The following DATA lines show the annual salaries of all the employees in Division 72 of the Manley Corporation. The last value (72) is an EOD tag.

   ```
   DATA 14000, 16200, 10195, 28432, 13360
   DATA 19300, 16450, 12180, 25640, 18420
   DATA 18900, 12270, 13620, 12940, 31200
   DATA 72
   ```

   Read these data into an array S, and then create a new array T as follows. For each subscript K, obtain T(K) by subtracting the average of all the salaries from S(K). Then display arrays S and T as a two-column table with appropriate headings.

9. Use the salary data shown in Problem 8 to create two arrays as follows. Array A is to contain all salaries less than $14,000 and B is to contain the rest. Display arrays A and B in adjacent columns with appropriate headings.

10. Input an undetermined number of values into arrays P and N so that array P contains those that are positive and N contains those that are negative. Ignore zeros and let 999 serve as the EOD tag. When the EOD tag is encountered, display the two lists in adjacent columns with the headings POSITIVES and NEGATIVES.

11. Read a list of words from DATA lines into arrays A$ and B$. Have array A$ contain all words beginning with a letter from A to M. Put the other words into B$. Display the contents of the two arrays in adjacent columns with appropriate column headings.

12. The following DATA lines show a name and four scores for each student in a psychology class:

    ```
    DATA ARDEN MARK,72,79,91,70
    DATA AUDEN WINN,95,92,86,82
    DATA BRICE SALLY ANN,90,80,70,84
    DATA BRANT EMILY,75,62,43,65
    DATA RANDALL TONY,52,54,50,33
    DATA RANDOLPH KIM,82,72,80,79
                .
                .
                .
    DATA XXX
    ```

    Create arrays S$ and A so that S$ contains the names and A contains the corresponding average scores. Then display two reports as follows. The first is to show the names and averages for students whose average is at least 60. The other students and their averages should be shown in the second report. Each report is to have an appropriate title and column headings.

13. Create arrays S$ and A exactly as described in Problem 12. Then allow the user to enter a string with one or more letters to obtain the names and averages of all students whose names begin with the letter or letters typed.

14. Write a program as described in Problem 13. This time assume the names in DATA lines are in

alphabetical order, and use this fact to reduce the number of string comparisons that must be made.

15. The names and precinct numbers of all residents of the town of Plymouth who voted in the last election are included in DATA lines in alphabetical order. Here are the first two DATA lines:

```
DATA ALDEN JOHN,1,ALDEN PRISCILLA,1
DATA BARTON JONATHAN,4,BARTON MARY,2
```

Plymouth has four precincts. You are to read the names into four arrays according to precinct, and then display the four lists as follows:

```
   PRECINCT 1           PRECINCT 2
- - - - - - - - - -    - - - - - - - - - -
ALDEN JOHN            BARTON MARY
ALDEN PRISCILLA          .
      .                  .
      .                  .
      .
   PRECINCT 3           PRECINCT 4
- - - - - - - - - -    - - - - - - - - - -
      .              BARTON JONATHAN
      .                  .
      .                  .
```

16. Let any three consecutive entries of an array L of size 40 be related to each other by the equation

$$L(J + 2) = L(J + 1) + L(J)$$

Input two integer values for $L(1)$ and $L(2)$ and generate $L(J)$ for $J = 3, \ldots, 40$. Display all 40 integers in four columns; the first column is to display $L(1)$ through $L(10)$, the second is to display $L(11)$ through $L(20)$, and so on.

17. A number of scores, each lying in the range from 0 to 100, are given in DATA lines. Use these scores to create an array C so that

$C(1) = $ a count of scores S satisfying $S \leq 20$
$C(2) = $ a count of scores S satisfying $20 < S \leq 40$
$C(3) = $ a count of scores S satisfying $40 < S \leq 60$
$C(4) = $ a count of scores S satisfying $60 < S \leq 80$
$C(5) = $ a count of scores S satisfying $80 < S \leq 100$

Display the results in tabular form as follows:

Interval	Frequency	
0– 20	C(1)	*[actually the value of C(I)]*
20– 40	C(2)	
40– 60	C(3)	
60– 80	C(4)	
80–100	C(5)	

18. Problem 17 asks for a count of the number of scores in each of five equal-length intervals. Instead of using five intervals, allow a user to type a positive integer N to produce a similar frequency table using N equal-length intervals.

19. For any input string, display two columns. In the first show the letters appearing in the string; in the second display how many times these letters occur in the string. For example, if the string constant "BOB,ROB,OR BO" is typed (quotation marks are included because of the commas), the output should be

```
B  4
O  4
R  2
```

276   *Chapter 15   Arrays*

If the string "Bob, Rob, or Bo" is typed, the output should be the same. Use F(1) to store the count of A's, F(2) for the B's, and so on, up to F(26). The method used in Example 16 of Section 14.6, to find the position in the alphabet of any letter, can be used here to find the appropriate subscript for any letter in the input string. It isn't necessary to use a second array to hold the letters of the alphabet. You may check that the letter whose count is stored in F(K) is CHR$(ASC("A") + K − 1).

20. Each of many DATA lines contains a single string (it may be long). The last string is the EOD tag END-OF-DATA. Produce a two-column table as described in Problem 19 for all letters that appear in all DATA lines but the last. Label the columns LETTER and FREQUENCY. Run your program with the following DATA lines:

```
DATA "QUICKBASIC IS FUN! ESPECIALLY WHEN I MUST CONVERT"
DATA "STRINGS TO NUMBERS AND NUMBERS TO STRINGS,"
DATA "AND SO ON, AND SO ON, AND SO ON,..."
DATA END-OF-DATA
```

21. A list of words terminated with an EOD tag is contained in DATA lines. Determine how many of the words begin with the letter A, how many begin with B, and so on. Display these counts in a two-column frequency table.

■ *15.4 Arrays in Procedures*

Many programming tasks that require processing arrays are well-defined subtasks that can be coded conveniently as SUB or FUNCTION procedures. The following are typical:

1. Read data into one or more arrays. (The procedure reads the data into arrays and passes these values back to the calling unit.)
2. Display a report from the values stored in one or more arrays. (The calling unit passes the array values needed to produce the report to the procedure.)
3. Search the contents of an array for a specific value. (The calling unit passes the array values and the object of the search to the procedure.)
4. Rearrange (sort) the entries in one or more arrays into a specified order: for example, string arrays into alphabetical order, and numerical arrays into ascending or descending order. (The calling unit passes the array values to the procedure that carries out the sort and returns the modified array or arrays back to the calling unit.)

Each of these four tasks involves entire arrays rather than single array values; this is the usual situation. To pass an *entire array* to a procedure, include the procedure name followed by empty parentheses ( ) as the argument in the procedure call. The corresponding parameter in the procedure definition must have the same form. Thus, if a procedure definition begins with

```
SUB DISPLAY (A( ), N)
```

the statement

```
CALL DISPLAY (NUMBERS( ), INDEX)
```

passes the entire array NUMBERS as the first argument and the variable INDEX as the second. In QuickBASIC, *entire arrays* are passed only by reference; that is, the communication between the array argument and the corresponding array parameter in the procedure definition is always a two-way communication. A single array value—that is, the value of a subscripted variable—is passed just as any other variable value is passed. Thus, if a procedure definition begins with

```
SUB VOLUME (X, Y, Z)
```

the statement

```
CALL VOLUME (X, Y, M(8))
```

passes the array value M(8) by reference as the third of three arguments. To pass M(8) by value, enclose it in parentheses.

Following are three examples that illustrate the use of arrays as procedure parameters. Example 7 includes a detailed discussion of how array values are passed between calling units and SUB procedures, Example 8 uses a FUNCTION procedure to calculate the average of all values in a numerical array, and Example 9 presents a FUNCTION procedure that searches arrays for specified values.

EXAMPLE 7 *Here is a program that uses two procedures: READ.ARRAY to read a list of words into a string array, and REVERSE.DISPLAY to display the contents of a string array in reverse order.*

```
'-----------------------------------------
'          MAIN PROGRAM UNIT

DATA 5                    : ' word count
DATA CAT, DOG, EEL
DATA BIRD, FISH

READ COUNT                'Read count.
DIM WORDS$(1 TO COUNT)    'Declare array.

CALL READ.ARRAY(WORDS$(), COUNT)
CALL REVERSE.DISPLAY(WORDS$(), COUNT)
END


'---------------------------------
'Procedure to read data into array
'
SUB READ.ARRAY (W$(), N)
   FOR INDEX = 1 TO N
      READ W$(INDEX)
   NEXT INDEX
END SUB

'---------------------------
' Procedure to display array
'
SUB REVERSE.DISPLAY (A$(), N)
   FOR INDEX = N TO 1 STEP −1
      PRINT A$(INDEX)
   NEXT INDEX
END SUB
```

Program output:
```
FISH
BIRD
EEL
DOG
CAT
```

The READ and DIM statements in the main program unit ensure that the array WORDS$ is dimensioned to exactly the size needed for the given data. The correspondence between arguments and parameters set up by the first CALL statement

```
CALL READ.ARRAY (WORDS$(), COUNT)
```

are as follows:

```
Main program unit        Procedure READ.ARRAY

       COUNT          ⟷   N
       WORDS$(1)      ⟷   W$(1)
       WORDS$(2)      ⟷   W$(2)
       WORDS$(3)      ⟷   W$(3)
```

```
          WORDS$(4)      ⟷   W$(4)
          WORDS$(5)      ⟷   W$(5)
```

When the procedure READ.ARRAY is first called, we have

```
    Main program unit        Procedure READ.ARRAY

        COUNT        =   5 =   N
        WORDS$(1)    = " " =   W$(1)
        WORDS$(2)    = " " =   W$(2)
        WORDS$(3)    = " " =   W$(3)
        WORDS$(4)    = " " =   W$(4)
        WORDS$(5)    = " " =   W$(5)
```

Recall that QuickBASIC automatically assigns the null string "" to each position in array WORDS$ when the program is run. Thus, when READ.ARRAY is called, the corresponding positions in array W$ also have the value "". The procedure then reads the five strings CAT, DOG, EEL, BIRD, and FISH into positions 1, 2, 3, 4, and 5, respectively, of W$. Because there is a two-way correspondence, these changes in array W$ are also changes in array WORDS$. At this point, we have

```
    Main program unit        Procedure READ.ARRAY

        COUNT        =   5 =   N
        WORDS$(1)    = CAT =   W$(1)
        WORDS$(2)    = DOG =   W$(2)
        WORDS$(3)    = EEL =   W$(3)
        WORDS$(4)    = BIRD =  W$(4)
        WORDS$(5)    = FISH =  W$(5)
```

Control then passes back to the calling unit (the main unit), and the next statement

```
    CALL REVERSE.DISPLAY(WORDS$(), COUNT)
```

calls the procedure REVERSE.DISPLAY with the following correspondences between arguments and parameters:

```
    Main program unit        Procedure REVERSE.DISPLAY

        COUNT        =   5 =   N
        WORDS$(1)    = CAT =   A$(1)
        WORDS$(2)    = DOG =   A$(2)
        WORDS$(3)    = EEL =   A$(3)
        WORDS$(4)    = BIRD =  A$(4)
        WORDS$(5)    = FISH =  A$(5)
```

The procedure displays the values A$(1) to A$(5) in reverse order to produce the output shown.

EXAMPLE 8   *Here is a program that uses a FUNCTION procedure AVERAGE to find the average of the numbers in an array. The action of the program is described by its comments.*

```
    '-----------------------------------
    '    D   A   T   A

    'First datum is number of scores
    DATA 4
    DATA CARL,70,70,80,80
    DATA MARK,70,70,60,70
    DATA MARY,65,75,75,80
    DATA SALLY,90,92,94,90
    DATA TOM,70,70,80,75
    DATA END-OF-DATA
```

```
'------------------------------------
'Read number of scores per student
'and declare the array SCORES.

READ COUNT
DIM SCORES(1 TO COUNT)

'------------------------------------
'Display a report of names and averages.

PRINT "NAME", "AVERAGE"
PRINT
READ NAME$
DO UNTIL NAME$ = "END-OF-DATA"
   FOR N = 1 TO COUNT
      READ SCORES(N)
   NEXT N
   PRINT NAME$, AVERAGE(SCORES(), COUNT)
   READ NAME$
LOOP
END

'------------------------------------
'FUNCTION procedure to find average
'of the values S(1),S(2), ... ,S(N)
'
FUNCTION AVERAGE (S(), N)
   LET SUM = 0
   FOR K = 1 TO N
      LET SUM = SUM + S(K)
   NEXT K
   LET AVERAGE = SUM / N
END FUNCTION
```

Program output:
```
NAME          AVERAGE

CARL          75
MARK          67.5
MARY          73.75
SALLY         91.5
TOM           73.75
```

The two statements

```
READ COUNT
DIM SCORES(1 TO COUNT)
```

that follow the DATA lines read the first datum 4 for COUNT and declare array SCORES to be of size four so that the four scores for any student can be read into the array.

The second program segment reads the name and four scores of each student to produce the output. The statement

```
PRINT NAME$, AVERAGE(SCORES(), COUNT)
```

in the DO loop displays a student's name and calls the FUNCTION procedure AVERAGE to obtain the average of the student's four scores.

At the outset of this section, we mentioned that the task of searching the contents of an array for a specified value is suited for coding as a procedure. The usual practice is to use a FUNCTION procedure, just as we have used FUNCTION procedures to search values included in DATA statements. To search the array values

```
A(1),A(2),A(3),...,A(MAXINDEX)
```

for the value X, we can compare X with the successive array values until it is found, or until the last array value A(MAXINDEX) has been tested. The following loop does this:

```
LET N = 1
DO UNTIL A(N) = X OR N = MAXINDEX
   LET N = N + 1
LOOP
```

After this loop, we can be sure that X was found if A(N) = X. The procedure in the next example uses this loop to carry out searches.

EXAMPLE 9   *Here is a search function SEARCH that searches any numerical array for any value specified. The comment lines describe the parameters and explain what value the function returns to a calling unit.*

```
' Function to search A(1) to A(MAXINDEX)
' for the value X.  The function returns
'
'      INDEX   such that A(INDEX) = X
'         0    if X is not found.
'
FUNCTION SEARCH (X, A(), MAXINDEX)
      LET N = 1
      DO UNTIL A(N) = X OR N = MAXINDEX
         LET N = N + 1
      LOOP
      IF A(N) = X THEN
         SEARCH = N                 'X found
      ELSE
         SEARCH = 0                 'X not found
      END IF
END FUNCTION
```

■ 15.5 Sorting

Many programming tasks require sorting (arranging) arrays according to some specified order. When lists of numbers are involved, this usually means arranging them according to size—from smallest to largest or from largest to smallest. For example, you may be required to produce a salary schedule in which salaries are displayed from largest to smallest. When lists of names are involved, you may wish to arrange them in alphabetical order. In this section, we'll describe the **bubble sort** and show how it can be used in applications that require sorting numerical arrays in ascending or descending order or sorting string arrays in alphabetical order.

The bubble sort algorithm described in this section is very inefficient (slow) when used to sort large arrays, but for small arrays (up to about 30 entries) it will execute as rapidly as most sorting algorithms. Moreover, the bubble sort algorithm is easy to understand and easy to code. Thus, it serves as an excellent introduction to the topic of sorting. A more comprehensive treatment of this topic is included in Chapter 18.

The idea behind the bubble sort is to compare adjacent array entries, beginning with the first pair and ending with the last pair. If two values being compared are in the proper order, we leave them alone. If not, we interchange them. Thus, to sort the short numerical array

	1	**2**	**3**	**4**
A	6	5	8	3

into ascending order, we begin the bubble sort by comparing the values in positions 1 and 2. Since these values (6 and 5) are not in order, they are swapped.

6 5 8 3   becomes   **5 6** 8 3

Next we compare the values in positions 2 and 3 in the same manner:

5 **6 8** 3   remains   5 **6 8** 3

Then we compare the values in positions 3 and 4:

5 6 **8 3**   becomes   5 6 **3 8**

The effect of these three comparisons is to move the largest value to the last position. If we repeat exactly the same process for the modified array

	1	2	3	4
A	5	6	3	8

the array entries will be rearranged as follows:

5 6 3 8   remains   **5 6** 3 8
5 **6 3** 8   becomes   5 **3 6** 8
5 3 **6 8**   remains   5 3 **6 8**

The effect of these three comparisons is to move the next-to-largest value (6) to the next-to-last position. Repeating the process a third time will move the third-from-largest value (5) to the third-from-last position, and the array will be in order:

5 3 6 8   becomes   **3 5** 6 8
3 **5 6** 8   remains   3 **5 6** 8
3 5 **6 8**   remains   3 5 **6 8**

You probably noticed that several of the comparisons shown are unnecessary. After the first three comparisons are made (we'll refer to these three comparisons as *a pass through the array*), we can be sure that the largest array value is in the last position. Hence, it isn't necessary to make further comparisons involving the last array entry. Similarly, after the second pass through the array, it isn't necessary to make further comparisons involving the next-to-last array entry. If we include these unnecessary comparisons, however, it is a simple matter to code the process described. Indeed, since the statement

```
SWAP A(I), A(I + 1)
```

interchanges the values of the adjacent entries A(I) and A(I + 1), we can cause a single pass through the array A of size 4, swapping values that are not in order, with a FOR loop of the form

```
FOR I = 1 TO 3
   IF A(I) > A(I + 1) THEN SWAP A(I), A(I + 1)
NEXT I
```

If the array A is of size N, we would simply change the FOR statement to

```
FOR I = 1 TO N - 1
```

The number of passes that must be made to sort an array depends on the array size and the array values. For an array of size N, at most N − 1 passes are required because on each pass another array value is moved to its proper position. But it isn't always necessary to make N − 1 passes through the array. For instance, to sort the four-element array

	1	2	3	4
A	5	3	8	6

we make one pass through the array to move the largest entry to the last position:

5 3 8 6	becomes	**3 5** 8 6
3 **5 8** 6	remains	3 **5 8** 6
3 5 **8 6**	becomes	3 5 **6 8**

Thus, for this array, one pass is enough. Rather than attempting to keep count of how many passes have been made, we'll simply repeat the process described until a pass is made in which no array entries are swapped—this will happen only if the array is in order. The procedure shown in Figure 15.1 accomplishes this by using the variable FLAG. Just before each pass through the array (that is, through the FOR loop), FLAG is set to 0. If a swap occurs in the loop, FLAG is set to 1. If the loop is completed with FLAG = 1, another pass is made; but if FLAG = 0 the array is sorted.

The bubble sort algorithm shown in Figure 15.1 can be used in any program to sort, in ascending order, any one-dimensional numerical array of size N. If you need to sort an array into descending rather than ascending order, simply change the IF condition $A(I) > A(I + 1)$ to $A(I) < A(I + 1)$.

```
'  ------------------------------------------------
'  Procedure to sort A(1) to A(N) into ascending
'  order by using the bubblesort algorithm.
'
SUB BUBBLESORT (A(), N)

   'Start each pass with FLAG = 0.
   'Set FLAG = 1 after each swap.

   DO
      LET FLAG = 0
      FOR I = 1 TO N - 1
         IF A(I) > A(I + 1) THEN
            SWAP A(I), A(I + 1)
            LET FLAG = 1
         END IF
      NEXT I
   LOOP UNTIL FLAG = 0

END SUB
```

Figure 15.1 Bubble sort procedure for numerical arrays

As we explained in the preceding analysis, the bubble sort we have devised makes many unnecessary comparisons. Even so, it is only a bit slower than a bubble sort that includes extra statements to avoid these comparisons. To increase speed, you should not try to improve the bubble sort. Rather, you should use a different and faster algorithm. Two very fast sorting algorithms (called Shellsort and Quicksort) are given in Chapter 18.

Any sorting algorithm used to sort numerical arrays is easily modified to sort string arrays. To modify the bubble sort in Figure 15.1 to sort strings, change the array name A to A$ or any other string array name. If the strings to be sorted can contain both upper- and lowercase letters, use the IF condition

```
UCASE$(A$(I)) > UCASE$(A$(I + 1))
```

We made this change to obtain the procedure BUBBLE.STRING shown in Figure 15.2. It can be used in any program to alphabetize any string array of size N.

```
' -------------------------------------------------
' Procedure to sort A$(1) to A$(N) into alphabetical
' order by using the bubblesort algorithm.
'
SUB BUBBLE.STRING (A$(), N)

   'Start each pass with FLAG = 0.
   'Set FLAG = 1 after each swap.

   DO
      LET FLAG = 0
      FOR I = 1 TO N - 1
         IF UCASE$(A$(I)) > UCASE$(A$(I + 1)) THEN
            SWAP A$(I), A$(I + 1)
            LET FLAG = 1
         END IF
      NEXT I
   LOOP UNTIL FLAG = 0

END SUB
```

Figure 15.2 Bubble sort procedure for string arrays

EXAMPLE 10

Let's write a program to alphabetize lists of names typed at the keyboard.

It is easy to write an algorithm for the specified task if we leave out the details. The following is appropriate:

THE ALGORITHM

a. Store all names typed at the keyboard in an array.
b. Sort the array of names into alphabetical order.
c. Display the alphabetized list of names.

Writing QuickBASIC code for Steps (a) and (c) is routine. For Step (b) we will use, without change, the procedure in Figure 15.2.

MAIN UNIT

```
' ---------------------------------------
' Data entry section: Store all names
' typed at the keyboard in array NAMES$.

DIM NAMES$(1 TO 50)
PRINT "Enter up to 50 names to be alphabetized."
PRINT "Use the form: LAST FIRST MIDDLE (no commas)"
PRINT "Enter FINI when done."
PRINT
LET C = 1                       'Array subscript
PRINT "NAME"; C;               'Prompt the user
INPUT NAMES$(C)                ' for a name.
DO UNTIL UCASE$(NAME$(C)) = "FINI" OR C = 50
   LET C = C + 1
   PRINT "NAME"; C;            'Prompt for the
   INPUT NAMES$(C)             ' next name.
LOOP
IF C = 50 THEN
   PRINT
   PRINT "Fifty names have been entered."
ELSE
   LET C = C - 1                'Actual name count
END IF

' ---------------------------------------
' Alphabetize the C entries of array NAMES$.
CALL BUBBLE.STRING(NAMES$(), C)
```

```
' -------------------------------------
' Display the alphabetized array NAMES$.

PRINT
PRINT "THE ALPHABETIZED LIST:"
PRINT
FOR N = 1 TO C
    PRINT NAMES$(N)
NEXT N
END
```

Program output:
```
Enter up to 50 names to be alphabetized.
Use the form: LAST FIRST MIDDLE (no commas)
Enter FINI when done.

NAME 1 ? Washington George
NAME 2 ? Adams John
NAME 3 ? Jefferson Thomas
NAME 4 ? Madison James
NAME 5 ? Monroe James
NAME 6 ? Adams John Quincy
NAME 7 ? fini

THE ALPHABETIZED LIST:

Adams John
Adams John Quincy
Jefferson Thomas
Madison James
Monroe James
Washington George
```

REMARK

This program does not allow the usual comma when names are typed with last names first. A simple way to allow commas is to use LINE INPUT instead of INPUT. Another common method used to enter names at the keyboard is to prompt the user twice for each name: first for the last name, and then for the first and middle names. For example, instead of

```
INPUT NAME$(C)
```

you can use

```
INPUT "Last name"; LAST$
INPUT "First and middle names"; FIRST$
LET NAME$(C) = LAST$ + ", " + FIRST$
```

Many applications that require arrays to be sorted involve more than one array. For example, suppose NAMES$ and SAL denote one-dimensional arrays with each pair NAMES$(I),SAL(I) giving a person's name and salary. If the contents of these two arrays must be displayed in a two-column report with the salaries appearing from largest to smallest, the list of pairs NAMES$(I),SAL(I) must be sorted so that the entries in SAL are in descending order. This is easily accomplished by modifying a bubble sort that sorts array SAL. Simply insert statements to interchange NAMES$(I) and NAMES$(I + 1) whenever SAL(I) and SAL(I + 1) are interchanged. If a second two-column report must be displayed with the names in alphabetical order, you would modify a bubble sort that alphabetizes NAMES$ by inserting statements to swap SAL(I) and SAL(I + 1) whenever NAMES$(I) and NAMES$(I + 1) are swapped. The next example illustrates this method of sorting.

EXAMPLE 11 *Several pairs of numbers are included in DATA lines. The first of each pair is a quality point average (QPA), and the second gives the number of students with this QPA. Write a program to produce a table with the column headings QPA and*

FREQUENCY. The frequency counts in the second column are to appear in descending order.

Two lists are given in the DATA lines. Let's use Q to denote QPAs and F to denote the frequency counts. The following algorithm shows the three subtasks that must be performed;

a. Read arrays Q and F.
b. Sort the two arrays so that the frequencies appear in descending order.
c. Display the two arrays as a two-column table and stop.

To code Step (a), we must remember that the lists are presented in DATA lines as pairs of numbers. Thus, we will read values for Q(I) and F(I) for I = 1, 2, and so on, until all pairs have been read. We'll use the dummy pair 0, 0 as the EOD tag.

To code Step (b), we will use a bubble sort to sort array F in descending order. However, since a pair Q(I), F(I) must not be separated, we will interchange Q values whenever the corresponding F values are interchanged. We made these changes to the procedure in Figure 15.1 to obtain the following procedure BUBBLE.PAIR to sort Arrays F and Q.

```
' --------------------------------------------
' Procedure to sort arrays Q and F so that
' the entries in F are in decreasing order.
'
SUB BUBBLE.PAIR (Q(), F(), N)

    'Start each pass with FLAG = 0.
    'Set FLAG = 1 after each swap.

    DO
       LET FLAG = 0
       FOR I = 1 TO N - 1
          IF F(I) < F(I + 1) THEN
             SWAP F(I), F(I + 1)
             SWAP Q(I), Q(I + 1)
             LET FLAG = 1
          END IF
       NEXT I
    LOOP UNTIL FLAG = 0

END SUB
```

The following main program unit uses this procedure to do the sorting.

```
' ----------------------------------------------------
'     Read arrays Q and F and find data count N.

DIM Q(1 TO 50), F(1 TO 50)
LET N = 1                             'Subscript
READ Q(N), F(N)                       'First pair
DO UNTIL Q(N) = 0 AND F(N) = 0
   LET N = N + 1                       'Increase subscript
   READ Q(N), F(N)                     'Next pair
LOOP
LET N = N - 1                          'Adjust count

' ----------------------------------------------------
' Sort arrays Q and F so that F entries are ordered.

CALL BUBBLE.PAIR(Q(), F(), N)

' ----------------------------------------------------
' Display arrays Q and F in a two-column table.

PRINT "QPA     FREQUENCY"
  F$ = "#.##       ###    "
PRINT
```

```
FOR I = 1 TO N
   PRINT USING F$; Q(I); F(I)
NEXT I
END

' ---------------------------------------------
'            D    A    T    A

DATA 4.00,  2, 3.75, 16,  3.40,  41, 3.20,  38
DATA 3.00, 92, 2.75, 162, 2.30, 352, 2.00, 280
DATA 1.70, 81, 1.50,  27
DATA 0,0
```

Program output:

QPA	FREQUENCY
2.30	352
2.00	280
2.75	162
3.00	92
1.70	81
3.40	41
3.20	38
1.50	27
3.75	16
4.00	2

■ 15.6 Problems

In Problems 1–20, write a program to perform each task specified.

1. Display, in ascending order, any five input values L(1), L(2), L(3), L(4), and L(5). Have your program process many such sets of five numbers during a single run. Test your program with the following input data:

5	4	3	2	1
5	1	2	3	4
−1	−2	−3	−4	−5
2	1	4	3	5
15	19	14	18	10
1	2	3	4	5

2. Modify your program for Problem 1 so that each group of five integers is displayed in descending order. (Only one line needs to be changed.)

3. Display any list of numbers typed at the keyboard in ascending order. Use the value 9999 to indicate that the entire list has been entered.

4. Input a list of numbers to obtain a two-column table with the column headings ORIGINAL LIST and SORTED LIST. Have the first column contain the list values in the order in which they are typed and the second column contain the same values displayed from largest to smallest. Use the following algorithm:

   a. Input the list values into identical arrays A and B.

   b. Sort array B into descending order.

   c. Display the two-column table as described.

5. Read several numbers, ranging from 0 to 100, and store them in two arrays A and B. Let array A contain numbers less than 50 and array B the others. Then sort arrays A and B in descending order and display them side by side with the column headings LESS THAN 50 and 50 OR MORE. Test your program by using the following data:

```
DATA 80,70,40,90,95,38,85,42,60,70
DATA 40,60,70,20,18,87,23,78,85,23
DATA 9999
```

6. A study of Tidy Corporation's annual reports for 1982–1992 yielded the following statistics:

Year	Gross sales in thousands	Earnings per share
1982	18,000	−0.84
1983	18,900	0.65
1984	20,350	0.78
1985	24,850	1.05
1986	24,300	0.68
1987	27,250	0.88
1988	34,000	2.05
1989	51,000	1.07
1990	46,500	0.22
1991	60,000	1.45
1992	49,500	0.87

Include the first and third columns of this table in DATA lines for a program to produce a two-column report with the same headings as those shown. However, have the earnings-per-share figures appear in ascending order.

7. Include all three columns given for the Tidy Corporation (Problem 6) in DATA lines for a program to produce a three-column table with the same headings. However, have the gross sales figures appear in descending order.

8. Compute the semester averages for all students in a psychology class. A separate DATA line should be used for each student and should contain the student's name and five grades. A typical DATA line might read

```
DATA LINCOLN JOHN,72,79,88,97,90
```

Produce the output in tabular form with the column headings STUDENT and SEMESTER AVERAGE. Have the names appear in alphabetical order.

9. Modify Problem 8 as follows: round averages to the nearest integer and give letter grades according to this table:

Average	Grade
90–100	A
80–89	B
70–79	C
60–69	D
Below 60	E

Read the five strings A, B, C, D, and E into an array. Produce the output in tabular form with the column headings STUDENT, SEMESTER AVERAGE, and LETTER GRADE. Have the names appear in alphabetical order.

10. Following is the weekly inventory report of a sewing-supply wholesaler:

Item	Batches on hand Monday	Batches sold during week	Cost per batch	Sales price per batch
Bobbins	220	105	$8.20	$10.98
Buttons	550	320	5.50	6.95
Needles—1	450	295	2.74	3.55
Needles—2	200	102	7.25	9.49
Pins	720	375	4.29	5.89
Thimbles	178	82	6.22	7.59
Thread—A	980	525	4.71	5.99
Thread—B	1424	718	7.42	9.89

Include all five columns in DATA lines by using one DATA statement for each item. Have your program produce a three-column report showing the item names and, for each item, the number of batches on hand at the end of the week and the income generated by that item. Have the income column appear in descending order.

11. Using the inventory report shown in Problem 10, produce a five-column report showing the item names, the cost per batch, the sales price per batch, the dollar markup per batch, and the percent markup per batch. Have the figures in the last column appear in descending order. [The percentages in the fifth column are given by (M/C) $*$ 100, where M denotes the markup and C denotes the cost.]

12. A program is to contain the following DATA lines.

```
DATA Marian Evans, James Payn, Joseph Conrad
DATA Emily Dickinson, Henry Thoreau, John Payne
DATA John Fox, Mary Freeman, George Eliot
DATA END-OF-LIST
```

Use the following algorithm to alphabetize the list of names:
a. Read the names into an array A$.
b. Create a new array B$ containing the names in A$ but with last names first.
c. Sort A$ into alphabetical order by comparing entries of B$.
d. Display A$.

13. A program is to contain the following DATA lines.

```
DATA Marian, Evans, James, Payn, Joseph, Conrad
DATA Emily, Dickinson, Henry, Thoreau, John, Payne
DATA John, Fox, Mary, Freeman, George, Eliot
DATA END-OF-LIST
```

(Note that these are the names given in Problem 12 but with first names and last names included as separate strings.) Have your program produce an alphabetical listing with each name appearing in the form

```
LAST, FIRST
```

with a space after the comma as shown. (*Suggestion:* Use the concatenation operator + to place the names in a single string array with each name in the form specified for the output. Then simply sort and display this array. No other arrays are needed.)

14. Display a list of words included in DATA lines in two adjacent columns with the column headings A–M and N–Z. Have the words in each column appear in alphabetical order.

15. Use the following DATA lines in a program to help chemistry students learn some of the abbreviations of the basic elements in the periodic table:

```
DATA ALUMINUM,AL,GOLD,AU,SILVER,AG
DATA BORON,B,BROMINE,BR,CARBON,C
DATA COPPER,CU,CALCIUM,CA,COBALT,CO
DATA CHROMIUM,CR,CHLORINE,CL,HYDROGEN,H
DATA XXX,XXX
```

The program should begin by displaying a list of all element names (no abbreviations) that you include in the DATA lines. The student should then be allowed to enter element names in any order. For each correctly spelled name typed by the student, the computer is to ask for the abbreviation. If the abbreviation is not correct, the correct abbreviation should be displayed before allowing the student to enter another name. If the student misspells an element name or enters one that is not included in the DATA lines, display a simple message such as I DON'T KNOW THAT ONE and prompt the user again. The list of element names displayed at the beginning will quickly scroll off the screen. It is to be displayed again only if the student types HELP when it is time to enter an element name. If the student types HELP when the computer is waiting for an abbreviation, the message HELP NOT AVAILABLE AT THIS TIME should be displayed and the student should be prompted again for the abbreviation.

16. A correspondence between x and y is given by the following table. (Each y entry corresponds to the x entry just above it.)

x	0	2	4	6	8	10	12	14	16	18	20
y	-5	3	27	67	123	195	283	387	507	643	795

Write a menu-driven program for the following menu:
1. To end the program.
2. To find the y value for any x value entered at the keyboard.
3. To use linear interpolation to find a y value for any x value entered at the keyboard.
In option 2, display NOT FOUND if the value typed is not in the table. In option 3, display VALUE IS OUT OF THE INTERPOLATION RANGE if x is less than 0 or greater than 20. The interpolation formula is

$$y = y_1 + \frac{x - x_1}{x_2 - x_1}(y_2 - y_1)$$

where x_1 and x_2 are successive values in the list of x values, with x lying between them; y_1 and y_2 are the corresponding y values.

17. If a set of N scores is arranged in either increasing or decreasing order, the *median* score is the middle score when N is odd and the average of the two "middle" scores when N is even. Thus the sixth score is the median for a set of 11 scores, whereas the average of the fifth and sixth scores is the median for a set of 10 scores. Determine the median for an undetermined number of scores typed at the keyboard.

18. Input an array L at the keyboard and display its contents. Then sort the array into ascending order and display the new ordering. Finally, modify L by deleting all values that appear more than once and display the modified array. For example, if L(1) = 7, L(2) = L(3) = 8, and L(4) = L(5) = L(6) = 9, then the new array is to have L(1) = 7, L(2) = 8, and L(3) = 9. Write your program so that many different lists of input values can be processed as described during a single program run.

19. Read N pairs of numbers so that the first of each pair is in array A and the second is in array B. Sort the pairs A(I), B(I) so that A(1) $\leq$ A(2) $\cdots \leq$ A(N) and so that B(I) $\leq$ B(I + 1) whenever A(I) = A(I + 1). Display the modified arrays in two adjacent columns with the headings LIST A and LIST B. [*Hint:* If A(I) > A(I + 1), a swap is necessary; if A(I) < A(I + 1), no swap is necessary; otherwise—that is, if A(I) = A(I + 1)—swap only if B(I) > B(I + 1).]

20. English prose can be written in DATA lines by representing each line of text as a string occupying a single DATA line:

```
DATA "When in the course of human events, it"
DATA "becomes necessary for one people to"
DATA "dissolve the political ............. "
                     .
                     .
                     .
DATA "END-OF-TEXT"
```

Write a program to determine some or all of the following statistics:
a. A count of the number of words of text.
b. A count of the number of N-letter words for N = 1,2,3, . . .
c. A two-column table giving each word used and its frequency. The column of words should be in alphabetical order.
d. A two-column table showing the number of sentences with one word, the number with two words, and so on.
e. A count of the number of words used from a list of words you include in DATA lines. For instance, to determine the number of times the author uses articles and conjunctions, your list might include A, AN, AND, BUT, HOWEVER, NOR, OR, THE, and others. If you were studying an author's use of color imagery, your list might be one of colors.

■ *15.7 Table Processing*

Several of the examples considered in previous chapters involved processing data given in tabular form. In each case, we used READ statements to read the data into simple variables for processing and RESTORE statements to allow us to reuse the data. Although this method can be used for many programming tasks, sometimes it is inadequate or at least very inconvenient. The examples in this section illustrate how the array data structure can provide a useful and convenient alternative to this method of processing tabular data.

EXAMPLE 12

The hourly pay rate of each employee in a certain business is determined by the employee's job classification. We must produce a report showing the week's gross pay for each employee.

We need more information. We need to know the name, job classification, and hours worked for each employee as well as the hourly pay rates for the job classifications. Let's assume this information is given to us in two tables as shown and that time and a half is paid for all hours over 32.

Hours-Worked Table

Name	Job class	Hours
Jane Arcus	3	40
Jonathan Beard	6	45
Sandra Carlson	3	32
Susan Dahlberg	1	24
Thomas Farrell	5	29
Heidi Graves	1	40
⋮	⋮	⋮

Hourly Rate Table

Job class	Rate of pay
1	$ 4.00
2	4.75
3	5.75
4	7.00
5	8.50
6	10.75

To produce the required report, we must look up the job class and hours worked for each employee from the Hours-Worked Table and the corresponding rate of pay from the Hourly Rate Table. There is a difference in how these two tables should be used. In particular, the Hourly Rate Table is needed each time the week's pay for an employee is being calculated— that is, each time we process a line from the Hours-Worked Table. Thus, the data in the Hourly Rate Table must be accessed many times whereas the data in the Hours-Worked Table is needed only once. For this reason, we will read the Hourly Rate Table into an array. If we name this array PAYRATE and if JOB denotes a job class (1 through 6), the rate of pay corresponding to job class JOB will be PAYRATE(JOB).

The discussion in the preceding paragraph allows us to give a precise description of the input data and how they should be organized. (The output is simply a two-column report showing the name and gross pay for each employee.)

Input: Six hourly pay rates corresponding to job classes 1–6.
          The name, job class, and hours worked for each employee.

All input data will be included in DATA statements. Since the Hourly Rate Table will be read into an array for use in determining the week's pay for each employee, the six hourly rate amounts should be first, before the data given in the Hours-Worked Table. To avoid having to count the employees, we will end this later table with XXX,0,0 and use XXX to detect the end of the data. Since each employee's name, job class, and hours worked will be read and immediately processed, there is no need to read these data into arrays.

At this point, it should not be difficult to write an algorithm for the task specified in the problem statement. To keep our algorithm concise, we will use these descriptive variable names:

PAYRATE	= array of hourly rates for job classes 1–6
EMPNAME$	= an employee's name
JOB	= job classification for EMPNAME$
HOURS	= hours worked this week by EMPNAME$
GROSSPAY	= week's gross pay for EMPNAME$

THE ALGORITHM

a. Read hourly rates for job classes 1–6 into array PAYRATE.
b. Display report title and column headings.
c. Read EMPNAME$, JOB, and HOURS.
d. Repeat the following until EMPNAME$ is XXX:
   d1. Calculate GROSSPAY for EMPNAME$.
   d2. Display EMPNAME$ and GROSSPAY.
   d3. Read EMPNAME$, JOB, and HOURS.
e. Stop

Writing QuickBASIC code for the individual steps in this algorithm should not be difficult. Notice, however, that Step (d1) involves two steps: determine the hourly rate for job classification JOB and then calculate the gross pay. As explained in the problem analysis, the hourly rate (we'll call it RATE) is given by the statement

```
LET RATE = PAYRATE(JOB)
```

Since time and a half is paid for all hours over 32, we can carry out the second step by using the following FUNCTION procedure, which calculates the gross pay given the hours worked HOURS and hourly rate RATE

```
FUNCTION PAY (HOURS, RATE)

    'Return gross pay if time and a half
    'is earned for all hours over 32.

    IF HOURS <= 32 THEN
       PAY = HOURS * RATE
    ELSE
       BASEPAY = 32 * RATE
       OVERTIME = (HOURS - 32) * 1.5 * RATE
       PAY = BASEPAY + OVERTIME
    END IF

END FUNCTION
```

Thus, by including this procedure in the program, we can code Step (d1) with these two lines:

```
LET RATE = PAYRATE(JOB)
LET GROSSPAY = PAY(HOURS, RATE)
```

MAIN UNIT

```
' ------------------------------------------
' Load Hourly Rate table into array PAYRATE.
' ------------------------------------------

DIM PAYRATE(6)
FOR JOBCLASS = 1 TO 6
   READ PAYRATE(JOBCLASS)
NEXT JOBCLASS
```

```
' ---------------------------------------
' Display report title and column headings
' and assign output format string F$.
' ---------------------------------------

PRINT "  SALARIES FOR CURRENT WEEK"
PRINT
PRINT "EMPLOYEE'S NAME       GROSS PAY"
 F$ = "\              \    ####.##"
PRINT


' ---------------------------------------
' Read Hours-Worked data to determine
' and display all names and salaries.
' ---------------------------------------

READ EMPNAME$, JOB, HOURS
DO UNTIL EMPNAME$ = "XXX"
   LET RATE = PAYRATE(JOB)
   LET GROSSPAY = PAY(HOURS, RATE)
   PRINT USING F$; EMPNAME$; GROSSPAY
   READ EMPNAME$, JOB, HOURS
LOOP
END


' ---------------------------------------
'      D    A    T    A
' ---------------------------------------

' Hourly rates for job classes 1 to 6:
DATA 6.00, 6.75, 7.75, 8.00, 8.50, 10.75

' (name, jobclass, hours worked)
DATA Jane Arcus, 3, 40
DATA Jonathan Beard, 6, 45
DATA Sandra Carlson, 3, 32
DATA Susan Dahlberg, 1, 24
DATA Thomas Farrell, 5, 29
DATA Heidi Graves, 1, 40
DATA XXX,0,0
```

Program output:

```
   SALARIES FOR CURRENT WEEK

EMPLOYEE'S NAME       GROSS PAY

Jane Arcus            341.00
Jonathan Beard        553.63
Sandra Carlson        248.00
Susan Dahlberg        144.00
Thomas Farrell        246.50
Heidi Graves          264.00
```

REMARK   It is worth noting that we decided on the organization of the input data by considering how the data were to be used, not by the form in which the data were given. Specifically, we decided to store the Hourly Rate Table in an array because the information it contains must be used each time an employee's pay is to be calculated. Also, we decided not to store the Hours-Worked Table in arrays because the information it contains needs to be processed only once, in the order given. In other programming tasks involving exactly the same data, you may find it convenient to use a different organization of these data. To illustrate, suppose you must produce listings of employees whose job class numbers are typed at the keyboard. If you read the entire Hours-Worked Table into arrays EMP$, JOBCLASS, and HRS and use the simple variable CLASSNUM for the job class number typed at the keyboard, it is a simple matter to produce the required listing. The following procedure does this:

```
SUB LISTING (COUNT, CLASSNUM, EMP$(), JOBCLASS())

   ' PROCEDURE TO LIST ALL EMPLOYEES
   ' WITH A SPECIFIED JOB CLASS NUMBER

   '    CLASSNUM = THE SPECIFIED JOB CLASS NUMBER
   '    EMP$     = ARRAY OF EMPLOYEE NAMES
   '    JOBCLASS = CORRESPONDING ARRAY OF JOB CLASSES
   '    COUNT    = COUNT OF ALL EMPLOYEES

   PRINT
   PRINT "LIST OF EMPLOYEES IN JOB CLASS"; CLASSNUM; ":"
   FOR N = 1 TO COUNT
      IF JOBCLASS(N) = CLASSNUM THEN PRINT EMP$(N)
   NEXT N

END SUB
```

Each time the program in Example 12 references the array PAYRATE, it does so by specifying a position in the array. This happens because the integers 1 through 6 are used to specify both job class numbers and the positions of the corresponding pay rate in the array— PAYRATE(1) is the pay rate for job class 1, PAYRATE(2) is the pay rate for job class 2, and so on. Tabular data, however, are not often so conveniently stored in arrays. A more common situation is to use two or more arrays to store a single table and to carry out a table search by searching one of the arrays for a specified value. This value is called the **search argument,** and the entries of the particular array being searched are called **table arguments.**

Searching an array for a specified value is not new to us. For instance, Example 9 presents the following FUNCTION procedure that can be used to search numerical arrays.

```
' Function to search A(1) to A(MAXINDEX)
' for the value X.  The function returns
'
'      INDEX   such that A(INDEX) = X
'        0     if X is not found.
'
FUNCTION SEARCH (X, A(), MAXINDEX)
      LET N = 1
      DO UNTIL A(N) = X OR N = MAXINDEX
         LET N = N + 1
      LOOP
      IF A(N) = X THEN
         SEARCH = N              'X found
      ELSE
         SEARCH = 0              'X not found
      END IF
END FUNCTION
```

In Example 13, we use this function in a program that uses multiple arrays to store a single table. The example illustrates the use of search functions in table look-up applications.

EXAMPLE 13   *Here is a program to display information about incoming flights whose flight numbers are entered at the keyboard. The comment lines describe the purpose and action of the program.*

MAIN
UNIT

```
'       AIRLINE FLIGHT INFORMATION PROGRAM

' -----------------------------------------------
'    Load incoming flight data into arrays.
' -----------------------------------------------

READ COUNT                      'Flight count
DIM FLIGHTNUM(1 TO COUNT)       'Flight numbers
DIM ORIGIN$(1 TO COUNT)         'Origination points
DIM ARRIVE$(1 TO COUNT)         'Arrival times
```

```
        FOR F = 1 TO COUNT
            READ FLIGHTNUM(F), ORIGIN$(F), ARRIVE$(F)
        NEXT F

        '  -----------------------------------------------
        '  Display available flight information for
        '  flight numbers entered at the keyboard.
        '  -----------------------------------------------

        INPUT "Flight number (0 when done)? ", FLIGHT
        DO UNTIL FLIGHT = 0

            'Search array FLIGHTNUM for FLIGHT.
            'Return index 0 for F if not found.

            LET F = SEARCH(FLIGHT, FLIGHTNUM(), COUNT)

            IF F = 0 THEN
                PRINT FLIGHT; "is not a listed flight number."
            ELSE
                PRINT
                PRINT "    Available information on Flight"; FLIGHT
                PRINT "    Origination point:         "; ORIGIN$(F)
                PRINT "    Expected time of arrival: "; ARRIVE$(F)
            END IF
            PRINT
            INPUT "Flight number (0 when done)? ", FLIGHT
        LOOP
        END

        '  -----------------------------------------------
        '  Incoming flight information data

        DATA   6                       : 'Flight count

        '(Flight number, Point of origin, Arrival time)
        DATA 53,MIAMI,"8:15 AM"
        DATA 172,ATLANTA,"9:20 AM"
        DATA 122,NEW YORK,"11:30 AM"
        DATA 62,MONTREAL,"2:20 PM"
        DATA 303,HOUSTON,"4:45 PM"
        DATA 291,CHICAGO,"6:15 PM"
```

The following display was produced when we ran this program with the keyboard input values 62, 281 (an incorrect flight number), and 291:

```
    Flight number (0 when done)? 62

        Available information on Flight 62
        Origination point:         MONTREAL
        Expected time of arrival: 2:20 PM

    Flight number (0 when done)? 281
     281 is not a listed flight number.

    Flight number (0 when done)? 291

        Available information on Flight 291
        Origination point:         CHICAGO
        Expected time of arrival: 6:15 PM

    Flight number (0 when done)? 0
```

15.8 Problems

In Problems 1–3, write a program for each task specified. In each problem, decide how to organize the data by considering how they are to be used.

1. The following DATA lines show a name and four scores for each student in a psychology class:

```
DATA ARDEN MARK,72,79,91,70
DATA AUDEN WINN,95,92,86,82
DATA BRICE SALLY ANN,90,80,70,84
DATA BRANT EMILY,75,62,43,65
DATA RANDALL TONY,52,54,50,33
DATA RANDOLPH KIM,82,72,80,79
        .
        .
        .
DATA XXX
```

Letter grades for the students are determined by specifying four cutoff values for the four passing grades A, B, C, and D. Write a program to display the names and letter grades of all students. Include the four cutoff values, as well as the student names and scores in DATA statements.

2. A produce wholesaler uses the following price table while preparing invoices. A typical invoice is shown after the price table:

Current Price Table

Item	Item code	Price per crate
Artichokes	ART	8.50
Carrots	CAR	5.20
Cabbage	CAB	5.40
Collard greens	COL	5.90
Cucumbers	CUK	11.00
Lettuce-Iceberg	LET1	14.00
Lettuce-Romaine	LET3	12.75
Lettuce-Boston	LET7	10.50
Turnips	TUR	3.75

```
                NORTH END PRODUCE, INC.
    CUSTOMER: RAINBOW VEGETABLE STAND
    DESCRIPTION        QUANTITY   PRICE   AMOUNT
    -------------------------------------------
    CABBAGE               3        5.40    16.20
    ARTICHOKES           10        8.50    85.00
    LETTUCE-ICEBERG      10       14.00   140.00
    -------------------------------------------
    TOTALS               23               241.20
```

Write a program to prepare an invoice for each produce order included in the following DATA statements. (The first of these contains the order for the invoice shown.)

```
DATA RAINBOW VEGETABLE STAND,CAB,3,ART,10,LET1,10,X,0
DATA WEST END MARKET,TUR,1,LET3,1,COL,3,X,0
DATA CASEY'S PUB,ART,1,CUK,1,LET7,1,LET1,1,X,0
        .
        .       (additional orders go here)
        .
DATA END-OF-ORDERS
```

The pair X, 0 is used to indicate the end of each order, and END-OF-ORDERS is used to indicate that all invoices have been completed.

3. Write a program to produce invoices as in Problem 2 but with the produce orders typed at the keyboard rather than included in DATA lines. A suitable display created while typing the order whose invoice is shown would be

```
CUSTOMER? RAINBOW VEGETABLE STAND
(ENTER X FOR ITEM WHEN ORDER IS COMPLETED)

ITEM? CAB
CRATES? 3
ITEM? ART
CRATES? 10
ITEM? LET1
CRATES? 10
ITEM? X
```

(A complete order must be entered before any part of the invoice is displayed. Thus, you will need either two arrays to store the order information as it is entered or one or more arrays to store the invoice as it is generated. Either method is appropriate.)

■ *15.9 Higher-Dimensional Arrays*

All arrays used to this point have been one-dimensional, a term indicating that the array entries are referenced by using a single subscript. As illustrated in Sections 15.1 through 15.7, programming tasks involving tables represent an important application of one-dimensional arrays. There are some table-processing applications, however, for which the one-dimensional array structure is inadequate. For example, consider the following table that summarizes the responses of 10 families to a product survey:

Product Survey Table

Key to table entries									
Rating		Survey response							
0		POOR							
1		FAIR							
2		GOOD							
3		VERY GOOD							
4		EXCELLENT							

		Family number								
		1	2	3	4	5	6	7	8	9	10
Product number	1	0	1	1	2	1	2	2	1	0	1
	2	2	3	3	0	3	2	2	3	4	1
	3	1	3	4	4	4	1	4	2	3	2
	4	3	4	2	4	3	1	3	4	2	4
	5	0	1	3	2	2	2	1	3	0	1
	6	4	4	4	3	2	1	4	4	1	1
	7	1	3	1	3	2	4	1	4	3	4
	8	2	2	3	4	2	2	3	4	2	3

To store these data in one-dimensional arrays, we could use a string array to store the responses (POOR, FAIR, and so on) corresponding to the rating keys 0 through 4, but it would not be convenient to use one-dimensional arrays to store the table of numerical ratings. Doing so would require eight numerical arrays, if a separate array is used for each product, or ten arrays, if an array is used for each family. The program would be unnecessarily complicated (each array would have a different name) and very difficult to modify to handle other than eight products and ten families.

What is needed is a convenient way to store such tables. QuickBASIC provides this capability by allowing you to declare arrays whose entries are referenced by using two subscripts. First, we will introduce some terminology to make it easier to refer to arrays used to store tables such as the Product Survey Table. To keep things as simple as possible, however, we will use the following smaller table for illustration. The data in this table summarize the responses of college students to a hypothetical opinion poll concerning the abolition of grades.

Class	In favor of abolishing grades	Not in favor of abolishing grades	No opinion
Freshman	207	93	41
Sophomore	165	110	33
Junior	93	87	15
Senior	51	65	8

A **two-dimensional array** is a collection of items arranged in a rectangular fashion. That is, there is a first (horizontal) row, a second row, and so on, and a first (vertical) column, a second column, and so on. An array with *m* rows and *n* columns is called an **m-by-n array** (also written *m* × *n array*). Thus the opinion-poll data are presented as a 4-by-3 array.

An item in a two-dimensional array is specified by giving its row number and column number. For example, the item in the third row and second column of the opinion-poll table is 87. By convention, the row number is specified first. Thus, in the opinion-poll table, 33 is in the 2,3 position and 51 is in the 4,1 position. In mathematical notation we could write

$$P_{1,1} = 207, \quad P_{1,2} = 93 \quad P_{1,3} = 41$$

to indicate the values in the first row of our table. Since the QuickBASIC character set does not include such subscripts, this notation is changed as it was for one-dimensional arrays. Thus, the values in the opinion-poll table would be written as follows:

P(1,1) = 207	P(1,2) = 93	P(1,3) = 41
P(2,1) = 165	P(2,2) = 110	P(2,3) = 33
P(3,1) = 93	P(3,2) = 87	P(3,3) = 15
P(4,1) = 51	P(4,2) = 65	P(4,3) = 8

We say that **P** is the **name** of the array, that P(1,1), P(1,2), . . . , are **doubly subscripted variables,** and that the numbers enclosed in parentheses are the *subscripts* of P. The symbol P(I,J) is read **P sub I comma J** or simply **P sub IJ.**

The 4-by-3 array P can be visualized as follows:

```
                    (Column)
            P   1     2     3
            ─────────────────────
            1 │ 207   93    41
            2 │ 165   110   33
   (Row)    3 │  93   87    15
            4 │  51   65     8
```

This schematic displays the array name P, the row number for each item, and the column numbers.

To declare to the computer that your program will use the 4-by-3 array P, you would include the statement

```
DIM P(1 TO 4, 1 TO 3)      [or DIM P(4, 3)]
```

so that it is encountered before any of the doubly subscripted variables P(1,1), P(1,2), and so on, are referenced. If instead you include the statement

```
DIM P(1 TO 100, 1 TO 100)
```

your program can reference any or all of the subscripted variables P(R,C) with R and C integers in the range 1 to 100—there are 10,000 (100 × 100) such subscript assignments.

The value of a doubly subscripted variable—that is, an array entry—is referenced in a program just as values of singly subscripted variables are referenced. The subscripts can be integer constants, variables, or expressions. For example, the FOR loop

```
FOR C = 1 TO 3
   LET P(1, C) = 5 * C
NEXT C
```

assigns the values 5, 10, and 15 to the first row, P(1,1), P(1,2), P(1,3), of P. Similarly,

```
LET C = 1
FOR R = 1 TO 4
   LET P(R, C) = P(R, C) + 6
NEXT R
```

adds 6 to each entry in the first column, P(1,1), P(2,1), P(3,1), P(4,1), of P.

EXAMPLE 14   *Here is a program segment to read the college students' opinion-poll data into an array P.*

```
' Read values for the 4-by-3 array P.
DIM P(1 TO 4, 1 TO 3)

FOR R = 1 TO 4
   'Read values for the Rth row of P.
   FOR C = 1 TO 3
      READ P(R, C)
   NEXT C
NEXT R

DATA 207,93,41
DATA 165,110,33
DATA 93,87,15
DATA 51,65,8
```

When the first FOR statement is executed, R is assigned the initial value 1. The C loop then reads the first three data values 207, 93, and 41 for the variables P(1,1), P(1,2), and P(1,3), respectively. That is, when R = 1, values are read into the first row of P. Similarly, when R = 2, values are read into the second row, P(2,1), P(2,2), P(2,3), of P, and so on, until all 12 values have been assigned to P.

The nested FOR loops in the program segment shown in Example 14 are easily modified to read values into two-dimensional arrays of any size. Simply change 4 to the number of rows and 3 to the number of columns. We made this change and included the code in the following procedure READ.ARRAY. The procedure can be used to read values into any two-dimensional numerical array.

```
' Procedure to read values for
' the R-by-C numerical array P.
'
SUB READ.ARRAY (P(), R, C)
   FOR ROW = 1 TO R
      FOR COLUMN = 1 TO C
         READ P(ROW, COLUMN)
      NEXT COLUMN
   NEXT ROW
END SUB
```

The procedure READ.ARRAY is easily modified to display the contents of two-dimensional arrays. The following procedure DISPLAY.ARRAY shows one way to do this.

```
' Procedure to display the R-by-C array P.
'
SUB DISPLAY.ARRAY (P(), R, C)
```

```
      FOR ROW = 1 TO R
         FOR COL = 1 TO C
            PRINT USING "###.## "; P(ROW, COL);
         NEXT COL
         PRINT
      NEXT ROW
   END SUB
```

If you include these two procedures in a program, the statements

```
READ R, C
DIM P(1 TO R, 1 TO C)
CALL READ.ARRAY(P(), R, C)
CALL DISPLAY.ARRAY(P(), R, C)

DATA 2, 5                       :' Array size
DATA 11, 12, 13, 14, 15
DATA 16, 17, 18, 19, 20
```

will cause the display

```
   11.00  12.00  13.00  14.00  15.00
   16.00  17.00  18.00  19.00  20.00
```

EXAMPLE 15   *Let's write a program to count the number of students in each class who partici-pated in the opinion-poll survey.*

PROBLEM ANALYSIS

By leaving out all the details, we can write the following algorithm to carry out the specified task.

a. Read the opinion-poll data into array P.
b. Determine and display how many students in each class participated in the survey.

Since all three entries in any one row of P correspond to students in one of the four classes, the task in Step (b) is to add the three entries in each row of P and display these four sums. Let's use S(1) to denote the sum of the entries in the first row and S(2), S(3), and S(4) for the other three row sums. These sums can be determined as follows:

```
LET S(1)=P(1,1)+P(1,2)+P(1,3)
LET S(2)=P(2,1)+P(2,2)+P(2,3)
LET S(3)=P(3,1)+P(3,2)+P(3,3)
LET S(4)=P(4,1)+P(4,2)+P(4,3)
```

However, note that S(R), for R = 1, 2, 3, and 4, is obtained by summing P(R,C) for C = 1, 2, and 3. This is exactly the order of subscripts determined by the nested FOR loops

```
FOR R=1 TO 4
   FOR C=1 TO 3
      .
      .
      .
   NEXT C
NEXT R
```

The following program shows one way to complete the code for Step (b). For Step (a), we will use the procedure READ.ARRAY shown above.

MAIN UNIT

```
' -----------------------------------
' Read values for the 4-by-3 array P.
' -----------------------------------

DIM P(1 TO 4, 1 TO 3)
CALL READ.ARRAY(P(), 4, 3)

' ---------------------------------------
' Determine and display the row sums of P.
' ---------------------------------------
```

```
        PRINT "PARTICIPATION IN SURVEY BY CLASS"
        PRINT "--------------------------------"
        DIM S(1 TO 4)
        ERASE S
        FOR R = 1 TO 4
           FOR C = 1 TO 3
              LET S(R) = S(R) + P(R, C)
           NEXT C
           SELECT CASE R
              CASE 1: PRINT "FRESHMEN",
              CASE 2: PRINT "SOPHOMORES",
              CASE 3: PRINT "JUNIORS",
              CASE 4: PRINT "SENIORS",
           END SELECT
           PRINT S(R)
        NEXT R
        END

        DATA 207,93,41
        DATA 165,110,33
        DATA 93,87,15
        DATA 51,65,8
```

Program output:

```
PARTICIPATION IN SURVEY BY CLASS.
--------------------------------
FRESHMEN        341
SOPHOMORES      308
JUNIORS         195
SENIORS         124
```

Many programming applications involve rearranging the entries in arrays. The next two examples illustrate the rearrangement of entries in two-dimensional arrays.

EXAMPLE 16   *Here is a program segment to interchange rows K and L of an N × N array A.*

```
        FOR J = 1 TO N
           SWAP A(K, J), A(L, J)
        NEXT J
```

When $J = 1$, the SWAP statement causes A(K,1) and A(L,1), the first entries in the Kth and Lth row of A, to be interchanged; when $J = 2$, the second entries A(K,2) and A(L,2) are interchanged; and so on.

EXAMPLE 17   *Here is a program to read a two-dimensional array and interchange the row with the largest first value with the first row. The action of the program is described by its comment lines. The procedures READ.ARRAY and DISPLAY.ARRAY are the procedures given earlier.*

MAIN
UNIT

```
        '  --------------------------
        '   Read the following data
        '   into an R-by-C array A.
        '  --------------------------

        READ R, C
        DIM A(1 TO R, 1 TO C)
        CALL READ.ARRAY(A(), R, C)

        DATA 4,4        : 'Array size
        DATA 22.25,21.75,28.63,29.84
        DATA 61.23,55.47,59.55,62.33
        DATA 33.35,42.78,39.25,48.62
        DATA 44.45,43.25,27.62,39.04
```

```
' --------------------------------
' Display array A, row by row.
' --------------------------------

PRINT "ORIGINAL ARRAY:"
PRINT
CALL DISPLAY.ARRAY(A(), R, C)   'Display array A.
PRINT


' --------------------------------
' Find the row number K of the row
' with largest first value A(K,1).
' --------------------------------

LET K = 1
FOR ROW = 2 TO R
    IF A(ROW, 1) > A(K, 1) THEN K = ROW
NEXT ROW


' --------------------------------
' Interchange row K and row 1.
' --------------------------------

FOR COL = 1 TO C
    SWAP A(K, COL), A(1, COL)
NEXT COL


' ------------------------------------------
' Display the modified array A, row by row.
' ------------------------------------------

PRINT "MODIFIED ARRAY:"
PRINT
CALL DISPLAY.ARRAY(A(), R, C)    'Display array A.
PRINT
END
```

Program output:
```
ORIGINAL ARRAY:

22.25   21.75   28.63   29.84
61.23   55.47   59.55   62.33
33.35   42.78   39.25   48.62
44.45   43.25   27.62   39.04

MODIFIED ARRAY:

61.23   55.47   59.55   62.33
22.25   21.75   28.63   29.84
33.35   42.78   39.25   48.62
44.45   43.25   27.62   39.04
```

QuickBASIC does not restrict you to one or two subscripts. For example, the statement

```
DIM A(1 TO 2, 1 TO 2, 1 TO 2)
```

specifies a three-dimensional array whose entries can be referenced by using A(I,J,K), where the subscripts I, J, and K can be either 1 or 2. Similarly,

```
DIM B(1 TO 3, 1 TO 3, 1 TO 3, 1 TO 3, 1 TO 3)
```

specifies a five-dimensional array whose entries can be referenced by B(I,J,K,L,M), where the five subscripts can be any of the values 1, 2, and 3.

Arrays with more than two dimensions are sometimes used in technical engineering and mathematical applications, but they are rarely used in nontechnical programming tasks. For this reason, they are not illustrated here.

We conclude this section with three points concerning the use of higher-dimensional arrays that were not specifically mentioned or illustrated in this section:

1. Every higher-dimensional array should be declared in DIM statements. As with one-dimensional arrays, however, failure to do so will cause a fatal error only if you use a subscript that's not in the range 0 to 10.

2. Both one- and higher-dimensional arrays can be declared with the same DIM statement. The following DIM statement properly declares a one-dimensional numerical array YEAR with subscripts 1993 to 2000, a two-dimensional numerical array TABLE with subscripts 1 to 10, and a one-dimensional string array PLANET\$ with subscripts 1 to 9:

```
DIM YEAR(1993 TO 2000), TABLE(1 TO 10, 1 TO 10), PLANETS$(1 TO 9)
```

3. Higher-dimensional string arrays are permitted. At the beginning of this section, we showed an 8-row-by-10-column Product Survey Table. Each entry in the table is a numerical rating whose meaning is as follows:

Key to table entries

Rating	Survey response
0	POOR
1	FAIR
2	GOOD
3	VERY GOOD
4	EXCELLENT

Thus, to store the given Product Survey Table in the two-dimensional array PRODUCT, we could declare PRODUCT as follows:

```
DIM PRODUCT(1 TO 8, 1 TO 10)
```

If we wanted to store the actual responses (POOR, FAIR, and so on) rather than the corresponding rating numbers in an array, we would specify a string array as follows:

```
DIM PRODUCT$(1 TO 8, 1 TO 10)
```

■ *15.10 Problems*

1. *Show the output of each program.*

a.
```
DIM M(1 TO 4,1 TO 4)
FOR R=1 TO 4
   FOR C=1 TO 4
      LET M(R,C)=R*C
   NEXT C
NEXT R
FOR K=1 TO 4
   PRINT M(K,K);
NEXT K
END
```

b.
```
DIM A(1 TO 3,1 TO 2),B(1 TO 2,1 TO 3)
FOR R=1 TO 3
   FOR C=1 TO 2
      READ A(R,C)
      LET B(C,R)=A(R,C)
   NEXT C
NEXT R
PRINT B(2,1);B(2,2);B(2,3)
DATA 1,2,3,4,5,6,7,8,9
END
```

c.
```
DIM S(1 TO 3,1 TO 3)
FOR K=1 TO 3
   FOR L=1 TO K
      READ S(K,L)
      LET S(L,K)=S(K,L)
   NEXT L
NEXT K
```

```
      FOR N=1 TO 3
         PRINT S(N,2);
      NEXT N
      DATA 1,2,3,4,5,6
      END

   d. DIM YESNO$(1 TO 4,1 TO 4)
      FOR R=1 TO 4
         FOR C=1 TO 4
            IF R<C THEN A$="N" ELSE A$="Y"
            LET YESNO$(R,C)=A$
         NEXT C
      NEXT R
      FOR R=1 TO 4
         FOR C=1 TO 4
            PRINT YESNO$(R,C);
         NEXT C
         PRINT
      NEXT R
      END

   e. DIM T$(1 TO 3),P$(1 TO 3,1 TO 4)
      FOR N=1 TO 3
         READ T$(N)
         FOR P=1 TO 4
            READ P$(N,P)
         NEXT P
      NEXT N
      FOR N=1 TO 3
         PRINT T$(N);":",
      NEXT N
      PRINT
      FOR P=1 TO 4
         FOR N=1 TO 3
            PRINT P$(N,P),
         NEXT N
         PRINT
      NEXT P
      DATA DEVILS,ED,JANE,JOHN,SUE
      DATA HOOFERS,ANN,JIM,RON,RUTH
      DATA SAINTS,DEB,DOT,RUSS,TIM
      END
```

In Problems 2–18, write a program to perform each task specified.

2. Read 16 values into the 4 × 4 array M. Then display the array. Further, display the four column sums below their respective columns.

3. Repeat Problem 2 for an N × N array M in which N can be any integer up to 6.

4. Read 16 values into the 4 × 4 array M. Then display the array. Have row sums appear to the right of their respective rows and column sums below their respective columns.

5. Repeat Problem 4 for an N × N array M in which N can be any number up to 6.

6. Read values into an N × N array A. Display the array and then display the sum of the entries in the upper-left to lower-right diagonal of A. This sum is called the *trace* of array A. (Assume that N will never exceed 6.)

7. The *transpose* of an N × N array A is the N × N array whose rows are the columns of A in the same order. Read the entries of A from DATA lines, and display A and the transpose of A. (Assume that N will be less than 6.)

8. The *sum* S of two N × N arrays A and B is the N × N array whose entries are the sums of the corresponding entries of A and B. Read A and B from DATA lines, and display arrays A, B, and S. (Assume that N will be less than 6.)

9. Create the following 5 × 5 array N

$$
\begin{array}{rrrrr}
0 & 1 & 1 & 1 & 1 \\
-1 & 0 & 1 & 1 & 1 \\
-1 & -1 & 0 & 1 & 1 \\
-1 & -1 & -1 & 0 & 1 \\
-1 & -1 & -1 & -1 & 0
\end{array}
$$

Determine the values N(R,C) during program execution without using READ or INPUT statements. Display array N. [*Hint:* The value to be assigned to N(R,C) can be determined by comparing R with C.]

10. A manufacturing company sends a package consisting of eight new products to each of ten families and asks each family to rate each product. Here are the survey results:

Product Survey Table

Key to table entries	
Rating	**Survey response**
0	POOR
1	FAIR
2	GOOD
3	VERY GOOD
4	EXCELLENT

		Family number									
		1	2	3	4	5	6	7	8	9	10
	1	0	1	1	2	1	2	2	1	0	1
	2	2	3	3	0	3	2	2	3	4	1
	3	1	3	4	4	4	1	4	2	3	2
Product number	4	3	4	2	4	3	1	3	4	2	4
	5	0	1	3	2	2	2	1	3	0	1
	6	4	4	4	3	2	1	4	4	1	1
	7	1	3	1	3	2	4	1	4	3	4
	8	2	2	3	4	2	2	3	4	2	3

Write a menu-driven program that will carry out any or all of the tasks listed. (Have your program read the given data into arrays. You may find it convenient to use a string array to store the possible responses POOR, FAIR, and so on, and a two-dimensional array to store the data given in the table of numerical ratings.)

a. Display the entire Product Survey Table essentially as shown.

b. Display a two-column report showing the average rating for each product.

c. Display a two-column report as follows: the first column gives the product numbers receiving at least six ratings of 3 or better; the second gives the number of these ratings obtained.

d. Display a two-column table showing how many times each of the five possible responses (POOR, FAIR, and so on) were made.

11. An N × N array of numbers is called a *magic square* if the sums of each row, each column, and each diagonal are all equal. Test any N × N array in which N will never exceed 10. Values for N and array values should be input. Be sure to display and identify all row, column, and diagonal sums, the array itself, and a message indicating whether or not the array is a magic square. Try your program on the following arrays:

a.
$$
\begin{array}{rr}
1 & 1 \\
1 & 1
\end{array}
$$

b.
$$
\begin{array}{rrrrr}
11 & 10 & 4 & 23 & 17 \\
18 & 12 & 6 & 5 & 24 \\
25 & 19 & 13 & 7 & 1 \\
2 & 21 & 20 & 14 & 8 \\
9 & 3 & 22 & 16 & 15
\end{array}
$$

c.
$$
\begin{array}{rrrrrr}
4 & 139 & 161 & 26 & 174 & 147 \\
85 & 166 & 107 & 188 & 93 & 12 \\
98 & 152 & 138 & 3 & 103 & 157 \\
179 & 17 & 84 & 165 & 184 & 22 \\
183 & 21 & 13 & 175 & 89 & 170 \\
102 & 156 & 148 & 94 & 8 & 143
\end{array}
$$

12. Input five numbers to produce a five-column table as follows. The first column is to contain the five numbers in the order they are input. The second column is to contain the four differences of successive values in the first column. For example, if the first column contains 2, 4, 8, 9, 3, the second column will contain 2, 4, 1, −6. In the same way, each of columns 3–5 is to contain the differences of successive values in the column before it. If the values 1, 5, 9, 6, 12 are input, the output should be

1	4	0	−7	23
5	4	−7	16	
9	−3	9		
6	6			
12				

In the following suggested algorithm, M denotes a 5 × 5 array:
   a. Input the first column of M.
   b. Generate the remaining four columns of M as specified in the problem statement.
   c. Display the table as specified.
13. Input N numbers to produce a table of differences as described in Problem 12. Assume that N is an integer from 2 to 10.
14. Read values into a 5 × 3 array N. Then display the subscripts corresponding to the largest entry in N. If this largest value appears in N more than once, more than one pair of subscripts must be displayed. Use the following algorithm:
   a. Read values for array N.
   b. Determine M, the largest number in array N.
   c. Display all subscripts R,C for which N(R,C) = M.
15. Read values into a 5 × 3 array N. Display the row of N with the smallest first entry. If this smallest value is the first entry in more than one row, display only the first of these rows. Then interchange this row with the first row and display the modified array N. Use the following algorithm:
   a. Read values for array N.
   b. Find the first K such that row K has the smallest first entry.
   c. Display row K.
   d. Interchange rows 1 and K.
   e. Display the modified array N.
16. Read values into a 5 × 3 array A. Rearrange the rows of A so that their first entries are in ascending order. Display the modified array row by row. (Use a bubble sort to place the first-column entries A(1,1), A(2,1), A(3,1), A(4,1), A(5,1) in ascending order. Instead of swapping only A(I,1) and A(I + 1,1) whenever they are out of order, you must interchange all of row I with row I + 1.)
17. Modify your program for Problem 16 to handle M × N arrays rather than just 5 × 3 arrays.
18. Read N pairs of numbers into an N × 2 array A. Sort these pairs (that is, the rows of A) so that first-column entries are in ascending order and so that A(I,2) ≤ A(I + 1,2) whenever A(I,1) = A(I + 1,1). Use a bubble sort that will place the first-column entries A(1,1), A(2,1), . . . , A(N,1) in ascending order with the following modification. If A(I,1) > A(I + 1,1), swap rows I and I + 1; if A(I,1) < A(I + 1,1), no swap is necessary; otherwise—that is, if A(I,1) = A(I + 1,1)—swap only if A(I,2) > A(I + 1,2).

■ *15.11 Review True-or-False Quiz*

1. The two programming lines

```
DIM A(1 TO 25)
LET A = 1
```

   will assign the value 1 to all entries in the array A.   T F
2. Once array L is assigned values in a program, the statement PRINT L is sufficient to cause the entire array to be displayed.   T F

3. If arrays A and B are declared by using DIM A(1 to 9), B(1 to 9), then the statement
LET A = B will replace all entries of A by the corresponding entries of B.   T   F

4. The statement LET A(7) = 25 can never cause an error message to be displayed.   T   F

5. If a noninteger subscript is encountered during program execution, an error message
will be displayed and the program run will terminate.   T   F

6. Array values may be assigned by READ, INPUT, and LET statements.   T   F

7. If both one-dimensional and two-dimensional arrays are to be used in a program, two
DIM statements must be used.   T   F

8. Two or more arrays are sometimes needed to store a single table of values.   T   F

9. If a program is needed to process data given in tabular form, it is always best to use
arrays.   T   F

10. The bubble sort can be used to arrange a list of numbers in either ascending or
descending order.   T   F

11. The bubble sort can be used to arrange a list of words in alphabetical order but not in
reverse alphabetical order.   T   F

12. The bubble sort is inefficient when it's used to sort arrays with fewer than 30 values.   T   F

13. If an array N$ of employee names and an array S containing the corresponding salaries
of the employees are to be used to produce a two-column salary report with the names
in alphabetical order, two loops will be needed, one to alphabetize the array N$ and
another to make the corresponding changes to array S.   T   F

16
Data Files

*I*n the preceding chapters, all data to be processed by programs have been included in DATA lines or entered at the keyboard, and all output has been directed to the display screen or to a printer. Although these methods of handling I/O are adequate for many programming applications, situations do arise for which they are inadequate. For example, the output values of one program might be required as the input values of another program, or even of several other programs. Also, it might be necessary to store extensive output for printing at a later time when the computer isn't otherwise being used—long reports can be generated very quickly by computers, but comparatively, printers are very slow. To make all of this possible, QuickBASIC allows for input data to come from a source external to the program (other than a keyboard), and for the output to be stored on secondary storage devices for later use. This is accomplished with data files.

A **data file** is a named collection of related data that can be referenced by a program. The principal storage device used for data files is the disk unit.

QuickBASIC allows you to use two types of data files: **sequential access files** (or simply *sequential files*) and **random access files** (or simply *random files*). The contents of both types of files are ordered in sequence—there is a first entry, a second entry, a third, and so on. There are two main differences in the uses of sequential and random access files:

1. Data in a sequential file are accessed in order, beginning with the first datum, whereas data in a random file can be accessed in any order.
2. Data are added only at the end of a sequential file. This means that to change an entry in an existing file, you would create a completely new file that contains this change. With random files, individual entries can be changed, and there is no need to create a completely new file each time a file must be changed.

In this chapter, we show how to create both sequential and random access files and explain how they are used in several programming applications. Sequential files are described first (Sections 16.1 through 16.5) because they are somewhat easier to use and are adequate for applications encountered by beginning programmers. Random access files are considered in Section 16.7.

■ 16.1 Sequential Access Files

Associated with each data file that you use in a program are a **name** and a **file number.** The statement

```
OPEN "SCORES" FOR OUTPUT AS #1
```

declares SCORES as the *name* and 1 as the *file number* of a sequential file to be used as an output file. If F$ = "SCORES" and N = 1, the statement

```
OPEN F$ FOR OUTPUT AS #N
```

does the same thing. The statement

```
OPEN "STUDENTS.DAT" FOR INPUT AS #3
```

declares STUDENTS.DAT as the *name* and 3 as the *file number* of a sequential file to be used as an input file.

File names have the form

name [.extension]

where **name** contains from 1 to 8 characters and **extension** contains up to 3 characters. DAT is often used as the extension for data files. As indicated by the brackets, the extension is optional. File numbers must be integers in the range from 1 to 255.

Brief descriptions of the QuickBASIC statements that are used most often to process sequential files are as follows.

OPEN	Establishes a communication link between a program and a file. As shown in the two examples above, the name and number of the file and its designation as an input or output file are specified in the OPEN statement.
INPUT #*n*,	Obtains input values from file *n*, rather than from the keyboard. The comma is required.
PRINT #*n*, and WRITE #*n*,	Transmit output values to file *n*. The comma is required. PRINT # writes exactly the same information on a file as would be displayed on the screen if PRINT were used. You can also use **PRINT #*n*, USING** to specify an output format. WRITE # encloses strings in quotation marks and inserts commas between output values. As explained in what follows, WRITE # is preferred if the file being created is intended for later use as an input file. PRINT # is preferred if the file is a formatted output document not intended for later use as an input file.
CLOSE #*n*	Terminates the communication link established by the OPEN statement. We say that file #*n* has been closed. More than one file can be closed by a CLOSE statement: CLOSE #2, #3 (or more simply CLOSE 2,3) closes files 2 and 3; CLOSE with no file numbers closes all active files. Every file that has been opened with an OPEN statement should be closed. Failure to do so may result in a loss of data.

Let's assume that a file named SCORES contains the following six lines. (The use of the term "lines" as it applies to sequential files will be explained shortly.)

```
NICKLAUS
206
MILLER
208
WATSON
205
```

In Example 1, we show how a program can access the data contained in this file, and in Example 2, we show how the file SCORES can be created.

EXAMPLE 1   *Here is a program to read and display the information stored in file SCORES.*

```
OPEN "SCORES" FOR INPUT AS #1
FOR N = 1 TO 3
   INPUT #1, A$        'File input
   INPUT #1, S         'File input
   PRINT A$, S         'Screen output
NEXT N
CLOSE 1
END
```

Program output:
```
NICKLAUS          206
MILLER            208
WATSON            205
```

The OPEN statement specifies SCORES and 1 as the name and number of the input file. Whenever the file is used by the program, it is referenced by its number, not by its name. Thus, each time the statements

```
INPUT #1, A$
INPUT #1, S
```

are executed, values for A$ and S are obtained from the file SCORES. The PRINT statement displays these two values, as shown in the output.

REMARK 1   When an INPUT # statement obtains a value from a file, we say that it *reads* the value, or that the value is *read*.

REMARK 2   You should not run this program until you have used the program in Example 2 to create the file SCORES. Any attempt to open a file for INPUT whose name is not in the disk's directory of files will cause a *File not found* error that halts program execution. How you can write your programs so that such fatal errors do not halt program execution is explained in Section 16.3.

EXAMPLE 2   *Here is a program that can be used to create the file SCORES.*

```
OPEN "SCORES" FOR OUTPUT AS #1

PRINT "Type X for NAME to stop."
PRINT
INPUT "NAME:"; N$             'Keyboard input
DO UNTIL UCASE$(N$) = "X"
   INPUT "SCORE"; S           'Keyboard input
   PRINT #1, N$               'File output
   PRINT #1, S                'File output
   INPUT "NAME:"; N$          'Keyboard input
LOOP
CLOSE 1
END
```

Program output:
```
Type X for NAME to stop.

NAME? NICKLAUS
SCORE? 206
NAME? MILLER
SCORE? 208
NAME? WATSON
SCORE? 205
NAME? X
```

The OPEN statement specifies SCORES and 1 as the name and number of the output file. If SCORES is the name of an existing disk file, its previous contents are lost. If SCORES does not already exist, the name SCORES is added to the disk's directory of files.

Each time an INPUT statement is executed, we type a name or a score as shown in the display that was produced when the program was run. The two statements

```
PRINT #1, N$
PRINT #1, S
```

transmit these values to file 1 (that is, to the file SCORES) rather than to the screen or printer. When a PRINT # statement transmits a value to a file, we say that it *writes* the value or that the value is *written*.

In the preceding example, each time either of the statements PRINT #1,N$ or PRINT #1,S is executed, a single value followed by a *return* and *line feed* character [CHR$(13) and CHR$(10)] is written to the file SCORES. Following is a schematic representation of how information is organized in the file scores. (← denotes the *return* character and **lf** the *line feed* character.)

NICKLAUS	←	**lf**	206	←	**lf**	MILLER	←	**lf**	208	←	**lf**	WATSON	←	**lf**	205	←	**lf**	. . .

Because it has the six return and line feed characters shown, this file is customarily visualized as containing six distinct lines. Indeed, if you issue the DOS command* TYPE SCORES, the screen will display:

```
NICKLAUS
 206
MILLER
 208
WATSON
 205
```

(Note the blank in front of each numerical value. Remember, PRINT# writes exactly the same information on a file as would be displayed if PRINT were used.)

If, in the program of Example 2, you replace the statements

```
PRINT #1, N$
PRINT #1, S
```

by the single statement

```
PRINT #1,N$;S
```

the program will create file SCORES with three lines:

```
NICKLAUS 206
MILLER 208
WATSON 205
```

If the intent is to save the file for later printing, you may want this form; but if the file is intended only as an input file, you should not use it. If SCORES has this form, the statement

```
INPUT #1,N$
```

will give

```
N$="NICKLAUS 206"
```

Unless a string that appears in a file is enclosed in quotation marks, QuickBASIC obtains a value for a string variable by using all characters on the current line up to the first comma.

_____
*DOS commands cannot be issued from QuickBASIC. You must first return control to DOS.

To obtain the intended values, you could include a separating comma

```
PRINT #1,N$;",";S
```

or you could enclose the string in quotation marks:

```
PRINT #1,CHR$(34);A$;CHR$(34);S
```

(34 is the numeric code for the quotation mark.) A simpler way is to use WRITE # instead of PRINT #. *The WRITE # statement encloses all strings in quotation marks and inserts commas between output values.* If you replace the two PRINT # statements in the program of Example 2 with the single statement

```
WRITE #1,N$,S
```

or equivalently,

```
WRITE #1,N$;S
```

the program will create file SCORES as follows:

```
"NICKLAUS",206
"MILLER",208
"WATSON",205
```

The statement

```
INPUT #1,N$,S
```

will now give the intended values for N$ and S.

If you consistently use WRITE # statements to create files that will be used as input files, you can think of the items as constituting a single list of input values (just as do the items appearing in DATA lines). INPUT # statements will access these items in order (just as items in DATA lines are accessed in order by READ statements.) That the file may consist of lines as described above is of no consequence if all strings are quoted. Thus in Quick-BASIC, the statement

```
INPUT #1,N$,S
```

is equivalent to the two statements

```
INPUT #1,N$
INPUT #1,S
```

All that matters is the order in which the input variables N$ and S appear. Note that this means that INPUT # does *not* obtain values from files in exactly the same way that INPUT obtains values from the keyboard. With keyboard input, the statement

```
INPUT N$,S
```

requires that you type two values with a separating comma. If you respond in any other way, QuickBASIC will display

```
Redo from start
```

and you must retype the input. The topic of how INPUT # obtains values from a file is considered in greater detail following Example 3.

EXAMPLE 3 *Here is a program to create a short file and then read it.*

```
'Create file CITIES from these DATA:

DATA 4
DATA MONTEREY,CA,93940
DATA BRIDGEWATER,MA,02324
DATA AUSTIN,TX,78731
DATA JOHNSON CITY,TN,37601
```

```
OPEN "CITIES" FOR OUTPUT AS #1
READ COUNT
FOR C = 1 TO COUNT
    READ CITY$, STATE$, ZIP$
    WRITE #1, CITY$, STATE$, ZIP$
NEXT C
CLOSE 1

'Read and display data stored in file CITIES.

OPEN "CITIES" FOR INPUT AS #1
FOR C = 1 TO COUNT
    INPUT #1, CITY$, STATE$, ZIP$
    PRINT CITY$; ", "; STATE$; " "; ZIP$
NEXT C
CLOSE 1
END
```

Program output:
```
MONTEREY, CA 93940
BRIDGEWATER, MA 02324
AUSTIN, TX 78731
JOHNSON CITY, TN 37601
```

The program has two parts, as indicated by the comment lines. The first part opens the file CITIES that is to be created. Then, on each pass through the FOR loop, the statement

```
READ CITY$, STATE$, ZIP$
```

reads values from the DATA lines and

```
WRITE #1, CITY$, STATE$, ZIP$
```

transmits these values with quotes and separating commas to the output file CITIES. After execution of this first part, the contents of the file CITIES will be as follows:

```
"MONTEREY","CA","93940"
"BRIDGEWATER","MA","02324"
"AUSTIN","TX","78731"
"JOHNSON CITY","TN","37601"
```

The second part of the program reopens CITIES but this time as an input file. Then, on each pass through the FOR loop, the statement

```
INPUT #1, CITY$, STATE$, ZIP$
```

reads values from the file CITIES and

```
PRINT CITY$; ", "; STATE$; " "; ZIP$
```

displays them as shown in the output.

REMARK

The CLOSE statement at the end of the first part of the program is necessary. Without it, the second OPEN statement will halt program execution and display a *File already open* dialogue box. The file number of an active file cannot be used in an OPEN statement.

There may be times when you need to process files that were created with PRINT # statements instead of WRITE # statements. In such situations, you should know more about how INPUT # obtains values from files. As we have already mentioned, string values that are enclosed in quotation marks are obtained as expected and, if a string input value is not quoted, the PC uses all characters up to the next comma or up to the end of the line. If the input variable is numerical, the PC uses all characters up to the next space or comma or up to the end of the line. If these characters do not represent a numerical constant, the value 0 is assigned to the input variable and program execution continues. The following table illustrates how INPUT # obtains values from files that were created by using PRINT # statements.

Statement	Contents of file#1	Values obtained
INPUT #1,A$,S	NICKLAUS 206 MILLER 208	A$="NICKLAUS 206", S=0 (The character string MILLER gives the value 0 for S.)
INPUT #1,A$,S	NICKLAUS,206	A$="NICKLAUS", S=206
INPUT #1,S,A$	206 NICKLAUS	S=206, A$="NICKLAUS"
INPUT #1,A$	NICKLAUS,JACK	A$="NICKLAUS"
INPUT #1,A$	"NICKLAUS,JACK"	A$="NICKLAUS,JACK"
INPUT #1,A,B,C	10 20 30	A=10, B=20, C=30
INPUT #1,A,B,C	10,,30	A=10, B=0, C=30 (As with keyboard input, the empty string gives value 0.)

■ *16.2 Detecting the End of a Sequential File*

Each file contains a special character, called an **end of file mark,** following its last datum. This end of file mark serves two purposes:

1. While reading data from a file, the computer senses the end of file mark. Any attempt to read information beyond this end of file mark produces a fatal *Input past end* error.
2. QuickBASIC includes the **end of file function EOF.** If n is the file number of an active sequential file, EOF(n) is true if the end of file n has been reached; otherwise, EOF(n) is false. Example 4 shows how you can use the EOF function to write programs that do not attempt to read beyond the ends of files.

EXAMPLE 4

Here is an illustration of the EOF function. The program displays the contents of a file named BIRTHS that contains these three lines:

```
SUE COREY,2,4,92
ADAM JONES,2,15,92
CANDY FOBES,2,28,92
```

THE
PROGRAM

```
OPEN "BIRTHS" FOR INPUT AS #1
LET N = 0              'Name count
DO UNTIL EOF(1)
    INPUT #1, N$, M, D, Y
    PRINT N$, M; "/"; D; "/"; Y
    LET N = N + 1
LOOP
PRINT
PRINT "THERE WERE"; N; "BIRTHS THIS MONTH."
CLOSE 1
END
```

Program output:
```
SUE COREY      2 / 4 / 92
ADAM JONES     2 / 15 / 92
CANDY FOBES    2 / 28 / 92

THERE WERE 3 BIRTHS THIS MONTH.
```

The statement

```
DO UNTIL EOF(1)
```

checks whether more data are available on file 1. If the end of file mark has not been reached, EOF(1) is false and the DO loop is entered. On each pass through this loop, the INPUT#,

PRINT, and LET statements read and display one line of the file and increase the name count N by 1. After the last line of file BIRTHS has been processed by this DO loop, the UNTIL condition EOF(1) is true; that is, the end of file mark has been sensed. Control then passes out of the loop to the PRINT statements that produce the last line shown in the output.

QuickBASIC contains the LINE INPUT# statement, which can be used with the EOF function to display the contents of any sequential file. The statement

```
LINE INPUT #1,A$
```

assigns to A$ all characters (including any commas) on the current line of file #1. It skips over the RETURN/line feed sequence that ends the line so that the next LINE INPUT# statement will read the next line of the file.

EXAMPLE 5   *Here is a program to display the contents of any sequential file.*

```
INPUT "Enter file name: ", F$
OPEN F$ FOR INPUT AS #1
DO UNTIL EOF(1)
    LINE INPUT #1, A$    'Get one line.
    PRINT A$             'Display it.
LOOP
CLOSE 1
END
```

REMARK   This program is easily modified to make copies of sequential files. Simply insert

```
INPUT "Enter name for new file: ",G$
```

after the INPUT statement,

```
OPEN G$ FOR OUTPUT AS #2
```

after the OPEN statement, and change the PRINT statement to

```
PRINT #2, A$           'Write it to file 2.
```

■ *16.3 Error Trapping: The ON ERROR GOTO Statement*

If you run the program in Example 5 and enter the name of a file that is not in the disk's directory of files, QuickBASIC will halt program execution and display the dialogue box:

```
┌─────────────────────────┐
│   File not found         │
├─────────────────────────┤
│  < OK >    < Help >      │
└─────────────────────────┘
```

The statement

```
OPEN F$ FOR INPUT AS #1
```

produces a fatal error condition whenever F$ does not specify the name of an existing file. In this section, we show how you can cause program execution to continue after run-time errors have occurred—that is, after QuickBASIC has detected a fatal error condition. The EOF function illustrated in Section 16.2 is different: it is used to *avoid* run-time errors, not to allow program execution to continue *after* the error has occurred.

If **linelabel** denotes a label for a line that follows the END statement in the main program unit, the main unit can also include these statements:

ON ERROR GOTO **linelabel**
RESUME
RESUME NEXT

Once the ON ERROR GOTO statement has been executed, any fatal error—that is, any error that would otherwise cause an error message and halt program execution—causes an immediate transfer of control to the line specified by **linelabel.** The program segment that begins at this label is called the **error-handler.** The statements in the error-handler are carried out until a RESUME statement is encountered. The statement

```
RESUME NEXT
```

transfers control back to the statement that follows the one that caused the error. Example 6 shows how the ON ERROR GOTO and RESUME NEXT statements can be used to modify the program of Example 5 so that it handles otherwise fatal *File not found* errors. The statement

```
RESUME
```

transfers control back to the statement that caused the error, and program execution continues from that point. Because the statement that caused the error is executed a second time, you must include code in the error-handler to ensure that the same error does not occur again. This form of the RESUME statement is illustrated in Example 7.

EXAMPLE 6

Here is a program to display the contents of any sequential file. The program is a slight modification of the program in Example 5.

```
ON ERROR GOTO HANDLE.ERROR

INPUT "Enter file name: ", F$
OPEN F$ FOR INPUT AS #1          'If error, F$=ERROR".
IF F$ <> "ERROR" THEN
    DO UNTIL EOF(1)
        LINE INPUT #1, A$         'Get one line.
        PRINT A$                  'Display it.
    LOOP
    CLOSE 1
END IF
END

HANDLE.ERROR:  PRINT F$; " not found."
               LET F$ = "ERROR"
               RESUME NEXT
```

If you enter the name of a file that is not in the disk's directory of files (say FILE12), the OPEN statement causes the *File not found* error and control passes to the error-handler that begins at the label HANDLE.ERROR. The error-handler displays

```
FILE12 not found.
```

and assigns the string ERROR to F$ before the RESUME NEXT statement transfers control back to the statement that follows the OPEN statement that caused the error. Since F$ now has the string value ERROR, the statements in the Block IF statement that read and display the contents of a file are not executed.

The method of handling errors illustrated in Example 6 is called **error trapping;** the error caused by the OPEN statement is *trapped* by the computer's error-trapping facility. QuickBASIC's error-trapping facility is turned on by executing an ON ERROR GOTO statement. The special form

```
ON ERROR GOTO 0
```

of this statement turns off the error-trapping facility. Example 7 shows how this feature can be used.

Any fatal error, not just *File not found* errors, can be trapped. There is a good reason for trapping errors: a user of your programs should not be confronted with unexpected error messages that are not understood and that halt program execution before the intended task has been carried out. To assist you in handling multiple errors, QuickBASIC provides an error-handling function:

ERR   returns the code (a number) of the most recent run-time error. Table 16.1 gives a list of the error codes associated with run-time errors.

Table 16.1   **Run-time error codes.**

Code	Description	Code	Description
2	Syntax error	53	File not found
3	RETURN without GOSUB	54	Bad file mode
4	Out of DATA	55	File already open
5	Illegal function call	56	FIELD statement active
6	Overflow	57	Device I/O error
7	Out of memory	58	File already exists
9	Subscript out of range	59	Bad record length
10	Duplicate definition	61	Disk full
11	Division by zero	62	Input past end of file
13	Type mismatch	63	Bad record number
14	Out of string space	64	Bad file name
16	String formula too complex	67	Too many files
19	No RESUME	68	Device unavailable
20	RESUME without error	69	Communication-buffer overflow
24	Device timeout	70	Permission denied
25	Device fault	71	Disk not ready
27	Out of paper	72	Disk-media error
39	CASE ELSE expected	73	Advanced feature unavailable
40	Variable required	74	Rename across disks
50	FIELD overflow	75	Path/File access error
51	Internal error	76	Path not found
52	Bad file name or number		

Example 7 shows how the function ERR allows you to handle more than one run-time error in your error-handler. It is common practice, however, to use ON ERROR GOTO to trap only those errors that cannot be handled conveniently in some other way. For instance, we consistently use the end of file function EOF to avoid run-time errors while reading from a file.

EXAMPLE 7   Here is a program with an error-handler that takes corrective action for more than one run-time error.

```
' THIS PROGRAM PRODUCES A PRINTED LIST OF ALL
' WORDS INCLUDED IN THESE DATA STATEMENTS.

DATA RED, BLUE, GREEN
DATA LAVENDER, MAGENTA

ON ERROR GOTO ERROR.HANDLER
```

```
LPRINT "LIST OF WORDS IN DATA LINES:"
LPRINT
DO
   READ X$                 '(Set to ERROR, on error)
   IF X$ = "ERROR" THEN
      EXIT DO
   ELSE
      LPRINT X$            'Print it.
   END IF
LOOP
END

ERROR.HANDLER:

   SELECT CASE ERR

      CASE 4                    'Out of DATA
         LET X$ = "ERROR"
         RESUME NEXT

      CASE 27                   'Out of paper
         PRINT "Out of paper."
         PRINT "Fix and press key."
         DO WHILE INKEY$ = "": LOOP
         RESUME

      CASE ELSE
         'Unanticipated error has occurred.
         'Turn off error trapping so that
         'QuickBASIC will display the normal
         'error message and stop the program.
         ON ERROR GOTO 0

   END SELECT
```

The error-handler takes corrective action in two cases:

ERR=4   An attempt to read from DATA statements after all data have been read. In this case, the error-handler assigns the string ERROR to X$ and then uses RESUME NEXT to transfer control back to the IF statement that follows the READ that caused the error. This IF statement causes an orderly exit from the DO loop, and the program ends with no error message.

ERR=27   An attempt to transmit output to a printer that is not ready. In this case, the error-handler displays an appropriate message, waits for the user to press a key after fixing the printer problem, and then uses RESUME to transfer control back to the LPRINT statement that caused the error. The LPRINT statement then prints the value of X$ (provided, of course, that the user fixed the printer problem), and program execution continues until an *Out of data* error occurs.

If any other error is encountered during run time, the statement

```
ON ERROR GOTO 0
```

in the CASE ELSE clause turns off error trapping so that the error will be handled in the usual way.

The following points concerning error trapping were not explicitly mentioned in this section. Except for items 1 and 2, the comments suggest error-handling techniques that are allowed but not recommended for beginners. You should find the comments helpful, even if they only point out practices to be avoided.

1. Because the error-handler is in the main program unit, the error-handler knows only the variables in that unit. Thus, if an error occurs in a procedure, you may not be able to change the values of variables that appear in the procedure. The error-handlers in Examples 6 and 7 do change variables (F$ in Example 6, and X$ in Example 7), but in each case the change is to a variable that appears in the main program unit.

2. The ON ERROR GOTO statement can appear in a program unit other than the main program unit. The error-handler, however, should be in the main program unit.

3. It is a common, but not required, practice to include error-handlers in the main program unit, as was done in each example. Writing error-handlers in any other way represents an advanced programming technique and is not recommended for beginners.

4. QuickBASIC allows a third form of the RESUME statement

RESUME linelabel

This form returns control from the error-handler to the line with the label **linelabel.** The label must not be in a procedure. Using this form of the RESUME statement represents an advanced programming technique and is not recommended for beginners.

■ 16.4 Problems

1. *Here is a program to create a file COMM.*

```
OPEN "COMM" FOR OUTPUT AS #1
READ N$,S,Q
DO UNTIL N$="XXX"
    WRITE#1,N$,S,Q
    READ N$,S,Q
LOOP
CLOSE 1
END
DATA J.D.SLOANE,13000,10000
DATA R.M.PETERS,5000,5000
DATA A.B.CARTER,7400,5000
DATA I.O.ULSTER,12000,10000
DATA XXX,0,0
```

Show the output of each program in parts (a) and (b).

```
a. OPEN "COMM" FOR INPUT AS #1
   DO UNTIL EOF(1)
       INPUT#1,N$,S,Q
       IF S>Q THEN
           PRINT N$
           PRINT "EXCESS:"; S-Q
           PRINT
       END IF
   LOOP
   CLOSE 1
   END
```

```
b. OPEN "COMM" FOR INPUT AS #2
   DO UNTIL EOF(2)
       INPUT#2,A$,S,Q
       IF S>Q  THEN C=0.10*(S-Q)  ELSE C=0
       LET W=265+C
       PRINT A$,W
   LOOP
   CLOSE 2
   END
```

2. *Here is a program to create a file GRADES.*

```
OPEN "GRADES" FOR OUTPUT AS FILE #1
READ A$,N1,N2
DO UNTIL A$="X"
    WRITE#1,A$,N1,N2
    READ A$,N1,N2
LOOP
CLOSE 1
END
DATA JOAN,80,90
DATA SAM,100,80
DATA GREG,80,40
DATA MARY,70,30
DATA MARK,50,90
DATA X,0,0
```

Show the output of each program in parts (a) and (b).

a.
```
OPEN "GRADES" FOR INPUT AS #1
DO UNTIL EOF(1)
    INPUT#1,B$,A,B
    IF A>B THEN PRINT B$
LOOP
CLOSE 1
END
```

b.
```
OPEN "GRADES" FOR INPUT AS #2
LET P$="PASS"
LET F$="FAIL"
DO UNTIL EOF(2)
    INPUT#2,N$,X,Y
    LET A=(X+2*Y)/3
    IF A>65 THEN PRINT N$,P$ ELSE PRINT N$,F$
LOOP
CLOSE 2
END
```

In Problems 3–23, write a program for each task specified.

3. Create a file named WORDS that contains whatever words are typed at the keyboard. After WORDS has been created, display its contents, three words per line. The file is to be used as an input file for Problems 4 and 5.

4. Given the file WORDS described in Problem 3, display all words beginning with a letter A through M, and follow this list by two counts—a count of how many words are in the file and a count of how many words were displayed.

5. Given the file WORDS described in Problem 3, create two files—one containing all words beginning with a letter A through M and the other containing the remaining words. Use appropriate names for the two files. After the two new files have been created, display their contents with appropriate titles.

6. Create a file NAMES containing up to 50 names typed at the keyboard. If a name is typed a second time, display an appropriate message, but do not store the name twice. If at any time LIST is typed, display all names entered to that point. If END is typed, halt program execution. (*Suggestion:* Input names into an array and create the file NAMES only after the user types END.)

7. Create two files named ALPHA and BETA. ALPHA is to contain all numbers from 1 to 200 that are multiples of either 2, 3, 5, or 7. The rest of the numbers from 1 to 200 go in file BETA. After the files have been created, display their contents with appropriate titles.

8. The following table describes an investor's stock portfolio. Create a file STOCKS that contains this information. The file STOCKS is to be used as an input file in Problems 9–11.

Name of stock	Number of shares	Last week's closing price	Current week's closing price
STERLING DRUG	800	16.50	16.125
DATA GENERAL	500	56.25	57.50
OWEN ILLINOIS	1200	22.50	21.50
MATTEL INC	1000	10.75	11.125
ABBOTT LAB	2000	33.75	34.75
FED NATL MTG	2500	17.75	17.25
IC GEN	250	43.125	43.625
ALO SYSTEMS	550	18.50	18.25

9. Produce a report displaying precisely the information contained in the file STOCKS. Be sure to label each column and to give the report a title.

10. Produce a five-column report with the first four columns as in Problem 9 and a fifth column showing the percentage increase or decrease for each security.

11. Produce a four-column report showing the stock name, the equity at the close of business last week, the equity this week, and the dollar change in equity. End the report with a message that shows the total net gain or loss for the week.

12. Create a file named LIBEL that contains the following information about employees of the Libel Insurance Company. The file LIBEL is to be used as an input file in Problems 13–18.

ID	Sex	Age	Years of service	Annual salary
012-24-2735	M	47	13	25,200.00
024-18-2980	F	33	6	19,300.00
018-26-3865	F	41	15	28,900.00
035-14-4222	M	22	2	16,400.00
026-21-4740	M	59	7	24,200.00
024-25-5200	F	25	3	18,000.00
018-17-5803	M	33	13	26,500.00
016-24-7242	F	28	4	18,400.00
021-18-7341	M	68	30	30,500.00
021-25-8004	M	35	6	19,300.00
031-42-9327	F	21	3	14,200.00

13. Produce a five-column report with a title and appropriate column headings displaying the employee information contained in the file LIBEL. (The sex column is to contain MALE or FEMALE, not M or F.)

14. Produce two reports that show the employee information contained in LIBEL by sex. Give each report a title and four appropriately labeled columns.

15. Produce a report that shows the ID numbers, years of service, and salaries of all employees who have been with the firm for more than 5 years.

16. Produce a two-column report that shows ID numbers and annual salaries of all employees whose annual salary exceeds $15,000. In addition to column headings, be sure the report has an appropriate title.

17. Produce a two-column report as described in Problem 16 for all employees whose annual salaries exceed the average annual salary of all Libel employees. Following the report, display the total annual salary earned by these employees. The title of the report should include the average salary of all Libel employees. (Do not read the file contents into arrays. Rather, read through the file to determine the total annual salary and average annual salary figures; then read the file a second time to produce the report.)

18. Write a menu-driven program to perform some or all of the tasks specified in Problems 13–17.

19. Create a file INVTRY containing the following inventory data. The file INVTRY is to be used as an input file in Problems 20–23.

Item code	Item type	Units on hand	Average cost per unit	Sales price per unit
ITEM 1	A	20500	1.55	1.95
ITEM 2	A	54000	0.59	0.74
ITEM 3	B	8250	3.40	4.10
ITEM 4	B	4000	5.23	6.75
ITEM 5	A	15000	0.60	0.75
ITEM 6	A	10500	1.05	1.35
ITEM 7	B	6000	7.45	9.89
ITEM 8	B	7500	5.10	5.43
ITEM 9	B	15500	3.10	4.10

20. Produce a five-column report that displays exactly the information in INVTRY.

21. Produce two separate reports, the first to display the given information for type-A items and the second for type-B items.

22. Produce a five-column report that shows the item code, the number of units on hand, and the total cost, total sales price, and total income these units represent (income = sales − cost). Conclude the report with a message that shows the total cost, total sales price, and total income represented by the entire inventory.

23. Write a menu-driven program to perform some or all of the tasks specified in Problems 20–22.

■ *16.5 Maintaining Sequential Files*

Updating existing data files is a common programming application. In this section, we give two examples to illustrate this practice. The first involves updating a short simplified inventory file and the second a short personnel file. It should be remarked, however, that data files usually are not short and require rather complicated programs to maintain them. Our objective is simply to show that file maintenance is possible. A complete discussion of the many techniques used in file maintenance programs is beyond the scope of this introductory book.

In Example 8, we will write a program to modify a file named INVTRY that contains these data:

```
"A10010",2000
"A10011",4450
"C22960",1060
"D40240",2300
"X99220",500
"X99221",650
"Y88000",1050
"Y88001",400
```

The first entry in each line denotes an item code, and the second entry gives the number of units on hand. The following program can be used to create this file:

```
OPEN "INVTRY" FOR OUTPUT AS #1
READ A$, N
DO UNTIL A$ = "XXX"
   WRITE #1, A$, N
   READ A$, N
LOOP
CLOSE #1
END
DATA "A10010", 2000, "A10011", 4450
DATA "C22960", 1060, "D40240", 2300
DATA "X99220",  500, "X99221",  650
DATA "Y88000", 1050, "Y88001",  400
DATA "XXX", 0
```

EXAMPLE 8   *We will write a program to allow a user to update the file INVTRY to reflect all transactions that have occurred since the last update.*

Let's assume that the user must specify, for each item to be changed, the item code, the number of units shipped since the last update, and the number of units received since the last update. Thus the user might come to the computer armed with a list like this:

Item code	Shipped	Received
A10010	1,200	1,000
A10011	1,000	550
D40240	1,800	2,000
Y88000	300	0

A person carrying out this task by hand might proceed as follows:

a. Read an item code.
b. Search the file INVTRY for this code, and change the units-on-hand figure as required.
c. If more changes are to be made, go to Step (a).
d. Have the updated copy of INVTRY typed.

There is a slight problem with this algorithm. Step (b) says to change a *single* number that appears on the file INVTRY, and this is not done when using sequential files. We will first input the data from INVTRY into two arrays and make the necessary changes in these arrays. After this has been done for each item that requires a change, Step (d) will involve creating a new copy of INVTRY by using the PRINT # or WRITE # statement. Since INVTRY is used as an input data file, we'll use WRITE #. Before rewriting the algorithm, let's choose variable names:

CODES$ = array of item codes from file INVTRY
UNITS   = corresponding array of quantities from INVTRY
COUNT = number of lines in the file INVTRY
X$ = item code to be typed
S   = quantity shipped
R   = quantity received

In the following algorithm, we require the user to type END after all changes have been made.

a. Input arrays CODES$ and UNITS from the file INVTRY.
b. Enter an item code X$.
c. Repeat the following until X$ is END.

    c1. Search for subscript P with CODES$(P) = X$.
    c2. If X$ is not found display an appropriate message, otherwise input quantities S and R and change UNITS(P) to UNITS(P) +R − S.
    c3. Enter next item code X$.

d. Make a new copy of INVTRY.
e. Stop.

Step (a) is easily coded. We simply open INVTRY as an input file and use a loop to read its contents into the arrays CODES$ and UNITS. We'll carry out this task in a SUB procedure with parameters that allow us to pass the following five values between the main program unit and the procedure:

1. Name of the file (to be passed to the procedure).
2. Array of item codes (to be returned).
3. Array of units on hand amounts (to be returned).
4. Number of items read from file (to be returned).
5. Dimension of the arrays (to be passed to the procedure).

```
SUB FILE.INPUT (F$, C$(), QTY(), COUNT, MAX.ARRAY.SIZE)

   'Read paired data from file F$ into arrays C$
   'and QTY and determine the number COUNT of pairs.

   OPEN F$ FOR INPUT AS #1
   LET COUNT = 0
   DO UNTIL EOF(1) OR COUNT = MAX.ARRAY.SIZE
      LET COUNT = COUNT + 1
      INPUT #1, C$(COUNT), QTY(COUNT)
   LOOP
   IF NOT EOF(1) THEN
      PRINT "ARRAY DIMENSIONS NOT ADEQUATE - SEE PROGRAMMER."
   END IF

   CLOSE #1

END SUB
```

Step (c) is also easily coded. We will include code that carries out Steps (c1) through (c3) in a DO loop that ends when the input value X$ is END. To keep the main program unit as uncluttered as possible, we'll write the code that carries out the search in Step (c1) as a FUNCTION procedure:

```
FUNCTION SEARCH (C$(), X$, COUNT)

   'Search array C$ of size COUNT for X$.

   '    If found, return subscript P for which C$(P)=X$.
   '    If not found, return 0.

   LET P = 1                            'Array position
   DO UNTIL C$(P) = X$ OR P >= COUNT    'Loop until X$ is found
      LET P = P + 1                     ' or all array entries
   LOOP                                 ' have been tested.
   IF C$(P) = X$ THEN                   'Was X$ found?
      LET SEARCH = P                    'Yes.
   ELSE
      LET SEARCH = 0                    'No.
   END IF
END FUNCTION
```

Code for Step (d) is also straightforward. We simply reopen INVTRY as an output file, and write the contents of arrays CODES$ and UNITS to the file. We'll use the following procedure for this task:

```
SUB UPDATE (F$, C$(), QTY(), COUNT)

   'Write the paired data included in
   'arrays C$ and QTY (of size COUNT)
   'to the file F$.

   OPEN F$ FOR OUTPUT AS #1
   FOR P = 1 TO COUNT
      WRITE #1, C$(P), QTY(P)
   NEXT P
   CLOSE 1

END SUB
```

PROGRAM MAIN UNIT

```
'                  INVENTORY UPDATE PROGRAM
'
DIM CODES$(50)       'Array of item codes
DIM UNITS(50)        'Array of quantities

'Input arrays CODES$ AND UNITS from file
'INVTRY and find the count COUNT of items.
```

```
          CALL FILE.INPUT("INVTRY", CODES$(), UNITS(), COUNT, 50)


          'Get keyboard changes and update arrays CODES$ and UNITS.

          PRINT "ENTER UPDATE INFORMATION AS REQUESTED."
          PRINT
          INPUT "ITEM(END WHEN DONE)"; X$          'Keyboard input
          LET X$ = UCASE$(X$)
          DO UNTIL X$ = "END"
             LET P = SEARCH(CODES$(), X$, COUNT)   'Position P of X$, or 0.
             IF P = 0 THEN                          'Found?
                PRINT X$; " NOT IN INVENTORY."      'No.
             ELSE
                INPUT "UNITS SHIPPED"; S            'Yes. Get changes
                INPUT "UNITS RECEIVED"; R           ' from keyboard.
                LET UNITS(P) = UNITS(P) + R - S     'Update array.
             END IF
             PRINT
             INPUT "ITEM(END WHEN DONE)"; X$
             LET X$ = UCASE$(X$)
          LOOP


          'Make a new copy of file INVTRY and stop.

          CALL UPDATE("INVTRY", CODES$(), UNITS(), COUNT)
          PRINT "INVTRY IS UPDATED."
          END
```

We ran this program with the file INVTRY shown at the outset of this section to obtain the following screen display:

```
ENTER UPDATE INFORMATION AS REQUESTED.

ITEM(END WHEN DONE)? A10010
UNITS SHIPPED? 1200
UNITS RECEIVED? 1000

ITEM(END WHEN DONE)? A10011
UNITS SHIPPED? 1000
UNITS RECEIVED? 550

ITEM(END WHEN DONE)? D40241
D40241 NOT IN INVENTORY.

ITEM(END WHEN DONE)? D40240
UNITS SHIPPED? 1800
UNITS RECEIVED? 2000

ITEM(END WHEN DONE)? Y88000
UNITS SHIPPED? 300
UNITS RECEIVED? 0

ITEM(END WHEN DONE)? END
INVTRY IS UPDATED.
```

REMARK 1   The last line, INVTRY IS UPDATED, is intended to reassure us that the file has been correctly updated. To see that this is so, we ran the program of Example 6, which displays the contents of any sequential file, to obtain the following display:

```
Enter file name: INVTRY
"A10010",1800
"A10011",4000
"C22960",1060
"D40240",2500
"X99220",500
```

```
"X99221",650
"Y88000",1050
"Y88001",400
```

REMARK 2   Notice that the number 50 used to dimension the arrays CODES$ and UNITS appears in the main program unit in three places: in the two DIM statements and in the statement

```
CALL FILE.INPUT("INVTRY", CODES$(), UNITS(), COUNT, 50)
```

Thus, to modify the program to handle larger files, all three of these instances of 50 must be changed to a larger number. In QuickBASIC, there are two ways to modify the program so that only one change needs to be made. You can insert the statement

```
LET MAX.ARRAY.SIZE = 50
```

at the beginning of the main program unit just before the DIM statements, and change each 50 to MAX.ARRAY.SIZE. Then, to have the program handle larger files, only this LET statement needs to be changed. The other way to modify the program is to use a CONST statement, such as

```
CONST MAX.ARRAY.SIZE = 50          'Global constant
```

instead of the LET statement. This statement declares MAX.ARRAY.SIZE as another name for the constant 50. Because it is a constant, it cannot be changed by the program. Any attempt to do so will result in a fatal error. As indicated by the comment, names declared as constants in CONST statements are global; that is, they have the same meaning in every program unit and do not have to be passed by using parameters.

In the next example, we modify an existing sequential file by adding data to the end of it. Changing a sequential file in this way does not require making a completely new copy of the file. The statement

```
OPEN "DATA5" FOR APPEND AS #1
```

opens DATA5 as an output file but positions the file at the end of any data already on the file. Subsequent output to this file will be written at the end of the file.

EXAMPLE 9   ***The ID numbers and names of all employees of the Land Foundry Company are stored in the personnel file EMPLOY.DAT. Typical lines are***

```
"23501","AHEARN JOHN F."
"53241","ANDERSON ALBERT G."
"15653","SIMPSON DONALD C."
"37671","HENDRIX SAMUEL D."
"49313","POST EDWARD L."
"44446","MURRAY HAROLD N."
"23786","SILVA JOSE R."
"83817","CONNORS FRANK P."
```

Let's write a program to allow a user to add new employees to the file.

PROBLEM ANALYSIS

Input: Data stored in the file EMPLOY.DAT
New names and ID numbers typed at keyboard

Output: File EMPLOY.DAT updated as specified in the problem statement

A person carrying out this task by hand might proceed as follows.

a. Get the employee file.
b. For each new employee:

　　b1. Select an ID not yet used.
　　b2. Add the employee to the file.

c. Return the file to the file cabinet.

Since each ID for a new employee must not already be in use, the first task in Step (b) requires that each new ID be compared with all IDs that are currently being used. We will not search the actual file each time these comparisons must be made. Rather, we will read all IDs into an array and use this array for each search. (Although information on a disk can be accessed very quickly, accessing information that is already in memory is much faster.) Of course, each new ID must be added to the array of ID codes so that the same code will not be used for two new employees. We'll read the IDs into an array by using a SUB procedure with parameters that allow us to pass the following values between the main program unit and the procedure:

1. Name of the file (to be passed to the procedure).
2. Array of IDs (to be returned).
3. Number of IDs read from the file (to be returned).
4. Dimension for the array (to be passed to the procedure).

The following procedure is a slight modification of the procedure FILE.INPUT of Example 8.

```
SUB FILE.IDS (F$, ID$(), ID.COUNT, MAX.ARRAY.SIZE)

   ' Read paired data from file F$:
   '
   '    Store first entry of each pair in array ID$.
   '    Determine the count ID.COUNT of pairs.

   OPEN F$ FOR INPUT AS #1
   LET ID.COUNT = 0
   DO UNTIL EOF(1) OR ID.COUNT = MAX.ARRAY.SIZE
      LET ID.COUNT = ID.COUNT + 1
      INPUT #1, ID$(ID.COUNT), OLD.EMP$
   LOOP
   IF NOT EOF(1) THEN
      PRINT "ARRAY DIMENSIONS NOT ADEQUATE - SEE PROGRAMMER."
   END IF
   CLOSE #1

END SUB
```

Step (b1) in the algorithm says to select an ID number not yet in use. Thus, we must search the array of IDs for each new ID number entered at the keyboard. To carry out this search, we'll use the same search function used in Example 8:

```
FUNCTION SEARCH (C$(), X$, COUNT)

   'Search array C$ of size COUNT for X$.

   'If found, return subscript P for which C$(P)=X$.
   'If not found, return 0.

   LET P = 1                        'Array position
   DO UNTIL C$(P) = X$ OR P >= COUNT 'Loop until X$ is found
      LET P = P + 1                 ' or all array entries
   LOOP                             ' have been tested.
   IF C$(P) = X$ THEN               'Was X$ found?
      LET SEARCH = P                'Yes
   ELSE
      LET SEARCH = 0                'No
   END IF

END FUNCTION
```

Step (b2) requires that we add information to the end of a file. To accomplish this, we will reopen the file as an APPEND file before new names and IDs are entered at the keyboard, and we will close it only after all new data have been written to the file.

The variable names shown in the procedures are local to the procedures and are not known to the main program unit. To allow us to write a detailed yet concise algorithm for the main program, we will use these variable names:

ID$	= array of ID numbers
COUNT	= actual number of entries in array ID$
NEW.EMP$	= name of new employee to be added to the file
NEW.ID$	= ID number assigned to employee NEW.EMP$

In the following algorithm, we require the user to type XXX after all new names have been entered.

THE ALGORITHM

a. Read the file EMPLOY.DAT to obtain the array ID$ of ID codes and the count COUNT of how many codes are included.

b. Enter a new NEW.EMP$.

c. While NEW.EMP$ is not XXX, do the following:

   c1. Enter NEW.ID$.

   c2. Search array ID$ for NEW.ID$.

   c3. If NEW.ID$ is found:

      Repeat Step (c1).

   Otherwise:

      Append NEW.ID$ and NEW.EMP$ to the file.

      Add 1 to COUNT.

      Assign NEW.ID$ to ID$(COUNT).

      Enter the next name NEW.EMP$.

d. Close EMPLOY.DAT and stop.

In the following program, we use two additional variable names:

F$	= Name of file
ARRAY.SIZE	= Dimension for array ID$

By assigning the file name EMPLOY.DAT to F$ and the array dimension (we use 50 in the program) to ARRAY.SIZE, we simplify the task of modifying the program to handle other files or files with more data than anticipated when the program was written.

PROGRAM MAIN UNIT

```
'                 PROGRAM TO UPDATE THE FILE F$

' Variable names used in main program unit:

'          F$ = Name of file
'         ID$ = Array of ID numbers
'  ARRAY.SIZE = Dimension for array ID$
'       COUNT = Actual number of entries in array ID$
'    NEW.EMP$ = Name of new employee to be added to the file
'     NEW.ID$ = ID number assigned to employee NEW.EMP$


' Read ID codes from file F$ into array ID$
' and store the actual size of ID$ in COUNT.

LET F$ = "EMPLOY.DAT"                        'Name of file
PRINT "PROGRAM TO UPDATE THE FILE "; F$
LET ARRAY.SIZE = 50                          'Array dimension
DIM ID$(ARRAY.SIZE)                          'Array of ID codes
CALL FILE.IDS(F$, ID$(), COUNT, ARRAY.SIZE)  'Read file F$ and
                                             ' return ID$
                                             ' and COUNT.

' Get new employee names and IDs from
' the keyboard and APPEND to file F$.
```

```
              OPEN F$ FOR APPEND AS #1                    'Open file for APPEND.
              PRINT
              PRINT "Enter each new employee with last name first."
              PRINT "Do not use commas.  Thus, type"
              PRINT "    DOE SUSAN B.  and not  DOE,SUSAN B."
              PRINT
              INPUT "NAME (XXX when done)"; NEW.EMP$
              DO UNTIL UCASE$(NEW.EMP$) = "XXX" OR COUNT = ARRAY.SIZE
                 INPUT "IDENTIFICATION CODE"; NEW.ID$
                 LET P = SEARCH(ID$(), NEW.ID$, COUNT)    'Search for NEW.ID$.
                 IF P > 0 THEN                            'Found?
                    PRINT NEW.ID$; " already in use."     'Yes. Don't use it.
                 ELSE
                    LET COUNT = COUNT + 1                 'No. Count it and
                    LET ID$(COUNT) = NEW.ID$              ' add it to ID$.
                    WRITE #1, NEW.ID$, NEW.EMP$           'Update the file.
                    PRINT
                    INPUT "NAME (XXX when done)"; NEW.EMP$
                 END IF
              LOOP
              IF COUNT = ARRAY.SIZE THEN
                 PRINT : PRINT "To add more names, see programmer."
              END IF
           CLOSE 1                                        'Update completed.
           PRINT
           PRINT "File "; F$; " has been updated."
           END
```

We obtained the following display when we ran the program to add two new employees to the file EMPLOY.DAT shown in the problem statement:

```
PROGRAM TO UPDATE THE FILE EMPLOY.DAT

Enter each new employee with last name first.
Do not use commas.  Thus, type
    DOE SUSAN B.  and not  DOE,SUSAN B.

NAME (XXX when done)? MANN HEATHER A.
IDENTIFICATION CODE? 63334

NAME (XXX when done)? JACKSON SALLY J.
IDENTIFICATION CODE? 23501
23501 is already in use.
IDENTIFICATION CODE? 33501

NAME (XXX when done)? XXX

File EMPLOY.DAT has been updated.
```

After this run, we used the program of Example 6 to obtain the following display:

```
Enter file name: EMPLOY.DAT
"23501","AHEARN JOHN F."
"53241","ANDERSON ALBERT G."
"15653","SIMPSON DONALD C."
"37671","HENDRIX SAMUEL D."
"49313","POST EDWARD L."
"44446","MURRAY HAROLD N."
"23786","SILVA JOSE R."
"83817","CONNORS FRANK P."
"63334","MANN HEATHER A."
"33501","JACKSON SALLY J."
```

REMARK   As it stands, the program in this example cannot be used to create the file EMPLOY.DAT. It can be used only to add new information to an existing file. If a file named EMPLOY.DAT does not exist (on the disk in the disk unit) when the program is run, the OPEN statement

```
           OPEN F$ FOR INPUT AS #1
```

in the procedure FILE.IDS that reads the file EMPLOY.DATA will cause a fatal *File not found* error condition. As mentioned in Section 16.3, only files that exist can be opened for INPUT. If, as explained in Section 16.3, you include the statement

```
ON ERROR GOTO ERROR.HANDLER
```

at the beginning of the program and the error-handler

```
ERROR.HANDLER:

    IF ERR = 53 THEN                'File not found error
        OPEN F$ FOR APPEND AS #1    'Put the name F$ in the
        CLOSE #1                    ' directory of files and
        RESUME                      ' return to OPEN for INPUT.
    ELSE
        ON ERROR GOTO 0             'Allow QuickBASIC to
    END IF                          ' handle other errors.
```

after the END statement, the program can be used either to add new data to the file F$ or to create a new file with that name.

16.6 Problems

In Problems 1–17, write a program for each task specified.

1. The Hollis Investment Company maintains a file EMPLOY containing the name, age, years of service, and monthly salary of salaried employees. Include the following information in DATA lines for a program to create the file EMPLOY. The file will be used as an input file in Problems 2–5.

Name	Age	Years of service	Monthly salary
Murray George	53	21	2,100.00
Ritchie Albert	41	13	1,850.00
Galvin Fred	62	35	2,475.00
Cummings Barbara	37	16	1,675.00
Gieseler Norma	41	20	2,200.00
Hughes Bette	52	18	2,050.00
Meland Ralph	29	5	1,550.00
Tibeau Betty	30	7	1,340.00

2. A 5% across-the-board salary increase has been negotiated for all Hollis employees. Write a program to update the file EMPLOY to reflect this increase.
3. Write a program to remove employees from the file or to add new employees. Use your program to delete Fred Galvin and add the following:

   BING MELINDA 23 0 1200
   DEREK SUSAN 24 0 1800

   (*Suggestion:* If you use an array to store the names, do not actually delete Fred Galvin. Rather, store a special value such as DELETE in place of the name. Then when you make an updated copy of the file EMPLOY, simply omit employees stored as DELETE.)
4. Using the file EMPLOY as an input file, create a file EMPLOY1 that contains precisely the information in EMPLOY but with the names in alphabetical order. After EMPLOY1 has been

created, display its contents. (*Suggestion:* Read the file contents into four arrays, sort the arrays so that the names are in alphabetical order, and then create EMPLOY1.)

5. Create a file EMPLOY2 that contains the same information as EMPLOY, but with monthly salaries in descending order. After EMPLOY2 has been created, display its contents.

6. A manufacturing company sends a package consisting of eight new products to each of ten families and asks each family to rate each product on the following scale:

$$0 = poor \qquad 1 = fair \qquad 2 = good \qquad 3 = very\ good \qquad 4 = excellent$$

Here are the results in tabular form:

		Family number									
		1	2	3	4	5	6	7	8	9	10
	1	0	1	1	2	1	2	2	1	0	1
	2	2	3	3	0	3	2	2	3	4	1
	3	1	3	4	4	4	1	4	2	3	2
Product number	4	3	4	2	4	3	1	3	4	2	4
	5	0	1	3	2	2	2	1	3	0	1
	6	4	4	4	3	2	1	4	4	1	1
	7	1	3	1	3	2	4	1	4	3	4
	8	2	2	3	4	2	2	3	4	2	3

Create a file RATE that contains the information in this table. Then use this file to produce a two-column report that shows the product numbers and the average rating for each product. (The file RATE will be used as an input file in Problems 7–9.)

7. Errors in the transcription of the numbers in the survey are discovered. The correct results for Families 1 and 7 are as follows:

Family 1	3	2	4	2	2	4	1	3
Family 7	2	3	4	4	2	4	3	2

Write a program to allow the user to change the eight ratings for any family. Use your program to correct the ratings for Family 1 and Family 7.

8. Use the file RATE to produce a report as in Problem 6. However, have the average ratings appear from smallest to largest.

9. Use the file RATE to produce a two-column report as follows: The first column is to give the product numbers that receive at least six ratings of 3 or better, and the second column is to give the number of these ratings obtained.

10. The Sevard Company maintains files SST and WEEKLY. Create these two files so that they contain the following information. The files are to be used as input files in Problems 11–13.

File SST

Employee ID number	Year-to-date income	Hourly rate
024-25-5200	18240.00	12.00
018-26-2980	16800.00	10.50
021-18-7341	21150.50	14.25
031-42-9327	35600.00	16.00
035-14-4222	57250.00	25.00
026-21-1274	54980.00	23.00

File WEEKLY

Employee ID number	This week's hours
024-25-5200	42
018-26-2980	36
021-18-7341	32
031-42-9327	52
035-14-4222	50
026-21-1274	48

11. A Social Security tax deduction of 7.65% is taken on the first 53,400 earned by an employee. Once this amount is reached, no further deduction is made. Using the files SST and WEEKLY, produce a report giving the ID number, the current week's gross pay, and the current week's Social Security deduction for each employee. Employees are paid time and a half for all hours over 32.

12. Modify the program written for Problem 11 to update the year-to-date income in the file SST.

13. Using the files SST and WEEKLY, display a list of the ID numbers of all employees who have satisfied the Social Security tax requirement for the current year. With each ID number, give the year-to-date income figure.

14. Write a program to allow the user to create a mailing list file by typing its contents at the keyboard. Organize the file so that each entry occupies six lines as follows:

Line 1	Last Name
Line 2	First Name and Middle Initial
Line 3	Street Address
Line 4	City or Town
Line 5	State
Line 6	Zip Code

After a file has been created, display its contents by using a standard three-line address format.

15. Write a menu-driven program to allow the user to create a mailing list file as described in Problem 14 and also to maintain the file by specifying changes at the keyboard. Since the user can modify the mailing list, you should store all mailing list entries in arrays (for instance, six string arrays) and make any changes in these arrays. This means that the file will be opened in only two situations: when any previously entered data must be read into the arrays (at the outset), and when the user specifies that the file should be updated (see UPDATE option below). Following is a suggested menu:
   1. To end the program. (In the procedure that carries out this option, remind the user that Option 5 is required to save the latest version of the mailing list. Then give the user the chance to cancel this option selection.)
   2. To add new names and addresses.
   3. To delete names from the mailing list. (To delete a name, you can change the array entry that stores the last name to DELETE; then, while updating the file, ignore any entries marked in this way.)
   4. To display the current mailing list entries with each entry occupying a single display line.
   5. To make a new copy of the mailing list file.

16. Write a menu-driven program as described in Problem 15. Then add the following options:
   6. To alphabetize the mailing list. (As explained in Problem 15, the array entries should be rearranged, not the file entries.)
   7. To display all or part of the mailing list in a standard address format. (This option should be preceded by Option 6. The procedure you write for Option 7 should prompt the user for two words and then produce an alphabetical listing of all entries between these two words. Do not display entries marked for deletion under Option 3.)

17. Write a menu-driven program as described in Problem 15 or 16. Then add the following options:
   8. To sort the mailing list by zip codes. (As explained in Problem 15, the array entries should be rearranged, not the file entries.)
   9. To display all or part of the mailing list in a standard address format. (This option should be preceded by Option 8. The procedure you write for Option 9 should prompt the user for a lowest and a highest zip code and then produce a listing of all entries with zip codes in this range. Do not display entries marked for deletion under Option 3.)

■ 16.7 Random Access Files

Data in random files are organized in equal-length subdivisions called **records.** The statement

```
OPEN "DATA5" FOR RANDOM AS #1 LEN = 40
```

specifies DATA5 as a random file with file number 1, in which each record contains 40 characters, or bytes.* If F$ = "DATA5", N = 1, and R = 40, the statement

```
OPEN F$ FOR RANDOM AS #N LEN = R
```

does the same thing. As explained shortly, you will not have to calculate the record length. You will simply specify one or more variables whose values will be stored in each record and allow the computer to calculate the number of bytes needed to store the values. The CLOSE statement closes a random file, just as it closes a sequential file.

The following points concerning random files and how they differ from sequential files are significant:

1. A random file that has been opened can be used for output or input. You will recall that sequential files must be opened with a mode specifier FOR INPUT, FOR OUTPUT, or FOR APPEND.

2. As just mentioned, data in random files are organized in equal-length subdivisions called records. Data in sequential files are organized in subdivisions called lines, that is, as sequences of characters that end with the return and line-feed [CHR$(13) and CHR$(10)] combination. (It is common to refer to these lines as records but, to avoid possible confusion, we will continue to refer to them as lines.) Unlike the records in a random file, which all have the same length, the lines in a sequential file can—and most often do—have varying lengths.

3. The records in a random file are numbered in sequence from 1 up to the number of records in the file. The records can be accessed in any order (that is, randomly) simply by specifying the record number. In a sequential file, the lines are not numbered, and data must be accessed in order (that is, sequentially) from the beginning of the file.

4. You can change any record in a random file without affecting the other records. With sequential files, changing any value in a file involves making an entirely new copy of the file.

5. The part of a random file record or a sequential file line that stores a single value is called a field. In a random file, each record contains the same number of fields, and each field is of fixed length. In sequential files, the lines can have varying numbers of fields, and the fields can be of varying length.

6. Numerical values written to random files are stored in a compressed binary form that saves disk space when compared to sequential files.

In addition to the OPEN and CLOSE statements, the following statements and functions are used with random files.

The TYPE and END TYPE Statements

These statements are used to specify a list of variables whose values will be stored in each record of a random file. The TYPE statement block

```
TYPE PAIR
      X AS INTEGER
      Y AS INTEGER
END TYPE
```

would be appropriate for a random file in which each record will contain two integer fields. This TYPE statement defines PAIR as the name of a new data type, called a **record type.** PAIR is a type (just as INTEGER is a type); it is not a variable. To declare variables as having the type PAIR, you would use the DIM . . . AS statement described below.

The variables listed between the TYPE and END TYPE statements (X and Y in the record type PAIR) must not include the suffixes (%, &, !, #, and $) that specify variable

---

*On the IBM PC, a *byte* is a sequence of eight bits (binary digits 0 and 1), and each character uses one byte for storage. Thus, *byte* and *character position* mean the same thing. It is also common practice to refer to the characters themselves as bytes.

Table 16.2 **QuickBASIC's numerical and string variable types.**
**(C denotes an integer numeral such as 15, or an integer constant declared
in a CONST statement.)**

Type	Suffix	Name	Length
Integer	%	INTEGER	2 bytes
Long integer	&	LONG	4 bytes
Single-precision real	!	SINGLE	4 bytes
Double-precision real	#	DOUBLE	8 bytes
Varying-length string	$	STRING	0 to 32767 bytes
Fixed-length string	none	STRING * C	C (a constant) bytes

types. Also, they must be of fixed length. Table 16.2 shows the names and lengths of QuickBASIC's numerical and string variables.

Other than the type STRING, all types listed in Table 16.2 are types of fixed-length variables, and they can be used as types of the fields that you specify between the TYPE and END TYPE statements. Here is a TYPE statement block that defines STOCKITEM as a record type with two fixed-length string fields, ITEM and CODE, and three fixed-length numerical fields, INSTOCK, COST, and PRICE.

```
TYPE STOCKITEM
    ITEM AS STRING * 15
    CODE AS STRING * 6
    INSTOCK AS INTEGER
    COST AS SINGLE
    PRICE AS SINGLE
END TYPE
```

Since integers use 2 bytes and single-precision reals use 4 bytes, a variable of type STOCK-ITEM will have length 31 (15 + 6 + 2 + 4 + 4). (You do not have to count bytes. As explained next, you can use the LEN function to count them for you.)

The DIM . . . AS Statement

If **v** denotes a variable name that does not end with a type specifier, and **vartype** denotes a variable type (any type), then the statement

DIM **v** AS **vartype**

declares **v** as a variable of type **vartype.** Thus,

```
DIM S AS STRING
DIM CODE AS STRING * 10
```

or, equivalently,

```
DIM S AS STRING, CODE AS STRING * 10
```

declares S as a varying-length string variable and CODE as a string variable of fixed length 10. If the type PAIR has been defined with the integer fields X and Y as shown above, the following DIM statement declares P as a variable of type PAIR:

```
DIM P AS PAIR
```

A variable **v** whose type is a record type (that is, defined by a TYPE statement block), is called a **record variable.** Moreover, its length is given by LEN(**v**). Thus, P is a record variable of length LEN(P), that is, 4. To store records of the type PAIR in a random file, say RANDFILE, you could use the following OPEN statement to specify exactly the record length needed:

```
OPEN "RANDFILE" FOR RANDOM AS #1 LEN = LEN(P)
```

The integer contents of the two fields X and Y in the record variable P are referenced by using the names P.X and P.Y. The statements

```
LET P.X = 5
LET P.Y = 7
PRINT "A PAIR OF INTEGERS: ";P.X ; P.Y
```

assign the values 5 and 7 to the integer variables P.X and P.Y to produce the output

```
A PAIR OF INTEGERS:  5   7
```

Generally, if **vartype** is defined by using a TYPE statement block that specifies **fieldname** as the name of a field, and if **v** has the type **vartype,** then the value in **v** corresponding to this field is referenced by using the expression **v.fieldname.**

The variables P.X and P.Y are integer variables and can be used in the same way that any other integer variables can. The record variable P, however, is not an integer variable. It is not even a numerical variable. It contains two integer fields; thus, its contents are a *pair* of integers.

There are only three operations that you can perform on the entire contents of a record variable such as P: you can write its contents as a record in a random file, read values for the record variable from a random file record, and assign the contents of one record variable to another of the same type. As explained below, the PUT # and GET # statements are used to write and read records in random files. To illustrate the second operation, let's declare a record variable Q of the same type as P. For this, you may use the two statements

```
DIM P AS PAIR
DIM Q AS PAIR
```

or the single equivalent statement

```
DIM P AS PAIR, Q AS PAIR
```

With P and Q both of the same record type, the statement

```
LET Q = P
```

copies the entire contents of P into Q. This statement is equivalent to the two statements

```
LET Q.X = P.X
LET Q.Y = P.Y
```

Similarly, the statement

```
SWAP P, Q
```

swaps the contents of P and Q. This single SWAP statement is equivalent to the two statements

```
SWAP P.X, Q.X
SWAP P.Y, Q.Y
```

The worked-out examples in this section illustrate how the assignment of the contents of one record variable to another can be used effectively in QuickBASIC programs.

The PUT # Statement

If RANDFILE has been opened with the statement

```
OPEN "RANDFILE" FOR RANDOM AS #1  LEN=LEN(P)
```

and if P.X and P.Y have the values 5 and 7, the statement

```
PUT #1,24,P
```

writes the contents 5 and 7 of the record variable P as record number 24 of file #1. If N = 1 and REC = 24, the following statement does the same thing:

```
PUT #N,REC,P
```

In general, if **r** denotes a positive integer, **v** a record variable (or any variable of fixed length), and **n** the file number of a random file of record length LEN (**v**), the statement

```
PUT #n,r,v
```

writes the contents of **v** as record **r** of file **n**. If the record number **r** is omitted in a PUT # statement, sequential record numbers are used. A common practice is to use the abbreviated form

```
PUT #n,,v
```

when creating a new file by writing its records in order from record number 1.

The GET # Statement

After the statement

```
PUT #1,24,P
```

has stored the contents 5 and 7 of P as record 24 of file #1, the statement

```
GET #1,24,Q
```

reads the contents of record 24 and copies them into the record variable Q; that is, 5 and 7 are assigned to Q.X and Q.Y. If N = 1, and REC = 24, the following statement does the same thing:

```
GET #N,REC,Q
```

In general, if **r** denotes a positive integer, **v** a record variable (or any variable of fixed length), and **n** the file number of a random file of record length LEN(**v**), the statement

```
GET #n,r,v
```

reads record **r** of file **n** and copies its contents into the variable **v**. As with the PUT # statement, records are accessed sequentially if you omit the record number and use the form

```
GET #n,,v
```

It is common practice to use this abbreviated form if all records are to be read in order from the beginning of a random file.

The LOF(n) Function

This is the **length of file** function. LOF(n) gives the number of bytes in the file currently opened as file #n. Moreover, if the file is opened as a random file of record length R, the expression

```
LOF(n) \ R
```

gives the number of records currently in the file.

CAUTION

LOF(n) \ R may not give the correct number of records if you use a PUT# statement to store the contents of a variable that does not have the fixed-length R.

The LOC(n) Function

This is the **record locator function.** If n denotes the number of an opened random file, LOC(n) gives the number of the last record written to or read from the file. When file #n is first opened, loc(n) is 0.

EXAMPLE 10   *Here is a program to create a random file that contains data included in DATA statements.*

```
TYPE LOCATION                 'Define the data type
   CITY AS STRING * 15        'LOCATION for records
   STATE AS STRING * 2        'in random file.
END TYPE

DIM PLACE AS LOCATION         'Record variable: PLACE


'Read data and store in the random file CITIES.

OPEN "CITIES" FOR RANDOM AS #1 LEN = LEN(PLACE)
FOR N = 1 TO 4
   READ PLACE.CITY, PLACE.STATE    'Read DATA.
   PUT #1, N, PLACE                'Store in file.
NEXT N
CLOSE 1
END

'Data to be stored in the random file CITIES

DATA MONTEREY,CA
DATA BRIDGEWATER,MA
DATA AUSTIN,TX
DATA JOHNSON CITY,TN
```

The TYPE and DIM statements declare PLACE as a record variable with two fields: the 15-byte field CITY, and the 2-byte field STATE. By using

```
LEN = LEN(PLACE)
```

in the OPEN statement, we ensure that each record in the random file CITIES will have exactly the length needed to store the 17-byte contents of the record variable PLACE.

On the first pass through the FOR loop, the READ statement reads the strings MONTEREY and CA from the DATA lines to give

```
PLACE.CITY  = "MONTEREY       "   (15 BYTES)
PLACE.STATE = "CA"                (2 bytes)
```

Notice that the 8-character string MONTEREY is stored left justified with trailing blanks in the 15-byte field CITY. Since $N = 1$, the PUT # statement writes the contents of PLACE (the fixed-length strings stored in PLACE.CITY and PLACE.STATE) as record 1 of file CITIES. Similarly, the other three passes through the FOR loop write information into records 2, 3, and 4 of the file CITIES.

REMARK 1   As mentioned previously, a record number is not needed in a PUT# statement when information is being stored in successive records beginning with record number 1. Thus, the PUT# statement can be changed to

```
PUT #1,,PLACE
```

REMARK 2   It would not be correct to replace the READ statement with

```
READ CITY,STATE
```

Remember, the fields in record variables are referenced by writing the record variable name followed by a period and then the field name.

■

EXAMPLE 11   *Here are two programs to read and display the contents of the file CITIES. Each program produces the following output:*

```
MONTEREY       CA
BRIDGEWATER    MA
```

```
AUSTIN          TX
JOHNSON CITY    TN
```

Program A
```
TYPE LOCATION                  'Define the data type
   CITY AS STRING * 15         'LOCATION for records
   STATE AS STRING * 2         'in random file.
END TYPE

DIM PLACE AS LOCATION          'Record variable: PLACE


'Read and display contents of random file CITIES.

OPEN "CITIES" FOR RANDOM AS #1 LEN = LEN(PLACE)
FOR N = 1 TO 4
   GET #1, N, PLACE
   PRINT PLACE.CITY; PLACE.STATE
NEXT N
CLOSE 1
END
```

The TYPE and DIM statements used to declare PLACE as a record variable are identical to those used in the program of Example 10 to create the file CITIES. On the first pass through the FOR loop, the GET # statement reads record 1 of file CITIES into the record variable PLACE to give

```
PLACE.CITY     "MONTEREY       "      (15 bytes)
PLACE.STATE = "CA"                    (2 bytes)
```

and the PRINT statement displays these values to produce the first line of the output. Similarly, the other three passes through the FOR loop read and display records 2, 3, and 4 of file CITIES.

Program B
```
TYPE ONEFIELD              'Define the data type
   ALL AS STRING * 17      'ONEFIELD for records
END TYPE                   'in random file.

DIM PLACE AS ONEFIELD      'Record variable: PLACE


'Read and display contents of random file CITIES.

OPEN "CITIES" FOR RANDOM AS #1 LEN = LEN(PLACE)
FOR N = 1 TO 4
   GET #1, N, PLACE
   PRINT PLACE.ALL
NEXT N
CLOSE 1
END
```

The TYPE and DIM statements in Program B declare PLACE as a record variable with one field, the 17-byte field ALL. Thus, each time the GET # statement is executed, the contents of a 17-byte record in file CITIES is read for the record variable PLACE and stored as the value of PLACE.ALL. On the first pass through the FOR loop, the GET # statement gives

```
PLACE.ALL = "MONTEREY       CA"      (17 bytes)
```

and the PRINT statement displays this 17-character string as shown in the output. Similarly, records 2, 3, and 4 are read and displayed on the other three passes through the FOR loop.

REMARK 1   The GET # in both Program A and Program B can be written

```
GET #1,,PLACE
```

Remember, it is not necessary to specify a record number in a GET # statement when records are accessed in order beginning with record number 1.

REMARK 2

If you change the FOR statement in either program to

```
FOR N=4 TO 1 STEP -2
```

the output will be

```
JOHNSON CITY   TN
BRIDGEWATER    MA
```

The records in a random file can be accessed or created in any order.

REMARK 3

In both Program A and Program B we use the FOR statement

```
FOR N = 1 TO 4
```

to ensure that exactly four records will be read from the file. Each program is significantly improved by inserting the statement

```
LET COUNT LOF(1) \ LEN(PLACE)
```

after the OPEN statement and changing the FOR statement to

```
FOR N = 1 TO COUNT
```

With this change, each program can be used even if the file CITIES does not contain exactly four records.

The TYPE statement block in Program A of Example 11 specifies that each record is to consist of two fields: the 15-byte field CITY and the 2-byte field STATE. The TYPE statement block in Program B specifies only a single 17-byte field ALL. It is common terminology to say that the records in a file are **fielded** by a TYPE statement block.

A file can be fielded in more than one way in the same program. We illustrate by modifying Program A of Example 11 as follows:

1. Add the additional TYPE and DIM statements

```
TYPE ABBREVIATION
   TWO AS STRING * 2
END TYPE
DIM ABBR AS ABBREVIATION
```

to declare ABBR as a record variable of type ABBREVIATION.

2. Follow the existing GET# statement with the statement

```
GET #1, N, ABBR
```

to assign the first two characters of record N to the 2-byte field ABBR.TWO of ABBR. The other 15 bytes in record N are simply not used. [Since LEN(ABBR)=2, we would not use ABBR to specify the record length in the OPEN statement.]

3. Change the PRINT statement to

```
PRINT PLACE.CITY; "First two letters are "; ABBR.TWO; "."
```

The modified program will produce the output:

```
MONTEREY       First two letters are MO.
BRIDGEWATER    First two letters are BR.
AUSTIN         First two letters are AU.
JOHNSON CITY   First two letters are JO.
```

In Program A of Example 11, the variable PLACE.CITY contains the name of a city followed by trailing blanks. If you need to display the name of the city without the trailing blanks, you must find the position P of the last letter in PLACE.CITY. The statement

```
LET X$ = PLACE.CITY
```

does not get rid of these blanks. This LET statement assigns all 15 characters of PLACE.CITY to X$. Nor can you use the statement

```
LET P = INSTR(PLACE.CITY," ") - 1
```

This will give the position P of the letter just before the first blank, but for JOHNSON CITY, this is not the letter we need. The following loop shows one way to find P.

```
LET P = 15
DO WHILE MID$(PLACE.CITY,P,1) = " "
   LET P = P - 1
LOOP
```

If you insert these lines in Program A just before the PRINT statement and change the PRINT statement to

```
PRINT LEFT$(PLACE.CITY,P);", ";PLACE.STATE
```

you will obtain the output

```
MONTEREY, CA
BRIDGEWATER, MA
AUSTIN, TX
JOHNSON CITY, TN
```

In this section, we have described the following statements and functions used with random files:

Statements	Functions
OPEN	LOF
CLOSE	LOC
TYPE..END TYPE	
DIM..AS	
PUT #	
GET #	

The preceding examples illustrate illustrate how these statements and functions are used to create random files and access the information they contain. The following two examples show how they can be used in file maintenance programs.

EXAMPLE 12 *Let's write a program to add new data typed at the keyboard to a student information file. The program must work for files that already exist and also be able to create new files.*

The information for each student is to be stored in a record as follows.

Field 1	9-digit identification number	Bytes 1–9
Field 2	Student's name	Bytes 10–34
Field 3	Student's local address	Bytes 35–80

PROBLEM ANALYSIS

We are told precisely how data are to be stored in records. The following TYPE statement block assigns the field names ID, SNAME, and ADDR to the three fields specified in the problem statement. (We use SNAME because NAME is a reserved word.)

```
TYPE RECTYPE
   ID AS STRING * 9         '9-digit ID number
   SNAME AS STRING * 25     '25-character student name
   ADDR AS STRING * 46      '46-character local address
END TYPE
```

If we use the statement

```
DIM STUDENT AS RECTYPE
```

to declare STUDENT as a record variable of type RECTYPE, the three fields can be referenced in the program by using the fixed-length string variables

```
STUDENT.SNAME    Student's name
STUDENT.ID       ID number for STUDENT.SNAME
STUDENT.ADDR     Local address of STUDENT.SNAME
```

The problem statement says that the program must allow the user to create new files or add to existing files. Thus, we will require that the user specify a file name at the keyboard. Notice also that if the file already exists, new student information must be written in unused records—that is, in records with larger record numbers than the largest record number in the file. With the variables

F$ = Name of file entered at the keyboard
RECNUM = Largest record number already used

we can open F$ as file #1 with record length LEN(STUDENT), and then find RECNUM by using the statement

```
LET RECNUM = LOF(1) \ LEN(STUDENT)
```

With these file considerations out of the way, it is not difficult to write an algorithm for the specified task, if we omit the details.

THE ALGORITHM

a. Use a TYPE statement block to define fields for any file to be processed.
b. Input a file name F$.
c. Open F$ as a random file, and find the number RECNUM of its last record.
d. Get input data from the keyboard, and write this information in file F$.
e. Close the file F$ and stop.

Only Step (d) requires further analysis; we have already shown how to carry out the other steps. Specifically, the TYPE statement block that defines the record type RECTYPE accomplishes Step (a); Step (b) requires only an INPUT statement; for Step (c), we will open F$ as random file #1 with record length LEN(STUDENT), and use the function LOF(1) to find the number RECNUM of its last record; and Step (e) requires only a CLOSE statement and an END statement. In the program, we will compare RECNUM found in Step (c) with 0 and display a short message telling whether the file name F$ typed at the keyboard is an existing file name or a new one.

We now consider how Step (d) can be refined to contain sufficient detail for coding into QuickBASIC. To obtain input for records that contain more than one field, the usual practice is to allow an end of data indicator as the value of the first field to be input. In the following refinement of Step (d), we require that the user enter the dollar sign character ($) to indicate that all new student information has been entered.

d1. Input STUDENT.SNAME
d2. Repeat the following until STUDENT.SNAME is $.

   d2.1. Input STUDENT.ID and STUDENT.ADDR
   d2.2. Add 1 to RECNUM
   d2.3. Write the contents of STUDENT as record RECNUM.
   d2.4. Input STUDENT.SNAME

To allow the user to include commas in names or addresses, we'll use LINE INPUT instead of INPUT to obtain names and addresses from the keyboard. This statement is similar to the LINE INPUT# statement used in Section 16.2 to obtain input from a sequential file. The statement

```
LINE INPUT A$
```

assigns to A$ all characters typed at the keyboard (including any commas) up to, but not including, the RETURN/line-feed combination caused when you press the Enter key.

We will add one more feature to the program. After the user has typed the information for a new student, we will display the prompt

```
                    ENTRY CORRECT(Y/N)?
```

The information will be written to the file if the user responds with Y; otherwise, it will be
ignored so that the user can reenter the correct information for that student.

THE PROGRAM

```
'         PROGRAM TO CREATE OR ADD TO STUDENT ADDRESS FILES


TYPE RECORDTYPE
    ID AS STRING * 9             '9-digit identification number
    SNAME AS STRING * 25         '25-character student name
    ADDR AS STRING * 46          '46-character local address
END TYPE

DIM STUDENT AS RECORDTYPE        'Record variable: STUDENT

'-----------------------------------------------------------------
' Enter file name F$ and count number RECNUM of records.
'-----------------------------------------------------------------

INPUT "Enter file name: ", F$                   'File name
OPEN F$ FOR RANDOM AS #1 LEN = LEN(STUDENT)      'Open it.
LET RECNUM = LOF(1) \ LEN(STUDENT)              'Last record
IF RECNUM = 0 THEN
    PRINT "The new file "; F$; " will be created."
ELSE
    PRINT F$; " contains"; RECNUM; "record(s)."
END IF

'-----------------------------------------------------------------
' Keyboard data entry: Add new student information to file F$.
'-----------------------------------------------------------------

PRINT
PRINT "Enter names as follows: LAST, FIRST INITIAL."
PRINT
LINE INPUT "NAME ($ to stop): ", STUDENT.SNAME   'Enter name.
DO UNTIL LEFT$(STUDENT.SNAME, 1) = "$"           'Loop until $
    INPUT "ID NUMBER:        ", STUDENT.ID        'Enter ID.
    LINE INPUT "ADDRESS:            ", STUDENT.ADDR 'Enter address.
    INPUT "Entry correct(Y/N)"; RESPONSE$         'Is entry ok?
    IF UCASE$(RESPONSE$) = "Y" THEN
        LET RECNUM = RECNUM + 1                  'Yes, write it
        PUT #1, RECNUM, STUDENT                  ' to the file.
    ELSE
        PRINT "Entry ignored!!!!!"               'No, ignore it.
    END IF
    PRINT
    LINE INPUT "NAME ($ to stop): ", STUDENT.SNAME 'Next name.
LOOP
CLOSE 1
END
```

We obtained the following screen display when we ran this program to create a new file
named STUDENTS. Notice that the incorrect entry PRICE, HARRY A. was noticed after
the ID number was typed. We simply pressed the Enter key for the address, typed N as
shown, and then retyped all three lines.

```
Enter file name: STUDENTS
The new file STUDENTS will be created.

Enter names as follows: LAST, FIRST INITIAL.

NAME ($ to stop): BYRON, SALLY ANN
ID NUMBER:        123456789
ADDRESS:          BIRCH 122, CAMPUS
Entry correct(Y/N)? Y
```

```
                       NAME ($ to stop): TREMONT, JOSEPH E.
                       ID NUMBER:        987654321
                       ADDRESS:          ASPEN 312, CAMPUS
                       Entry correct(Y/N)? Y

                       NAME ($ to stop): HAVERLY, BARRY A.
                       ID NUMBER:        012333012
                       ADDRESS:          123 SUMMER ST., DEVON CT
                       Entry correct(Y/N)? Y

                       NAME ($ to stop): PRICE HARRY A.
                       ID NUMBER:        412444321
                       ADDRESS:
                       Entry correct(Y/N)? N
                       Entry ignored!!!!!

                       NAME ($ to stop): PRICE HARRY O.
                       ID NUMBER:        412444321
                       ADDRESS:          ASPEN 226, CAMPUS
                       Entry correct(Y/N)? Y

                       NAME ($ to stop): $
```

REMARK 1

We specified a file name STUDENTS that was not already in the disk's directory of files. Thus, after the run shown, the file contained four records. The DOS command TYPE can be used to see these records. (Numerical fields are written to files in a compressed binary form that will not be displayed as readable numbers by the TYPE command. The contents of string fields, however, are readable when displayed by TYPE commands.) A record length of 80 was specified in the problem statement so that each record would occupy one line of a display screen with 80-character lines.

```
A>TYPE STUDENTS
123456789BYRON, SALLY ANN         BIRCH 122, CAMPUS
987654321TREMONT, JOSEPH E.       ASPEN 312, CAMPUS
012333012HAVERLY, BARRY A.        123 SUMMER ST., DEVON CT
412444321PRICE HARRY O.           ASPEN 226, CAMPUS
```

REMARK 2

If you respond to the line

```
    INPUT "ID NUMBER          ";STUDENT.ID
```

by entering an identification number with fewer than 9 digits, the number will be stored in STUDENT.ID with trailing blanks. If you enter more than 9 digits, all digits other than the first 9 are ignored. Although the program allows you to reject incorrect entries, an incorrect 8-digit ID number or an incorrect 9-digit number obtained by truncating an entry with more than 10 digits could easily go unnoticed. To help avoid errors made while typing ID numbers, you can replace the INPUT statement with the following lines that reject input values that do not contain exactly 9 characters.

```
    DO
        INPUT "ID NUMBER          ";ID$
    UNTIL LEN(ID$) = 9
    LET STUDENT.ID = ID$
```

The varying-length string variable ID$ is needed because LEN(STUDENT.ID) is always 9.

REMARK 3

The block IF statement

```
    IF RECNUM = 0 THEN
        PRINT "The new file "; F$; " will be created."
    ELSE
        PRINT F$; " contains"; RECNUM; "record(s)."
    END IF
```

is important. If you intend to create a new file but inadvertently enter the name of an existing file, all new student information will be written to the existing file—even if its contents have nothing to do with student information. Programs should not let this happen. The program in this example accomplishes this with the block IF statement that tells you something about the file name selected. If this information indicates that another file name should be selected, you can type $ in response to the prompt

```
NAME ($ to stop):
```

The program will halt without changing the file in any way. You can then run the program again and specify another file name.

As mentioned at the outset of this section, any record or any part of a record can be changed without affecting other records in the file. This is possible because a file can be fielded in any way you wish and also because the PUT# statement can write to any record in the file. Thus, programs used to maintain random files should allow for changes in individual records as well as for the addition of new records, as illustrated in the preceding example. File maintenance programs should also allow for the deletion of records. As illustrated in the next example, deleting a record does not necessarily remove it from the file. Rather, a special character is written in a record (usually as the first byte) to indicate that the record is no longer in use.

EXAMPLE 13   *Let's write a program to allow the user to modify records in a student information file. Specifically, the user should be allowed to change the name and address of any student or to delete a student from the file.*

PROBLEM ANALYSIS

We will use the same variable names used in the preceding program to create and add to student information files. If we omit details, we can write the following algorithm for the stated task. Notice that Steps (a), (b), (c), and (e) are identical to the corresponding steps in the algorithm of Example 12. Only Step (d) is new.

a. Use a TYPE statement block to define fields for the file to be modified.
b. Input the file name F$.
c. Open F$ as a random file and find the number RECNUM of records in F$.
d. Modify file F$ as described in problem statement.
e. Close the file F$ and stop.

We require that the user identify students by ID number rather than by name because two students might have the same name. If the record identified by an ID number is to be modified, we will prompt the user for a new name and address and then write the new information to the file. If record number R is to be deleted, we will write the character CHR$(255) as the first byte of the record by using the two statements

```
LET STUDENT.ID = CHR$(255)
PUT #1,R,STUDENT
```

This will leave the name and address fields as they were but will erase the ID number and replace it with CHR$(255) followed by 8 spaces. In subsequent processing of the file, records with CHR$(255) as the first character will be ignored. We chose CHR$(255) as the *delete character* simply because it is rarely used for another purpose. The following refinement of Step (d) of the algorithm carries out the process just described.

d1. Input an ID number ID$.
d2. Repeat the following until $ is entered for ID$.
    d2.1. Specify whether the record is to be deleted or modified.
    d2.2. If the record is to be deleted, write CHR$(255) as the first character of the record.
    d.2.3. If the record is to be modified, input a new name and/or address and write the new information to the file.
    d.2.4. Input another value for ID$.

<table>
<tr><td>THE
PROGRAM</td></tr>
</table>

```
' PROGRAM TO CHANGE ENTRIES IN STUDENT INFORMATION FILES.

   TYPE RECORDTYPE
      ID AS STRING * 9               '9-digit identification number
      SNAME AS STRING * 25           '25-character student name
      ADDR AS STRING * 46            '46-character local address
   END TYPE

DIM STUDENT AS RECORDTYPE           'Record variable: STUDENT

'-------------------------------------------------------------------
'Enter file name F$ and count number RECNUM of records.
'-------------------------------------------------------------------

INPUT "NAME OF FILE TO BE MODIFIED? ", F$    'File name
OPEN F$ FOR RANDOM AS #1 LEN = LEN(STUDENT)  'Open it.
LET RECNUM = LOF(1) \ LEN(STUDENT)           'Record count
IF RECNUM = 0 THEN
   PRINT "File "; F$; " not found"
   END                                       'EXIT ON NO FILE.
END IF

'----------------------------------------------------------
'Keyboard changes: delete or modify student addresses.
'----------------------------------------------------------

PRINT
PRINT "You can change current information for any"
PRINT "student whose identification number you type."
PRINT
INPUT "ID NUMBER(type $ when done)"; ID$
DO UNTIL ID$ = "$"
   LET R = SEARCH(ID$, RECNUM)     'Record number R of ID$.
   IF R = 0 THEN
      PRINT "No student with the ID: "; ID$
   ELSE
      GET #1, R, STUDENT                                'Get record R.
      PRINT "STUDENT'S NAME:       "; STUDENT.SNAME     'Display name
      PRINT "STUDENT'S ADDRESS:    "; STUDENT.ADDR      ' and address.
      INPUT "Is student to be removed (Y or N) "; C$
      IF UCASE$(C$) = "Y" THEN                          'Delete?
         STUDENT.ID = CHR$(255)                         'Yes.
         PUT #1, R, STUDENT                             'Update file.
         PRINT "Student has been deleted."
      ELSE                                              'No.
         PRINT "Press the Enter key to indicate no change."
         LINE INPUT "ENTER NEW NAME: ", N$              'Get changes
         IF N$ <> "" THEN STUDENT.SNAME = N$            ' for name
         LINE INPUT "ENTER NEW ADDRESS: ", ADDR$        ' and address
         IF ADDR$ <> "" THEN STUDENT.ADDR = ADDR$       ' from KB.
         PUT #1, R, STUDENT                             ' Update file.
         PRINT "Any changes have been recorded."
      END IF
   END IF
   PRINT
   INPUT "ID NUMBER(type $ when done)"; ID$             'Get next ID.
LOOP
CLOSE 1
PRINT "Changes to file "; F$; " have been made."
END

FUNCTION SEARCH (ID$, RECNUM)

   DIM STUDENT AS RECORDTYPE

   'Search the ID field of records 1 to RECNUM
   'of any random file of records of type RECORDTYPE
   'for the string ID$.
```

```
          LET R = 1
          GET #1, R, STUDENT
          DO UNTIL ID$ = STUDENT.ID OR R = RECNUM
             LET R = R + 1
             GET #1, R, STUDENT
          LOOP
          IF STUDENT.ID = ID$ THEN SEARCH = R ELSE SEARCH = 0

       END FUNCTION
```

We ran this program to modify the file STUDENTS created by the run shown in Example 12. As shown in the following output, the student TREMONT was marked for deletion, and the address of the student PRICE was changed. Notice that the ID number for PRICE was first typed incorrectly and had to be reentered.

```
    NAME OF FILE TO BE MODIFIED? STUDENTS

    You can change current information for any
    students whose identification number you type.

    ID NUMBER(type $ when done)? 987654321
    STUDENT'S NAME:     TREMONT, JOSEPH E.
    STUDENT'S ADDRESS:  ASPEN 312, CAMPUS
    Is student to be removed (Y or N) ? Y
    Student has been deleted.

    ID NUMBER(type $ when done)? 412444432
    No student with the ID: 412444432

    ID NUMBER(type $ when done)? 412444321
    STUDENT'S NAME:     PRICE, HARRY O.
    STUDENT'S ADDRESS:  ASPEN 226, CAMPUS
    Is student to be removed (Y or N) ? N
    Press the Enter key to indicate no change.
    ENTER NEW NAME:
    ENTER NEW ADDRESS: 226 GROVE AVE., DEVON CT
    Any changes have been recorded.

    ID NUMBER(type $ when done)? $
    Changes to file STUDENTS have been made.
```

Before the run shown, we used the DOS command TYPE STUDENTS to obtain:

```
    A>TYPE STUDENTS
    123456789BYRON, SALLY ANN          BIRCH 122, CAMPUS
    987654321TREMONT, JOSEPH E.        ASPEN 312, CAMPUS
    012333012HAVERLY, BARRY A.         123 SUMMER ST., DEVON CT
    412444321PRICE, HARRY O.           ASPEN 226, CAMPUS
```

After the run, we obtained the following screen display.

```
    A>TYPE STUDENTS
    123456789BYRON, SALLY ANN          BIRCH 122, CAMPUS
             TREMONT, JOSEPH E.        ASPEN 312, CAMPUS
    012333012HAVERLY, BARRY A.         123 SUMMER ST., DEVON CT
    412444321PRICE, HARRY O.           226 GROVE AVE., DEVON CT
```

(On the display screen, CHR$(255) appears as a blank space.)

REMARK

Each new record added to a file causes the file to get longer, but deleting a record by writing CHR$(255) as the first byte does not decrease the size of the file. Thus, after a file has been in use for some time, you may have to remove the "deleted" records. To modify the program so that deleted records are actually removed, you can insert the following programming lines just before the CLOSE statement at the end of the main program unit:

```
    OPEN "TEMPFILE.TMP" FOR RANDOM AS #2 LEN = LEN(STUDENT)
```

```
            FOR REC = 1 TO RECNUM
               GET #1, REC, STUDENT
                  IF ASC(STUDENT.ID) <> 255 THEN PUT #2, , STUDENT
            NEXT REC
            CLOSE 1, 2
            KILL F$                               'Remove from directory.
            NAME "TEMPFILE.TMP" AS F$             'Name modified file F$.
```

This program segment opens a temporary file TEMPFILE.TMP as file #2 and with the same record length as F$. On each pass through the FOR loop, the GET # statement reads a record from F$ and the PUT # statement copies this record to TEMPFILE.TMP, but only if the first character in the ID field STUDENT.ID is not CHR$(255). After all records that were not marked for deletion have been written to the temporary file, both files are closed, the file F$ is deleted rom the disk's directory, and the temporary file is renamed as F$. A KILL statement must be used to remove F$ from the disk's directory because the NAME command cannot be used if F$ is the name of an existing file.

The REMARK in the preceding example shows how to delete records whose first byte is the character CHR$(255). But the method will not work if TEMPFILE.TMP happens to be the name of an existing file. Instead of using a name such as TEMPFILE.TMP, it is a common practice to use the name obtained by changing any extension F$ may have to the extension .TMP. The following statements show how to assign this name to G$.

```
            LET G$ = F$                          'Assign F$ to G$.
            LET P = INSTR(1, G$, ".")            'Does G$ have period?
            IF P > 0 THEN G$ = LEFT$(G$, P - 1)  'Yes, delete extension.
            LET G$ = G$ + ".TMP"                 'Add extension .TMP.
```

If you always use the same character, say CHR$(255), as the first byte of records marked for deletion, you may find it helpful to have a program that will delete such records from any random file. The program given in the next example can be used for this purpose. The program uses QuickBASIC's INPUT$ function. If *n* denotes a numerical expression whose value is a positive integer, and if file #1 has been opened as a sequential file, then

```
            INPUT$(n, #1)
```

returns an *n*-character string consisting of the next *n* characters from file #1.

EXAMPLE 14   *Here is a program to remove each record whose first character is CHR$(255) from any file.*

```
            PRINT "This program deletes records from files that were"
            PRINT "created as RANDOM files.  Each record that begins"
            PRINT "with the character CHR$(255) is deleted."
            PRINT
            INPUT "Enter name of file to be processed: ", F$
            INPUT "Enter record length for the file:   ", L

            LET G$ = F$                          'Assign F$ to G$.
            LET P = INSTR(1, G$, ".")            'Does G$ have period?
            IF P > 0 THEN G$ = LEFT$(G$, P - 1)  'Yes, delete extension.
            LET G$ = G$ + ".TMP"                 'Add extension .TMP.
            OPEN F$ FOR INPUT AS #1               'Open given file for input.
            OPEN G$ FOR OUTPUT AS #2              'Open TMP file for output.

            LET NUMRECS = LOF(1) \ L              'Number of size L records
            FOR K = 1 TO NUMRECS
               LET X$ = INPUT$(L, #1)                'Get one record.
               IF ASC(X$) <> 255 THEN PRINT #2, X$;   'Keep if not CHR$(255).
            NEXT K
            CLOSE 1,2
            KILL F$                               'Delete original file.
            NAME G$ AS F$                         'Rename file G$ as F$.
            PRINT "Records marked for deletion have been removed."
            END
```

Notice that F$ is opened as a sequential file, even though it gives the name of a random file. It is necessary to do this because the INPUT$ function is designed to work only with sequential files.

We ran this program specifying the file STUDENTS modified by the program of Example 13 to obtain the display:

```
This program deletes records from files that were
created as RANDOM files.  Each record that begins
with the character CHR$(255) is deleted.

Enter name of file to be processed: STUDENTS
Enter record length for the file:   80
Records marked for deletion have been removed.
```

After this run, we used the TYPE command to obtain:

```
A>TYPE STUDENTS
123456789BYRON, SALLY ANN        BIRCH 122, CAMPUS
012333012HAVERLY, BARRY A.       123 SUMMER ST., DEVON CT
412444321PRICE, HARRY O.         226 GROVE AVE., DEVON CT
```

The student TREMONT marked for deletion by the run shown in Example 13 has actually been removed.

REMARK   We could have opened file F$ as a random file of record length L, but we could not have declared a record variable of the fixed-length L. The statement

```
DIM V AS STRING * L
```

generates a fatal error condition unless L is the name of a constant. This is the reason that the program opens all files as sequential files.

We conclude this section with six points concerning the use of random files that were not previously mentioned. You should find these points useful while writing programs to process random files and while testing your programs.

1. QuickBASIC stores the contents of record variables as fixed-length strings. For this reason, they cannot be used as arguments in statements that call SUB procedures or reference FUNCTION procedures.

2. The variable names that appear in a TYPE statement block should be used elsewhere in the program in only two ways: the type name can be used in any program unit to specify types of record variables being declared in DIM . . . AS statements; the field names are used in expressions such as *var.fieldname* to reference the field *fieldname* of the record variable *var.*

3. QuickBASIC allows you to use the variable names that appear in TYPE statement blocks for purposes other than the two uses mentioned in item 2. However, the use of a variable name for more than one purpose is not recommended. For example, if A is the name of a type defined by a TYPE statement block, the statement LET A = 237 can be used in the same program unit to assign 237 to the numerical variable A. This usage of A as a type name and as a variable name is allowed, but this double meaning of the variable name A is confusing and should be avoided.

4. If V has the record type RECTYPE, you can use LEN(V) to specify the length of a record of type RECTYPE. If W has the same type, you can use LEN(W) instead of LEN(V). But, it makes no sense to use LEN(RECTYPE). RECTYPE is the name of a type, it is not a record variable. As mentioned in item 3, QuickBASIC will treat this use of the name RECTYPE as a single-precision numerical variable and will return 4 as the value of LEN(RECTYPE). This will not be the correct record length unless, by coincidence, LEN(V) happens to be 4.

5. The fields specified in TYPE statement blocks can have record types. For example, the TYPE and DIM statements

```
TYPE STUDENT
   LAST AS STRING * 20
   FIRST AS STRING * 20
END TYPE

TYPE STUDENTRECORD
   STUDENTNAME AS STUDENT
   SCORE AS INTEGER
END TYPE

DIM SREC AS STUDENTRECORD
```

declare SREC as a record variable with two fields STUDENTNAME and SCORE that are referenced by using the expressions

```
SREC.STUDENTNAME
SREC.SCORE
```

The field SREC.SCORE stores an integer, but SREC.STUDENTNAME stores a record of type STUDENT. The two fields LAST and FIRST in this record are referenced by using the expressions

```
SREC.STUDENTNAME.LAST
SREC.STUDENTNAME.FIRST
```

6. QuickBASIC allows you to declare arrays whose elements are records. For example, the TYPE and DIM statements

```
TYPE STUDENT
   LAST AS STRING * 20
   FIRST AS STRING * 20
END TYPE

DIM A(1 TO 100) AS STUDENT
```

declare A as the name of an array in which the subscripted variables A(1), A(2), . . . , A(100) are record variables of the type STUDENT. The two fields stored in A(N) are referenced by using the expressions

```
A(N).LAST
A(N).FIRST
```

■ 16.8 Problems

1. Write a program to create a random access file INVTRY that contains the following information.

Item code	Units on hand	Warehouse number
A2000	7	39
A3500	25	39
C2255	0	39
D4296	100	46
E7250	19	46
P2243	5	39

The information in this table is to be stored in records 1-6.

2. Write a menu-driven program to allow a user to modify the file INVTRY created in Problem 1. The user should be able to choose options from this menu:

   1. to end the program

   2. to add new items to the file

   3. to display the warehouse number and units-on-hand figure for any item code

3. First, write a menu-driven program for the menu in Problem 2. Then, modify the program by adding these additional options:

   4. to obtain a printed report of the entire contents of the file

   5. to change the units-on-hand figure for any item code

   For option 4, instruct the user to turn on the printer. For option 5, ask for an item code and a number and whether the number represents additions to or deletions from the inventory.

4. Write a program to allow the user to create a mailing list file MAIL.LST by typing its contents at the keyboard. Each record is to contain six fields as follows:

Field 1	Byte 1	Contains CHR$(255) for "deleted" records.
Field 2	Bytes 2–26	Name
Field 3	Bytes 27–58	Street address
Field 4	Bytes 59–73	City or town
Field 5	Bytes 74–75	State (two-letter code)
Field 6	Bytes 76–80	Zip code

   After the file has been created, its contents are to be displayed by using one 80-character display line for each record.

5. Write a program to allow the user to add new entries or delete existing entries in the file MAIL.LST created in Problem 4.

6. Write a program to display the contents of the file MAIL.LST by using a standard address format. Ignore entries that are designated for deletion.

7. Write a program to allow the user to change any part of any existing record in the file MAIL.LST.

8. Write a menu-driven program to perform all of the tasks specified in Problems 4–7.

9. First, write a menu-driven program for Problem 8. Then, add an option to sort the records in the file so that zip codes are in numerical order.

■ *16.9 Review True-or-False Quiz*

1. At most two files can be referenced in a program—one for input data and one for output data. T   F

2. If a program uses a file as an input file, then the program cannot also use this file as an output file. T   F

3. Input data to a program cannot be read from a file and also from DATA lines. These two methods of supplying input data are incompatible. T   F

4. Any attempt to read data from a sequential file after the end of file mark has been detected by the computer will cause a fatal error condition. T   F

5. The contents of a sequential file can be displayed in a readable form by using the DOS command TYPE. T   F

6. If a file named F1 does not exist, the statement

   ```
   OPEN "F1" FOR INPUT AS #1
   ```

   places the name F1 in the disk directory of files. T   F

7. The only difference between sequential files and random files is that data in sequential files must be read in order, whereas data in random files can be read in any order. T   F

8. If a file named F2 does not exist, the statement

   ```
   OPEN "F2" FOR RANDOM AS #1 LEN=50
   ```

   will cause a *File not found* error. T   F

9. The TYPE statement block

```
TYPE REC
   FIELD1 AS STRING * 20
   FIELD2 AS STRING * 15
END TYPE
```

defines REC as a record variable with LEN(REC) = 35.   T   F

10. The two statements

```
LET L = 12
DIM A AS STRING * L
PRINT LEN(A)
```

will display the number 12.   T   F

17
Random Numbers and Their Application

*I*f you toss a coin several times, you'll obtain a sequence such as HTTHTHHHTTH, where H denotes a head and T a tail. We call this a **randomly generated sequence** because each letter is the result of an experiment (tossing a coin) and could not have been determined without actually performing the experiment. Similarly, if you roll a die (a cube with faces numbered 1 through 6) several times, you'll obtain a randomly generated sequence such as 5315264342. The numbers in such a sequence are called **random numbers.**

QuickBASIC contains a built-in function called **RND** used to generate sequences of numbers that have the appearance of being randomly generated. Although these numbers are called random numbers, they are more accurately referred to as **pseudorandom numbers** because the RND function does not perform an experiment such as tossing a coin to produce a number; rather, it uses an algorithm carefully designed to generate sequences of numbers that emulate random sequences. This ability to generate such sequences makes it possible for us to use the computer in many new and interesting ways. Using "random number generators," people have written computer programs to simulate the growth of a forest, to determine the best location for elevators in a proposed skyscraper, to assist social scientists in their statistical studies, to simulate game playing, and to perform many other tasks.

In this chapter we describe the RND function and illustrate its use in several areas.

■ 17.1 The RND Function

The RND function is used somewhat differently from the other built-in functions. For any number X, RND(X) has a value between 0 and 1.

$$0 < RND(X) < 1$$

If X > 0, the value assumed by RND(X) is unpredictable—it will appear to have been selected randomly from the numbers between 0 and 1. In this section, we illustrate the use of RND(X) for the case X > 0. The use of RND(X) with X ≤ 0 is considered in Section 17.2.

EXAMPLE 1   *Here is a program to generate six random numbers that lie between 0 and 1.*

```
PRINT "A LIST OF RANDOM NUMBERS:"
PRINT
FOR N = 1 TO 6
    PRINT RND(1)
NEXT N
END
```

Program output:
```
A LIST OF RANDOM NUMBERS:

.7055475
.533424
.5795186
.2895625
.301948
.7747401
```

Observe that each time the statement PRINT RND(1) is executed, a different number is displayed, even though the same expression RND(1) is used.

REMARK

If you run this program a second time, the same list of six numbers will be displayed. How you obtain different lists on each run is explained following Example 3.

When X > 0 in RND(X), QuickBASIC allows the use of the abbreviated form RND. The expressions RND, RND(1), RND(2), and RND(any positive number) are equivalent. For instance, in Example 1, you can replace RND(1) by RND(2) or even by RND(.125) and get exactly the same result. In what follows, we'll use the shortened form RND; nothing is gained by using RND(X) with X > 0.

EXAMPLE 2

Here is a program to generate 1,000 random numbers between 0 and 1 and determine how many are in the interval from 0.3 to 0.4.

```
LET C = 0          'C does the counting.
FOR K = 1 TO 1000
   LET R = RND
   IF R > .3 AND R < .4 THEN C = C + 1
NEXT K
PRINT
PRINT "OF 1000 NUMBERS GENERATED,"
PRINT C; "WERE BETWEEN .3 AND .4."
END
```

Program output:
```
OF 1000 NUMBERS GENERATED,
 106 WERE BETWEEN .3 AND .4.
```

Each time LET R = RND is executed, RND takes on a different value, which is then assigned to R. The IF statement determines whether R lies in the specified interval. In this example, it was necessary to assign the value of RND to a variable R so that the comparisons could be made. If we had written

```
IF RND > .3 AND RND < .4 THEN C = C + 1
```

the two occurrences of RND would have different values—which is not what we wanted in this situation.

The numbers generated by the RND function are nearly uniformly distributed between 0 and 1. If many numbers are generated, approximately as many will be less than 0.5 as are greater than 0.5, approximately twice as many will be between 0 and 2/3 as are between 2/3 and 1, approximately one-hundredth of the numbers will be between 0.37 and 0.38, and so on. The examples throughout the rest of this chapter illustrate how this property of random number sequences can be put to use by a programmer.

EXAMPLE 3

Let's write a program to simulate tossing a coin 20 times. An H is to be displayed each time a head occurs and a T each time a tail occurs.

PROBLEM ANALYSIS

Since RND will be less than 0.5 approximately half the time, let's say that a head is tossed whenever RND is less than 0.5. The following program is then immediate:

```
PRINT "RESULT OF TOSSING A COIN 20 TIMES:"
PRINT
```

```
FOR N = 1 TO 20
   IF RND < .5 THEN PRINT "H"; ELSE PRINT "T";
NEXT N
END
```

Program output:
```
RESULT OF TOSSING A COIN 20 TIMES:

TTTHHTHTTTHHTTHTTHTH
```

REMARK

If you wish to simulate tossing a bent coin that produces a head twice as often as a tail, you could say that a head is the result whenever RND < 0.66667. Thus, one change in the IF condition allows the same program to work in this case.

The programs shown in Examples 1 through 3 generate the same sequence of random numbers each time they are run. Thus, they always produce the same output. Although this result might be useful while testing a program, it does not reflect what actually happens in real-life situations. QuickBASIC provides the RANDOMIZE statement that can be used to cause different and unpredictable sequences to be generated each time a program is run. If **expr** denotes a numerical expression, the statement

```
RANDOMIZE expr
```

will cause subsequent values of RND to follow a sequence that depends not only on the number of times RND has already been encountered but also on the value of **expr.** This value is called a **random number seed** and can be any numerical value allowed in QuickBASIC. A common choice for **expr** is QuickBASIC's numerical function TIMER. If your PC has an internal clock, TIMER returns the number of seconds elapsed since midnight; otherwise, it returns the number of seconds elapsed since the computer was turned on. Thus, if you include the statement

```
RANDOMIZE TIMER
```

in your programs so that it is executed before RND is encountered, your programs will generate random numbers that depend only on the value of TIMER when the RANDOMIZE statement is executed. This should ensure different and unpredictable sequences each time you run your programs.

The following program and output illustrate what has just been said. The output of each run is different because the value of TIMER was different each time the RANDOMIZE statement was executed.

```
RANDOMIZE TIMER
PRINT "First five values of RND:"
FOR N = 1 TO 5
   PRINT USING ".######   "; RND;
NEXT N
END
```

Program output:
```
First five values of RND:
.541805   .602775   .637090   .319973   .601341
```

Program output:
```
First five values of RND:
.614971   .055153   .264333   .485119   .965278
```

If you use RANDOMIZE without including an expression such as TIMER, the computer will display the prompt

```
Random-number seed (-32768 to 32767)?
```

and you must enter a seed in the range shown. This form is rarely used. Not only does the prompt clutter the output, it also requires an unnecessary action of the user.

The next example shows how the RND function can be used to simulate a real-life situation.

EXAMPLE 4   *A professional softball player has a lifetime batting average of .365. Assuming that the player will have four official times at bat (walks are not official at bats) in each of the next 100 games, estimate the number of games in which 0, 1, 2, 3, and 4 hits are made.*

PROBLEM ANALYSIS

To simulate one time at bat, we will generate a number RND and concede a hit if RND < .365. For any one game, we will compare four such numbers with .365. If AVG = .365, the following FOR loop accomplishes this:

```
'Find the number H of hits in one game.
LET H = 0
FOR ATBAT = 1 TO 4
   IF RND < AVG THEN H = H + 1
NEXT ATBAT
```

We must repeat this program segment 100 times (once for each of the 100 games), keeping counts of the number of games in which H is 0, 1, 2, 3, and 4. If we declare array COUNT with the statement

```
DIM COUNT(0 TO 4)
```

we can use COUNT(0) to count the number of hitless games, COUNT(1) the number of games with one hit, and so on. Thus, we should follow the FOR loop shown above with the statement

```
LET COUNT(H) = COUNT(H) + 1
```

This problem analysis shows how to code Step (b1) of the following algorithm. Coding the other steps is routine. Note that the algorithm allows the user to specify any batting average AVG (not just the average .365 given in the problem statement) and to obtain simulation results for any number of batting averages.

THE ALGORITHM

a. Input a batting average AVG.
b. Repeat the following until AVG = 0.

    b1. Simulate 100 games to obtain the counts COUNT(0) to COUNT(4).
    b2. Display the results of the simulation.
    b3. Input a batting average AVG.

c. Stop

THE PROGRAM

```
PRINT "This program simulates the performance in"
PRINT "one hundred games of any batter whose batting"
PRINT "average you specify.  The program assumes four"
PRINT "official times at bat in each game."
PRINT

'*****************************************************
COLUMN HEADINGS$ = "HITS PER GAME     FREQUENCY"
  OUTPUT.FORMAT$ = "       #            ###      "

DIM COUNT(0 TO 4)            'Declare counting array.
RANDOMIZE TIMER             'Select random sequence.

'*****************************************************
' CARRY OUT SIMULATION FOR AVERAGES TYPED AT KEYBOARD.

INPUT "Batting average (0 to stop)"; AVG

DO UNTIL AVG = 0                    'Exit on 0 input.
   ERASE COUNT                      'Initialize counters.

      '---------------------------------------------
      'Simulate 100 games with batting average AVG.
```

```
FOR GAME = 1 TO 100
   'Find the number H of hits in one game.
   LET H = 0
   FOR ATBAT = 1 TO 4
      IF RND < AVG THEN H = H + 1
   NEXT ATBAT
   LET COUNT(H) = COUNT(H) + 1      'Count H.
NEXT GAME

'-------------------------------------
'Display the result of the simulation
'and input next batting average.

PRINT
PRINT COLUMN.HEADINGS$
FOR H = 0 TO 4
   PRINT USING OUTPUT.FORMAT$; H; COUNT(H)
NEXT H
PRINT
INPUT "Batting average (0 to stop)"; AVG
LOOP
END
```

Program output:

```
This program simulates the performance in
one hundred games of any batter whose batting
average you specify.  The program assumes four
official times at bat in each game.

Batting average (0 to stop)? .365

HITS PER GAME      FREQUENCY
      0                18
      1                44
      2                26
      3                11
      4                 1

Batting average (0 to stop)? .223

HITS PER GAME      FREQUENCY
      0                39
      1                42
      2                18
      3                 1
      4                 0

Batting average (0 to stop)? 0
```

REMARK   In this example, we concede a hit if the condition RND < AVG is true. If we change this condition to RND <= AVG, essentially the same results will occur; it is extremely unlikely that RND will ever take on the exact value AVG, whatever the value of AVG. But even if it does, it will happen so rarely that no significant change in the simulation being carried out will occur.

17.2 Repeating a Random Process

In this section, we show how zero and negative arguments for RND can be used to repeat previously generated random numbers.

A zero argument always produces the last random number that was generated by the program. Thus, the two statements

```
PRINT RND
LET B = RND(0)
```

will display the value generated by RND and then assign this value to B. Similarly, the following line will display a single random number three times:

```
PRINT RND; RND(0); RND(0)
```

Since you can always use a variable to "remember" the most recent random number, you will have little need to use RND(0). Instead of using RND(0), assign RND to R and then use R. As we now show, negative arguments for RND can be helpful.

Each negative argument of RND has associated with it a fixed number between 0 and 1. If you execute the statement

```
PRINT RND(-1); RND(-2); RND(-3.2)
```

you will always obtain the same (predictable) numbers. We did this and got the numbers

```
.224007   .7133257   .8111894
```

These particular values are of no significance, however. What is important is that using RND with a negative argument will cause subsequent random numbers generated with RND[or RND(X) with X > 0] to follow a sequence associated with this negative argument. For example, note that the two FOR loops in the following program produce exactly the same output.

```
PRINT "Value of RND(-1):"; RND(-1)
FOR N = 1 TO 4: PRINT RND; : NEXT N
PRINT
PRINT
PRINT "Value of RND(-1):"; RND(-1)
FOR N = 1 TO 4: PRINT RND; : NEXT N
```

Program output:
```
Value of RND(-1): .224007
 3.584582E-02  8.635235E-02  .1642639  .1797358

Value of RND(-1): .224007
 3.584582E-02  8.635235E-02  .1642639  .1797358
```

It is not necessary that RND(−1) be output; it simply must be used. For instance, if you change both occurrences of

```
PRINT "Value of RND(-1):"; RND(-1)
```

to

```
LET Q = RND(-1)
```

the two FOR loops will again produce exactly the same random numbers.

The preceding program produces the same output each time it is run. To cause a different output for each run, you can begin the program with

```
LET NEGATIVE = -TIMER
```

and change each occurrence of RND(−1) to RND(NEGATIVE). The next example illustrates the method.

EXAMPLE 5   *Here is a program to illustrate the use of RND with a negative argument in a program that generates different random sequences each time it is run. The action of the program is described by the comments that begin the two sections of the program.*

```
LET NEGATIVE = -TIMER
LET SEED = RND(NEGATIVE)              'Select random sequence.

'-------------------------------------------------------------
'     Find average AVG of next 10 random numbers.
'-------------------------------------------------------------
```

```
            LET S = 0
            FOR N = 1 TO 10
               LET S = S + RND
            NEXT N
            LET AVG = S / 10
            PRINT
            PRINT USING "AVERAGE OF TEN RANDOM NUMBERS: #.######"; AVG
            PRINT


            '-----------------------------------------------------------
            '     Display the same ten random numbers and their
            '     values reduced by the average AVG of all ten.
            '-----------------------------------------------------------

            LET SEED = RND(NEGATIVE)      'Select same random sequence.

            PRINT "   THE TEN        THEIR VALUES REDUCED BY"
            PRINT "   NUMBERS        THE AVERAGE OF ALL TEN"
            PRINT "-----------       -----------------------"
             F$ = " #.######           #.###### "

            FOR N = 1 TO 10
               PRINT USING F$; RND; RND(0) - AVG
            NEXT N
            END
```

Program output:
```
AVERAGE OF TEN RANDOM NUMBERS: 0.530198

    THE TEN        THEIR VALUES REDUCED BY
    NUMBERS        THE AVERAGE OF ALL TEN
    -----------    -----------------------
    0.958938            0.428740
    0.175901           -.354297
    0.756641            0.226443
    0.507037           -.023161
    0.215503           -.314694
    0.898637            0.368439
    0.361139           -.169059
    0.625427            0.095230
    0.314678           -.215519
    0.488075           -.042122
```

REMARK

We could have stored the random numbers in an array and used the array values to produce the table displayed by the second part of the program. By using RND with the same negative argument in both parts of the program, we avoided the need for an array.

Example 5 shows how you can use RND with a negative argument to obtain different sequences of random numbers each time a program is run. The method illustrated, however, should be used only if you need to generate a random sequence a second time. In every other situation, the common practice is to use the RANDOMIZE statement.

■ *17.3 Problems*

1. *Approximately how many asterisks are displayed by each program segment?*

   a.
```
   FOR I=1 TO 100
        IF RND<0.8 THEN PRINT "*";
   NEXT I
```

   b.
```
   FOR K=1 TO 100
        LET X=RND
        IF X<0.4 OR X>0.7 THEN PRINT "*";
   NEXT K
```

```
c. FOR K=1 TO 100
       IF RND>0.4 AND RND(0)<0.7 THEN PRINT "*";
   NEXT K

d. FOR J=1 TO 10
       IF RND=RND THEN PRINT "*";
   NEXT J

e. FOR L=1 TO 100
       IF RND<>0.5 THEN PRINT "*";
   NEXT L

f. LET X=RND(-4)
   FOR L=1 TO 10
       LET A(L)=RND
   NEXT L
   LET Y=RND(-4)
   FOR N=1 TO 10
       LET Z=RND
       IF Z=A(N) THEN PRINT "*";
   NEXT N
```

2. Which of these logical expressions are always true? Which are always false? Which may be true or false?

a. `RND>0` **b.** `4*RND<4`
c. `RND<RND` **d.** `RND+RND<3*RND`
e. `RND+1>RND` **f.** `INT(RND)=0`

In Problems 3–12, write a program to perform each task specified.

3. Display approximately one-fourth of all values that appear in DATA lines. Make a decision to display or not to display as the number is read.

4. Display approximately 1% of all integers from 1,000 to 9,999, inclusive. Select the integers randomly.

5. Simulate tossing two coins 100 times. The output should be a count of the number of times each of the possible outcomes HH, HT, TH, and TT occurs.

6. Simulate tossing three coins 10 times. The output should be a list of 10 terms such as HHH, HTH, HHT, and so on.

7. Simulate tossing K coins N times. The output should be a list of N terms in which each term is a sequence of K H's and T's. N and K are to be input.

8. A game between players A and B is played as follows. A coin is tossed three times or until a head comes up, whichever occurs first. As soon as a head comes up, player A collects $1 from player B. If no head comes up on any of the three tosses, player B collects $6 from player A. In either case, the game is over. Have your program simulate this game 1,000 times to help decide whether A or B has the advantage (or if it is a fair game).

9. Generate an array L of 500 random numbers between 0 and 1. Using L, determine an array C as follows: C(1) is a count of how many entries of L are between 0 and 0.1, C(2) a count of those between 0.1 and 0.2, and so on. Display a two-column table showing the intervals and the corresponding counts stored in array C.

10. The first three hitters in the Bears' batting order have lifetime batting averages of .257, .289, and .324, respectively. Simulate their first trip to the plate for the next 100 games, and tabulate the number of games in which they produce zero, one, two, and three hits. Allow the user to specify the three batting averages during program execution.

11. Jones and Kelley are to have a duel at 20 paces. At this distance Jones will hit the target on the average of two shots in every five, and Kelley will hit one in every three. Kelley shoots first. Who has the best chance of surviving? Use a FOR loop to run the program 20 times and display the results.

12. (Drunkard's walk.) A poor soul, considerably intoxicated, stands in the middle of a 10-foot-long bridge that spans a river. The inebriate staggers along, either toward the left bank or toward the right bank, but fortunately cannot fall off the bridge. Assuming that each step taken is exactly 1 foot long, how many steps will the drunkard take before a bank is reached? Assume that it is just as likely that a step will be toward the left bank as toward the right.

You must do three things:

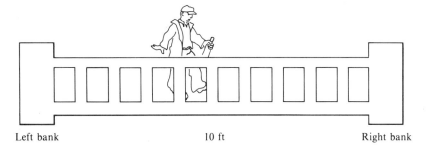

Left bank   10 ft   Right bank

a. Find how many steps are taken in getting off the bridge.
b. Tell which bank is reached.
c. Let the drunkard go out for several nights and arrive at the same point (the center) on the bridge. Find, on the average, how many steps it takes to get off the bridge.

■ *17.4 Random Integers*

Many computer applications require generating **random integers** rather than just random numbers between 0 and 1. For example, suppose a manufacturer estimates that a proposed new product will sell at the rate of 10 to 20 units each week and wants a program to simulate sales figures over an extended period of time. To write such a program, you must be able to generate random integers from 10 to 20 to represent the estimated weekly sales. To do this, you can multiply RND, which is between 0 and 1, by 11 (the number of integers from 10 to 20) to obtain

$$0 < 11 * \text{RND} < 11$$

If many numbers are obtained using 11 * RND, they will be nearly uniformly distributed between 0 and 11. This means that the value of INT(11 * RND) will be one of the integers $0, 1, 2, \ldots, 10$. Thus, if you add 10 to this expression, you will get an integer from 10 to 20:

$$10 \leq \text{INT}(11 * \text{RND}) + 10 \leq 20$$

The important thing here is that integers generated in this way will appear to have been chosen randomly from the set of integers $\{10, 11, 12, \ldots, 20\}$.

In general, if A and B are integers with $A < B$,

$$\text{INT}((B - A + 1) * \text{RND})$$

will generate an integer from 0 to $B - A$. (Note that $B - A + 1$ gives the number of integers between A and B, inclusive.) Thus, adding A to this expression, we obtain

$$\text{INT}((B - A + 1) * \text{RND}) + A$$

whose value is an integer chosen randomly from the set $\{A, A + 1, A + 2, \ldots, B\}$. The following table illustrates how to obtain random integers within specified bounds:

Expression	Value of the expression
`INT(10*RND)`	A random integer from 0 to 9
`INT(N*RND)`	A random integer from 0 to $N - 1$
`INT(N*RND)+1`	A random integer from 1 to N
`INT(51*RND)+100`	A random integer from 100 to 150
`INT(11*RND)-5`	A random integer from -5 to 5

EXAMPLE 6

Let's write a program to generate 15 numbers randomly selected from the set {1, 2, 3, 4, 5}.

PROBLEM ANALYSIS

From the preceding discussion, we know that the expression INT(5 * RND) will be an integer from 0 to 4. Thus, INT(5 * RND) + 1 will be an integer from 1 to 5, as required.

```
PRINT "15 INTEGERS SELECTED RANDOMLY"
PRINT "FROM THE SET {1, 2, 3, 4, 5}:"
PRINT
RANDOMIZE TIMER
FOR I = 1 TO 15
   PRINT INT(5 * RND) + 1;
NEXT I
END
```

Program output:
```
15 INTEGERS SELECTED RANDOMLY
FROM THE SET {1, 2, 3, 4, 5}:

 2  1  5  3  2  2  2  3  1  2  2  4  1  3  4
```

EXAMPLE 7

Let's write a program to generate 15 numbers randomly selected from the set {100, 101, 102, . . . , 199}.

PROBLEM ANALYSIS

The technique used in Example 6 is also applicable here. Since INT(100 * RND) is an integer from 0 to 99, we add 100 to obtain an integer from the specified set. Thus, the program required is that of Example 6 with the PRINT statement in the FOR loop changed to

```
PRINT INT(100 * RND) + 100;
```

■ 17.5 Simulation

Example 4 of Section 17.1 shows how the RND function can be used to simulate a ball player's future performance based on past performance. The example illustrates a major category of simulation problems encountered in computer programming—namely, the simulation of future events based on data obtained by observing the results of similar or related previous events. In this section, we show how such a simulation can be used to advantage in a business setting.

EXAMPLE 8

A retail store will soon handle a new product. A preliminary market survey indicates that between 500 and 1,000 units will be sold each month. (The survey is no more specific than this.) Write a program to simulate sales for the first 6 months. The retail store management is to be allowed to experiment by specifying two values: the number of units to be purchased initially and the number to be purchased on the first of each subsequent month.

PROBLEM ANALYSIS

The input values are:

IPUR = initial inventory purchase
PUR = inventory purchase for subsequent months

The problem statement does not specify the nature of the output. Let's agree to produce a four-column report showing the following items:

MONTH = month (1, 2, . . . , 6)
SALES = estimated sales (500–1,000) for 1 month

FIRST = quantity on hand at beginning of month (initially, IPUR)
LAST   = quantity on hand at end of month

For each month we must generate a random integer SALES from 500 to 1,000. There are 501 integers to choose from (501 = 1,000 − 500 + 1). Thus, we can use the following expression to select an integer randomly from 500 to 1,000:

```
INT(501 * RND) + 500
```

After the initial and periodic purchase quantities (IPUR and PUR) are input, we will display column headings and then assign the input value IPUR to FIRST so that the simulation can begin. The actual simulation of sales for each of the 6 months (MONTH = 1 to 6) can be carried out as follows:

1. Estimate sales for 1 month (SALES = INT(501 * RND) + 500).
2. Determine the quantity on hand at the end of the month (LAST = FIRST − SALES).
3. Display MONTH, SALES, FIRST, LAST.
4. Determine the quantity on hand at the start of the next month (FIRST = LAST + PUR).

Since the problem statement specifies that the store management is to be allowed to experiment, we must have the program generate different sequences of random numbers each time it is run. As usual, we will use RANDOMIZE TIMER for this purpose.

THE PROGRAM

```
'              NEW PRODUCT SIMULATION

'        PUR = MONTHLY INVENTORY PURCHASE
'      MONTH = MONTH (1,2,...,6)
'      FIRST = ON HAND - BEGINNING OF MONTH
'      SALES = SALES FOR ONE MONTH (500-1000)
'       LAST = ON HAND - END OF MONTH

' **********************************************************
'                 KEYBOARD INPUT

INPUT "INITIAL INVENTORY PURCHASE"; IPUR
INPUT "SUBSEQUENT MONTHLY PURCHASE"; PUR
PRINT
' **********************************************************
'       DISPLAY HEADINGS AND ASSIGN OUTPUT FORMAT F$.

PRINT "                      INVENTORY"
PRINT "                 -------------------"
PRINT "MONTH     ESTIMATED   START OF    END OF"
PRINT "NUMBER     SALES       MONTH      MONTH"
 F$ = "  ##        ####       #####      #####"
PRINT
' **********************************************************
'         SIMULATE AND DISPLAY SALES FOR SIX MONTHS.

RANDOMIZE TIMER                      'Select random sequence.
LET FIRST = IPUR                     'On hand first month
FOR MONTH = 1 TO 6
   LET SALES = INT(501 * RND) + 500  'Sales for the month
   LET LAST = FIRST - SALES          'On hand end of month.
   PRINT USING F$; MONTH; SALES; FIRST; LAST
   LET FIRST = LAST + PUR            'On hand start of month
NEXT MONTH
END
```

Program output:
```
INITIAL INVENTORY PURCHASE? 1000
SUBSEQUENT MONTHLY PURCHASE? 900
```

```
                                     INVENTORY
                                --------------------
         MONTH     ESTIMATED    START OF    END OF
        NUMBER       SALES       MONTH      MONTH

           1          674        1000         326
           2          512        1226         714
           3          919        1614         695
           4          656        1595         939
           5          921        1839         918
           6          664        1818        1154
```

REMARK

■

A user would run this program several times and use the results as a guide to determine a reasonable purchasing strategy. The increasingly larger values in the last two columns suggest that a monthly purchase of 900 units is excessive.

We wrote the new-product simulation program so that sales of 500 to 1,000 units would be selected with equal likelihood. We did this not because it is realistic, but because the preliminary market analysis gave no further information. A more careful market analysis would probably show that the number of units would range from 500 to 1,000—with sales near 750 more likely than sales near the extremes 500 and 1,000. We'll now show how random numbers that cluster about a specific number can be generated.

The FUNCTION procedure

```
FUNCTION RAN
   LET R = 0
   FOR K = 1 TO 5
      LET R = R + RND
   NEXT K
   LET RAN = R / 5
END FUNCTION
```

returns a random number between 0 and 1 each time the function reference RAN is encountered. The random number is determined by averaging five random numbers RND. If many numbers are generated by using the function RAN, they will tend to cluster about the midpoint 0.5 of the interval 0 to 1, with fewer occurring toward the endpoints 0 and 1. If a number larger than 5 is used in the function definition, the numbers generated will cluster more closely around the midpoint 0.5.

If we include this FUNCTION procedure in a program, the statement

```
LET SALES = INT(501 * RAN) + 500
```

will generate random integers SALES from 500 to 1,000. Since the RAN values will cluster about the midpoint 0.5 of the interval 0 to 1, the corresponding SALES values will cluster about the midpoint 750 of the interval 500 to 1,000. The new-product simulation program given in Example 8 is easily modified to generate sales by this method. Simply include the FUNCTION procedure RAN and replace

```
LET SALES = INT(501 * RND) + 500
```

by

```
LET SALES = INT(501 * RAN) + 500
```

Here is a run of the program after the changes were made:

```
INITIAL INVENTORY PURCHASE? 1000
SUBSEQUENT MONTHLY PURCHASE? 900
```

```
                          INVENTORY
                       - - - - - - - - - - - - - - - - - -
   MONTH    ESTIMATED   START OF     END OF
   NUMBER     SALES       MONTH      MONTH

     1         701        1000         299
     2         774        1199         425
     3         686        1325         639
     4         757        1539         782
     5         761        1682         921
     6         760        1821        1061
```

Note that the estimated sales figures are nearer 750 than before. Note also that the figures in the last column give more evidence that purchasing 900 units per month is excessive.

■ *17.6 Problems*

1. *Write a single PRINT statement to display each of the following:*
   a. A nonnegative random number (not necessarily an integer) less than 4
   b. A random number less than 11 but greater than 5
   c. A random number less than 3 but greater than -5
   d. A random integer between 6 and 12, inclusive
   e. A random number from the set {0, 2, 4, 6, 8}
   f. A random number from the set {1, 3, 5, 7, 9}

2. *What values can be assumed by each of the following expressions? For each expression, tell whether the possible values are all equally likely to occur.*

   a. `INT(2*RND+1)`   b. `3*INT(RND)`
   c. `INT(5*RND)-2`   d. `INT(2*RND+1)+INT(2*RND+1)`
   e. `INT(6*RND+1)+INT(6*RND+1)`   f. `INT(3*RND+1)*(INT(3*RND)+1)`

3. If two coins are tossed, two heads, two tails, or one of each may result. The following program was written to simulate tossing two coins a total of 20 times. If it is run, the output will not reflect what would happen if the coins were actually tossed. Explain why, and then write a correct program.

```
    FOR I=1 TO 20
       LET R=INT(3*RND)
       IF R=0 THEN PRINT "TWO HEADS"
       IF R=1 THEN PRINT "TWO TAILS"
       IF R=2 THEN PRINT "ONE OF EACH"
    NEXT I
    END
```

In Problems 4–18, write a program to perform each task specified.

4. Display a sequence of 20 letters that are selected randomly from the word RANDOM.

5. Randomly select and display an integer from 1 to 100 and then another integer from the remaining 99.

6. Create an array B of exactly 20 different integers from 1 to 100. Choose the integers randomly. Display the array, but only after it is completely determined.

7. Read 20 different English words into an array A$. Then create another array B$ that contains exactly 10 different words randomly selected from those in array A$.

8. Starting with D(1) = 1, D(2) = 2, D(3) = 3, . . . , D(52) = 52, rearrange the entries of array D as follows: select an integer K from 1 to 52 and swap D(K) with D(52), select K from 1 to 51 and swap D(K) with D(51), select K from 1 to 50 and swap D(K) with D(50), and so on. The last step in this process is to select K from 1 to 2 and swap D(K) with D(2). Then, display the entries of D in four adjacent columns, each containing 13 numbers. Explain in what sense your program shuffles a standard bridge deck and deals one hand in bridge.

9. A retail store will soon carry a new product. A preliminary market analysis indicates that between 300 and 500 units will be sold each week. (The survey is no more specific than this.) Assuming that each unit costs the store $1.89, write a program to simulate sales for the next 16 weeks. Allow the store management to specify the selling price to obtain output showing the week, the estimated sales in number of units, the total revenue, the income (revenue − cost), and the cumulative income. Allow the user to try many different selling prices during a single program run.

10. Carry out the task specified in Problem 9, but this time assume that the market analysis says the number of units sold per week (300–500) will cluster about the midpoint (400), as described in Section 17.5.

11. Juanita Fernandes is offered the opportunity to transfer to another sales territory. She is informed that, for each month of the past year, sales in the territory were between $18,000 and $30,000, with sales of $25,000 or more being twice as likely as sales under $25,000. A 4% commission is paid on all sales up to $25,000, and 8% on all sales above that figure. Simulate the next 6 months' sales, and print the monthly sales and commission to give Juanita some information on which to base her decision to accept or reject the transfer.

12. The IDA Production Company will employ 185 people to work on the production of a new product. It is estimated that each person can complete between 85 and 95 units each working day. Experience shows that the absentee rate is between 0 and 15% on Mondays and Fridays and between 0 and 7% on the other days. Simulate the production for 1 week. Display the results of this simulation in four columns showing the day of the week, the number of workers present, the number of units produced, and the average number produced per worker.

13. Two knights begin at diagonally opposite corners of a chessboard and travel randomly about the board but always make legitimate knight moves. (The knight moves either one step forward or backward and then two steps to the right or left or else two steps forward or backward and one step to the right or left.) Calculate the number of moves before one knight captures the other. However you number the squares, each knight's move should be displayed as it is taken.

14. A single trip for a knight is defined as follows. The knight starts in one corner of the chessboard and randomly makes N knight moves to arrive at one of the 64 squares of the chessboard. (See Problem 13 for a description of an admissible knight move.) Write a program to simulate 1,000 such trips for a knight to determine how many times each square was reached at the end of a trip. These counts should be presented as an 8 × 8 table that displays the counts for the 64 squares. Allow the user to obtain a frequency table for many values of N during a single program run.

15. SIM is a game in which two players take turns drawing lines between any two of the six dots numbered 1 through 6 in the following diagram:

```
        1    2
        .    .
  6 ·    .    .    · 3
        .    .
        5    4
```

The first player's lines are colored red; the second player's are colored blue. The loser is the first player to complete a triangle with three of these six dots as vertices. For example, if the second player draws a line (blue) between dots 2 and 4, 6 and 4, and 2 and 6, this player has completed a blue triangle and hence loses. Write a program in which the computer is the second player. The computer is to record all moves and announce the end of each game with a message stating who won. [*Hint:* Use a 6 × 6 array H(I,J) to record the moves. If the first player types 3,5 to indicate that a red line is drawn between these two dots, set H(3,5) and H(5,3) to 1. If the computer picks 2,6 (to be done randomly), then set H(2,6) and H(6,2) to 2. Note that a triangle of one color has been completed when there are three different numbers I, J, K for which H(I,J), H(J,K), and H(K,I) are all 1 or all 2.]

16. Write a program for the game of SIM described in Problem 15, but this time with a person as the second player, not the computer.

17. Write a function to generate random numbers between 0 and 1 by averaging N random numbers rather than 5 as in Section 17.5. Include this function in a program that allows the user to specify a positive integer N to obtain a frequency table showing counts of how many of 500 random numbers generated by the function are in each of the 10 intervals 0–0.1, 0.1–0.2, . . . , 0.9–1.

The user should be allowed to obtain tables for many positive integers N during a single program run.. The program should halt when the user types zero. (Be sure to try the cases N = 1, 10, and 20.)

18. Display 20 sets of three integers D, L, and F with $0 \le D < 360$, $5 \le L \le 15$, and $1 \le F \le 4$. (*Note:* If you interpret D as a direction and L as a length, you can create a design using these numbers. Starting at a point on a piece of paper, draw a line of length L in the direction given by D. At the end of this line segment draw one of four figures as specified by F—for example, different colored circles the sizes of a dime, nickel, quarter, and half dollar. Using the end of this first line segment as a new starting point, repeat the process by using the second of the 20 triples D, L, F. This process illustrates, in a very elementary way, what some people refer to as random art.)

■ *17.7 A Statistical Application*

Programmers are often confronted with tasks that simply cannot be programmed to run within a specified time limit. When this happens, it is not always necessary to abandon the task. Sometimes satisfactory results can be obtained by doing only part of the job. The following example, which illustrates one such situation, makes use of the statistical fact that the average of a large collection of numbers can be estimated by taking the average of only a fraction of the numbers, provided that the numbers are chosen randomly.

EXAMPLE 9

A researcher has compiled three lists A, B, and C of 500 measurements each and wishes to determine the average of all possible sums obtained by adding three measurements, one from each of the three lists. We are to write a program to assist the researcher in this task.

PROBLEM ANALYSIS

On the surface, this appears to be a simple programming task. For each set A(I), B(J), C(K) of measurements, we can add A(I) + B(J) + C(K) to a summation accumulator SUM and then divide SUM by the number of sets A(I), B(J), C(K) used. The following program segment will do this:

```
LET SUM = 0
FOR I = 1 TO 500
   FOR J = 1 TO 500
      FOR K = 1 TO 500
         LET SUM = SUM + A(I) + B(J) + C(K)
      NEXT K
   NEXT J
NEXT I
PRINT "REQUIRED AVERAGE IS"; SUM / 500 ^ 3
```

If you use this program segment to find the required average, you'll have a long wait. To see that this is so, precede the program segment shown with the line

```
DIM A(1 TO 500), B(1 TO 500), C(1 TO 500)
```

and issue the run command. (The PC takes just as long to add zeros—which is what will happen here—as other numbers.) We did this and, after one minute, used Ctrl-Break to stop program execution. The immediate mode command

```
PRINT I,J,K
```

gave the values I = 1, J = 12, and K = 472. This means that J × 500 + K = 6,472 passes through the triply nested loops were made in one minute. Since $500^3 = 125,000,000$ passes must be made in all, the estimated execution time is $125,000,000 \div 6,472 = 19,313.97$ minutes—which is approximately 322 hours, or thirteen 24-hour days.

About the only way out of this dilemma is to treat only a fraction of the 125 million sets A(I), B(J), C(K) and use the average of *their* sums as an estimate of the average desired.

Using 1 in 10,000 of these sets will take approximately 1.9 minutes (19,313.97 ÷ 10,000). To ensure that the average obtained will be a reliable estimate of the average desired, the sets A(I), B(J), C(K) must be chosen randomly. In the following program segment, we use the expression INT(500 * RND) + 1 to select subscripts from 1 to 500 randomly. The statement FOR N = 1 to 12500 is appropriate, since using 1 in 10,000 of the sets A(I), B(J), C(K) means that a total of 125,000,000 ÷ 10,000 = 12,500 sets will be used.

```
LET SUM = 0
FOR N = 1 TO 12500
   LET I = INT(500 * RND) + 1
   LET J = INT(500 * RND) + 1
   LET K = INT(500 * RND) + 1
   LET SUM = SUM + A(I) + B(J) + C(K)
NEXT N
PRINT "ESTIMATED AVERAGE IS"; SUM / 12500
```

REMARK 1   When this program segment is executed, the same subscripts I, J, K may be selected more than once. Since each set A(I), B(J), C(K) has an equal chance of being selected, however, the effect on the final average will be statistically insignificant.

REMARK 2   It is not necessary to use 12,500 of the sets A(I), B(J), C(K) to obtain a reliable estimate of the average desired. Indeed, random number generators used with QuickBASIC will eventually repeat the sequence of random numbers being produced. If you use only 2,500 of the sets (1 in 50,000), you will probably get just as accurate an estimate of the average as you would with 12,500 sets.

■ 17.8 Monte Carlo

The speed of modern computing machines, together with their ability to generate good random sequences, allows us to approach many problems in ways not previously possible. The following example illustrates one such method, called the **Monte Carlo method.** When you complete the example, you should have little difficulty explaining why this name is applied to the technique involved.

EXAMPLE 10   *Consider the following figure of a circle inscribed in a square.*

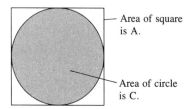

Area of square is A.

Area of circle is C.

If darts are randomly tossed at this figure and tosses landing outside the square are ignored, we can expect the number of darts falling within the circle to be related to the number falling on the entire square as the area C of the circle is related to the area A of the square. We will use this observation to approximate the area C of a unit circle (circle of radius 1).

PROBLEM ANALYSIS   Let's suppose that N darts have landed on the square and that M of these are in the circle. Then, as noted in the problem statement, we will have the approximation

$$\frac{M}{N} \approx \frac{C}{A}$$

or, solving for C,

$$C \approx M \times \frac{A}{N}$$

The more darts thrown (randomly), the better we can expect this approximation to be. The problem, then, is to simulate this activity and keep an accurate count of M and N. To simplify this task, let's place our figure on a coordinate system with its origin at the center of the circle:

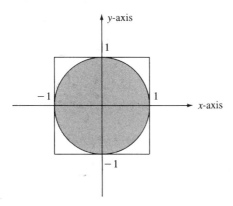

A point (x, y) will lie in the square if both x and y lie between -1 and $+1$. Such a point will lie within the circle if

$$x^2 + y^2 < 1$$

To simulate tossing a single dart, we randomly generate two numbers x and y between -1 and $+1$. The following algorithm describes this process for N = 10,000 tosses. The approximate area of the circle M × A/N is displayed for the values N = 1,000, 2,000, 3,000, . . . , 10,000.

a. Let M = 0. (M counts the darts falling within the circle.)
b. For N = 1 to 10,000, do the following:

    b1. Generate x and y between -1 and 1.
    b2. If $x^2 + y^2 < 1$, add 1 to M.
    b3. If N is a multiple of 1,000, display N and M × A/N.

c. Stop.

Since 2 * RND − 1 gives a random number between -1 and $+1$, and since the area A of the square is 4, the above algorithm translates rather easily into the following program:

<table>
<tr><td>

THE PROGRAM

</td><td>

```
'              A MONTE CARLO SIMULATION

' *****************************************************
' DISPLAY HEADINGS AND ASSIGN OUTPUT FORMAT STRING.
' *****************************************************

PRINT " NUMBER OF    ESTIMATED AREA"
PRINT "DARTS THROWN  OF UNIT CIRCLE"
PRINT "------------  --------------"
 F$ = "    #####         #.#####"

' *****************************************************
'          SIMULATE TOSSING 10,000 DARTS.
' *****************************************************

RANDOMIZE TIMER
LET M = 0                    'Darts falling in circle
LET A = 4                    'Area of square
```

</td></tr>
</table>

```
FOR N = 1 TO 10000
   LET X = 2 * RND - 1
   LET Y = 2 * RND - 1
   IF X ^ 2 + Y ^ 2 < 1 THEN      'Dart in circle?
      LET M = M + 1                'Yes, count it.
   END IF
   IF N / 1000 = N \ 1000 THEN    'Multiple of 1000?
      LET C = M * A / N            'Yes - estimate
      PRINT USING F$; N; C         ' area of circle.
   END IF
NEXT N
END
```

Program output:

NUMBER OF DARTS THROWN	ESTIMATED AREA OF UNIT CIRCLE
1000	3.12800
2000	3.16200
3000	3.19733
4000	3.16900
5000	3.15760
6000	3.15133
7000	3.14971
8000	3.15100
9000	3.15289
10000	3.14840

REMARK

Since we know that the area of a circle of radius 1 is π (approximately 3.1416), we see that the final estimate is accurate to two decimal places. To obtain greater accuracy, you might be tempted to use more than 10,000 points. Indeed, if RND were a true random number generator—that is, if it actually performed a random experiment such as tossing coins to generate numbers—you could expect to obtain any degree of accuracy desired by taking N large enough. The fact that RND is not a true random number generator places a limit on the accuracy obtainable.

17.9 Modular Arithmetic and Random Numbers

The realization that the use of random numbers in computer programs makes possible new and promising applications of the computer brought about an intensive search for ways to generate sequences of numbers that possess the attributes of random sequences. In this section, we describe a method for generating such sequences that has its basis in modular arithmetic. The method is one of the very first tried and is still one of the most widely used.

To illustrate the method, let us start with 33 as the first number in a sequence to be generated. To obtain the second number in the sequence, we multiply the first by 33 to obtain $33 * 33 = 1089$; however, we will keep only the last two digits, 89, of this product. To obtain the third number, multiply the second by 33 to obtain $89 * 33 = 2937$, and again keep only the 37. (To keep the last two digits of any product, divide the product by 100 to obtain a quotient and a remainder; the remainder will be the last two digits. Thus, if $89 * 33 = 2937$ is divided by 100, the quotient is 29 and the remainder is 37. When we divide the product by 100 and keep only the remainder, we say we are multiplying modulo 100; 100 is called the *modulus*.) Continuing to multiply each new number obtained by 33 modulo 100, we get

$$33 * 33 = 89 \bmod 100$$
$$89 * 33 = 37 \bmod 100$$
$$37 * 33 = 21 \bmod 100$$

The first 20 integers in the sequence so generated are

33 89 37 21 93 69 77 41 53 49 17 61 13 29 57 81 73 9 97 1

Although these numbers were not randomly generated (we know exactly how they were produced), they are rather uniformly distributed between 0 and 100. For example, the interval 0 to 25 contains five integers as do the intervals 25 to 50, 50 to 75, and 75 to 100. If we want numbers between 0 and 1, we can divide each of these twenty numbers by 100, the modulus, to obtain

.33 .89 .37 .21 .93 .69 .77 .41 .53 .49 .17 .61 .13 .29 .57 .81 .73 .09 .97 .01

The process just described can be generalized by using numbers other than 33 and 100. In the following algorithm, S (for seed) denotes the starting value and M the modulus. (In the preceding discussion, S = 33 and M = 100.) The product of two integers A and B modulo M is the remainder R obtained when the product A $\times$ B is divided by M. In QuickBASIC, R is given by

```
LET R = A * B MOD M
```

Algorithm to Generate Sequences of Numbers Between 0 and 1

a. Assign values to M and S with S < M.
b. Let A = S.
c. Replace A with A * S modulo M.
d. A/M is the next number.
e. Go to step (c) if another number is desired.

Notice that if Step (c) assigns 0 to A, then all subsequent A values will also be 0. It can be shown, however, that if S and M have no common factor, then the algorithm will never give A = 0. The program in Example 11 uses this algorithm with M = 2^{15} and S = 3^7. These two numbers have no common factors, so the algorithm will never give A = 0.

EXAMPLE 11   *Here is a program to display the first 100 pseudorandom numbers generated by the modular arithmetic algorithm.*

```
' ---------------------------------------------------
' Generate and display 100 pseudorandom numbers RAND.
' ---------------------------------------------------

LET M = 2 ^ 15                      'Modulus
LET S = 3 ^ 7                       'Integer Seed

LET A = S                          'Starting integer
FOR I = 1 TO 100
    LET A = A * S MOD M             'Next integer
    LET RAND = A / M                'Next random number
    PRINT USING ".######   "; RAND;
    IF I / 5 = I \ 5 THEN PRINT
NEXT I
END
```

Program output:

```
.964630   .646088   .993683   .184418   .321564
.259857   .307648   .825531   .436310   .209564
.316925   .115082   .683868   .620209   .396515
.178070   .439240   .616791   .921417   .139496
.077423   .324310   .266632   .124359   .973419
.867767   .807159   .257660   .502228   .372162
.917999   .664398   .038849   .962494   .974152
.469574   .958282   .763763   .350616   .798187
.635529   .900970   .422394   .775238   .445587
```

```
.499115    .564484    .525726    .763458    .683197
.151886    .174652    .964142    .578217    .559601
.847015    .422638    .309174    .162628    .667816
.513947    .001068    .335968    .762054    .613068
.778900    .454620    .254730    .095001    .767670
.893585    .270844    .334747    .092377    .027863
.935394    .707306    .878021    .232452    .373383
.587677    .249603    .882355    .709808    .350861
.332123    .352570    .069672    .371857    .250580
.018097    .577972    .025665    .129974    .253937
.359711    .687286    .095306    .435089    .539886
```

REMARK

The statement

```
LET A = A * S MOD M
```

introduces a limitation to this program. The MOD operator cannot be used for values that exceed the maximum 2,147,483,647 ($2^{31} - 1$) allowed for long integers. Thus, M and S must be chosen so that the two operands M and A * S of the MOD operator do not exceed this number. If you always choose S < M as specified in the algorithm, you can check that the values of both S and A in the program will always be less than M. Thus, M must satisfy the condition

$$M * M \le 2^{31} - 1$$

This condition is satisfied for the value $M = 2^{15}$ used in the program.

The algorithm shown for generating pseudorandom numbers can be used to devise a FUNCTION procedure that will return the next number generated each time it is referenced. To do this, you need to understand the STATIC attribute. If you place the keyword STATIC after a FUNCTION or SUB statement, all local variables (those used to define the procedure) will retain their values between procedure calls. In each procedure to this point, all local variables have been initialized because we did not include the STATIC attribute. In the following FUNCTION procedure, which we name RAND, the local variables S, M, and A have the same meaning as in the algorithm for generating a random number:

```
FUNCTION RAND STATIC
   IF A = 0 THEN       'First reference?
      M = 2 ^ 15       'Yes. Assign
      S = 3 ^ 7        ' starting values
      A = S            ' of M,S, and A.
   END IF
   LET A = A * S MOD M
   LET RAND = A / M
END FUNCTION
```

When the function RAND is called for the first time, A will have the value 0 and the Block IF statement will assign M and S, and the value of S to A. The next two LET statements generate and return the first pseudorandom number as the value of RAND. On subsequent calls, A, S, and M will retain their previous values. Moreover, as mentioned previously, A will not be 0. Thus, on each call other than the first, only the two statements

```
LET A = A * S MOD M
LET RAND = A / M
```

are executed. These statements determine the next pseudorandom number. If you include this FUNCTION procedure in a program, you can use RAND in the same way that you use RND to generate pseudorandom numbers. For example, the following loop will produce the output shown for Example 11.

```
FOR I = 1 TO 100
   PRINT USING ".######    "; RAND;
   IF I / 5 = I \ 5 THEN PRINT
NEXT I
```

Whether the numbers generated using particular values for M and S emulate random numbers is of course a very relevant question. Problem 2 of Section 17.10 describes one of the many statistical tests that can be used in making this evaluation.

To assist you in making promising choices for M and S, we state the following guidelines that, experience has shown, increase the likelihood that "good" random sequences will be obtained.

1. M should be large. (For a variety of reasons, powers of 2 are popular.)
2. M and S should have no common factors. (We used 2^{15} and 3^7 for these values.)
3. S should not be too small in comparison to M.

The method described in this section is called the **power residual method:** "power" because successive powers of a single number S are used and "residual" because the numbers used are residues (remainders) upon division by a fixed number M. The RND function provided with QuickBASIC generates random numbers using a method not unlike the power residual method.

■ *17.10 Problems*

In Problems 1–3, write a program for each task specified.

1. A principle of statistics tells us that the mean (average) of a large collection of numbers can be approximated by taking the mean of only some of the numbers, provided that the numbers are chosen randomly. Generate a one-dimensional array L containing 500 numbers (any numbers will do), and display the mean M of these 500 numbers. To test the stated principle of statistics, randomly select approximately 30 numbers from L and display their mean. Use a loop to repeat this process 20 times. The 20 means obtained should cluster about M.

2. Let L be an array of N numbers between 0 and 1. Using array L, determine an array C as follows: C(1) is a count of how many entries of L are between 0 and 0.1, C(2) a count of those between 0.1 and 0.2, and so on. If L emulates a random sequence, we can expect each C(J) to be approximately E = N/10. In statistics, the value

$$X = \frac{(C(1) - E)^2}{E} + \frac{(C(2) - E)^2}{E} + \cdots + \frac{(C(10) - E)^2}{E}$$

is called the *chi-square statistic* for C. If it is small, it means that the C(J) do not differ drastically from the expected value E. For the present situation, statistics tells us that if $X \geq 16.92$, we can be 95 percent confident that L does not emulate a random sequence. Thus, unless $X < 16.92$, we should reject L as a potential random sequence.

   a. Assuming that N and the list C are known, write a subroutine to compute and display the chi-square statistic X.

   b. Use the subroutine of part (a) in a program to test RND as a random number generator. For any positive integer $N \geq 200$, the program is to determine the counts C(1), C(2), . . . , C(10) for N numbers generated by RND and then determine and display the chi-square statistic. The program should halt if a value of N less than 200 is typed. [*Note:* If C gives a count of numbers in intervals other than (0, 0.1), (0.1, 0.2), and so on, a critical value other than 16.92 must be used. The test described here is called a *chi-square goodness-of-fit test* and is described in most introductory statistics books.]

3. In Section 17.5, we used the following function to generate random numbers that lie between 0 and 1 but that cluster about the midpoint (0.5).

```
FUNCTION RAN
   LET R = 0
   FOR K = 1 TO 5
      LET R = R + RND
   NEXT K
   LET RAN = R / 5
END FUNCTION
```

a. Include this function in a program that generates 500 random numbers R and displays a frequency table showing counts of how many of the 500 numbers are in each of the intervals 0–0.1, 0.1–0.2, . . . , 0.9–1.

b. Modify the given function so that it averages N numbers generated by RND instead of 5. Repeat Part (a) using the modified function. Arrange things so that a user can specify several different values for N during a single program run. The program should halt when the user types 0 for N. Input values of N that are not 0 or positive integers should be rejected and the user should be allowed to make another entry.

c. Run the program written for Part (b) for the values N = 1, 2, 3, . . . , 10. Explain the output.

4. Use the function given in Problem 3 in a program that generates 500 random integers in the range 1–30. The results are to be displayed as a two-column frequency table showing how many times each of the integers from 1 to 30 was generated.

5. Let a function $y = f(x)$ have positive values for all x between A and B as in the following diagram:

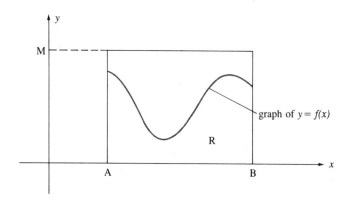

A point (x, y) with $A < x < B$ will lie in the region R if $0 < y < f(x)$. If M is a number such that $f(x) \leq M$ for all such x, the area of the rectangle of height M shown in the diagram is $M * (B - A)$. Use the Monte Carlo method to approximate the area R. Try your program for the following cases:

a. $y = 1 - x^3$, A = 0, B = 1
b. $y = \sin(x)$, A = 0, B = $\pi/2$
c. $y = \sin(x)/x$, A = 0, B = 1

■ *17.11 Review True-or-False Quiz*

1. The RND function generates sequences of numbers by using a well-defined algorithm.   T   F
2. If 100 numbers are generated by the statement LET R = RND, then approximately half these numbers will be less than 50.   T   F
3. With equal likelihood, the expression INT(2 * RND) will have the value 0 or 1.   T   F
4. With equal likelihood, the expression INT(3 * RND) + INT(2 * RND) will have one of the values 1, 2, 3, 4, or 5.   T   F
5. Let L$ be an array of 100 different names. If we wish to select exactly 20 of these names randomly, we can generate 100 random numbers between 0 and 1 and select the Ith name in array L$ if the Ith number generated is less than 0.2.   T   F
6. A certain experiment has two possible outcomes: Outcome 1 and Outcome 2. To simulate this experiment on the computer, you can generate a number R = RND and specify that Outcome 1 occurs if R is less than 0.5 and Outcome 2 occurs otherwise.   T   F
7. RND/RND = 1.   T   F

8. The value of the expression INT(17 ∗ RND) + 1 is an integer from 1 to 17.   T   F

9. The value of the expression INT(5 ∗ RND) + 5 is an integer from 5 to 10.   T   F

10. The loop

```
FOR N=1 TO 10
    PRINT RND(-5)
NEXT N
```

will display ten negative random numbers.   T   F

11. The loop

```
LET S=0
FOR K=1 TO 100
   LET S=S+RND
NEXT K
```

will generate random numbers S between 0 and 100. Moreover, the S values will cluster about the midpoint 50 of this interval.   T   F

18
Sorting

*I*n Section 15.5, we described the bubble sort algorithm and showed how it could be used to alphabetize lists of strings such as names and to rearrange lists of numbers according to size. The bubble sort is one of the easiest sorting algorithms to understand, to remember, and to code. For this reason many beginners tend to use it exclusively. This is fine if the lists to be sorted are short and the program will see only limited use, but the bubble sort is very inefficient for long lists. Using the version of the bubble sort given in Section 15.5, a program running on an IBM PC takes about 18 seconds to sort a list of 50 numbers, but it takes over half an hour for a list of 500 numbers and over 2 hours for a list of 1,000 numbers. These sorting times are unacceptably slow and show the need for a faster sorting algorithm.

Much attention has been given to the problem of sorting, and many fast sorting algorithms have been developed. The reasons for this activity go deeper than the need to produce well-formatted output documents with values printed in a certain order. A common task is that of searching an array A(1), A(2), . . . , A(N) for some specified value V. If the array is not arranged in a known order, the best we can do is to compare V with A(1), then with A(2), and so on, until V is found or the entire list has been examined. This method of searching is called a sequential search and is easily coded. (See Chapter 15, Example 9, for a FUNCTION procedure that carries out sequential searches.)

If a long array A is to be searched for many different values V (a common situation), and if you use a sequential search, you and others waiting to use the computer may have a long wait. However, if the array A is sorted (say, in ascending order), a much more efficient search can be made for V. (To turn to page 216 of this book, for instance, you would not start from page 1 and turn pages until you found page 216; you would use a more efficient method.) Principally, it is this need for a fast searching algorithm that prompted much of the attention given to sorting algorithms.

In this chapter, we will describe some of the techniques used to write efficient sorting algorithms and present two very fast sorts: the Shellsort (Section 18.2) and the quicksort (Section 18.4). The material on recursion presented in Section 18.3 will help us describe and code the quicksort algorithm. The insertion sort described in Section 18.1 is included not for its speed but because the sorting method is used in the Shellsort. In Section 18.5, we describe the binary search algorithm, a very fast search algorithm that is used with data that have previously been sorted. A comprehensive treatment of all topics covered in this chapter, and many more, can be found in *Sorting and Searching,* by Donald Knuth.*

The following table shows comparative sorting times on an IBM PC for a bubble sort and the two fast-sorting algorithms Shellsort and quicksort presented in this chapter. The times shown are for sorting lists of numbers generated by using the RND function.

---

* The Art of Computer Programming, Vol. 3: Sorting and Searching, by Donald E. Knuth (Reading, Mass.: Addison-Wesley, 1973).

List length	Bubble sort	Shellsort	Quicksort
25	4 sec.	2.5 sec.	1.5 sec.
50	19 sec.	6.1 sec.	3.2 sec.
100	1.3 min.	15 sec.	7.5 sec.
300	11.7 min.	1.1 min.	27 sec.
500	33 min.	1.7 min.	51 sec.
1000	2 hrs	4.5 min.	1.9 min.
5000	54 hrs	30 min.	12 min.

■ 18.1 Insertion Sort

The sorting algorithm described in this section is called an *insertion sort* and is somewhat more efficient than the bubble sort (about twice as fast). Although it is not one of the fastest sorting algorithms, it is easy to understand and will help us describe an algorithm that is very fast.

Suppose the list $A(1), A(2), \ldots, A(N)$ is to be sorted in ascending order. We start with a list that contains only the one entry $A(1)$. Then we compare the next term $A(2)$ with $A(1)$, and these are swapped, if necessary, to give a list with the two entries

A(1), A(2)

in the proper order. Next A(3) is compared with A(2) and, if necessary, with A(1) to determine where it should be inserted. We illustrate with the following list:

3 2 5 4 1

Start with a single entry list:	3
Insert the 2 before the 3:	2, 3
Place 5 after the 3:	2, 3, 5
Insert 4 between 3 and 5:	2, 3, 4, 5
Insert 1 before the 2:	1, 2, 3, 4, 5

Let us examine this process of insertion more carefully. Suppose the first I entries of array A

$A(1), A(2), A(3), \ldots, A(I)$

are in order and $A(I + 1)$ is to be inserted in its proper place. Temporarily assigning the value of $A(I + 1)$ to the variable T, we proceed as follows.

If $T \geq A(I)$	no swap is necessary and no further comparisons are required.
If $T < A(I)$	let $A(I + 1) = A(I)$. (This moves A(I) one position to the right.) Note that T "remembers" the original value of $A(I + 1)$.
If $T \geq A(I - 1)$	let $A(I) = T$ and the insertion is complete.
If $T < A(I - 1)$	let $A(I) = A(I - 1)$. (This moves A(I − 1) one position to the right.) T still remembers the original value of $A(I + 1)$.
$\vdots$	$\vdots$

[Continue this process until T—that is, $A(I + 1)$—has been inserted in its proper place.] This process describes a loop in which we make the comparisons

T < A(J)

for J = I, I − 1, I − 2, and so on until the proper position J + 1 for T, the original value of $A(I + 1)$, is found. If T is less than each of the other entries A(J), we will eventually obtain J = 0, and even in this case J + 1 = 0 + 1 = 1 gives the proper position for T. The following algorithm shows a concise way to carry out the process described.

a. Let T = A(I + 1).   (Number to be inserted.)
b. Let J = I.   (Compare T with A(I) first.)
c. Repeat until T ≥ A(J) or J = 0:
    c1. Let A(J + 1) = A(J)   (Move A(J) to the right.)
    c2. Let J = J − 1   (Next subscript for comparison.)
d. Let A(J + 1) = T.   (Insert T in proper position.)

To sort a list A(1), A(2), . . . , A(N), this procedure must be repeated for each value of I from 1 to N − 1. The flowchart in Figure 18.1 describes this process, and the procedure in Figure 18.2 that was coded directly from the flowchart can be used in any program to sort an array A of N numbers into ascending order. In the procedure, we introduce the variable DONE to avoid the LOOP condition

UNTIL T >= A(J) OR J = 0

indicated in Step (c) of the algorithm. If the correct position for T is A(1), the statement LET J = J − 1 will repeatedly subtract 1 from J until J = 0. In that case, the comparison T >= A(J) would be meaningless.

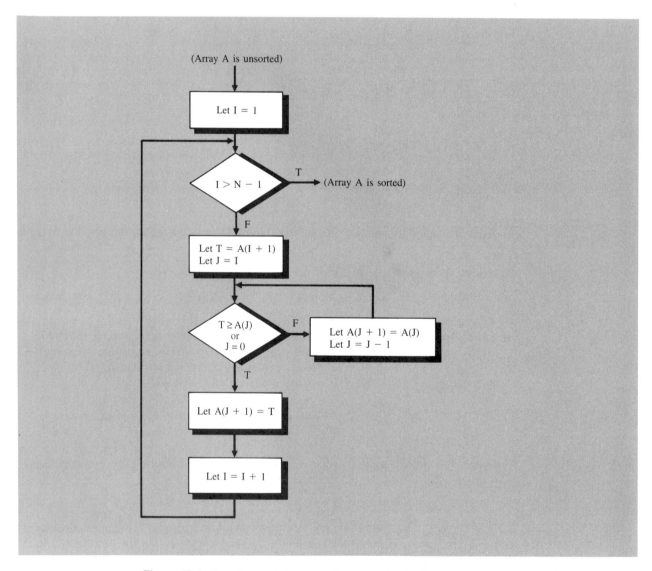

Figure 18.1 Insertion sort algorithm. Sort array A with N entries into ascending order.

```
SUB INSERTIONSORT (A( ), N)

' Sort array A of size N into ascending order.

FOR I = 1 TO N - 1
   LET T = A(I + 1)              'Value to be inserted
   LET J = I                    'Compare T with A(I) first.
   LET DONE = 0                 'Position for T not yet found.
   DO
      IF T < A(J) THEN
         LET A(J + 1) = A(J)    'Move A(J) up 1 position.
         LET J = J - 1          'Position for next comparison.
      ELSE
         LET DONE = 1           'Position for T found.
      END IF
   LOOP UNTIL J = 0 OR DONE = 1
   LET A(J + 1) = T             'Correct position for T.
NEXT I

END SUB
```

Figure 18.2 Insertion sort procedure.

Following are five comments concerning the insertion sort:

1. To sort the array A into descending order, change the comparison $T < A(J)$ to $T > A(J)$.
2. If a list of N strings (for instance, names) is to be alphabetized, simply use string variable names for A and T.
3. The insertion sort is very fast for sorting lists that are "almost" in order. Can you see why?
4. Although the insertion sort is not one of the most efficient sorting algorithms, it is ideally suited for sorting lists that are to be entered by using a slow input device such as your keyboard. If you input your unsorted list directly into A(1), A(2), and so on, the computer will have adequate time to insert the last value you entered in its proper position while you are preparing to type the next input value.
5. The code for the procedure INSERTIONSORT can be simplified by using A(0) instead of T to temporarily store the value to be inserted in its correct position. If you do this, the extra variable DONE will not be needed and the DO loop will simplify to

```
DO
   LET A(J+1) = A(J)
   LET J = J - 1
LOOP UNTIL A(0) >= A(J)
```

We use the slightly more complicated form with DONE because it will allow us to use almost identical code in the Shellsort procedure presented in the next section. The simplified form would not allow us to do this.

■ *18.2 Shell's Method (Shellsort)*

A principal reason for the inefficiency of the bubble sort is that it moves array entries at most one position at a time. [Recall that in the bubble sort, all comparisons involve adjacent array entries A(I) and A(I + 1), which are swapped if they are out of order.] The insertion sort improves slightly on this technique, but not much. For example, consider the following list.

4 2 3 1 7 8 9

Either of the two methods will make numerous comparisons and swaps to sort this list, even though only one swap is actually needed. Certainly, no sorting algorithm should be expected to recognize this one swap. However, the example does suggest that we might do better than the two methods presented. The key is to allow comparisons and swaps between list entries that are not next to each other. The method we now describe does this. It is called **Shell's method,** after Donald Shell who discovered it.*

The idea behind Shell's method is to precede the insertion algorithm by a process that moves "smaller" values to the left and "larger" values to the right more quickly than could be accomplished by making comparisons involving adjacent entries only. To illustrate the method, we'll sort the following list.

    7   1   6   3   4   2

First, think of the list as divided into two parts

    7   1   6   and   3   4   2

and compare the first, second, and third entries of these sublists, swapping the pairs of numbers that are not in order. We will indicate the comparisons to be made as follows:

    7   1   6   3   4   2

Thus, 7 and 3 will be swapped, 1 and 4 will not, and 6 and 2 will. This gives us a new list:

    3   1   2   7   4   6

Note that these three comparisons resulted in moving the "small" values 2 and 3 to the left and the "large" values 6 and 7 to the right, each by more than one position.

We now have a rearrangement of the given list in which entries three positions apart are in order. Similarly, we can rearrange the list so that entries two positions apart are in order. First, we make the comparisons

    3   1   2   7   4   6

to give

    2   1   3   7   4   6

and then the comparisons

    2   1   3   7   4   6

to give

    2   1   3   6   4   7

Note that this step involves sorting two sublists. First

    3   2   4   (1st, 3rd, and 5th entries)

and then

    1   7   6   (2nd, 4th, and 6th entries)

With Shell's method, these sublists are sorted by using an insertion sort. If we now make the comparisons

    2   1   3   6   4   7

from left to right—swapping pairs that are not in order—we will obtain the sorted list

    1   2   3   4   6   7

These comparisons are also made by using an insertion sort. But since the list is "almost" in order—entries two positions apart and entries three positions apart are in order—this insertion sort will be very fast.

---

* "A High-Speed Sorting Procedure," by Donald L. Shell. *Communications of the ACM,* 2 (July 1959), pp. 30–32.

Let's summarize the process just used to sort a list of length 6:

A(1), A(2), A(3), A(4), A(5), A(6)

First, the list was rearranged so that entries *three* positions apart were in order—that is, each of the following two-element lists was sorted.

A(1), A(4)
A(2), A(5)
A(3), A(6)

Next, the list obtained was rearranged so that entries *two* positions apart were in order—that is, each of the following three-element lists was sorted.

A(1), A(3), A(5)
A(2), A(4), A(6)

Finally, the list was rearranged so that entries *one* position apart were in order, which resulted in a completely sorted list. While carrying out this process, each partial list was sorted by using the insertion method.

We now describe Shell's method for sorting an array A of length N.

a. Select an integer S from 1 to N/2.
b. Sort the array A so that entries S positions apart are in order.
c. If S = 1, stop. The array is sorted.
d. Pick a new and smaller S (S ≥ 1), and go to step (b).

For the list with six entries, the values S = 3, S = 2, and S = 1 were chosen. The successive values S = 3, 2, 1 are not always to be used. The sequence of S values that yields the fastest sort is not known. The most common practice, and one that gives a fast algorithm, is to use the successive S values INT(N/2), INT(N/4), INT(N/8), and so on, until the value S = 0 is reached. The flowchart in Figure 18.3 displays the steps in the algorithm for this sequence of S values.

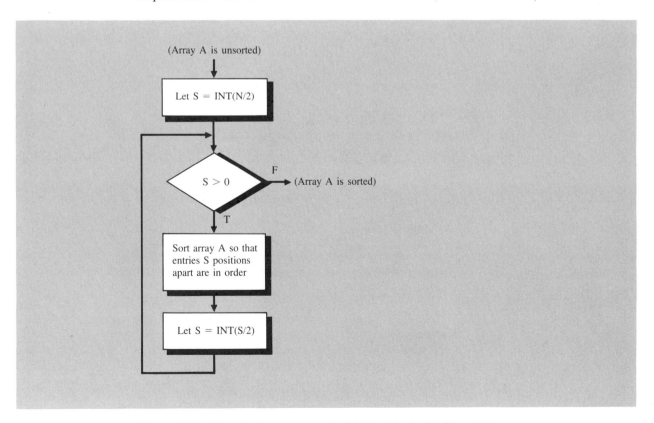

Figure 18.3 Flowchart to sort array A with N entries by Shell's method.

The only part of this flowchart that may be difficult to code is the box corresponding to step (b) of the written algorithm. To accomplish this, each of the following lists must be sorted.

$$A(1), A(1 + S), A(1 + 2S), A(1 + 3S), \ldots$$

$$A(2), A(2 + S), A(2 + 2S), A(2 + 3S), \ldots$$

$$\vdots$$

$$A(S), A(S + S), A(S + 2S), A(S + 3S), \ldots$$

As indicated in the worked-out example, these partial lists will be sorted by using the insertion method. Note that each of these partial lists can be written

$$A(K), A(K + S), A(K + 2S), \ldots$$

where K is an integer from 1 to S. The flowchart in Figure 18.4, which sorts lists of this form, is identical to the insertion-algorithm flowchart (Figure 18.1) except that it uses increments of S rather than increments of 1. In particular, a value T being inserted in its proper place is compared with A(J) for J = I, I−S, and I−2S, and so on, until T ⩾ A(J) or J < K.

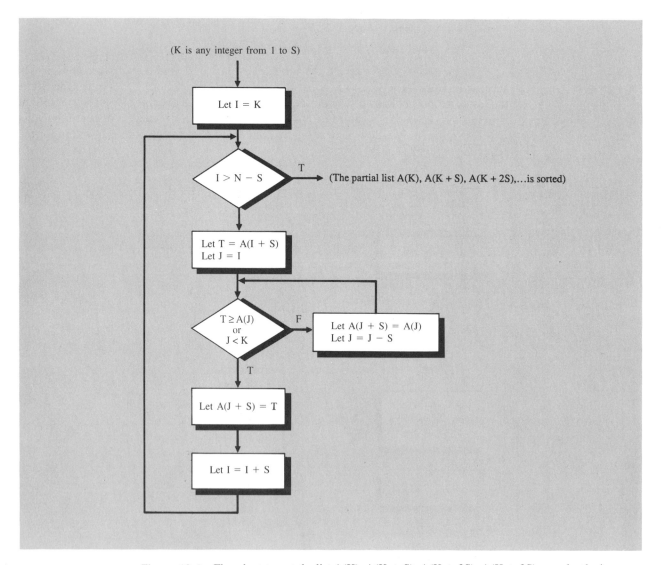

Figure 18.4   Flowchart to sort the list A(K), A(K + S), A(K + 2S), A(K + 3S), . . . , by the insertion method.

```
SUB SHELLSORT (A( ), N)

' Sort array A of size N into ascending order.

S = INT(N / 2)
DO WHILE S > 0

   ' Sort array A so that all entries that
   ' are S positions apart are in order.
   FOR K = 1 TO S
     FOR I = K TO N - S STEP S
       LET T = A(I + S)           'Value to be inserted
       LET J = I                  'Compare T with A(I) first.
       LET DONE = 0               'Position for T not yet found.
       DO
         IF T < A(J) THEN
           LET A(J + S) = A(J)    'Move A(J) up S positions.
           LET J = J - S          'Position for next comparison.
         ELSE
           LET DONE = 1           'Position for T found.
         END IF
       LOOP UNTIL J < K OR DONE = 1
       LET A(J + S) = T            'Correct position for T
     NEXT I
   NEXT K
   LET S = INT(S / 2)
LOOP

END SUB
```

Figure 18.5   Shellsort procedure.

To sort all of the lists indicated, we must carry out the process shown in Figure 18.4 for all values of K from 1 to S. The Shellsort procedure shown in Figure 18.5 uses a FOR loop initiated by the statement FOR K = 1 TO S to accomplish this. This procedure was coded directly from the flowcharts shown in Figures 18.3 and 18.4. It can be used to sort any list of numbers in ascending order. It is very fast.

■ *18.3 Recursion*

The material covered in this section will allow us to describe and code a very fast sorting algorithm called quicksort. Recursion is a fundamental concept in the science of computing. In many programming languages, including QuickBASIC, the definition of a procedure can contain a call to the procedure being defined; that is, a procedure can call itself. Such procedures are called **recursive** (they recur). The term **recursion** refers to the action caused by procedures that call themselves.

Perhaps the best way to acquire an understanding of the concept of recursion is to trace through the action caused by simple recursive procedures. In this section, we give detailed descriptions of two such procedures, a recursive SUB procedure (Example 1) and a recursive FUNCTION procedure (Example 2). In Section 18.4, we present the recursive quicksort algorithm.

EXAMPLE 1   *Here is a SUB procedure to produce a number display determined by a single positive integer. The procedure is recursive because the CALL statement in the ELSE block is recursive, that is, it calls the same procedure. (We end each PRINT statement with a semicolon so that the output will appear on as few lines as possible.)*

```
SUB DISPLAY (N)
   IF N = 1 THEN
      PRINT N;
   ELSE
```

```
            PRINT N;
            CALL DISPLAY(N - 1)
            PRINT N;
        END IF
    END SUB
```

If you include this procedure in a program, the statement

```
    CALL DISPLAY(NUM)
```

will execute the procedure with NUM supplying the value of the parameter N. With NUM = 1, the IF condition N = 1 will be true, and the procedure will simply display the value 1 of N and return control to the calling unit. If NUM = 2, the IF condition N = 1 will be false and the ELSE block

```
    PRINT N;
    CALL DISPLAY(N - 1)
    PRINT N;
```

will be executed. The first PRINT statement will display the value 2 of N. The CALL statement will then call the procedure DISPLAY again, this time with the value 1 of N − 1 as the argument. As we have already seen, calling the procedure with the argument 1 simply causes 1 to be displayed. The third statement again displays the value 2 of N. Thus, with NUM = 2, the output is

```
    2  1  2
```

Similarly, if NUM = 3, the IF condition N = 1 will be false and the ELSE block will be executed. With N = 3, the three statements in the ELSE block are effectively

```
    PRINT 3;
    CALL DISPLAY(2)
    PRINT 3;
```

As we have just seen, the CALL statement displays 2 1 2, so the output for NUM = 3 will be

```
    3  2  1  2  3
```

At this point, it should not be difficult to see that for any positive integer NUM greater than 1, the procedure will display the value of NUM, followed by the output produced for the case NUM − 1, followed by the value of NUM. Thus, with NUM = 4, the output will be

```
    4  3  2  1  2  3  4
```

with NUM = 5, it will be

```
    5  4  3  2  1  2  3  4  5
```

and so on.

REMARK 1 An essential property of every recursive procedure is that it must stop. The procedure DISPLAY meets this requirement for any positive integer N because, each time it is called, it is with an argument one less than the previous call. This means that for any positive integer N, however large, the procedure eventually will be called with the argument 1. When this happens, the THEN clause will display 1 and, since it does not call the procedure, the process of recursion will stop.

REMARK 2 The procedure DISPLAY has a limitation. It is designed to handle only positive integers N. Thus, a program that calls the procedure should pass only positive integers as arguments. You can code the procedure to reject arguments that are not positive integers. The following block IF statement does this:

```
    IF N < 1 OR N <> INT(N) THEN
        PRINT "Bad argument for DISPLAY!"
    ELSEIF N = 1 THEN
        PRINT N;
```

```
        ELSE
            PRINT N;
            CALL DISPLAY(N - 1)
            PRINT N;
        END IF
```

REMARK 3

As mentioned in Remark 2, the procedure DISPLAY will not work if N is not a positive integer. In such cases, the IF condition N = 1 will never be true. Thus, each call to the procedure will execute the ELSE block and the procedure will be called again. Although this is an infinite loop, the program will soon halt and display the error message

```
Out of stack space
```

You may also get this error message if N is a large positive integer. What the message means and ways to avoid it are explained following Example 2.

EXAMPLE 2

Let's write a FUNCTION procedure that returns the Nth number of the following sequence. Notice that each term beginning with the third is the sum of the two before it.

1   1   2   3   5   8   13   21 . . .

The sequence is known as the Fibonacci sequence, so we will call the function FIB. Since the function must calculate the Nth number in the sequence for different values of N, we'll use N as a parameter. As stated in the problem statement, the first two values of FIB must be

FIB(1) = 1
FIB(2) = 1

and each value from FIB(3) on must be the sum of the two preceding values: FIB(3) = FIB(2) + FIB(1), FIB(4) = FIB(3) + FIB(2), and so on. Thus, we can define FIB as follows:

Definition of FIB(N) for positive integers N:

1. If N = 1 or 2, FIB(N) = 1
2. If N > 2, FIB(N) = FIB(N − 1) + FIB(N − 2)

This is a recursive definition: for each value of N greater than 2, the second step defines FIB(N) recursively in terms of FIB for smaller values of N. Since QuickBASIC allows a function to call itself, we can code FIB as a recursive FUNCTION procedure. The two-step definition of FIB shows how to do this:

```
FUNCTION FIB(N)
    IF N = 1 OR N = 2 THEN
        FIB = 1
    ELSE
        FIB = FIB(N - 1) + FIB(N - 2)
    END IF
END FUNCTION
```

Notice that the THEN clause corresponds to Step 1 of the definition and the ELSE clause corresponds to Step 2. Note, however, that the formulas

```
FIB(N) = 1
FIB(N) = FIB(N - 1) + FIB(N - 2)
```

in Steps 1 and 2 of the definition are changed to the LET statements

```
FIB = 1
FIB = FIB(N - 1) + FIB(N - 2)
```

in the FUNCTION definition. Remember, QuickBASIC requires that you use LET statements to assign to the name of the function the value to be returned by that function. Other than this difference dictated by the syntax of the QuickBASIC language, the two-step definition of FIB and the definition of the FUNCTION procedure FIB are the same.

Let's examine the details of the action caused by calling the function FIB. If you include this function in a program, and if K has a positive integer value, the statement

```
PRINT FIB(K)
```

will display the Kth Fibonacci number. With K = 1 or 2, the IF condition will be true and the LET statement FIB = 1 will return 1 as the value of FIB(K). If K = 3, the IF condition will be false and the LET statement

```
FIB = FIB(N - 1) + FIB(N - 2)
```

will be executed. This statement recursively calls the function FIB twice: first with 2, the value of N - 1, as the argument; and then with 1, the value of N - 2. Thus, effectively, the LET statement is

```
FIB = FIB(2) + FIB(1)
```

Since each of the recursive calls FIB(2) and FIB(1) returns the value 1, their sum 2 is returned as the value of FIB(K). Similarly, if K = 4, the LET statement in the ELSE block is

```
FIB(4) = FIB(3) + FIB(2)
```

which gives the sum 3 of 2 [FIB(3)] and 1 [FIB(2)]. Notice that you don't have to trace through the entire process that calculates FIB(4). Indeed, having found that FIB(4) = 3 and FIB(3) = 2, we know that FIB(5) will be their sum 5; FIB(6) will be 8, the sum of FIB(5) and FIB(4); and so on. The actual process carried out by the computer is complicated and can be difficult to follow. For example, the following analysis describes all of the details involved in calculating FIB(4):

$$
\begin{aligned}
\text{FIB} &= \text{FIB}(3) + \text{FIB}(2) && \text{(ELSE block with N = 4)}\\
&= [\text{FIB}(2) + \text{FIB}(1)] + \text{FIB}(2) && \text{(ELSE block with N = 3)}\\
&= [\,1 + \text{FIB}(1)] + \text{FIB}(2) && \text{(IF block with N = 2)}\\
&= [\,1 + 1\,] + \text{FIB}(2) && \text{(IF block with N = 1)}\\
&= 2 + \text{FIB}(2) && \text{(Arithmetic)}\\
&= 2 + 1 && \text{(IF block with N = 2)}\\
&= 3 && \text{(Arithmetic)}
\end{aligned}
$$

Each time a program calls a procedure, QuickBASIC saves the values of variables in the calling unit so that after the procedure performs its task, program execution can continue with the correct variable values. The values are temporarily stored in a portion of memory called a **stack.** Programs that contain recursive procedures can use up the allocated stack space very quickly. For example, we used the statement

```
CALL DISPLAY(NUM)
```

to call the procedure DISPLAY given in Example 1. The procedure produced the correct output for each value of NUM less than 80, but for NUM = 80, we obtained the following dialogue box:

```
┌─────────────────────────┐
│ Out of stack space      │
├─────────────────────────┤
│ < OK >    < Help >      │
└─────────────────────────┘
```

If you obtain this display, you should make sure that each recursive procedure in the program provides the means for the recursion to stop. If it does not, the program will cause the same error condition each time it is run. If the procedure seems correct, you can try increasing the stack size. QuickBASIC provides the function FRE and the statement CLEAR that can be used to increase the stack size. The function reference FRE(−2) returns the number of bytes currently available in the stack. By placing the statement

```
PRINT FRE(-2)
```

at the beginning of a program, you can determine the number of bytes initially allocated for the stack. We did this and obtained 1,200 bytes. The CLEAR statement can be used to specify a new stack size. The statement

```
CLEAR , , 2000
```

(the two commas are necessary) initializes all program variables and allocates a stack with 2,000 bytes. To increase the stack size by N bytes, use the statement

```
CLEAR , , FRE(-2) + N
```

Thus, if a recursive program causes the *Out of stack space* error, you can use a CLEAR statement to increase the stack size. For instance,

```
CLEAR , , FRE(-2) + 2000
```

will increase the stack size by 2,000 bytes. If you still get the error, try a number larger than 2,000.

Since the CLEAR statement initializes all program variables, it should be either executed in immediate mode before you run a program or placed near the beginning of the program before any values are assigned to variables. The new stack size will be in effect until you change the current program. Thus, QuickBASIC reallocates the stack space each time you issue an Open or a New command.

■ *18.4 Quicksort*

As mentioned at the outset of this chapter, much attention has been given to the topic of sorting, and many sorting techniques have been developed. The bubble sort is an example of an **exchange sort**—pairs of list entries are compared and, if they are not in order, they are *exchanged.* The insertion sort and the Shellsort are examples of **insertion sorts**—values are *inserted* into previously sorted lists or sublists. In this section, we present the **quicksort,** a very fast sorting algorithm that uses a method significantly different from the exchange and insertion methods. Quicksort is a "divide and conquer" algorithm. The entries in an array are rearranged in such a way that the array is partitioned into two parts, a left part and a right part, with each part occupying the array positions that it will have in the final ordering. Quicksort uses the same divide and conquer method to partition the two smaller parts into four even smaller ones, and continues this subdivision process until each part contains only one array entry. Since each part obtained in the process occupies the array positions that it will have in the final ordering, the array will be in order. The quicksort algorithm was discovered by C. A. R. Hoare.*

The quicksort algorithm, like the bubble, insertion, and Shellsort algorithms, is a **comparison sort**—that is, sorting is carried out by comparing pairs of list entries. The average sorting time of quicksort is less than that of any other comparison sort. It is perhaps the most widely used sorting algorithm.

The heart of quicksort is a procedure that rearranges the entries in an array so that one of the values—for now we'll use the first—is moved to the position that it will occupy in the final ordering, and also so that all entries to its left will precede it in the final ordering, and all entries to its right will follow it. For example, if you are sorting numbers into increasing order and rearrange the entries in the list

```
5   4   3   8   1   9   2   6
```

to obtain the ordering

```
2   4   3   1   5   9   8   6
```

---

* "Quicksort," by C. A. R. Hoare. *Computer Journal, 5,* 1 (1962).

you will have moved the first entry 5 to the position it will occupy in the final ordering, with the sublist {2 4 3 1} to its left containing all numbers less than 5, and the sublist {9 8 6} to its right containing those greater than 5. Having done this, you can use the same method of subdivision for each of the two shorter sublists to obtain four even shorter ones. By continuing this process of rearranging the entries of shorter and shorter lists, the original list will be sorted into ascending order.

From the preceding discussion, we see that the procedure that does the rearranging must work for any sublist of the original list. We will specify such a sublist by giving its leftmost and rightmost subscripts, LEFT and RIGHT. After the specified sublist entries have been rearranged, we will need to know the position to which the first entry has been moved. We'll use the variable INDEX for this subscript. If we use the name PARTITION for the procedure that does the rearranging, a call to PARTITION will have the form

```
CALL PARTITION (A(), LEFT, RIGHT, INDEX)
```

where A is the name of the array being sorted. The value A(LEFT) that must be moved to the position it will occupy in the final ordering is called the **pivot value.** As just explained, the procedure that we write must rearrange the entries from A(LEFT) to A(RIGHT) by moving the pivot value A(LEFT) to its final position A(INDEX) in such a way that each entry to its left is less than or equal to A(INDEX) and each entry to its right is greater than or equal to A(INDEX).

Once we write the procedure PARTITION, we will be able to use the following procedure QUICKSORT to sort any numerical array A so that the entries from A(LEFT) to A(RIGHT) are in ascending order. If LEFT = 1 and RIGHT = N, the entries from A(1) to A(N) will be sorted.

```
SUB QUICKSORT (A(), LEFT, RIGHT)
  IF LEFT < RIGHT THEN
    CALL PARTITION(A(), LEFT, RIGHT, INDEX)
    CALL QUICKSORT(A(), LEFT, INDEX - 1)     'Sort left part.
    CALL QUICKSORT(A(), INDEX + 1, RIGHT     'Sort right part.
  END IF
END SUB
```

With this procedure (and with PARTITION, which we'll write shortly) in a program, the statement

```
CALL QUICKSORT(A(), 1, N)
```

will pass 1 and N as the values of the QUICKSORT parameters LEFT and RIGHT. If LEFT < RIGHT (that is, if N is at least 2), the first CALL statement will cause the procedure PARTITION to rearrange the entries from A(LEFT) to A(RIGHT)—that is, from A(1) to A(N). PARTITION will move the pivot value A(LEFT) to its final position A(INDEX). Moreover, for each subscript I less than INDEX, we'll have A(I) ≤ A(INDEX), and for each subscript J greater than INDEX, we'll have A(J) ≥ A(INDEX). Thus, the sort can be completed by separately sorting the two sublists

```
A(LEFT) TO A(INDEX - 1)
```

and

```
A(INDEX + 1) to A(RIGHT)
```

The second CALL statement is a recursive call to QUICKSORT. It will sort the first of these sublists. After this has been done, the third CALL statement calls QUICKSORT again, this time to sort the second of these sublists. Each call to QUICKSORT may cause many other calls. However, the sublists to be sorted get shorter and shorter. Since additional recursive calls are made only when the IF condition LEFT < RIGHT is true—that is, only when the sublists contain two or more entries—eventually the recursion will stop.

We now consider how to carry out the task described for the procedure PARTITION. We'll illustrate the method by rearranging the entries in the following array A of size 8.

	1	2	3	4	5	6	7	8
A	5	4	3	8	1	9	2	6

↑
Pivot value P

We'll use P to denote the pivot value 5. Since P must be moved to the position it will have in the final ordering, we must compare it with every other entry. Notice that all entries that must be compared with P are to its right. We will make the comparisons from right to left until we encounter a value less than P, that is, until we encounter a value that must be to the left of P in the final ordering. [If there were no such value, we would stop when we got to A(1), the current position of P.] Since P < 6, we compare P with 2. Since P > 2, we must move 2 to the left of P. We'll do this by swapping them. At this point, the array is as follows:

	1	2	3	4	5	6	7	8
A	2	4	3	8	1	9	5	6

↑
Pivot value P

We must still compare P with the entries in the partial list {4 3 8 1 9}. Notice that now all of the values yet to be compared with P are to its left. We will make the comparisons from left to right until we encounter a value greater than P, that is, until we encounter a value that must be to the right of P in the final ordering. [If there were no such value, we would stop when we got to A(7), the current position of P.] The values 4 and 3 are not greater than P, but 8 is. Since 8 > P, we must move 8 to the right of P. We'll do this by swapping them. At this point, the array is as follows:

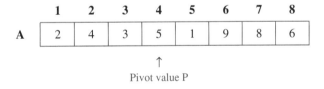

	1	2	3	4	5	6	7	8
A	2	4	3	5	1	9	8	6

↑
Pivot value P

Notice that all values yet to be compared with P (1 and 9) are again to its right, just as in the beginning. As in the beginning, we will make the comparisons from right to left. The entry 9 is not less than P, but 1 is. Since 1 < P, we swap 1 and P. This gives us the ordering

	1	2	3	4	5	6	7	8
A	2	4	3	1	5	9	8	6

↑
Pivot value P

We have now compared P, the first value 5 in the original array, with every other array entry. Moreover, P is in the position it will occupy in the final ordering, each value to its left is less than P, and each value to its right is greater than P.

It is important to note that in the process just used to rearrange the 8 entries of array A, the value of P and the array entries not yet compared with P were always in consecutive array positions, with P either in the left or in the right position. When P was in the left position, we compared it with the other values from right to left. With P in the right position, the comparisons were made from left to right. If we begin the entire process with the statements

```
LET P = A(1)        'Pivot value
LET I = 1           'Left subscript
LET J = 9           '1 more than right subscript
```

the DO loop

```
DO
    J = J - 1
LOOP UNTIL A(J) < P OR I = J
```

will carry out the comparisons of P with array values from right to left. Looping will stop if a value $A(J) < P$ is found—that is, a value $A(J)$ that must be to the left of P in the final ordering. If such a value $A(J)$ is found, it must be swapped with $A(I)$, the current position of P. If no value smaller than P is encountered, the loop will stop with $I = J$, and no harm will be done if we swap $A(I)$ and $A(J)$ in this case as well. Thus, we will follow the DO loop with the statement

```
SWAP A(I), A(J)
```

At this point, $P = A(J)$, and the partial array

```
A(I+1), A(I+2), ... , A(J-1), A(J)
```

contains all values yet to be compared with P followed by P. If $I = J$, there are no such values and the process must stop. If there are comparisons to be made, they will be made from left to right by following DO loop:

```
DO
    I = I + 1
LOOP UNTIL A(I) > P OR I = J
```

If a value $A(I) > P$ is encountered, it must be swapped with $A(J)$, the current position of P. If no value larger than P is encountered, the loop will stop with $I = J$, so in either case we can use

```
SWAP A(I), A(J)
```

At this point, $P = A(I)$ and the partial array

```
A(I), A(I+1), A(I+2), ... , A(J-1)
```

contains P followed by all values yet to be compared with P. If $I = J$, there are no such values and the process must stop. If there are values not yet compared with P, they all lie to the right of P, just as in the beginning. Thus, the comparisons can be made from right to left with the same DO loop

```
DO
    J = J - 1
LOOP UNTIL A(J) < P OR I = J
```

used at the outset. By placing both DO loops inside another loop that begins with the statement

```
DO UNTIL I = J
```

all comparisons will be made and looping will stop with $I = J$. Since the procedure PARTITION must return the final position of the pivot value P as the value of INDEX, we must assign the final value of I (or J, which is the same) to INDEX. We can now code the procedure PARTITION as shown in Figure 18.6.

With the two procedures QUICKSORT and PARTITION, a CALL statement to sort an array A of size N must have the form

```
CALL QUICKSORT (A( ), 1, N)
```

That is, you must include the first subscript 1 as well as the array size N as an argument. The usual situation is to write sorting procedures so that only two arguments are needed, the name and size of the array to be sorted. To allow you to call the quicksort algorithm in this way, include the following short procedure:

```
SUB QSORT (A( ), N)
    CALL QUICKSORT(A( ), 1, N)
END SUB
```

```
SUB PARTITION (A(), LEFT, RIGHT, INDEX)

  LET P = A(LEFT)                  'Pivot value
  LET I = LEFT                     'Left subscript
  LET J = RIGHT + 1               '1 more than right subscript

  DO UNTIL I = J

    DO                                          'Compare with P from
      J = J - 1                                 ' right to left.
    LOOP UNTIL A(J) < P OR I = J
    SWAP A(I), A(J)                             'P is now A(J).

    IF I < J THEN                               'Done, if I = J.
      DO                                        'Compare with P from
        I = I + 1                               ' left to right.
      LOOP UNTIL A(I) > P OR I = J
      SWAP A(I), A(J)                           'P is now A(I).
    END IF
  LOOP
    INDEX = 1                                   'Final position of P

END SUB
```

Figure 18.6   The procedure PARTITION.

With the three procedures QSORT, QUICKSORT, and PARTITION in a program, you can sort an array A of size N by using the more common form

```
CALL QSORT(A(), N)
```

As mentioned at the outset of this section, the average sorting time of quicksort is less than that of any other comparison sort. The algorithm works best for arrays whose entries are in a more or less random order. The performance of the version of quicksort presented to this point is poor for arrays whose entries are nearly in order (or nearly in reverse order). This happens because, in such cases, PARTITION divides sublists into two parts unevenly, with one part very small and the other large. An extreme case is when the array to be sorted is already in order. Suppose, for example, that an array of size 1,000 is already in order. Since the pivot value is already in its final position, the first call to PARTITION will give the sublist of all entries from the 2nd to the 1,000th. When QUICKSORT is called to sort this sublist, PARTITION will give the sublist of all entries from the 3rd to the 1,000th. Another call will give the sublist of all entries from the 4th to the 1,000th, and so on. In each of these calls to PARTITION, the pivot value is compared with every other value. The first call to PARTITION will make 999 comparisons, the call with LEFT = 2 and RIGHT = 1,000 will make 998 comparisons, and so on. Not only is this process time consuming, but all of the recursive calls to QUICKSORT for these sublists must be active at the same time, and the program will quickly run out of stack space (see Section 18.3).

A simple modification to the procedure PARTITION will significantly improve the performance of QUICKSORT when nearly ordered arrays are sorted. As illustrated in the preceding paragraph, poor sorting times and excessive stack requirements occur when the procedure PARTITION repeatedly divides sublists into two parts unevenly, with one part very small and the other large. The trick is to modify PARTITION so that it does this less often. We can do this by randomly selecting a pivot value, instead of always using the first entry. Since each list to be subdivided by PARTITION is specified by LEFT and RIGHT, its first and last subscripts, the following three statements will randomly select a subscript R in the range LEFT to RIGHT and interchange the two values A(LEFT) and A(R).

```
LET S = RIGHT - LEFT + 1       'Size of sub array
LET R = LEFT + INT(S * RND)    'A random subscript
SWAP A(R), A(LEFT)             'Swap with first entry.
```

The rest of PARTITION remains unchanged. The pivot value A(LEFT) is whatever value was formerly in A(R). This simple change to the procedure PARTITION will significantly reduce the sorting times for arrays whose entries are not in a more or less random order. We ran both versions for an array whose entries were already in order. With the array size 50, the sorting time was cut from 9.5 seconds to 3 seconds. With the array size 100, the sorting time was cut from 36 seconds to 7 seconds. For larger arrays, the percentage reduction in the sorting times will be even greater. The same change will also significantly reduce the stack size requirements, making it much less likely that you will have to increase the stack size when using QUICKSORT. (How to increase the stack size is explained in Section 18.3.) The improved version of PARTITION and the procedures QUICKSORT and QSORT are shown together in Figure 18.7. To sort arrays in descending order, change A(J) < P to A(J) > P in the procedure PARTITION. To sort string arrays, change the array name A to A$ and the pivot value P to P$.

```
SUB PARTITION (A(), LEFT, RIGHT, INDEX)

   LET S = RIGHT - LEFT + 1        'Size of sub array
   LET R = LEFT + INT(S * RND)     'A random subscript
   SWAP A(R), A(LEFT)              'Swap with first entry.

   LET P = A(LEFT)                 'Pivot value
   LET I = LEFT                    'Left subscript
   LET J = RIGHT + 1               '1 more than right subscript

   DO UNTIL I = J

     DO                           'Compare with P from
       J = J - 1                  ' right to left.
     LOOP UNTIL A(J) < P OR I = J
     SWAP A(I), A(J)              'P is now A(J).

     IF I < J THEN               'Done, if I = J.
       DO                        'Compare with P from
         I = I + 1               ' left to right.
       LOOP UNTIL A(I) > P OR I = J
       SWAP A(I), A(J)           'P is now A(I).
     END IF
   LOOP
   INDEX = I                     'Final position of P

END SUB


SUB QSORT (A(), N)
  CALL QUICKSORT(A(), 1, N)
END SUB


SUB QUICKSORT (A(), LEFT, RIGHT)
  IF LEFT < RIGHT THEN
    CALL PARTITION(A(), LEFT, RIGHT, INDEX)
    CALL QUICKSORT(A(), LEFT, INDEX - 1)      'Sort left part.
    CALL QUICKSORT(A(), INDEX + 1, RIGHT)     'Sort right part.
  END IF
END SUB
```

Figure 18.7   Procedures for the quicksort algorithm.

■ *18.5 Binary Search*

In this section, we present the binary search algorithm that is used to search arrays whose entries have been sorted. We will describe the method for a numerical array A whose entries are in ascending order. The first step in a "binary" search for a specified value V is to compare V with the "middle" term A(M). When this is done, one of three things will happen.

V = A(M), in which case V is found.
V < A(M), in which case V is in the left half of the list, if at all.
V > A(M), in which case V is in the right half of the list, if at all.

Thus, if V is not found by these comparisons, the search may be confined to a list half the length of the original list. The next step would be to compare V with the "middle" term of this smaller list. If this "middle" term is V, the search is complete. If not, the number of terms to be considered is again halved. Continuing in this manner, we could search the entire list very quickly. We illustrate by searching the following list of 13 numbers for the value V = 67.

28   31   39   43   48   52   **60**   62   67   73   77   86   89

V = 67 is compared with the middle term, 60. Since it is larger, only the last six terms need be considered.

62   67   **73**   77   86   89

This shorter list has two "middle" terms. When this happens, let's agree to use the leftmost of these. Thus, V = 67 is compared with 73. Since it is smaller, the search is confined to the two values

62   67

These final two values are both "middle" terms, so 62 is used. V = 67 is larger than 62, which leaves only the term 67. This final comparison results in a match, and V = 67 is found.

Note that V was compared with just four "middle" terms. In the same manner, a search for any value V can be completed by comparing V with at most four such "middle" terms. If none of these four values is V, it must be concluded that V is not in the list. Using this method on any list with fewer than 2^N terms, we will either find V by comparing it with at most N "middle" terms or be sure that V is not in the list. Thus, a list with $1023 = 2^{10} - 1$ terms requires 10 or fewer steps to find V or to conclude that it is not present. In contrast, a sequential search for values V known to be in a list with 1023 terms require 1023/2 comparisons, on the average. If V is not in the list, 1023 comparisons must be made to determine this fact.

As simple as a binary search may appear, care must be taken to state the algorithm precisely so that it can be programmed (coded) without bugs. Perhaps the safest way to do this is to use two variables, say L and R (for left and right), to store the leftmost and rightmost positions yet to be searched. Thus, at the outset L = 1, R = N, and the middle term is M = INT((1 + N)/2). If V < A(M), only the terms in positions L through M − 1 need be considered, so R will be replaced by M − 1. Similarly, if V > A(M), L will be replaced by M + 1. The position of the next middle term is M = INT((L + R)/2). If L ≤ R, the comparison of V with A(M) must be repeated. However, if L > R, no more comparisons are required and we must conclude that V is not in the list. The flowchart shown in Figure 18.8 displays an algorithm for carrying out this process. The binary search function shown in Figure 18.9 was coded directly from this algorithm.

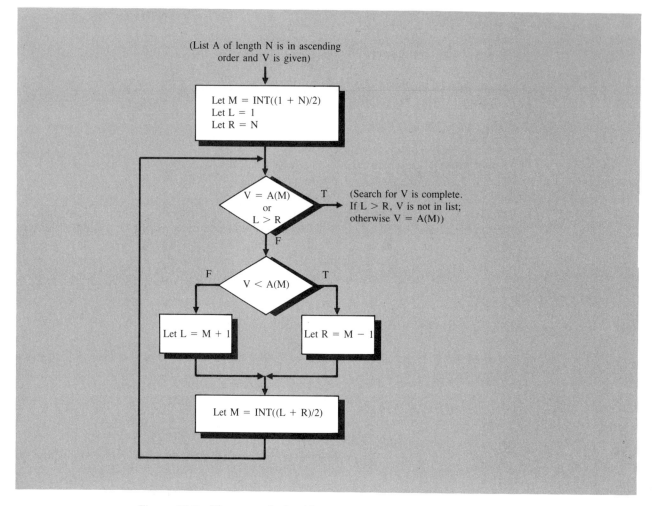

(List A of length N is in ascending
order and V is given)

Let M = INT((1 + N)/2)
Let L = 1
Let R = N

V = A(M)
or
L > R

T (Search for V is complete.
If L > R, V is not in list;
otherwise V = A(M))

F

F   V < A(M)   T

Let L = M + 1   Let R = M − 1

Let M = INT((L + R)/2)

Figure 18.8 Binary search algorithm.

```
FUNCTION BINARYSEARCH (V, A(), N)

  ' Search array A of size N for V.
  ' Return the subscript M such that
  '
  '    V = A(M)
  '
  ' Return 0 if V is not in array A.

  LET L = 1                    'Left subscript
  LET R = N                    'Right subscript
  LET M = INT((1 + N) / 2)     'Middle subscript
  DO UNTIL A(M) = V OR L > R   'Test A(M).
     IF V < A(M) THEN
        R = M − 1              'New right subscript
     ELSE
        L = M + 1              'New left subscript
     END IF
     LET M = INT((L + R) / 2)  'New middle term
  LOOP
  IF L > R THEN M = 0          '0 if not found

  BINARYSEARCH = M

END FUNCTION
```

Figure 18.9 Binary search function.

Following are three comments concerning the use of the binary search algorithm:

1. If an alphabetized list of words, such as names, is to be searched for a given name, simply use A$ and V$ rather than A and V.
2. If the array A is in descending order, change the condition $V < A(M)$ to $V > A(M)$.
3. If you know that the entries in a list are in ascending order, but know nothing else about the list, then the binary search algorithm is the fastest search algorithm available to you.

■ *18.6 Problems*

1. Modify SHELLSORT or the quicksort procedures to sort arrays A and B so that the A entries are in ascending order. The pairs A(K),B(K) must not be separated.
2. Use the method described in Steps (a) through (e) to modify arrays A and B as described in Problem 1. The basic algorithm can be either the bubble sort, Shellsort, or quicksort algorithm. The idea of the method is to rearrange the entries in a numerical array of subscripts, instead of rearranging the array entries themselves. The method is especially useful when large amounts of data must be moved each time a SWAP or LET statement is executed. In such cases, the reduction in the sorting time can be significant.
   a. Begin by setting $S(K) = K$ for $K = 1$ to N, where N is the size of the arrays A and B. The array S will be used to supply subscripts for A and B.
   b. If a comparison involves A(K), change A(K) to A(S(K)).
   c. Instead of swapping array A and B values, swap array S values. For instance, you would replace the two statements

      ```
      SWAP A(K), A(L)
      SWAP B(K), B(L)
      ```

      by the single statement SWAP S(K), S(L).
   d. Instead of assigning array A and B values, assign the corresponding array S values. For instance, you would change the statement LET T = A(K) to LET T = S(K). Similarly, you would change the two statements

      ```
      LET TA = A(K)
      LET TB = B(K)
      ```

      to the single statement LET T = S(K).
   e. The array S of subscripts must be returned to the calling unit. The array values must not be changed in any way.

Write a program for each task specified in Problems 3–10.

3. Input a list of integers into identical arrays A, B, and C. Sort array B by using the bubble sort algorithm, and sort array C by using either the Shellsort or quicksort algorithm. Display the three arrays in a three-column table with the headings INPUT ORDER, SORTED BY BUBBLE, and SORTED BY SHELLSORT (or QUICKSORT). Before each sorting procedure is called, display which sort is about to be carried out and assign the value of TIMER to the variable START. After the CALL statement, display the value of TIMER − START which gives the sorting time in seconds.
4. Create an array A of N numbers by using the RND function and copy the array into a second array B. (Do this in one loop.) Sort array A by using the bubble sort algorithm, and sort array B by using either the Shellsort or quicksort algorithm. Be sure to include PRINT statements before and after each CALL statement, as suggested in Problem 3. Allow the user to try many different values of N in the range 1 to 1,000 during a single program run.
5. Create an array A of 1,000 numbers with

   $$A(K) = K * (K - 1) + 1, \qquad \text{for } K = 1 \text{ to } 1000.$$

   Search this array for each of the following 16 numbers (include them in DATA statements).

133	135	241	300	450	507	517	600
601	900	993	2450	2451	6000	9900	9901

Display each of these numbers with the K value that gives its position in the array. If a number is not in the array, display an appropriate message. Use a binary search function to do the searching. You don't have to sort array A; it is in ascending order.

6. Create an array A of 500 integers randomly selected from the integers 1 to 1,000 [The expression INT(1001 * RND + 1) gives a random integer in the specified range.] Your program should search array A for any integer N typed at the keyboard and display the subscript K for which A(K) = N or a message that N is not in the array. Have the program end only when the user enters 0 for N. Use a sequential search function to do the searching; the array entries will not be in order. (For input values N in the range 1 to 1,000, the searches should be successful about half the time.)

7. Write a program as specified in Problem 6 with this difference: sort array A into ascending order and use a binary search function to search for the input values.

8. Create an array A of 500 random integers as described in Problem 6, and search the array for each of the integers 1 to 50. Your output should be a two-column table showing the numbers that were found, with the corresponding subscripts of array A. Use a sequential search function to do all of the searching; the array will not be ordered.

9. Write a program as described in Problem 8, with this difference: sort array A into ascending order and use a binary search function to do the searching.

10. Input a list of numbers into an array A, and then display the input values in ascending order by using the following modification of the insertion sort:
   a. Start with COUNT = 0.
   b. Input X.
   c. While X <> 0, do the following
      c1. Add 1 to COUNT.
      c2. Insert X in the list A(1), A(2), . . . , A(COUNT − 1) so that A(1), A(2), . . . , A(COUNT) contain the COUNT input values entered thus far, but in ascending order.
      c3. Input X.
   d. Display array A.
   Use a procedure to carry out Step (c2).

■ *18.7 Review True-or-False Quiz*

1. It is desirable to use sorting algorithms that compare and swap only adjacent entries, because such algorithms will not only be easier to understand but will also generally be very efficient.   T F

2. Sorting algorithms are useful in producing printed reports in which lists of numbers appear in ascending or descending order or in which names appear in alphabetical order. Such tasks represent the principal and only major application of sorting.   T F

3. An array must be sorted in ascending or descending order before a sequential search can be made.   T F

4. A binary search can be made only on lists that are sorted.   T F

5. Each step in a binary search for a value V involves comparing V with an array entry A(M) to determine if V = A(M), V < A(M), or V > A(M). At most, 15 such steps are required to determine if a value V is included in an array of length 30,000.   T F

6. The idea behind the insertion sort is to build a list by starting with one value and then placing each successive value in its proper position relative to all values included to that point.   T F

7. The idea of the Shellsort is to use the insertion method on shorter and shorter partial lists.   T F

8. One reason the Shellsort is efficient is that "small" values are moved to the left by more than one position at a time.   T F

9. The Shellsort and quicksort are "divide and conquer" algorithms.   T F

10. A recursive procedure is a procedure that calls another procedure.   T F

11. The procedure PARTITION is a recursive procedure.   T F

19
Graphics

*A*ll screen displays thus far have been produced by displaying up to 25 horizontal lines, each with up to 80 characters chosen from the PC character set. This is referred to as operating in **text mode**—only *text* (that is, letters, digits, and other character symbols) is displayed. In QuickBASIC, text mode is called Mode 0. If your computer has a graphics capability, you can also operate in one or more of QuickBASIC's graphics modes. In this chapter, we show how to create displays that contain both text and a wide variety of other shapes and patterns by using QuickBASIC's medium- and high-resolution graphics modes:

Medium-resolution graphics (Mode 1) allows you to produce graphic images in color on a screen of 200 lines with each line containing up to 320 points.

High-resolution graphics (Mode 2) allows you to produce black and white graphic images on a screen of 200 lines with each line containing up to 640 points.

If your computer has either a built-in graphics capability, or a graphics card, such as the Color/Graphics Monitor Adapter (CGA), Enhanced Graphics Adapter (EGA), or Video Graphics Array (VGA), you can use the following statements to produce graphic displays:

SCREEN	The statement SCREEN 0 selects text mode, SCREEN 1 selects medium-resolution graphics mode, and SCREEN 2 selects high-resolution graphics mode.
PSET	Used to plot individual points.
COLOR	Used to specify colors to be used in medium-resolution graphics. The COLOR statement is not allowed in high-resolution graphics mode.
LINE	Used to draw lines and boxes.
CIRCLE	Used to draw circles and ellipses.
PAINT	Used to color selected areas of the screen.
GET/PUT	Used to move graphic images from one part of the screen to another.

The use of these statements to produce medium-resolution graphics displays is described in Sections 19.1 through 19.8. Each of these statements, other than COLOR, can also be used in high-resolution graphics mode. The same forms are used in both graphics modes, but there are differences in the displays produced. In medium-resolution graphics mode colors can be displayed, text will appear in the WIDTH 40 size, and points will be spaced so that a horizontal line across the entire screen contains 320 points. In high-resolution graphics mode all displays will be in black and white, text will appear in the smaller WIDTH 80 size, and points will be spaced so that a horizontal line across the entire screen contains 640 points. These differences are described in greater detail in Section 19.10.

■ *19.1 Medium-Resolution Graphics: Getting Started*

In **medium-resolution graphics mode,** the screen is divided into a 320-column by 200-row grid of points, called **picture elements** (or **pixels**). The columns in the grid are numbered 0 to 319 from left to right; the rows are numbered 0 to 199 from top to bottom (Figure 19.1).

An individual point is specified by giving its column number followed by its row number. As shown in Figure 19.1, (0, 0) identifies the point in the upper-left corner, the point (0, 100) is located 100 point positions below this corner point, (220, 65) is the point in column 220 and row 65 (since positions are numbered from zero, this is the two hundred twenty-first column and sixty-sixth row), and (160, 100) is located at about the center of the screen.

The two numbers used to specify a point in the grid are called its *coordinates*. The first is the *x*- or *horizontal* coordinate; the second is the *y*- or *vertical* coordinate. This terminology is borrowed from mathematics. We can also refer to the top row as the *x*-axis (labeled 0 to 319 from left to right), the left-hand column as the *y*-axis (labeled 0 to 199 from top to bottom), and the point (0, 0) in the upper-left corner as the origin.

To enter the PC's medium-resolution graphics mode of operation, use the statement SCREEN 1; to return to text mode, use SCREEN 0. (All graphics statements can be issued in either immediate mode or deferred mode.)

SCREEN 1   Sets the output screen to Mode 1 (medium-resolution graphics mode). In this operating mode, you can use all previously introduced QuickBASIC statements, as well as the graphics statements to be introduced in this chapter. Text will still be displayed on the screen but in the larger WIDTH 40 characters. Each character uses the same space as an 8 × 8 block of points.*

SCREEN 0   Sets the output screen to Mode 0 (text mode). Each time you issue a Run, New, Open, or Exit command,** QuickBASIC sets the output screen to its normal text mode—that is, Mode 0 with up to 80 white on black characters per line. Thus, the only time you should need SCREEN 0 in a program is when you want the program to operate in the normal text mode after it has been operating in a graphics mode. To return the output screen to the normal text mode, use the statement

```
SCREEN 0: WIDTH 80
```

The SCREEN statement clears the output screen, but only if it specifies a new screen mode. Since QuickBASIC automatically selects Mode 0 when you issue the RUN command, the screen will always be cleared when SCREEN 1 is first encountered.

Once in medium-resolution graphics mode (SCREEN 1) you can use the statement

```
PSET (X, Y)
```

---

*The width of the screen is 320 points or 40 characters, and the height is 200 points or 25 characters. Since 320/40 = 8 and 200/25 = 8, each character is 8 points wide and 8 points high. Most video screens display more points per inch in the horizontal direction than the vertical direction, so this 8 × 8 block of points will be slightly higher than it is wide.

**Many versions of QuickBASIC allow you to return temporarily to DOS by using the DOS Shell command Alt F D. If you issue this command with the output screen in Mode 1, you will return to DOS with the larger WIDTH 40 characters. Also, if you have specified colors for your graphic displays (as explained shortly), DOS will use these colors instead of the normal white on black. There are many ways to return temporarily to DOS with width 80 characters. One way is to save the current program and issue the New program command Alt F N before typing Alt F D. This will give you the normal text screen. Another way is to execute WIDTH 80 in immediate mode before typing Alt F D. This will give you the smaller width 80 characters but keep the current color specification.

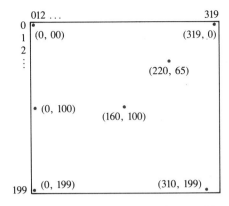

Figure 19.1 Medium-resolution graphics screen.

to illuminate any one of the 64,000 (320 × 200) points (X, Y) on the screen. Illuminating a specific point is called **plotting the point** (another term borrowed from mathematics). For example,

    PSET (319, 0)

plots the point with coordinates (319, 0). If X = 319 and Y = 0, the statement PSET (X, Y) plots the same point. As shown in Figure 19.1, this point is in the upper-right corner of the screen. The general form of the PSET statement is given at the end of this section.

EXAMPLE 1   *Here is a program to plot the four corner points and the center point of the screen.*

```
'Display 5 points and a caption in Graphics Mode 1.

SCREEN 1                          'Graphics Mode 1

PSET (0, 0)                       'Upper left corner
PSET (319, 0)                     'Upper right corner
PSET (319, 199)                   'Lower right corner
PSET (0, 199)                     'Lower left corner
PSET (160, 100)                   'Center of screen

LOCATE 19, 9
PRINT "CENTER AND CORNER POINTS"

DO: LOOP WHILE INKEY$ = ""        'Wait for key.
END
```

The statement SCREEN 1 gets you into graphics mode with a clear screen; the five PSET statements plot the points indicated by the comments; and the PRINT statement displays the figure caption CENTER AND CORNER POINTS beginning at the screen position specified in the LOCATE statement.

REMARK 1   You can use LOCATE and PRINT statements in graphics mode exactly the way they are used in text mode. The output, however, will be in the larger WIDTH 40 characters. If you want the smaller WIDTH 80 characters in graphic displays, you must use the high-resolution graphics mode as explained in Section 19.10. In this program, the statement LOCATE 19, 9 specifies text line 19 for the caption. Since each text character occupies the same space as an 8 × 8 block of points, the bottom line of the caption is the horizontal line whose points have the y-coordinate 152 (19 × 8). Thus, the caption is displayed in the horizontal bar consisting of all points with the eight y-coordinates 145 to 152 (top line to bottom line of caption). As shown in the output, this is approximately halfway between the horizontal line (y = 100) that contains the center point (160, 100) and the horizontal line (y = 199) along the bottom of the screen.

REMARK 2   QuickBASIC erases everything on text line 25 when it displays the message *Press any key to continue.* The DO loop just before the END statement keeps the program running so that you can view the graphic output before QuickBASIC erases the two bottom points—they lie along the bottom of text line 25. If you avoid text line 25 in your graphic displays, you will not need to include this DO loop at the end of your programs. Simply allow the *Press any key to continue* message to be displayed, press a key, and then use Function key F4 to view the output screen without the message.

You can also specify the coordinates of a point to be plotted by indicating the number of units by which the *x*- and *y*-coordinates of the most recently plotted point must be changed to arrive at this new point. If (X, Y) has just been plotted, the statement

```
PSET STEP(A, B)
```

will plot the point (X + A, Y + B). For example, the statements

```
PSET (50, 70): PSET STEP(10, −30)
```

will plot the point (50, 70) and then the point (50 + 10, 70 − 30) or (60, 40). The numbers 10 and −30 are called the *X-offset* and *Y-offset* values, respectively. The coordinates in the first PSET statement are said to be in **absolute form** (the actual coordinates 50 and 70 are specified), whereas the second PSET statement gives coordinates in **relative form** [STEP(10, −30) specifies coordinates *relative* to the most recently plotted point].

If the PC encounters the statement

```
PSET STEP(A, B)
```

before any point has been plotted, it uses the screen's center (160, 100) as the starting point and plots (160 + A, 100 + B) as the first point. The usual practice, however, is to plot at least one point before using STEP(A, B) to specify coordinates in relative form. In Example 2 we use

```
PSET (90, Y)
```

to plot the point (90, Y) and then execute the loop

```
FOR DOT = 1 TO 46
    PSET STEP(3, 0)
NEXT DOT
```

to plot 46 more points along the line specified by Y, with each point three pixels to the right [STEP(3, 0)] of the previous one.

EXAMPLE 2   *Here is a program to display a rectangle by plotting every third point in a rectangular region of the screen.*

```
SCREEN 1                'Graphics Mode 1

' ---------------------------------------------
'    Display a rectangular array of points.

LET Y = 45              'First line of graphic
FOR YLINE = 1 TO 25     'Display 25 lines.
   PSET (90, Y)         'First point on line
   FOR DOT = 1 TO 46
      PSET STEP(3, 0)   '3 pixels to the right
   NEXT DOT
   LET Y = Y + 3        'Move down 3 pixels.
NEXT YLINE

' ---------------------------------------------
'        Display a figure caption.

LOCATE 18, 13: PRINT "A RECTANGLE WITH";
LOCATE 20, 9:  PRINT "EVERY THIRD POINT PLOTTED"
END
```

Program output:

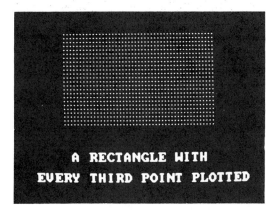

The first program segment begins with Y = 45 and then executes the body of the outer FOR loop 25 times. On the first pass through this loop, PSET(90, Y) plots the point (90, 45) and then the inner FOR loop plots 46 additional points on the same line with each point 3 pixels to the right of the previous one. Since $90 + 3 \times 46 = 228$, the first pass through the outer loop displays the following 47 points on the line with y-coordinate Y = 45:

$$(90,Y), (93,Y), (96,Y), \ldots, (228,Y)$$

The statement LET Y = Y + 3 then increases Y by 3 and the body of the outer loop is repeated with this new Y value. Since the outer loop is repeated first with Y = 45 and then 24 more times, each time increasing Y by 3, the program will display 25 similar lines for the Y values $45, 48, 51, \ldots, 117$ ($117 = 45 + 24 \times 3$).

The second part of the program displays the caption beginning on text line 18 as specified by the statement LOCATE 18, 13. Since each text character uses an 8×8 block of points, the caption will begin on the line with y-coordinate 137 ($17 \times 8 + 1$). But since points on the bottom line of the rectangle have the y-coordinate 117, the caption will be displayed 20 ($137 - 117$) pixels (or $20/8 = 2.5$ characters) below the rectangle.

REMARK

As suggested in Remark 2 of Example 1, we caused no output to text line 25 (y-coordinates 192 to 199) so that we could use function key F4 to view the graphic display without the *Press any key to continue* message.

If you run the programs shown in Examples 1 and 2, you will obtain white output on a black background. To display images in color, you will need to understand how the COLOR statement is used in medium-resolution graphics mode. (It is not used as explained in Chapter 10 for text mode.) The form used for medium-resolution graphics is

COLOR **back, palette**

where **back** is an integer from 0 to 15 and **palette** is 0 or 1:

back   This first parameter specifies one of 16 colors (numbered 0 through 15 in Table 19.1) as the background color. The entire background, but not points or text already on the screen, is colored as soon as the color statement is executed. If **back** is omitted, the background color is not changed—this color is black when SCREEN 1 is executed.

palette   This second parameter specifies one of two palettes (numbered 0 and 1 in Table 19.2) from which the colors of images to be displayed will be chosen. If **palette** = 0 you can create images using four colors: the background color, and the three palette colors green (1), red (2), and brown (3). If **palette** = 1 you can use the background color and the

Table 19.1   **Medium-resolution background colors**

Number	Color	Number	Color
0	Black	8	Gray
1	Blue	9	Light blue
2	Green	10	Light green
3	Cyan (medium blue)	11	Light cyan
4	Red	12	Light red
5	Magenta (purple)	13	Light magenta
6	Brown	14	Yellow
7	White	15	High-intensity white

Table 19.2   **Medium-resolution palettes**

Color	Palette 0	Palette 1
1	Green	Cyan
2	Red	Magenta
3	Brown	White
(Color 3 is used for text and is called the foreground color.)		

palette colors cyan (1), magenta (2), and white (3). If **palette** is omitted, the palette is not changed—SCREEN 1 selects palette 1.

We now explain how points and text are colored.

Color for Text

All text output (output produced by PRINT statements) will appear in color 3 of the palette (0 or 1) selected. As indicated in Table 19.2, this color is called the **foreground color.** For example, the statements

```
SCREEN 1              'Graphics Mode 1
COLOR 1, 0            'Blue (1) background—palette 0
PRINT "BROWN ON BLUE"
```

will display the string BROWN ON BLUE in brown (color 3 of palette 0) on a blue (1) background. If you continue with the statement

```
COLOR 4, 1
```

to specify palette 1 with red (4) as the background, the text BROWN ON BLUE will immediately change to white (color 3 of palette 1) and the background to red. To see that everything is as explained, run the following short program. You will have to press a key to change colors. As we have already explained, the output screen will return to the normal WIDTH 80 white on black characters when you issue a Run, New, Open, or Exit command. Until you do this, you can use function key F4 to view the last color display produced by the program.

```
SCREEN 1                         'Graphics Mode 1
COLOR 1, 0                       'Blue (1) bkgrd.—palette 0
LOCATE 12, 1
PRINT "BROWN ON BLUE"
DO WHILE INKEY$ = "": LOOP
COLOR 4, 1                       'Red (4) bkgrd.—palette 1
END
```

Color for Points

A color for a point displayed by a PSET statement can be specified by using the forms

```
PSET (X, Y),   color
PSET STEP(A,B),   color
```

where **color** denotes an integer from 0 to 3. The value 0 specifies the background color—to *erase* a point, plot it in the background color. The values 1, 2, and 3 specify colors from the current palette. For example,

```
COLOR 2, 1
PSET (0, 100), 1
```

will plot the point (0, 100) in cyan (color 1 of palette 1) on a green (2) background. Similarly,

```
COLOR 2, 1
PSET (0, 100), 1
FOR N = 1 TO 159: PSET STEP(2, 0), 1: NEXT N
```

will plot every other point on the horizontal line with *y*-coordinate 100 in cyan on a green background. If you now issue the statement

```
COLOR 4, 0
```

the dotted line will immediately change to green (color 1 of palette 0) and the background to red (4). To see that everything is as explained, run the following short program.

```
SCREEN 1                        'Graphics Mode 1
COLOR 2, 1                      'Green (2) bkgrd.—palette 1
PSET (0, 100), 1                'Display a point in cyan.
FOR N = 1 TO 159
    PSET STEP(2, 0), 1          '2 pixels to the right
NEXT N
DO WHILE INKEY$ = "": LOOP      'Wait for key.
COLOR 4, 0                      'Red (4) bkgrd.—palette 0
END
```

The general forms of the PSET statement are

PSET (**x,y**), **c**

or

PSET STEP(**a,b**), **c**

where **x, y, a, b,** and **c** are numerical expressions that are rounded, if necessary, to obtain integer values X, Y, A, B, and C. The integers X and Y specify the coordinates of a point to be plotted; the integers A and B are the offset values—if the previous point plotted has coordinates (X, Y), the point (X + A, Y + B) will be plotted. The integer C selects a color from the current palette; if C = 0 the background color is selected. The following rules apply:

1. If **c** is omitted, the foreground color (color 3 of the current palette) is used.
2. The rounded value C should be an integer from 0 to 3. If C > 3, the foreground color (color 3 of the current palette) is used. C must be in the range 0 to 32,767.
3. X and Y can be any numerical values allowed in QuickBASIC. However, if they do not specify a point in the graphics view area, nothing is plotted.

COMMENT

When producing color displays in medium-resolution graphics mode, the usual practice is to include a COLOR statement to select a background color and either palette 0 or palette 1. As mentioned previously, a background of black and palette 1 are used if these are not specified in a COLOR statement. Thus, even without the COLOR statement, you can produce displays in the palette 1 colors cyan, magenta, and white, on a black background. All text will appear in white (the foreground color) and points will appear in the color specified in PSET statements. If the color parameter is omitted in a PSET statement, the point will also appear in the foreground color white. This explains why the programs in Examples 1 and 2 produce white output on a black background.

The general form of the COLOR statement as used in *medium-resolution graphics mode* is

   COLOR **back, palette**

where **back** and **palette** denote numerical expressions that are rounded if necessary to integer values, which we'll call BACK and PALETTE. These integers specify the background color and palette of colors, respectively, to be used in color displays. The following rules apply.

1. BACK and PALETTE must be in the range 0–255.
2. If BACK is greater than 15 then BACK MOD 16 is used.
3. Any even value of PALETTE selects palette 0 and any odd value selects palette 1.
4. Each of the color parameters **back** and **palette** is optional. Omitting a color parameter means it will not be changed.

19.2 Drawing Lines and Rectangles: The LINE Statement

In this section, we describe the LINE statement and show how a single LINE statement can be used to plot an entire line segment, an entire rectangle, or an entire rectangular area. We first describe how lines are drawn.

The simplest form of the LINE statement is

```
LINE (X, Y)-(Z, W)
```

This statement plots a line segment joining the points (X, Y) and (Z, W) in the default color (color 3 of the current palette). To specify a different color, simply add a color parameter as was done with the PSET statement. If C is 0, 1, 2, or 3, the statement

```
LINE (X, Y)-(Z, W), C
```

plots the same line in color C of the current palette or in the background color if C = 0.

EXAMPLE 3   *Here is a program to plot the triangle with vertices (160, 10), (260, 90), and (60, 90).*

```
SCREEN 1              'Graphics Mode 1
COLOR 1, 0            'Blue bkgrd.-palette 0

' -------- DRAW A GREEN TRIANGLE -----------

LINE (160, 10)-(260, 90), 1
LINE (260, 90)-(60, 90), 1
LINE (60, 90)-(160, 10), 1

' ------- DISPLAY A FIGURE CAPTION --------

LOCATE 14, 13
PRINT "A GREEN TRIANGLE"
END
```

Program output:

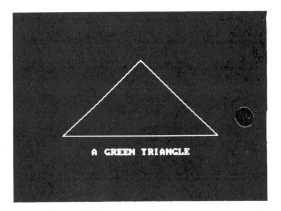

The COLOR statement specifies a blue background (color 1) and palette 0. Since each LINE statement specifies the color parameter 1, the three lines are drawn in green (color 1 of palette 0) on a blue background. The figure caption is displayed in the foreground color brown (color 3 palette 0).

REMARK 1   LOCATE 14, 13 specifies screen line 14 for the caption A GREEN TRIANGLE. Since each text line of the screen is 8 points high, displaying the caption below the 13th text line means that it will not be above the line with y-coordinate $13 \times 8 = 104$. This is below the triangle; the y-coordinate for each point on the bottom edge of the triangle is 90.

REMARK 2   Notice that the two upper edges of the triangle are not straight. You will find that only horizontal, vertical, and 45-degree lines [STEP(1,1)] consist of points that actually lie on a straight line. All other lines will have a more or less jagged appearance. The reason for this discrepancy is that the number of different points that can be plotted on the PC's video screen is inadequate for displaying most line segments. Consider, for example, the statement

```
LINE (0, 0)-(50, 1)
```

As the PC plots the segment from (0, 0) to (50, 1), the only y-coordinates available are 0 and 1. Since these two y-coordinates designate adjacent horizontal lines on the screen, each point displayed will lie on one of these lines. If you execute this LINE statement, the PC will display a broken line as follows.

⎯⎯⎯⎯⎯⎯⎯⎯⎯⎯⎯⎯⎯⎯⎯⎯⎯⎯⎯⎯

If the first point in a LINE statement is the last point referenced in the program, it can be omitted. For example, the line plotted by the statement

```
LINE (243, 50)-(84, 148)
```

can also be plotted by using

```
PSET (243, 50)
LINE -(84, 148)
```

The second of these statements plots a line from the last point referenced—in this case, (243, 50)—to the point (84, 148). With this new form of the LINE statement, the three LINE statements of the preceding program (which plot a triangle) can be replaced by

```
PSET (160, 10)
LINE -(260, 90)
LINE -(60, 90)
LINE -(160, 10)
```

thus simplifying somewhat the job of typing the program.

The form

```
LINE (X, Y)-(Z, W)
```

is most often used when isolated line segments are to be plotted. The form

```
LINE -(Z, W)
```

is intended for applications requiring a sequence of connecting line segments for which the coordinates of the endpoints must be determined during program execution.

The expression **last point referenced,** used in the preceding discussion, needs clarification—it does not necessarily refer to the last point plotted. After execution of each graphics statement (PSET, LINE, and others described later in this chapter), the PC stores the coordinates of a point called the *last point referenced.* After the statement

```
PSET (X, Y)
```

is executed, the *last point referenced* is (X, Y)—in this case, the last point plotted. After the statement

```
LINE (X, Y)-(Z, W)
```

is executed, the *last point referenced* is (Z, W), which may or may not be the last point plotted. If you execute the statement

```
LINE (319, 100)-(0, 0)
```

and look carefully, you may be able to detect that the line is plotted from (0, 0) to (319, 100) and not from (319, 100) to (0, 0). There are more compelling reasons than this for using the expression *last point referenced* rather than last point plotted. Indeed, as shown in Section 19.4, the *last point referenced* can be a point you specify in a graphics statement that is not plotted at all. With each graphics statement described in this chapter, we will indicate what point is stored as the *last point referenced.*

The coordinates of either or both points in a LINE statement can be specified in relative form by using STEP just as it was used in the PSET statement. For example, the statement

```
LINE (50, 75)-STEP(100, 0)
```

plots a horizontal line segment connecting (50, 75) to (50 + 100, 75 + 0) or (150, 75). If the next statement is

```
LINE STEP(0, 2)-(50, 77)
```

STEP (0, 2) specifies coordinates relative to (150, 75), the point specified by STEP(100,0) in the first LINE statement. Thus, STEP(0, 2) gives the point (150 + 0, 75 + 2) or (150, 77), and the line segment connecting (150, 77) to (50, 77) is plotted. Note that this second line segment is also horizontal (both endpoints have y-coordinate 77) and lies two points below the first line segment (its points have y-coordinate 75). The next example uses coordinates in relative form to display a design centered at the point (160, 100).

EXAMPLE 4   *Here is a program to create a graphics display consisting of several lines emanating from the screen's center.*

```
SCREEN 1              'Graphics Mode 1
COLOR 3, 1            'Cyan bkgrd.-palette 1

'Draw magenta (purple) lines that emanate
'from the center (160,100) of the screen.

LET S = -90
DO WHILE S <= 90
   LINE (160, 100)-STEP(90, S), 2
   LINE (160, 100)-STEP(-90, S), 2
   LET S = S + 10
LOOP
END
```

Program output:

Each time through the loop, the first LINE statement displays one of a sequence of line segments from the point (160, 100) directed toward the right. The second point that determines each line segment always has an *x*-coordinate of 160 + 90 = 250, but the *y*-coordinates range from 100 + (−90) = 10 to 100 + 90 = 190 in increments of 10. Similarly, the second LINE statement displays the line segments directed to the left.

At the outset of this section, we mentioned that a single LINE statement can be used to plot an entire rectangle or an entire rectangular area. This is accomplished by including a final parameter B (for box) or BF (for filled box). The statement

```
LINE (X, Y)-(Z, W), C, B
```

plots the rectangle whose diagonally opposite corners are at (X,Y) and (Z,W) in color C of the current palette. The statement

```
LINE (X, Y)-(Z, W), C, BF
```

plots the same rectangle and its interior in color C of the current palette. Thus, the statements

```
COLOR 8, 1
LINE (20, 30)-(100, 80), 2, B
```

color the background in gray (color 8) and plot the four edges of the following rectangle in magenta (color 2 of palette 1).

(20, 30) ┌───────────────┐ (100, 30)
         │   │
         │   │
         │   │
         │   │
(20, 80) └───────────────┘ (100, 80)

The statement

```
LINE (20, 30)-(100, 80), 2, BF
```

colors not only the edges of this rectangle in magenta, but its interior as well. Since the second point (100, 80) is 80 points to the right and 50 points below the first point (20, 30), this LINE statement may be written as

```
LINE (20, 30)-STEP(80, 50), 2, BF
```

This equivalent form shows explicitly that the rectangle has width 80 and height 50.

The next two examples illustrate the B and BF options in LINE statements.

EXAMPLE 5   *Let's write a program to display*

PROBLEM ANALYSIS

Since CAPTION contains 7 letters, and since each letter uses the same space as an 8×8 block of points, the required box must be at least $7 \times 8 = 56$ points across and 8 points high. So that the box will not touch the letters, we'll use a width of 58 and a height of 10. Thus, once we have determined the upper-left corner (X, Y) for the box, we'll draw it with the statement

```
LINE (X, Y)-STEP(58, 10), C, B
```

Before selecting the upper-left corner (X, Y), we must know where on the screen CAPTION will be displayed. Let's center it on screen line 5 by using

```
LOCATE 5, 16: PRINT "CAPTION"
```

The bottom edge of the fourth text line has y-coordinate 31 ($4 \times 8 - 1$; minus 1 because point positions are numbered beginning with 0). Similarly, the right edge of the 15th character position on a line has x-coordinate 119 ($15 \times 8 - 1$). Thus, (119, 31) is the point just above and to the left of the caption. So that the box doesn't touch the letters we'll use $(X, Y) = (118, 30)$. (We allowed for this by using a box size of 58×10 rather than 56×8.)

THE PROGRAM

```
SCREEN 1                            'Graphics Mode 1
COLOR 1, 0                          'Blue bkgrd.—palette 0
LOCATE 5, 16: PRINT "CAPTION"       'Display CAPTION.
LINE (118, 30)-STEP(58, 10), 1, B   'Box it in.
END
```

CAPTION is displayed in the foreground color brown (color 3 of palette 0) on a blue background. The LINE statement then draws the box in green (color 1 of palette 0).

EXAMPLE 6   *Here is a program to display a rectangle centered in the graphics area. Colors for the rectangle and the background are specified by the user. The action of this program is described by its comments.*

```
' Descriptions of program variables:
'
'    B  = NUMBER FOR BACKGROUND COLOR
'    B$ = BACKGROUND COLOR
'    P  = PALETTE NUMBER (0 OR 1)
'    S  = COLOR NUMBER FROM PALETTE P
'    S$ = COLOR FOR BOX TO BE DISPLAYED

' ----------------------------------------
'  Keyboard input: Get colors for design.

DO
   INPUT "BACKGROUND COLOR (0-15)"; B
LOOP UNTIL B >= 0 AND B <= 15

DO
   INPUT "PALETTE (0 OR 1)"; P
LOOP UNTIL P = 0 OR P = 1

DO
   INPUT "COLOR OF THE RECTANGLE (1-3)"; S
LOOP UNTIL S = 1 OR S = 2 OR S = 3

' -------------------------------------------------------
'   Select graphics mode and color the background.

SCREEN 1                            'Graphics Mode 1
COLOR B, P                          'Background B and Palette P
```

```
'    ----------------------------------------------------
'    Color rectangular box in color S of palette P.

LINE (100, 50)-(220, 150), S, BF


'    ----------------------------------------------------
'    Select a title from DATA lines and display it.

FOR C = 0 TO B
   READ B$
NEXT C
IF P = 0 THEN RESTORE PALETTE0
IF P = 1 THEN RESTORE PALETTE1

FOR C = 1 TO S                     'Get color number S
   READ S$                         ' from the palette
NEXT C                             ' specified by P.

LET COL = (37 - LEN(S$) - LEN(B$)) / 2  'Position for
LOCATE 22, COL                          'figure caption
PRINT S$; " ON "; B$
END


'    ----------------------------------------------------
'              D    A    T    A
' Background colors
DATA BLACK,BLUE,GREEN,CYAN,RED,MAGENTA,BROWN,WHITE
DATA GRAY,LIGHT BLUE,LIGHT GREEN,LIGHT CYAN,LIGHT RED
DATA LIGHT MAGENTA,YELLOW,HIGH INTENSITY WHITE

PALETTE0:
DATA GREEN,RED,BROWN

PALETTE1:
DATA CYAN,MAGENTA,WHITE
```

Program output:
```
BACKGROUND COLOR (0-15)? 1
PALETTE (0 OR 1)? 0
COLOR OF THE RECTANGLE (1-3)? 2
```

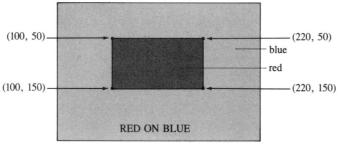

The general form of the LINE statement is

LINE **Point 1-Point 2,c,s**

where **Point1** and **Point2** specify points in the absolute form (**x,y**) or in the relative form. STEP (**a,b**), **c** denotes the color parameter, and **s** is either B (for box) or BF (for filled box). **Point1, c** and **s** may be omitted. The symbols **x, y, a, b,** and **c** denote numerical expressions that are rounded, if necessary, to obtain integer values X, Y, A, B, and C, respectively. The following rules govern the use of LINE statements:

1. As with PSET, points whose coordinates are not screen coordinates are not plotted. In QuickBASIC, there is no wraparound.

2. If **Point1** is omitted, the *last point referenced* is used.
3. If **s** is omitted, a line segment connecting **Point1** and **Point2** is plotted. If **s** = B, a rectangle with **Point1** and **Point2** as opposite vertices is plotted. If **s** = BF, the same rectangle and its interior are plotted.
4. If **c** is omitted, the line, rectangle, or rectangular area is plotted in the default color 3 of the current palette. If **c** is included, its integer value C must be a valid color parameter as described in Section 19.1. C specifies a color from the current palette or the background color.
5. Since most video screens display more points per inch in the horizontal direction than in the vertical direction, a "square" plotted by the statement

    ```
    LINE (X, Y)-STEP(R, R), , B
    ```

    will appear slightly longer from top to bottom than from left to right.
6. After execution of the LINE statement, the *last point referenced* is set to **Point2.**

We conclude this section with two examples further illustrating the use of the LINE statement. The first concerns plotting a bar chart showing grade distribution of students; the second uses the RND function to generate changing kaleidoscopic designs.

EXAMPLE 7
The number of students receiving the grades of A, B, C, D, and E at Easy University are given below. Write a program to display a bar chart showing the relative sizes of the five groups.

Number of students	Grade
432	A
567	B
673	C
123	D
53	E

PROBLEM ANALYSIS

To keep things as simple as possible, we'll include the five input values (432, 567, 673, 123, and 53) in a DATA statement. Since no specific details of the output are given in the problem statement, let's agree to produce a chart like the one shown here. (The column numbers 100, 140, 180, 220, and 260, and the row number 160 are for reference only.) Let's also agree to leave 10 positions between each of the vertical bars, thus making each bar 30 positions wide.

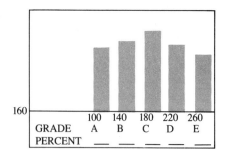

A simple two-step algorithm to produce this output is as follows.

a. Display the vertical bars using lines 0–160 of the graphics screen.
b. Display labels below the vertical bars as shown.

To display the bars, we need to know the height of each rectangle. The height should represent the fraction F of students receiving a particular grade. If we use $160 \times F$ vertical points, we can be sure that each rectangle will fit in the graphics area above line y = 160. (A fraction F is between 0 and 1, so $160 \times F$ is between 0 and 160.)

Step (b) of the two-step algorithm is not difficult. It requires only that data be output in specified rows and columns. We will use LOCATE and PRINT USING statements to display the two lines. Step (a) requires more detail. To this end let's choose variable names:

NUM = number of students receiving a certain grade
TTL = total number of grades given
F = fraction of TTL receiving a certain grade (F = NUM/TTL)
COL = column position of the left side of a vertical bar
HGT = height of vertical bar to be constructed.

THE ALGORITHM (REFINED)

a1. Add the five counts NUM to obtain TTL.
a2. For each of the five counts NUM:
    a2.1 Calculate F = NUM/TTL.
    a2.2 Calculate HGT = 160 × F.
    a2.3 Display a vertical bar HGT points high.
b. Display the two lines of text below the bar chart and stop.

From the diagram, we see that the bars begin at positions COL = 100, 140, 180, 220, and 260. To display them 30 columns wide we'll use the LINE statement

```
LINE (COL, 160)-(COL + 30, 160 - HGT), 1, BF
```

for each of the column positions COL.

THE PROGRAM

```
' ************** GRADE REPORT BAR CHART **************
' Program to display a bar chart based on the following
' data showing numbers of students earning grades A-E.

DATA 432,567,673,123,53
' -------------------------------------------------------
'         Find the total number TTL of grades.

LET TTL = 0
FOR K = 1 TO 5
   READ NUM: TTL = TTL + NUM
NEXT K
RESTORE


' -------------------------------------------------------
'         Display a bar for each grade.

SCREEN 1                      'Graphics Mode 1
COLOR 8, 0                    'Gray bkgrd.-palette 0
LET COL = 100                 'Position of first bar
LET K = 1 TO 5
   READ NUM
   LET F = NUM / TTL
   LET HGT = 160 * F
   LINE (COL, 160)-(COL + 30, 160 - HGT), 1, BF
   LET COL = COL + 40         'Position of next bar
NEXT K
RESTORE


' -------------------------------------------------------
'     Display identifying text for the bar chart.

LOCATE 22, 1
PRINT "GRADE         A    B    C    D    E"
LOCATE 24, 1
PRINT "PERCENT    ";
FOR K = 1 TO 5
   READ NUM
   PRINT USING "  ###"; 100 * NUM / TTL;
NEXT K
END
```

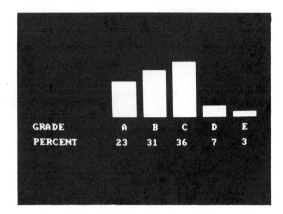

EXAMPLE 8   *Kaleidoscope designs.*

Kaleidoscopic designs make use of reflections to produce symmetrical sets of images. In this example, we obtain the required symmetry as follows. First, we divide the graphics area into four quadrants by means of imaginary horizontal and vertical lines that meet in the center:

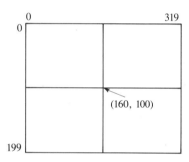

Next, we select a point (X, Y) in the upper-left quadrant and plot the following four symmetrical points:

(X, Y)	=	point selected
(319 − X, Y)	=	reflection of (X, Y) in the vertical line
(X, 199 − Y)	=	reflection of (X, Y) in the horizontal line
(319 − X, 199 − Y)	=	reflection of (319 − X, Y) in the horizontal line

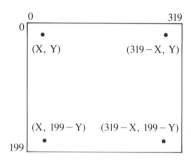

The following steps show one way to produce changing kaleidoscopic designs with the symmetries just described:

a. Randomly select a point (X, Y) in the upper-left quadrant.
b. Randomly select a color (0−3) from current palette or background.
c. Plot the four symmetrical points associated with (X, Y).
d. Go to Step (a).

The design that results from a program written from these steps is slow to develop because of the very small size of the individual points plotted. To speed the development and also enhance the appeal of the design, we will plot 8×8 blocks rather than individual points. To do this, we modify Step (a) so that the only points chosen in the upper-left quadrant are those with coordinates that are multiples of 8.

$$X = 0, 8, 16, \ldots, 152$$
$$Y = 0, 8, 16, \ldots, 96$$

Note that the statements

```
LET X = 8 * INT(20 * RND)
LET Y = 8 * INT(13 * RND)
```

will randomly select X and Y values from these sets.

Step (c) must also be modified to display 4 symmetrical 8×8 blocks as the following diagram illustrates.

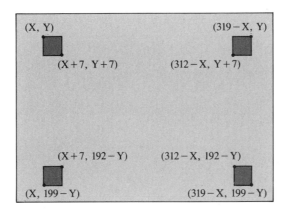

Such blocks are easily plotted by using LINE statements with the BF option. In the following program, which incorporates these two changes, we specify the coordinates of the inner vertex of each rectangle in relative form. Notice also that we choose only Y values that are 8 or greater. This will give $199 - Y < 192$, which means that all blocks will appear above text line 25.

```
' *************** KALEIDOSCOPE PROGRAM *****************

RANDOMIZE TIMER
SCREEN 1                    'Graphics Mode 1
COLOR 0, 0                  'Black bkgrd.—palette 0

DO WHILE INKEY$ = ""        'Loop until key is pressed.

    ' RANDOMLY SELECT A POINT IN UPPER-LEFT QUADRANT
    '      AND A COLOR PARAMETER FROM 0 TO 3.

    LET X = 8 * INT(20 * RND)     'Random X coordinate
    LET Y = 8 * INT(13 * RND) + 8 'Random Y coordinate
    LET C = INT(4 * RND)          'Random color

    '       DISPLAY FOUR SYMMETRIC BLOCKS

    LINE (X, Y)-STEP(7, 7), C, BF               'Upper left
    LINE (319 - X, Y)-STEP(-7, 7), C, BF        'Upper right
    LINE (X, 199 - Y)-STEP(7, -7), C, BF        'Lower left
    LINE (319 - X, 199 - Y)-STEP(-7, -7), C, BF 'Lower right
LOOP
END
```

Program output:

■ 19.3 Problems

1. *What graphics display results from each program?*

   a.
```
SCREEN 1
FOR N=0 TO 90 STEP 10
    LINE (N,0)-STEP(5,5),,BF
NEXT N
END
```

   b.
```
SCREEN 1
LET X=30 : Y=50
LINE (X,Y)-(X+20,Y+40),,BF
LINE (X+5,Y)-(X+20,Y+35),0,BF
END
```

   c.
```
SCREEN 1
LET X=30: Y=90
LINE (X,Y)-STEP(5,-40),,BF
LINE (X,Y)-STEP(20,-5),,BF
END
```

   d.
```
SCREEN 1
FOR N=0 TO 99
    LINE (0,99-N)-(N,0)
    LINE (100+N,0)-(199,N)
NEXT N
END
```

In Problems 2–10, write a program to produce each display described.

2. On a white background, color the left half of the graphics area cyan and the right half magenta.

3. Divide the graphics area into four quadrants. Color the upper-left quadrant black, the upper-right green, the lower-left red, and the lower-right brown. Do this on a black background.

4. Divide the graphics area into 10 equal rows, each 20 points thick. On a background of yellow, color every other row green, beginning with the first. Color the remaining rows red.

5. Divide the graphics area into 20 equal columns, each 16 points wide. On a background of green, color every other column magenta, beginning with the first. Color the remaining columns white.

6. Display a sequence of twenty 8×8 squares: the upper-left corner of successive squares should be at the points (0, 0), (8, 8), (16, 16), and so on. Choose any background color and palette; let the rectangles be plotted in the foreground color.

7. Display the word HALT in large red block-letters centered in the graphics area on a yellow background.

8. Fill the graphics area with an 8×8 checkerboard pattern of 40-point $\times$ 20-point rectangles. A background color and two colors from palette 1 for the checkerboard should be specified by the user during program execution.

9. Fill the graphics area with a 40 × 40 checkerboard pattern of 8-point × 5-point rectangles. A background color and two colors from palette 0 for the checkerboard should be chosen by the user during program execution.

10. Produce a design consisting of three squares whose sides are 150, 100, and 50 points. All three squares have the common center (160, 100). You may use any background color, and the three squares should be in the three colors of whatever palette is chosen. (The smallest square is "on top" and the largest is on the "bottom.")

In Problems 11–13, write a program for each task specified.

11. Produce a bar chart to display the following sales figures graphically. The years and the sales amounts should be displayed below the chart. (Assume that a bar 160 points high represents the sales amount $1500 million.) Include the given data in DATA lines so that the program can be used for five other years and five different sales figures.

Year	Sales in millions
1988	$1,235
1989	1,421
1990	1,251
1991	1,025
1992	843

12. Produce a design consisting of filled squares of various sizes in one of three colors by the following method. For each square to be plotted, choose four random numbers: the first (from 1 to 50) represents the size of the square, the second (from 1 to 3) gives the color, and the last two (from 0 to 319 and 0 to 199) are coordinates for the upper-left corner of the square. If the position specified for the square is not entirely in the graphics area, reject the corner coordinates and randomly select others. Each square is to remain on the screen unless it happens to be covered by subsequent squares. The display should end only when a key is pressed.

13. Produce changing kaleidoscopic designs by modifying the program of Example 8 in one or more of the following ways:
    a. If a randomly selected point (X, Y) satisfies the condition X + Y < 160, reject it and select another. (The designs will no longer occupy the full graphics area.)
    b. If a randomly selected point (X, Y) satisfies the condition

$$(X - 160)^2 + (Y - 100)^2 > 75^2$$

reject it and select another. (The designs will appear in a circle centered on the screen. If you change > to <, the designs will appear outside this circle.)
    c. Rather than 8 × 8 squares, use 4 × 4 squares and *x*- and *y*-coordinates that are multiples of 4.

■ *19.4 Drawing Circles and Ellipses: The CIRCLE Statement*

In this section, we describe the CIRCLE statement and show how a single CIRCLE statement can be used to plot an entire circle or ellipse, or an arc of a circle or ellipse. We first describe how circles are drawn.

The simplest form of the CIRCLE statement is

```
CIRCLE (X, Y), R
```

This statement plots the circumference of the circle with center (X, Y) and radius R in the foreground color (color 3 of the current palette). After this statement is executed, the *last point referenced* is the center (X, Y)—which is *not* plotted. To specify a different color, simply add a color parameter as was done with the PSET and LINE statements. If C is 0, 1, 2, or 3, the statement

```
CIRCLE (X, Y), R, C
```

plots the same circle in color C of the current palette or in the background color if C = 0.

EXAMPLE 9   ***Here is a program to display the Olympic symbol.***

```
SCREEN 1              'Graphics Mode 1
COLOR 1, 0            'Blue bkgrd.—palette 0

' --------------------------------------
' Display Olympic symbol and a caption.

CIRCLE (100, 80), 25, 2
CIRCLE (160, 80), 25, 2
CIRCLE (220, 80),25, 2
CIRCLE (130, 100), 25, 2
CIRCLE (190, 100), 25, 2
LOCATE 20, 14
PRINT "OLYMPIC SYMBOL"
END
```

Program output:

The five circles are colored red (color 2 of palette 0), the figure caption is brown (the foreground color), and the background is blue (color 1 is specified in the COLOR statement).

The radius R in the statement

```
CIRCLE (X, Y), R, C
```

specifies the radius in points in the horizontal *x*-direction. A radius in the vertical *y*-direction will contain (5/6) × R points. To see that this is so, run the following program, which displays a circle of radius 50 and a box with the same center with width 100 and height (5/6) × 100.

```
SCREEN 1                          'Graphics Mode 1
LET R = 50                        'Radius for circle
LET S = 5 / 6 * R                 '5/6 of radius
CIRCLE (160, 100), R              'The circle
LET X = 160 — R                   'Left edge of box
LET Y = 100 — S                   'Top edge of box
LINE (X, Y)—STEP(2 * R, 2 * S), , B  'Box—same center
END
```

Program output:

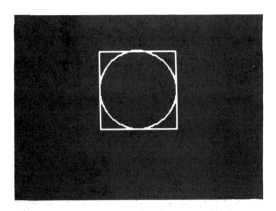

A vertical radius of (5/6) × R is used to accommodate screens on which 6 adjacent points in the horizontal direction have the same length as 5 adjacent points in the vertical direction. On such screens, circles will actually appear as circles. If your screen does not faithfully display circles, you may be able to adjust the Vertical Size control on the back of the display unit so that it does.

The coordinates of the center of a circle can be specified in relative form by using STEP just as with PSET and LINE statements. For example, the statements

```
CIRCLE (160, 100), 20
CIRCLE STEP(15, 5), 20
```

plot two circles of radius 20. The first plots the circle with center (160, 100) of radius 20 and sets (160, 100) as the last point referenced. Thus, the center of the second circle is at (160 + 15, 100 + 5) or (175, 105). In the next example, we use STEP (8, 0) to specify centers along a horizontal line for ten circles.

EXAMPLE 10   *Here is a program to display ten circles with centers (8, 100), (16, 100), (24, 100), . . . , (80, 100). The respective radii are 8, 16, 24, . . . , 80.*

```
SCREEN 1                      'Graphics Mode 1
COLOR 1, 0                    'Blue bkgrd.—palette 0

PSET (0, 100), 2              'Set last point referenced.
FOR N = 1 TO 10
   CIRCLE STEP(8, 0), 8 * N, 2   'Next circle
NEXT N
END
```

Program output:

On the Nth pass through the FOR loop, the circle with center (8 * N, 100) and radius 8 * N is plotted. Since the radius is measured in points in the horizontal *x*-direction, the point (0, 100) lies on each circle as shown.

An arc of a circle can be plotted with the CIRCLE statement by adding a *start* and an *end* parameter to specify the angles at which the arc is to begin and end. The angles are positioned according to standard mathematical usage (see Figure 19.2), beginning at the right with 0° and increasing counterclockwise to 360°. The angles in the CIRCLE statement must be in radian measure. Since

$$1° = \frac{\pi}{180} \text{ radians}$$

the number of radians in D° is given by the formula

$$D° = \frac{\pi}{180} \times D \text{ radians}$$

Those more comfortable thinking in terms of degrees can continue to do so, if you remember to convert to radians in the program before using the CIRCLE statement. For example, if PI = 3.141593 the statement

```
CIRCLE (X, Y), R, C, 0, (PI / 180) * 45
```

will plot the 45° arc (0–45°) of the circle with center (X, Y) and radius R. Since (PI/180) * 45 = PI/4 it is easier to write (type)

```
CIRCLE (X, Y), R, C, 0, PI / 4
```

Either form plots the same arc

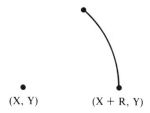

(X, Y)   (X + R, Y)

The arc produced by

```
CIRCLE (X, Y), R, C, PI / 4, 0
```

is different. The PC always plots the arc obtained by moving in the counterclockwise direction beginning at the first angle (the *start* parameter) and ending at the second (the *end* parameter). Thus, with *start* = PI/4 and *end* = 0, you will get the following 315° arc.

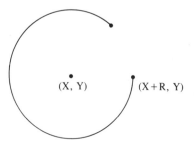

(X, Y)   (X+R, Y)

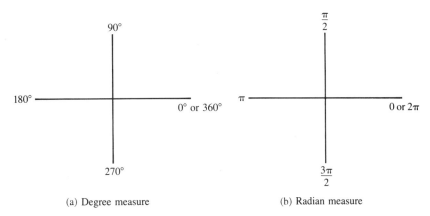

(a) Degree measure   (b) Radian measure

Figure 19.2   Angles used in CIRCLE statements.

EXAMPLE 11   *Here is a program to display six labeled arcs.*

```
SCREEN 1                                'Graphics Mode 1
LET PI = 3.14159                        'Approximation for pi
COLOR 0, 1                              'Black bkgrd.—palette 1

LOCATE 8, 1: PRINT "0 to PI"
CIRCLE (30, 30), 20, 3, 0, PI           '180 deg. arc (0 to 180)
LOCATE 8, 16: PRINT "PI to 0"
CIRCLE (150, 30), 20, 3, PI, 0          '180 deg. arc (180 to 360)
LOCATE 8, 31: PRINT "0 to PI/2"
CIRCLE (270, 30), 20, 3, 0, PI / 2      '90 deg. arc (0 to 90)
LOCATE 17, 1: PRINT "PI/2 to 2PI"
CIRCLE (30, 100), 20, 3, PI / 2, 2 * PI '270 deg. arc (90 to 360)
LOCATE 17, 16: PRINT "3PI/2 to 0"
CIRCLE (150, 100), 20, 3, 3 * PI / 2, 0 '90 deg. arc (270 to 360)
LOCATE 17, 31: PRINT "PI to PI/2"
CIRCLE (270, 100), 20, 3, PI, PI / 2    '270 deg. arc (180 to 90)
END
```

Program output:

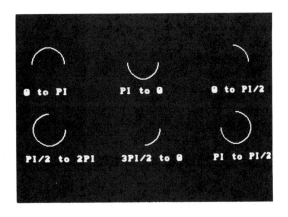

REMARK   The COLOR statement is not needed. It specifies the default background (0) and default palette (1). The color parameter 3 in each CIRCLE statement is also not needed, since the default color is color 3 of the current palette.

EXAMPLE 12   *Here is a program to display a "Horn of Plenty" design by drawing arcs of concentric circles.*

```
SCREEN 1                    'Graphics Mode 1
COLOR 1, 0                  'Blue bkgrd.—palette 0
LET PI = 3.141593          'Approximation for pi

LET R = 0                  'R gives radius of arcs.
FOR A = 0 TO PI STEP .1
   LET R = R + 3
   CIRCLE (160, 100), R, 2, PI, PI + A
NEXT A
END
```

Program output:

For angle A between 0 and PI (180°), the circle statement plots the arc from PI to PI + A of the circle with center (160, 100) and radius R.

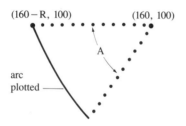

On each pass through the FOR loop, the radius R and angle A are increased (R by 3 and A by 0.1), so the arcs are plotted from shortest to longest to produce the design.

REMARK 1   If you display the arcs farther apart, you will be able to distinguish between them more easily. If you increase successive radii by 6 instead of 3 and use STEP 0.2 instead of STEP 0.1 in the FOR statement, you will obtain a design of the same size and shape but with twice the distance between adjacent arcs.

REMARK 2   If you begin the FOR loop with

```
FOR A = 0 TO PI STEP (.1) / 3
   LET R = R + 1
```

the design will again have the same size and shape, but the arcs will be so close that the entire design will be colored except for scattered points. The missing points occur because the number of points that can be plotted on the screen in medium-resolution graphics is insufficient for displaying circles (just as for displaying most lines).

The *start* and *end* parameters for arcs can be any numbers in the range -2π to 2π. Negative values, however, do not specify negative angles. Rather, a negative parameter $-A(0 < A \le 2\pi)$ specifies that the arc is to be connected to the center of the circle by a radial line segment at the angle A.

EXAMPLE 13 *This example illustrates the effect of negative* start *and* end *parameters in CIRCLE statements.*

Starting value	Ending value	Output
$-\dfrac{\pi}{2}$	$-\pi$	
$-\dfrac{\pi}{2}$	-2π	
0	$-\pi$	
$-\dfrac{3\pi}{2}$	π	

REMARK

The angle specifier -0 is the same as 0. To connect an arc at angle 0 to the center, you must use -2π as in the second illustration.

EXAMPLE 14 *Let's write a program to display a circle partitioned into 12 equal sectors.*

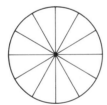

PROBLEM ANALYSIS

Since a circle contains 360° (2π radians), the arc for each sector must be a 30° arc ($\pi/6$ radian arc). If we start at 0° and move in the counterclockwise direction, the first arc will be from 0° to 30°, the second from 30° to 60°, and so on. To plot the first sector, we can use

```
CIRCLE (X, Y), R, C, 0, -PI / 180 * 30
```

This statement displays the required 30° arc and connects it to the center at the angle 30°.

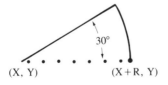

The next sector can be plotted by using the same CIRCLE statement with different *start* and *end* values.

```
CIRCLE (X, Y), R, C, PI / 180 * 30, -PI / 180 * 60
```

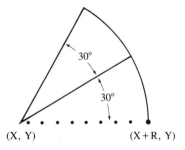

(X, Y)   (X + R, Y)

Although it would be correct to use the start value −PI/180 ∗ 30, it is not necessary to do this, since the radial line segment at 30° was plotted when the first sector was plotted.

If we plot the 12 sectors in counterclockwise order, the starting angle for each sector other than the first will be the ending angle of the preceding sector. In the following program, we use S to specify the starting angle and E for the ending angle. However, −E is used in the CIRCLE statement to plot the radial line segment at angle E. After a sector is plotted, we set S to E and increase E by PI/6 (that is, 30°) to obtain starting and ending angles for the next sector.

THE PROGRAM

```
SCREEN 1                            'Graphics Mode 1
COLOR 1, 1                          'Blue bkgrd.—palette 1

'    S = Starting angle (radians) for arcs
'    E = Ending angle (radians) for arcs

LET PI = 3.14159      'Approximation for pi
LET S = 0

FOR DEGREES = 30 TO 360 STEP 30
   LET E = PI / 180 * DEGREES       'Convert to radians
   CIRCLE (160, 100), 50, 1, S, −E  'Plot a sector
   LET S = E                        'Next starting angle
NEXT DEGREES
END
```

REMARK 1

By using (X, Y) to specify the center instead of (160, 100), the diagram can be displayed elsewhere on the screen. By using R instead of 50 to specify the radius, diagrams of different sizes can be displayed. Nothing else in the program needs to be changed except that values must somehow be assigned to X, Y, and R.

REMARK 2

The method illustrated in this example can be used to display "pie charts" with sectors of different sizes. For example, suppose A(1), A(2), A(3), A(4), and A(5) have been assigned values and their sum has been assigned to the variable SUM. The following modification of the FOR loop in the program will display a pie chart with 5 sectors whose sizes show the relative sizes of the numbers A(1), A(2), . . . , A(5).

```
FOR N = 1 TO 5
   LET E = A(N) / SUM * 2 * PI + S
   CIRCLE (160, 100), 50, 1, S, −E  'Plot sector
   LET S = E                        'Next starting angle
NEXT N
```

The numerical expression A(N)/SUM ∗ 2 ∗ PI gives the angular size of the sector; it does not give the sector's ending angle. Thus, we add this value to S to obtain the angle E that ends the sector.

Following Example 9 of this section, we mentioned that circles actually appear on the screen as circles. (What you see is called the **visual circle.**) This is because QuickBASIC makes adjustments to compensate for the way that points are displayed on the screen. You will recall that 6 adjacent points in the horizontal direction have the same length as 5 adjacent points in the vertical direction. The ratio 5/6 is called the **aspect value.**

The CIRCLE statement allows one final parameter so you can specify different aspect values. The statement

CIRCLE (X, Y), R, *color, start, end,* V

specifies the numerical value of V as the aspect value. The center (X, Y) and the radius R are required. To specify an aspect value V but accept the default values 3, 0, and 2π for *color, start,* and *end,* simply omit these parameters and write

```
CIRCLE (X, Y), R, , , , V
```

The PC uses the default aspect value 5/6 if you omit this final parameter, as we have done to this point.

If you specify an aspect value V other than V = 5/6, the visual circles will be ellipses. For aspect values less than 5/6, each ellipse will have a longer *x*-radius than *y*-radius. For aspect values greater than 5/6, each ellipse will have a longer *y*-radius.

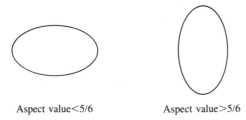

Aspect value<5/6   Aspect value>5/6

The actual *x*- and *y*-radii (in screen points) of a visual circle depend on both the radius R and the aspect value V specified in the CIRCLE statement:

$V \leq 1$ The *x*-radius is R points long, and the *y*-radius is V∗R points long.

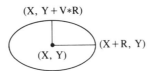

As explained previously, these screen lengths are the same only if V = 5/6. (The case V = 1 is of interest: the vertical and horizontal radii are both R points long, but the vertical radius is actually longer because points in the vertical direction are farther apart than points in the horizontal direction.)

$V > 1$ The *y*-radius is R points long, and the *x*-radius is R/V points long.

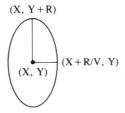

The following table illustrates how changing the aspect value results in variously shaped ellipses.

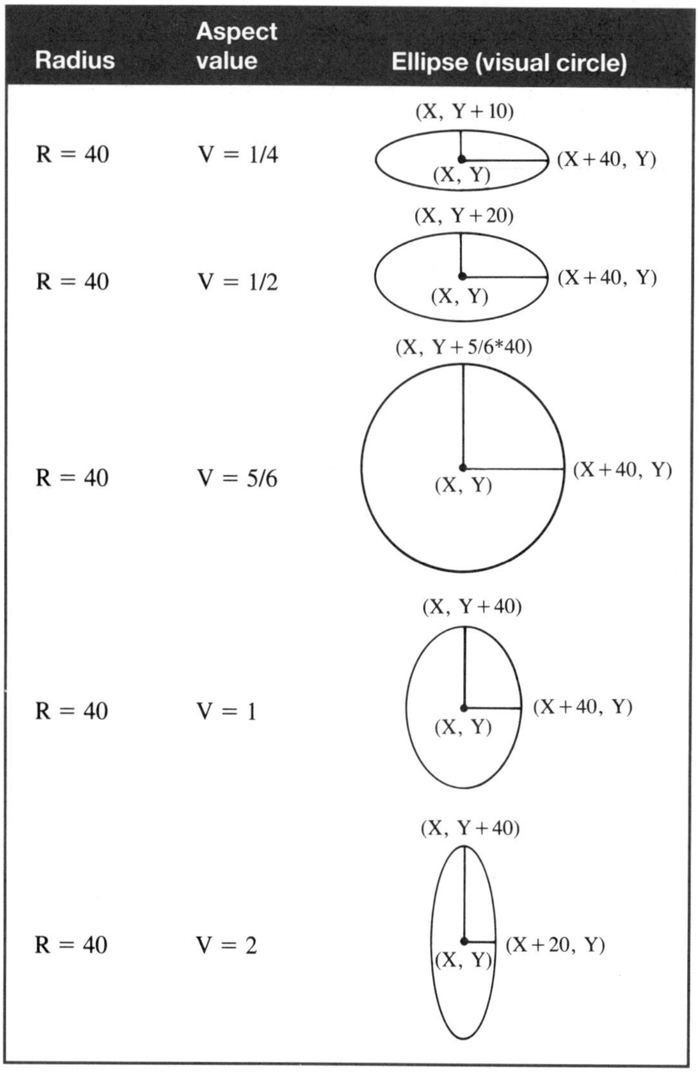

Radius	Aspect value	Ellipse (visual circle)
R = 40	V = 1/4	(X, Y + 10) ... (X, Y) ... (X + 40, Y)
R = 40	V = 1/2	(X, Y + 20) ... (X, Y) ... (X + 40, Y)
R = 40	V = 5/6	(X, Y + 5/6*40) ... (X, Y) ... (X + 40, Y)
R = 40	V = 1	(X, Y + 40) ... (X, Y) ... (X + 40, Y)
R = 40	V = 2	(X, Y + 40) ... (X, Y) ... (X + 20, Y)

The general forms of the CIRCLE statement are

> CIRCLE **(x, y)**, **r, c, start, end, aspect**
> CIRCLE STEP**(a, b)**, **r, c, start, end, aspect**

The symbols **x, y, a, b, r,** and **c** denote numerical expressions that are rounded if necessary to obtain integer values X, Y, A, B, R, and C, respectively. (X, Y) and STEP(A, B) specify coordinates of the center of a circle, R the radius of this circle, and C a color from the current palette or the background color. The last three parameters **start, end,** and **aspect** are also numerical expressions, but these values are not converted to integers. The parameters **start** and **end** give the starting and ending positions (in radian measure) for an arc of the specified circle. The last parameter **aspect** specifies the aspect value to be used by the PC while plotting the circle.

The following rules apply:

1. The parameters **c, start, end,** and **aspect** are optional. Their respective default values are 3, 0, 2π, and 5/6. A CIRCLE statement must not end with a comma. (If it does, a fatal error results.) To omit a parameter, you would omit the comma preceding the parameter only if it violates this rule.

2. Points whose coordinates are not screen coordinates are not plotted.

3. The radius R must be in the range 0 to 32767; otherwise a fatal *Overflow* error results. Because of Rule 2, it makes little sense to use most of these values. (Note: the PC calculates coordinates for all points on specified circles, whether or not it plots them. When we tried R = 32767, the PC took 20 seconds to execute the CIRCLE statement, even though it produced no visible output.)

4. The **start** and **end** parameters that specify angles in radian measure for circular arcs must be in the range -2π to 2π. A negative value $-A$ does not indicate a negative angle; rather it specifies that a radius is to be plotted at the angle A. If either **start** or **end** is not in the range -2π to 2π, a fatal *Illegal function call* error results.

5. The aspect value parameter **aspect** should be positive. If you adjusted the Vertical Size control on the back of the display unit as described following Example 9 of this section, the aspect value 5/6 (.8333333) gives visual circles that look like circles. Other aspect values give ellipses as explained previously. (Because of the limited number of points that can be displayed on screens, positive aspect values that are close to zero will give horizontal line segments and large aspect values will give vertical line segments.)

6. After a CIRCLE statement is executed, the *last point referenced* is the center specified by (X, Y) or STEP(A, B).

19.5 *Coloring Areas of the Screen: The PAINT Statement*

The PAINT statement fills in a region of the screen with a color that you select from the current palette and background colors. To "paint" a region, you must know two things: the color B of the boundary of the region, and a point (X, Y) within the region whose color differs from the boundary color B.

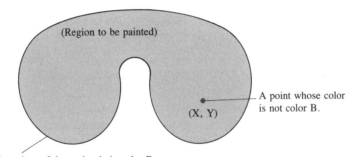

With color B and point (X, Y) as described, the statement

```
PAINT (X, Y), P, B
```

colors the entire region in color P. P can specify any of the four available colors.

Consider, for example, the program segment

```
SCREEN 1                  'Graphics Mode 1
COLOR 8, 0                'Gray bkgrd.—palette 0
CIRCLE (160, 100), 50, 2  'Draw a red circle.
PAINT (160, 100), 1, 2    'Paint its interior green.
```

Since the point (160, 100) specified in the PAINT statement is inside the red circle, and since its color is not red (it is gray), the PAINT statement colors the interior of the circle green (color 1 of palette 0). The color (red) of the circle is not changed—only interior points are painted. To color both the circle and its interior green, use

```
CIRCLE (160, 100), 50, 1
PAINT (160, 100), 1, 1
```

As mentioned above, the painting color can be any of the four available colors, including B. The only requirement for painting is that the color of the point (X, Y) specified in the PAINT statement differ from the boundary color B.

A more precise description of the effect of the statement

```
PAINT (X, Y), P, B
```

is as follows (you will notice that the description does not use the word *boundary*): if the current color of the point (X, Y) is different from the color B, the PC begins painting in color P at the point (X, Y) and continues painting until all points in the graphics area that can be reached from (X, Y) without passing through a point of color B have been painted. If the current color of (X, Y) is color B, nothing is painted.

Either or both of the color parameters P and B can be omitted. The default for P is the foreground color (color 3 of the current palette). You will recall that this is the default value for color parameters omitted in PSET, LINE, and CIRCLE statements. If you omit B, however, the PC uses the painting color P for B.* Thus, the statements

```
CIRCLE (160, 100), 50, 2
PAINT (X, Y), 2
```

plot a red circle and paint its interior red as well. The PAINT statement

```
PAINT (160, 100), 2
```

is equivalent to

```
PAINT (160, 100), 2, 2
```

If both P and B are omitted, P defaults to the foreground color (as already mentioned), and B defaults to P. Thus the statements

```
CIRCLE (160, 100), R
PAINT (160, 100)
```

plot a circle and its interior in the foreground color. The PAINT statement

```
PAINT (160, 100)
```

is equivalent to

```
PAINT (160, 100), 3, 3
```

EXAMPLE 15   *This example further illustrates the use of the PAINT statement to color regions of the screen. In each of parts (a)–(c), we assume that the given program lines are preceded by these two lines:*

```
SCREEN 1        'Graphics mode
COLOR 0, 1      'Black bkgrd.—palette 1
```

This will allow us to refer to the following colors:

Black	The background
Cyan	Color parameter 1
Magenta	Color parameter 2
White	Color parameter 3 (foreground color)

a.
```
LINE (160, 0)–(160, 199), 1  'Partition the screen.
LOCATE 1, 1
INPUT "X,Y ? ", X, Y                'Input a point.
PAINT (X, Y), 1, 1                  'Paint part with point.
```

The LINE statement draws (in cyan) a vertical line that completely divides the graphics area into a left half and a right half. If the input values specify a point (X, Y) in the left half, the

---

*The boundary parameter in PAINT statements and the two parameters in COLOR statements are the only color parameters in graphics statements that do not default to color 3 of the current palette.

paint statement will color the entire left half (also in cyan). Similarly, the right half is colored if (X, Y) lies to the right of the vertical line. Nothing happens if (X, Y) lies on the vertical line.

REMARK 1   If the vertical line were shortened by only one point—for instance, if the statement

```
LINE (160, 0)-(160, 199), 1
```

were changed to

```
LINE (160, 1)-(160, 199), 1
```

this would no longer be a boundary and the entire screen except for this line would be painted.

REMARK 2   Since the boundary color defaults to the painting color, the PAINT statement can be written in the equivalent form

```
PAINT (X, Y), 1
```

REMARK 3   If each color parameter is changed to 3, the display will be in white on black instead of cyan on black. But then the color parameters wouldn't be needed: the default color for the LINE statement is 3, the default for the painting color is 3, and the default for the border is the painting color, which happens to be 3. When producing black and white displays, color parameters in PSET, LINE, CIRCLE, and PAINT statements are needed only if black points are to be plotted. As mentioned previously, points are plotted in black to erase them or to create black images on a white background.

```
b. PSET (160, 10), 2        'Draw a magenta
   LINE -(260, 90), 2       'triangle.
   LINE -(60, 90), 2
   LINE -(160, 10), 2
   PAINT (160, 11), 2       'Color its integer.
```

The point (160, 11) specified in the PAINT statement lies inside the triangle (one point below the top vertex). Hence, the interior of the triangle is painted in magenta.

REMARK 4   To color the region outside of the triangle, simply change the point (160, 11) in the PAINT statement to (160, 9) or to any other point outside the triangle.

```
c. 'Color regions formed by a circle
   'drawn inside a rectangle.

   LINE (0, 0)-STEP(120, 120), 1, B    'Cyan rectangle
   CIRCLE (60, 60), 40, 1              'Inner cyan circle
   PAINT (101, 60), 1                  'Paint outside of circle
   PAINT (60, 60), 3, 1                'Paint inside of circle
   LOCATE 8, 6:  PRINT "White"
   LOCATE 14, 6: PRINT "Cyan"
   LOCATE 17, 1: PRINT "Black background"
```

The point (101, 60) in the first PAINT statement is inside the rectangle and outside the circle, so this region is colored in cyan. The point (60, 60) in the second PAINT statement is at the center of the circle, so this PAINT statement colors the circle's interior in white (3). The three captions are in white (the foreground color) on a black background. The black background for each letter is what allows you to see the word "white" displayed in white letters within a white circular region.

The next example illustrates how a display can be altered by systematically changing the colors.

EXAMPLE 16   *Here is a program to alternately color the upper and lower halves of a circle.*

```
SCREEN 1                    'Graphics Mode 1
COLOR 1, 1                  'Blue bkgrd.—palette 1
' -------------------------------------------------
' Draw boundaries for upper and lower semicircles.

CIRCLE (160, 100), 50, 3
LINE (110, 100)—(210, 100), 3


' -------------------------------------------------
'    Assign points in upper and lower halves.

LET X = 160              'X for both points
LET Y = 99               'Y for upper half
LET Y1 = 101             'Y1 for lower half


' -------------------------------------------------
' Alternately color the upper and lower semicircles
' using colors 0, 1, and 2 of the current palette.
'

LET P = 0                        'Starting color
DO WHILE INKEY$ = ""
   PAINT (X, Y), P, 3
   FOR N = 1 TO 100: NEXT N      'Delay
   LET P = (P + 1) MOD 3         'Next color
   SWAP Y, Y1                    'Get Y for other half
LOOP
END
```

The CIRCLE statement draws a circle in the center of the screen and the LINE statement draws a horizontal diameter to divide the circle into a top and bottom half. The circle and the line are colored white (color 3 of palette 1).

The LET statements in the second section of the program assign coordinates for two points, one in the top and the other in the bottom half of the circle.

The third part of the program starts with the painting color P = 0 and then repeatedly executes the three statements

```
PAINT (X, Y), P, 3
LET P = (P + 1) MOD 3
SWAP Y, Y1
```

until a key is pressed. The LET statement assigns the successive painting colors 0, 1, 2, 0, 1, 2, and so on, to P. The SWAP statement interchanges Y and Y1 so that (X,Y) alternates between (160,99) in the top half of the circle and (160,101) in the bottom half. Thus, the PAINT statement alternates in painting the upper and lower semicircles in the colors specified by P. The FOR loop that causes the delay simply slows the transition from one color to the next.

REMARK   Since the boundaries of the half circles were colored white and remain white, we avoided white as a painting color. Had we not done so, a half circle that was painted white would stay that way—the interior point specified in the PAINT statement would be white, the same color as the boundary, so the PAINT statement would do nothing.

The general forms of the PAINT statement are

PAINT(x,y),**paint,border**
PAINT STEP(a,b),**paint,border**

where **x, y, a, b, paint,** and **border** are numerical expressions that are rounded to integer values X, Y, A, B, P, and BORD, respectively. (X, Y) and STEP(A, B) specify the coordinates of a point within the region to be painted. P and BORD specify colors from the current palette or the background color. P specifies the color with which to paint, and BORD gives the color of the boundary of the region to be painted. The following rules apply:

1. If the point specified by (X, Y) or STEP(A, B) has the same color as the border (color BORD), nothing is painted. Otherwise, the PC paints in color P all points in the graphics area that can be reached from the specified point without passing through a point with color BORD.
2. If **paint** is omitted, the foreground color (color 3 of the current palette) is used.
3. If **border** is omitted, the painting color **paint** is used.
4. After a PAINT statement is executed the *last point referenced* is the point whose coordinates are given by (X, Y) or STEP(A, B).

■ *19.6 Problems*

In Problems 1–11, write a program to produce the display described. The PAINT statement is not needed.

1. Plot ten circles in a row across the display screen. They should be equally spaced, have the same radius, and should not touch each other.
2. Plot ten circles as in Problem 1, but in a vertical column rather than a row.
3. Plot ten circles as in Problem 1, but have their centers lie along the line joining the points (0, 0) and (199, 199).
4. Display a smiling face, centered on the screen; the eyes and mouth should be arcs of ellipses.
5. For R in the range 1 to 115, display a circle with center (160, 100) and radius R. Also display a rectangle that encloses the circle and touches it at four points. R is to be input and is to be rejected if not in the specified range. (Do not specify an aspect value in the CIRCLE statement.)
6. For V in the range 0.7 to 1.1, use a CIRCLE statement with aspect value V to display an ellipse with center (160, 100) that fits on the screen. At the bottom-left corner of the screen, inform the user what radius was used. V is to be input and is to be rejected if not in the specified range.
7. Display an ellipse as in Problem 6 and also a rectangle that encloses the ellipse and touches it at four points.
8. Divide the screen into four parts by drawing horizontal and vertical lines through the center (160, 100). In each part, display a "Horn of Plenty" design as described in Example 12. Use the four points (80, 50), (240, 50), (80, 150), and (240, 150) as centers for the four designs.
9. Display four "Horn of Plenty" designs one after the other. The user will press a key to see the next design. All four designs are to be centered at (160, 100), but they are not to be identical. The first should be as in Example 12, and each successive design is to be the preceding one rotated 90°.
10. Divide the screen into four parts by drawing horizontal and vertical lines through the center (160, 100). Display the four "Horn of Plenty" designs described in Problem 9, one in each of the four parts. Use the four points (80, 50), (240, 50), (80, 150), and (240, 150) as centers for the four designs.
11. Display a circle partitioned into N equal sections. The integer N is to be input and is to be from 1 to 360 (input values that are not integers in this range are to be rejected). The method used in Example 14 can be used for this problem as well.

In Problems 12–16, write a program to produce the display described. The PAINT statement should be used.

12. Plot a square, circle, and triangle as shown in the diagram.

The numbers indicate the colors from the palette to be used to color the four regions of the display. (Use the BF option to plot the square.)

13. Display interlocking ellipses as shown in the diagram. The numbers indicate colors from the current palette to be used to color the regions.

14. Display three interlocking circles as shown in the diagram.

The numbers indicate colors from the current palette to be used to color the eight regions of the display. The circles themselves should be plotted in color 3.

15. Display a pie with a piece removed but placed just next to it, as shown in the diagram.

Choose one color for the background and one for both parts of the pie.

16. Divide the graphics area into eight parts by drawing four lines through the center as shown. The numbers indicate colors from the current palette to be used. Use color 3 for the four lines.

■ *19.7 Moving Objects: The GET and PUT Statements*

While in graphics mode, the GET and PUT statements are used to move objects (rectangular screen images) from one part of the screen to another. This is accomplished by first using GET to store a numerical representation of the object to be moved in an array, and then using a PUT statement to specify a new position for the image represented by the array.* We will first describe the GET statement.

If (X1, Y1) and (X2, Y2) give valid screen coordinates, and if the numerical array A has been dimensioned (as will be explained shortly), the statement

```
GET (X1, Y1)-(X2, Y2), A
```

stores a numerical representation of the rectangular region with (X1, Y1) and (X2, Y2) as opposite corners in the array A. We will say, more simply, that the screen image is stored in array A. [The rectangular region is the same region that is colored by the statement LINE (X1, Y1)−(X2, Y2),C,BF.] The numerical representation stored in A consists of the dimensions of the rectangular region and the color numbers of all points in this region.

Consider, for example, the following program segment:

```
SCREEN 1                          'Graphics mode
COLOR 1, 0                        'Blue bkgrd.-palette 0
LINE (0, 0)-(8, 8), 1, BF        'Green rectangular area
LINE (2, 2)-(6, 6), 2, BF        'Smaller red rectangular area
DIM A(7)
GET (0, 0)-(8, 8), A             'Store image in array A.
```

The first two statements get you into medium-resolution graphics mode with a clear blue screen, and the two LINE statements produce the following display:

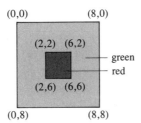

The GET statement then stores this 9 × 9 rectangular image in array A. The DIM statement is necessary even though 7 does not exceed 10. An array specified in a GET statement must be dimensioned before the GET statement is executed. That the dimension 7 is adequate to store the 9 × 9 screen image is explained following the next example.

Having stored this rectangular screen image in array A, you can use the PUT statement to display it elsewhere on the screen. The statement

```
PUT (20, 0), A
```

will display it with its upper-left corner at the point (20, 0). If you execute the same PUT statement again, however, the image will disappear. The statement

```
PUT (X, Y), A
```

plots a point in the color specified by array A only if the point currently has the background color. If the current color of the point is the same as the color specified by array A, you get the background color. (What happens when the current color is some other color is explained later in this section.)

---

* As described in Section 16.7 on random access files, while in text mode, GET assigns data from a file to a record variable (rather than a screen image to an array), and PUT copies the contents of a record variable to the file (rather than the contents of an array to the screen).

EXAMPLE 17 *Here is a program that uses GET and PUT to display the following line drawing at several screen positions.*

```
SCREEN 1                          'Graphics Mode 1
COLOR 1, 1                        'Blue bkgrd.—palette 1

' --------------------------------------------------
'            Display a line drawing.

LINE (160, 115)—STEP(0, —17), 3     'Body
LINE (140, 100)—STEP(40, 0), 3      'Arms
LINE (160, 115)—STEP(—20, 20), 3    'Left leg
LINE (160, 115)—STEP(20, 20), 3     'Right leg
CIRCLE (160, 92), 6, 3              'Head

' --------------------------------------------------
'  Store line drawing in array F and then erase it.

DIM F(135)
GET (140, 87)—(180, 135), F        'Store image in F.
PUT (140, 87), F                   'Erase image

' --------------------------------------------------
'   Display several drawings next to each other.

FOR X = 0 TO 250 STEP 41
   PUT (X, 0), F                   'Display image at (X,0)
   FOR N = 1 TO 200: NEXT N        'Delay
NEXT X
LOCATE 23, 1: PRINT "Press a key to erase figures."
DO WHILE INKEY$ = "": LOOP         'Wait for key.
LOCATE 23, 1: PRINT SPACE$(40)

' --------------------------------------------------
'      Erase the drawings (one at a time).

FOR X = 0 TO 250 STEP 41
   PUT (X, 0), F                   'Erase image at (X,0)
   FOR N = 1 TO 200: NEXT N        'Delay
NEXT X
END
```

The first two lines get you into medium-resolution graphics mode with a clear blue screen. The rest of the program is divided into four sections, as indicated by the comments.

The first section displays the specified figure in a 41 × 49 rectangular region as follows. (The dotted lines are for reference only.)

(140,87)

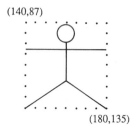

(180,135)

Note that the CIRCLE statement plots the head with center (160, 92) and radius 6, but that the top point of this circle has y-coordinate $87 = 92 - 5$, and not $86 = 92 - 6$. Remember that the y-radius of a visual circle is 5/6 times the specified radius if the aspect value parameter is omitted. Since $5/6 \times 6 = 5$, the y-radius of the head is 5.

The second section is self-explanatory. (The choice of 135 as the dimension of F is explained just after the example.) The PUT statement erases the figure because it was already in the rectangular region specified in the PUT statement.

The third section displays the figure seven times in rectangular regions with upper-left corners (0, 0), (41, 0), (82, 0), (123,0), (164, 0), (205, 0), and (246, 0). Since each rectangle is 41 points wide, the figures touch. Following is the display produced by these lines. The delay FOR loop allows us to see the effect of each PUT statement.

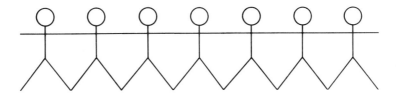

The fourth section erases these seven figures one at a time, beginning at the left. This leaves you, once again, with a clear blue screen. (Note that this FOR loop that erases the figures is identical to the FOR loop that displays them.)

REMARK

The point specified in a PUT statement must be chosen so that the entire rectangular image to be displayed lies on the screen. If it does not, a fatal *Illegal function call* error occurs. For example, if you replace

```
FOR X = 0 TO 250 STEP 41
```

in the third section by

```
FOR X = 0 TO 319 STEP 41
```

the statement PUT (X, 0),F will be executed an eighth time with X = 287. Since the image to be displayed is 41 points wide, the x-coordinates 287–327 would be needed. But points with x-coordinates greater than 319 lie off the screen, so an *Illegal function call* error will occur.

The following formulas can be used to obtain the array dimension N needed to store a rectangular screen region of size $x \times y$ (x points in the horizontal direction and y in the vertical direction). First calculate

$$B = 4 + y \times INT((2\,x + 7)/8)$$

and then use

$$N = INT(B/4) \qquad \text{(for single-precision arrays—such as A)}$$

You needn't carry out these calculations by hand. Simply precede the statement

```
GET (X1, Y1)-(X2, Y2), A
```

by the statements

```
LET X = X2 — X1 + 1
LET Y = Y2 — Y1 + 1
LET B = 4 + Y * INT((2 * X + 7) / 8)
DIM A(INT(B / 4))
```

For an integer array A%, use

```
DIM A%(INT(B / 2))
```

COMMENT

The number B is precisely the number of bytes the PC needs to store the information contained in an $x \times y$ rectangular screen region that is produced while in medium-resolution graphics mode. (You will recall that a byte is the memory space needed to store a single character.) To store a 9×9 rectangular screen image in an array A, you will get

$$B = 4 + 9 * INT((2 * 9 + 7)/8) = 31$$

But you don't have to dimension A to be of size 31. Each entry in a single-precision numerical array consists of four bytes. This means that array A must have at least B/4 entries. Since B/4 = 31/4 = 7.75, you could use DIM A(7) to give the eight entries A(0), A(1), . . . , A(7). The value N = 7 is precisely what the formula N = INT(B/4) gives for N when B is 31. To store a 41×49 image in an array F (as was done in Example 17), you would get

$$B = 4 + 49 * INT((2 * 41 + 7)/8) = 543$$

In this case, N = INT(543/4) = INT(135.75) = 135, so you could use DIM F(135) as was done in the example. If B happens to be a multiple of 4, the formula N = INT(B/4) gives a dimension N one larger than needed. This causes no difficulty; dimensions larger than needed to store a screen image are admissible. The second formula shown above for N is used if integer arrays are specified in GET statements. Each entry in an integer array consists of two bytes, so the dimension must be at least as large as B/2. Thus, just as the dimension N = INT(B/4) is adequate for single-precision arrays, the dimension N = INT(B/2) suffices for integer arrays.

We now describe precisely how PUT statements create displays. As we have already mentioned, the statement

    PUT (X, Y), A

plots a point in the color specified in array A if the point currently has the background color; if the current color is the same as the color specified in A, you get the background color. The following table shows how this statement colors any point, whatever its current color.

		Color specified in array			
		0	**1**	**2**	**3**
Current	**0**	0	1	2	3
screen	**1**	1	0	3	2
color	**2**	2	3	0	1
	3	3	2	1	0

The first row (current color 0) says that the color specified in the array is used when the current color is the background color. By using this table you can verify that executing the same PUT statement twice restores any point (not just points with the background color) to its original color. For instance, if the array specifies color 3 for a point with color 2, the table shows that you get color 1 the first time and then color 2 back again.

The PUT statement allows one additional parameter called the *action parameter.*

    PUT (X, Y), A, **action**

For **action** you can use XOR, PSET, PRESET, AND, and OR. The parameter XOR gives screen displays as just described. That is, the statements

    PUT (X, Y), A   and   PUT (X, Y), A, XOR

are equivalent. (XOR stands for *exclusive OR.*) The colors displayed when the other action parameters are used are given in Table 19.3. Note that PSET causes the colors specified in the array to be used regardless of what colors are currently on the screen. Thus, in Example 17, we could have used the PSET parameter in the PUT statements that create the display, but not in those that erase it. PRESET also gives colors that depend only on the array colors.

Table 19.3   Colors produced by using action parameters in PUT statements

PSET
Color specified in array

		0	1	2	3
Current screen color	0	0	1	2	3
	1	0	1	2	3
	2	0	1	2	3
	3	0	1	2	3

PRESET
Color specified in array

		0	1	2	3
Current screen color	0	3	2	1	0
	1	3	2	1	0
	2	3	2	1	0
	3	3	2	1	0

AND
Color specified in array

		0	1	2	3
Current screen color	0	0	0	0	0
	1	0	1	0	1
	2	0	0	2	2
	3	0	1	2	3

OR
Color specified in array

		0	1	2	3
Current screen color	0	0	1	2	3
	1	1	1	3	3
	2	2	3	2	3
	3	3	3	3	3

Images produced by using PRESET are called *negative images*. The AND parameter is used to produce images only where images exist—this is called *masking*. The OR parameter is used to superimpose an image onto an existing image.

■ *19.8 Simulated Motion*

By repeatedly displaying an image with a PUT statement, erasing it with the same PUT statement, and displaying it again in a nearby position, you can use the display screen for animation. The following algorithm describes how computers can simulate a moving object.

Motion Algorithm

a. Select a starting position P.
b. Display the object at position P.
c. Delay (leave object on screen).
d. Erase the object.
e. Change P slightly.
f. Go to Step (b) until done.

This is precisely how film projectors simulate motion. By using this algorithm, you will display "snapshots" of the object at different positions so quickly that the object will appear to be moving.

The delay in Step (c) can be caused by a loop that does nothing but loop:

```
FOR D = 1 TO 10: NEXT D
```

If a moving image flickers excessively, you can sometimes include a delay to reduce the flicker. Delays can also be used to help control the speed of a moving image.

EXAMPLE 18   *Here is a program to move a small 2 × 2 block across the top edge of the screen.*

```
SCREEN 1                       'Graphics Mode 1
DIM A(1)                       'For storing a 2 x 2 block
LINE (0, 0)-(1, 1), 3, BF      'Display the block.
GET (0, 0)-(1, 1), A           'Store it in A.

LOCATE 23, 1: PRINT "Press a key to start the block."
DO WHILE INKEY$ = "": LOOP
LOCATE 23, 1: PRINT SPACE$(40)
PUT (0, 0), A                  'Erase the block.

FOR X = 0 TO 318 STEP 2
   PUT (X, 0), A               'Display a block at (X,0).
   PUT (X, 0), A               'Erase it.
NEXT X
END
```

On the first pass through the FOR loop, the 2 × 2 image stored in array A is plotted at (0, 0) and immediately erased. On the successive passes through the loop, the same thing happens two points to the right (STEP 2).

REMARK 1   If you run this program, you will see that the 2 × 2 image moves across the screen in about 2 seconds, with little flickering. A good way to change this speed is to plot fewer points for greater speed, and more points for less. If you change the STEP value in the FOR statement from 2 to 4, you will approximately double the speed. If you change STEP 2 to STEP 1 you will approximately halve the speed.

REMARK 2   The speed can also be reduced by including a delay. If you insert the loop

```
FOR D = 1 TO 10: NEXT D
```

between the two PUT statements in the FOR loop, the image will take about 6 seconds to cross the screen. Delays should be executed while the image is on the screen. If you insert the delay loop after the two PUT statements instead of between them, the image will not be on the screen during the delay. This will increase the flicker.

REMARK 3   If you change the two PUT statements in the FOR loop to

```
PUT (X, X), A
PUT (X, X), A
```

the motion will be along the line sloping down to the right that contains the points (0, 0) and (199, 199). If you make this change, you must also change the terminal value 318 in the FOR statement to a number 198 or less. Otherwise, the attempt to use PUT to display the image off the screen will result in an *Illegal function call* error.

REMARK 4   Motion can be simulated without using GET and PUT. For instance, you could replace

```
PUT (X, 0), A
PUT (X, 0), A
```

with

```
LINE (X, 0)-STEP(1, 1), 3, BF    'Display block at (X,0).
LINE (X, 0)-STEP(1, 1), 0, BF    'Erase it.
```

There are at least two good reasons for using GET and PUT. Most often, images are displayed more quickly with PUT statements than with PSET, LINE, CIRCLE, and PAINT statements. Also, the coding process can be simplified considerably by using GET and PUT. For instance, a complex image can be displayed once, stored in an array by using GET, and then displayed anywhere on the screen and as often as needed simply by specifying a single point and the array name in a PUT statement. To do this by using PSET, LINE, CIRCLE, and PAINT statements can be a formidable coding task.

In the rest of this section, we show how the PUT statement can be used to simulate the motion of a ball that moves along straight lines in an area enclosed by four walls and that rebounds whenever a wall is reached. The ball will be represented by a filled circle. In addition, we'll place a stationary target (also a filled circle) on the screen and detect a collision, should the ball strike the target.

Let's begin by displaying the filled circle that will represent the ball and storing it in an array for later use in PUT statements. Rather than using the default aspect value 5/6, we will specify the aspect value 1 in all circle statements. This will give us a visual circle whose horizontal and vertical radii have the same number of points. As you will see, this will somewhat simplify the task of detecting when the ball reaches a wall, and will greatly simplify the task of detecting when the target is hit. By using the aspect value 1, the ball and target will appear as ellipses that are taller than they are wide. To make them look like circles, simply adjust the Vertical Size control on the back of the display unit.

In what follows, we will use R to denote the radius of the circle that represents the ball and BALL% as the name of the array that stores an image of the ball. Here is a program segment to store a representation of the ball in the array BALL%.

```
SCREEN 1                        'Graphics Mode 1
COLOR 1, 1                      'Blue bkgrd.—palette 1

'Display a ball image and store it in array BALL%.

R = 4                           'Radius of ball
CIRCLE (4, 4), R, 3, , , 1
PAINT (4, 4), 3, 3
B = 4 + 9 * INT((2 * 9 + 7) / 8)   'Bytes needed in BALL%
DIM BALL%(INT(B / 2))
GET (0, 0)—(8, 8), BALL%        'Store ball in BALL%.
PUT (0, 0), BALL%               'Erase it.
```

The CIRCLE and PAINT statements display a white-filled circle of radius 4 on a blue background. The GET statement stores in array BALL% the 9 × 9 region with (0, 0) and (8, 8) as opposite vertices. Because the CIRCLE statement specifies the aspect value 1, this region is as follows. (The dotted lines enclosing the circle and the labels are for reference only.)

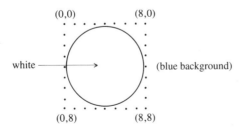

The following program segment uses the motion algorithm that precedes Example 18 to move the ball across the screen from left to right. (To execute this program segment, simply add it to the lines above.)

```
LET X = 0: Y = 100                    'Starting point
DO WHILE X <= 311
    PUT (X, Y), BALL%                 'Display the ball.
    FOR D = 1 TO 5: NEXT D            'Delay
    PUT (X, Y), BALL%                 'Erase the ball.
    LET X = X + 4                     'Select next position.
LOOP
```

The programming delay in the DO loop helps reduce flicker. Note that the ball is on the screen during the delay. If you find the motion too slow, plot fewer images. For instance, if you use LET X = X + 8, half as many images will be displayed, so the speed will be doubled. To cut the speed in half, use LET X = X + 2.

The DO loop simulates a ball moving from left to right along the horizontal line Y = 100 (actually the upper-left corner of the rectangle stored in BALL% moves along the line Y = 100). If you keep X fixed and vary Y, the ball will move along a vertical line. By changing both X and Y, the ball can be made to move in directions other than the horizontal and vertical. For example, the program segment

```
LET X = 30: Y = 180                   'Starting point
DO WHILE X <= 311 AND Y >= 0
    PUT (X, Y), BALL%                 'Display the ball.
    FOR D = 1 TO 5: NEXT D            'Delay
    PUT (X, Y), BALL%                 'Erase the ball.
    LET X = X + 4: Y = Y - 3          'Select next position.
LOOP
```

simulates a ball moving from the lower-left screen position (30, 180), along the line that contains the successive points (30, 180), (34, 177), (38, 174), (42, 171), and so on.

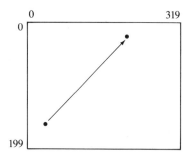

The WHILE condition ensures that the PUT statements will be executed only if the ball fits in the graphics area. As with horizontal and vertical motion, the speed can be increased by plotting fewer points and decreased by plotting more. Thus, if you change

```
LET X = X + 4: Y = Y - 3
```

to

```
LET X = X + 8: Y = Y - 6
```

the speed will double, but the direction will remain the same. If you use

```
LET X = X + 2: Y = Y - 3 / 2
```

the speed will be cut in half.

Many video games involve a moving ball capable of rebounding off a wall. The following program segment shows one way to build a wall surrounding the graphics screen.

```
FOR W = 0 TO 4
    LINE (W, W)-(319 - W, 191 - W), 1, B
NEXT W
```

(We use 191 instead of 199 to avoid screen line 25, in which QuickBASIC displays the *Press any key to continue* message.) These five rectangles, drawn one inside the other, give us four walls along the four edges of the graphics area. The inside boundaries of the left and right walls occur at X = 4 and X = 315, respectively. The inside boundaries of the top and bottom walls occur at Y = 4 and Y = 187, respectively.

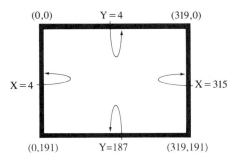

Assume now that a ball approaches one of these walls. To simulate a rebounding ball, two things must be done: we must detect when a wall has been encountered, and then we must start the ball off in a new direction just as if it were a real ball meeting a barrier.

To determine when a wall is encountered, remember that the statement

```
PUT (X, Y), BALL%
```

displays the following 9 × 9 region:

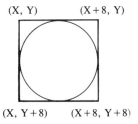

The circle touches all four edges of the region because we specified the aspect value 1 while drawing the filled circle stored in BALL%. Because of this, the ball will hit the left wall when the left side of the rectangle (X) encounters the left wall (4)—that is, when X ≤ 4. Similarly, the top wall is hit when Y ≤ 4. The ball will hit the right wall when the right side of the rectangle (X + 8) encounters the right wall (315)—that is, when X + 8 ≥ 315. Similarly, the bottom wall will be hit when Y + 8 ≥ 187. These last two conditions can be written more simply as X ≥ 307 and Y ≥ 179, respectively.

In summary, a wall is encountered when the next position (X, Y) of the upper-left corner of the rectangle satisfies one of the following conditions:

X ≥ 307   right wall is encountered
X ≤ 4   left wall is encountered
Y ≥ 179   bottom wall is encountered
Y ≤ 4   top wall is encountered

To describe a method for selecting a new direction for a rebounding ball, let's assume that the ball moves by changing its coordinates X and Y by the respective amounts XCHANGE and YCHANGE. Having just plotted the ball in position (X, Y), we give the next position by the statements

```
LET X = X + XCHANGE: Y = Y + YCHANGE
```

Let's assume that X ≥ 307—that is, the ball has reached the right vertical wall. To start it in the opposite direction, we'll let X = 306 and continue it in the new direction by letting XCHANGE = −XCHANGE. Similar remarks apply as the ball approaches the other three boundaries. The following program segment simulates the motion of a ball that starts at the screen's center point (160,100). The four IF statements in the DO loop ensure that the ball will rebound when it reaches any of the four boundaries. The simulated motion will continue until you type the key combination Ctrl-Break.

```
LET X = 160: Y = 100
DO
    PUT (X, Y), BALL%                          'Display the ball.
    FOR DELAY = 1 TO 10: NEXT DELAY            'Delay
    PUT (X, Y), BALL%                          'Erase it.
    LET X = X + XCHANGE: Y = Y + YCHANGE       'Next position

    ' ----------- TEST FOR REBOUND ------------
    IF X >= 307 THEN X = 306: XCHANGE = -XCHANGE   'Right wall
    IF X <= 4 THEN X = 5:     XCHANGE = -XCHANGE   'Left wall
    IF Y >= 187 THEN Y = 186: YCHANGE = -YCHANGE   'Bottom wall
    IF Y <= 4 THEN Y = 5:     YCHANGE = -YCHANGE   'Top wall
LOOP
```

This program segment does not simulate the motion of a bouncing ball exactly. The method presented here gives an approximation of this motion that is adequate for beginning programming tasks. To improve significantly on this method would require a detailed mathematical analysis that is beyond the scope of this book.

EXAMPLE 19   *A simple video game.*

The program in this example makes use of the rebounding ball simulation and introduces one other element. There is a target on the graphics screen in the shape of a circle whose center (X1, Y1) and radius R1 are chosen randomly by the computer. The ball is given an initial position and a direction and then allowed to rebound off the four walls until it hits the target or until a predetermined number of rebounds has occurred. The following algorithm was used to write the program. You will note that code for much of the algorithm has already been described.

a. Display instructions for the user.
b. Display a ball image and store it in array BALL%.
c. Select the center (X1, Y1) and the radius R1 of the target.
d. Select a starting position (X, Y) for the ball.
e. Select a starting direction (XCHANGE and YCHANGE) for the ball.
f. Simulate the motion of the ball until the target is hit or until 20 rebounds have occurred.
g. Display the results of the simulation and stop.

We discuss these seven steps in order:

Step (a). This is routine. The necessary code, however, can be written only after the interaction that will take place between the user and the computer has been decided. We'll use a procedure named INSTRUCTIONS for this task.

Step (b). Code for this step has already been described.

Step (c). As already stated, the position and radius of the target will be chosen randomly by the computer. The following code is used in the program.

```
RANDOMIZE TIMER
LET X1 = INT(201 * RND) + 60      'From 60 to 260
LET Y1 = INT(101 * RND) + 40      'From 40 to 140
LET R1 = INT(11 * RND) + 10       'From 10 to 20
```

You may check that this will give the center (X1, Y1) and radius R1 of a circle (the target) that lies well within the screen area bounded by the vertical lines X = 4 and X = 315 and the horizontal lines Y = 4 and Y = 187. (The walls drawn previously are also used in this video game program.) We'll use procedures DRAWBOUNDARIES and DRAWTARGET to draw the four walls and the target.

Step (d). The starting position of the ball [the 9 × 9 rectangular region with its upper-left corner at (X, Y)] will be along the left wall; hence X = 5. The user will select the *y*-coordinate by typing a value from 25 to 160. This will ensure that the ball lies in the region surrounded by the four walls. The limits 25 and 160 are used to avoid cluttering the user prompts and the directions that the program displays on text lines 2, 3, 22, and 23. Since $8 \times 3 = 24$, 25 specifies a *y*-coordinate just below text line 3; since $8 \times 21 = 168$, 160 specifies a *y*-coordinate 8 points above the bottom of text line 21.

Step (e). A starting direction for the ball is determined by giving values to XCHANGE and YCHANGE. Since the ball starts at the left wall, XCHANGE should be positive: 0 gives the vertical direction, which makes no sense in this simulation, and negative XCHANGE values will start the ball off to the left directly into the wall. YCHANGE, however, can be negative, positive, or 0. A negative value starts the ball off with a positive inclination (upward and to the right), 0 gives the horizontal direction, and positive values give negative inclinations (downward to the right). The user will select the starting direction by typing a value for YCHANGE in the range -8 to 8. The computer will then determine XCHANGE by using the statement

```
LET XCHANGE = 15 - ABS(YCHANGE)
```

This ensures that the starting XCHANGE value will be positive. Note that the second ball plotted will be XCHANGE points to the right and YCHANGE points above or below the first ball—above if YCHANGE is negative, and below if it is positive. For instance, if the user types 6 for YCHANGE, XCHANGE will be 9, so the second ball will be 9 points to the right and 6 points below the first ball. The numbers 9 and 6 not only determine the direction but also influence the speed of the moving image. If, instead of using XCHANGE and YCHANGE, we had used 2 * XCHANGE and 2 * YCHANGE, we would get 18 and 12 instead of 9 and 6; the direction would be the same, but the speed would be doubled, since only half as many points would be plotted. In general, if you assign a positive value to the variable SPEED and use SPEED * XCHANGE and SPEED * YCHANGE instead of XCHANGE and YCHANGE, you will get the same directions, but the speed will be changed by a factor of SPEED. The motion will be faster if SPEED is greater than 1 and slower if SPEED is less than 1.

Step (f). Everything needed to code the actual simulation has been explained except for how to detect when the ball hits the target. Recall that PUT(X, Y),BALL% displays the ball with its center at $(X + 4, Y + 4)$. The center of the target is always at $(X1, Y1)$.

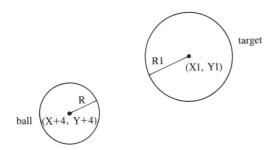

The distance D1 between these two centers is given by

```
D1 = SQR((X + 4 - X1) ^ 2 + (Y + 4 - Y1) ^ 2)
```

If the distance D1 is greater than the sum $R + R1$ of the two radii, the ball and target do not touch. If $D1 <= R + R1$, the target has been hit and the simulation should stop. Since at most 20 rebounds are to be allowed, we should also stop the simulation if C, the number of rebounds, reaches 20. In the program, we will set $D2 = R + R1$ and continue the simulation until the following condition is true:

```
D1 <= D2 OR C = 20
```

Step (g). The results of the simulation will be a message telling whether or not the target was hit and a count of how many rebounds occurred. Also, since the simulation is a visual simulation (you are "seeing" the motion of the ball rather than being told what happens), a visual effect should be produced if the ball hits the target. The program does this by displaying an array of lines through the center of the target when the target is hit.

REMARK   The method described in Step (f) to detect when the ball hits the target can be used only if the aspect value 1 is specified in CIRCLE statements. With the default aspect value 5/6, the horizontal radii of the ball and target will be R and R1 as before, but the vertical radii will be 5/6 × R and 5/6 × R1. Thus, if you don't specify the aspect value 1, you will need a method to detect when two ellipses, rather than two circles, meet. This is more difficult.

```
' *********************** A VIDEO GAME ***************************

CALL INSTRUCTIONS                          'Display game instructions

SCREEN 1                                   'Med. res. graphics
COLOR 1, 1                                 'Blue bkgrd.—palette 1

' ----------------------------------------------------------------
'          Display a ball image and store in array BALL%.

LET R = 4                                  'Radius of ball
CIRCLE (4, 4), R, 3, , , 1                 'Display a circle.
PAINT (4, 4), 3, 3                         'Paint its inside.
LET B = 4 + 9 * INT((2 * 9 + 7) / 8)       'Bytes needed to
DIM BALL%(INT(B / 2))                      ' store the ball.
GET (0, 0)-(8, 8), BALL%                   'Store it in BALL%.
PUT (0, 0), BALL%                          'Erase ball image.

' ----------------------------------------------------------------
'     Select a center (X1,Y1) and radius R1 for the target
'        and display the target and the boundary walls.

RANDOMIZE TIMER
LET X1 = INT(201 * RND) + 60               'From 60 to 260
LET Y1 = INT(101 * RND) + 40               'From 40 to 140
LET R1 = INT(11 * RND) + 10                'From 10 to 20

CALL DRAWBOUNDARIES
CALL DRAWTARGET(X1, Y1, R1)

' ----------------------------------------------------------------
'   KEYBOARD INPUT:  Select a starting position along the
'                    left wall and a starting direction.

LET X = 5                                  'Select left wall.
DO
   LOCATE 2, 2: PRINT SPACE$(38)           'Clear prompt line.
   LOCATE 2, 2
   INPUT "SELECT STARTING POSITION (25-160) ", Y
LOOP UNTIL Y >= 25 AND Y <= 160

DO
   LOCATE 3, 2: PRINT SPACE$(38)           'Clear prompt line.
   LOCATE 3, 2
   INPUT "SELECT STARTING DIRECTION (−8 TO 8) ", YCHANGE
LOOP UNTIL YCHANGE >= −8 AND YCHANGE <= 8

LET XCHANGE = 15 − ABS(YCHANGE)            'XCHANGE is 7 TO 15.
```

```
'  --------------------------------------------------------------------
'          Display starting position and direction of ball
'          and prepare the screen for the simulation.

LOCATE 22, 5
PRINT "STARTING POSITION AND DIRECTION"           'Display
PUT (X, Y), BALL%                                 ' ball and
LINE (X + R, Y + R)—STEP(3 * XCHANGE, 3 * YCHANGE)   ' direction
LOCATE 23, 2
PRINT "Press any key to begin the simulation."

DO WHILE INKEY$ = "": LOOP                        'Wait for key.
CLS                                               'Clear screen.
CALL DRAWBOUNDARIES                               'Redraw the walls.
CALL DRAWTARGET(X1, Y1, R1)                       'Redraw the target.

'  --------------------------------------------------------------------
'          Start the ball in motion --- simulation begins.

LET D2 = R + R1                   'Radius of ball + radius of target
LET C = 0                         'C counts number of rebounds.
DO
    PUT (X, Y), BALL%                             'Display the ball.
    FOR DELAY = 1 TO 10: NEXT DELAY               'Delay
    PUT (X, Y), BALL%                             'Erase the ball.
    LET X = X + XCHANGE: Y = Y + YCHANGE          'Next position

    '-----------------------------------------------------------------
    'Check if wall is met. If so, beep the speaker, add 1 to C,
    'select next position for ball and change its direction.

    IF X >= 307 THEN                                      'Right
       BEEP: C = C + 1: X = 306: XCHANGE = —XCHANGE       'wall

    ELSEIF X <= 4 THEN                                    'Left
       BEEP: C = C + 1: X = 5: XCHANGE = —XCHANGE         'wall

    ELSEIF Y <= 4 THEN                                    'Top
       BEEP: C = C + 1: Y = 5: YCHANGE = —YCHANGE         'wall

    ELSEIF Y >= 179 THEN                                  'Bottom
       BEEP: C = C + 1: Y = 178: YCHANGE = —YCHANGE       'wall
    END IF

    D1 = SQR((X + R — X1) ^ 2 + (Y + R — Y1) ^ 2)   'Hit if <= D2

LOOP UNTIL D1 <= D2 OR C = 20     'Loop until hit or 20 rebounds.

'  --------------------------------------------------------------------
'          Motion has stopped.  Check if the target was hit
'          and display the results of the simulation.

IF C < 20 THEN                                    'Target hit?
   LINE (X1 — 30, Y1)–(X1 + 30, Y1), 1            'Yes—display
   LINE (X1 — 20, Y1 + 20)–(X1 + 20, Y1 — 20), 1 ' some rays
   LINE (X1 — 20, Y1 — 20)–(X1 + 20, Y1 + 20), 1 ' emanating
   LINE (X1, Y1 — 30)–(X1, Y1 + 30), 1           ' from target.
   LOCATE 23, 8
   PRINT "A HIT AFTER"; C; "REBOUND";
   IF C = 1 THEN PRINT "." ELSE PRINT "S."
   FOR I = 1 TO 3: BEEP: NEXT I                   '3 beeps.
ELSE
   LOCATE 23, 8                                   'No—display
   PRINT "20 REBOUNDS WITH NO HIT!"              ' a message.
END IF
END                                               'End program.
```

```
SUB DRAWBOUNDARIES

   FOR W = 0 TO 4
      LINE (W, W)-(319 - W, 191 - W), 2, B
   NEXT W

END SUB


SUB DRAWTARGET (X, Y, R)

   CIRCLE (X, Y), R, 1, , , 1: PAINT (X, Y), 3, 1
   CIRCLE (X, Y), 2 * R / 3, 1, , , 1
   CIRCLE (X, Y), R / 3, 1, , , 1
   CIRCLE (X, Y), 0, 1

END SUB

SUB INSTRUCTIONS

CLS
PRINT "            BOUNCING BALL AND TARGET GAME"
PRINT
PRINT "In this game a ball bounces off the boundary walls of a"
PRINT "region until it hits a target whose size and location are"
PRINT "chosen randomly by the computer."
PRINT
PRINT "The object of the game is to select a starting position"
PRINT "and direction for the ball so that it hits the target"
PRINT "after the fewest number of rebounds.  At most 20 rebounds"
PRINT "will be made."
PRINT
PRINT "You will select a starting position along the left wall"
PRINT "by typing a number from 25 (near the top of the screen)"
PRINT "to 160 (near the bottom of the screen)."
PRINT
PRINT "You will select a starting direction by typing a number"
PRINT "from -8 to 8 (-8 gives the greatest inclination)."
PRINT
PRINT "Press any key to continue."
DO WHILE INKEY$ = "": LOOP

END SUB
```

■ 19.9 Problems

In Problems 1–11, write a program to produce each display described.

1. Store a representation of this arrow in an array. The arrow is to be 25 points long.

   ⟶

   Then display 15 rows of arrows as follows: The odd-numbered rows are each to contain 6 arrows with adjacent arrows 25 points apart. The even-numbered rows are each to contain 5 arrows, also 25 points apart. The first arrow in each odd-numbered row is to begin in the column position at which the first arrow in the row above it ends.

2. Produce the display described in Problem 1, but with the arrows in the even-numbered rows pointing to the left. (You should use a second array to store the left-pointing arrow.)

3. In this problem, you are to display an image of a star-filled sky and then simulate motion for shooting stars. Begin by displaying 1,000 stars at randomly generated screen positions. Approximately 99% of the stars should be single points, and the others should consist of the two diagonals of a 3 × 3 square. After all 1,000 stars have been displayed, the program is to select ran-

domly a position in the upper half of the screen for a larger star (four line segments inside a 5 × 5 square and passing through its center will do). This larger star is to move downward to the right if its starting *x*-coordinate is less than 160; otherwise, it is to move downward to the left. Many such shooting stars should be simulated, one at a time. The simulation should stop when the user presses any key.

4. Write a program for the simulation described in Problem 3 but with one additional feature incorporated into the program. Each time a new shooting star is created, generate a random number R in the range 5–15, and use this number to determine the speed of the star. [If the current position of the star is (X, Y), use (X + R, Y + R) as the next position if the star is to move downward to the right. If it is to move downward to the left, change the sign of R before starting the motion.]

5. In this problem, you are to simulate simple horizontal motion for the arrow shown in Problem 1. The arrow is to begin at the left margin of the screen and move toward a target you will display at the right (a rectangle plotted with the B or BF option is good enough). As soon as the arrow-head has embedded itself in the target, the motion is to stop, but the arrow is to remain in its final position until a key is pressed to halt the program. Be sure that the target is thick enough to hold the entire arrowhead.

6. Simulate horizontal motion for an arrow that can change speeds while in flight. Do this as follows. With XC = 3, plot the first arrow at its starting position (X, Y), and then change X to X + XC so that (X, Y) now specifies the next position for the arrow. Before plotting the next arrow, change XC by generating a random number R in the range −1/4 to 1/4 and adding R to XC. If R is positive, the speed is increased slightly (not abruptly); if R is negative, the speed is decreased slightly. (Note that if R were always positive, the arrow would move faster and faster. Thus, R can be thought of as the acceleration. Negative R would give deceleration.) If XC should become negative, the arrow will move backward. Make sure that this doesn't happen. The program should halt as described in Problem 5.

7. Simulate the simultaneous motion of three arrows, one under another, that start off together at the left edge of the screen and head toward a vertical line drawn near the right edge. The speed of each arrow should vary as described in Problem 6. When one of the arrows reaches the vertical line, motion is to stop with the arrows in their final positions, and a message should be displayed telling which arrow reached the line first. The program should halt when the user presses a key.

8. In this problem (and the next two as well) you are to simulate motion by using the following three images.

Start by storing representations of the three images in three arrays—we'll call them P1, P2, and P3. Simulate a mouth that opens and closes by repeatedly displaying and erasing P1, P2, and P3, always with their centers at the point (160, 100). Allow the user to specify a common radius R for P1, P2, and P3 during program execution. R is to be rejected if it is less than 5 and also if it specifies positions for the three images that are not on the screen. Use a delay if you find that it gives a better simulation.

9. In this problem, you are to simulate horizontal motion to the right by repeatedly displaying P1, P2, and P3 along the horizontal line with *y*-coordinate 100 beginning at the left edge of the screen. (P1, P2, and P3 are described in Problem 8). As the image moves across the screen, its mouth should open and close. The program should halt when the right edge is reached.

10. Write a program for the simulation described in Problem 9 but with one additional feature incorporated into the program. Along the horizontal line on which the centers of P1, P2, and P3 are displayed, there is to be a row of dots (these can be placed as far apart as you wish, but they must appear as dots and not as a solid line). As the image created by P1, P2, and P3 moves through the points, they are to disappear. [*Suggestion:* Use the form PUT (X, Y),A,PSET to display images and the form PUT (X, Y),A to erase them.]

11. Simulate the motion of two rebounding balls in search of a target (see Example 19). The game ends when one of the balls hits the target (a winner) or when the two balls strike each other (a draw). The user should specify starting positions and directions for the two balls during program execution. One ball (L) is to start along the left wall and the other (R) along the right. The program should announce at the end whether the game is a draw or which ball is the winner. [If the two balls are in the shape of circles with centers (x, y) and (z, w) and radii $r1$ and $r2$, respectively, there is a collision when $(x - z)^2 + (y - w)^2 \leq (r1 + r2)^2$, provided you specify the aspect value 1 in CIRCLE statements.]

■ 19.10 High-Resolution Graphics

In this section, we'll assume that you are familiar with the PC's medium-resolution graphics mode. As mentioned at the outset of this chapter, all graphics statements except for the COLOR statement are allowed in either medium-resolution or high-resolution graphics mode. We also mentioned that although the same forms of these statements can be used in both modes, there are differences in the displays produced. These differences are summarized in Table 19.4. If you understand how graphics statements are used in medium-resolution graphics mode, you will find that this table contains the only additional information needed to produce high-resolution graphics displays. The table describes only differences. Items not mentioned in the table are the same in both modes.

In high-resolution graphics, the 640 columns are numbered 0 to 639 from left to right and the 200 rows are numbered 0 to 199 from top to bottom (see Figure 19.3). As in medium-resolution graphics a point is specified by giving its column number followed by its row number. Several labeled points are shown in Figure 19.3. Note that (320, 100) is approximately at the center of the graphics screen.

Table 19.4   Medium-resolution and high-resolution differences

Topic	Medium-resolution	High-resolution
Mode selection	SCREEN 1	SCREEN 2
Points	A horizontal line contains 320 points numbered 0–319.	A horizontal line contains 640 points numbered 0–639.
Text	All characters are displayed in the WIDTH 40 form.	All characters are displayed in the smaller WIDTH 80 form.
COLOR statement	Used to specify a background color and a palette number.	Not used. The background color is black (0) and the foreground color is white (1).
Color parameter	Specifies a color from current palette, but 0 specifies the background color. The default is color 3 of the current palette except in PAINT, where the default for the boundary color is the painting color.	0 and 2 specify black; 1 and 3 specify white. The default is white except in PAINT, where the default boundary color is the painting color.
Color of text	Color 3 of the current palette.	White (1).
Aspect value	Default is 5/6.	Default is 5/12. (This gives visual circles that look like circles, just as 5/6 does in medium-resolution mode.)
Dimension needed to store an X × Y screen image by using a GET statement.	With B given by `B=4+Y*INT((2*X+7)/8)` use INT(B/2) for integer arrays, and INT(B/4) for single-precision arrays.	With B given by `B=4+Y*INT((X+7)/8)` use INT(B/2) and INT(B/4) just as in medium-resolution graphics mode.

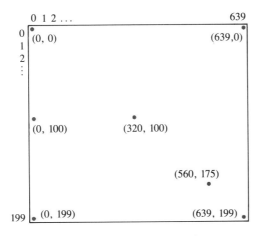

Figure 19.3   High-resolution graphics screen.

All displays produced while in high-resolution graphics mode (SCREEN 2) will be black and white displays. An attempt to execute a COLOR statement will give a fatal *Illegal function call* error. You can, however, include color parameters in PSET, LINE, CIRCLE, and PAINT statements just as in medium-resolution mode. These specify not colors from a palette, but rather black or white, as explained in Table 19.4.

We conclude this chapter with three short programs that illustrate the use of graphics statements in high-resolution graphics mode. After reading through these examples, you may find it informative to modify some of the medium-resolution graphics programs from the preceding sections so that they will produce high-resolution displays. To do this, simply change SCREEN 1 to SCREEN 2 and delete all COLOR statements. You will get black and white displays that fit in the left half of the screen. (Some circles may be partially off the screen if CIRCLE statements specify aspect values: as explained in Table 19.4, high-resolution graphics mode uses the aspect value 5/12.) All text will be white. Points will be white if color 1 or 3 is specified and black for color 0 or 2.

EXAMPLE 20   *Here is a program to display an underlined title.*

```
SCREEN 2                        'Graphics Mode 2

LOCATE 2, 20                     'Text line 2
PRINT "MICROSOFT"               'Display a title.
LINE (152, 16)–(223, 16), 1     'Underline it.
END
```

Program output:

```
MICROSOFT
```

The SCREEN statement gets you into high-resolution graphics mode with a clear (black) screen. The LOCATE and PRINT statements display the title MICROSOFT in character position 20 of text line 2. With SCREEN 2 in effect, the WIDTH 80 size is used for text output.

The LINE statement underlines the title by drawing a line segment between the points (152, 16) and (223, 16) that lie just below the ends of the title. The coordinates of these two points are determined exactly as in medium-resolution graphics—each text character is 8 points high (200/25 = 8) and 8 points wide (640/80 = 8). Since the title appears on line 2, the y-coordinate of the bottom edge of the title is $2 \times 8 - 1 = 15$ (minus 1 because point positions are numbered beginning with 0 just as before). We used 16 as the y-coordinate of the underscore so that it would be below the title and not on its bottom edge. By using a similar analysis, you can verify 152 as the x-coordinate for the left edge of the title and 223 as the x-coordinate for the right edge.

REMARK

The title is displayed in white (1), as is all text in high-resolution graphics. The color parameter 1 in the LINE statement specifies white for the underscore as well. This parameter, however, is not needed since the default color is also white. In high-resolution graphics, color parameters are needed in only two situations: to erase images previously plotted in white or to display black points on a white background. (Displaying black images on a white background is not unusual. It's what you do when writing on white paper with black ink.)

EXAMPLE 21   *Here is a program to display four concentric circles on a white background.*

```
SCREEN 2                        'Graphics Mode 2

LINE (0, 0)-(639, 199), , BF    'Color screen white.
PSET (320, 100), 0              'Color center point black.
FOR R = 50 TO 200 STEP 50
   CIRCLE (320, 100), R, 0      'Black circle, radius R
NEXT R
END
```

SCREEN 2 gets you into high-resolution graphics mode with a clear (black) screen and the LINE statement colors the entire screen white.

The last circle drawn by the FOR loop has center (320, 100) and radius R = 200. Since an aspect value is not specified in the CIRCLE statement, the PC used the default aspect value 5/12. Thus, the horizontal radius contains 200 points, but the vertical radius contains only 83 ($5/12 \times 200 = 83.3333$ is rounded to 83). This means that the x-coordinates of points on this circle lie in the range 120 to 300, and the y-coordinates are from 17 (100 − 83) to 183 (100 + 83), so the circle fits on the screen.

REMARK 1   It would not be correct to omit the color parameter 0 in the PSET and CIRCLE statements. Remember, the default value is 1 (white) and not 0 (black).

REMARK 2   If the aspect value 1 were specified

```
CIRCLE (320, 100), R, 0, , , 1
```

both the horizontal and vertical radii of the circle would be R. In this case, only the first circle (R = 50) would fit entirely on the screen. If you specify the aspect value 1 while SCREEN 2 is in effect, visual circles will be considerably elongated—in high-resolution graphics, 5 points in the vertical direction have the same length as 12 points in the horizontal direction. Adjusting the Vertical Size control on the back of the display unit, we were unable to make these ellipses look like circles.

EXAMPLE 22   *Here is a program to plot concentric circles and alternately color the ringed regions formed by the circles in black and white.*

```
' ---- CONCENTRIC CIRCLES - FILLED IN BLACK AND WHITE ----

SCREEN 2                        'Graphics Mode 2

LET C = 1                       'C MOD 2=1,0 for white,black.
FOR R = 200 TO 0 STEP -20
   CIRCLE (320, 100), R, C MOD 2   'Draw a circle of radius R.
   PAINT (320, 100), C MOD 2        'Paint the circle.
   LET C = C + 1                    'Increment C to change color.
NEXT R
END
```

In this program, C takes on the values 1, 2, 3, 4, and so on; hence, C MOD 2 assumes the values 1, 0, 1, 0, ... The first time through the loop, the CIRCLE statement draws a white circle, and the PAINT statement colors its interior white. (Remember, the default boundary color in a PAINT statement is the painting color—in this case, C MOD 2.) The next time through the loop, a smaller circle is drawn in black and colored black. This process continues until, on the last pass when R = 0, the circle is plotted as a single point.

■ *19.11 Problems*

Write a program to perform each task.

1. Draw a white boundary, 10 points wide, around the graphics area.
2. Color the region of the graphics area below the upper-left to lower-right diagonal white.
3. Color the upper-left and lower-right quadrants of the graphics area white.
4. Color the triangular region bounded by the three line segments connecting (320, 0), (0, 199), and (639, 199) white.
5. Divide the graphics area into five regions by drawing four rectangles that have the point (0, 0) as a common corner point. The sizes of the rectangles should be 40 × 128, 80 × 256, 120 × 384, and 160 × 512.
6. First, divide the graphics area into five regions as in Problem 5, and then color adjacent regions in alternating colors with the smallest region white.
7. Divide the graphics area into quadrants by coloring the upper-left and lower-right quadrants white and leaving the other two black. A star is to move clockwise through the four quadrants. When it appears in a white quadrant, it should be black (and vice versa). Make sure the star is centered in each quadrant. Include a delay so that the star is easily seen. After this delay, erase the star before going on to the next quadrant.
8. Allow the user to use the following method to create line drawings in the upper three-fourths of the graphics area. The lower portion of the screen is to be used to display any dialogue between the user and the computer. After entering a starting point, the user should be allowed to enter L, R, U, or D (for left, right, up, or down) and a number for the length of a line segment. A segment of the chosen length and direction should be drawn from the starting point. The user should then be allowed to specify a direction and length for another line segment that should be drawn from the end point of the previous segment. If, instead of entering L, R, U, or D, the user types A, the graphics area should be cleared and the user allowed to create another line drawing. If the user types S, program execution should terminate. Any entry other than L, R, U, D, A, or S should be ignored and a new entry requested. If the direction and length specify a line segment that will extend out of the viewing area, they should be rejected and a new entry requested.
9. Transform the 640-column by 200-row high-resolution graphics area into a Cartesian coordinate system whose origin is at the point (320, 100) in the graphics area. Draw horizontal and vertical axes through this point. Display the graphs of each of the following functions. [Point (X, Y) in the Cartesian coordinate system will have coordinates (320 + X, 100 − Y) in the graphics area.]
   a. $Y = 10 * SGN(X)$ $-200 \leq X \leq 200$
   b. $Y = ABS(X)$ $-75 \leq X \leq 75$
   c. $Y = 10 * INT(X/10)$ $-75 \leq X \leq 75$
   d. $Y = 75/X$ $-75 \leq X \leq 75, \quad X \neq 0$
   e. $Y = 5\sqrt{X + 30}$ $-30 \leq X \leq 200$
   f. $Y = 10X^2/(100 - X^2)$ $-200 \leq X \leq 200, \quad X \neq -10, X \neq 10$
   g. $Y = X(X - 50)(X + 50)/1000$ $-60 \leq X \leq 60$

■ *19.12 Review True-or-False Quiz*

1. The two programming lines

   ```
   SCREEN 1 : COLOR 4,0
   ```

   and

   ```
   COLOR 4,0 : SCREEN 1
   ```

   are equivalent.   T F
2. In high-resolution graphics, the COLOR statement determines whether points are plotted in black or in white.   T F

3. The statement SCREEN 0 will return you from medium-resolution graphics to text mode with 40-character lines.   T F

4. In medium-resolution graphics, the statements COLOR 1,0 : PSET(20,20) will always result in a white point at position (20, 20).   T F

5. The statements

```
LINE(23,130)-(85,35)
```

and

```
LINE(85,35)-(23,130)
```

result in the same display. Subsequent output, however, may depend on which of these forms is used.   T F

6. The statements PSET(X1, Y1) : LINE $-$ (X2, Y2) are equivalent to the single statement LINE(X1, Y1) $-$ (X2, Y2).   T F

7. In graphics mode, the statement

```
LOCATE 1,1 : PRINT "FIRST LINE"
```

will display FIRST LINE at the top of the graphics area.   T F

8. In high-resolution graphics, you are limited to white images on a black background.   T F

9. In medium-resolution graphics mode, the default for any color parameter omitted from a PSET, LINE, CIRCLE, or PAINT statement is color 3 of the current palette.   T F

10. The statement PAINT (X, Y),P,B will color only points that can be joined to (X, Y) by a straight line segment that contains no point of color B.   T F

A
The Disk Operating System (DOS)

*T*he IBM Personal Computer's disk operating system (DOS) includes programs that allow you to use the disk unit as an external storage device. This appendix shows how to load DOS and explains how you can use it to perform certain tasks necessary for efficient use of the disk unit. The process of loading the disk operating system is called *starting* or *booting* DOS.

■ *A.1 Starting DOS from a Hard Drive*

To start DOS, carry out these three steps:

1. Make sure that drive A (and B if there is one) contains no disk.
2. If the video display unit has a separate power switch, turn it on.
3. If the PC's power switch is in the off position, turn it on. If the PC's power is already on, do one of the following:

    a. Turn the PC off and then on again.
    b. Press the Del key while holding down the Ctrl and Alt keys. This process is called a *system reset.*

At this point, the *in use* light for the hard disk unit will glow, and after a short time, one of three things will happen:

- The PC will display the DOS prompt C: \>, indicating that DOS has been loaded and is operational.
- The PC will display a menu from which you must make a selection. Choosing DOS will give you the DOS prompt C: \>, indicating that DOS is operational.
- The PC will prompt you first for the date and then for the time. In each case, you can simply press the Enter key to leave the date and time as displayed by the PC. Having done this, the PC will display the DOS prompt C: \>, indicating that DOS is operational.

The letter C in the DOS prompt C: \> indicates that drive C is the default drive. This means that a disk command will be carried out on the hard disk in drive C unless a command specifies a different drive. For instance, if a file named *fname* is to be specified in a DOS command but the file is stored on the disk in drive A, you would use A: *fname* to specify the file.

DOS allows you to change the default drive. To change it to drive A, simply type A: after the prompt C: \> and press the Enter key. Thus,

    C:\>a: (you type a: and press the Enter key)
    A:\>   (displayed by the PC)

gives drive A as the default drive, as indicated by the new DOS prompt A: \>.

■ *A.2 Starting DOS from a Disk in Drive A*

If your system does not have DOS installed in a hard drive, insert a DOS system disk in drive A, close the door on the disk unit, and carry out Steps 2 and 3 in Section A.1. After Step 3, the *in use* light for drive A will glow. After a short time one of two things will happen:

1. The PC will display the DOS prompt A>, indicating that DOS has been loaded and is operational.
2. The PC will prompt you first for the date and then for the time. In each case, you can simply press the Enter key to leave the date and time as displayed by the PC. Having done this, the PC will display the DOS prompt A>, indicating that DOS is operational.

The letter A in the DOS prompt A> indicates that drive A is the default drive. This means that a disk command will be carried out on the disk in drive A unless a command specifies a different drive. For instance, if a file named *fname* is to be specified in a DOS command but the file is stored on the disk in drive B, you would use B:*fname* to specify the file.

DOS allows you to change the default drive. To change it to drive B, simply type B: after the prompt A> and press the Enter key. Thus,

```
A>b:        (you type b: and press the Enter key)
B>          (displayed by the PC)
```

gives drive B as the default drive, as indicated by the new DOS prompt B>.

■ *A.3 Formatting and Copying Disks: The FORMAT and DISKCOPY Commands*

Before a new disk can be used to store information, it must be **formatted** by using either the FORMAT or the DISKCOPY command. FORMAT writes information on a disk that initializes it to a recording format acceptable to DOS. Formatting a disk destroys any information that may previously have been stored on the disk. DISKCOPY is used to make new copies of existing disks. The disk being created is formatted before any files are copied; hence, any information previously stored on the disk is destroyed. To issue either of these commands, DOS must be operational and the DOS system (actually, only the file names FORMAT.COM and DISKCOPY.COM) must be in the disk directory of the default drive. In what follows, we assume that the default drive is drive C for systems with a hard disk, and drive A for systems with no hard drive. Thus, we assume the DOS prompt

```
C:\>        (for systems with DOS installed in hard drive C)
A>          (for systems with DOS on the disk in drive A)
```

To format a disk, type FORMAT A: and press the Enter key. You will obtain the display

```
Insert new diskette for drive A:
and strike any key when ready
```

When the drive A *in use* light is off, insert the disk to be formatted in drive A and press the Enter key. The PC will display

```
Formatting...
```

and after some whirring of the disk unit, you will obtain a message similar to

```
Formatting complete
Format another (Y/N)?
```

To format another disk, type Y (or y). If only one disk is to be formatted, type N (or n) to get back the DOS prompt C:\> or A>.

To issue the DISKCOPY command, type

```
DISKCOPY A: B:
```

and follow the instructions displayed by the PC. (The instructions you get will depend on the hardware configuration of your system.) The disk you are copying is called the *source disk,* and the disk being created is called the *target disk.*

A.4 The Directory and Delete Commands: DIR and DEL

To obtain a listing of all file names included in the current default disk directory, type DIR and press the Enter key. The display will show for each file the file size (in bytes) and the date and time the file was created. There are many forms of the DIR command. You should find the following two forms useful:

```
DIR *.ext
DIR fname.*
```

The first will produce a listing of all files with the extension *ext,* and the second will list each file whose name without the extension is *fname.*

The DEL command is used to delete file names from disk directories. The command

```
DEL fname.ext
```

deletes *fname.ext* from the default disk directory. As with the DIR command, there are many forms of the DEL command. You should find the following two forms useful:

```
DEL *.ext
DEL fname.*
```

The first deletes all files with the extension *ext* from the default disk directory, and the second deletes each file whose name without the extension is *fname.*

A.5 Disk Directories

As mentioned at the outset of this appendix, the disk operating system DOS includes programs that allow you to use the disk unit as an external storage device. A principal function of the operating system is to keep track of the files stored on disks. DOS uses letters to designate disk drives. On most computers, C denotes a hard disk, and A and B denote 5¼ and 3½ inch disks. Each disk contains a file directory, called the **root directory.** Most 5¼ and 3½ inch disks have only this root directory, but hard disks usually have directories other than the root directory. If you issue the DIR command with hard drive C as the default drive, you should obtain a screen display with

```
C:\>DIR
```

followed by a list of files and directories. The directory names are those indicated by the designation <DIR>. We did this and obtained, among others, the directory names

```
DOS        <DIR>
QB45       <DIR>
```

The first indicates that the DOS system is stored in a directory named DOS. The second, QB45, is the name of the directory that contains the QuickBASIC system. DOS contains the commands MD, CD, and RD that allow you to make new directories (MD), change the default directory (CD), and remove directories (RD). The DOS manual that comes with your system explains how to use these three commands.

■ *A.6 File Names and Path Names*

Each DOS file name can contain from 1 to 8 letters and digits followed by an optional period and an optional extension of up to 3 letters and digits. The following are admissible DOS file names:

```
FILENUM1        NAMES           123JUMP
321             TEMP            TRY.TMP
SCORES.DAT      PROG1.BAS       LETTER.12
```

The extension is often used to designate the type of a file. For instance, if you are using QuickBASIC and specify a file name without an extension, the QuickBASIC system will automatically add the extension .BAS.

The complete identifier for a file is called its **path name.** If a file named *fname* is in the root directory of a disk, say the disk in drive C, its path name is

```
C:\fname
```

If the root directory of disk drive C contains the directory CLASS1 and if file *fname* is in the directory CLASS1, the path name for the file *fname* is

```
C:\CLASS1\fname
```

Similarly,

```
C:\LABS\CLASS1\fname
```

is the path name for the file *fname* in the directory CLASS1, contained in the directory LABS. LABS is in the root directory of disk drive C.

Thus, the path name for a file contains the disk drive designation (such as C:), followed by the various directories, followed by the file name, with successive items separated by backslashes.

B
QuickBASIC Reserved Words

ABS	CSNG	EXIT
ACCESS	CSRLIN	EXP
ALIAS	CVD	FIELD
AND	CVDMBF	FILEATTR
ANY	CVI	FILES
APPEND	CVL	FIX
AS	CVS	FOR
ASC	CVSMBF	FRE
ATN	DATA	FREEFILE
BASE	DATE$	FUNCTION
BEEP	DECLARE	GET
BINARY	DEF FN	GOSUB
BLOAD	DEF SEG	GOTO
BSAVE	DEFDBL	HEX$
BYVAL	DEFINT	IF
CALL	DEFLNG	IMP
CALLS	DEFSNG	$INCLUDE
CALL ABSOLUTE	DEFSTR	INKEY$
CALL INTERRUPT	DIM	INP
CASE	DO	INPUT
CDBL	DOUBLE	INPUT #
CDECL	DRAW	INPUT$
CHAIN	$DYNAMIC	INSTR
CHDIR	ELSE	INT
CHR$	ELSEIF	INTEGER
CINT	END	IOCTL
CIRCLE	ENDIF	IOCTL$
CLEAR	ENVIRON	IS
CLNG	ENVIRON$	KEY
CLOSE	EOF	LBOUND
CLS	EQV	LCASE$
COLOR	ERASE	LEFT$
COM	ERDEV	LEN
COMMAND$	ERDEV$	LET
COMMON	ERL	LINE
CONST	ERR	LINE INPUT
COS	ERROR	LINE INPUT #

LIST	POINT	$STATIC
LOC	POKE	STEP
LOCAL	POS	STICK
LOCATE	PRESET	STOP
LOCK	PRINT	STR$
LOF	PRINT #	STRIG
LOG	PSET	STRING
LONG	PUT	STRING$
LOOP	RANDOM	SUB
LPOS	RANDOMIZE	SWAP
LPRINT	READ	SYSTEM
LSET	REDIM	TAB
LTRIM$	REM	TAN
MID$	RESET	THEN
MKD$	RESTORE	TIME$
MKDIR	RESUME	TIMER
MKDMBF$	RETURN	TO
MKI$	RIGHT$	TROFF
MKL$	RMDIR	TRON
MKS$	RND	TYPE
MKSMBF$	RSET	UBOUND
MOD	RTRIM$	UCASE$
NAME	RUN	UEVENT
NEXT	SADD	UNLOCK
NOT	SCREEN	UNTIL
OCT$	SEEK	USING
OFF	SELECT	VAL
ON	SETMEM	VARPTR
OPEN	SGN	VARPTR$
OPTION BASE	SHARED	VARSEG
OR	SHELL	VIEW
OUT	SIGNAL	WAIT
OUTPUT	SIN	WEND
PAINT	SINGLE	WHILE
PALETTE	SLEEP	WIDTH
PCOPY	SOUND	WINDOW
PEEK	SPACE$	WRITE
PEN	SPC	XOR
PLAY	SQR	
PMAP	STATIC	

C
IBM PC Numeric Codes

Numeric code	Character	Numeric code	Character
000	(null)	033	!
001	☺	034	"
002	●	035	#
003	♥	036	$
004	♦	037	%
005	♣	038	&
006	♠	039	´
007	(beep)	040	(
008	■	041	)
009	(tab)	042	*
010	(line feed)	043	+
011	(home)	044	,
012	(form feed)	045	–
013	(carriage return)	046	.
014	♪	047	/
015	☼	048	0
016	►	049	1
017	◄	050	2
018	↕	051	3
019	‼	052	4
020	¶	053	5
021	§	054	6
022	▬	055	7
023	↨	056	8
024	↑	057	9
025	↓	058	:
026	→	059	;
027	←	060	<
028	(cursor right)	061	=
029	(cursor left)	062	>
030	(cursor up)	063	?
031	(cursor down)	064	@
032	(space)	065	A

Numeric code	Character	Numeric code	Character
066	B	118	v
067	C	119	w
068	D	120	x
069	E	121	y
070	F	122	z
071	G	123	{
072	H	124	¦
073	I	125	}
074	J	126	~
075	K	127	⌂
076	L	128	Ç
077	M	129	ü
078	N	130	é
079	O	131	â
080	P	132	ä
081	Q	133	à
082	R	134	å
083	S	135	ç
084	T	136	ê
085	U	137	ë
086	V	138	è
087	W	139	ï
088	X	140	î
089	Y	141	ì
090	Z	142	Ä
091	[	143	Å
092	\	144	É
093	]	145	æ
094	^	146	Æ
095	—	147	ô
096	`	148	ö
097	a	149	ò
098	b	150	û
099	c	151	ù
100	d	152	ÿ
101	e	153	Ö
102	f	154	Ü
103	g	155	¢
104	h	156	£
105	i	157	¥
106	j	158	Pt
107	k	159	*f*
108	l	160	á
109	m	161	í
110	n	162	ó
111	o	163	ú
112	p	164	ñ
113	q	165	Ñ
114	r	166	ª
115	s	167	º
116	t	168	¿
117	u	169	⌐

Numeric code	Character	Numeric code	Character
170	¬	213	╒
171	½	214	╓
172	¼	215	╫
173	¡	216	╪
174	«	217	┘
175	»	218	┌
176	░	219	█
177	▒	220	▄
178	▓	221	▌
179	│	222	▐
180	┤	223	▀
181	╡	224	α
182	╢	225	β
183	╖	226	Γ
184	╕	227	π
185	╣	228	Σ
186	║	229	σ
187	╗	230	μ
188	╝	231	τ
189	╜	232	Φ
190	╛	233	Θ
191	┐	234	Ω
192	└	235	δ
193	┴	236	∞
194	┬	237	φ
195	├	238	ε
196	─	239	∩
197	┼	240	≡
198	╞	241	±
199	╟	242	≥
200	╚	243	≤
201	╔	244	⌠
202	╩	245	⌡
203	╦	246	÷
204	╠	247	≈
205	═	248	°
206	╬	249	●
207	╧	250	·
208	╨	251	√ⁿ
209	╤	252	²
210	╥	253	²
211	╙	254	∎
212	╘	255	(blank 'FF')

D QuickBASIC Statements

Statement	Purpose	Text reference
CALL	To execute a QuickBASIC SUB procedure	Sections 12.1, 12.4
CD	To change the current directory	Appendix A.5
CIRCLE	To plot a circle in graphics mode	Section 19.4
CLOSE	To terminate communication between a program and a file	Section 16.1
CLS	To clear the display screen	Sections 4.5, 4.7
COLOR (graphics mode)	To select a background color and palette for graphic displays	Section 19.1
COLOR (text mode)	To select colors for screen displays	Section 10.3
CONST	To declare a symbolic constant	Section 16.5
DATA	To include input data as part of a program	Section 11.1
DEF FN	To define a function	Sections 13.3, 14.7
DIM	To specify dimensions for arrays	Sections 15.1, 15.2, 15.9
DIM . . . AS	To declare a variable as a certain type	Section 16.7
DO	To initiate a DO loop	Section 6.1
END	To terminate execution of a program	Section 3.5
END FUNCTION	To end a function definition	Section 12.5
END SELECT	To end a SELECT CASE definition	Section 8.5
END SUB	To end a SUB definition	Section 12.1
ERASE	To reinitialize the entries of a static array	Section 15.2
EXIT FOR	To exit a FOR loop	Section 9.1
FOR	To initiate a FOR loop	Section 9.1
FUNCTION	To declare a FUNCTION procedure	Section 12.5
GET (files)	To read a record from a random file into a record variable	Section 16.7

Statement	Purpose	Text reference
GET (graphics mode)	To store an image from the graphics screen in an array	Section 19.7
IF-THEN-ELSE (single line)	To execute one sequence of statements if a specified condition is true and another if it is false	Section 8.1
IF-THEN-ELSE (block)	To execute one sequence of statements if a specified condition is true and another if it is false	Section 8.4
INPUT	To obtain input data from the keyboard	Section 5.1
INPUT #	To obtain input data from a sequential file	Section 16.1
LET	To evaluate an expression and assign its value to a variable	Section 3.5
LINE	To plot line segments and rectangles in graphics mode	Section 19.2
LINE INPUT	To read an entire line from the keyboard	Section 5.1
LINE INPUT #	To read an entire line from a sequential file	Section 16.2
LOCATE	To position the cursor at a specified row and column on the screen	Section 10.1
LOOP	To terminate a DO loop	Sections 6.1, 6.5
LPRINT	To transfer output to printer	Section 4.10
MID$	To replace part of one string with another string	Section 14.1
MD	To create a new directory	Appendix A.5
NEXT	To terminate a FOR loop	Section 9.1
ON ERROR GOTO	To transfer to a specified line when a fatal error occurs	Section 16.3
OPEN	To establish communication between a program and a file	Sections 16.1, 16.7
OPTION BASE	To select 0 or 1 as the smallest allowable subscript in a program	Section 15.2
PAINT	To color a region of the graphics screen	Section 19.5
PRINT	To transfer output to the video screen	Sections 3.6, 6.2 Chapter 7
PRINT USING	To transfer output to the video screen according to a specified format	Section 7.6
PRINT #	To transfer output to a sequential file	Section 16.1
PSET	To plot a point on the graphics screen	Sections 19.1, 19.10
PUT (files)	To store the contents of a record variable in a random file	Section 16.7

Statement	Purpose	Text reference
PUT (graphics)	To display on the graphics screen an image stored by a GET statement	Section 19.7
RANDOMIZE	To reseed the random number generator	Section 17.1
READ	To obtain input data from DATA lines	Section 11.1
REDIM	To change the size of a dynamic array	Section 15.2
REM	To include comments in a program and to improve its readability	Section 3.7
RESTORE	To restore the data pointer to the first or to a specified DATA line	Section 11.3
RESUME	To continue program execution after an error recovery procedure	Section 16.3
RD	To remove an existing directory	Appendix A.5
SCREEN	To select text, medium-resolution graphics, or high-resolution graphics mode of operation	Sections 19.1, 19.10
SELECT CASE	To execute one of several statement blocks, depending on the value of an expression	Section 8.5
STATIC	To preserve values of local variables between procedure calls	Section 17.9
SUB	To declare a SUB procedure	Sections 12.1, 12.4
SWAP	To interchange the values of two variables	Section 14.5
TYPE	To define a data type	Section 16.7
WIDTH	To specify the number of characters in an output line	Section 7.1
WRITE#	To transfer output to a sequential file	Section 16.1

E
QuickBASIC Functions

Function	Purpose	Text reference
ABS(*x*)	Returns the absolute value of *x*	Section 13.1
ASC(*x$*)	Returns the ASCII code of the first character in *x$*	Section 14.6
ATN(*x*)	Returns the arctangent of *x*	Section 13.1
CDBL(*x*)	Converts *x* to a double-precision value	Section 13.1
CHR$(*n*)	Returns the character whose ASCII code is *n*	Section 10.4
CINT(*x*)	Converts *x* to an integer by rounding	Section 13.1
CLNG(*x*)	Converts *x* to a long integer by rounding	Section 13.1
COS(*x*)	Returns the cosine of *x*	Section 13.1
CSNG(*x*)	Converts *x* to a single precision value	Section 13.1
EOF(*f*)	Indicates the end of the file condition on file *f*	Section 16.2
ERR	Returns the code of the most recent run-time error	Section 16.3
EXP(*x*)	Raises *e* to the power *x*	Section 13.1
FIX(*x*)	Truncates *x* to an integer value	Section 13.1
INKEY$ *variable*	To read a single character from the keyboard	Section 10.1
INSTR(*n*, *x$*,*y$*)	Returns the position of the first occurrence of *y$* in *x$* starting at position *n*	Section 14.3
INT(*x*)	Returns the greatest integer less than or equal to *x*	Section 13.1
LCASE$(*x$*)	Converts uppercase letters in *x$* to lowercase	Section 6.2
LEFT$(*x$*,*n*)	Returns the first *n* characters of *x$*	Section 14.1
LEN(*x$*)	Returns the number of characters in *x$*	Section 14.1
LOC(*f*)	Returns the record number of last record accessed in file *f*	Section 16.7
LOF(*f*)	Returns the length of file *f*	Section 16.7
LOG(*x*)	Returns the natural logarithm of *x*	Section 13.1
MID$(*x$*,*n*, *m*)	Returns *m* characters from *x$* beginning at position *n*	Section 14.1
RIGHT$(*x$*,*n*)	Returns the last *n* characters from *x$*	Section 14.1
RND	Returns a random number between 0 and 1	Chapter 17

Function	Purpose	Text reference
SGN(x)	Returns +1, 0, or −1 depending whether x is positive, zero, or negative	Section 13.1
SIN(x)	Returns the sine of x	Section 13.1
SPACE$(n)	Returns a string of n spaces	Section 10.4
SPC(n)	Skips n spaces	Section 7.4
SQR(x)	Returns the principal square root of x	Section 13.1
STR$(x)	Converts x to a string	Section 14.6
STRING$(n,m)	Returns the character whose ASCII code is m, repeated n times	Section 10.4
STRING$(n, x$)	Returns the first character of x$, repeated n times	Sections 10.1, 10.4
TAB(n)	Tabs to position n	Section 7.4
TAN(x)	Returns the tangent of x	Section 13.1
UCASE$(x$)	Converts lowercase letters in x$ to uppercase	Section 6.2
VAL(x$)	Returns the numerical value of x$	Section 14.6

F
Answers to Selected Problems

■ *Section 1.3*

1. F	**2.** F	**3.** T	**4.** F	**5.** F	**6.** T
7. T	**8.** F	**9.** F	**10.** F	**11.** F	**12.** F

■ *Section 2.3*

1. 5% discount
2. Decide whether the discount is applicable.
3. 693.50
4. 250.00
5. 80.00 and 0, 128.00 and 0, 176.00 and 48.00, 206.00 and 78.00
6. $4
7. $6 per hour
8. Step (c) is used to determine whether there is any overtime. G denotes gross pay. B denotes pay for overtime hours.
9. 21
10.   1   1
       2   2
       3   6
       4   24
       5   120
       6   720
11. 55
12. 2, 4, 7, 8, 14, 28, 64
13. Process will *never* stop, since SUM is always less than 2.
14. Process will *never* stop, since N is always less than 10.
15. Variable names:

NAME	= name of an item
COST	= cost for the item NAME
PRICE	= sale price for the item NAME
QTY	= number of units of NAME sold
GROSS	= gross sales for the item NAME
INCOME	= income from the item NAME

Algorithm:

a. Print column headings as specified.
b. Read NAME and values for COST, PRICE, and QTY, for one item.
c. Assign the value of the product QTY × PRICE to GROSS.
d. Multiply QTY times (PRICE − COST) to obtain a value for INCOME.
e. Enter NAME and the values GROSS and INCOME under the appropriate column headings.
f. Return to Step (b) until the report is complete.

17. Variable names:

CORP = corporation name
SHARES = number of shares
PRICE = current price for one share
EARN = earnings for one share
EQTY = equity represented by all shares of corporation CORP
PE = price/earnings ratio for one share

Algorithm:

a. Print column headings as specified.
b. Read CORP and values for SHARES, PRICE, and EARN.
c. Assign the value of the product SHARES × PRICE to EQTY.
d. Divide PRICE by EARN to obtain a value for PE.
e. Enter CORP and the values SHARES, PRICE, EARN, EQTY, and PE under the appropriate column headings.
f. Return to Step (b) until the report is complete.

19. Algorithm:
a. Start with SUM = 0 and COUNT = 0
b. Add the number on the top card to SUM, and add 1 to COUNT.
c. Remove the top card and return to Step (b) until all cards have been processed.
d. Divide SUM by COUNT to obtain the average AV, and proceed to Step (e) with the original stack of cards in hand.
e. If the number on the top card exceeds AV, write the letter G on the card; otherwise write the letter L.
f. Remove the top card and return to Step (e) until all cards have been examined.

20. Algorithm:
a. Press the CLEAR key.
b. Insert your ID card into reader as shown.
c. Enter your four-digit code and press ENTER.
d. Enter amount of check and press ENTER.
e. Place check in punch unit, blank side toward you.
f. Remove check and ID card when these items are released by the machine.

■ Section 2.4

1. F   **2.** T   **3.** F   **4.** F   **5.** T   **6.** T   **7.** T   **8.** F   **9.** T

■ Section 3.4

1. **a.** 17   **b.** 33   **c.** −2   **d.** −6   **e.** −15   **f.** −9   **g.** 17
    h. 9   **i.** 0.25   **j.** −9   **k.** 64   **l.** −12.3   **m.** −12   **n.** 12300000
    o. 0.00075   **p.** 4.5   **q.** 3   **r.** 3   **s.** 2   **t.** 0   **u.** 5

2. a. 3.5   **b.** 5   **c.** 0.75   **d.** 0.75   **e.** 10   **f.** 25   **g.** 4.5   **h.** 1.666667
i. 10   **j.** 3   **k.** −8   **l.** −8   **m.** 1   **n.** 2   **o.** 2

3. a. * missing between (Y + Z) and X.
c. 7B is not admissible as an expression or variable name.
e. KEY is a reserved word.
f. 2B is not admissible as an expression or variable name.
g. 2X is not admissible as an expression or variable name.

4. a. 0.06*P   **b.** 5*X+5*Y   **c.** A^2+B^2
d. 6/(5*A)   **e.** A/B+C/D   **f.** (A+B)/(C+D)
g. A*X^2+B*X+C   **h.** (B^2−4*A*C)^0.5   **i.** (X^2+4*X*Y)/(X+2*Y)

5. a. X+1+Y   **b.** A^2−B^2   **c.** A^3+A^2*B+A
d. A*B/C   **e.** A/B/C   **f.** X^4+X^3*D+X^2*C+X*B+A
g. P^Q^R   **h.** 1/A/B/C/D

■ *Section 3.9*

1. a. LET M=7   **b.** LET B=B+7
c. LET H=2*H   **d.** LET C2=(A−B)/2
e. LET A=(1+R)^10   **f.** LET X=X−2*Y
g. LET C$="COST"   **h.** LET A$="DOE,JANE"
i. LET Q$=P$ **j.** LET S$="*****"

2. a. LET X=(A+B)*C   **b.** admissible
c. LET S=A+B   **d.** LET DEPT5=17
e. admissible   **f.** LET M5=2+7*X
g. admissible   **h.** admissible
i. LET Z=4*10^2.5   **j.** LET AREA=LENGTH*WDTH
k. LET SUM=SUM+NXT   **l.** admissible
m. LET A$="SAMMY"   **n.** LET NME$="JANE DOE"
o. admissible   **p.** LET D$="DEPT#7"
q. LET M$="MONTHLY RENT" **r.** admissible

3. a. PRINT "SO-AND-SO"   **b.** admissible   **c.** admissible
d. PRINT SPC$;X   **e.** admissible   **f.** admissible
g. PRINT WDTH   **h.** admissible

4. a. RESULT 12   **b.** AMOUNT= 108   **c.** RESULT−2   **d.** RESULT 5
e. VOLUME 200   **f.** LIST PRICE 45   **g.** BOBBY LOVES   **h.** 1
Be careful.   DISCOUNT 4.5   MARY   3
VOLUME 200   SELLING PRICE 40.5

5.

a. A	B	C	**b.** N	Output	**c.** X	Y	Z	Output
1	2	1	1	1	0	0	0	
1	2	3	2	2	0	7	0	
4	2	3	6	6	0	7	7	
4	5	3	42	42	0	7	7	7
4	20	2	42		7	7	7	
2	20	11			7	343	7	
2	20	11			7	343	7	343
					7	343	7	

6. a.

S	A	Output
0	25	
25	25	25
50	25	50
25	25	25
25	25	

b.

X	Y	Output
1.5	0	
1.5	0.6	
1.5	0.6	.6
−1.5	0.6	
−1.5	0.6	−1.5
−1.5	0.6	.6
−1.5	0.6	

c.

N	C	S	G	P	Output
130	0	0	0	0	
130	3	0	0	0	
130	3	3.6	0	0	
130	3	3.6	468	0	SALES 468
130	3	3.6	468	78	PROFIT 78
130	3	3.6	468	78	

d.

A	P	Output
0	0	NTH POWERS OF 10
10	10	
10	10	FOR N = 1 10
10	100	
10	100	FOR N = 2 100
10	1000	
10	1000	FOR N = 3 1000
10	10000	
10	10000	FOR N = 4 10000
10	10000	
10	10000	

Section 3.10

1. F	**2.** F	**3.** F	**4.** T	**5.** F	**6.** T	**7.** F
8. F	**9.** T	**10.** T	**11.** F	**12.** T	**13.** T	**14.** F

Section 4.12

1. Syntax: LET D=23000
Programming: LET R=0.06
Syntax: LET A=R*D

Output: ANSWER IS 1380

2. Programming: LET A=(N1+N2)/2
Syntax: PRINT "AVERAGE IS";A

Output: AVERAGE IS 19.5

3. Programming:
T=5   ' T=TAX RATE
P=120   ' P=PRICE

Output: TOTAL COST: 126

4. Syntax and programming:
Replace LET A*X+B=0
with LET X=−B/A

Output: SOLUTION IS −6.28571

5. Programming:
   Replace
   ```
   LET A$=B$
   LET B$=A$
   ```
   with
   ```
   LET T$=A$
   LET A$=B$
   LET B$=T$
   ```

   Output:
   ```
   A$=STOCK
   B$=BOND
   A$=BOND
   B$=STOCK
   ```

6. Syntax:
   Replace PRINT TAX ON FIRST CAR IS T with PRINT "TAX ON FIRST CAR IS"; T
   and   PRINT TAX ON SECOND CAR IS T with PRINT "TAX ON SECOND CAR IS"; T
   Programming:
   Insert · LET T=V*R after LET V=5700

   Output: TAX ON FIRST CAR IS 297
              TAX ON SECOND CAR IS 376.2

■ *Section 4.13*

1. F	**2.** T	**3.** F	**4.** T	**5.** F	**6.** T	**7.** F
8. F	**9.** T	**10.** T	**11.** T	**12.** T	**13.** T	**14.** F

■ *Section 5.3*

```
1. LET A=100*(1.06)^X          3. LET A=X+0.045*X
5. LET A=X/19.2                7. LET A=X/(52*40)
9. LET A=2667.50+28*(X−17850)  12. LET A=X/133.84
14. LET A=X/1.8045             16. LET A=(1.8045/133.84)*X
18. LET A=(4*X/3.14159)^0.5    20. LET A=X/2.54
```

■ *Section 5.4*

1. T	**2.** F	**3.** T	**4.** F	**5.** F	**6.** T	**7.** F	**8.** T	**9.** F	**10.** T	**11.** F

■ *Section 6.4*

1. a.		**b.**		**c.**		**d.**	
1	1	1	1	1	64	1	
2	3	2	2	2	32	1	
4	7	3	6	3	16	2	
8	15	4	24	4	8	3	
16	31	5	120	5	4	5	
32		6	720	6	2	8	
				7	1	13	

2. a, b, d, and f are true.

3. a. X is never less than X − 0. Loop is never entered.

   b. OK must be quoted. Syntax error.

   c. A ∗ A is always greater than or equal to 0. Infinite loop.

   d. "DONE" is not a proper condition. Syntax error.

   e. Condition always true. Loop is never entered.

   f. Condition always true. Loop is never entered.

■ Section 6.6

1. a.		**b.**	
1	3	1	25
2	9	2	12
3	27	3	6
4	81	4	3
		5	1

c.		**d.**
3	1	5
4	3	4
7	4	3
11	7	2
		1
		2
		3
		4
		5

e.		
A	B	C
B	A	C
C	A	B
A	C	B
B	C	A
C	B	A

■ Section 6.7

1. T   **2.** F   **3.** F   **4.** F   **5.** T   **6.** F   **7.** T   **8.** F   **9.** T

■ Section 7.3

1. a. BASEBALL'S HALL OF FAME   **b.** PASCAGOULA RIVER
       COOPERSTOWN, NY 13326   BAYOU COUNTRY, U.S.A.

   c. 5 TIMES 8 = 40

   d.
```
0     5     10     15     20
25    30    35     FINI
```
   e. IF A= 5 A+2= 7
       IF A= 10 A+2= 12
       IF A= 15 A+2= 17

2. a. PRINT X;"/";Y;"=";X/Y

   c. PRINT "X −";Y;"= ";−X

   e. PRINT "DEPT. NO.";Y+Y+X

3. a. Prints TEAFORTWO
  b. Replace "Sleeping"; by "Sleeping "; and "Bear"; by "Bear ";
  c. Change PRINT 7; "A" to PRINT "7A"
  d. Insert the statement PRINT between the two DO loops.

■ Section 7.5

1. a.
SALES	COMMISSION
2000	200
2500	250
3000	300
3500	350
4000	400
4500	450
5000	500

b. BASIC BASIC BASIC BASIC

c.
```
1234567890
0
 -1
  -2
   -3
    -4
THAT'S ENOUGH
```

d.
```
7777777
7
7
7
7
7
7
```

e.
```
1234567890
*
 *
  *
   *
```

f.
X	X^2
1	1
2	4
3	9
4	16

2. a. PRINT TAB(6); "B"; TAB(9); 3
  b. PRINT X; SPC(13); 2*X; SPC(13); 3*X; SPC(13); 4*X
  c. PRINT TAB((80−N)/2); "...*name*..." where N = number of characters in *name*.
  d. PRINT 0; SPC(10); 0; SPC(10); 0; SPC(10);
     0; SPC(10); 0; SPC(10); 0; SPC(10); " 0"
  e. PRINT "0 "; SPC(10); 0; SPC(10);
     0; SPC(10); 0; SPC(10); 0; SPC(10); 0; SPC(10); 0

■ Section 7.7

1. a.
```
9.00
4.50
2.25
1.13
```

b.
```
RIVERBOAT
        BOATSWAIN
```

c.
```
1/8=12.5 CENTS
3/8=37.5 CENTS
5/8=62.5 CENTS
7/8=87.5 CENTS
```

d.
```
TIME 1 A= 0.00
TIME 2 A= 0.01
TIME 3 A= 0.01
```

e.
```
1234567890
 23.60
 23.6
```

f. POPEYE

g.
```
BOBBY LOVES JUDITH
JUDI LOVES BOB
```

h. TAX-RATE 15   TAX-RATE 25   TAX-RATE 35

■ Section 7.8

1. F	2. F	3. F	4. T	5. T	6. F	7. T
8. F	9. F	10. F	11. T	12. T		

■ Section 8.3

1. a, b, d, and f are true.
2. a. IF R=7 OR R=11 THEN PRINT "OK"
   b. IF A<B THEN C=A ELSE C=B
   c. IF X>A AND X>B THEN C=C+1
   d. IF 2<=S AND S<=8 THEN PRINT "BETWEEN"
   e. IF P<50 OR P>75 THEN PRINT "BAD DATA"
   f. IF 0<=R AND R<=100 AND R<>50 THEN D=D−1
   g. IF R<>2 AND R<>7 AND R<>11 AND R<>12 THEN PRINT "CONTINUE"
   h. IF UCASE$(C$)<>"Y" AND UCASE$(C$)<>"N" THEN PRINT "TRY AGAIN"
   i. IF UCASE$(C$) = "RED" OR UCASE$(C$) = "BLUE" THEN PRINT C$
   j. IF X$=UCASE$(X$) THEN PRINT X$
   k. IF Y$=UCASE$(Y$) OR Y$=LCASE$(Y$) THEN PRINT Y$
   l. IF A$=UCASE$(A$) AND A$=LCASE$(A$) THEN PRINT "NO LETTERS"

3. a. ```
   5 5 8
   5 5 6
   ```

   b. ```
   1  5
   2  12
   2  9
   ```

   c. ```
   20 10
   15 10
   10 10
   ```

   d. ```
   0  62
   1  52
   ```

   e. ```
   11 12 13 14 15
   16 17 18 19 20
   21 22 23 24 25
   ENOUGH
   ```

## ■ Section 8.6

1. a. −1

   b. ```
   1  0
   2  3
   3  9
   4  16
   ```

   c. ```
   8
   6
   3
   2
   1
   0
   ```

2. a. 10  18
   b. 8  5
   c. 6  24
   ```

d. YYY
   XXX
   XXX
   YYY
   ZZZ

e. CBADAB

3. a.
```
IF X > Y THEN
    PRINT X
    TOTAL = TOTAL + X
ELSE
    PRINT Y
    TOTAL = TOTAL + Y
END IF
```

b.
```
IF A$="BOTH" THEN
    PRINT X; Y
ELSEIF X<Y THEN
    PRINT X
ELSE
    PRINT Y
END IF
```

c.
```
IF X<Y THEN
    PRINT X
    PRINT Y
ELSEIF Y<X THEN
    PRINT Y
    PRINT X
ELSE
    PRINT X
END IF
```

d.
```
IF H<=40 THEN
    PRINT "GROSS SALARY"; D*H
ELSE
    PRINT "OVERTIME PAY"; 3/2*D*(H-40)
    PRINT "GROSS SALARY"; 40*D+3/2*D*(H-40)
END IF
```

e.
```
IF GRADE < 50 THEN
    PRINT "POOR"
ELSEIF GRADE <= 80 THEN
    PRINT "GOOD"
ELSE
    PRINT "EXCELLENT"
END IF
```

f.
```
IF X$=UCASE$(X$) THEN
    PRINT "ALL UC"
ELSEIF X$=LCASE$(X$) THEN
    PRINT "ALL LC"
ELSE
    PRINT "UC AND LC"
END IF
```

```
4. a. SELECT CASE LEVEL$
         CASE "E"
            PRINT "ELEMENTARY SCHOOL"
         CASE "M"
            PRINT "MIDDLE SCHOOL"
         CASE "H"
            PRINT "HIGH SCHOOL"
         CASE "C"
            PRINT "COLLEGE"
         CASE ELSE
            PRINT "Bad Value - must be E, M, H, or C."
      END SELECT

   b. SELECT CASE CLASS$
         CASE "A"
            RATE = 5.25
         CASE "B"
            RATE = 7.95
         CASE "C"
            RATE = 11.45
         CASE "D"
            RATE = 14.50
         CASE ELSE
            PRINT "Bad Value - must be A, B, C, or D."
      END SELECT

   c. SELECT CASE ABBREV$
         CASE "CT"
            PRINT "Connecticut"
         CASE "ME"
            PRINT "Maine"
         CASE "MA"
            PRINT "Massachusetts"
         CASE "NH"
            PRINT "New Hampshire"
         CASE "RI"
            PRINT "Rhode Island"
         CASE "VT"
            PRINT "Vermont"
         CASE ELSE
            PRINT "Bad Value - must be CT, ME, MA, NH, RI, or VT."
      END SELECT

   d. SELECT CASE QTY
         CASE 1 TO 49
            COST = .99 * QTY
         CASE 50 TO 99
            COST = .89 * QTY
         CASE 100 TO 199
            COST = .75 * QTY
         CASE IS >= 200
            COST = .62 * QTY
      END SELECT
```

■ Section 8.7

1. T	**2.** F	**3.** T	**4.** T	**5.** T	**6.** F	**7.** F
8. T	**9.** F	**10.** T	**11.** F	**12.** T		

■ Section 9.2

1. a. 4
5
6

b. 5
1
−3

c. TIMES THROUGH LOOP= 2

d. +++///   **e.** LOOP   **f.** No output   **g.** 5   2
12   10
34   24

h. ITEM1   ITEM2   ITEM3   ITEM4
  1   2   3   4

i. 123456789
V   V
  V   V
    V   V
    V V
      V

2. a. Syntax error: Change NEXT X to NEXT N.

b. Programming error: LET C = 0 should precede the FOR statement.

c. Programming error: Change X to some other variable name in the two statements INPUT X and LET S=S+X.

d. Programming error: STEP S is admissible but the step value cannot be changed within the loop. Rewrite the program.

```
LET S=0
FOR N=1 TO 5
   LET S=S+N
    PRINT S
NEXT N
```

■ Section 9.4

1. a. 2   3   2   3   2   3   **b.** 13   16   11   14

c. 2   3   4   5
3   4   5
4   5
5

d. 108   **e.** 7   7   7
9   9   9
11   11   11
13   13   13

2. a. Syntax error: Interchange NEXT I and NEXT J.

b. Programming error: Include STEP −1 in both FOR statements.

c. Programming error: Change I<>J in the IF statement to I<J.

d. Programming error: Change R>=C in the first IF statement to R<=C.
Change R<C in the second IF statement to R>C.
Insert the line PRINT between NEXT C and NEXT R.

■ Section 9.5

1. F	**2.** F	**3.** T	**4.** F	**5.** T	**6.** F
7. T	**8.** F	**9.** F	**10.** T	**11.** F	

■ *Section 10.2*

1. a.
<pre>
                    BASIC   (The first B displayed is in row 2, column 40.)
           BASIC   BASIC
    BASIC   BASIC   BASIC
</pre>

b. IBM   (The first I displayed is in row 1, column 21.)

<pre>
        IBM

            IBM

        IBM

    IBM
</pre>

c.
<pre>
H   H   (The first H displayed is in row 15, column 8.)
H   H
H   H
HHHHH
H   H
H   H
H   H
</pre>

d. The word GOOD is displayed successively 6 times on lines 10 through 15, each beginning in column 15. After all six GOOD's are displayed, the screen is cleared. A similar block of GRIEF's is then displayed on the same lines but beginning in column 20, and the screen is cleared again. This same sequence is repeated 50 times.

■ *Section 10.5*

1. a.
<pre>
        NORMAL
        NORMAL   ← (normal)
        NORMAL
        NORMAL
        NORMAL
                    REVERSE
                    REVERSE
    (reverse →   REVERSE
    image)   REVERSE
                    REVERSE
</pre>

b. BASIC
<pre>
    BASIC
    BASIC
   |BASIC| ← (blinking)
    BASIC
    BASIC
</pre>
(The first B is displayed in row 11, column 38.)

c. The 10-row by 10-column block in the upper-left corner of the display area is white, and the rest of the screen is black.

d. The first 16 rows are colored by using color codes 0–15. The rest of the display area is white.

2. a.

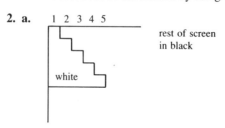

b.

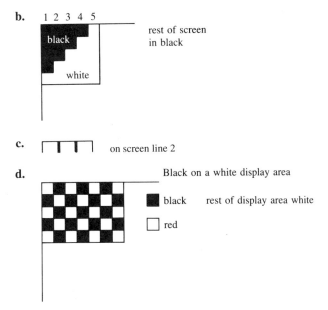

c. on screen line 2

d. Black on a white display area

■ black   rest of display area white

□ red

■ *Section 10.6*

1. T   **2.** F   **3.** F   **4.** T   **5.** F   **6.** T   **7.** T   **8.** T
9. F   **10.** F   **11.** T   **12.** F   **13.** T   **14.** F   **15.** T

■ *Section 11.2*

1. a. 2 −3   **b.** CATWOMAN   **c.** 7   **d.** BAD VALUE: 22
5 0   3   BAD VALUE: 84
0 −5   18   2 BAD VALUES.
                           −5
                           4

2. a. Change the DATA line to DATA 1, A
   b. Replace ; in the first line by ,
   c. Replace GOODBYE in the second line by "GOODBYE"
   d. Change the first DATA line to DATA "TOM DOOLEY, JR"

3. a. Interchange the statements in lines 3 and 4 of the program.
   b. The statements between the comment and the PRINT statement should read as follows:

```
LET SUM=0
LET N=0
READ X
DO WHILE X<>IE-30
    LET SUM=SUM+X
    LET N=N+1
    READ X
LOOP
```

   c. The statements between the comment and the PRINT statement should read as follows:

```
LET C=0
READ V
DO WHILE V<>999
    LET C=C+1
    READ V
LOOP
```

■ *Section 11.4*

1. a. 9
   3
   5

b. 3
   5
   3
   5

c. ROBINHEAD

d. 10 20 30
   10 20 30

e. ALLEN 40
   ALLEN 40

■ *Section 11.5*

1. T **2.** F **3.** F **4.** F **5.** T **6.** F **7.** T **8.** T
9. T **10.** T **11.** F

■ *Section 12.3*

1. CROWBAR
   RIP SAW
   TAPE50

2. Last datum: XXX
   Data count: 5

3. 40
   10
   100
   25
   100
   5   275

4. CROWBAR   200
   RIP SAW   75
   TAPE25   445
   TAPE50   250
   YARDSTICK   279
   TOTAL $1249

■ *Section 12.6*

1. X = 7
   Y = 9
   Z = 3
   U = 7
   V = 9

2. S = 8
   T = 4
   U = 5
   A = 4
   B = 5

3. X = 4
   Y = 9
   Z = 7

4. A = 9
   X = 5
   Y = 7
   Z = 9

5. A = 9
   X = 9
   Y = 7
   Z = 9

6. A = 6
   X = 1
   Y = 3
   Z = 1

7. 9 3 2 9
   4 6 3 6
   0 2 4 4

8. 1 1
   2 3
   3 6

9. 1 1
   2 3
   3 6

■ *Section 12.7*

1. F   **2.** F   **3.** F   **4.** T   **5.** F   **6.** T
7. F   **8.** F   **9.** T   **10.** F   **11.** T

■ *Section 13.2*

1. **a.** 9   **b.** 6   **c.** 18   **d.** 26   **e.** −43   **f.** 1200
   g. 124   **h.** −124   **i.** 123   **j.** −123   **k.** 4   **l.** 3

2. **a.** 4   **b.** 5   **c.** 6   **d.** −4   **e.** 2865   **f.** 2860
   g. 2900   **h.** 3000   **i.** 2864.714   **j.** 4   **k.** 4   **l.** 59

3. **a.**
```
0   8
1   8
2   6
3   2
4   4
```
b.
```
1.1      1
1.21     1
1.331    1
1.4641   1
```
c.
```
XX
XXXX
XX
```
d.
```
X
X
X
X
X
X
X
X
```

e.
```
XX
X
XXX
X
X
```
f. `1  3  7  9  21`
g.
```
*
**
*****
```
h.
```
13.990  13.99
13.993  13.99
13.996  14.00
13.999  14.00
```

4. **a.** `IF ABS(A+B)=ABS(A)+ABS(B) THEN PRINT "EQUAL"`
   c. `IF (INT(X)=X) AND (X>0) THEN PRINT "OK"`
   e. `IF (INT(L/2)=L/2) AND (INT(L/25)=L/25) THEN PRINT`

5. **b.** `LET X=INT(1000*X+0.5)/1000`
   d. `LET X=1000*INT(X/1000+0.5)`

■ *Section 13.4*

1. **a.** Programming error: Change `LET V=FNZ(U)` to `LET V=FNZ(X)`.
   b. Programming error: Change `DEF FNS(I)=X^2` to `DEF FNS(X)=X^2`.
   c. Syntax error: Change `DEF BONUS(S)=200+0.02*S` to `DEF FNB(S)=200+0.02*S`.
        Change `LET B=BONUS(S)` to `LET B=FNB(S)`.
   d. Programming error: Change `DEF FNR(X)=X/N` to `DEF FNR(N)=X/N`.

2. **a.**
```
200
1400
0
```
b. `.5  2  .5`
c.
```
0  3
1  4
2  5
3  6
```
d.
```
1   2   3   4
 .5  1  1.5  2
```
e.
```
10
15
20
25
```

3. **a.** `DEF FNT(L)=L+0.05*L`
   b. `DEF FNI(R)=100*(R/100)*(1/4)`
   c. `DEF FNC(L,W)=(L*W/9)*12.95`
   d. `DEF FNT(E)=E*(27/1000)`
   e. `DEF FNF(C)=9/5*C+32`
   f. `DEF FNC(F)=5/9*(F−32)`

```
g. DEF FNM(F)=F/5280
h. DEF FNM(K)=K/1.6093
i. DEF FNK(M)=1.6093*M
j. DEF FNR(X)=INT(1000*X+0.5)/1000
k. DEF FNS(D,T)=D/T
l. DEF FNS(X,Y)=X-(X*Y/100)
m. DEF FNC(X,Y)=X/15*Y
n. DEF FNA(R)=3.14159*R^2
o. DEF FNV(R)=4/3*3.14159*R^3
p. DEF FNS(A)=SIN(3.14159/180*A)
```

Section 13.5

1. T	**2.** T	**3.** F	**4.** F	**5.** F	**6.** F
7. F	**8.** F	**9.** T	**10.** T	**11.** T	**12.** T

Section 14.4

1. a. CYBER   **b.** Z TO A   **c.** CONSULTATION   **d.** BIOPHYSICS

e. Great   **f.** ADD   **g.** 3 STEP
Salt   LIST   2 LIST
Lake   STOP   4 STOP
Desert,   STEP   1 ADD
Utah

2.
```
a. PRINT LEFT$(A$,1)
b. PRINT MID$(A$,2,1)
c. PRINT RIGHT$(A$,1)
d. PRINT LEFT$(A$,3)
e. PRINT RIGHT$(A$,3)
f. PRINT LEFT$(A$,1);RIGHT(A$,1)
g. IF LEN(A$)=LEN(B$) THEN N=N+1
h. IF LEFT$(A$,1)=RIGHT$(A$,1) THEN PRINT LEFT$(A$,1)
i. IF LEFT$(A$,1)=MID$(A$,2,1) THEN X$="SAME"
j. IF INSTR(A$,",")>O THEN PRINT "COMMA"
k. IF INSTR(A$," ")=O THEN PRINT "NO SPACES"
l. LET B$=LEFT$(A$,N)
m. LET B$=RIGHT$(A$,1)+LEFT$(A$,1)
n. LET T$=MID$(S$,2,1)+LEFT$(S$,1)+RIGHT$(S$,LEN(S$)-2)
o. LET F$=LEFT$(G$,3)+RIGHT$(H$,3)
p. IF LEFT$(A$,1)+MID$(B$,2,1)+MID$(C$,3,1)="YES" THEN PRINT "OK"
q. MID$(A$,4,1)="Y"
```

Section 14.8

1. a. M   **b.** CATDOG   **c.** HARRY
A   1010   ALICE
            BEASTBEAST   LAST
                            LAST

d. 31+31=62   **e.** E 5   **f.** 7 7   **g.** 0123456789:

h. 42 WINS AND 21 LOSSES GIVES A PERCENTAGE OF .667
i. CORRECT
j. 9876543210
k. COUNT: 50

■ *Section 14.9*

1. F   **2.** F   **3.** T   **4.** T   **5.** T   **6.** F   **7.** F   **8.** F
9. T   **10.** T   **11.** T   **12.** T   **13.** F   **14.** F   **15.** T

■ *Section 15.3*

1. a. 5   **b.** TO BE OR NOT TO BE   **c.** 8   **d.** IRAQGATE
    4

e. PAYCHECK, JOHN   **f.** SAM
    DENVER, JOHN   JESS
    JOHN, ELTON   SANDI
    CASH, JOHN

■ *Section 15.10*

1. a. 1   4   9   16   **b.** 2   4   6   **c.** 2   3   5   **d.** YYYY
                                                     NYYY
                                                     NNYY
                                                     NNNY

e. DEVILS: HOOFERS: SAINTS:
    ED   ANN   DEB
    JANE   JIM   DOT
    JOHN   RON   RUSS
    SUE   RUTH   TIM

■ *Section 15.11*

1. F   **2.** F   **3.** F   **4.** F   **5.** F   **6.** T   **7.** F
8. T   **9.** F   **10.** T   **11.** F   **12.** F   **13.** F

■ *Section 16.4*

1. a. J.D.SLOANE   **b.** J.D.SLOANE   565   **2. a.** SAM   **b.** JOAN   PASS
      EXCESS: 3000   R.M.PETERS   265   GREG   SAM   PASS
                          A.B.CARTER   505   MARY   GREG   FAIL
      A.B.CARTER   I.O.ULSTER   465   MARY   FAIL
      EXCESS: 2400   MARK   PASS

      I.O.ULSTER
      EXCESS: 2000

■ Section 16.9

1. F   2. F   3. F   4. T   5. T   6. F   7. F   8. F   9. F   10. F

■ Section 17.3

1. **a.** 80   **b.** 70   **c.** 30   **d.** 0   **e.** 100   **f.** 10
2. **a.** T   **b.** T   **c.** either   **d.** either   **e.** T   **f.** T

■ Section 17.6

1. **a.** PRINT 4*RND
   b. PRINT 6*RND+5
   c. PRINT 8*RND-5
   d. PRINT INT(7*RND)+6
   e. PRINT 2*INT(5*RND)
   f. PRINT 2*INT(5*RND)+1

2. **a.** 1, 2, (equally likely)
   b. 0
   c. -2,-1,0,1,2, (equally likely)
   d. 2, 3, 4 (3 about half the time; 2 and 4 each about one-fourth the time)
   e. 2,3,4,...,12 (not equally likely—simulates rolling a pair of dice)
   f. 1,2,3,4,6,9 (not equally likely)

3. ONE OF EACH, TWO HEADS, and TWO TAILS will be displayed about the same number of times. In practice, ONE OF EACH will occur about half the time.

■ Section 17.11

1. T   2. F   3. T   4. F   5. F   6. F
7. F   8. T   9. F   10. F   11. T

■ Section 18.7

1. F   2. F   3. F   4. T   5. T   6. T   7. F   8. T
9. F   10. F   11. F

■ Section 19.3

1. **a.** A row of 10 white 6 × 6 blocks, five points apart.
   b. A block letter L with upper-left corner at (30, 50).
   c. Same as part (b).
   d. A white arch created by drawing 200 line segments. The first LINE statement draws the left half and the second draws the right.

■ Section 19.12

1. F   2. F   3. T   4. F   5. T   6. T
7. T   8. F   9. F   10. F

Index